THE INSEAD GLOBAL MANAGEMENT SERIES: STRATEGY AND MANAGEMENT IN ASIA PACIFIC

The INSEAD Global Management Series

STRATEGY AND MANAGEMENT IN ASIA PACIFIC

Philippe Lasserre and Hellmut Schütte

McGraw-Hill Publishing Company

London · New York · St Louis · San Francisco · Auckland · Bogotá · Caracas
Lisbon · Madrid · Mexico · Milan · Montreal · New Delhi · Panama · Paris
San Juan · São Paulo · Singapore · Sydney · Tokyo · Toronto

Published by

McGraw-Hill Publishing Company

Shoppenhangers Road, Maidenhead, Berkshire, SL6 2QL, England
Telephone 01628 23432
Facsimile 01628 770224

British Library Cataloguing in Publication Data
The CIP data of this title is available from the British Library

Library of Congress Cataloging-in-publication Data
The CIP data of this title is available from the Library of Congress,
Washington DC, USA

Further information on this and other McGraw-Hill titles is to be found at
http://www.mcgraw-hill.co.uk

Publisher: Alfred Waller
Desk Editor: Alastair Lindsay
Produced by PSP Publishing Services
Cover by: Hybert Design

Typeset by Mackreth Media Services, Hemel Hempstead
Printed and bound in Great Britain at the University Press, Cambridge

CONTENTS

Acknowledgements

With this book we are trying to pull together many years of research on Asian management matters with the insight we have gained in the inner workings of companies in Asia. These are either of Western, Japanese or Asian origin.

Writing cases in the field of international management is never an easy matter. It requires interviews to be carried out in different company locations around the world—in our case often 10,000 km apart. This can only be done with substantial financial support. Equally, logistic and cultural barriers have to be bridged, and cooperation with many executives in companies assured.

Fortunately, we are both working in an environment which enables us to overcome many of those and other hurdles. INSEAD and its Euro-Asia Centre have provided us with the financial resources for travel and assistance. Two of our collaborators, Charlotte Butler and Jocelyn Probert have been for many years our main case writers or co-writers as well as editors. Through our active involvement in other research projects, consulting assignments and executive seminars, we have been able to access many companies and to convince their executives to spend some of their valuable time discussing their problems with us. A number of our MBA students such as Marc Canizzo, Claire Chai, Deborah Clyde-Smith, Pierre Courbon, Eric Dugulay, Lisbeth Froman, Qionghua Hu, Eriko Ishida, Michele Jurgens, Jens Kjar, Huong-Giang Nguyen, Jake Vigoda and Elizabeth Withell have also contributed to the exploration and writing of cases.

To all of them we would like to express our sincere thanks.

We are also grateful to our colleagues, Professor Henri-Claude de Bettignies, Professor Wilfried Vanhonacker and Professor Peter Williamson for allowing us to include some of their own case material in this book. It is the shared expertise on Asia assembled in our school in Fontainebleau which has made this project possible.

Last, but not least, we have to thank Joan Lewis for keeping the text (and us) on track and under control. Coordinating a project between so many parties, most of them not located in France, or travelling extensively, is a task requiring exceptional skills and patience.

PREFACE

This case and text book series was conceived to meet a need felt by business school faculty for a set of volumes comprising recent international cases which have shown to be effective by the hard test of actual classroom use. Although cases were the motivation, the series' editorial board insisted that there be an accompanying text that would guide the reader, whether professor, student, or just interested party, through the fundamental concepts the case authors wanted to illustrate. There is logic for this insistence.

Learning with cases is learning inductively. The student reads and thinks about one or more specific observation, participates in a class discussion, and then tries to draw some generalizations useful in a different setting. This is the classical method of science; the method of Ptolemy, Maxwell, and Newton. As is true with their work, however, even a large number of observations can never prove the truth of any generalization. Many favourable observations under precisely defined and controlled conditions can only raise the researcher's confidence in his or her theory even if it is still unproved.

The business academic using cases, and the student learning from them, must appreciate early on that theirs is a field where large numbers of observations are impossible to make, and that conditions of observation cannot be controlled sufficiently to conduct anything close to experimental work. It might often seem to students that they are pushed to make generalizations from single cases. Worrisome in addition is the fact that the cases are not chosen randomly. They are typically selected to demonstrate a point or to suggest a generalization to the student. Rarely does a professor look for disconfirming evidence.

This is why business cases alone can rarely drive a convincing argument and why in this series the editorial board has sought to give considerable attention to accompanying text. The author's point must be woven of several fabrics: logic, examples (including brief reference to examples typically known to the reader), theories borrowed from formal disciplines such as economics, psychology, or sociology, and a draw on the reader's own experiences and intuition. The case itself is vital but not sufficient alone. It is perhaps the frame on which to weave the analysis.

We trust the reader will find the themes of these volumes well supported, and we thank the various authors for their enthusiasm and hard work.

H. Landis Gabel
Series Editor
10 September 1998

The Strategic Importance of Asia Pacific

Part
1

The Asia Pacific region

In the early decades of the twentieth century, much of Asia was still called the Far East – a region remote from its European colonial masters and the USA. It provided the West with raw materials and in exchange received small quantities of manufactured goods. Trading houses established in the nineteenth century flourished; enterprising industrialists set up factories in Japan, China and other countries; otherwise the Far East remained on the edge of the world economy.

Japan became an industrial country in the 1920s and 1930s, exporting massive quantities of cheap watches and textiles to the West. By 1941 it felt strong enough to attack the world's most powerful nation, the USA. Japan was an exception in the region: China, once a leader in many technologies, was in a shambles, and most other Asian countries had been exploited rather than developed by the colonial powers.

After the war, Japan had to rebuild its shattered manufacturing base. Mao's communists had taken over Shanghai, driving out entrepreneurs to Taiwan and Hong Kong. Korea, with an average income lower than Sudan's, was split in two after a devastating war. Manila, Rangoon and Saigon, however, flourished, promising a new era in Asia.

Much has changed since then:

- Japan has become a highly developed country, challenging US leadership in a number of industries. The newly industrialized economies (NIEs) of South Korea, Taiwan, Hong Kong and Singapore are among the most successful economies in the world; with sustained growth rates of 7–8%, their gross national product (GNP) doubled each decade. Today, they are the only developing economies likely to catch up with industrialized Europe and North America in terms of technology, infrastructure and per capita income.

- ASEAN member countries Indonesia, Thailand and Malaysia also showed a consistently good economic performance. By improving their infrastructure and building up substantial manufacturing sectors, they reduced their dependency on raw materials and agriculture. People in these countries, as well as in the Philippines, today enjoy much better standards of living than those in the overwhelming majority of Third World nations. Vietnam, which recently joined the ASEAN group, shows equally strong growth.

- In the late 1970s China opened its borders to foreign technology, trade and investment. As pragmatism increasingly overruled ideology, it became the fastest growing economy in the region (it did admittedly start from a very low base, like Vietnam).

Economists, journalists and business professionals widely use the term 'Asia Pacific', though which countries they refer to is often unclear. Japan, the NIEs, the five ASEAN members (ASEAN 5) and China are what we call Asia Pacific. This term is widely accepted – even if implying that Singapore lies on the shores of the Pacific stretches geographic credibility.

The division of Asia Pacific into four groups (Japan, the NIEs, the ASEAN 5 and China) reflects economic development patterns rather than political affiliations. Singapore – an ASEAN member but whose development followed more closely the model of newly industrialized countries – we place in the same subgroup as South Korea, Taiwan and Hong Kong.

Economic and political systems in Asia Pacific are by no means homogeneous. Officially at least, the Chinese economy still follows socialist principles, while Hong Kong and others are a capitalist's paradise. Macroeconomic data also vary widely. In 1995 Indonesia had 190 million people with per capita income of US$980; neighbouring Singapore had a population of less than three million with an average income of US$26,730. Japan, with 16% of the world's economy, has only 2.3% of the world's people while China, with more than a fifth of the world's population, contributed a mere 2.3% to world economy.

Despite these huge variations, a number of common characteristics can be found:

- Asia Pacific countries all aim at improving economic well being through individual efforts. They share a high degree of entrepreneurship, a determination to progress, high savings rates and substantial private investment in assets and in education.

- They are led by business-minded, outward-looking governments that support wealth creation through moderate intervention and policies orientated towards economic growth.

- These countries are consensus-orientated: efforts and results are shared within the nation, the local community, the firm or the family; income distribution is relatively even.

- A rather vague feeling of 'Asianness' – best described as being neither Caucasian nor African nor Latin American – is emerging, encouraged by regional media and growing contacts among communities.

The economies of Australia and New Zealand, while deeply intertwined with Asia Pacific, are not Asian in culture and don't have the same growth momentum. India is not part of Asia Pacific either, because of geographical distance, and a lack of economic and political ties. India, which opened up to the outside world only recently, has shown little interest in closer involvement with Asia Pacific.

Western firms and economists find it difficult to determine which countries to include in the region. Some follow our rather narrow definition; others include Australia and New Zealand. Alternatively, they use the much broader term of 'Asia'. But what is Asia? If it begins in Turkey and ends with New Zealand to the south and Japan, or even Siberia, to the north, it is not a very useful concept from a business perspective.

This book deals mainly with Asia Pacific – only a part, though by far the most dynamic, of Asia. With 1,700 million people, it is home to 31% of the world's population. Asia Pacific reaches from the cold deserts of northern China to the tropical belt of the ASEAN countries; it is so spread out that a direct flight from Singapore to Tokyo takes more than seven hours. Indonesia alone extends over an area wider than the distance from Paris to New York. As the millennium nears its end, however, Asia Pacific accounts for 25% of the world's output. This figure is due to increase, but not overnight.

The role of Asia Pacific in the world economy

Economic size compared

The easiest way to compare the size of economies is to look at their gross national product (GNP). This is arrived at by adding up the income of all participants: wages and salaries, rents, interest, profits and so on. This income is either spent on private or public consumption, or on investments, or is saved. Consumption and investments is the demand for products and services in the economy. Income saved is channelled back as demand, as long as the savings are given to financial institutions which in turn lend to domestic creditors. This simplified economic model allows us to use GNP data as overall indicators of demand.

According to the World Bank, Asia Pacific's total GNP in 1995 was about US$7.1 billion – about the same as that of the USA, and about 90% of that of the 15 economies of the European Union (see Figure 1.1 which shows GNP levels for the Asia Pacific countries and India). The problem with these comparisons is that the USA, and even the European Union, are fairly homogeneous markets while in Asia Pacific, the multinational firm faces 11 distinct markets with substantial geographic distances and differences in industrial sophistication, purchasing power and consumer behaviour.

Most Asian countries either have a large population, but with relatively little spending power, or a small, fairly affluent population. Apart from Japan (which accounts for over 70% of Asia Pacific's GNP), individual economies are relatively small (see Figure 1.2). The GNP of Singapore or Malaysia is probably not much larger than that of Boston or Munich, and Indonesia's economy smaller than that of New York.

These two traits do not make Asia Pacific attractive for the Western firm (except Japan, of course, but it is often seen as a closed market). A series of small markets, each with its own structure and regulations, requires a lot of management attention, and that usually implies high overheads. There are several reasons, however, why Western firms should not ignore the region:

- GNP data must be interpreted with great care, even if they come from institutions such as the World Bank, the International Monetary Fund (IMF) or the Asian Development Bank.

4

Figure 1.1   Total GNP in US$billion, 1995 (Source: World Bank)

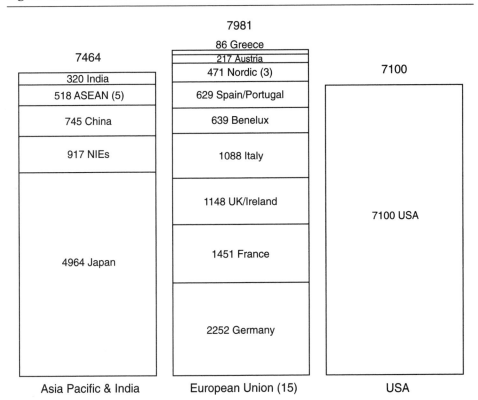

- Assessing present and future growth in the region calls for a long-term perspective.
- A trend towards regionalization in Asia may reduce some of the 'separateness' of the individual economies.
- There is more to the value of an economy than the size of its market. Asia Pacific is a major supplier of natural resources (tin, rubber, edible oil, crude oil, gas), of cheap labour and, more recently, of technology in the broadest sense (although only in Japan so far).
- Purely competitive reasons may advise being present in the home region of world-class Asian competitors. As global companies reassess the region's attractiveness, the need to pre-empt, match or follow competitors also grows.

Economic size reconsidered

According to the World Bank, only three of the 11 Asia Pacific countries are high-income economies, and only Japan and South Korea belong to the Organization for Economic Cooperation and Development (OECD), the 'rich countries' club'. China and Indonesia are low-income economies; the rest fall into the middle income category. But there are several reasons why the Bank's classification should be reconsidered:

5

Figure 1.2   Economic size of Asia Pacific countries, 1995 (Source: World Bank Atlas, 1997 and authors' estimates

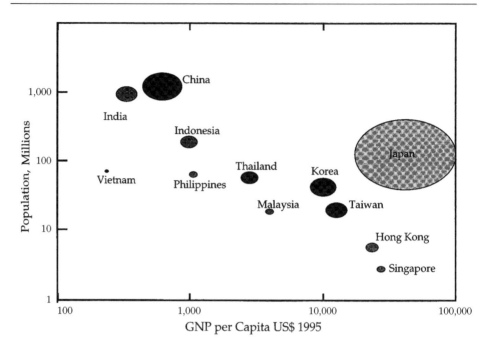

- As a rule, less developed countries have a comparatively larger informal sector, where the exchange of products and services is not recorded in official statistics. (An example would be farmers producing for their own consumption.)

- The statistics released by governments of developing countries tend to underestimate economic activity. (In some cases they deliberately under-report economic size so as to qualify for foreign aid and trade concessions.)

- To compare national economies with one another, statistics are converted into a single currency, usually the US dollar. This means that in countries with soft currencies, the dollar-denominated GNP can go down even during periods of impressive growth, as was the case for China through much of the 1980s.

- Theoretically, when economies open up to international trade, exchange rates start moving towards a point where price levels across countries become more or less aligned. In practice, major price differentials remain across countries for non-traded goods such as housing, transport services or education. Governments in developing countries usually keep these prices low; they may even subsidize them. As a result, US$100 buys far more local goods in Jakarta or Shanghai than it would in Tokyo or New York City.

For all these reasons, international institutions are now recalculating income and GNP figures using purchasing power parities (PPP) to make their data more realistic. The results show staggering differences, especially for countries such as China and Indonesia (see Table 1.1 and Figure 1.3).

Overall, the wide income differentials between rich and poor nations are narrowing, although they still exist. Taking PPP into account, China is the world's second largest economy. Even if the new PPP data are somewhat inaccurate, they describe activity in developing countries far better. If one considers China's consumption of commodities such as steel and cement, or consumer durables such as bicycles and television sets, its ranking as one of the largest economies in the world seems more than appropriate. Similarly, revaluing the size of the Indonesian, Thai or Philippine economies seems justified.

Assessing the size of an economy based on PPP measures comparable quantities of output. For the foreign firm, it is the first indication of the volume of business it can expect in a given country. It also allows for better comparisons of per capita

Table 1.1 Income comparison 1995 in US$

Country	GNP per capita	GNP per capita PPP
Japan	39,640	22,110
Singapore	26,730	22,770
Hong Kong	22,990	22,950
Taiwan*	13,000	N/A
South Korea	9,700	11,450
Malaysia	3,980	9.020
Thailand	2,740	7,540
Philippines	1,050	2,850
Indonesia	980	3,800
China	620	2,920
In comparison:		
Switzerland	40,630	25,860
USA	26,980	26,980
UK	18,700	19,920
India	290	1,250

*Own estimates.

Source: World Bank (1997).

Figure 1.3 Economic size of Asia Pacific countries based on PPP, 1995 (Source: World Bank Atlas, 1997 and authors' estimates)

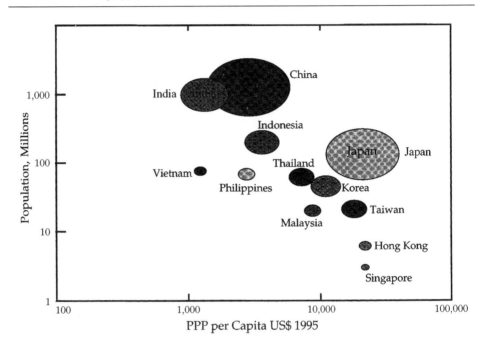

consumption. PPP statistics, however, lose their relevance once local profits are converted into the home country currency. In this case, it is current exchange rates that matter. The same is true when imports into a given country must be paid for in hard currency, or when investment decisions must be made based on revenues and expenses in both local and foreign currencies. In other words, while traditional statistics considerably underestimate the economic size of developing countries in Asia Pacific, in their accounts multinational firms must only consider values based on current exchange rates.

Growth as a driver and the Asian crisis

Economic growth refers to the increase in output, measured in terms of total GNP or GNP per capita. High growth rates are seen as positive, as long as they are not so high as to cause an economy to overheat. During the years 1965–1996, a period of more than three decades, Asia Pacific grew considerably faster than any other region in the world. A long-term rate of over 7.2%, which would allow the total size of an economy to double within a decade, was seen as normal in developing Asia, though unrealistic for Japan or any other mature economy in the world.

In a rare show of unity, international institutions, Asian governments, business forecasters and scholars around the world were optimistic about the region's future in the middle of the 1990s. The World Bank, for example, foresaw growth in the developing countries of Asia Pacific of nearly 8% a year until 2005. Any growth projection of this kind implied that Asia Pacific as a region would overtake both the USA and the European Union within the next few years. Based on PPP statistics, it already had.

The record of past growth and prospects for future growth created an environment of over-optimism and over-investment. When on July 2, 1997, the Bank of Thailand caved in to currency traders and unpegged the Thai baht from the US Dollar, the Asian crisis began to unfold. Financial turmoil spread from Thailand to Malaysia, Indonesia, the Philippines and later to South Korea. Stock markets, financial institutions, and finally many of Asia's heavily indebted companies were devastated.

Three main explanations can be given for the sudden and totally unexpected turn of events.

- As growth was almost taken for granted and economic success had come relatively easily, many businessmen in Asia had become growth maniacs. Projects were undertaken without due consideration of market risks. The result was the build-up of enormous over-capacities in many industries across the region, from empty office blocks to idle car factories. In financing their new investments, businessmen neglected basic practice: debt/equity ratios of 4:1 became the rule rather than the exception. Funds borrowed short-term were invested long-term. In addition a large percentage of those funds was raised in foreign currency, US dollars in particular, but was invested in domestic projects expected to produce a stream of income denominated in local currency.

  All of this worked well—until the moment that banks, especially foreign banks, refused to roll over short-term funds any longer. The depreciation of Asian currencies inflicted a heavy toll on companies unable to match their foreign debt service obligations with incoming cash flows in foreign currencies.

- Equity investments from abroad which had flooded into the five countries mentioned above slowed down when the banks stopped financing. While direct investment in 1997 remained at almost the same level as the preceding year portfolio investment, that previously had exceeded direct investment flows by almost 100%, turned negative.

  Commercial banks, attracted by high growth rates and pressured by peers not to miss out on the Asian boom, had provided the region with easy credit of more than US$ 50 billion in both 1995 and 1996. The same banks in 1997 took fright and withdrew US$ 27 billion. Proper credit evaluation could have avoided these excessive movements.

- Governments, themselves caught in the strong belief in an ever expanding economy, had neglected good housekeeping. Budgets were inflated, current accounts out of control, and supervision of the financial sector was weak or non-existent. Senior officials' vested interests in the economy made governments reluctant to undertake corrective measures quickly. The IMF and World Bank, hanging on to their earlier assessment of the region as the 'Asian miracle' came late with technocratic solutions for what had in 1998 become not only economic but also political problems.

In the second half of 1998, the situation in Asia Pacific looked grim. The Asian crisis had moved from financial shocks to the real economy and begun to inflict social pain on large parts of the population in terms of falling standards of living. The first hunger crisis for decades was reported in Southeast Asia. After unprecedented high growth rates over three decades, unprecedented high negative growth rates were forecast for the year. Japan, itself caught in a self-inflicted domesticated financial crisis, is finding it difficult to provide funds and lacks the political will to lead Asia out of its misery. The USA and Europe cautiously support Asia, though primarily through the levers of the IMF and the World Bank.

Very few Western companies are starting to withdraw. Many try to delay expansion plans and to survive by cutting costs, switching to local production and local sourcing. A few MNCs are vigorously pursuing acquisitions, an avenue of expansion that was practically closed in the past.

The overall perception of opportunities among Asian businessmen and representatives of the MNCs remains surprisingly positive. It is thought that growth will return to Asia, though it may take time. The period to recovery and future growth rates will probably vary considerably from country to country.

Strong belief in the long-term growth opportunities in Asia is based on two assumptions:

- Three decades of high growth across the region represent more than a short-term statistical phenomenon. The same people and resources that created the additional wealth over all these years are still around. Governments and businessmen will have learned from their mistakes. More transparency, greater competence, fewer market distortions can be expected in future, probably leading to a higher degree of international competitiveness.

- The fundamental strength of the region is also still around. It compares well with other parts of the world and is characterized by:

  high savings rates
  entrepreneurship
  young population
  low taxes
  high work ethic
  flexible labour markets

The limits of long-term growth

In the 1970s the Club of Rome warned that the world would soon reach the limits of growth. Since then, Asia Pacific has been a textbook example in the growth of limits.

This, however, does not mean that its long-term future as a fast-growing region is assured. If the growth in output of Asia's developing economies was based mainly on a higher input of labour and capital, there is a risk that they will experience diminishing returns, and therefore lower growth rates.

There are others reasons for concern. While governments strive to remove infrastructure bottlenecks, the lack of some basic services and facilities may already be slowing down growth momentum. The planned improvements may be 'too little, too late'.

A major worry is the dramatic deterioration in the environment. Bangkok's traffic congestion is notorious, as is industrial pollution in Seoul and Taipei, and even more so in the industrial centres of China. As long as industrialization and urban agglomeration continue to increase, living conditions are unlikely to improve markedly. In rural areas, aggressive logging and expansion of arable land have caused soil erosion with consequent flooding, or even changes in weather patterns. This is forcing millions of farmers into increasingly overcrowded and unmanageable cities.

Population growth, while lower in percentage terms than in parts of Africa or Latin America, results in unbearably high population density. China grows by 16–18 million people a year – as much as the entire current population of Scandinavia. The annual increase for Indonesia is 3–4 million – the total population of New Zealand.

More careful use of energy is needed in order to sustain growth and save vital natural resources. Both China and Indonesia are on the way to becoming energy importers, thus joining Japan, the Asian NIEs and the Philippines in their dependence on Middle East oil supplies, with serious consequences for their foreign exchange balances.

Rapid growth of income gives rise to feelings of unfairness. Ostentatious consumption is envied or detested, materialistic goals are questioned. Industrialization and the liberalization of markets bring efficiency gains and higher productivity, but also the danger of growing unemployment, as in China and Indonesia. Governments must work hard to maintain a delicate balance between economic growth and the risk of social upheaval.

Quality of life is another important issue. GNP figures only reflect the creation of material wealth; they fail to measure the extent to which human lives are enriched. It is only this broader concept of increase in quality of life which one may call development. In other words, high growth rates do not necessarily lead to substantial development, though they certainly can help. Depletion of natural resources and exploitation of cheap labour can result in high growth rates, as can the accumulation of wealth through corruption among the elite.

The vision of governments as regards the future of their society, the way in which they invest in development and take care of the needs of people and the environment are foremost in assessing sustainable growth potential. The analysis of macro-economic data is insufficient for this purpose. But any broader perspective leads us into uncharted waters. How does one measure quality of life? How does one weigh the limited availability of space in Japan against its low crime rate, and compare these two aspects with those in the USA? What role do climate, traffic conditions, the chance of a fair trial, the quality of services play?

The United Nations Development Program (UNDP) has tried to get to grips with this topic for years. It stresses the importance of an equitable distribution of the benefits of economic growth and the sharing of opportunities between individuals and generations. It also argues that the creation and accumulation of wealth do not necessarily fulfil important human choices: it is the use of wealth, not wealth itself that determines the quality of life. Respect for the law, maintenance of minority rights, equal treatment of men and women do not depend on wealth. Some Asia Pacific countries do not grant these conditions to their people, even if they claim to do so.

In an attempt to compare countries with each other, the UNDP has created a Human Development Index (see Table 1.2) with only three components: longevity, education and standard of living. Longevity is taken as an indication of health care, education as an indicator of providing people and society with an opportunity to improve themselves, and standard of living as an indicator of well-being. The UNDP ranks a total of 173 countries around the world, first using the HDI, then using income per capita. About half the countries in the region see their standing considerably improved when the HDI is applied. This means that they have been comparatively more successful in pursuing development in a broader sense than in simply improving their people's income in dollar terms.

Table 1.2 HDI ranking versus GDP per capita ranking

	HDI* world ranking	GDP per capita world ranking
Japan	7	7
Hong Kong	22	5
Singapore	26	11
South Korea	32	37
Thailand	59	51
Malaysia	60	47
Philippines	98	110
Indonesia	99	92
China	108	111
Vietnam	121	147
India	138	143

*This is a composite of three parts: longevity (measured by life expectancy), knowledge (measured by adult literacy and years of schooling) and standard of living (measured by GDP per capita adjusted to PPP).

Source: UNDP (1997)

Internal stability

A country's internal stability depends on its leadership structure, degree of social cohesion, and institutional and legal framework. In Asia, the debate about internal stability is dominated by a deeply-seated belief that a strong government matters more than a stable constitution. A strong government is seen as essential to launching and implementing successful development policies. This view implies that political liberalism is not compatible with economic growth (since it is difficult for governments to make policy choices, such as privileging investment rather than consumption, under pressure from special interest groups). China, Hong Kong, Indonesia, South Korea, Singapore and Taiwan have all prospered under authoritarian governments, while democratic India and the Philippines fared comparatively poorly.

This view needs some qualification. China and Indonesia certainly prospered, although not during all periods of authoritarian rule. The Philippines has experienced swings between democratic and authoritarian rule, but has always provided more public services and justice for its people than China, for example. While India enjoyed political freedom, endless controls hampered economic activity. And how does one explain the economic success of democracies such as Japan and Malaysia, or the failure of authoritarian regimes in Myanmar or North Korea?

Two lines of thought emerge in the dispute between the supporters of democracy and those of authoritarianism. The first argues for a staged approach: authoritarianism, it says, is needed to catapult poor, agriculturally-based countries into industrialization and a degree of prosperity. Only once societies become more complex do the shortcomings of authoritarian governments – often cornered in a closed political system by big business, the military and bureaucracy – become apparent. The better educated workforce and the emerging middle class will then face more demanding jobs that can be filled only by 'grown-up', responsible citizens whose active involvement in the economy inevitably spills over into society and government.

This change is accelerated by the media and increased contact with Western political culture. Germany made the transition to democracy during its phase of industrialization. Similar changes are taking place in South Korea, Taiwan and Thailand – countries that are laying the basis for a stable future where their citizens can actively participate in further development.

According to the second line of thought, it does not really matter whether a government is authoritarian or democratic as long as it is good. But what is a 'good' government? One that cares about its people and ensures that food, health services, housing and schooling are available at affordable prices. One that is honest and competent, safeguards its people's security, and acknowledges the civil rights of the individual and his or her right to own property.

An appreciation of authority is fundamental in Asia; conversely, the accountability of governments is not widely thought essential. The role of law and the independence of the judiciary are controversial subjects. Supporters of authoritarianism see both as undue limitations of the power of the government. Democrats argue that

13

such a system of checks and balances is not enough and call for freedom of expression, a free press, a multi-party system and an elected parliament. Authoritarians see these requirements as unreasonable restrictions imposed on leaders who are trying to do their best. They add that good governments listen to their citizens while non-benevolent leaders are automatically removed by their peers.

Unfortunately, even a long-serving benevolent leader may change and turn against his people. He may also die unexpectedly with his succession unresolved, and chaos will follow. Blind belief in authoritarian leaders does not ensure internal stability. Ethnic and religious divisions and economic disparities demand continuous and responsible government. This is best anchored in a strong legal and institutional framework that includes provisions for accountability. In the long run it is laws and institutions, not individual leaders, that give citizens trust in their future and encourage them to identify themselves as a nation rather than with their racial or ethnic group. This aspect of internal stability must be taken into account when assessing the risks associated with foreign investments in Asia Pacific.

Asia Pacific and the outside world

During the first half of this century much of Asia Pacific was under either colonial rule, or strong foreign influence. Malaysia and Singapore, then still united as Malaya, were British; Indonesia was ruled by the Dutch. The Americans governed the Philippines, the French Vietnam, the Japanese Korea and Taiwan. Colonial rule came to an end in the decade after the Second World War (except in Malaya, in 1957, and Hong Kong in 1997). While Europeans have generally left the region, US influence has expanded.

Relations between newly-independent countries and their former rulers are mixed. The Dutch have had difficult times in Indonesia, as have the Americans in the Philippines. The British sometimes find cooperation with Malaysia hard, and the Japanese are occasionally exposed to unfriendly gestures in Korea. As a new generation replaces those who lived through colonial times and occupation, relations become shaped by today's economic and political realities, as well as the influence of the international media and tourism. Dutch and French have become irrelevant languages in Indonesia and Vietnam. English is the dominant language of business in Asia Pacific, even among Asians, and the US dollar is the currency most frequently used.

There is a paradox here, bearing in mind Japan's overwhelming influence: as largest foreign investor as well as provider of technology, capital and aid in the region, largest foreign employer and number one exporter to most Asia Pacific countries. Japan, which occupied most of Asia during the war, had to withdraw completely, later re-establishing itself through trade and investment links. But the USA remains strongly committed, too (see Table 1.3). About 50% of all foreign investment in Japan is American.

Exports have made a major contribution to regional growth, rising faster than anywhere else in the world: by 1995, Asia Pacific accounted for 26% of world exports (compared with 11% in 1965). While Japan is by far the region's largest exporter, its

Table 1.3 Ranking of foreign investors in Asia Pacific*

Host country	No. 1 foreign investor	No. 2 foreign investor	No. 3 foreign investor
Japan	USA	Netherlands	Switzerland
South Korea	Japan	USA	Netherlands
Taiwan	Japan	USA	Netherlands
Hong Kong	Japan	USA	UK
Singapore	USA	Japan	UK
Indonesia	Japan	USA	UK
Thailand	Japan	USA	UK
Malaysia	Japan	USA	UK
Philippines	USA	Japan	UK
China	Japan	USA	UK

*Cumulative Direct Foreign Investment; the picture is somewhat distorted as regional investors (from Hong Kong, Taiwan, China and Singapore) are excluded, though they play a very important role as investors in Hong Kong, China and all the ASEAN countries. The true origin of such neighbourly investment is often unclear. Foreign investment is often redirected domestic investment.

Source: UNDP (1996)

share in total Asian exports is dropping. This is due to the trade activities of Korean and Chinese firms, and to a shift of export-orientated manufacturing from Japan to other countries in the region.

By far the most important non-Asian destination for exports is the USA, which runs a major trade deficit with Asia Pacific; Japan runs a major trade surplus (see Table 1.4). Because the USA is a major market, it exerts significant power over regional trade policies, as its endless trade disputes with Japan testify. Past arguments over the extension of Most Favored Nation (MFN) status to China, intellectual property rights in Taiwan and Thailand illustrate these countries' dependence on the USA. As the only remaining superpower and with a military presence in Japan and South Korea, the USA also provides security to the region, balancing the influence of Japan and the growing assertiveness of China. This gives Americans additional weight in government negotiations and explains why their taking a leading role in APEC (Asia Pacific Economic Cooperation) has been accepted.

Inter-regional cooperation

Asia Pacific has had far less success than Europe and North America in institutionalizing economic and political cooperation. Historical legacies, gross disparities among countries and alliances with different superpowers still prevent the region from

Table 1.4 Main trading partners

Imports		Exports	
Into:	**From:**	**From:**	**To:**
Japan	USA	Japan	USA
S. Korea	Japan	S. Korea	USA
Taiwan	Japan	Taiwan	USA (Hong Kong)
Hong Kong	China (Japan)	Hong Kong	China (USA)
Singapore	Japan	Singapore	USA
Malaysia	Japan	Malaysia	USA (Singapore)
Indonesia	Japan	Indonesia	Japan
Thailand	Japan	Thailand	USA
Philippines	Japan	Philippines	USA
China	Hong Kong (Japan)	China	Hong Kong (Japan)

NB: Figures in brackets give second largest trading partners.
*Both countries are equally important.
Source: Asian Development Bank (1996)

speaking with a common voice in international negotiations and reaching a consensus on important issues.

The APEC group is one of many recent initiatives to increase cooperation. Structured as a debating club whose decisions are not binding, it certainly lacks teeth. Representing 50% of the world's population, 50% of its output and 40% of global trade, it is closer to a mini-World Trade Organization than a regional forum based on common interests. APEC cannot even claim to be a truly Asia Pacific body, since its members include the USA and Canada. No wonder that some governments (Malaysia in particular) feel that their efforts to promote greater Asian unity have been hijacked.

ASEAN, formed in 1967, groups Thailand, Malaysia, Singapore, Indonesia, the Philippines and Brunei. A tightly knit anti-communist group, for many years it was effective mainly in security matters. Despite many attempts to foster inter-ASEAN trade and investments, member countries still do most of their business with outside partners. To avoid becoming irrelevant when communism faded and Vietnam became a potential new member rather than a common enemy, ASEAN launched AFTA, the ASEAN Free Trade Association. AFTA is supposed to convert the area into a free trade zone in the future, but so many exceptions and exemptions were built into the last agreement that it should not be expected to give much of a boost to member economies, nor to greatly influence business investment decisions. The admittance of two new members (Myanma and Laos) in addition to Vietnam did not add to its clout.

The failure of governments to bind their countries together is in sharp contrast with the increase in inter-regional trade and investments. The close links between China, Taiwan and Hong Kong are the best example of the conflict of interests between governments and business communities.

The leading forces for regional economic integration are the Overseas Chinese, with their nationless enterprises and multinational firms, mainly of Japanese and more recently also of Korean and Taiwanese origin. The Overseas Chinese are the dominant investors in China, and Hong Kong and China are each other's largest trading partner. Taiwanese and Korean firms are important investors in Vietnam, while Singaporeans play an important role in Malaysia and the Philippines.

While inter-regional trade and investment is growing considerably, one cannot talk of the emergence of a third large trade bloc: trade with, and investment in, other parts of the world are also expanding. Exchanges with European countries often exceed those with next-door neighbours. Most of developing Asia is increasingly dependent on funding and technology from Japan – whose exports and investment are still overwhelmingly directed at the USA. The role of Singapore and Hong Kong as transshipment centres also leads to artificially high inter-regional trade figures. The increase of activity within the growth triangle of Singapore, Johore (Malaysia) and Batam (Indonesia) reflects the integration of adjacent localities rather than an increase in inter-Asian trade and investment. Similarly, the intensification of exchanges between Hong Kong and southern China was only the prologue to the former colony's integration into China.

Much of the trade and investment flow within Asia Pacific is based on a division of labour, in the sense that different countries carry out different activities in the value chain. The country of destination and final consumption is frequently a third one, often the USA. For example, Matsushita's 14 plants in Malaysia are financed by the Japanese and induce exports of machinery, parts and components from Japan; however, their main objective is to establish 'triangular trade' with the USA so as to capitalize on Malaysia's Generalized System of Preferences (GSP) status and the absence of quotas for certain products from Japan. While statistically such investments and exports from Japan count as inter-regional trade, it is doubtful that they lead to closer regional integration.

External stability and sources of conflict

The boundaries of some Asian countries result from historical accident rather than long-standing national identities. In a decade that has witnessed the disintegration of the Soviet Union and Yugoslavia, the foundation of many new states and the reunification of Germany, the inviolability of countries or nation states is called into question. Neither separatist movements nor unifying forces in Asia Pacific should be underestimated. One cannot help thinking of Indonesia, Malaysia and the Philippines, although none is under imminent threat.

China is a special case because of its size and history. In contrast with the ASEAN countries, it is racially rather homogeneous with tightly controlled minorities, and religion has no important role. This, and the strong desire of the Chinese leadership to re-establish itself as a superpower, argues strongly against the probability of a break-up such as happened in the former Soviet Union. However, minorities harbour dissidents who may be prepared to fight for independence; economic disparities between China's coastal regions and its hinterland could also threaten the country's unity in the long run. With potential disintegration looming in the background, China has reintegrated Hong Kong, will soon bring home Macao, and is actively pursuing the reunion with Taiwan. The latter raises by far the most critical issues, in terms of sovereignty and self-determination. Taiwan's fate will have a strong impact on the stability of the whole region.

In the split nation of Korea, the border between North and South will eventually disappear. While South Korean officials draw up plans for a slow, smooth transition, crisis management will probably be needed once the physical and ideological barriers that keep an homogeneous people apart are dismantled. A united Korea will be internally unstable and externally weak, to the relief of its neighbours who fear the emergence of an assertive and militarily strong united country.

There are several territorial disputes in the region, some of them between ASEAN countries, others between China and its neighbours. The major bones of contention are the Kurile Islands in the north of Japan and various small islands in the China Sea. The Kuriles, currently occupied by Russia, belong historically to Japan; they are the cause for cool bilateral relations. China's seizing of the Spratly Islands, which are claimed by several countries, raises suspicions about further expansionist moves.

Ideological differences have lost significance since the end of the Cold War. With the exception of North Korea, the probability of a conflict between communist and non-communist nations has receded. Pressure to improve the economic well-being of their people has pushed governments towards pragmatism, while the major communist powers have withdrawn their support from smaller countries and underground movements in the region.

Internally, however, ideological antagonism still exists. In China and Vietnam the authorities persecute those who dare question the monopoly of the Communist party. Hard-line anti-communist countries such as Indonesia suppress even movements vaguely leaning towards socialist ideas. In Cambodia, a civil war based on ideological differences rages on.

Great power rivalries continue to shape the foreign policies of Asia Pacific countries, though in a new way. The former Soviet Union has faded away. Although Russia remains geographically an Asia Pacific country, its influence has become negligible. This decline is more than compensated for by the re-emergence of China. A nuclear power in the 1960s, a permanent member of the security council of the UN at the beginning of the 1970s, China has taken a truly leading role in the region since internal turmoil and ideological warfare with its neighbours subsided. Today, with Hong Kong, Taiwan and the Overseas Chinese in its orbit, China is undoubtedly a superpower.

China's influence is only partly balanced by Japan – a country often described as an economic giant but a political dwarf. The subliminal rivalry between the two rarely surfaces, but clearly exists. It is complicated by a long relationship, embittered by Japan's invasion of China in the 1930s and 1940s. Since the Japanese emperor's visit to China in 1992, the two countries openly acknowledge their mutual economic dependence, and bilateral relations have warmed considerably. Japanese capital is pouring into China. Japan, however, remains wary of China's recent political assertiveness and the newly belligerent orientation of its armed forces.

With large military bases in Japan and South Korea and a naval fleet, the USA balances the influence of Japan and the growing assertiveness of China, and provides a security umbrella for the whole of Asia Pacific. Politically, it has close bilateral ties with a number of Asian countries and tries to direct their governments towards US ideals such as democracy, human rights or market liberalization. Through its membership of APEC, the USA has found a way to extend its influence multilaterally.

Culturally, US influence ranges from Hollywood films and hard rock cafés to hamburgers, chewing gum and, more importantly, its prestigious universities where Asian families are proud to enroll their brightest children. In none of these dimensions can China or Japan match the influence of the USA, although its efforts to impose its own values on Asian societies lead to occasional anti-American outbursts. Asia, however, largely acknowledges the stabilizing role of the USA. Japan simultaneously opposes and appreciates its interdependence with the USA. China rejects Americans meddling in its affairs, but at the same time admires its enormous financial, military and technological power. Deep down, the other Asia Pacific powers trust neither Japan nor China to secure their future. As a neutral, non-Asian superpower in Asia, the USA thus remains welcome, if only as a lesser evil.

As the twentieth century ends, Asia finds itself dominated by one non-Asian and two Asian superpowers. It is doubtful whether this constellation can provide the stability which the region needs to continue its rapid economic development. Suspicions are that two of the players will collude to undermine the position of the third.

The move towards Asianization

As the awareness of being Asian and a critical stance towards the West increase, the influence of the USA on Asia may fade. It has been argued that future conflicts will be primarily rooted in cultural differences, and will thus occur between different civilizations. A civilization in this context is defined as a cultural grouping at the broadest level with which people can identify – beyond religion, race and nationality. As interactions between different civilizations increase, so does the awareness of differences between cultures.

The question then is: is there a single or several Asian civilizations? Where are the similarities and differences within the region, or between Asia Pacific and the West?

Asia Pacific is home to three of the seven or eight major civilizations: they are Confucian, Japanese and Islamic groupings. (Hindu civilization is a separate civilization dominating the Indian sub-continent.)

The division of Asia between various civilizations may have serious consequences for any attempts to integrate the region economically and politically. As long as Japan considers itself unique, it will not be able to integrate fully and emerge as a regional leader. By joining the G7 (the group of the seven most influential economic powers), it has become an associate of the West and set itself apart.

China, on the other hand, could become the new epicentre of the region through its Confucian roots which naturally connect it to Taiwan and the Overseas Chinese in Southeast Asia. Should Confucian thought regain influence in China, it could also find common ground with the Korean and Vietnamese cultures. At this level of abstraction, the differences between a Confucian-orientated, but Chinese-led, civilization and the Japanese world become arbitrary and give way to commonalities. One could then envisage a single Asian civilization solidly underpinning a far-reaching regionalization process under Chinese leadership.

Such an East Asian civilization would leave others stranded. India would not join the region; nor would Australia. What choices, however, would there be for Christian Filipinos whose culture resembles that of Latin America? And where would countries with several civilizations such as Malaysia, Singapore and Thailand see their destiny?

In Asia itself the present debate emphasizes commonalities rather than differences. The strongest advocates of Asianization today come from neither China nor Japan, but Singapore and Malaysia. Led by Lee Kuan Yew, they depict Asian values as superior to those of the West, and often talk of 'Western decadence'. Malaysia's prime minister Mahathir still argues for an East Asian Economic Caucus which would bring together only Asian nations. Not surprisingly, Malaysia emphasizes good relationships with Asian neighbours, even with China, and loses no opportunity to complain loudly about supposedly Western interference in its internal affairs.

Asianness is clearly visible in daily life: Asians continue to prefer Asian music to Western pop stars; Japanese, Chinese, even Indian soap operas are staple evening entertainment across much of Asia. Karaoke bars dot the urban landscape and holidays abroad are increasingly taken in neighbouring countries.

Asian values provide a common thread across the region. While for the West the inviolability of the individual is dogma, in East Asia the individual exists only in the context of family and society. In contrast to the European welfare state, East Asian societies rely on the mutual support of families. Asians favourably compare their own thriftiness and deferment of present enjoyment for future gain with American-style overspending and indebtedness. Asians, they argue, make every effort to educate themselves; they display a strong work ethic and thrive in a morally healthy, consensus-orientated environment.

This somewhat idealized picture begs several questions:

- Will the so-called Asian values still hold once Singapore or Malaysia reach the same standard of living as Switzerland or Japan?

- How much of a morally healthy, consensus-orientated environment does one find in China or Indonesia today?

- How much are Asian values truly accepted across Asia's diverse cultures and religions?

- If 'Asian values' are equally valid and ingrained among Confucian Chinese, Buddhist Thais, Shintoist Japanese, and Muslims from Indonesia and Malaysia, then what is so special about them? Are they in any way specifically Asian, or are they simply common sense that can be shared by anybody in the world?

Learning about and learning from Asia Pacific

The conviction is growing in Asia that Asian values are not only different but also better then those in the West. Outspoken advocates point to drug abuse, crime, indecency, the decay of the inner cities or inferior economic performance in the West to support their case. They hardly mention the fact that some Asian societies also struggle with exploitation of women, child prostitution, excessive speculation and corruption in high places.

For Western business the confrontation with this newly confident, sometimes arrogant, Asia is a major challenge. The colonial times may be over, yet many Western firms still pay fat remuneration packages to expatriates from Europe or the USA while refusing to do so for an equally qualified Singaporean sent to China. They still talk about transfer of technology rather than best practice – implying a handing down of know-how to the ignorant, and often insist on 51% ownership in a joint venture in order to keep things under (their) control.

Asians find this behaviour patronizing and unacceptable. Increasingly, Western firms will be confronted with demands for equal treatment and partnership at any level. They will have to adapt their management practices, and change the way in which they think and act.

The West will get used to Asia's growing assertiveness. It has to accept that Asia Pacific has a different definition of human rights and that, for some time to come, Asian economists will continue to favour a strong government role in the economy.

Asia Pacific wants not only to be recognized as an economic success, but also to be taken seriously – politically, technologically and culturally – on equal terms with the USA and Europe. It resents being told what to do, and it is beginning to express its own ideas more openly and in more critical fashion than ever before.

The West will also be exposed to increasingly negative comments about its decline. Asians will expect it, not only to learn *about* Asia, but also to listen to and learn *from* the region. Western nations will witness the emergence of China as a military power and, sooner or later, they will give in to Japan's request for a permanent seat in the security council.

Asia Pacific is changing and modernizing rapidly, but as Japan's development over the last century has shown, it is possible to modernize without losing one's own identity and culture. Managing this change is an enormous task and will bring setbacks and disasters. The region's confidence in its new-found strength, however, will help it overcome the many obstacles that lie ahead. It will be crucial for managers and firms who want to be successful in Asia Pacific to constantly challenge their own perceptions and attitudes.

Implementing global strategies in the region will not be easy. It will create problems for those who believe in a simple, uniform world. Not many global consumers are at home in Asia Pacific. Only on a superficial level does one witness a convergence in beliefs and practices. Bearing in mind its recent successful development, the region cannot be expected to move towards Western societal, economic and management models soon – if ever. As Rudyard Kipling said 100 years ago, 'Asia is not going to be civilized after the methods of the West. There is too much Asia, and she is too old.'

References

Huntington, Samuel P., 'The Clash of Civilizations?', *Foreign Affairs*, Summer 1993, pp. 22–49. See also *Foreign Affairs*, September/October 1993, pp. 2–26, and November/December 1993, pp. 186–94.

Kipling, Rudyard, 'The Man Who Was', *Life's Handicap*, first published 1891.

Koh, Tommy, 'The 10 Values That Undergird East Asian Strength and Success', *International Herald Tribune*, 11 December 1993, p. 6.

Krugman, Paul, 'The Myth of Asia's Miracle', *Foreign Affairs*, November/December, 1994, pp. 62–78.

Lee Kuan Yew, *The Economist*, 29 June 1991, pp. 18–19.

Mahbubani, Kishore, 'The Pacific Way', *Foreign Affairs*, January/February 1995, pp. 100–111.

Probert, Jocelyn, 'The Investment Climate in the Asia Pacific Region', *INSEAD Euro-Asia Center Research Series*, No.9, Fontainebleau, April 1992.

UNDP, *Human Development Report 1997*, Oxford University Press, New York, 1997.

World Bank, *East Asia's Trade and Investment*, Washington, 1994.

World Bank, *Global Economic Prospects and Developing Countries*, Washington, 1994.

World Bank, *The East Asian Miracle: Economic Growth and Public Policy*, Oxford University Press, New York, 1993.

Zakaria, Fareed, 'Culture in Destiny – A Conversation with Lee Kuan Yew', *Foreign Affairs*, April/March 1994, pp. 109–126.

Developing Strategies for Asia Pacific

Part

2

ormulating strategies for Asia Pacific revolves around four major issues: defining the company's corporate ambition in the region, positioning the business, investing in new capabilities and creating an organization. The strategic framework in Figure 2.1 takes in all four.

An ambition for Asia Pacific

A company's objectives in Asia Pacific will depend on its global strategy. Other regions (North America, Eastern Europe, Latin America) and activities (diversifying, new products, new technologies) are also vying for the firm's resources. Companies should consider Asia Pacific for three strategic reasons: because of its importance as a market, as a resource base, and as a source of inspiration.

The importance of Asia as a market

In 1995, Asia Pacific produced an estimated 25% of the world's total output. For most Western firms, however, it accounts for barely 10% of direct sales or exports. (Figure 2.2 shows the relative importance of sales in Asia Pacific for major European and US companies.)

Before defining a strategy for Asia Pacific, a company should chart its position

Figure 2.1 Strategic framework

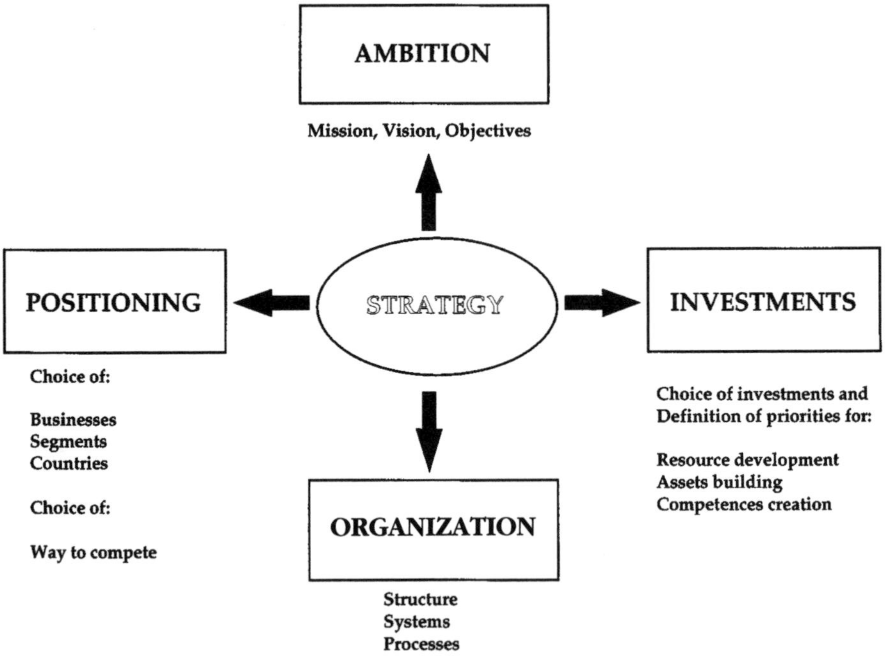

AMBITION

Mission, Vision, Objectives

POSITIONING ← STRATEGY → **INVESTMENTS**

Choice of:

Businesses
Segments
Countries

Choice of:

Way to compete

Choice of investments and
Definition of priorities for:

Resource development
Assets building
Competences creation

ORGANIZATION

Structure
Systems
Processes

Figure 2.2   Share of Asia Pacific for major western firms

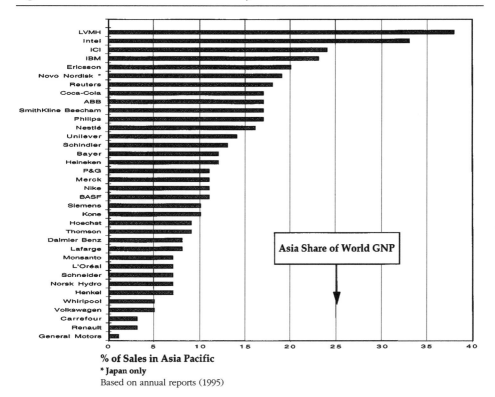

% of Sales in Asia Pacific
* Japan only
Based on annual reports (1995)

there *vis-à-vis* its sector as a whole, and each individual competitor. Does it have a higher proportion of its sales in Asia Pacific than the industry average? Is Asia, on the contrary, under-represented in its portfolio of activities? This will help it in several ways:

■ To measure the gap between its actual position in Asia, that of its industry, and the industry's objectives for the future.

■ To benchmark its position.

■ To reflect on the costs and benefits of such a position in both the short and long term.

Let's consider a major player in the electric appliances sector, where 1995 world sales amounted to 190 million units, including 56 million in Asia. This company, with 1% of the Asian market (some 600,000 units equivalent to 3% of its total turnover) had the ambition of selling 10% of all appliances sold in the region by 2005. To achieve this objective – which would amount to 12 million units, or 30% of its turnover, the company needs to devote approximately two-thirds of its overall investment in Asia.

The benefits of having a market presence in Asia are qualitative as well as quantitative. Because Asian customers are hard to please, markets such as Japan offer Western firms an opportunity to increase their corporate goodwill. A Western automobile components maker that supplies Toyota or Nissan gains a reputation for quality that can be turned to account in other markets. An increasing number of companies use success in Asian markets as a benchmark or reference in the rest of the world.

The importance of Asia Pacific as a resource base

Asia Pacific is a vast pool of natural, human and technological resources. Southeast Asia is rich in many raw materials, both mineral (bauxite, tin, manganese, natural gas, petroleum) and agricultural (timber, palm oil, rubber, fisheries, cocoa, coconuts). The region also enjoys a comparative advantage in terms of labour. Asian governments realized this in the 1960s and created export processing zones to attract foreign investment. The first industrial estates, located in Singapore, Korea, Malaysia, Indonesia, the Philippines and Taiwan, served as models for China's Special Economic Zones (SEZs). While productivity and discipline may vary, wages are far lower than Western standards and these zones have attracted labour-intensive industries as diverse as electronic assembly, textiles, and shoe manufacturing.

Technology is another key resource. Until recently, Japan was the only Asian country where Western firms wanted to set up research and development (R&D) centres. This is no longer the case: a Scientific Park opened at Hsinchu in Taiwan in 1980, followed by one at Kent Ridge in Singapore (1984). These parks offer infrastructure and skilled personnel at lower costs to attract Western research laboratories.

These resources all add to the region's appeal in terms of cost, quality, time and flexibility – the four major dimensions of competitive advantage. For example, a study found that a printing plant in Singapore had higher productivity (by 30%), faster time to market (over 50%), better quality (10–15%) and two or three times more models than a similar facility in the USA.

The importance of Asia Pacific as a source of learning

A presence in Asia Pacific exposes Western firms to a major, fast-paced industrial battlefield. Talented competitors, demanding customers and contact with a wide range of suppliers test their capabilities and force them to stay fit: Asia Pacific is a permanent industrial Olympics. Such a demanding environment develops strong competitive capabilities that are essential to long-term profitability. To use Michael Porter's terminology, some Asian markets are 'global platforms' where any company that wants to stay 'in the race' must be present. This is particularly true for new materials, opto-electronics, biotechnology or mechatronics in Japan; however, Indonesia is also a candidate for petrochemicals and process engineering, Thailand for food processing, Hong Kong for financial engineering.

Asia's business culture and approach to competition force Western companies to re-evaluate and adapt their own strategies and concepts. Success in Asia will depend to a large extent on their capacity to learn: from new kinds of relationships with suppliers, new approaches to managing people, innovative ways of packaging tenders in view of establishing long-term customer relationships, different ways of thinking about consumer behaviour. These lessons may be transferred back to the parent company in Europe or the USA with great profit – particularly in the fields of customer service, flexibility, total quality and human resource management.

Positioning in Asia Pacific

Positioning consists in a set of choices: does the company want access to resources, or markets, or both? Which countries does it want to operate in? Which entry mode will it choose – wholly owned subsidiaries, or partnerships such as joint ventures, licensing and franchising agreements? Which activities will it establish? Which segments will it compete in? Should it integrate its activities across the region, or country by country?

Resource-based, or market-based, strategies?

If the Western company's primary strategy is access to resources, it will target countries with the best and cheapest sources of supply, setting up sourcing offices or production plants in areas that have cheap labour (south China) or which specialize in processing raw materials (Sumatra, Kalimantan). There is a danger, however, in focusing exclusively on resources and neglecting Asia's potential in terms of markets, learning and competitiveness, as some US companies learned in the 1960s and 1970s. Their strategy of setting up assembly plants in export processing zones backfired as conditions in terms of labour costs and government policies towards foreign business can change quickly in the region.

A company with a market-based strategy will set up marketing, maybe manufacturing activities, either wholly-owned or with local partners. Its choice will depend on market potential, the competitive climate, government policies and its own capabilities.

Far from having to choose 'either resources or markets', Western firms should adopt an appropriate mix of the two so that the search for resources and markets form a mosaic of activities across the entire region.

Choice of countries

Western firms should consider several factors when deciding how to enter a market in Asia Pacific: its overall attractiveness; costs; their own ability to enter and develop the resources, assets and competencies needed in good time; government requirements; the competitive situation; political and operational risks. A firm will choose its country (or countries) of operations based on the attractiveness of:

■ its market: in terms of size, growth rate, segmentation, sophistication of demand, intensity and nature of competition;

- its resources: the availability, quality and cost of raw materials; the costs, productivity and attitude of labour; supplier networks; quality of information; financing; infrastructure; logistics;

- political and monetary stability, regulations, price and exchange controls.

While political and economic developments make some countries more popular with Western firms, conditions should obviously be assessed industry by industry. Each company must design its own criteria. This assessment is frequently made in two steps: first an evaluation of the political and regulatory climate (this is known as country-risk analysis); then a business analysis covering both market and resources for specific projects.

Choosing an entry mode and a development model

Before a company decides to enter a new market, it must decide what type of operation it needs there. Once it has become established, further decisions must be made in order to develop and consolidate. These decisions must be based on the company's experience and capabilities, as well as on the strategic appeal of different industrial sectors or countries.

An important decision is whether to enter a market alone, by setting up a new operation or acquiring an existing business, or through a partnership (joint venture, licensing or franchising agreement).

Countries in Asia Pacific command different entry strategies:

- **Platform countries** such as Singapore or Hong Kong can be used as bases at the entry stage for gathering intelligence and initiating contacts; later they can be regional hubs. Medium-sized companies new to the region can establish listening posts in these cities.

- In **emerging countries** such as Vietnam, Myanmar or Cambodia, it may be a good idea to set up a presence through a local distributor and a representative office; these will build the relationships needed to set up either a direct local operation or a joint venture.

- In **growth countries** such as China and the ASEAN 5, Western companies should expand quickly to take advantage of the opportunities offered by rapid economic development.

- In **maturing** and **established countries** such as Korea, Taiwan and Japan, a significant economic infrastructure is already in place; so are local and international competitors. The challenge is to build the operational capabilities needed to catch up with these competitors through either a joint venture, an acquisition or a large investment.

Choice of business segments and competitive approach

Segmenting in Asia Pacific is complex because there are many different marketing environments. At one extreme Japan has a very sophisticated and unique segmentation; at the other, Indonesia or the Philippines have largely rural economies and pyramidal markets. In between, the segmentation of the fast-growing economies of the NIEs is increasingly similar to Western markets. In China and Vietnam, it is still in its infancy but it evolves rapidly.

Literature on strategic management usually advocates an 'either/or' competitive strategy: *either* a company positions itself as the cost leader in its industry by offering lower prices, *or* it tries to differentiate itself through better technology, quality or services. In Asia Pacific this approach is inadequate: Western firms must offer low prices *and* good quality, *and* good service, *and* a short response time, *and* appropriate financing. The expectations of Asian customers usually range far wider than Western firms are used to. In Japan, customers are very exigent in terms of product and service quality. Elsewhere in Asia, consumers want the best of both worlds: great price and great performance. In other countries still, the decisive factor is relationships and indirect services. This variety calls for flexibility and sensitivity from the Western manager.

Orientation: regional strategy versus country-by-country strategy

In positioning a business in Asia Pacific, a company must decide whether to adopt a regional or country-by-country strategy. Asia Pacific is so diverse that there are as many differences between Japan and Indonesia as between Germany and Tunisia. The only regional economic group, ASEAN, is a long way from becoming a common market. Differences in habits, religion, government policies and regulations erect solid barriers between countries.

There are, however, several arguments in favour of a regional approach:

- Business functions such as strategic intelligence, financial engineering, R&D, training, and specialized services, only achieve economies of scale if they are in a central location from which it is possible to service the whole region.

- It is still possible for Western firms to achieve a regional or a sub-regional coordination of activities, particularly for components, spare parts and semi-finished products.

- Certain industries must serve regional customers and compete with regional competitors in order to make a regional strategy worthwhile.

- Because the directors of Western multinationals are used to thinking in terms of large regions such as North America or Europe instead of individual countries, managers in Asia Pacific often find it easier to obtain adequate investment resources if they present a regional perspective rather than a collection of country strategies.

Therefore strategies for Asia Pacific must combine a regional approach and a country-by-country approach.

Creating capabilities in resources, assets, competencies

The most salient characteristics of doing business in the region are the following:

- It is difficult to get reliable information.

- Maintaining smooth and regular contacts with government officials is essential.

- China and Vietnam lack a strong legal framework; the region has a general resistance to rely on the legal system to resolve disputes.

- Corruption is a frequent practice in some countries.

- Personal relationships, called *guanxi* in China, play a greater role in Asia than anywhere else in the world.

- Business cultures are hard to decode in terms of values, norms, behaviours and operational practices; the firm must invest in cultural understanding and develop a talent for learning.

- Financial profits are usually slow to come; this calls for patience.

- Western management approaches must be adapted without losing strengths such as quality, integrity, and technological expertise.

- Products or trademarks may be copied – with no legal redress available.

Western firms must then make specific, tailored strategic investments in resources, assets and competencies in order to meet the challenges raised by the environment and to build capabilities in Asia Pacific (Figure 2.3).

Developing resources

In practice, competitive advantage depends on six major strategic resources: financing, people, supplies, information, location, sponsorship. Western firms operating in Asia Pacific are at a relative disadvantage as regards all six, particularly people and information. Developing these resources requires continuous efforts: forming links with schools and universities, financing scholarships, sponsoring social and cultural events, cultivating relationships with journalists, lobbying, compiling and updating intelligence reports... All these cost money; the returns are difficult to estimate, but they are sure to take a long time.

Figure 2.3   Required strategic capabilities in Asia Pacific

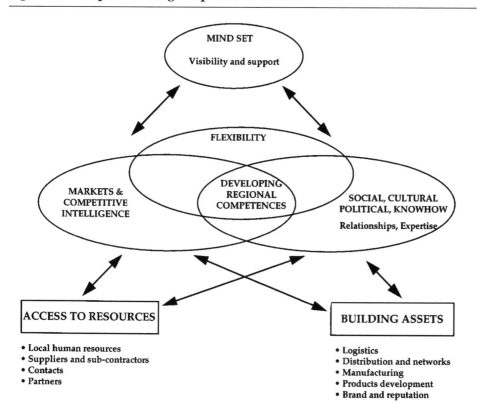

Access to resources is often complicated by the tendency of certain governments to grant preferential advantages to local firms.

Building assets

The two critical assets for success in Asia Pacific are technology and marketing. In order to create an operation, a Western firm will need to transfer technology to local subsidiaries or joint ventures. Downscaling operational infrastructure and adapting technology to local conditions also requires particular attention: the small size of many Asia Pacific markets makes it uneconomical to build large specialized plants. In the late 1970s, Western aluminium producer Alcan built a rolling mill in Malaysia. For all its growth potential, the Malaysian market could not justify a state-of-the-art mill. Alcan's efforts to design a small-scale plant were enormously difficult: its US and European engineers were used to thinking big. Finally, after 18 months of internal strife, a downsized plant was designed by engineers brought over from Alcan's subsidiary in India.

Marketing assets are often the hardest to develop, especially goodwill and distribution networks. In consumer segments, goodwill depends on the company's image and reputation; in industrial segments it is a function of relationships with customers. Asian consumers are acutely sensitive to image and services; Western firms must make a long, unflagging effort to develop a reputation. Building distribution networks and personal relationships is not easy because many local and multinational traders, Japanese and Western manufacturers and services firms have been actively cultivating Asian markets for 20 years or longer.

Creating competencies

Competencies in strategy are particularly important; Asia Pacific requires three sets of specific competencies:

- intelligence building (the ability to decode the business, political and sociological environment and use this as a basis for relevant business recommendations);

- a flexible decision-making process, capable of accepting solutions that differ from the corporation's core organizational norms or accepted practices;

- networking (the ability to partner and manage relationships with Asian firms in different cultural contexts).

To cultivate these three sets of competencies, the Western company must invest in:

- a cultural understanding of language, history and sociology. Asian cultures are at the junction of countless religious streams. China's 50-century-old heritage, the rich traditions and social norms of Japan, Korea, Thailand and the Indonesian islands, have long fascinated the West. The French and British diplomatic services trained civil servants specifically for Oriental postings. Modern executives who graduated from schools of engineering or business often lack the cultural sensitivity needed to operate effectively in this tangled web of cultures. It is top management's task to develop a cultural, technical and business sensitiveness to Asia. This involves training managers with specific competencies for the region, but also disseminating understanding and respect for these skills throughout the organization;

- gathering information. Publicly available sources are few and unreliable. Investing in intelligence does not mean simply buying a database or commissioning market research: it requires a physical presence and putting in the time to create a network of contacts and systematically cross-check information;

- relationships. Doing business in Asia Pacific, where great importance is attached to personal contacts, requires special skills in developing partnerships and acquaintances. Building relationships with suppliers, distributors, partners, officials requires appropriate policies and takes time. It is also a good idea to set up a communications network to foster cooperation and information exchanges among the company's managers across the region.

Organizational capabilities

When Western firms reach the point of designing an organization that will carry out their strategy choices, several questions are likely to arise. Should they adopt a country-by-country structure, a regional organization, or one that is global? Do they need a regional headquarters? Should Asia Pacific as a region be represented on the board of directors? What degree of autonomy should country managers enjoy? To what extent must planning, budgeting and performance evaluation systems be adapted to fit regional specifications? How should local managers be recruited and trained? How should expatriate managers be managed?

It has been argued that Western companies in Asia are weak because they lack adequate organizational support mechanisms. In many Western businesses, top management is unfamiliar with the region. (Top executives usually have held previous positions in businesses and countries that account for large shares of the company's business.) The company's norms, systems and procedures are often not adapted to the Asian context.

To implement Asian strategies it is advisable:

- to place a powerful senior executive in charge of the region;

- to create a regional focus through networking and, in some cases, by establishing regional headquarters;

- to try to infuse managers with an entrepreneurial spirit;

- to quickly develop a local 'elite' of managers who will spearhead the company's regional expansion;

- most importantly, to transform management systems and processes in a way which fits with the regional environment.

In Asia Pacific, Western firms must not only speak foreign languages and adapt to local cultural contexts, but also think differently (see Figure 2.4). To become players in the Japanese market, it is not enough for Western managers to learn Japanese; they must learn how to play Japanese in a Japanese game, according to a strategic logic that is often at odds with their own.

P&G is a good example. Its success at developing and marketing products in the USA and Europe was undeniable; however, when P&G applied its marketing expertise to a new subsidiary in Japan, the results were so appalling that it nearly closed down the operation. The company transformed its approach, and became so successful that P&G Japan is now a model of innovation for the entire group.

Figure 2.4   Transforming management practices for strategic success in Asia

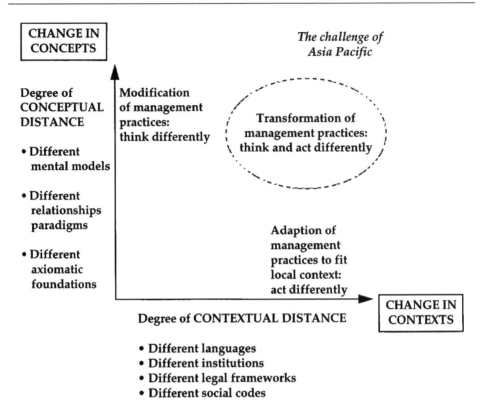

Putting strategy for Asia Pacific into action

The signs are there: the Asia Pacific century has already begun. Western firms must speed up their development in the region if they want to survive and prosper in the new global business environment. For companies already established in Asia, the challenge is to keep up with regional growth. For newcomers, it is to find and exploit a beachhead from which to establish and develop a presence in the region.

This has several practical implications; all companies need:

1. a strategic mandate for the region: rather than the simple addition of country-by-country strategies, it should express an overall corporate ambition for the region, supported by adequate resources; this mandate can be designed by using the framework proposed here;

2. an energetic approach: Asia is part of the global battlefield and must mobilize all corporate capabilities. The region is no longer marginal; it

becomes central to the corporation's strategic effort. ABB expresses this by saying it has to 'Win the Battle of Asia';

3. a special emphasis on developing people: the game is no longer to post a maverick expatriate speaking the local language to the Far East, but to create a many-layered population of managers capable of turning the corporate ambition into results. This involves:

■ identifying and appointing international managers able to pioneer business development in Asia by building networks, recruiting local talent and generating business opportunities;

■ rapidly developing local managers who can learn the corporate culture and manage local operations (some of them will later develop into international corporate managers);

■ that a product manager, plant manager or technician should welcome a posting in Asia and see it as a normal stage in an international career, not a waste of time;

■ that managers at headquarters should be convinced of the strategic importance of Asia Pacific, and familiar with its business practices and logic: only in this way will they understand and support development in the region. Just as the general manager must understand finance, marketing or leadership, he or she must understand Asian business.

References

Asian Business, 'Competition in Asia', October 1992, p. 4.

Hamel, Gary and C.K. Prahalad, 'The Core Competence of the Corporation', *Harvard Business Review*, May–June 1990, pp. 79–91.

Lasserre, Philippe, 'Why are Europeans Weak in Asia?', *Long Range Planning*, Vol. 21, No. 4, 1988, pp. 25–335.

Lasserre, Philippe, 'Gathering and Interpreting Strategic Intelligence in Asia Pacific', *Long Range Planning*, Vol. 26, No. 3, 1993, pp. 56–66.

Lasserre, Philippe and Jocelyn Probert, 'Human Resources Management in the Asia Pacific Region: A Comparative Assessment', *INSEAD Euro-Asia Center Research Series* No 25, Fontainebleau, January 1994.

Porter, M.E., *The Competitive Advantage of Nations*, Macmillan, London, 1990.

Case 1

This case was prepared by Philippe Lasserre of Strategy and Asian Business at INSEAD. It is intended to be used as a basis for class discussion rather than to illustrate either effective of ineffective handling of an administrative situation. Copyright © 1997 INSEAD-EAC, Fontainebleau, France

Chemical Corporation of America: the Asian Push

'As you know, we've been putting Asia at the top of our list for years, but until now we just haven't put our money where our mouth is.' Bill Ruthven remembered it well – he had stood there in front of the board, anxious to create a good impression, and contrary to his better judgement he had started his slide presentation with that attack. The annual board meeting for 1995, was held in Houston and attended for the first time by the new chairman. His presentation of an Asia Pacific Strategic Review was the culmination of nearly two years of work trying to convince the Chemical Corporation of America ('Chemco') group that Asia was vital to their long-term survival. With the looks he had received after that opening line, he had had a few desperate thoughts about his own survival.

As the meeting wore on, it became clear that many of the board members were preoccupied by other problems. By the time the discussion following his presentation had finished, Bill realized that there was still a great deal of work ahead for him and his team. Not only did it seem likely that the board members would give him long lists of questions to answer in a follow-up meeting in the new year, he also felt that he hadn't inspired them with the overriding enthusiasm he wanted them to have for Asia. But how could he do it? How could he convince them of the importance of this dynamic, difficult region in face of the complacency they seemed to have developed from decades of dealing with familiar markets in the USA and Europe?

THE RISE OF CHEMCO

Originally a small oil business, Chemco was set up in Texas in the early 1930s by John R. Lytle. Lytle was a 'wildcatter' whose initial assets were a few holes in the ground and some associated drilling equipment and supplies with questionable resale value. Lytle's enterprise benefited from one of the first recorded instances of project financing. It was clear that the oil in the ground represented a prospective value as a future revenue stream, and there were banks prepared to loan to Lytle based on the projected revenues without looking exclusively at his company's balance sheet or production assets for credit support.

Due to a run of bad luck in exploration activities Lytle's oil business ran into trouble in the late 1930s. He was bought out by a rapidly growing chemicals company but due to his financial expertise retained as chief financial officer of the merged firm, renamed Chemical Corporation of America. New exploration leases were purchased with the new capital and all of the oil went into the production of industrial chemicals and lubricants. When the USA entered the Second World War in 1941, the company obtained government contracts and grew with exceptional speed.

The big strategic change came in the 1960s and 1970s when through a series of bold acquisitions, Chemco transformed itself into an international chemicals conglomerate entering new markets in speciality and consumer products particularly in Europe. The oil crises in the 1970s reinforced Chemco's commitment to its diversification strategy.

In the mid-1980s Chemco's 20 or so companies were reorganized into six business divisions. As six new HQs sprang up in Chemco's Houston head office, the result was organizational complexity, increased bureaucracy and an immense burden on top management. Subsequently, through a programme of mergers and divestments, Chemco reduced its portfolio to four main international strategic business units (SBUs): Chemco Oil for oil and gas activities; Chemco Petroleum for lubricants and petroleum products; Chemco Chemicals for chemicals and speciality products; and Chemco Consumer Products, a diversified portfolio of companies in pharmaceuticals, cosmetics and health care. The results of the business sectors over the decade from 1985 are shown in Exhibit CS1.1.

Chemco was thus the parent company of a large, diversified group of companies in the oil and chemicals industries. In 1996 the group employed a total of 25,000 people in 15 countries.

THE CHEMCO ORGANIZATION

Chemco's top management in Europe praised the matrix-style organizational structure formulated at the Swiss/Swedish giant ABB in the late 1980s, and convinced Houston head office to adopt a similar structure for Chemco's companies. From 1990 onwards, any one manager reported to a product-line boss and a functional boss (in sales, manufacturing, R&D, etc.). Unlike the ABB model, geographical regions were not formally taken into account in Chemco's matrix structure, principally because Chemco was present in a small number of relatively homogenous countries. This, however, proved to be a disadvantage when it came to entering a new country or transferring learning within or between SBUs in a specific country. Chemco's four SBUs acted autonomously and there was little communication between them. Senior managers rarely met to discuss cross-business issues.

In early September 1995, Mike Kaplan was appointed chairman and chief executive of the group. He had comprehensive plans for the transformation of the Chemco companies through the imposition of a coherent strategy. He began delayering the organization by cutting the swollen middle tier of management and, through a policy of decentralization, empowered the SBUs. The Chemco head office also underwent a fundamental reorganization, aiming for a significantly downsized corporate centre.

It was against this background of organizational upheaval that Bill Ruthven's Asia Pacific Region team was struggling to convince the board and the SBUs to act in a coordinated manner in Asia.

CHEMCO IN ASIA

The company's earliest experience of Asia was in Japan in the 1960s. Japan, then well into a phase of long-term economic growth, represented a huge market for basic petroleum-based chemicals. In 1964, the year of the Tokyo Olympics, Chemco set up an office in Yokohama. This trading connection continued throughout the next 30 years, but with little attempt on Chemco's behalf to build an asset base in Japan, in part because of local regulations restricting foreign investment.

In the mid-1970s, Chemco Petroleum, under pressure from the US government, opened a small blending plant outside Manila to supply motor oil to the Philippine market. The business flourished, largely due to the availability of competent English-speaking local staff the operation worked well. In 1980 Chemco Petroleum opened a similar plant in Singapore after one of its Manila-based expatriates, Jack Shrigley, made a visit to the island-state and recognized the pace of development of its oil refining and trading activities. This activity aroused the interest of several executives at Chemco Oil, who conducted a number of investigative missions in ASEAN countries in the mid-1980s. But preoccupied with problems in the USA, Chemco ultimately failed to make substantial investments in the region, preferring to continue its piecemeal approach.

Prompted by a group in the head office corporate planning department, interest in Asia was revived in 1990. To them, it was clear that Chemco was missing out by not building up a presence in the region and their arguments convinced some board members. A regional coordination group, known as Asia Operations, was set up in Houston. The Asia Operations team prepared an internal study painting Asia as a region of opportunity. They attempted to promote investment by the SBUs in the region by focusing on specific markets. Breaking from the design of the newly imposed matrix structure, Chemco's head office opened small business development offices in South Korea, Hong Kong, Taiwan, China and Indonesia to complement the existing presence in Japan, the Philippines and Singapore. These offices had limited success due to conflicts over funding and country responsibility that arose between the staff in these offices and those in SBUs.

In 1991, the Asia Operations team tried to influence resource allocation by setting a target of 10% of group assets in Asia by the year 2000. Again and again the team drew attention to the group's overall portfolio, both in a business and in a regional sense, underlining the lack of investment in Asia and trying actively to steer the group in that direction. One positive result was that SBU management now felt impelled to include Asia when proposing a budget or a worldwide strategic plan. However, on the whole it appeared that the target was insufficiently focused.

By 1993, only three of the four SBUs had significant operations in Asia Pacific (Exhibit CS1.2). Overall the region represented 10% of group sales and 3% of group assets. Yet the region accounted for nearly 20% of world demand for oil and chemicals and was likely to account for approximately 30% by the year 2000.

At the September 1993 annual meeting to review group strategy, the Asia Operations team convinced Chemco's top management to make a firm commitment to increasing the group's presence in Asia. Yet, there remained a big gap between the rhetoric and concrete investments in the region. The task of pushing the necessary changes through the Chemco businesses was given to a newly formed Asia Pacific Region (APR) team that replaced the war-weary Asia Operations group.

THE APR TEAM AND THEIR TASK

The team that emerged was led by Bill Ruthven. He was assisted by Phil Lavers and Dave Aymer who had both worked in business development offices in Asia – in Indonesia and Taiwan, respectively. The quality of the team was augmented considerably by the addition of Sharon Marsing, an economist who had been in corporate planning since 1989. Later to become Chemco's head of economic studies, she was responsible for country reports and the economic side of the regional strategy.

The APR team soon discovered the depth of the opposition they faced in achieving even simplest attitudinal changes. For many of the managers, Asia was something of an unknown quantity and Asian projects were seen as high risk. Compared with the fast returns available in the familiar and still-lucrative markets of the USA and Europe, investments in Asia involved long time horizons with no immediate prospects of pay back or profit. The prospect of explaining early losses to shareholders was an intimidating one.

THE CAMPAIGN TO 'SELL ASIA PACIFIC'

Between 1994 and March 1995, the APR team battled to counter the SBUs' negative attitudes towards further investment in Asia. Almost daily Bill Ruthven, Dave Aymer, Phil Lavers and Sharon Marsing stalked the corridors of the Chemco business head offices, meeting chief executives, finance managers, human resource managers and so on down the line. As Bill Ruthven recalled, 'we were effectively running a crusade, trying to make the people in the businesses warm to the idea of Asia'. A set of slides, carefully developed to demonstrate the potential of the burgeoning Asia Pacific markets was shown and reshown. Gradually, managers became convinced.

In retrospect, Bill saw the process of getting a coordinated response to Asia throughout the Chemco group as a combination of preparing convincing country studies, providing courses on Asia Pacific, holding conferences, and finally preparing an authoritative and detailed Asia Pacific strategic review to be presented to the board.

1. Country studies

The APR team started by adding an innovative dimension to the individual country studies that had been regularly produced by the Asia Operations group. At the insistence of Sharon Marsing, intelligence was gathered by a group of 3–4 people recruited from the SBUs who visited each country and conducted exhaustive interviews with bankers, government officials and representatives of foreign and local companies. This provided a mechanism for tying the businesses together, and the high proportion of on-site research gave the studies credibility.

Each study gave a background history of the country concerned, its political structure, trade and economic policies, as well as opportunities for Chemco. It looked at each of the Chemco business operations, how these activities fitted together, and highlighted the main issues for the future. The results of these studies were presented to the chairman and several levels of SBU top management.

2. Courses on Asia Pacific

Another mechanism for raising awareness was to provide seminars on the Asia-Pacific region. From early 1994 onwards, a series of tailor-made courses held in the USA and Asia brought together high-potential middle managers from each SBU who had not hitherto been exposed to the region. Even if the managers in this group were unlikely ever to work in Asia, it was felt that exposure to the region was important. In February, Chemco's internal Senior Management Program devoted a whole day to Asia, inviting an outside consultant to lead the discussion and talk about opportunities in the region, where Chemco should be and where it actually was, and the reasons behind the gap. The same tactics were used in Chemco's lower level international courses.

3. Asia Pacific regional conferences

Two major conferences were held, the first being in Manila in March 1994 and the second in Bali in March 1995. Attended by SBU heads, BDMs and the APR team, the conferences were deliberately designed to bring together relevant decision makers and give them a feel for the region.

The Bali conference was the more important of the two. In his introductory speech, Bill Ruthven outlined what had been achieved since 1990 on a country-by-country basis, including growth in people on the ground and in assets. No one, he believed, could ignore top management's encouragement for investment in most Asia Pacific countries. However, he added, unless the businesses were clear on what they wanted to do together in the region and gave support for a coherent strategy for Asia, the group was in danger of falling into the trap of 'missing the boat in Asia' (Exhibit CS1.3). Was Chemco, he asked, really prepared to push into Asia seriously?

Central to the debate was the question: 'Is it really worth it?' The businesses had slowly begun to invest a little more in the region, as opposed to their former trade-only stance. However, their experiences had not encouraged them to view the region with optimism. Considerable investments in China and Indonesia by Chemco Oil had not yet been rewarded by an oil find, while Chemco Petroleum was still smarting over the failure of a South Korean venture.

The latter experience had, however, provided a salutary lesson by demonstrating to those at the top the importance of getting the right people involved in local projects. This meant having people who knew the country and how it worked, who knew how to contact government officials and senior business people, and above all who knew the market. In general, Chemco's efforts in the region had been expatriate-led with very little local management involvement. The expatriate managers stayed only a short time, eager to be posted to a 'more important' part of the group. This rapid turnover meant that little ongoing local expertise was being built up within Chemco.

The final day of the conference, therefore, was all about people. The SBUs were urged to look at their recruitment policies, with the aim of encouraging continuity among staff. The importance of recruiting local people who could provide essential local expertise was heavily underlined. After the conference, a database of all those in Chemco who had worked in Asia or spoke an Asian language was created, although there was no coordinated effort or master plan for the development of local staff.

4. Preparation of an Asia Pacific strategic review

In March 1995, the influence of the APR team was reinforced by the appointment of a former head of Chemco Petroleum, Jack Shrigley, to the board. Shrigley had been one of the first to take concrete action in penetrating the Asia Pacific region, having set up Chemco's Singapore office from Manila. He was given responsibility for both Asia Pacific and the Middle East, and Bill Ruthven and the team were to report to him.

Described as 'by nature a strategic thinker', Shrigley's immediate impulse was to urge the team to produce, in conjunction with people from corporate planning and with each SBU, an Asia Pacific strategic review for the board. Strategic reviews for Europe and USA were already well under way, so one for Asia should not be delayed. Over the next six months, he oversaw the preparation of the review, which included a political and economic survey of the region and an analysis of the strategic options open to Chemco in Asia.

At an early meeting it was decided that in order to appeal to SBU top management, it would not be sufficient to merely portray Asia as a region of opportunity. To catch the imagination and competitive instincts of the SBU chiefs, the message should be: 'If we don't get in there now ourselves, we'll get eaten alive by the competition when we try in a few years' time'.

The analysis of the strategic options available to Chemco in Asia began with a review of the implications of the current investment projections of the SBUs. In 1995, about US$440 million or 4% of the group's asset value lay in Asia, mainly in Singapore and the Philippines. A consolidation of the individual 1995 business plans indicated that in the next 10 years (to 2005), assets in Asia would roughly double to about US$1 billion or 6% of projected worldwide assets. In other words, if the businesses were left to implement their own individual plans without any head office intervention, in the year 2005 Asia would still only represent a fraction of the group's assets.

The team looked at a much wider range of competitors than it would normally consider in its traditional markets. For example it examined the Asian national oil and chemicals companies. Operating predominately within their own borders, their 1995 assets averaged about US$7–8 billion. The team also examined Japanese companies and calculated that their assets fell within a range of US$10–15 billion each. The assets of Korean competitors, which included Samsung and Lucky Goldstar, were estimated to be roughly the same. Compared with the giant international oil companies, Chemco was, of course, far behind. Placed in this context, it was obvious that even if Chemco doubled its assets in Asia to US$1 billion by 2005, the group would still be seen as a small operator and therefore be less credible as a potential joint venture partner than its rivals.

The inescapable conclusion was that Chemco needed to grow substantially faster than current business plans were proposing. The APR team, together with corporate planning staff, outlined four possible strategic routes for Chemco to follow over the next 10 years (see Exhibit CS1.4). Shrigley and the team preferred Option 1 and presented it in substantial detail in their final report.

Option 1 involved building up Chemco's presence in Asia in small steps, by devoting ever-increasing resources to the region in order to increase the pace of development. By doubling its investment annually, Chemco would follow the existing business investment plans, but at a faster pace. Chemco's growth would result from a combination of getting more people in, increasing its spending and above all, building up knowledge of the region.

The team calculated that the financial outcome of this strategy would be that group assets in Asia would grow to US$3 billion by the year 2005. This made Chemco a middle-market player and a suitable partner for growth in the 21st century. Remarkably, the SBUs agreed that the growth projections were feasible, and that suitable projects existed on the drawing board, however, they warned of a possible reoccurrence of the price slump which had eroded margins in the oil and chemicals industries in the early 1990s and which could render some of the projects unprofitable.

In addition to an evaluation of strategic options, the Asia Pacific strategic review contained detailed work on potential partners for Chemco, competitors' positioning, and a review of some of the cultural aspects of doing business in Asia. It emphasized the need for Chemco to get into Asia quickly while the competitive scene was still largely open and there were no significant barriers to entry. In this context, the team considered how windows of opportunity might open and close at different speeds in different countries. Would China, for example, be 'ready' in the late 20th or early 21st century? Finally, the report reiterated that the human resources dimension was absolutely vital. The key to success would be properly developed and managed relationships.

5. Presentation to the board

Bill Ruthven presented his team's Asia Pacific strategic review to the board in Houston in September 1995, complete with his famous opening line. Although there was a general acceptance that 'it seemed a good idea' and that 'Asia was an attractive proposition, given the group's portfolio', the board declared that it needed time to consider the strategy and compare it with the other regional reviews.

The timing of the presentation was not ideal, as it followed the inauguration of Mike Kaplan as the new chairman and chief executive of the Chemco group. Although a staunch supporter of the move towards Asia, Kaplan also had plans for an extensive reorganization of the group, news of which had just begun to circulate around the Chemco companies at the time of the launch of the Asia Pacific Strategic Review.

Nevertheless, the board discussed the proposals and came back with a number of questions. First, it asked the individual SBUs to prepare specific individual strategies for Asia. Could they look at the potential for greater investment, and show what they would actually do? What exactly, the board asked, were those additional prospects that appeared on the business investment lists but never made it to the final plans?

The second set of questions, posed by both internal and external directors, was whether Chemco had the number and variety of 'soft' resources necessary to achieve the profit opportunity and potential. Did Chemco have adequate US and European staff with the cultural adaptability to operate in Asia? Did it have the quality of local staff needed to assist and guide the businesses through the learning process? Externally, Chemco would need local advisors, political and cultural contacts, legal and tax consultants to help it through the Asian minefield. Did it have potential partners lined up to cover all this, and did Chemco have enough credibility with the various governments to obtain the licenses necessary to operate in different countries?

The final set of questions posed by the board concerned the focus of Chemco's efforts in the region. Clearly, Asia Pacific was not a homogeneous unit. Was the APR team saying that all countries in Asia were 'wonderful', or had certain targets been carefully lined up for the Chemco businesses? In retrospect, translating macroeconomic growth into individual business opportunities was pinpointed by the APR team as one of its most difficult problems.

Between October 1995 and February 1996, Bill Ruthven and his team went back to address these questions. With regards to the human resources issue, for example they planned a major initiative to encourage Chemco companies to recruit and train their own staff so as to be less reliant on expatriates. In principle, the business executive directors on the board agreed to this, and gave their go-ahead. First to take action was Chemco Oil, which designed a programme to allow local employees to undertake short-term job-related training at US and European universities.

In the end, Bill Ruthven's anxieties about how to fundamentally convince the board members of the importance of Asia were quelled by the new chairman. To set an example for external analysts and observers, as well as for the benefit of internal disbelievers, Mike Kaplan announced in February 1996 that he was taking the whole board with him on a visit to the region. News of the intended visit rocketed through the Chemco group, a clear signal that Asia was really on the investment map. For the APR team, it was a final endorsement of actions that had been taking place for some time. In March 1996, an updated Asia Pacific strategic review was presented to the board in Singapore.

THE SINGAPORE BOARD MEETING

Since the first presentation, the Asia Pacific strategic review had been refocused on specific potential opportunities for the individual businesses. The document presented in Singapore included, for each SBU, a graph contrasting the degree of opportunity in each Asian country with that SBU's capabilities. (Exhibit CS1.5 shows the chart prepared for Chemco Chemicals.)

For the first time all relevant information had been pulled together and included the revised report which also showed the extent of Chemco's HR experience in the region. Four 'softer' critical success factors were also identified: relationship management, localization, commitment and the ability to withdraw gracefully. The last was stressed because 'even when we have failed, as in Korea, we have built up goodwill that we can use if we try again later with the right partner and opportunity'.

After the meeting the board divided into four parties, visiting Japan, China, the NIEs (Taiwan, Hong Kong and South Korea), and the ASEAN five (Singapore, Malaysia, Indonesia, the Philippines and Thailand). During their travels, members of the board met government ministers over dinner, talked to external contacts and potential partners, and noted the reaction to the Chemco name. They also met local and expatriate staff in the region. The board returned to the USA very impressed by its experiences. As Bill Ruthven and his team realized, no mere Houston presentation could have given the board the same degree of confidence in their strategy.

**Exhibit CS1.1 Chemical Corporation of America financial results 1985–95
(US$ billion)**

Sales revenues	1985	1990	1995
Chemco Oil	2.5	3.2	3.3
Chemco Petroleum	3.5	4.0	4.1
Chemco Chemicals	1.5	2.5	4.6
Chemco Consumer Products	0.5	0.8	2.0
Total	8.0	10.0	14.0
Distribution of sales			
USA	70%	58%	50%
Europe	23%	28%	31%
Asia Pacific	2%	7%	11%
Rest of the world	5%	7%	8%
Total assets	**6.0**	**7.0**	**11.0**
Distribution of assets			
USA	65%	60%	55%
Europe	28%	30%	30%
Asia Pacific	1%	2%	4%
Rest of the world	6%	8%	11%

Exhibit CS1.2 Chemco activities in Asia, 1993

Chemco Oil

Presence in:

– China since 1990 (exploration)

– Indonesia since 1990 (exploration)

By 1993 Chemco Oil had spent over US$100 million in China, without success. Its efforts in Indonesia, however, proved more rewarding.

Chemco Petroleum

Presence in:

– The Philippines since 1976 (processing plant)

– Singapore since 1980 (processing plant)

– South Korea since 1990 (joint venture then representative office only)

– Taiwan since 1993 (representative office)

In 1990, Chemco Petroleum took a 40% interest in a new US$20 million blending factory being built near Seoul. Unfortunately, due to partnership difficulties the Korean project subsequently collapsed, with significant costs. This experience tended to reinforce the belief within Chemco Petroleum that it was 'better to build on what you have got', rather than begin long-term investments in new Asian countries.

Chemco Chemicals

Presence in:

– Japan since 1964 (sales only)

– South Korea since 1990 (sales only)

– China since 1992 (sold licence to Chinese state-owned enterprise)

– Hong Kong since 1993 (representative office)

It was estimated that by the year 2000, the Asian chemical industry would be the same size as the Western European and US markets. However there was 'a mentality gap' among the Chemco Chemicals managers: they thought of Asia 'only as a place to sell spare product if they were making too much'.

Chemco Consumer Products

No presence in Asia. Some products sold through agents.

Case 1

Exhibit CS1.3 Missing the boat in Asia

Problems

– Eager to talk about opportunities but not to develop concrete strategies to tap potential.

– Actual performance falls well short of realizing available opportunities.

– No clear regional vision and no long-term commitment to achieve such a vision.

– Fear of short-term losses while establishing operations – fear disproportionate to actual risk when compared with investing in other regions of the world.

– In contrast, main competitors take a long-term view (patient money).

– Little willingness to adapt to local business conditions and trust locals.

Result: Wasted Opportunities

– De facto strategy of sum of incremental decisions by business units.

– Fragmented presence – lack of synergy.

– Weak corporate image – limited visibility.

– Chemco companies are or will be latecomers in most countries.

Exhibit CS1.4 Asia Pacific Region strategic options

Strategic option	Strengths	Weaknesses
1. ASEAN and China		
Concentrate on ASEAN countries	Focus on key opportunities for growth	Weak presence in Japan
China push	Phased penetration of markets, manageable pace	Poor competitiveness if asset build-up too slow
Emphasize joint ventures	Establish strong positions for long-run growth	Long time to overall pay-off
	Project image of coordinated effort	
2. Pan Regional		
Push into all countries	Quick build-up of strength *vis-à-vis* competitors	Possible lack of shareholder support
Emphasize M&A	Earlier cash-flow generation	Complex implementation and logistics
	Includes Japan	Risk of spreading too thin
3. Japan First		
Build joint venture or alliance to strengthen position in Japan	Position in region's largest consumer market	Late entrant problems in rest of region
Longer term build-up in other countries	Build-up of know-how re Japan Strong scope for global alliances	Mature market in Japan Lose opportunities in China and ASEAN
4. Withdrawal		
Divest existing positions	Releases cash for alternative investments	Reduced global strategic flexibility
	Focuses HR on familiar markets	Major long-run competitive threats
		Lose access to regional skills
		Will be called 'chicken'

Case 1

Case 1

Exhibit CS1.5   Opportunites for Chemco Chemicals in Asia Pacific

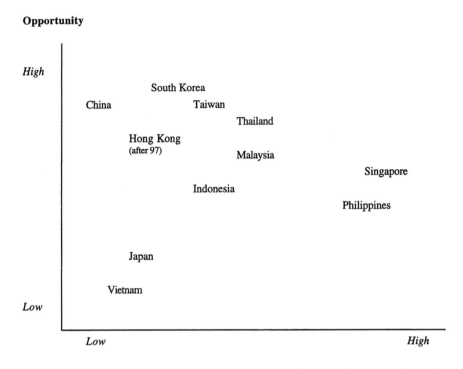

Opportunity

Case 2

This case was written by Jens Kjar (MBA '92) and edited by Huong-Giang Nguyen (MBA '93) under the supervision of Philippe Lasserre, Professor at INSEAD. It is intended to be used as a basis for class discussion rather than to illustrate either effective or ineffective handling of an administrative situation.

Gemplus Technologies Asia

In February 1993, six months after his arrival in Singapore as the newly appointed managing director of Gemplus Technologies Asia (GTA), Rémy de Tonnac, a 33-year-old French engineer, was reviewing the company's achievements. GTA had been created in 1989 to produce and market 'smart cards' in the Asia Pacific region. Originally a joint venture between Gemplus Card International from France and the Singapore Technology Industrial Corporation, the company had recently been transformed into a wholly owned subsidiary of Gemplus Card International.

The market in the Asia Pacific region was still in its infancy, with sluggish sales but good long-term prospects. De Tonnac had been appointed to promote the development of the company's operations in the region, and he gave himself to the task with great relish and optimism. However, since he was confronted with the dual challenge of penetrating a fragmented and diverse market with an emerging technology, the future was filled with imponderables.

GEMPLUS CARD INTERNATIONAL

Gemplus Card International was created in 1988 by five engineers from the French multinational Thomson, a manufacturer of a wide range of military and consumer electronics. In early 1993, four of the original entrepreneurs were still with the company: Marc Lassus, Daniel Legal, Philippe Maes, and Jean-Pierre Glotoh. With headquarters located near Marseille in southern France, the company employed more than 500 people worldwide. It was a private limited company with equity capital of FF36 million (around US$7 million) owned by a holding company and a range of other investors (Exhibit CS2.1). In 1991, turnover was FF350 million (US$70 million) of which 55% was exported. Gemplus had been profitable since year one, and in 1991 the company's net profit was equal to 15% of revenues (Exhibit CS2.2). Gemplus was a rapidly growing organization, and, according to the director of sales and marketing, Amedeo d'Angelo, the company's organizational structure was constantly changing.

The Gemplus management style was informal and the organization flat, and managers often had many employees under their charge. The general manager, Marc Lassus, concentrated on the long-term aspects of the business. Day-to-day operations were delegated to nine directors, who had a high degree of authority and were basically empowered to make any decisions within their

Case 2

given budgets. The general atmosphere of the company was congenial and very international. Altogether, 19 different languages were spoken at Gemplus!

International operations

Gemplus' declared strategy was to be a supplier of quality products and to promote, through the establishment of joint ventures or subsidiaries, the expansion of international markets for its card products. In selecting foreign partners, Gemplus tried to identify the most developed market segment and then find a partner who was potentially strong in that segment.

To date, most of the company's international development had been focused on Europe. A subsidiary had been established in Stuttgart to take responsibility for production and sales in the German market, and had a staff of 50 people. There were also sales subsidiaries in London and Milan, and a joint venture in Madrid.

Gemplus had a presence in the USA, South Africa, and, of course, Singapore. The US office was staffed by six sales people and three technicians who were in charge of developing the markets of North and Central America. In South Africa Gemplus had an exclusive distribution arrangement with a local firm, Net One Product (whose software Gemplus also supplied to its French customers). Gemplus Technologies Asia in Singapore was charged with developing Asian markets (with the exception of Japan and Korea) as well as those of Australia and New Zealand.

The remaining geographical markets in Europe, South America, and Asia (i.e. Japan and Korea) were served by a direct sales force operating out of Gemplus' headquarters in southern France. All of the foreign subsidiaries reported to both the Gemplus sales director Amedeo d'Angelo and the production director J.P. Avenier.

THE CARD PRODUCTS

Gemplus produced a variety of wallet-sized plastic cards containing microchips. These cards, also known as Integrated Circuit (IC) cards, were invented in 1975 by a Frenchman, Roland Moreno.

There were two different types of cards, each containing a different sort of chip.

1. *Memory cards*

   Memory cards contained a simple memory-only chip. There were several varieties:

   – Simple memory cards without logic protection.

   – Controlled memory cards with wired logic controlling access to the memory (using a PIN code).

   – Personalized memory cards, in which a specific area of memory, protected by a fuse, contained identification data that could never be altered once the fuse was blown. Access to the rest of the memory could be controlled by wired logic or be free.

Memory cards were typically used as pre-paid telephone cards (called 'Telecartes' in France).

2. *'Smart' cards*

'Smart' Cards, like memory cards, were based on a chip – but in this case a microprocessor chip rather than a memory-only chip, which meant that a Smart card was a computer (see Exhibit CS2.3). Smart cards had an operating system and a central processing unit (CPU), as well as internal memory. They were, however, inert: they operated only when a special read/write device provided them with power and exchanged coded commands with their operating systems.

Smart cards had multiple uses, and the number of possible applications was constantly growing.

The term 'Smart card' was often used as a generic term to describe memory and microprocessor cards when there was no need to emphasize the type of technology used in the cards.

Smart cards were commonly compared with magnetic stripe cards, but this comparison was misleading. A magnetic stripe card was merely a data medium. Comparing a memory or Smart card to a magnetic stripe card would be similar to comparing a PC with a floppy disk.

Information stored on Smart cards was highly secure. To access information, a person would need to know computer chip commands, personal identification numbers (PINs), and encryption keys. If a person found or stole a Smart card and attempted to guess a PIN, the card's computer would disable itself automatically after a specified number of incorrect PIN entries (usually three). The threat of reading or altering card information without authorization was almost totally eliminated, as was the possibility of card forgeries. The security provided by Smart cards was far greater than that of magnetic stripe cards; the latter, which in 1993 were widely used in banking, were plagued by fraud.

Standards set by the International Standards Organization (ISO) had been applied to Smart cards' size, electronic signals, and transmission protocols, but not to operating systems. Before being issued to final users, cards received logos to establish their visual identity.

Patents and licensing for Smart cards were managed by Roland Moreno's company, Innovatron, which also received royalties for the worldwide production of cards and readers.

Substitute products

Smart cards had a number of 'competitors', the biggest of which was cash, still by far the most widely used form of payment. Tokens for laundries, vending machines, and so forth could also be considered as competing products. In addition the Optical card was available. An Optical card was a read-only card that was able to store large quantities (up to 200 Mo) of information. Some of its disadvantages included the cost of production, the time it took to read the information, and the fact that it was not programmable.

Case 2

Gemplus' product offerings

Gemplus' product range included more than 40 products. In addition to a full range of Smart cards, there were four main product and service categories: hardware, software, development tools and customer support services (see Exhibit CS2.4).

1. *Hardware* products were primarily couplers and readers, i.e. the electronic devices which read and wrote on Smart cards, and which could be programmed for the user. Gemplus supplied couplers and readers both for immediate use and as inputs for original equipment manufacturers. The company also provided a number of personalization tools that enabled users to initialize, personalize and print graphically on cards. These tools were designed either for a manufacturing or office environment, and were driven by a standard DOS PC.

2. *Software* products provided the interface between the reader or coupler and application programs, enabling the user to send commands to the cards and receive information from them.

3. *Development tools* enabled users to develop subroutines in order to modify a card's chip operating system to fit a specific application.

4. *Customer support services*, mostly in the form of training seminars and workshops, were offered to help users customize chip operating systems.

In 1991, approximately 60% of Gemplus' revenues came from Telecartes, 20% from Smart cards, and the remaining 20% from hardware, software, services, and so on.

THE CARD INDUSTRY

Market size

The Smart card industry was young but growing rapidly. Worldwide production in 1992 amounted to 400 million cards with a total value of US$266 million. Memory card production was expected to grow 34% over the four years from 1991 to 1994 in the European market (see Table CS2.1), and some industry analysts foresaw one Smart card per human being in Europe by the year 2000.

Table CS2.1 Memory card market growth in Europe*

	Bank cards	Mobile phones	Telephone cards	Pay television	Others	Total production	Total value (US$)
1991 actual	3.87	0.00	40.70	0.38	2.39	47.34	16.30
1994 forecast	18.00	4.80	91.00	17.00	20.50	151.30	139.00

* All units in millions.

In the year ending March 1989, some 300 million prepaid cards (most of them magnetic stripe cards) were issued in Japan. These had a production value – as opposed to a face value – of 10 billion yen. The Japanese market was experiencing an annual growth rate of 50–60%, and it was estimated that it would be worth 220 billion yen by 1995.

Market players

Approximately 120 production licenses had been issued by Roland Moreno. However, only about 11 manufacturers produced and marketed Smart cards on a large scale.

In 1992 four European companies produced around 240 million cards for a value of US$160 million. Together, the four represented around 60% of the world market. All four were French companies: Gemplus (120 million cards), Schlumberger (65 million), Sligos (35 million) and Bull (20 million). In addition, two German firms produced a total of some 20 million cards. Other major producers included one firm in the UK, one in the USA, and three in Japan.

Gemplus' two largest competitors, Schlumberger and Bull, also supplied hardware and software products. However, both were large, diversified corporations, and the Smart card businesses accounted for a very small portion of their total revenues. The same held for most other manufacturers.

According to a 1990 study,[1] the Japanese had adopted a unique approach in order to overtake their European competitors. While the French were concentrating solely on the market which had the best long-term potential, i.e. Smart cards, the Japanese were focusing their efforts on the market which was largest at present, i.e., memory cards.

Card applications

Applications for Smart cards included: payment for telephones, parking meters, and vending machines; payment for leisure activities such as ski resorts, tanning centres, and pay television; bank cards and credit cards; city cards – for use of a city's medical and transportation services, for example security and access control; and so forth. Exhibit CS2.5 shows the range of applications for which Gemplus' Smart cards were used in 1993. Exhibits CS2.6, CS2.7 and CS2.8 provide further information about three specific applications: electronic voting in Norway, Sky Television in the UK, and Telecarte in France.

In Europe, applications were dominated by prepaid telephone cards, followed by banking and pay television. One big advantage of the telephone segment was that the demand could be fulfilled with a standardized product. In the banking segment, in contrast, cards needed a high degree of local adaptation, as each country had its own standards for banking transactions and transfers.

Amedeo d'Angelo estimated that Gemplus' 1992 revenues were generated as follows: 60% from the telecommunications segment, 20% from banking, 7% from health, 5% from pay television, 1%

---

[1] Steve Worthington and Ronald Brown, 'Plastic Cards in Japan', Institute for Retail Studies, University of Stirling, Scotland.

from transportation, and the remaining 7% from miscellaneous sources. The fastest growth was expected to occur in the banking segment in 1993 and the health care segment in 1995.

Sources of competitive advantage

Building and sustaining a competitive advantage in the card industry was not simple. According to Gemplus executives, a manufacturer producing large quantities of cards could achieve the required level of manufacturing quality relatively easily. In contrast, it was much harder, yet much more important for long-term viability, to build a durable advantage in the provision of hardware and software to complement the cards, or in distribution, sales and customer service.

Gemplus executives also pointed to the importance of providing 'complete solutions' to card system operators. Operators, who included telecommunications companies, local and national governments or state-owned enterprises, universities, banks, and golf clubs, were, in reality, a card manufacturer's primary clients. In order to offer a Smart card service to their own customers, operators needed not just cards and readers but also marketing tools, maintenance services, and so forth. Thus a card manufacturer, lacking the know-how to provide a complete package, often needed to form partnerships with other companies who could supply the missing services. Competence in forming such partnerships could provide the manufacturer with an important competitive advantage.

GEMPLUS IN ASIA

The creation of GTA

Gemplus Technologies Asia PTE Ltd (GTA) was initially established in 1989 as a 50/50 joint venture between Gemplus Card International and the Singapore Technology Industrial Corporation (STIC).

STIC was a diversified, government-controlled corporation with activities in shipbuilding, computer systems integration, industrial automation, aerospace and venture capital. In 1991 its total revenues were Singapore $1.2 billion (approximately US$700 million). Its principal markets were in Singapore, Malaysia and Indonesia, but it also had active operations in other Asian countries. STIC was organized into several subsidiaries, some of which were listed on the Singapore stock market. The initial contact with Gemplus was made when STIC's venture capital subsidiary, Vertex, acquired a minority stake in Gemplus' equity, although it was the systems integration subsidiary, STIC SI, that was interested in entering into a joint venture.

One of the original objectives of STIC in establishing the joint venture was to transfer technology from Gemplus to GTA. STIC envisaged this would occur through the establishment of local production facilities which would supply regional as well as domestic markets – most of the potential sales volume in Singapore was in prepaid cards for telephones or banking. The Singapore government was also interested in encouraging local production.

Gemplus had two principal objectives in establishing GTA. The first was to initiate a presence in a south-east Asian country and from this base slowly develop commercial coverage of the whole region. As with any new technology, considerable sales and marketing efforts would have to be directed towards educating the market, and STIC seemed to be a partner that possessed the necessary level of enthusiasm. Gemplus' second objective was to get closer to Japan and the Japanese 'sphere of interest' in order to learn about and better understand the Japanese competitors.

An agreement was made at the beginning to renegotiate the joint venture agreement after the first three years, which made both sides more relaxed about the set-up phase.

GTA's initial organizational structure

During its first three years, GTA employed 16 people. Two worked on specific application development, four provided technical support to customers, and five formed the marketing team that visited agents and partners around the region. The remaining five were support staff.

STIC's primary role was to provide manpower, including a local manager, and hence give guidance to the foreign staff on how to conduct business in Asia. STIC was also able to provide contacts with customers, although only in its own lines of business.

Gemplus Card International contributed the technology, detailed knowledge about present and potential applications, and, of course, the products themselves (cards, hardware and software). Gemplus also provided technical and marketing training for GTA's employees in both Singapore and France. All capital requirements were shared 50/50 between the two partners. Offices were rented.

It was Gemplus, rather than STIC, which had the greater operational control over GTA. Gemplus monitored GTA's activities through a variety of regular reports and meetings. Weekly reports covered customer contacts and ongoing problems, and monthly reports contained information on sales volumes, revenues and financial results. Board meetings took place four times annually with representatives from STIC, Gemplus and GTA, and were held alternately in Singapore and southern France. Technical and marketing meetings involved only personnel from Gemplus and GTA.

The first three years

The potential of the Singapore Smart card market had in fact been miscalculated in the initial plans. With a population of fewer than 3 million and an initial penetration level of no more than one card per person, demand was much lower than the minimum of 12 million a year required for a local plant to be economical. Thus, contrary to the wishes of STIC, products initially had to be imported from France. GTA's sales did not really take off until the second half of 1991 when a large contract in the banking segment in Singapore was obtained. GTA produced losses in 1990, 1991 and 1992, although profits were expected in 1993.

From the perspective of both parties, the joint venture faced several problems during the first three years.

According to Daniel Legal, Gemplus director of strategic planning:

We discovered how difficult it was to support an operational team so geographically far from headquarters. This was not only valid for the activities in Singapore, but also for those in the USA. A thing like the time difference between headquarters and the foreign operations proved to be a de facto limitation in the cooperation. We also found that it is not so easy to transfer know-how. It can be difficult to train someone else when you are an expert yourself. What is a detail to you may be critical for the understanding of the other person.

Gemplus also realized that the Asian market – which looked very homogeneous when seen from France – was in fact highly fragmented. There were big cultural differences between the countries in the region. Sending a Chinese person from Singapore to Thailand or Indonesia to do business with Thais or Indonesians often did not work. However, the cultural distance between the French and Singaporeans, which had been anticipated as a potential difficulty, turned out to be less problematic than expected.

After a while, Gemplus became concerned that potential customers might perceive GTA as part of the STIC 'constellation'. In cases where those same potential customers were in competition with one or more of STIC's businesses, they were often reluctant to engage in close business relationships with GTA.

Both parties felt that the French staff of the joint venture were not sufficiently committed. They felt that entrepreneurs were needed to create demand for a new technology, and that Gemplus was not supplying the right sort of people. Gemplus was relying too heavily on its local Asian partner.

The 1992 change in GTA's ownership structure

In 1992, when the joint venture's initial three-year term expired, Gemplus and STIC mutually decided to transform the joint venture into a full, 100% subsidiary of Gemplus International. STIC would continue to participate in the development of the Smart card and other related technologies by converting its equity in the joint venture into an equity participation in Gemplus Holdings, the controlling mother company.

All local personnel remained in the company, and a new managing director, Rémy de Tonnac, came to Singapore in September 1992. De Tonnac had been associated with the growth of Gemplus since its beginnings. From 1988 to 1990 he had served as marketing manager based in southern France, and from 1990 until his appointment to Singapore he had been director of sales for France.

The markets for cards in Asia

In early 1993, according to de Tonnac, the various potential Asian markets were at different stages of development. These markets could be grouped into five categories:

1. *'Take-off' markets*

   These were countries in which Smart card applications were materializing and where projects were beginning to be implemented. These included Taiwan, Singapore, and Australia.

In Singapore, Gemplus was engaged in a project with Singapore Telecom for the supply of Smart cards. A banking project for universal electronic payment was under way, and institutional and corporate applications for physical access and multiservice payment systems were also in the offing.

In Taiwan, where GTA had established a liaison office and a partnership with a local software company, a project for telephone applications had been started.

In Australia, Gemplus had initiated projects in pay television, telephone cards and banking.

2. *'On the Runway' markets*

These were countries in which contacts had been established, tests were under way, and applications were likely to take off in the near future. They included Indonesia and China.

In Indonesia, Gemplus had an exclusive agent, a software company that had developed a bank card application to be implemented in 1993. Technical assistance had also been given to upgrade public telephone booths designed by an Indonesian manufacturer, with the view that this collaboration would help Gemplus penetrate the telephone market.

In China, Gemplus had appointed four value-added resellers (distributors who provided additional services such as training). Projects in the field of banking, pay phones and radio telecommunications were being discussed. The local manufacture of fully equipped public telephone booths was a possible future outcome.

3. *'Ready to Board' markets*

These were countries in which initial contacts showed promising possibilities, for example Malaysia and Hong Kong.

In Malaysia, small-scale university student card systems had been implemented in thirteen educational institutions.

4. *'To be Confirmed' markets*

These were countries with potential but which had so far been disappointing. Thailand and the Philippines were in this situation.

5. *'Be Cautious' markets*

These were countries where potential was large, but where competitors were well-placed to benefit from any take-off in the card market. They included Japan and South Korea.

In Japan, NTT had purchased one million cards from Gemplus with the intention of testing them. It was considered likely that if Smart cards were to become widely used in Japan, Japanese competitors would quickly match Gemplus' products. The same would apply in South Korea. Matsushita was already active in the card industry and Korean firms such as Samsung were showing signs of interest.

Case 2

The future

Of the many items on de Tonnac's agenda, four were calling for special attention.

1. *Developing partnerships*

   Market penetration in Asia implied that a network of agents, value-added distributors and partners needed to be established. It was important to identify companies which possessed the right contacts, were capable of understanding the nature of the Smart card business, and were willing to back up their commitment with the necessary investment.

2. *Strengthening the marketing effort*

   A strong, creative, marketing effort was needed in order to convince potential customers of the benefits of Smart cards. The problem would be to recruit, train, and motivate local people in this respect.

3. *Organizational changes*

   It appeared that GTA in Singapore would need to evolve into a regional headquarters controlling and supporting national sales and marketing units.

4. *Dealing with Japan and South Korea*

   Although not one of de Tonnac's immediate responsibilities, Gemplus had to develop a strategy for Japan and South Korea. It would be particularly dangerous to ignore the huge Japanese market and potential Japanese competitors.

Case 2

Exhibit CS2.1   Gemplus Group – ownership overview

Exhibit CS2.2 Gemplus Card international financial results

	1989	1990	1991	Forecast 1992
Turnover (MFF)	150	227	350	450
% Export	32	45	55	65
Investments (MFF)	32	25	35	40
Patents applied	8	17	28	–
Employees	174	287	410	450

Exhibit CS2.3

What is a Smart Card?

The smart card is the size of a standard plastic "credit card" with an embedded computer chip. The chip holds various types of information in electronic form with sophisticated security mechanisms.

There are two types of smart cards:

- **Contact smart cards** require insertion into a smart card reader.

- **Contactless smart cards** require only close proximity to an antenna.

Some advantages of the smart card:

- Proven to be more reliable than the magnetic stripe card.

- Can store up to 100 or more times the information than the magnetic stripe card.

- Reduces tampering and counterfeiting through high security mechanisms.

- Can be disposable or reusable.

- Performs multiple functions.

- Has wide range of applications (e.g., banking, transportation, healthcare...).

- Compatible with portable electronics (e.g., PCs, telephones...).

- Evolves rapidly applying semi-conductor technology.

Exhibit CS2.4   Gemplus product offerings

■ **HARDWARE**

- Couplers
- Readers
- Personalization tools

■ **SOFTWARE**

- Pilot
- Drivers
- Tool-box

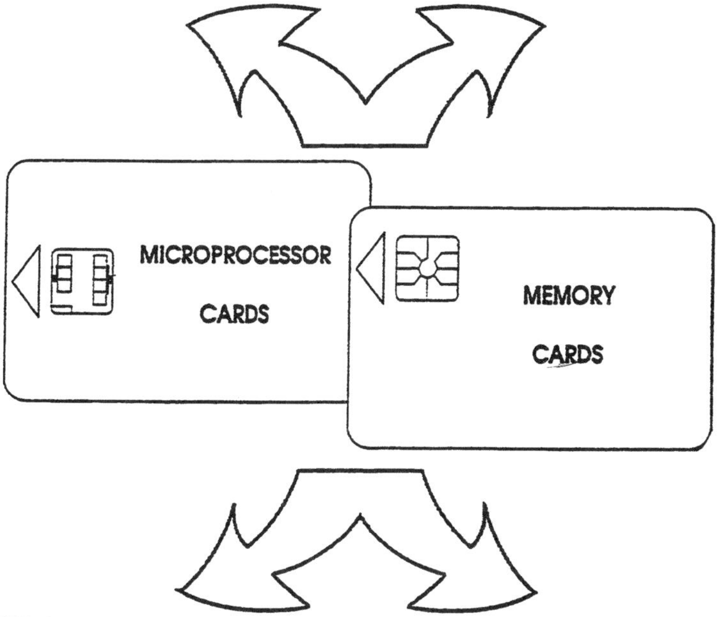

MICROPROCESSOR CARDS

MEMORY CARDS

■ **DEVELOPMENT TOOLS**

- Smart cards evaluation kit
- Smart cards programming kit
- Reader programming kit

■ **SERVICES**

- Specific code development
- COS subroutines development
- Personalization workshop
- Technical support and training

Case 2

Exhibit CS2.5 Applications using Gemplus' Smart cards

Application	Customer	Descriptions
Telecom	France Telecom	Prepaid telephone cards
	Bundespost	Prepaid telephone cards
	Telecom Eirean	Prepaid telephone cards
	GPT Lybie	Prepaid telephone cards
	Land Radio	Prepaid telephone cards
	France Telecom	Mobile telephone cards
	NR-GSM	Mobile telephone cards
Pay TV	Sky Television	Subscriber card for pay-TV channels (UK, Australia, New Zealand)
Banking and retail	CONF Commercio	Retail card for payments and services
	Keyline	Teleshopping card
	Banque Regional de l'Ain	Banking card and services
Company cards	CEA	Physical and logical access control
	French Treasury	Physical and logical access control
	CNES	Physical and logical access control
	Arthur Andersen	Physical and logical access control
	Aerospatiale	Physical and logical access control
	Seel	Physical and logical access control

City cards	Vitrolles (FR)	Access and payment for city services
	Courcouronnes (FR)	Access and payment for city services
	Chilly-Mazarin (FR)	Access and payment for city services
	Cergy-Pontoise (FR)	Access and payment for city services
	Jersey (UK)	Access and payment for city services
Leisure	La Plagne	Electronic purse and ski-station services
	Micro-BE	Prepaid cards for tanning services
	International Golfers Club	Portable file and services in interactive golf clubs
Transport	URBA 2000 (RATP)	Prepaid cards for transport
	Ivoir	Card against car thefts
	French Home Secretary	Identification card for cars
	Department of French Industry	Identification card for lorries
Health	Hippocarte	Medical portable file
	Biocarte	Medical portable file and insurance card
	Federation des Mutuelle de France	Medical portable file and payment automation
	Mutuelle des Alpes	Reimbursement of prescriptions
Logical access control	CMSA Sintra	High security for military computer applications
	French Foreign Office	Access to computer networks

Exhibit CS2.6   Electronic Voting in Norway

CIVIS

The most civic-minded smart card

- Cost reduction
- Elimination of fraud
- Confidentiality
- Quick results of votes

ELECTRONIC VOTING
CIVIS

Exhibit CS2.7   Pay TV in UK

The Sky Television Card

- Eliminate fraud
- Simplified system management
- Extremely convenient to subscribers
- Effective advertising medium
- Unlimited expandability

PAY T.V.
THE SKY TELEVISION CARD

Exhibit CS2.8   Pay Phone Card in France

The smart card for public telephones

- Suppression of vandalism and fraud
- Public telephones which are more reliable, convenient and profit making
- High-tech advertising medium which targets the general public
- State-of-the-art and evolving technology

TELECOMMUNICATION
THE PAY-PHONE CARD

Case 3

This case was written by Jocelyn Probert, Research Analyst at INSEAD Euro-Asia Centre, and Hellmut Schütte, Affiliate Professor of International Management at INSEAD. It is intended to be used as a basis for class discussion rather than to illustrate either effective handling or ineffective handling of an administrative situation. Copyright © 1996 INSEAD-EAC, Fontainebleau, France

Otis Elevator in Vietnam

It was summer 1995, and Mr Vu Trong Hiep, general director of Otis Vietnam, was reviewing progress in establishing the Otis name in Vietnam. Today he was in Ho Chi Minh City, the main hub of business activity in Vietnam, and one of three locations he spent his time shuttling between. If not there, he would be in Hanoi, the political capital of Vietnam, or in Singapore where the Otis operational headquarters for the Pacific Asia region – known as PAO – was based. In Singapore he had been (and remained for the time being) responsible for PAO market development in Indochina, and had initially surveyed prospects for the three countries of the former French territory from there.

Like all US companies, Otis had been shut out of the Vietnamese market until the US embargo on trade and investment in Vietnam was lifted in February 1994. Meanwhile, companies from Asian countries had actively sought business opportunities and some European firms were also beginning to establish toeholds. However, Vu had taken advantage in late 1992 of outgoing President Bush's decision to relax the complete ban on US business dealings, by seeking prospective partners in Vietnam and preparing the ground for opening a representative office as soon as the embargo was lifted. During the 18 months since February 1994 he had signed two joint venture agreements, but was still waiting to receive the investment operating licence for one of them.

Vu was convinced that Otis was in a leading position among the foreign elevator companies in Vietnam. It was the only company to have a direct presence in the country. Was this first mover advantage sustainable? How could he raise the entry barriers to competitors?

THE ELEVATOR INDUSTRY

During the late 1970s and 1980s the elevator industry worldwide underwent significant restructuring. By the early 1990s the market had consolidated into the hands of a few dominant firms. These included Otis, Schindler of Switzerland and Kone of Finland, as well as Mitsubishi Electric, Toshiba and Hitachi of Japan, and Goldstar of Korea. Most companies are strongest in their domestic or regional markets. Although Otis is the market leader in the USA and Europe, Mitsubishi Electric has the dominant position in Asia thanks to its strength in Japan. The fastest growing demand for elevators is in Asia, where market size in 1995 is expected to be around 80,000 units (of which 23–24,000 units will be installed in China), or roughly half of new installations worldwide.

The elevator business comprises three important elements: new equipment supply and installation; servicing and maintenance of installed units; and refurbishment of existing equipment. The first of these involves close coordination with a building's architects to establish the job's specifications, followed by negotiation and bidding for the installation contract. The maintenance element is conducted under long-term contract and properly maintained elevators will operate for decades. Given the sophistication of today's elevators, it is rare for a company to service the lifts of another company. It is not unusual that elevators are sold on a cost basis, and even with loss provisions. The service and refurbishment elements of the business are where elevator companies make their money.

The elevator market in Vietnam

The elevator market in Vietnam in 1995 is small and undeveloped. There is also very little industry data available. An accurate picture of the market therefore requires a painstaking collection of individual pieces of information – on existing installations, new projects in the pipeline, potential projects (for example construction projects for which financing has yet to be arranged) and new markets such as medium-height buildings requiring small, slow lifts. The chances of acquiring such proprietary information are improved if the interested party has a permanent presence in Vietnam. General estimates suggest a current market size of 200–300 unit installations per year, rising in a best case scenario over the next 10 years to 1,500–2,000 units.

In 1995, Ho Chi Minh City and Hanoi were effectively the only cities in Vietnam with construction projects requiring lift installations. Even in these cities most projects are likely to be 6–10 storey office blocks and hotels, with a small number of 20–30-storey buildings. In perhaps five years' time, some of the regional cities – Danang, Nha Trang, Haiphong – will begin to take over as Vietnam's fastest-growing markets for elevators. Maybe as few as 10–20 units will be installed in the central city of Danang during the next three years, however. Given the coastal setting of many of these cities (Exhibit CS3.1), most demand is expected to be from high class, low rise (three storey) resort complexes requiring lifts operating at, and finished to, a high standard. There will be fewer high rise office buildings of the type under construction in the main cities. Later, the government may build low cost, high rise social housing projects of the type common in Hong Kong and Singapore – a highly cost-conscious market in which to compete.

In the absence of any significant local manufacturing of elevators, Vietnamese import tariffs on complete lifts are 0%. Although this may change over time, government policy at present is to encourage general investment by keeping construction costs relatively low. On the other hand, duties are imposed on elevator parts and components at rates of 5–15% according to their import category (steel components, electric switchboards, and so on). Spare parts for maintenance work, therefore, are dutiable items.

In the wake of a number of serious accidents involving elevators, the Vietnamese government has implemented an elevator safety code and established an inspectorate to check on proper installation. It has also drawn up guidelines on approved manufacturers: a building with a lift made by a company that does not figure on the list will not be penalized but may find the inspection process a tougher proposition. Moreover, in order to import its product to Vietnam, an elevator manufacturer must get authorization from the Ministry of Labour, Invalids and Social Affairs.

At present, the distinguishing feature between the northern Vietnamese and southern Vietnamese markets for elevators is that very few of the projects in Hanoi are private sector or privately funded. Most are for government-linked organizations, so political connections are important. In the south, the majority of projects are either for private domestic companies or for foreign investment-related ventures, and winning contracts for these jobs requires a real marketing approach.

JOINT VENTURING IN VIETNAM: THE REGULATORY ENVIRONMENT

The foreign investment law in Vietnam requires the domestic partner to hold a minimum 30% share of any joint venture. This share usually represents the value of the land, in the form of land use rights, contributed by the Vietnamese company to the joint venture. Few state-owned companies have assets – cash, technology, machinery – to contribute other than the land they have traditionally occupied. Land values are calculated on the basis of official rental prices (for example in parts of Ho Chi Minh City, rents are US$12 per square metre per year) multiplied by the agreed duration of the joint venture. 'Goodwill' (or cash lent by the foreign partner, repayable out of the domestic partner's share of future earnings) makes up any shortfall in the local side's contribution to the venture's capital. The majority partner may have daily operational control, but Vietnamese law requires unanimity of decision making on such issues as capital increases, business plan approvals, financing commitments, and the appointment of the general director and the two deputy general managers. The minority partner can, therefore, play a blocking role.

State-owned enterprises are administered either by a central government agency – such as the Ministry of Heavy Industry, the Ministry of Light Industry, the Ministry of Construction, and so on – or by a provincial or municipal People's Committee. There may be intense competition and rivalry between centrally run and locally run state-owned firms. The Ho Chi Minh People's Committee is particularly powerful, by virtue of the amount of business activity that takes place in the city. State-owned enterprises dominate many industrial sectors. The role of private business was formally recognized only in the 1992 Constitution, and most privately run firms are young and relatively small. Joint ventures formed by foreign investors have 98% state firms as their local partners.

The State Committee for Cooperation and Investment (SCCI) in Hanoi is responsible for the final decision on granting or withholding business licences for all foreign-invested firms. Only foreign firms who manufacture in Vietnam may form joint ventures or (sometimes) establish wholly owned subsidiaries; firms that wish simply to distribute their products in Vietnam may only open a representative office and do not have the right to enter into contracts with customers directly.

Despite these various constraints, Otis felt that joint venturing was its best course of action. It had experience of joint ventures in other parts of Asia, notably in China, and was confident that it could handle the cultural issues and regulatory obstacles that were bound to arise. Based on Vu's research, which revealed the fundamental differences in the markets of northern and southern Vietnam, he identified and signed joint ventures with two separate companies. By summer 1995 Otis had the investment licence from the SCCI – giving the operational green light – for its venture with Lilama in Hanoi. It was still waiting for the licence for the Ho Chi Minh City venture with CEC, with whom negotiations had begun later. Vu was confident the licence would arrive soon.

THE PARTNERS

Otis Elevator

Part of the United Technologies Group, Otis Elevators is one of the world's leading manufacturers and installers of elevators, escalators, travelators and shuttles. It has 1,700 offices in about 140 countries and its products are sold in virtually every country of the world. In its ambition to be a truly global company, Otis moved quickly into China where it already has four joint ventures, and even aims to have a presence in the smallest markets such as Cambodia and Laos.

The manufacturing of Otis products takes place in two stages. A relatively small number of factories – in the USA, in Japan, Spain, Berlin, and Gien (France), among others – manufacture key components which are supplied to the company's many contract factories worldwide. Key components include the machinery, controller, door mechanisms and cars. The role of a contract factory is to assemble the lifts for local installation according to job specifications, but manufacturing or buying in the non-essential components such as wall panels which are much more cost-effective to source locally. The contract factory must have a strong network of reliable suppliers from which to source its non-critical components. Each contract factory also has a list of authorized Otis factories from which to acquire key components.[1]

Lilama

The Union of Erection Companies, commonly known as Lilama, is a group of 18 state-owned companies answering to the Ministry of Construction in Hanoi. It employs 15,000 people, which makes it one of the largest companies in Vietnam. It was founded as a single unit in the 1960s to install a steel mill. Subsequently, for each new large project in a new location, a separate company was established, leaving the older ones to sink into oblivion unless they found new business. Today Lilama's companies are spread all over Vietnam and are involved in heavy industrial equipment installations ranging from cement and steel mills to hydroelectric power stations and dams. The strongest and most profitable Lilama unit is based in Ho Chi Minh City. Some Lilama companies have experience of installing lifts – and had even tried to manufacture them, despite their lack of knowledge of safety requirements, using the 'learn by doing' approach which is common in Vietnam.

The affiliation between the various units is loose. Each member company has a general director and the Union has a small management team operating a peer management system. There is no consolidation of accounts. Each company manages its own accounts, and there is no obligation

---

[1] Otis Pacific Asia Operations (B): Regionalization, Harvard Business School case study N9-393-010, 1992.

for one unit to balance another's losses. This system may change in future, as the government pursues plans to form 'general companies', and a more bureaucratic, formal system of management may be imposed.

Otis was interested in a partnership with Lilama, both for its importance in the industrial framework of Vietnam and for its experience in elevator-related activity.

Construction and Elevator Co. (CEC)

Before 1975, the agent for Otis in the south of Vietnam was a private company called Engenico. Through them, around 200 Otis elevators were installed, mainly in Ho Chi Minh City. Engenico was nationalized in 1975 following the defeat of the South Vietnamese regime and the unification of the country. It was then renamed CEC and placed under the administration of the Ho Chi Minh City People's Committee. Twenty years later, some of the former staff still work for the company. Although moral and sentimental values played their part, Otis's choice of CEC as a southern partner is based on its good technical knowledge of the elevator business. Compared with Lilama, CEC is very small, employing only 70 people, but the company has a good reputation in the south.

Since signing their joint venture agreement in August 1994, Otis and CEC have been waiting to receive their investment licence from the authorities.

OTIS IN VIETNAM: NEGOTIATING THE JOINT VENTURE AGREEMENTS

Negotiating the joint venture with Lilama raised delicate issues. Specifically, Otis insisted on signing the agreement with the overall Lilama management team, rather than with one of the constituent companies of the Union. Included in the contract is a clause of non-competition, which prevents any of the member firms from forming joint ventures with other elevator companies. (Lilama is, however, free to make agreements with firms in other businesses. Among others it has already negotiated ventures with the LG Group – which includes Goldstar – and Posco, both of South Korea, for the manufacture of steel structures.) In light of the strength of Lilama's Ho Chi Minh City-based unit, Vu was particularly keen to preempt competition from that quarter.

Vietnam is clearly divided for Otis business purposes at Danang, which falls into the southern sector. Hue and northwards are covered by the Hanoi operation. The non-competition clause also prevents the northern and southern joint ventures from competing in each other's area. Again, Lilama was deeply opposed to being closed out of the market in the south, given the strength of its Ho Chi Minh City unit. Mr Vu was eventually able to prevail, on the grounds that competition between the two joint ventures for the same business would be self-destructive.

As the first foreign elevator company intending to establish a direct presence in Vietnam, Otis has seized the first mover advantage by forming joint ventures with two partners. It has chosen the companies it regards as the best in the country, and has removed both from the pool of potential partners for competitors. Its choice also allows Otis to address the crucial issue of competing political power structures. The backing of a company by a central government agency such as the Ministry of Construction is important in Hanoi, but carries significantly less weight in Ho Chi Minh City, where the People's Committee is largely able to set the agenda. A joint venture with a company under the aegis of the local People's Committee is likely to make more rapid progress in Ho Chi Minh City than one formed with a centrally run partner. The Ho Chi Minh City unit of Lilama lacked this local power.

Royalty payments

A sticking point in negotiations between Otis and the Vietnamese authorities, specifically the Ministry of Science, Technology and the Environment (MOSTE), is over the issue of royalty payments by Otis Vietnam to the Otis parent company. Under the Otis internal accounting system used worldwide, factories supply elevators at cost price to the sales subsidiaries, which book the revenues and pay a technical assistance contract (TAC) fee to headquarters. The TAC covers the ongoing Otis R&D programme and permits open and continuous access by all sales offices to Otis' technological developments. Disagreements with MOSTE centre on the application base for the royalty and on the royalty rate itself. Vietnam's laws on the transfer of technology propose a rate of 2% which is too low for Otis as well as most other foreign investors in Vietnam. The issue is even more serious for car manufacturing joint ventures. Some overcome the problem by charging the technology transfer fee in the import price of components. Otis does not want to resort to this arrangement and is still looking for the best solution.

Organizational issues

The Otis share in each of its joint ventures is 70%. Both joint ventures are structured in exactly the same way, as shown in the organization chart in Exhibit CS3.2. The organization differs from most foreign-invested joint ventures in Vietnam, in that the general manager and two deputy general managers out of three are expatriates. (Mr Vu is an overseas Vietnamese who has lived for many years in France. He has a French, a South African and a Japanese as his expatriate colleagues.) The standard joint venture organization in Vietnam has a local general director, supported by one Vietnamese and one expatriate deputy general manager. Within three to five years, Otis expects to localize all except the general manager position, and even this post should be held by a local Vietnamese as soon as Otis considers the succession capability is satisfactory.

More unusual than the organization chart *per se*, however, is that the Otis expatriate management team of four (including the training manager) is responsible for both joint ventures, with members shuttling between Hanoi and Ho Chi Minh City. The two operations are almost identical in terms of size and staffing, which makes it relatively easy for the expatriates to switch offices. Since each joint venture requires full-time attention, the four are kept busy but are thoroughly versed in the progress at both companies. The volume of business in Vietnam is not large enough at present to justify the expense of two expatriate teams. Even though the shared team reduces the cost of operations, Vietnam will still not quickly become profitable.

By the end of 1996 each joint venture will have 50–70 staff. The Vietnamese deputy general director of each company comes from the respective local partner. An important role for the Vietnamese deputy director is to manage relationships with the authorities, a time-consuming but essential task which can only be fulfilled satisfactorily by a local person.

Department heads are sourced either from the partner or hired externally. Although the partners were disappointed not to supply all the department heads, personnel with the necessary skills – for example to be the chief accountant or the finance manager – did not exist within their organizations. The management information systems (MIS) person, the sales manager and the estimator were all hired externally. 'We were lucky to find them', says Vu, reflecting on the shortage of skilled staff. Although local unemployment rates are high, rather few people have the market-oriented or technical skills sought by foreign firms. The person in charge of MIS ensures that both offices work on the same computer system. This has already involved changing all the software at the southern office (the newer venture) to assure compatibility with the Hanoi operation.

An inherent difficulty of Vietnam is the different concept of doing business. In other Otis joint ventures in Asia (with the exception of China), the local partners are simply interested in progress made and only want to be kept informed. Here, Vu feels that the partners are constantly tempted to comment on any information and interfere in the running of the business. They always want to know exactly what is happening. 'I don't need my shadow, I have a partner for that', he says. Vu has resisted suggestions from the local partners that, when he is away, the Vietnamese deputy should assume his responsibilities. He hopes that, if they meet the business plan, and after one or two audits by the Ministry of Finance, the partners will become less suspicious.

APPROACHING THE MARKET

In the initial stages, Otis is importing elevators on a project basis from France, Malaysia, Japan, even from the USA. The local team installs the elevator system, puts it into commission, and eventually expects to maintain it over a period of many years.

The Vietnamese authorities place great emphasis on persuading foreign firms to manufacture their products locally, in the belief that the transfer of technology takes place during the manufacturing process. The Otis stance, however, is that the real technology transfer in the elevator business takes place at the maintenance stage, since an engineer may take 10 or even 20 years to learn perfectly the workings of the equipment. A trained engineer is a highly skilled technician, who is not only able to troubleshoot but can also conceive the inner workings of the machinery. In contrast, any manufacturing that Otis would do in Vietnam would be simple sheetbending work, requiring relatively little skill and limited transfer of technology.

It will not be profitable for Otis to manufacture an entire elevator system in Vietnam, because the import of components that cannot be sourced locally would bear customs duties while imported complete elevators bear none. There are rumours that an Asian elevator manufacturer is preparing to establish an elevator manufacturing facility in Vietnam, but Vu cannot see how this could be cost effective. The risk is that a foreign elevator company prepared to manufacture in Vietnam will demand that the Vietnamese authorities raise import duties to give it market protection.

THE COMPETITION

Otis has won contracts for 60 elevators and escalators in the 18 months since February 1994. The majority of its jobs are in Hanoi, which Otis targeted first and where it has better market coverage. The competition is also less intense than in Ho Chi Minh City, where Mr Vu describes the contest between the world leaders in the elevator industry to win high profile projects as 'cut-throat'. Through Otis Lilama and CEC elevators have been installed in the guest house belonging to the Central Committee of the Vietnam Communist Party (supplied from Gien), in the Ministry of Energy and in the SCCI, as well as two escalators at the Saigon Superbowl bowling centre in Ho Chi Minh City.

Otis has not been successful in winning the largest, high profile projects in Ho Chi Minh City. The contract for the Landmark building, an office and apartment block on the waterfront, was signed (by Fujitec of Japan) before the US trade embargo was lifted, automatically barring Otis from tendering. Other contracts for office buildings and hotels have been lost to companies proposing exceptionally low prices – and therefore apparently taking on huge loss provisions – to buy their way into the market. Observation suggests that the Japanese elevator manufacturers (notably Mitsubishi and Toshiba) and Goldstar of Korea have certain advantages in winning projects invested by firms from Japan and Korea, although this does not prevent Otis from bidding aggressively even on these contracts. In general, Otis continues to compete hard for all available projects, but is not prepared to commit itself to the extent of taking significant losses on the product installed.

Competitors present in the market include:

- *Mitsubishi Electric* – won the largest project to date, the Saigon Trade Centre. It will also install elevators in the Hai Thanh Kotobuki development, a joint venture between another Japanese company and the Vietnamese navy.

- *Toshiba* – installed the elevators in the New World Hotel, a Hong Kong-invested project creating Ho Chi Minh City's largest hotel. Toshiba was introduced by the Hong Kong company Chevalier. It also has projects in Cholon, the Chinese area of Ho Chi Minh City.

- *Schindler Elevator K.K.* (formerly Nippon Elevator) – Schindler's majority-owned Japanese subsidiary has been active in Vietnam since 1987, which makes it the market leader in terms of number of lifts installed. The product it has been supplying (alternative current, variable voltage elevators) uses rather outmoded technology, suggesting that its market leadership will be lost in the next couple of years to Otis, Mitsubishi, Goldstar and others unless it upgrades its offering.

- *Goldstar* – actively supplying Korean investors, Goldstar is very much present in the market.

- *Schindler* – operating in Vietnam under its own name as well as through Nippon Elevator. The company beat Otis on bids for both Saigon Centre and Hanoi Centre Towers. It proposes to send Vietnamese people to Singapore for two years for training in elevator maintenance.

- *Thyssen* – present through its French subsidiary Soretec. Competitive and aggressive, the company has installed elevators in a number of the new hotels in Ho Chi Minh City.

The big companies are 'hitting hard at the upper end of the market range', according to Vu, offering top-of-the-range, high-speed lifts for 22–30 storey buildings. At the lower end of the product spectrum several companies – Thyman of Thailand and some smaller Italian and French firms, among others – are competing. Otis's goal is to challenge both ends of the market.

Of the 200 Otis elevators installed in the south before 1975, about half are still operational despite the lack of maintenance during the last 20 years. Otis is in the process of surveying these relics and proposing a modernization scheme. There is resistance, due to lack of money at the banks, hospitals and a few old hotels where they are installed. Nevertheless, Otis believes it is well positioned to capture not only this specific replacement market but also contracts related to general building renovations. Many of the older buildings in Vietnam are of French design, with narrow lift shafts of the type found in many Parisian buildings. The Otis factory at Gien in France is the only facility in the world to continue to produce lifts for this size of elevator shaft for the French market. It is technically feasible for any other elevator company to make small lifts specially, but they would not be competitively priced.

Otis's largest contract to date, worth US$1 million, is to install eight escalators at a municipal wholesale trade centre in Lang Son, on the border with China. Although the escalators have been delivered and Otis has been paid in full (it was a cash agreement, good until March 1994, made under a permitted execution contract before the US trade embargo was lifted), the escalators have yet to be installed. The case highlights some of the uncertainties of construction projects in Vietnam: the municipality began construction of the trade centre before negotiating the acquisition of additional land occupied by individuals and companies. The occupants have steadily increased the compensation they require for vacating their land in line with progress on the construction site. By the time the issue is resolved, Otis will need another contract to refurbish the escalators before they can be installed.

THE OTIS SERVICE ORGANIZATION

In normal market conditions, the prices and products offered by the principal elevator companies are similar. Firms differentiate themselves through their service organizations – which is also where they make their money. The Otis strategy in Vietnam is to begin to build a service organization immediately even though it has no service contracts yet. (Most installations are either still in progress or are still within the free one-year new installation service contracts.) Otis believes this long-term policy will distinguish it significantly from its rivals in the future, and contribute to its credibility and reputation in Vietnam.

To establish a credible maintenance operation to service the lifts installed will be difficult without a firm commitment to Vietnam: without a joint venture or wholly owned subsidiary, companies will not be allowed by the Vietnamese authorities to build a service-based organization. To bring engineers in on demand from Hong Kong or Singapore is also unsatisfactory and does not solve the problem of emergency calls.

Vu has a delicate balancing act to perform, between the need to win sufficient new installation contracts in order to build up a sufficient maintenance portfolio, and the strong wish not to burden the fledgling operation with excessive loss provisions. 'The Vietnamese market is the choice between cholera and the plague', he says. In his view, a company basically has two choices:

To accept heavy loss provisions in order to build a portfolio of an absolute minimum of 500–600 units installed. It must accept also that customers tend to be unwilling at first to spend much on maintenance and that they will be reactive, for example when breakdowns occur, rather than

Case 3

pro-active. In the long run it must also add the costs of establishing a proper service organization to the pain of the heavy losses taken on installed units.

The alternative is to take the initially more expensive path of establishing a direct presence and creating a service organization at the start, while at the same time building a portfolio of installed units carrying some profit margin to offset costs incurred. It will take longer to reach critical mass, but the organization will be more solid. Otis headquarters has already accepted that its Vietnam operations will not be profitable for many years, whereas other elevator firms may not be prepared to countenance such a situation.

According to Vu, Otis has also lost projects in Vietnam due to its unwillingness to 'play the game' or 'accommodate itself to the market'. Internal corporate rules require Otis to withdraw from any project where there is even a hint of 'under the table' money. The fact that Otis is present throughout the Asia Pacific region, including countries where bribery is certainly not unknown, suggests to Vu that the company will be able to survive in this country too. Nevertheless, its partners put pressure on Otis to win orders under all circumstances, in the interests of earning profits quickly. Vu has been able so far to resist this pressure on the grounds that good ethical behaviour eventually prevails. At the same time he is trying to educate them to recognize that service and maintenance activity is the best generator of revenue over the long term. 'We are not targeting 100% of the Vietnam market', he says. 'I tell my staff that they shouldn't panic if they lose contracts. They should do their best on each negotiation, look after our existing customers well, and they will come back for more units, not just the maintenance contracts'. Both the northern and the southern partners are difficult to convince on this point.

The sophistication of the elevators Otis installs for its customers requires its engineers to undergo intensive training. 'Once someone is trained, he becomes a scarce resource', comments Vu. Engineers become experts in Otis products, not in – for example – Mitsubishi lifts. Because each manufacturer's lifts are technically so refined (even though the quality of offering is similar) an expert service engineer leaving to work for a competitor needs months of retraining before becoming an asset to the new employer. Nevertheless, it is difficult for Otis to avoid some staff turnover.

In addition to technical training, the staff needs education in the culture and mentality of business. Vu believes that the mass of people have become passive in reaction to long years of war and a centrally planned economy. They have become used to having all their work checked by a manager. Vu wants them to exercise initiative and become more independent in the way they work. He also sees the labour relations environment in Vietnam as potentially hazardous, based on language problems and cultural misunderstandings. Already a number of foreign-invested companies have faced protest strikes by their workforce.

Vu intends to establish a rounded compensation package with a properly organized human resource structure. As in all Otis joint ventures, he wants the Vietnamese staff to feel part of the Otis 'family'. The policy of United Technologies – and therefore of Otis – is to build a team spirit, respect the human resource environment and offer very high standards of health and safety protection. For example, Otis adds extra safety dispositions for its engineers over and above industry norms, at its own expense (in order to remain competitively priced), with the result that engineers feel safer and are more confident in their work, and fewer working hours are lost.

ISSUES FOR THE FUTURE

Otis has won first mover advantage in commercial terms through setting up its joint ventures before any of its competitors and by entering a market devoid of service industries. In other respects there has been no benefit in arriving first, neither politically from the Vietnamese authorities, nor in business access terms since latecomers are profiting from the pioneering of the early birds. Competition is significantly more fierce than Vu had anticipated: his assumption was that Vietnam would initially be a high margin market for new equipment sales, during which time Otis would have the time to get established, and that prices would trend down thereafter. Instead, contracts are already being exchanged at more than 20% below cost.

Having people on the spot – by virtue of its Lilama joint venture – Otis has better understanding of the market than firms without a direct presence. Partnership with a Ministry of Construction company provides access to information held within the ministry. Otis is also better positioned generally to collect essential market data, not available from neutral sources as in other countries, on existing and future contracts for elevators.

Looking at Otis in Vietnam today, Mr Vu can see a number of threats or challenges that must be faced:

- ■ *Partnership issues*

- ■ One of the two partner companies, Lilama or CEC, may seek to form a joint venture with a strong competitor in the territory not covered by the JV with Otis.

- ■ The partner companies, Lilama and CEC, may try to exert pressure on Otis to maximize short-term profits, and to interfere in the day-to-day management of the joint ventures. Otis must work continually towards consensus.

- ■ *Contractual issues*

- ■ The royalty issue must be resolved. Otis cannot continue to bring in elevators from overseas on a project basis without upsetting its partners.

- ■ Otis must find a way of persuading the authorities to issue the second investment licence (for the joint venture in the south) without further delay.

- ■ *Competitive issues*

- ■ How can Otis raise entry barriers to its competitors in Vietnam?

- ■ How should Otis act in the cut-throat competitive environment of Vietnam to take full advantage of its knowledge and its organization in the market?

Exhibit CS3.1   Map of Vietnam

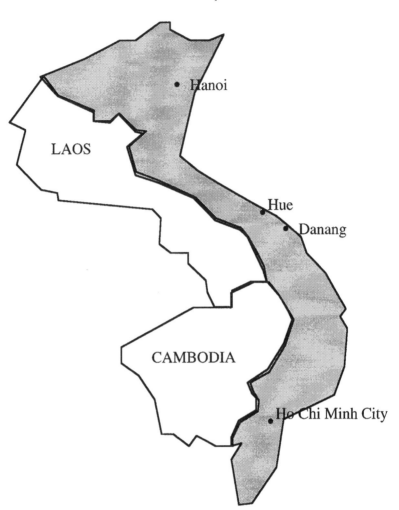

Exhibit CS3.2   Organizational chart of Otis in Vietnam

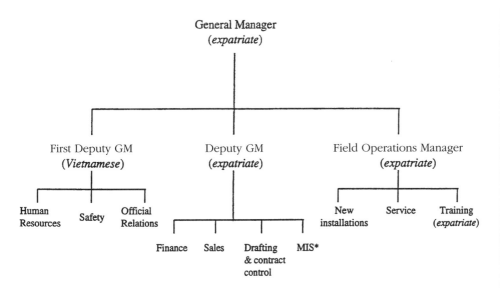

*Management Information Systems
Source: Otis Vietnam

Case 4

Case 4

This case was written by Jocelyn Probert, Research Analyst at INSEAD Euro-Asia Centre, and Philippe Lasserre, Professor of Strategy and Management at INSEAD. It is intended to be used as a basis for class discussion rather than to illustrate either effective handling or ineffective handling of an administrative situation. Copyright © 1995 INSEAD-EAC, Fontainebleau, France.

Ahlstrom Korea

On 5 February 1995 in Meggen, Switzerland, Thorleif Blok, president and CEO of Ahlstrom Paper, Ed Leinss, general manager of the filter division, and B.M. Chung, president of Ahlstrom Korea, were discussing the results of the Korean operations since their inception in 1987. They were also debating future plans for Korea and for Southeast Asia. Among the subjects for discussion was the location of a new filter plant: should it be part of an expanded Ahlstrom Korea site, or should it be constructed in Indonesia?

A FIRST VISIT TO KOREA

In autumn 1986 the head of business development at Ahlstrom Paper, Paul Olof Meinander, was on an exploration trip in Asia, a region of the world where the company was represented only by a sales office in Singapore and agents in places such as Japan and Korea.

The company was moving out of the commodity paper business and into speciality papers, and it harboured ambitions to become a global player in the engine filtration business. Negotiations were going on in Brazil to raise the profile of the company there, and they had a target in North America. Asia was recognized to be a potentially important market, but understanding of the region was very limited.

This was Meinander's second visit to the region. He had just been to Japan for the second time, where he met several local manufacturers of engine filter papers, but realized it would be a difficult market to penetrate. Then he moved on to Korea. This was a country about which he knew nothing – in fact he was only there because Seoul was not very far from Tokyo and Ahlstrom Paper's agent, Mr Chung, had been able to arrange some meetings for him. He hoped he might find a company that would be interested in forming some sort of cooperative agreement with Ahlstrom Paper. Meinander was amazed at the advanced state of development of Korea: the modern buildings, the air of affluence in Seoul, the large numbers of vehicles clogging the streets of the capital. Clearly, here was a potentially important market for Ahlstrom Paper's engine filter papers.

Case 4

Chung arranged for Meinander to meet the Korean company Jeonil. This was a family company run by Mrs Choi, who had inherited the paper mill on her husband's death. Intense questioning by the Koreans of Ahlstrom Paper's technical capabilities left Meinander feeling as though he had just sat an exam. By the following morning it was clear that he – and Ahlstrom – had passed: a telephone call from Chung announced that Jeonil believed Ahlstrom would be a better partner than the US or German companies which had been paying assiduous court to Mrs Choi. On the other hand, she was expecting to sign a joint venture agreement with Gessner in Germany in two weeks' time...

Only now did Meinander realize how far Ahlstrom Paper was behind its global competitors in researching the Korean market. He could see that the economy was extremely dynamic, with the automobile industry growing by 30% per annum. He had learned as well that Koreans liked to change their car engine filters more frequently than the Western norm. He also recognized that there was room for only one modern filtration company making engine filter papers in Korea. Unless Ahlstrom Paper moved fast it would be shut out of the market.

Mrs Choi was persuaded to postpone her visit to Germany, and to visit Ahlstrom's production sites and offices in France, Italy and Finland in December, with Mr Chung. Impressed with what she saw, by only the second day of her trip Mrs Choi was ready to sign a letter of intent to establish a joint venture between Jeonil and Ahlstrom Paper. Tradition, however, did not allow a Korean woman to take final decisions without consulting a male relative and, back in Korea, her brother-in-law refused his consent to the proposed joint venture. This was Ahlstrom Paper's first lesson in the intricacies of Korean business practice.

THE SEARCH FOR A PARTNER

Convinced of the existence of a market in Korea, but acutely aware of the interest also shown by competitors, Ahlstrom Paper had to begin again its search for a partner in January 1987. A clause in the letter of intent with Mrs Choi barred Jeonil from signing an agreement with a competitor during 1987, thus preventing the company from reverting to its originally proposed German partner. With the help of Ahlstrom Paper's agent, Mr Chung, and Ahlstrom Machinery's agent and the Finnish Embassy in Seoul, several possible joint venture partners were evaluated and two candidates shortlisted on the basis of structural fit with Ahlstrom Paper and business reputation. Few other details were available.

In early March 1987 Meinander visited Korea with Pekka Rantala, vice president of the Ahlstrom Group and CEO of the paper division, to meet both shortlisted companies. On the Monday they met the first prospect, Han Reyo, a trading company very enthusiastic about the idea of a partnership, and agreed to meet again over dinner on Tuesday evening. During the day on Tuesday they met Mr Lee, the head of the On Yang Pulp Company, and visited the company's paper factory. So strongly did Meinander and Rantala believe Mr Lee and On Yang would be the right partners for Ahlstrom Paper, that they telephoned Helsinki the same afternoon to speak to Krister Ahlstrom, the group CEO, and the corporate legal adviser to get agreement on a letter of intent and find the name of a Korean lawyer. At 18.00 they met the recommended lawyer to brief him on the proposed agreement – and they were only slightly late for dinner with the Han Reyo representatives.

Late the next morning, Meinander and Rantala reconvened with the lawyer to agree to the document he had drawn up in discussion with Helsinki – the time difference meant Mr Shin worked through the night to complete the task. At midday Mr Lee arrived to read and sign the letter of intent, 15 minutes later they were all enjoying a celebratory lunch. By this time they had known Mr Lee for only just over 24 hours.

Meinander and Rantala then returned to Helsinki, without informing Han Reyo of these developments. They hoped to keep the agreement with On Yang secret for at least one week, for fear that Han Reyo would cause problems. This was when they learned their second lesson about business practices in Korea: that Korea is a transparent society, where all information is readily 'knowable' and known. A fax from Han Reyo waiting for them in Helsinki demonstrated full awareness of all that had been agreed with On Yang, thanks to information received from a university friend working in the lawyer's office.

The next phase took place with equal rapidity. Mr Lee and the lawyer, Mr Shin visited Helsinki in May, two months after the letter of intent was signed. To the surprise of the Ahlstrom Paper team, On Yang was very happy to use the same legal adviser. Mr Lee believed that having an agreement *per se* was more important than the specific details contained within it. In a single 12-hour session all the paperwork related to the shareholders' agreement was concluded, and the Korean ambassador was invited to attend the signing ceremony at midday the following day. Four months after the formal agreement was signed, the joint venture was finally established on 2 October 1987.

THE PARTNERS

Ahlstrom Paper

The Ahlstrom Group of Finland is organized into four business sectors, with operations in 23 countries, sales of US$1.9 billion in 1993, and 12,900 employees (Exhibit CS4.1). Reflecting the highly decentralized nature of the group, both the Ahlstrom Paper and the Ahlstrom Pyropower sectors have their headquarters overseas (in Meggen, Switzerland and San Diego, USA, respectively).

Ahlstrom Paper, from its headquarters in the mountains west of Zurich, manages business units in Finland, Germany, Italy, Korea and the USA and has an important partnership with Sibille-Dalle of France, in which it has a 47% direct stake. A significant feature of Ahlstrom Paper, which differentiates it from all other paper companies, is its multicultural nature and its heritage as a family-run group. Several different nationalities are represented on the board of Ahlstrom Paper.

The company is today the world's largest producer of engine filter papers, with a 50% share of the market in North America, Europe and Korea (Exhibit CS4.2). It also produces self-adhesive papers, packaging materials and industrial-use papers (Exhibit CS4.3). Oil and water filter papers are made for use in cars, trucks, earthmovers and excavation units. An engine filter normally lasts 20–30,000 km, so that on average around five filters would be required during the lifetime of a car. Ahlstrom Paper's main competitors in the engine filtration business are two German companies, two US firms and a number of smaller Japanese producers.

In 1987 the Bosso paper mill in Italy was the sole source of engine filter papers made by Ahlstrom Paper, and was therefore the home of the company's proprietary technology in this field. Having established a presence in Korea, the company added production facilities in the USA in 1989 via the acquisition of Filtration Sciences (a former US competitor) and thus was equipped for global coverage of the engine filter market.

Although Ahlstrom Paper's drive to form a joint venture in Korea was initiated by Meinander, the proposal was strongly supported by both Rantala and the sales representative in Singapore, Christer Sundell, and fully endorsed by the chairman of the Ahlstrom Group, Krister Ahlstrom. Luigi Gai, then in charge of the Bosso filtration operations, was slightly ambivalent towards the planned joint venture, but basically supported the move. His concern was that the technology on which their global ambitions rested would be lost to the Koreans. It was also not in the short-term interests of Bosso to shift a portion of filter paper output to Korea.

Once the decision was taken to invest in Korea, hitherto a blank page for the company, the management team of Ahlstrom Paper underwent a series of briefings about Korean culture and business practices. They also read widely on Korean history and literature.

On Yang

The On Yang Pulp Company is part of what is now known as Shin Ho Paper, Korea's second largest paper-maker. Group profits in 1993 were Won 5,190 million (US$6.7 million on sales of Won 439,954 million (US$564 million). Shin Ho has a highly diversified range of businesses in the paper industry and has recently expanded its interests into electronics, steel, machinery and colour monitors. Nevertheless, it is still a family-run company, and this was one of the aspects that originally attracted Ahlstrom Paper. Mr Lee also seemed a straightforward man to deal with, and because On Yang was in the paper business anyway, there would be a ready pool of people for Ahlstrom Korea to draw upon.

Mr Lee, the founder of On Yang, has created the Shin Ho group over the course of the last 20 years through a mixture of acquisitions of small paper businesses, joint ventures and internal growth. In 1987, the scale of Lee's business was considerably smaller than it is today. The joint venture between On Yang and Ahlstrom Paper was his first partnership with a foreign company and a source of immense pride: despite being a minority shareholder, Lee gave Ahlstrom Korea a high profile in all his company brochures. It was also his first venture into high technology paper-making and Ahlstrom Korea thus represented for him a status symbol and a matter of prestige. He subsequently entered joint venture and alliance agreements with other Western firms, both domestically and overseas, though not in the engine filter paper business.

Because Lee was only in his mid-40s at the time – younger than some of his middle managers – he needed an older person in the background to command the necessary respect and discipline from his staff. Mr Kang was Lee's brother-in-law and also his business adviser. His background was that of a high government official, and his father had been professor at Seoul National University, the most prestigious academic institution in Korea. He was very much a conservative. Mr Kang was to be the first president of Ahlstrom Korea.

THE START-UP PHASE

Under the terms of the joint venture agreement, Ahlstrom Paper held 41% of the shares and On Yang 39% of the shares in Ahlstrom Korea. CNB Technology Finance Company (a Korean financial institution) held the remaining 20%, in the form of non-voting shares, and was effectively a sleeping partner. Total capital of the joint venture was US$10 million, of which the factory represented US$5.5 million. On the insistence of Mr Lee, the equity share of the investment was only 10%, leaving US$9 million to be debt-financed. His operations were usually highly leveraged, and he was not prepared to increase his initial cash injection. By Western standards, the newly found company was financially vulnerable. In 1987, moreover, the Korean economy was overheating, and money was in short supply domestically; the Korean government also imposed stringent restrictions on international financing. Interest rates were a punitive 11–15%. Eventually leasing companies were the prime source of financing for Ahlstrom Korea. Initial production capacity of the factory was 6,000 tonnes of filter paper per year, later to be increased to 9,000 tonnes.

The four-month period between the signing of the formal agreement in June and the founding of the company in October was the longest interval in the whole process. At the time the formal agreement was made, the two partners had made only tentative business plans. This interval was therefore used to formulate plans together and to conduct thorough research of the Korean filter market. The first group of Koreans from On Yang also visited Ahlstrom Paper's Bosso mill in Italy during the summer.

Market research in Korea was carried out by Mr Chung, who had been appointed vice-president of Ahlstrom Korea, and Christer Sundell from the Singapore office. Together they interviewed every engine filter producer who could be a customer for Ahlstrom filter papers to discover their paper consumption. From this they calculated that the market size was 3,000 tonnes per year, of which 1,000 tonnes was already supplied by the only existing competitor in Korea. This left Ahlstrom a potential market size of 2,000 tonnes.

Work on the Hyun Poong paper mill outside Taegu (Exhibit CS4.4) began in October 1987, with completion promised by On Yang for May 1988. To the Europeans, this seemed an exceptionally short construction period. The site was a former box-board factory which Lee had bought in a bankrupt state, on an industrial site surrounded by rice paddies and which offered little of the infrastructure necessary for specialized paper production, particularly lacking a water supply. Effectively, it was a greenfield site.

The project team was managed by the Korean side, using know-how from Bosso. There were no permanent on-site Europeans: a Finnish financial controller, Timo Harju, was based in Seoul, 280 km away, and the Italian technical director would come from Bosso for lengthy visits. Meinander also visited regularly, to see how the project was advancing. Progress, however, was hampered by friction between the Italian expert and the Korean team, and the fact that Lee's best people were quickly reassigned to another of his investments. Poor interaction with the technical director reinforced the Koreans' belief that Westerners do not respect them. The expected completion date slipped to the end of June.

When the president of the Ahlstrom group, Krister Ahlstrom, made his very first visit to the Korean site in mid-May he was completely unprepared for the chaotic state of affairs: work on the site hardly appeared to have begun. His confidence in the project was shaken and he described the whole business as 'not a disaster but a total disaster', despite the best efforts of Mr Kang to assure him of the Koreans' good faith. The project nevertheless continued, with Meinander pressing hard for rapid completion but otherwise keeping a low profile. The paper machines finally began turning in early August 1988, just 10 months after the joint venture was formed – a tremendous achievement from a greenfield site, given that in Italy it would take six months even to have a single new machine running smoothly.

The Ahlstrom Paper team learned several things from this experience: that apparently such projects in Korea were routinely completed half a year late, but that Koreans were capable of working night and day to turn chaos into order; and that exerting too much pressure could be counter-productive because the Koreans felt they lost face in such circumstances.

The difficulty in finding Koreans with the necessary expertise forced Ahlstrom Paper to bring in a Finn to help out in the early phase of operations, although as a company the philosophy was to build confidence and cooperation with local managers. Mr Chung was in effect in charge of the factory from the very beginning, but his skills lay in sales, marketing and finance rather than in manufacturing. Jussi Toivonen, who had spent two years at a Swedish-financed paper mill in northern Vietnam, became the engineer supporting the efforts of Mr Seo, the mill manager. From the beginning, it was made clear that Toivonen would spend only two years at Hyun Poong.

FROM START-UP TO MATURITY

Between August 1988 and early 1992, Ahlstrom Korea went through what Thorleif Blok called 'Death Valley' (see Exhibit CS4.5), a difficult period during which the company was confronted by three interdependent problems. Marketing and sales were below expectation; the operations were making heavy losses; and the relationship with the local partner was somewhat shaky.

The *marketing and sales* difficulties were attributed to four factors, three domestic and one overseas:

■ In Korea:

- Overestimation of market potential: during their market research, Chung and Sundell did not take into account the fact that customers based their consumption on 100% operating rates, whereas actual operating rates were no more than 70%. Once Ahlstrom Korea's operations began, it rapidly became clear that the market the joint venture could hope to reach was only half the anticipated size. This created initial over-capacity and affected profitability. Nevertheless, annual market growth was 30% in 1987–88.

- Quality problems: these were caused both by the learning curve and by employee attitudes. As time passed and employees became more skilled technically (for example in achieving the correct degree of porosity in the filter paper), the first of these factors disappeared, but the second issue proved more intractable. It seemed that Koreans generally were content to manufacture products of 'good enough' quality and it was difficult to encourage Ahlstrom Korea employees to manufacture to truly high quality standards – particularly since most of their customers in Korea were tiny backyard operators with no technical understanding of the needs of engine manufacturers. A real notion of quality awareness would depend on the Korean venture coming to trust Ahlstrom Paper's knowledge of the demands of world markets. The indifferent quality initially encouraged sales people to rely on price alone as a marketing tool, and this also hampered profitability.

– Under-capitalization: given the elevated debt/equity ratio (9:1), the cost of covering interest payments was high and allowed Ahlstrom Korea little flexibility in granting customers generous credit terms.

■ In the export markets of Southeast Asia:

– Unsuitable sales organization: export sales from Korea were handled by a European expatriate in the Singapore sales office. He worked hard, travelling widely throughout the region to meet customers, but he was expensive to employ relative to the results achieved. Quality problems also hampered his efforts. Ahlstrom's engine filter papers were not penetrating Asian markets quickly enough.

Profitability problems were due to:

■ Under-capitalization: this led to high financial costs, as described above.

■ Over-capacity: paper production generally is a capital-intensive business. Until Ahlstrom Korea's filter papers penetrated the market, the company had to bear high unamortized fixed costs on the installed machinery. They resorted to producing what is known in the paper industry as 'filler' goods in order to keep the paper mill turning: low quality paper, such as wrapping paper, on which they were happy even to cover the costs of the raw materials.

■ Pricing policy: the whole pricing issue was not in focus, but this reflected the Korean attitude that price is more important than quality. Prices in Korea were set low by the joint venture partly in order to break into the market, but also on reflection of the poor quality of the product. Ahlstrom Korea did not engage in price competition with the only other local producer but concentrated on taking a share from imported filter papers which bore customs duties.

Finally, issues related to the joint venture partner can be summarized as follows:

■ Unclear motivation: the Ahlstrom Paper team recognized that Mr Lee viewed the joint venture as a matter of prestige (after all, it was to be the only modern engine filter paper plant in Korea). On the other hand, in view of his method of expanding his own business interests by acquisition and the formation of new joint ventures, he was unwilling to commit many of his own resources to Ahlstrom Korea, in terms either of money (it was he who insisted on the low capitalization) or of people (he promised his best people to the venture, but then withdrew them to work on other projects). Mr Kang, for example, was soon sent to Thailand and then to Canada to manage Mr Lee's new business ventures. Mr Chung, Ahlstrom Paper's 'man' then took over the presidency of Ahlstrom Korea.

Also the Ahlstrom Korea mill was built on Lee's land. He received rent for its use, but was keen to sell it to the joint venture.

■ Poor support: overall, it seemed that the only support Ahlstrom Korea received from Mr Lee and On Yang Pulp was initial connections and introductions for doing business. Having the right connections is an important aspect of the business environment in Korea, and Ahlstrom Paper as a novice in the Asia Pacific region would not have been able to make its own way. When the joint venture needed a new injection of capital in 1989, however, Mr Lee was not in a position to participate. Ahlstrom Paper was forced to put up all the extra capital and thus increased its shareholding to 70% (Exhibit CS4.6). The capital of Ahlstrom Korea was again increased in 1990. By this time Mr Lee's group, Shin Ho, had financial difficulties of its own and Ahlstrom Paper increased its shareholding to 90%, leaving Mr Lee and On Yang simply as equity shareholders and landlords. Mr Kang, though, remained a strong supporter of Ahlstrom Korea.

The overall assessment of the relationship with Mr Lee and On Yang is 'tricky but not difficult'. Mr Lee is 'a very skilled negotiator'. In fact, since 1990 there has been rather little contact between Mr Lee and Ahlstrom Paper. As a shareholder he collects dividends, but Ahlstrom Paper has the freedom to take the critical decisions. In other words, although his underlying motivation may have been hard for Ahlstrom Paper to fathom, his initial involvement in the joint venture was by no means negative.

In addition, both sides needed to make cultural adjustments to the other. Neither side was familiar with the other's approach to issues for discussion and decision. The Koreans also had to cope with the multicultural Western management team of Ahlstrom Paper, which included Italians and Americans as well as Scandinavians. At least On Yang was represented by a homogeneous group of managers! Ahlstrom Paper people also had to get used to their 'own' people in Korea, including Mr Chung. The Koreans seemed very formal and disciplined, compared with the more relaxed behaviour of the Europeans.

Finally, it should be stated that 'Death Valley' for Ahlstrom Korea coincided with a period when the Ahlstrom Group as a whole was undergoing a difficult transition phase in global operations. The pulp and paper industry worldwide was struggling under the impact of low raw material and finished product prices during 1990–91, affecting not only Ahlstrom Paper but also Ahlstrom Machinery. In 1991 the Ahlstrom Group was deeply loss making.

ESCAPE FROM DEATH VALLEY, 1992–95

The decisive moment for Ahlstrom Korea came when top management in Helsinki concluded that, with all the problems the joint venture was facing, it would be better to cut its losses and withdraw. Krister Ahlstrom's confidence in the venture wavered during his disastrous visit to Korea in May 1988; two years later, as the situation in Korea and elsewhere deteriorated, he replaced the original Ahlstrom Paper management team. Thorleif Blok became the CEO of the paper division in October 1990 and soon encountered negative criticism about the joint venture, based largely on hearsay.

Once in possession of the facts, however, he could see the potential of the joint venture and argued against its closure on the following points:

■ it would be more expensive to disengage than to stay;

■ the market for engine filter papers in Korea and Southeast Asia was already significant and was growing considerably faster than markets in North America and Europe;

■ Ahlstrom Paper was forming a new global management structure that would facilitate problem solving in Korea;

■ quality problems were being resolved; and finally,

■ the learning process in Korea had been difficult but the lessons had been absorbed, and it would be a shame to abandon the venture now.

The turnaround

Global reorganization: Late in 1991 Ahlstrom Paper's business activities were reorganized into global product divisions. Although Blok was CEO of the company, responsibility specifically for engine filter papers – and hence for Ahlstrom Korea – was given to Ed Leinss, a larger-than-life American based in Chattanooga in the USA. This was one of the keys to the successful turnaround of the Korean operations. Leinss had originally been with Filtration Sciences, the US engine filter paper competitor acquired by Ahlstrom Paper in 1989. The Americans were specialists in the filtration business, and they had laboratories and technicians to support their work. Leinss began to visit Ahlstrom Korea regularly. The relationship between the Americans and the Koreans was good, and Leinss got on well with both Kang and Chung. Now, Ahlstrom Korea was no longer a standalone operation.

At about the same time, Blok decided to move the position of financial controller into the filter division. Timo Harju, who had been in Korea for the last three years, thus moved to Chattanooga and into the filter division's management team, where he could also promote the interests of the Korean operation.

Improved quality of output: Leinss and his technicians worked hard with the Koreans to improve the quality of output from the Hyun Poong mill. More than in other industries, speciality paper production relies on the skills of the workforce. Slowly the Americans overcame the lack of ambition among Korean employees to produce top quality papers and the Koreans began to understand why it was so difficult to sell their filter paper in Japan, where Ahlstrom Paper's engine filter papers occupied 10% of the market (800 tonnes/year) after 2–3 years of effort: technical quality which 'almost' met customer specifications was not good enough for the Japanese filter makers. Whereas in the beginning they were forced to concentrate sales on the less demanding domestic market, once quality improved it became easier to sell products overseas.

Better pricing strategies: The world market price per tonne of engine filter paper is around US$3,000 (slightly less in the USA), but in Japan it costs US$6,000/tonne and in Korea US$4,000. The high price in Japan reflects both the extended distribution chain (it must be a question of time how long this will continue) and high quality standards. In Korea, however, the price is above world levels because of nationalistic pride (domestically produced papers must be the best), protectionism (punitive tariffs are imposed on imported paper products) and regulatory requirements. Ahlstrom Korea's pricing structure was reworked by Blok's team in

1992, to reflect these characteristics and to correct the overly aggressive (low) price strategy of the start-up years. It would have been impossible to do this earlier, because of the low quality and the need to penetrate the market: they had had to pay an 'entrance fee'.

Korean market growth: Today, approximately 50% of Ahlstrom Korea's volume sales are in the domestic market, down from 60% in 1990–91 (Exhibit CS4.7). The market itself has trebled in size since 1988, when the company began operations, to an estimated 4,140 tonnes in 1995 and Ahlstrom Korea's market share has expanded from 64% in 1989 (the first full year of operations) to a commanding 80% share in 1994. Clearly, the scope to further expand domestic market share is limited, nor is it particularly desired by the management. Meanwhile, the market itself is expected to continue to grow at 5–10% per annum.

Export sales reorganization: In 1992 Blok decided to close the Singapore sales office, send the expatriate home and give full responsibility for export sales throughout Asia to Mr Chung. Mr Chung rose to the challenge. He produced a budget only one-third the size of that required to run the Singapore office but, much more importantly, he found a man who 'looks like a Chinese' to manage the export sales effort from Seoul. Mr Jin was actually Korean, and was well in tune with the requirements for selling into regional markets although he had no previous experience in the paper business. He was very easy to communicate with.

To relocate a regional sales operation from Singapore to Korea is an unusual move, and it encountered strong resistance in Helsinki. Blok is, however, '100% convinced' that this was another key to the successful turnaround of Ahlstrom Korea. Chung was highly motivated by this step, and extremely proud of the confidence shown in him and his organization.

Ahlstrom Paper measures success by the share of the market its products hold. Today for example via its operations in Korea, it has 50% of the market in Thailand and is well entrenched in Malaysia, Singapore and Indonesia, where many filter producers are located. Customers in Southeast Asia are bringing knock-on advantages too, as they recommend Ahlstrom Paper engine filters to their sister companies in North America. China represents between 500 and 1,000 tonnes per year of sales. Japan remains a difficult market even today, and for Blok this means that quality levels are still not high enough.

Ultimately, Ahlstrom Paper believes that Ahlstrom Korea has become a successful company today because of the mutual trust and respect built up between the two sides, rather than because of the excellence of the managers or the engineers. Such a relationship only became possible once Ahlstrom Paper had realized how psychologically difficult it was for the Koreans to accept their need for Western technology, but that pride would be restored if they undertook its implementation. It was a question of 'finding the right tune'.

CURRENT ISSUES

With engine filter paper production in Korea running smoothly and export sales well established, Blok felt it was time to expand Ahlstrom Paper's presence in the region. Although he knew that China had to be broached, he felt it was a large enough market to be treated as a standalone operation. In fact, the company had signed a memorandum of understanding with a Chinese company in Jinan, south of Beijing, although it was unclear what might materialize as a result. For

Case 4

the moment, however, Blok was going to leave that issue to one side in order to reach some decisions on how to develop from the base established by Ahlstrom Korea.

The *first project*, in 1994, was to establish a branch office of Ahlstrom Korea in Seoul, which would sell other Ahlstrom Paper and Sibille-Dalle products. It would have been impossible for the company to envisage such an operation without the penetration of the market already achieved through Ahlstrom Korea. The sales target for 1995 was US$5 million.

The *second project* involves establishing glass fibre production in Korea. Ed Leinss is heading a task force drawn from the filter division, the glass fibre division (based in Finland) and Ahlstrom Korea, to assess the potential. Glass fibre is used in Korea among other things for the backings of floor materials. Ahlstrom Paper's glass fibre is already imported from Finland and sold in Korea by the new branch office, suggesting that a market exists for the company's product. The manufacturing technology for glass fibre is similar to paper-making, in that both are manmade fibres, and the required infrastructure (water, electricity) is the same. There is room to build a glass fibre tissue line on Ahlstrom Korea's present site.

The *third project* is to finalize a decision on a second filter paper machine. This would add 10,000 tonnes of production, doubling present capacity in Korea. Together, this machine and the glass fibre machine would involve Ahlstrom Paper in an investment of US$30 million.

At issue is the location of the second filter paper machine. It would be easier and quicker to build it in Korea, but a strategic investment in, say, Indonesia would pre-empt competitors from establishing a direct presence in Southeast Asia. Until now, competitors have all preferred to export, rather than invest, in the region. Blok's decision on location had to be based on both a market perspective and the capability of the company.

In favour of Korea is the fact that Ahlstrom Paper has followed the learning curve and is now comfortable with operations there. A second machine would put pressure on the organization to work harder at penetrating the Japanese market, where Blok believes they should have one-third of the market (a direct presence in Japan is not an option). The China market is also close by, and there would be potential opportunities in the future reunification of North and South Korea. The surrounding markets are certainly large enough to support doubled capacity. To put in a second machine would, however, necessitate moving Ahlstrom Korea to a completely different site, since there is no room to put both a new filter paper line and a glass fibre machine on the existing plot of land. The installation of the engine filter paper machine would certainly take priority over the glass fibre facility if Ahlstrom Korea is to stay at Hyun Poong. With the approval of the government, Chung has examined a large site closer to Seoul. Proximity to Seoul, where the branch office is based, would be an advantage. Moving to a new site would give Ahlstrom Paper the option of adding yet another facility in the future, for example to produce backing paper for self-adhesive materials. This is a major product line for the company, and the anticipated market size in Asia is very high. Economies of scale in terms of administrative facilities and the training of personnel could be realized if all such operations were grouped together in one large complex of 300–400 people. Chung naturally favours the Korean option as does Leinss, who is keen to move the project forward.

On the other hand, if Ahlstrom Paper were to invest in a filter paper machine in Indonesia within the next two years it would safeguard its position in Southeast Asia *vis-à-vis* Western competitors, whereas two machines in Korea would leave the rest of Asia wide open to the likes of Gessner of Germany or H&W of the USA. Fast-growing markets in Indonesia, Malaysia and Thailand would also be more easily reached than from Korea. Indonesia represents a more attractive environment than Thailand, because it has everything to make it a big 'paper country': raw materials and a large population with low per capita paper consumption at present. Installation of a filter paper machine there would represent a second entrance point to Southeast Asia for all Ahlstrom Paper's product range: the effect would be to more than double the company's presence in a region where some countries already exhibit high paper consumption characteristics and others have significant growth potential (Exhibit CS4.8). In the short term, investment in Indonesia would be the more expensive option to take, but it would not necessarily be more costly in the longer term.

Two major issues would arise from the selection of Southeast Asia for the second filter machine: identification of a local partner, and the impact on Mr Chung and his team in Korea. Ahlstrom Paper's investigation of potential partners in both Thailand and Indonesia so far have borne no fruit. Large conglomerates dominate the industrial scene in such countries and these have shown no more than a passing interest in a 10,000-tonne paper plant. Blok and his team have yet to find smaller companies that would be more natural partners for Ahlstrom Paper. If, however, this issue were solved and production began in, say, Indonesia, all export sales of filter papers from Korea to the area would cease. Blok fears this would demotivate Mr Chung's people even more than if a similar step had to be taken in Europe, by virtue of the Korean character. Some compensation would be development of the glass fibre operations, which will definitely be sited in Korea.

Blok and Leinss were in agreement over the glass fibre plant for Korea, but its location would depend on the second decision they took: where to put the new engine filter paper plant, in Korea or in Indonesia?

Case 4

Case 4

Exhibit CS4.1   The Ahlstrom group: key data (*Source*: Ahlstrom Annual Report)

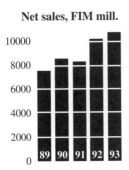

Net sales, FIM mill.

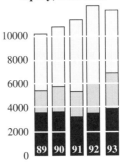

Net income, FIM mill.

Net debt as a percentage
of net sales

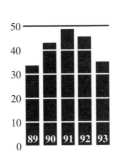

Liabilities and shareholders'
equity, FIM mill.

☐ **Interest bearing liabilities**
☐ **Non-interest bearing liabilities**
■ **Shareholders' equity**

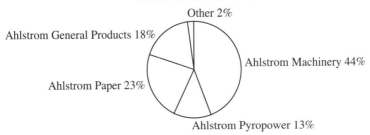

Distribution of net sales

Other 2%

Ahlstrom General Products 18%

Ahlstrom Machinery 44%

Ahlstrom Paper 23%

Ahlstrom Pyropower 13%

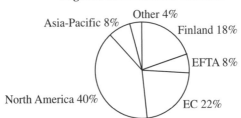

Regional distribution of net sales

Other 4%

Asia-Pacific 8%

Finland 18%

EFTA 8%

EC 22%

North America 40%

Exhibit CS4.2   Engine filter paper, worldwide markets ('000 tonnes/year)
(*Source*: Ahlstrom Paper)

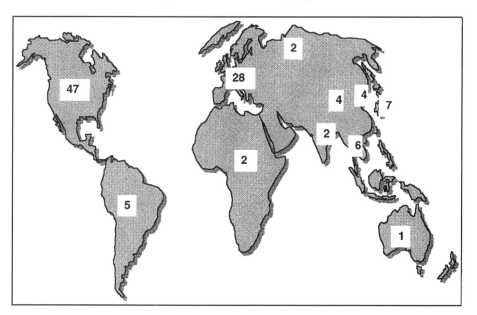

Case 4

Exhibit CS4.3   Ahlstrom product breakdown (*Source*: Ahlstrom Paper)

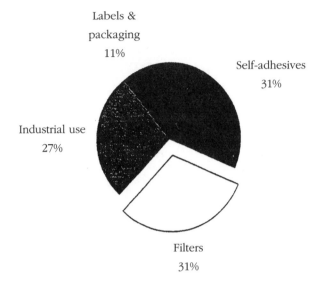

Labels &
packaging
11%

Self-adhesives
31%

Industrial use
27%

Filters
31%

*Filter Division, Annual Production
(total: 51,000 tonnes)*

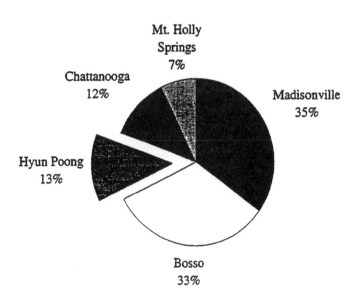

Mt. Holly
Springs
7%

Chattanooga
12%

Madisonville
35%

Hyun Poong
13%

Bosso
33%

Exhibit CS4.4   Republic of Korea

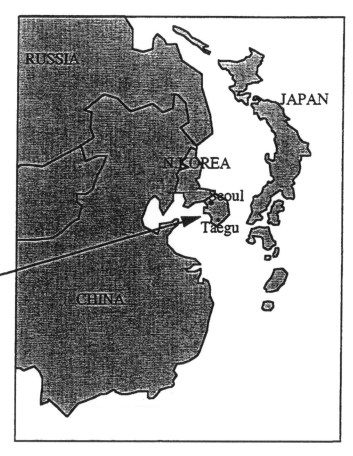

- Land area   9.9 million ha
- Population   44 million
- GDP (1993)   265,900 billion Won
                              (US$ 330.7 billion)
- Real GDP growth (%)

1990	1991	1992	1993
9.2	8.5	5.1	5.5

Case 4

Exhibit CS4.5   Ahlstrom Korea: results since inception (millions of Won)

	1988	1989	1990	1991	1992	1993	1994	1995
Net sales	680	4,504	7,039	9,516	11,716	14,142	15,812	19,863
Operating profit	−259	−634	175	1,816	2,470	3,539	3,282	3,881
Net Income	−620	−1,592	−761	651	1,552	2,505	2,2352	2,391
Current assets	1,390	2,584	5,034	5,286	7.845	10,036	12,641	12,252
Fixed assets	4,912	5,037	4,223	5,015	4,800	4,507	5,968	6,113
Total assets	6,842	7,621	9,257	10,301	12,645	14,543	18,609	18,635
Current liabilities	1,696	1,439	2,484	2,061	3,422	3,558	4,726	4,107
Long term liabilities	3,776	4,394	5,736	3,218	2,649	1,906	2,452	2,480
Shareholders' equity	1,380	1,788	1,037	5,022	6,574	9,079	11,431	11,778
Total liabilities & shareholders' equity	6,842	7,261	9,257	10,301	12,645	14,543	18,609	18,365

Case 4

Exhibit CS4.6   Shareholdings in Ahlstrom Korea (*Source*: Ahlstrom Paper)

			Shareholding %

June 1987

100,000 shares

- 80,000 common stock
  - 40 800 Ahlstrom Paper — 40.8
  - 39 200 On Yang Pulp — 39.2
- 20,000 non-voting stock
  - 20 000 CNB Technology Finance — 20.0

April 1988

200,000 shares

- 160,000 common stock
  - 81 600 Ahlstrom Paper — 40.8
  - 78 400 On Yang Pulp — 39.2
- 40,000 non-voting stock
  - 20 000 CNB Technology Finance — 10.0
  - 20 000 CNB-No.1 — 10.0

October 1989

400,000 shares

- 300,000 common stock
  - 221 600 Ahlstrom Paper — 70.4 *
  - 78 400 On Yang Pulp — 19.6
- 100,000 non-voting stock --
  - 20 000 CNB Technology Finance — 5.0
  - 20 000 CNB-No.1 — 5.0
  - 60 000 Ahlstrom Paper

1990

800,000 shares

- 700,000 common stock
  - 621 600 Ahlstrom Paper — 85.2 *
  - 78 400 On Yang Pulp — 9.8
- 100,000 non-voting stock --
  - 20 000 CNB Technology Finance — 2.5
  - 20 000 CNB-No.1 — 2.5
  - 60 000 Ahlstrom Paper

December 1993

800,000 shares

- 700,000 common stock
  - 621 600 Ahlstrom Paper — 89.6 *
  - 78 400 On Yang Pulp — 10.4 *
- 100,000 non-voting stock
  - 95 520 Ahlstrom Paper
  - 4 480 On Yang Pulp

*Includes share in non-voting (preference) stock.

Case 4

Exhibit CS4.7   Ahlstrom Korea's volume sales trend (*Source*: Ahlstrom Paper)

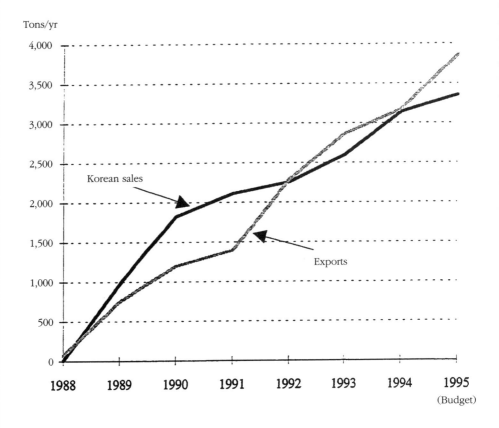

Exhibit CS4.8 Per capita paper and board consumption, 1992/93 (kg)

	1992		1993
Singapore	217.4	USA	317.3
Taiwan	187.8	Finland	262.0
Hong Kong	179.8	Japan	225.4
Korea	123.3	Canada	218.9
Malaysia	60.8	Belgium	213.7
Thailand	27.2	UK	169.5
China	15.0	France	154.4
Indonesia	9.0	Italy	127.8
India	3.2	Spain	120.3
Vietnam	0.9	Portugal	68.8
		Greece	63.1
Asia region average	**14.6**	**World average**	**44.0**

Source: Ahlstrom Paper

Marketing to Asian Consumers

Part

3

Japan

Commitment to the Japanese market

With 125 million affluent customers, Japan should be every marketing manager's dream. Yet for many it remains a nightmare. Most Western firms have trouble coming to terms with the intricacies of a market rife with 'different' rules, which, they feel, are rigged against them.

Some foreign firms have succeeded in Japan. IBM boasted annual profits of US$1 billion in the early 1990s. Western pharmaceutical firms and oil companies also performed well. Counter to all expectations, even McDonald's hamburgers have conquered Japan. In the 1980s, demand for French luxury goods and German cars surged. In the 1990s, US PC producers made major inroads into the market. Overall, however, the record is more than mixed. Manufacturers of international class – including those mentioned above – have rarely matched their market shares in the USA or Europe, often settling for less than half, even in industries where Japanese competitors were initially offering far lower standards. Their frustration, paired with Japan's consistently high trade surpluses, has caused protracted trade disputes since the early 1980s.

Many Japanese observers blame the dismal performance of foreign firms on their lack of commitment. The presence of Western firms in Japan is indeed minimal: the number of all foreign businesses is only a fraction of the number of Japanese businesses abroad. On a per capita basis, foreign investment is far lower in Japan than in other industrial countries. Rather than lack of commitment, however, these asymmetries are the result of past restrictive foreign investment policies, the difficulty of market entry, and the prohibitive costs of keeping expatriate staff in Japan today. Investing in Japan is very expensive (land prices are especially high); it also requires considerable time, since opportunities for acquisitions are rare, and foreign firms are forced to build up their operations from scratch.

Aside from flows of capital, there are several other indicators of corporate commitment:

- the degree to which foreign firms are prepared to change the way in which they run their business and adapt to the Japanese environment;

- their efforts to meet Japanese expectations, especially in terms of quality and service;

- the degree to which they adjust their marketing mix to the traits of the Japanese market.

Competition in Japan

Corporate rhetoric about the globalization of markets may actually have hindered foreign firms in Japan: too often, they simply tried to replicate strategies that had worked in Europe and the USA. It took P&G 11 years to realize that marketing strategies imported from the USA did not work. Club Med was almost as slow in learning that easy-going, somewhat hedonistic, holidays have little appeal for the Japanese. By emphasizing opportunities to learn new sports, however, it substantially increased its Japanese clientele in the 1990s.

Not only do foreign firms overestimate their own strengths: they also underestimate their Japanese competitors. P&G, and other Western firms, tended to look down on the capabilities of Japanese firms, considering they were weakened by collusion and cozy relations with government. Reality is quite different: in many sectors competition is intense. Japanese newspapers regularly publish the market shares of many companies in industries ranging from steel to advertising. Nowhere else does one find more than ten local manufacturers of air-conditioners, cameras, copiers, audio or video equipment and trucks, eight national car manufacturers, six mainframe computer producers or 34 semiconductor companies, all competing with each other and against foreign firms in their own local market.

Western firms often fail to grasp the precise nature of Japanese competition. In the West, price wars and noisy advertising battles are seen as indicators of intense rivalry. In Japan price wars were unusual, although new, aggressive retail chains are changing this. Competition is measured more qualitatively: through a constant flow of new or improved products, and unrelenting efforts to differentiate offerings in terms of performance, quality and service. In the early 1990s, more than 1,000 new soft drinks were launched in Japan every year, and leading producers of television sets had up to 100 different models on the market at any given moment. Both strategies are clear signs of acute competition.

Foreign firms usually enter the Japanese market with new products and services, or with goods promising superior performance and prestige. (Because of higher operating costs, there is no point for them to offer 'me-too' products; they can only afford to sell undifferentiated products at lower prices in cooperation with retail chains, as in the case for Belgian beer or Agfa's film.) However, market success achieved with new or superior products is sustainable only if they are constantly upgraded. Japanese competitors will seize the first opportunity to counter any new product introduction from abroad, either with improved versions or with more appropriate, cheaper products. The response of Japanese companies, supported by dedicated distribution networks and cooperative long-term suppliers, can be devastating, especially if the foreign firm is unprepared.

Consumer behaviour

Two cultural and social factors have traditionally shaped the behaviour of Japanese consumers, and made the Japanese market unlike any other:

- because of Japan's long isolation and idiosyncratic culture, consumer behaviour differs greatly from other world markets. A good example is the emphasis on service rather than price;

■ differences in behaviour among individual consumers are negligible: the overwhelming majority of the Japanese belong to the middle class, or rather the middle of the middle class. Similar wage packages and living conditions, a lack of minorities and sub-cultures, a high degree of education and omnipresent media have created very homogeneous standards of living and reinforced a tendency to act in conformity with the group.

These two traits have resulted in the past in a distinctively 'Japanese' market. Today, however, Japan's growing integration in the world economy, the offer of foreign products and services and the exposure of consumers to different cultures through the media and foreign travel have blurred the distinction, once clear, between 'Japanese' and 'foreign'. Western firms now offer typical Japanese goods with Japanese specifications and Japanese names, while Japanese firms sell foreign novelties under foreign names. The confusion over product origin, brand images and perceptions has created a sense (at least superficial) of internationalization, both in the marketplace and in the minds of consumers.

Among those Japanese consumers open to these new influences, the younger generation unsurprisingly comes first. Known as *shinjinrui* (rebellious youth), they increasingly question traditional Japanese values and replace with more modern values. (Figure 3.1 sets out some shifts in values and behaviour.) The *shinjinrui* – the first generation to experience neither war nor reconstruction – have come of age in a fairly affluent society, with widespread ownership of consumer durables and a sense of a financially secure future.

In marked contrast to their elders, they purchase on credit and spend on fads and fashions, entertainment and leisure. They have made Japanese markets more fickle and shortened product life cycles. Very lifestyle-orientated, they are strongly influenced by the specialized media. They are conspicuous consumers, concerned with expressing their individuality and impressing their immediate peer group. From the marketing perspective, two groups clearly stand out: young men prior to their first 'career ladder' job, and young women ('Office Ladies') before marriage and childbearing. Consumption patterns within these groups exhibit a high degree of conformity.

This trend towards consumption and the expression of individuality does not necessarily mark the end of an era in Japan: the new generation may well turn back to traditional values once they become *shakaijin* (full members of society with responsibilities to their families and firms).

In Japan, as in Korean and Chinese societies, group conformity and saving face remain strong forces in consumer markets, even among the young. Most decisions are strongly influenced by the group one belongs to and by fear of losing face. For instance, the brand, price and packaging of presents must reflect the status of both giver and recipient.

As in other East Asian societies, the individual is judged on his or her relationship to the group, rather than individual personality or performance. Western

Figure 3.1   Values in Japan

Traditional	Modern
Work	Leisure
Diligence	Quality of life
Thrift	Conspicuous consumption
Deferred gratification	Instant gratification
Non-material	Material

Conformity	Differentiation
Collectivism	Individualism
Loyalty	Independence
Security	Risk taking
Age	Youth
Position	Performance
Dedication	Detachment
Japaneseness	Eclectic/imitative

ego-driven consumption which thrives on self-fulfilment remains the exception. The driving force is still a desire to give a positive image of oneself by adopting prestigious consumer goods – as the success of brands such as Louis Vuitton, Waterman and BMW testifies.

Other observers argue that a new category of lifestyle-orientated consumers with a strong desire to assert their independence from society – maybe trendsetters for tomorrow – is emerging in Japan. It is premature, however, to expect truly Western-style individualism.

Yet another approach posits that in Japan, self-fulfilment is more socially-orientated: it is a desire to enhance one's position by contributing to society, in contrast with the egotistical, accumulative individualism typical of the West. This disparity in interpretation should serve as a warning to foreign firms: the Japanese market challenges many common Western assumptions about collectivism and individualism in the marketplace.

Market trends

The maturing of the Japanese economy, increased competition in many industries, political changes and the impact of foreign pressure are changing Japan's markets dramatically. Barriers to foreign influence have fallen and are likely to be dismantled further. Those foreign firms who persevere will attain insider status, although the increased sophistication of the Japanese market will not make success any easier. Government policy, more concerned in the past with the welfare of industry than with that of consumers, makes markets more demand-led rather than supply-driven, but this will also increase competitive pressure.

Three more specific trends will shape the future of the Japanese market:

- Japan's population is aging rapidly. By 2010, it will have the world's highest percentage of people over 65. This rapid transition raises several questions. Will this fast-growing 'silver generation' be as active a driver of markets as it has been in the USA, for example, or will its members remain traditional passive consumers? What will be the impact of this change on saving rates, health insurance and pensions? How will housing and healthcare services be affected?

- Despite the commonly accepted image of a staunchly middle-class Japan, the rich are now numerous enough to make a new market segment. This group comprises entrepreneurs, doctors and artists, and all those whose real estate investments soared in the 1980s: farmers who sold their land at the right time, or ordinary middle-class people lucky enough to have purchased the right house or apartment. All have income available for conspicuous consumption on prestigious foreign goods.

- The changing role of women, who already make up over 40 per cent of Japan's workforce. Some 70 per cent of young women work; this proportion falls after they marry, then rises again once their children have grown up. It will probably be higher in the future. The stereotype of the caring Japanese housewife is no longer valid. Japanese women have long been in charge of the family's finances; their power is even greater now that they contribute an increasing share to the budget themselves. In the future, therefore, men will make or even influence fewer and fewer purchasing decisions. As women become increasingly busy, the demand for supporting services and convenience products should continue to accelerate.

Distribution

The changing role of Japanese women and the continuing deregulation of trade will accelerate change in the distribution system. The Japanese have shopped traditionally at local stores so small that retailers need frequent supplies from wholesalers, also small, located nearby. These buy from larger, regional wholesalers who in turn are supplied by primary wholesalers often working exclusively with a particular manufacturer or importer. Close relationships are built over years, or decades, and include services such as credit, sales promotion support, and reimbursement of returned goods.

While this system suited neighbourhood customers, it drove up prices and excluded new players and practices. Large chains of convenience stores are now replacing the old-fashioned shops. With changes in the retail law in 1990, firms such as Toys'R'Us have moved into Japan, squeezing out layers of middlemen. New discount stores have also opened; instead of forging close links with manufacturers or importers, they purchase from the lowest-cost sources, often under private label, offer no services and use lower prices to undercut competitors.

The opening of larger outlets makes it easier for newcomers to enter the Japanese market and shift the balance of power from manufacturers to distributors, as has been happening in the West for over a decade. Nevertheless, the deeply-rooted traditional retail sector will not go out of business overnight; it is likely to coexist with modern forms of distribution for some time.

ASEANIEs*

Demographic changes

Dramatic demographic changes will take place in the ASEANIEs in coming decades; this will have a decisive impact on future market opportunities. The chief change is slower population growth. However, this does not mean that the size of Asia's populations is stabilizing. Indonesia's population for example will increase from about 190 million in 1995 to 283 million in 2025. Declining population growth is primarily due to reduced childbearing, although infant mortality has also fallen, and life expectancy increased. As a consequence, the structure of the population is changing: the proportion of young people is falling (see Table 3.1). The impact on consumption will be as follows:

- As the number of young adults with disposable income goes up, so will the number of households. They will require lodgings and equipment, ensuring that demand for housing and consumer durables remains strong.

- Relative spending power is slowly shifting from the younger to the more mature households who have completed their family and who will start buying transportation, better housing, entertainment and education, instead of daily necessities.

- Women, freed of maternal responsibilities, will continue to join the workforce. This will increase demand for labour-saving goods and eating out.

The trend towards urbanization will also continue. Marketing products and services will be easier, with consumers in closer reach. Urban dwellers, while on average much better off than country people, will nevertheless see their income

---

*This is the group of middle-sized developing and industrializing countries made up by the ASEAN group and the NIEs.

Table 3.1 Percentage of population 25 years and older

Country	1995	2020
Hong Kong	67	76
Japan	69	75
Singapore	62	69
Taiwan	58	69
South Korea	58	69
China	56	66
Thailand	50	61
Indonesia	46	59
Malaysia	44	59
Philippines	42	53

Source: *World Population Register: Estimates on Projection, Cult Related Demographic Statistics 1994–95,* World Bank, Johns Hopkins University Press, 1994

considerably dented by expensive housing. Traffic congestion in big cities will worsen and the existing infrastructure will be stretched to the limit, forcing governments to spend heavily just to keep up with the demand for utilities and public services. With fewer children, households will save more for their retirement – this is already mandatory in Singapore; parents will rely less on their children in their old age. As an increasing percentage of adults reach retirement age, they will begin to draw on their savings rather than accumulate more wealth; this could reduce the net saving rate.

Consumer segmentation

Demographics, income levels and distribution, expenditure and saving rates, geographic dispersion of the population, psychographic and behavioural characteristics – all these variables influence the make-up of segments for consumer goods. These segments must be defined differently for each of the ASEANIEs and for each product category.

Market research generally divides the consumer population into segments A, B, C, D and E according to income levels. In developing countries with low average income, the top segments are obviously very small, while an overwhelming majority still lives in relative poverty. The simplified segmentation for a less developed country (LDC) in Figure 3.2 may be typical of Indonesia; it is quite different from segmentation for an NIE such as Singapore, which now has a large group of fairly affluent spenders.

Figure 3.2   Class structures through different development stages

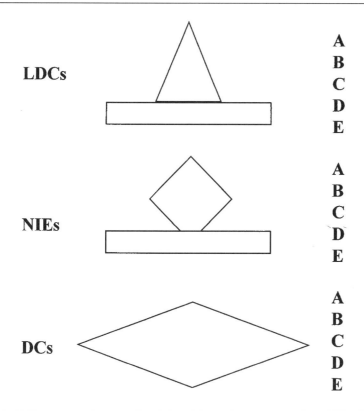

(Segments always relate to each other within one given country: an E consumer in Singapore is probably better off than a C or even a B in Indonesia.)

Only in developed countries (DCs) such as the USA or Germany does segmentation take the shape of a diamond, with most consumers belonging to the middle class, and a few either above or below that level. It is interesting to note that a less developed country does not become an NIE and later a DC through rapid growth of the D segment, but rather through an increase in B and C consumers, while relative conditions for the E segment remain unchanged for quite some time.

Bearing in mind the heterogeneity of economies and markets in the ASEANIEs, a segmentation into three types of consumer may suffice for a first overview.

The elite segment

This tiny minority of business, government and military leaders are rich by any Western standard. They live in the capital but travel abroad frequently. Their consumer behaviour and tastes resemble those of the rich in the West and Japan. Although their total number is small, their public appearances and their role as trendsetters make them important in marketing terms.

Western firms who target exclusively this segment do not need to make a major marketing effort in each country: the prestige value of their brands creates the necessary pull. Regional promotional activities, combined with controlled distribution in Singapore and Hong Kong, should be enough: brands with a strong appeal will find their way into the other countries through indigenous channels, thereby avoiding high tariff barriers.

The transition segment

Its members – mainly city-dwellers with above-average incomes – have benefited from recent economic growth. They are open-minded, active, consumption-orientated and modern without necessarily being Westernized. The world they live in is completely unlike that of their parents 20 or 30 years ago. They neither inherited nor accumulated substantial wealth but live well thanks to their managerial and technical skills. They are well educated, often thanks to sacrifices their parents made, and belong to the sector of the workforce which is currently most in demand in the ASEANIEs. A majority of Singaporeans fall into this segment, as do perhaps 10–15% of all Indonesians. The proportions for other ASEANIEs lie in between.

Demand from the transition segment creates the most dynamic markets in the region for goods from up-market clothing to motor bikes and cars, and services such as insurance and travel. These non-essential products, aimed at improving the quality of life, are the chief beneficiaries of income growth in this segment. As more and more people have access to higher education, move into cities and join the workforce of the modern sector, this segment keeps getting bigger.

The transition segment will require more marketing effort from foreign firms. The sales response function of Figure 3.3 shows the shape of the classical S-curve. The marketing mix must usually be adapted to each individual market, and positive results will take time. Early entrants will enjoy a considerable head start over latecomers. Western firms are established most firmly in the fields of food, cosmetics and pharmaceuticals; in consumer durables, the offer is almost exclusively Japanese, although competition from Korea and Taiwan is emerging.

The traditional segment

Traditional consumers can only afford basic necessities and the occasional cheap durables. They include most country dwellers, as well as the urban poor. Modernization and industrialization have largely passed them by. They are very price-conscious and lag in adopting new products.

This segment's sales response function also follows an S-curve, but flatter and more stretched. Consumers in this segment are reluctant to switch to new products: they are extremely risk-averse. They are also more loyal to traditional products, preferring tea to soft drinks, for example. Foreign firms who want to penetrate this segment must keep their costs well under control; they will also need elaborate

Figure 3.3   Sales response function

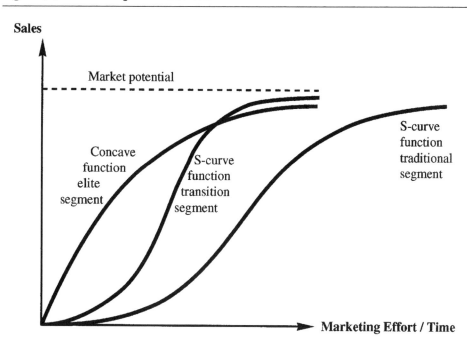

distribution systems to reach consumers in the countryside; this involves a major effort which only produces returns after a long time.

The distribution revolution

Nowhere in the markets of the ASEANIEs has change been more dramatic or visible than in the distribution sector. Japanese department stores dominate the shopping areas of Singapore and Hong Kong, Bangkok and Malaysia; hypermarkets attract large crowds in Taipei; shopping malls have been turned into entertainment centres in Manila and Jakarta, with everything from ice-skating rinks to cinemas. The traditional sector of small family-run shops, market traders and itinerant vendors, is retreating fast in big cities.

This trend is the result of increasingly mobile consumers with higher purchasing power who want to find a wider range of goods and services in a single location. Shopping has become a major social activity. Shopping centres are combinations of department and specialty stores, restaurants and fast-food stalls, art galleries, discos and cinemas. Small, traditional Mom-and-Pop shops lack both the capital and expertise to compete.

Small outlets are at a disadvantage because they have higher overheads and cannot match the buying power of chain stores. In suburban neighbourhoods and in the countryside, however, there have been no major changes; nor are there likely to be in the near future: consumers want access to a local shop where they can buy small amounts of fresh food daily and take it home easily. What matters is the personal relationship with the store owner, who extends credit without need for a credit card.

Western manufacturers operating in Asian countries other than Singapore and Hong Kong can rarely go into distribution themselves: they use local distributors instead, limiting themselves to sales promotions at the point of sale. Most countries, however, have taken steps to liberalize the distribution sector. Western distribution companies also face restrictions, although some have overcome them through franchise operations, licenses and joint ventures. Benetton (Italy), Esprit (USA) and Marks & Spencer (UK) sell garments in most ASEANIEs; IKEA (Sweden) and Habitat (UK) have outlets in Singapore and Hong Kong, where Galeries Lafayette and Le Printemps of France also compete head-on with Japanese department stores. In convenience stores, 7-Eleven (USA/Japan) leads across the region. The Asian outlets of fast-food chains such as McDonald's and Kentucky Fried Chicken are among their most successful. Carrefour (France) brought hypermarkets to Taiwan, later expanding from there into other Asian countries. Makro (Netherlands) introduced cash-and-carry in Thailand, then started operations in other ASEANIEs. Amway (USA) evaded restrictions on distribution activities in Korea by engaging customers to sell its products to friends and neighbours for a commission. The Singaporean bookstore chain, Times Publishing, is in fact a joint venture with a majority Indonesian partner; it now operates the first foreign bookstores in Indonesia.

Relationships between foreign manufacturers and appointed importers are bound to run into trouble when products enter through parallel channels the latter's exclusive territory where unauthorized agents sell them at lower prices. This happens frequently in the ASEANIEs. Official importers who shoulder the cost of sales promotions and advertising cannot compete with parallel imports, often bought from the cheapest sources world-wide, and brought through customs at less than full duty. To stop this, manufacturers must check their order processing procedures, keep track of products and should not resort to differential pricing.

China

The shift from state planning to market forces

Of all Asia Pacific nations, China is the most extreme case of a country in flux. When it opened its economy in 1978–79, Western business saw it as the world's biggest untapped market. The opening of the country to foreign investment – particularly in the SEZs – brought in technological expertise. Links with the outside world were urgently needed to export and earn foreign exchange. The influx of foreign exchange in turn allowed in imports, although in strictly regulated fashion.

Major industrial reforms began in the mid-1980s, slowly phasing out mandatory and guidance planning in many sectors, reducing the influence of the state's centralized administration, and moving towards market prices that reflect supply and demand. The results have been spectacular: standards of living have visibly improved and China has become a major player in world trade. The objective of quadrupling GNP between 1980–2000, which experts once declared impossible, has been reached in 1996.

However, China's political ideology continues to contradict its new-found economic pragmatism. The goal of reform has already changed from a 'planned economy with the market as auxiliary regulator' and 'socialism with Chinese characteristics' towards an undefined 'socialist market economy' in just a few years. Temporary setbacks cannot be ruled out: it will not be easy to slacken 50 million party members' and 30 million state bureaucrats' grip on power. Many Chinese have benefited from the dramatic growth, particularly in the cities. Farmers – the overwhelming majority of Chinese – may resent the growing disparity in income.

While China is an attractive market, it remains rife with uncertainties. Its huge population and land mass raise the question: should China be seen as a single market, or as a number of warring provinces competing for scarce resources and eager to promote their own well-being? An investment in booming Guangdong, for example, does not guarantee access to markets in the Chinese hinterland; building a plant in Shanghai does not ensure preferential treatment from a Beijing bureaucrat. While there is a tendency towards decentralization, other forces are promoting a Greater China that would take over Taiwan after Hong Kong; this could require a much more coordinated strategy from the Western firm.

As China moves away from bureaucratic allocations and targets towards market mechanisms, there are often doubts about which government officials remain in charge of which industries, and to what extent. The lack of information and a tendency to classify even basic economic data as state secrets make it difficult to carry out feasibility studies and market research. While China's willingness to provide information slowly improves, data are unreliable and liable to becoming quickly outdated. Ever-changing regulations and the weak legal system may provide flexibility for those who yield influence and can 'massage' the system; they have also led to a high degree of uncertainty in Western firms, used to operate in a legalistic environment.

Stratification of consumers

Until recently, communist ideology ensured that income differentials in China remained small, making the segmentation we use for the ASEANIEs inappropriate. As an example, China's most highly qualified specialists still earn about the same as unskilled workers. However, the high income growth in the SEZs, Guangdong province and urban areas of the coastal belt has created a group of 60–80 million people with incomes estimated at three times the Chinese average. These relatively affluent consumers are close to the standards of the ASEANIEs' transition segment. Another, much smaller group of entrepreneurs or speculators have become rich enough to afford cars and expensive electronic gadgets. Their number is variously estimated between a few hundred thousand and five million, although it is impossible to check: flaunting one's wealth is still seen as risky, should the political winds change. At the other end of the spectrum, many people live in poverty, either in isolated rural areas, or because they are unemployed. Estimates range from 50–150 million but, again, official data are not available.

This leaves the marketing people with one billion average income Chinese (see Figure 3.4) who display a strong appetite for goods such as bicycles, watches, television sets and cameras. As their income increases, they start buying video recorders, air-conditioners and motorcycles. Consumption of soft drinks, more up-market food products, cosmetics, toys and ready-to-wear apparel has grown substantially despite fairly high prices. Japanese manufacturers try to capture the demand for consumer durables; Western firms such as Nestlé, Coca-Cola, P&G, and Unilever are also building up major operations in China. Almost all international brewers have set up operations as well.

Foreign firms, mostly in joint venture with Chinese companies, charge more because import duties and operating costs are high. Chinese consumers don't seem to mind provided they get better product presentation and quality despite their relatively low average income. Their high propensity to spend lies in the fact that one's spending power often depends more on one's family rather than on one's income. Housing, health, education and transportation are still largely subsidized; as a consequence, a very high percentage of the Chinese income is disposable.

Increased contact with foreign firms has stimulated an ever growing number of local manufacturers to improve the quality of their own products as well as their marketing techniques. Others find it increasingly difficult to compete. The enormous influx of foreign investment and the upgrading of existing local firms has led to significant overcapacity in some industries. Better informed and more sophisticated consumers are becoming more discriminating, especially in Shanghai, the fashion centre of China, and in Guangdong province, where largely urban consumers are strongly influenced by constant exposure to Hong Kong television and radio.

The Hong Kong-ization of Guangdong – very visible in the Shenzhen SEZ – is a caricature of Chinese consumerism. While the more open-minded consumers are ready to adopt new, modern, foreign brands, the vast majority of consumers still live in the countryside and stick to traditional Chinese products (see Figure 3.5). There are also important differences in purchasing behaviour. While some people flaunt their wealth to differentiate themselves from neighbours and colleagues; others, who still adhere to

Figure 3.4   Income segmentation in China

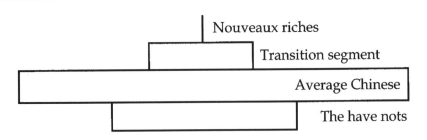

Figure 3.5   Psychographic segmentation in China

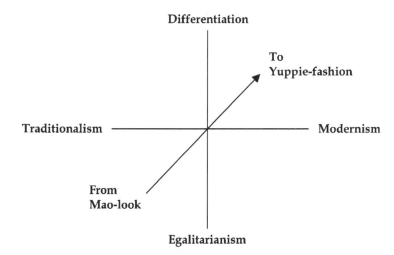

egalitarian principles, try not to be conspicuous. As the Maoist ideology fades, however, they are likely to become a minority.

Marketing instruments

There are few restrictions on advertising, which makes heavy use of television, radio, magazines and newspapers. The national television station, Central TV, claims an audience of 600 million for its evening news, and advertising hoardings dot the countryside. Direct mail campaigns are carried out. Advertising rates have increased but remain reasonable. Foreign firms are charged higher prices and must pay in foreign currency; joint ventures pay in local currency, but more than local firms.

Because of a general lack of information and reading material, advertising is followed with great interest. Simple explanatory messages seem to work best. Word-of-mouth is important, as are the recommendations of direct salespeople or department store assistants. Avon has successfully used part-timers to sell cosmetics directly to the consumer in southern China, primarily through traditional networks of friends and neighbours. Mary Kay has achieved a similar success in the Shanghai region.

Distribution, a critical marketing-mix factor for the foreign firm, can be problematic in terms of logistics and channel structure. The large distances, provincial self-interest, the overburdened transportation and telecommunications infrastructure and the lack of independent flexible transport companies are major hurdles. It takes at least a week to drive newly-built Volkswagen Santanas on bad roads from the plant in Shanghai to customers in Sichuan Province. When they arrive they need a good overhaul if they are not to be considered used cars. It is easier to ship coal from Australia to the coastal regions of China than to transport it on the single railway line from the hinterland.

Distribution channels are no less chaotic. While formerly the government allocated output from factories to a network of state wholesalers and retailers, a new breed of private distributor has emerged. This enables Western firms to bypass red tape; however, it is difficult to evaluate alternatives and the streamlining channels is slowed down by *guanxi*.

For most products, several parallel distribution systems are now available. Some state-owned department stores supply themselves directly from the producers. Cooperative stores run by local governments compete with factory outlets and an increasing number of specialized private retailers. Joint ventures such as Nike, Esprit and Benetton have set up their own retail outlets, and chain stores such as 7-Eleven and department stores such as Yaohan have started to do so too.

References

Chai, Joseph C.H., 'Consumption and Living Standards in China', *The China Quarterly*, 1992, pp. 721–749.

Fields, George, *Gucci on the Ginza*, Tokyo and New York, Kodansha 1989, pp. 235–255.

Lee, Chol, 'Modifying an American Consumer Behavior Model For Consumers in Confucian Culture: The Case of Fishbein Behavioral Intention Model', *The Journal of International Consumer Marketing*, Vol. 3, 1990, pp. 27–50.

Malayang, Ruth. V., 'The Distribution Industry in Asian NIEs and ASEAN Countries and the Effects of the Entry of Japanese Retailers', *Management Japan*, Vol. XXI, No. 2, 1988, pp. 15–28.

Palia, Aspy and Keown, Charles, 'Combating Parallel Importing: Views of US Exporters to the Asian Countries', *Industrial Marketing Management*, No. 12, 1983, pp. 113–123.

Roberto, Eduardo L., *Applied Marketing Research*, Ateneo de Manila University Press, Manila.

Schütte, Hellmut and Ciarlante, Deanne, *Consumer Behaviour in Asia*, Macmillan, 1998.

Case 5

This case was prepared by Pierre Courbon, MBA participant, under the supervision of Philippe Lasserre, Professor of Strategy and Management at INSEAD. It is intended to be used as the basis for class discussion rather than to illustrate either effective or ineffective handling of an administrative situation. Copyright © 1994 INSEAD Euro-Asia Centre, Fontainebleau, France.

Carrefour in Asia
Taiwan: A Bridgehead into Asia

In June 1993 as he was leaving Taiwan to move to his new office in Hong Kong, Gérard Clerc, the new Carrefour CEO for Asia, considered Carrefour's first operations in Asia. He had been building those stores from scratch in Taiwan. Five were already open, and two bigger ones were to open before the year's end. The results of his formula were so far quite satisfactory, but competition was fierce and increasing.

Reflecting on his six years' experience in Taiwan, Clerc wondered if Carrefour would be able to sustain an increasing level of competition coming from well-established mass retailers such as Makro, or new comers from the USA and Europe, or from local firms. He also asked himself whether he could have done things differently, and if the experience he had gained in Taiwan would be applicable to other countries in Asia.

THE FIRST STEPS

A Carrefour missionary

In the summer of 1986, Gérard Clerc was sent to Taiwan to prospect the local market. The 'Republic of China', as it calls itself, was then largely unknown to the general public (Exhibit CS5.2). But Jacques Fournier, the founder and chairman of Carrefour, and his partners, Denis and Jacques Defforey, all thought that this little island – where Chiang Kai-Shek had sought refuge in 1949 – had great potential.

Clerc, a business graduate, was an auditor with the French news magazine *L'Express* until 1971, when he joined Carrefour. Clerc was a store manager for six years. He was then in charge of a 5–10 year development plan at headquarters and was finally a regional manager for five years in Paris and Bordeaux.

The feasibility study

When he arrived in Taiwan Gérard Clerc accompanied by two department heads was planning a one and a half month feasibility study. He spent some time analysing the local conditions against the set of criteria usually used by Carrefour to determine if it should enter a new market. The retail business was in its infancy in Taiwan, which was one of the factors in favour of entering. If the legal environment was not satisfactory, the country seemed politically stable, and inflation was low. In addition, Taiwan was very open to foreign investors, although the language barrier was a problem.

Basic facts and figures were gathered about population, GNP per capita growth, road network, motorization rate and so on, although the data were very often unreliable. A population of 20 million could support the development of many stores and would be worth the effort. With a GNP per capita of around US$4,000 (Exhibit CS5.3), food consumption sophistication was actually still low, but with the potential for high growth. The motorization rate is also always a key criterion, and although it was still low in Taiwan, there were plenty of motorcycles and scooters (Exhibit CS5.2).

Clerc also had to check real estate prices and evaluate expected price differentials with the local competitors already operating, as well as payment terms, so as to produce income and cash flow projections. This approach was, of course, artificial and conservative, but was necessary to evaluate the potential return on investment of the project.

Other countries might also at first glance have offered favourable conditions. However, Hong Kong and Singapore were too urbanized and too small in market terms for Carrefour's ambitions, while Korea had a lower GNP per capita, and Japan seemed largely closed to foreign retailers and therefore much too difficult a country to start with.

In spite of the uncertainty inherent in any overseas investment decision, Clerc had a good feeling about the country. He presented his study to the Executive Board in October 1986, and a positive answer came a month later. Clerc was asked to head the development of Carrefour in Taiwan.

PRESICARRE CORPORATION

A partnership

Clerc settled in Taipei on 15 February 1987. His first task was to find a local partner. The Carrefour management felt this was necessary in a country such as Taiwan, far from the home base and so culturally different. The Crédit Lyonnais branch in Taiwan had introduced President Enterprises to Carrefour before 1986, and President had actually given some help to Clerc for his feasibility study. President was the island's largest foodstuff manufacturer.

Clerc met President again in February 1987, and the principle of a joint venture leaving the management to Carrefour was agreed. President already had a foothold in retailing and was interested in vertical integration so as to have preferential outlets to which it could sell its products.

The agreement was eventually signed in August, and a new company – PresiCarre Corp – was set up with an invested capital of FF120 million (about US$20 million). President Enterprises had a 40% share, the remaining 60% being Carrefour's. Gérard Clerc became president of the new company. From the beginning, President accepted the role of a sleeping partner. Clerc has always avoided resorting to President Enterprises so as not to be liable to them in any way. Still, the simple fact that President is such a well-known company and that Mr Kao, its chairman, is also the head of the local union of industrialists, has considerably helped Carrefour in its integration in the local networks. The case has been very clear in Tainan, from which the group originates.

Carrefour

Carrefour Supermarchés SA has been a pioneer in the setting up of hypermarkets in France.

Hypermarkets are mass retailing stores applying the principle of self-service, but on a much larger scale than supermarkets. While a typical supermarket would have a sales area of between 400 and 2,500 square metres and would carry over 5,000 to 10,000 items, a hypermarket would carry 40,000 to 50,000 items on a sales area much above 2,500 square metres. Large Carrefour stores in France have more than 20,000 square metres of sales space offering fresh vegetables as well as PCs and mountain bikes and it is not unusual to see sales assistants moving around on roller skates! (Exhibit CS5.4.)

Carrefour opened its first store in 1963 in a suburb of Paris and has expanded rapidly ever since. It is the largest retailing organization in France, operating some 114 stores with an average area of 9,400 square metres, for a total of more than one million square metres. Consolidated worldwide sales of Carrefour amount to FF123 billion (about US$20 billion).

The original principles on which Carrefour has built its development still underpin the company today:

- one-stop shopping
- self-service
- discount
- quality products
- free car park

Carrefour started going international at the end of the 1960s in Europe. Its most successful foreign operations are in Spain, where under the name Pryca it is the second largest retailer in the country, and in Brazil (Exhibit CS5.5). Carrefour has, however, had to pull out from the UK, from Belgium and Switzerland for lack of room for expansion and from the USA where the results have not been good.

Carrefour has been successful thus far not so much in mature markets, but rather when it has entered markets which, like France in the 1960s, showed dramatic changes in consumers' buying habits. These combined a set of characteristics that included high growth of the GNP per capita, sub-urbanization, higher participation of women in the labour force, and a large increase in ownership of cars and refrigerators.

Case 5

President Enterprise Corporation

Founded in 1967, President was initially a small company of 80 employees, producing flour and animal feed. Twenty-five years later, it ranks number one in the Taiwan agribusiness sector, and is the tenth largest company on the island, as well as the fifth largest employer (Exhibit CS5.6).

In 1992, the group had a consolidated gross revenue of NT$49.7 billion (more than US$1.7 billion). President's strength is not only in its food and beverage ranges, but also in its distribution network. In addition to its bakeries and automatic vending machines, President, in cooperation with Southland Inc. manages the 7-Eleven convenience stores, which, with its 824 outlets is the largest chain store on the island.

A large part of President's power stems from a sustained strategy of partnership with foreign groups, either as agent/importer in Taiwan ('Budweiser' beer from Anheuser Busch, 'Lu' biscuits from BSN, 'Welsh' fruit juice from National Grape-Coop), as shareholder in joint ventures as with the local subsidiaries of Pepsico, Frito Lay, Kentucky Fried Chicken, Kikkoman, or abroad with the giant Filipino agribusiness company San Miguel, to which President Enterprises is transferring technology.

If President is not yet a world leader in its field, it is clearly ambitious to join this elite group by the year 2010, and already has numerous investments in mainland China, the world's largest market. According to its last annual report, President Enterprises pursues, 'a long term goal of establishing a Food Kingdom, thus achieving once again a new miracle in the history of the President Enterprises operations'.

A slow start

Although initial plans were to build 10,000 square metre stores with over 1,000 car park spaces quickly, ambitions had soon to be scaled down. In February 1987, during a tender by the government for a large plot of land, the price reached twice the amount initially expected. This revealed the underestimation of land prices in Taiwan and the start of a real estate boom. Prices increased by five to ten times within two years. Carrefour was at that time negotiating the purchase of land for the stores, but prices were increasing by 20 to 30% every two to three months. Most negotiations were very lengthy, and prices were starting to be too high. The revaluation of the New Taiwan Dollar (NT$) made prices in French francs even higher. At that point, Clerc decided on renting land instead of buying it, something without precedent for Carrefour. Rent then represented only 1 to 2% of the price of the land and was thus affordable. Renting would also minimize the financial risk.

After 19 months, Clerc finally found a good location in Kaohsiung, south of Taiwan. He negotiated a 10-year contract, which was later increased to 20 years as the landlord became confident. Out of the 7,000 square metres available, Carrefour could actually build on only 3,500 square metres. The rest was to be used for car parks.

In the meantime, Mme Thirion, who was Clerc's assistant, and two other expatriate section heads, plus three Taiwanese staff hired in France one year earlier, arrived in Kaohsiung to assist Clerc in opening the store. When it opened, the store was partly in a basement, with a total of only 3,500 square metres of sales area – quite different from the large stores in France, and on two floors – another innovation for Carrefour. Some managers in France thought that a Carrefour store was a single floor rectangular store with a car park on proprietary land. They were reluctant to accept what they thought was a new concept. Clerc, however, made a point: the essence of the Carrefour concept worldwide is discount, freshness, car park, and nothing else.

The first store opened in December 1989 (Exhibit CS5.7) and was immediately successful. A second store was built in Kaohsiung in cooperation with the same landlord, and opened a year later at the same time as the first Taipei store. Break-even came as early as the first year, which was reassuring for both partners, especially Carrefour at a time when its US stores were facing problems.

The initial phase was, however, a difficult one because of the general mistrust from suppliers, real estate promoters and local government authorities. And as Clerc says, for the local retail industry, 'it was as if the Huns had arrived in Taiwan'.

THE CARREFOUR ADAPTATION IN TAIWAN

Carrefour wanted to avoid simply transferring to Taiwan a concept that had proved successful in France and in other countries. The choice was rather to take into account the particularities of the local environment, and adapt the Carrefour concept.

Adapting the store

One of the most difficult problems to solve at the beginning was finding the right place to open a store. Given the complicated regulations regarding the utilization of land and the distinction made between land for industrial use and land for commercial use, Carrefour could not open in vast spaces in the suburbs. Land is rare in Taiwan, and Carrefour had to operate in urban areas, on rented land. In addition, new stores were to be located not on flat open land, but in buildings, basements or ground floors in high population density areas.

In most Taiwanese stores, investment has usually been very limited in terms of decoration and layout. The shelves are all standard in contrast with France, and none is product-specific. The floor is usually of plain painted cement, with white tiles in the most luxurious stores.

On their first visit to the Taiwan stores the founding fathers of Carrefour actually felt these new stores looked a lot like the first very basic stores they had built in France 30 years before.

As far as possible, Carrefour managers have tried to create in their stores an atmosphere with which Taiwanese clients are familiar. In the fresh products section, for example the lamps hanging above the food stall are exactly the same as those found on traditional 'wet markets'.

Adapting the offer

Carrefour's policy in Taiwan has been to leverage its decision to limit the assortment and buy greater volumes so as to be in a position to obtain competitive prices from its suppliers.

Product choice at Carrefour is much more limited than at Makro which has larger stores. Carrefour mineral water and wines are still imported from France, and wines are sold only in one store located close to expatriate apartments. Given the difficulty of ensuring regular quality supply from manufacturers in Taiwan, no locally produced own labels have been launched so far as Carrefour does not want to damage its good reputation. Generics were, however, launched in 1991, and have been very successful, especially rice which is the top selling item, but also for babies' nappies priced at NT$159 a pack as against NT$459 for Pampers.

Carrefour promotions are held regularly, at individual stores or nationwide, with flyers or advertising in the press. In contrast to the situation in France, few promotions are launched by local manufacturers – even by the large companies such as Weichuan, I-Mei Foods, Foremost or President – unless Carrefour asks for it. Large multinationals such as Procter & Gamble and Unilever are, however, very present on the market and promote their products heavily. L'Oréal has recently introduced some products at Carrefour.

Tracking rapidly changing shopping habits and educating the customers

Given the population density, the specific urban location of the stores, and the traffic on the streets, Carrefour outlets in Taiwan are in fact more proximity stores attracting customers from a radius of 3 km, rather than the larger poles of attraction they can be in France. Carrefour studies have shown that the average rate of visit to a store is twice a week in Taiwan, compared to 1.2 times per month in France. The average value of a client basket is NT$680–700 or FF150, compared to FF500 in France (1 FF = 4.6 NT$, May 1994). A majority of Taiwanese customers are therefore still in a pattern of more frequent, smaller value proximity purchase, in line with traditional buying patterns.

The Taiwanese market changes very quickly. In 1991, the favourite flavours in food products were peanut and lemon. In 1994, the top selling flavours were vanilla, chocolate and strawberry. These would have been in total opposition with local tastes a few years before, and in practice not saleable. Retailers actually have a very important role of educating the Taiwanese consumers in terms of service concept, as well as in terms of products. In some respects a degree of westernization of local tastes is occurring.

Whereas previously there was only necessity purchasing, impulse buying is on the rise. A visit to the 'French' hypermarket is actually, for many families, like a Sunday 'day trip', and buying for pleasure has become normal.

All stores now constantly have pilot departments which introduce new ranges of products. The conclusions of these studies are then introduced on a national scale by all Carrefour stores in Taiwan. This cross learning is very important as it enables managers to learn about the market, follow its evolution closely, and proceed to market tests as well as spread the know-how within the company.

By being closer to the client, Carrefour has been able to promote new ranges of products which are contributing in a larger proportion to the turnover. In France, any increase in sales from one year to the next is purely incremental. What improves the results of stores in Taiwan is the opposite – the introduction in stores of new product categories that were not sold previously, at a time when demand is booming. Carrefour has in this way recently heavily promoted articles such as barbecue equipment, home decoration, cars, gear for swimming and camping and all kinds of outdoor sports, hi-fi equipment, microwave ovens, large screen TVs and so on. Basically,

Figure CS5.1   Carrefour's virtuous circle

one has to follow the market very closely: many articles are under-exploited and the top selling ones change at least every six months. In practice, for foreign management, it means that French patterns have to be forgotten, and the market has to be learnt from scratch. The virtuous circle at Carrefour, however, remains the same as shown in Figure CS5.1.

MANAGEMENT ADAPTATION

Carrefour has also had to adapt the way store management is traditionally run in France.

Human resources management

Management of the stores is extremely decentralized in Taiwan. Department heads are much more autonomous than they would be in France. They handle the relationship with suppliers entirely on their own, selecting products and negotiating prices. They fix the retail prices in their department themselves. Department heads in Taiwan have not only economic but also social power as they are in charge of recruiting employees and negotiating salaries with them, a function that would in France be devoted to a human resources division. The department head will be the one who at the end of each month will give each of the employees in his or her department their paycheque. They will also determine the possibilities of promotion of their staff, and have a say about bonuses. The pressure for sales and profit is put on department heads.

Store managers were initially all French expatriates. The situation has progressively changed: three out of eight are now Taiwanese. Women are given equal opportunities in Carrefour in Taiwan, two of the local managers are women.

Carrefour has a reputation for paying its employees well: a department head at Carrefour earns 20% more than he would with other supermarkets, a section head 25 to 40% more. Salaries for local store managers range from NT$120,000 to NT$200,000 per month (about FF26,000 to FF43,500 or US$4,400 to US$7,400), equivalent to that of a US-educated financial manager in a large company. In comparison, a cashier is paid NT$17,000 per month (about FF3,600 or US$625) for 48 hours a week, against FF7,000 (about NT$32,500 or US$1,200) in France for 39 hours. In France, a participation scheme allows employees to complement their salaries. A bonus linked to the results of each store is also added. In Taiwan, a maximum of three months' salary is given at the time of the Chinese New Year, for all levels of employees, according to the results of their store, their section and their department.

In addition, potential for internal promotion is very high given the rate of development of the operations in Taiwan.

Human resources management is a very serious problem in Taiwan for all local and foreign companies. Given the very low unemployment rate (1.15% in 1993) and the preference of young unskilled people to work in 'clean' services (karaoke bars, coffee shops, restaurants), it is very difficult to find – and to keep – employees. Carrefour stores in Taiwan have an average staff turnover of 65% per year, with 40% of their staff under 18 years old, most of them part-time. That means that the sense of belonging to the organization is usually very limited. It also means that the training effort – both technical and in terms of personal development – is central to the store management policy.

Managing the relationship with suppliers

Managing relations with suppliers is very different from the standard practice in France.

Taiwanese suppliers usually lack rigour, organization, equipment and aggressiveness, but their flexibility is much higher than in the West.

Suppliers usually totally lack information regarding such basic data as their sales in either volume or value, their inventory level, and even simple internal accounting or invoicing information. List prices are not determined according to any cost base, but rather to an ideal selling price. Suppliers can sometimes even lose money. General selling conditions are also very different from one retailer to another. When Procter & Gamble took over its former agent in 1992, it discovered that 123 different conditions were being offered to the market. There is no search for productivity gains nor development strategy. The only clear preoccupation is with the retail price which suppliers would like to remain stable and similar in all retail outlets in competitive chain stores. A few foreign-owned companies are just starting to segment their customer base by a distribution network, offering for example different packing sizes to different retailers.

Equipment is another problem. Only 10% of suppliers deliver their goods on pallets, and there is no standard pallet size on the market. Although Taiwan is one of the largest producers in the world of plastic, blister-pack was extremely hard to find on the local market. Manufacturers are just starting to realize they might have a market in their own country as companies such as Carrefour approach them. Salespeople visiting Carrefour to present their product will often have samples but no catalogues, product reference numbers, sometimes even no order forms.

Surprisingly, and in contrast with the habits of Taiwanese exporters, local suppliers have to be called on the phone for them to come and show their products, a clear difference with western countries where retailers are constantly assailed by manufacturers. Taiwanese suppliers sell products, not services. In Taiwan, the retailers are often in a position of solicitation. Product innovation is limited and can sometimes be initiated by Carrefour remarks or requirements. Many local manufacturers are solely exporting and largely ignore the local market, which offers lower margins and imposes on them smaller and more frequent deliveries as well as a right to return unsold products.

Suppliers in Taiwan are, however, very flexible regarding delivery terms – the following day is never a problem – or with the payment terms. Unsold goods can also be easily returned to the original supplier. Establishing good relationships with suppliers – as with all stakeholders – including foreign-owned companies, is always important. and the best business deals are seldom made in an office but rather in karaoke bars and around a few bottles of quality XO Cognac or local liquor.

Taiwan specific management problems

For French expatriate managers, communication is the number one problem. Taiwan is so far the only country for Carrefour where the working language is not the local language. Foreign managers cannot learn Chinese as fast as they have been able, in other countries, to learn Portuguese, Spanish or English. They usually do not even try to learn Chinese, given the time it takes and their long working hours. Taiwan is also the only country where all documents are written in two languages: Chinese and English. All minutes of meetings, performance reports, in fact all documents, including, of course, the company policy, are bilingual. This problem of communication between foreign managers and local employees naturally has important consequences.

It often means that competent department deads may have more difficulties getting promoted to section heads if they are not able to communicate in basic English with the expatriate store manager. Although this may change as more store manager positions are given to local Taiwanese, further promotion from section head to store manager will again be possible only for English-speaking staff.

In terms of training, it can be difficult to communicate clearly company policy, as well as the corporate culture. Things very often drag out: mass retailing is not only a relatively new concept in Taiwan, but the language barrier can make it difficult to communicate such ideas as the strategy, the goals, and the reasons behind the Carrefour way of doing things. It has been, and still is, extremely difficult for foreign managers to communicate the central message that the smaller the assortment is, the higher the turnover will be. Having fewer products means more sales per product, better buying prices, therefore cheaper induced selling prices, more sales ... and less chance of being out of stock (Exhibit CS5.8).

A second problem is the cultural gap. According to the experience of a local French store manager, Philippe Ravelli, the key difference between the French and the Chinese culture lies in the priority given to three basic elements in the daily life. For the Chinese, emotion (qing) comes first, followed by reason (li) and law (fa). For the French, the law comes first, and in Carrefour that means the company policy is the golden rule. Reason comes second, and emotion comes last. This inverse order between the two cultures is a source of misunderstanding in the management of local operations.

In France, in the distribution sector, it is the duty of managers to train their staff. In Taiwan, the tendency of managers is towards retention of information rather than knowledge sharing. They have been given much more autonomy than is usual at Carrefour, but they themselves delegate very little of their power to their subordinates.

A third problem very specific to Taiwan has been the relationship with new stakeholders, namely with the neighbours – most of the Carrefour hypermarkets being located in urban areas – but also with the local Triads.[1] Some kind of 'protection' has had to be negotiated, and a very strict client circulation and scheduling of deliveries has had to be organized for each store in cooperation with the suppliers. In practice, this has also meant educating the Taiwanese suppliers who were not used to such constraints in their usual operations with other less demanding clients.

What Carrefour has done in Taiwan, as Clerc says, is 'learning how to walk by walking'.

CARREFOUR HAS BEEN SUCCESSFUL IN TAIWAN BUT IS NOT ALONE

The key success factors in Taiwan

Carrefour is today a success in Taiwan. Not only have the financial results shown a profit during the third year (Exhibit CS5.6), but Carrefour contributes with other retailers to shaping new Taiwanese consumer habits.

Philippe Ravelli, store manager, considers the 'basics' of the Carrefour concept as the real competitive advantage of the company in Taiwan, namely free parking, one-stop shopping and competitive prices.

For Jean-Luc Chereau, who in 1993 took Gérard Clerc's position as managing director of the Taiwan operations, the key factors of Carrefour's success in Taiwan are different. They are threefold, and their implementation has been the difficult part:

- Entry at a time of development of a consumer market, when the disposable income was increasing considerably and the country opening up to the outside world.

- Choice of the people who were to constitute the backbone of the Taiwan operations, as well as the French-Chinese mix in the local management.

- Adaptation of a concept that had proved successful to the particularities of a local environment that was very different from the French market.

Customer satisfaction

Figures seem to show that customers like Carrefour, because they are coming back and purchasing, though that still might not be enough to measure actual satisfaction.

The hypermarket is a relatively new concept in Taiwan and customer service is still not well ingrained in the minds of consumers. Therefore although the waiting time at the cashier is shorter in Taiwan than in France, customers are still more attracted by the low prices.

In March 1993, Carrefour launched a nationwide customer survey to understand better the perception of the company. To the question 'What is your main reason for shopping at

---

[1] The Triads are secret societies which became powerful in central and southern China during the eighteenth century, but which today exercise wide influence among Chinese communities worldwide. They are sworn brotherhood groups, sharing a common tradition, initiation rites, secret signs and languages. Activities range from mutual aid organizations to gang-related business.

Carrefour?', price was the unprompted first answer (51%), followed by freshness (25%) and one-stop-shopping (24%). Customer surveys are now done twice a year on a panel of 1,000 customers.

Following the first survey, Carrefour designed a 'Customers' Suggestions Form' available at the information desk of each store. To maintain the image of the company, the department head concerned by the suggestion or complaint has an obligation to answer within 48 hours. Complaints and inquiries are being filed regularly. This useful tool provides excellent feedback from clients on a continuous basis.

Competition is tough

Carrefour is, however, not alone in Taiwan. The growth of western-style supermarkets has been dramatic. There were 189 supermarkets in Taiwan in 1989, and there should be 600 in 1995. With a history of about six years, Taiwan's mass retailing industry is currently dominated by foreign companies, but local companies are increasingly showing a strong interest in the industry.

The 'supermarket league' has been very active in Taiwan.

- *Wellcome* opened its first outlet in Taiwan in 1987, and now operates 72 stores on the island. A recent independent study found that 95% of Taiwanese recognize the Wellcome name, making it the best known of Taiwan's supermarket chains.

- The second largest player is *Park 'N Shop* which opened its first store in 1989. Park 'N Shop plans to open approximately 12 new stores each year for the next four to five years.

- Capturing an increasing market share among Taiwan's supermarkets are the so-called hypermarkets. At present, Taiwan counts two main players in this segment of the market, Carrefour and Makro.

- *Makro* has emerged as Taiwan's largest retailing operation.

If Makro has higher turnover per store than Carrefour, these stores are all much bigger than the Carrefour downtown stores. With five stores operating, Makro is the most successful mass retailing chain in Taiwan in terms of sales.

Makro has recently had to close down its Kaohsiung and Wuku stores which were illegally located in an industrial area not suited for commercial activities according to local regulations. All five of the other stores are in fact in similar situations, as Makro has in all cases opened its huge outlets as warehouses which clients can access only with membership cards. Changes in the regulations should soon solve the problem and open more largely industrial areas for Makro and its competitors. That is why Carrefour has recently opened two warehouse stores (called 'green stores') in the same way.

Continent from France (Promodès company) has set up a joint venture with the Far Eastern Group and is building its first store in Taiwan, which should open at the end of 1994.

So far, Carrefour managers rather welcome competitors. The market is far from saturated, and all will contribute to further educate the clients and get them used to doing their shopping in hypermarkets rather than in traditional wet markets or small stores.

INCREASING THE PACE

In 1993, Gérard Clerc was promoted to the position of chief executive officer for Asia and nominated onto the Carrefour board in France. He moved to Hong Kong to set up his new office and oversee from there Carrefour's activities in Asia. Jean-Luc Chereau took Clerc's position in Taipei and further developed and reorganized the Taiwan operations.

Coordination of the existing operations

In April 1993, Taiwan was divided into two regions (North and South) both headed by a French regional director. Regional managers were supposed to coordinate the activities of the stores. Human management, including training, is a central activity, followed by more centralized merchandising. The goal is to limit the number of wholesalers, concentrate the purchasing of the same product on one or on a few suppliers, to reduce further buying prices and pass on the savings to the consumers. However, with the increase in total sales, some suppliers are no longer in a position to supply the quantities demanded by Carrefour. Diversification of the supply source – with possible imports – is also the only way that Carrefour can presently cope with some of its problems. The trend is in any case towards more centralized buying to improve the terms of purchase and to compensate for the large staff turnover which often disrupts the operations.

Drawing up plans for further expansion in their respective areas is another responsibility for the regional directors. The focus is now so heavily on development that planning the expansion takes 50% of their time.

Development: the 'green stores'

Carrefour had been constantly opening in commercial (and legal) areas which are smaller urban stores compared to Makro's real hypermarkets in industrial suburban areas. The answer 'to the clients – not to Makro', says a Carrefour executive, was the opening in 1993 of the first Carrefour Warehouse in San-Chung, with a sales area of 9,600 square metres and a new distinctive red and green logo. A second Warehouse opened in 1994 with a sales area of 12,400 square metres (Exhibit CS5.6). Both these stores have been opened in industrial areas. Given the local zoning regulations, retailers cannot open stores in industrial areas. Although Carrefour has a business licence and a factory licence, a membership card is required to enter these warehouse stores, as in Makro stores, and the fiction of a Carrefour Warehouse Club instead of a standard hypermarket is maintained. The San-Chung store has already distributed over 200,000 cards.

Large hypermarkets are now definitely the trend for Carrefour in Taiwan, as this is the real area of expertise of the company, rather than the large supermarkets they have been operating so far. The new zoning regulations enacted in July 1994 will facilitate this kind of development. Other large stores are presently in construction in Tamshui, Taichung and Tainan, but smaller urban stores will still be opened provided good locations are found.

Despite good results, the Taiwan operations still represented in 1993 only 1.4% of Carrefour

Case 5

total consolidated turnover (Exhibit CS5.4). The relatively low ratio of sales per store can be explained by the limited size of the Taiwan stores. With a total of five stores in 1993 with an overall sales area equivalent to that of the two Portuguese stores, Carrefour Taiwan had approximately the same sales turnover. After the new openings, Taiwan is now ahead of Portugal.

With the arrival of new entrants and the development of existing competitors, new openings are vital: the pre-emption of market by the first mover is important because space is difficult to find and saturation will ultimately come.

Since his promotion as CEO for Asia, the most important thing on Gérard Clerc's mind had been the expansion of Carrefour into other Asian markets. Difficulties in Taiwan had been numerous, especially at the beginning. It had been a combination of legal, relational, cultural, communication and other problems. Mistakes had been made, but many things had been learnt. Reflecting on his experience, Clerc wondered how much it would help him and his assistants in developing the Carrefour business in the region.

Exhibit CS5.2   Map of Taiwan R.O.C.

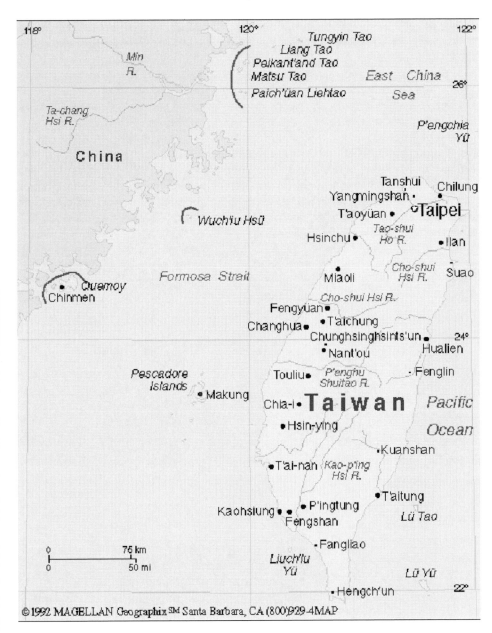

© 1992 MAGELLAN Geographix℠ Santa Barbara, CA (800)929-4MAP

Exhibit CS5.3 **Economic data of Taiwan R.O.C. (*Source*: Statistical Yearbook of the Republic of China)**

Year	Population ('000)	GNP growth (%)	GNP per capita (US$)
1985	19,258	5.0	3,144
1986	19,455	10.8	3,784
1987	19,673	11.9	4,989
1988	19,904	7.8	6,048
1989	20,107	7.3	7,571
1990	20,353	5.0	7,954
1991	20,557	7.2	8,788
1992	20,752	6.0	10,215
1993	20,944	5.9	10,566

Motorization in Taiwan

Year	Number of sedans registered for private use	Number of registered motorcycles
1985	830,315	6,588,854
1986	956,625	7,194,202
1987	1,159,701	5,958,754
1988	1,480,478	6,810,540
1989	1,868,389	7,619,038
1990	2,225,174	8,460,138
1991	2,535,277	9,232,889
1992	2,932,796	10,057,307
1993	3,317,580	10,948,972

Changes of household expenditures in Taiwan

Expenditure (%)/Year	1964	1976	1987	1991
Food, beverages and tobacco	59.7	46.4	36.5	30.9
Clothes and footwear	6.3	6.8	6.0	5.9
Rent, fuel and power	17.2	21.5	23.0	25.7
Family furniture and equipment	3.4	3.9	4.4	4.3
Transportation and communication	2.0	5.0	8.5	8.9
Education and recreation	1.2	6.4	10.6	12.8
Medical care and health expenses	–	4.6	5.3	5.4
Others	4.9	5.5	5.6	5.9

Exhibit CS5.4   The concept of hypermarkets (*Source:* **LSA, 29 April 1993**)

The difference between a supermarket and a hypermarket is not always clear. The term 'hypermarket' was introduced in 1969 by Jacques Pictet, founder of Libre Service Actualités (LSA), a self-service retail trade publication, to describe large supermarkets with a sales area of more than 2,500 square metres, or the exact surface of Carrefour's store in Sainte Geneviève at that time.

A hypermarket was supposed to have the following characteristics:

- a sales area of at least 2,500 square metres;
- a large variety of food and general merchandise;
- a large free car park (min. 1,000 cars);
- self-service and payment at central checkouts

The term hypermarket imposed itself very rapidly, but for 25 years its definition did not change while large chain retailers such as Carrefour were building larger stores with a sales area of over 10,000 or even 15,000 square metres. According to René Brillet, CEO for Carrefour in North Europe (including France), a hypermarket should supply 80% of consumers' needs. Below 5,000 square metres, this would be impossible: under these conditions, a store could only offer a few home appliances and a limited textile assortment. Only dry and fresh foodstuffs would be handled reasonably well. To take into account the changes in the trade, in 1993 LSA decided to change the definition and to retain as hypermarkets in its figures only those stores with sales areas of more than 5,000 square metres. Stores with an area of 2,500 to 5,000 square metres are considered as 'large supermarkets'.

Following is a paper written in 1969 by Marcel Fournier, founder and president of Carrefour, explaining his money-making discounting strategy.

> In front of those clients who want to get the best prices to increase their living standard, what do we find? Old-fashioned shopkeepers with medieval thinking who want to sell as high as possible and are so happy when they can take very high margins. It was maybe the best way to build a fortune when goods were scarce, but it is not the case anymore when modern industries can supply so many different articles and so much of them on the market. But there is a barrier between the flow of merchandises and the clients. It is the barrier of brains ridiculously blurred by the absurd and antiquated concept of gross profit margin. US retailers had accomplished a great step the day discounters replaced this traditional concept by the modern idea of return on invested capital. When we understood the importance of the change, we got rid of the formula:
>
> $$\frac{gross\ profit}{sales\ turnover}$$
>
> to replace it by the new formula:
>
> $$\frac{net\ profit}{invested\ capital}$$
>
> For the operation to be profitable, this ratio has to be as high as possible. Both terms of the ratio have to be acted upon: net profit will have to be maximised, while invested capital will have to be minimised. To obtain a high net profit while selling at discount rates, it is imperative to sell a lot and to limit overheads. Selling huge volumes, that is our first law at Carrefour . . .

Exhibit CS5.5   Carrefour in the world (*Source*: Carrefour 1993 Annual Report)

Country	Number of stores	Net turnover (MF)	Net turnover (%)
France	114	81,991	66.5
Spain	43	21,226	17.2
Brazil	29	10,191	8.3
Argentina	7	5,545	4.5
Taiwan	7	1,752	1.4
Portugal	2	1,657	1.3
Italy/Turkey	2	–	0.7

Case 5

Exhibit CS5.6   Organizational chart of President Enterprise Corporation

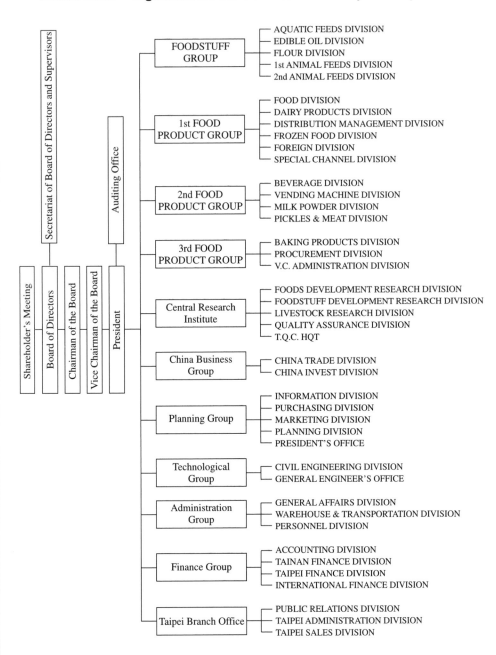

Case 5

Exhibit CS5.7   Carrefour stores in Taiwan (*Source*: PresiCarre Corporation)

Opening date	Location	Type	Sales area (square metres)	Parking
December 1989	Ta-Shun (Kaohsiung)	Store	4,500	220 car spaces
January 1991	Nan-Kang (Taipei)	Store	5,600	240 car spaces
February 1991	Shih-Chuan (Kaohsiung)	Store	5,400	370 car spaces
October 1991	Tien-Mou (Taipei)	Store	4,300	350 car spaces
July 1992	Pan-Chiao (Taipei)	Store	5,200	300 car spaces
November 1993	Chung-Hua (Tainan)	Store	7,500	390 car spaces
November 1993	San-Chung (Taipei)	Warehouse	9,600	720 car spaces
March 1994	Tao-Yuan (Taipei)	Warehouse	12,400	720 car spaces
Extension 84	To other		6,000	400 car spaces

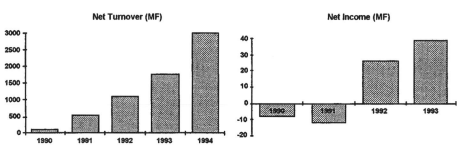

After two new store openings in 1993, sales are up 53.1% to NT $8 billion. Net income increased 46.8% in 1993 to NT * 18

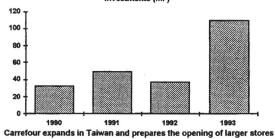

Carrefour expands in Taiwan and prepares the opening of larger stores

Case 5

Exhibit CS5.8   The Carrefour concept

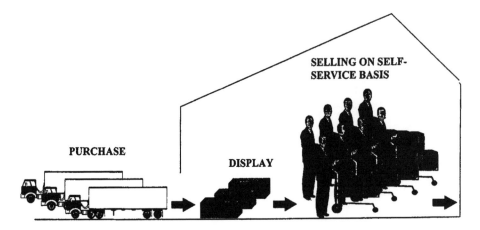

Focus on high rotation. 快速流通

The key success factors: 成功的關鍵因素：

■ **One-stop shopping**   ■ 一次購足
■ **Low selling price**   ■ 超低售價
■ **Freshness**   ■ 新鮮
■ **Free parking**   ■ 免費停車

Case 6

This case was written by Jocelyn Probert, Research Analyst at INSEAD Euro-Asia Centre, and Hellmut Schütte, Affiliate Professor of International Management at INSEAD. It is intended to be used as a basis for class discussion rather than to illustrate either effective handling or ineffective handling of an administrative situation. Copyright © 1996 INSEAD-EAC, Fontainebleau, France.

Cartier Japan

It was December 1995, and the end-of-year shopping season well under way. Mr Guy Leymarie, president of Cartier Japan, was looking forward to the visit the next week of Mr Alain-Dominique Perrin, president of Cartier International, Mr Richard Lepeu, managing director of Cartier International, and their team. Perrin and Lepeu came to Tokyo every year in December to discuss the marketing plans put together by Leymarie and his team, and continued from there to visit other Cartier subsidiaries in Asia. His style of leadership was already familiar to Leymarie, who had been secretary general of Cartier International in Paris until his posting to Japan in February 1992.

Leymarie knew that Perrin would have thoroughly read the documents he had already sent to Paris, and that the meeting would be more of a discussion than a presentation. He had made substantial changes to the operations of Cartier in Japan during the past four years, a period which had also seen a severe recession by Japanese standards, and he was confident that the company was now well attuned to Japanese consumer attitudes.

BACKGROUND

Cartier was founded in 1847 in Paris and by the early years of the 20th century had established itself as 'the jeweller of kings and the king of jewellers'. Its jewels and watches were worn by the world's most famous people. Despite a difficult period in the post-war years of the 1940s and 1950s Cartier is once again one of the world's most renowned creators of 'haute joaillerie'. Many of the pieces offered to the discerning consumer of the modern day echo the designs and concepts created during Cartier's golden era, such as the range of 'Tank' and 'Pasha' watches. A more affordable line of products, 'les Must de Cartier', was launched in 1972 offering pens and cigarette lighters, and later leather goods and watches, for a younger age group.

Today, Cartier is an important element of the Vendôme Luxury Group, which also includes the wristwatch companies Baume & Mercier and Piaget, Montblanc pens and Dunhill leather goods, menswear and watches. Vendôme itself is part of the Swiss-based Richemont group, the luxury goods, tobacco and media conglomerate of South African origin which acquired Cartier in 1983. Vendôme's operating profits rose 15% to £113.3 million on turnover of £699.5 million in the first half of the 1995/6 year (Exhibits CS6.1 and CS6.2). Cartier's contribution to group results is not revealed.

The name of Cartier was first introduced to Japan in the early 1970s through the Swiss trading company Liebermann Waelchli, which acted as agent for several prestigious names in the luxury goods sector. For the next 15 years Liebermann continued to represent Cartier in the Japanese market, and built a strong image of the company as a producer of quality leather goods, cigarette lighters and pens. A separate company, Sanki Shoji, handled watch distribution since Liebermann already represented Rolex.

By 1986 the decision had been taken at Cartier's headquarters in Paris to establish a more direct presence in Japan, which was rapidly emerging as an enormous market for luxury consumer goods. A joint venture was established between Cartier, Liebermann and Sanki Shoji, and management of the new entity was undertaken by Cartier's partners.

This arrangement was short-lived. In 1989, Cartier bought out its partners and established a wholly owned subsidiary. It also moved into a building next to the Okura Hotel, one of the best known hotels in Tokyo. Cartier Japan began with Japanese management and quickly developed into a very 'Japanese' company. Sales grew strongly during the period 1989–90 as the 'bubble' economy of the late 1980s reached its apogee, but mutual communication difficulties between the subsidiary in Tokyo and headquarters in Paris compounded misunderstandings over the changing economic environment of Japan. In February 1992 Guy Leymarie arrived in Tokyo to take over the management of Cartier Japan, and to establish a new strategy for development in the face of the bursting of the economic bubble.

THE DISTRIBUTION SYSTEM AND CONSUMER ATTITUDES IN JAPAN

Perhaps 90% of Japan's 120 million people may fairly be described as middle class, and they enjoy high purchasing power. Shopping is a major pastime in a country where space and time for leisure is limited, and on any day of the week (but especially at weekends) consumers crowd the streets and stores. Department stores have developed into luxury emporia, offering enormous ranges of high quality goods and excellent service in addition to cultural events such as art exhibitions and lessons on *ikebana* and the tea ceremony. An important service for the very richest clients is offered by the department store's *gaisho* or external sales staff, who manage corporate accounts and – important for luxury goods manufacturers – the accounts of a select number of wealthy individuals. For these customers the *gaisho* select the most exquisite items to propose to clients in the comfort of their own home.

The role of the group in Japanese society is paramount, and has important implications for consumer behaviour. Membership of a group, whether it be family, university, or work related, requires conformity with its social values. Japanese consumers also demonstrate an extraordinary capacity to study and to learn about a product before acquiring it. They are trend followers, and the press has greater influence over consumer behaviour than in other countries, precisely because of the nature of society and pressure for conformity. The consequences of such group pressure are that every Japanese knows, for example which jewel it is appropriate to wear on which occasion, or which gift, beautifully wrapped in the paper of a prestigious department store, to offer to whom under which circumstances. For producers of luxury goods, the homogeneity of demand creates the risk that their brands will lose their exclusive cachet.

The 1980s

The 1980s was the decade when Japanese people first began to really spend the money they had worked so hard since 1945 to accumulate. The 1985 Plaza Accord, which created the conditions for a substantial revaluation of the yen against the dollar, unleashed the start of a major asset boom in Japan. People began purchasing property, and stocks and bonds as never before. Young working women (known as office ladies, or OLs), unmarried but still living at home, had substantial disposable income to spend. They acquired a fascination for western luxury and designer products, and the brands that symbolized these desires – Louis Vuitton, Chanel, Dior – took an important place in the Japanese market. As the cost of buying a home rose to unattainable levels, some consumers turned to hedonistic purchases of luxury goods as substitutes (though strict social codes helped to avoid the worst potential excesses). Department stores vied to bring new western labels into their ground floor 'in-shop' boutiques. By the end of the decade Japan had become more important than the USA as a market for luxury goods. Some brands retailed in Japan at up to two times the price in their country of origin, and the foreign manufacturers enjoyed high profit margins.

During the late 1980s the strength of demand in Japan for luxury goods presented a challenge for traditional producers of such items: how to balance the desire to maintain a brand's exclusivity (for example by limiting the amount available) while at the same time achieving sufficient volume to be the market leader. Success in this delicate balancing act would allow the marque to become the point of reference in the marketplace. Myths began to emerge. Perhaps the best known was the notice reputedly pinned on the door of the Louis Vuitton boutique in Paris saying 'No Japanese' once the daily quota of handbags and luggage had been sold, or the tale of students being paid to queue to buy extra bags for eager Japanese visitors to France. Amid the fever for designer goods, it became easy to establish a luxury marque in Japan, and Japanese companies themselves participated either by launching their own brands with European names, or by acquiring the Japanese production and distribution licence for a true European brand.

By the end of the 1980s Japanese consumers were sufficiently well travelled and knowledgeable to recognize the difference between a licensed product and 'the real thing'. They also knew that prices in Japan were substantially higher than those for the same goods in the west. This did not necessarily matter. Some sectors of society displayed a certain pride, not so much in the possession of a particular object but in the price they paid for it: it was a means of demonstrating their purchasing power. Epitomizing this attitude was the owner of a Japanese paper company, who in 1990 paid a world record price of US$82.5 million for Van Gogh's 'Portrait of Dr Gachet', with the intention of having it buried with him when he died.

The 1990s

The bursting of the asset bubble in 1991 and the onset of long-lasting recession ushered in new trends in consumer behaviour. Discount stores began to appear, often offering imported goods brought in through parallel channels at prices far below prevailing domestic levels. They were encouraged by the Ministry of International Trade and Industry, which regarded these upstarts both as a means of reducing Japan's trade surplus with the USA and of demonstrating to US trade negotiators the openness of the Japanese market. The strength of the yen further contributed to the flood of competitively priced imported goods onto the marketplace. Department stores began to lose market share to discounters and supermarkets.

A second element in the restructuring of the market was a review of the Large Scale Retail Stores Law, effectively removing much of the power of local retailers to block consent for new supermarkets and department stores that had been given to them 20 years earlier. The LSRSL revisions of the early 1990s led to many new store openings and intensified competition within the supermarket sector and between department stores. The US toy chain Toys-'R'-Us also challenged the traditional distribution system by demanding direct dealings with Japanese toy manufacturers, thus forcing a shift in Japan's traditional balance of power between manufacturer and retailer in favour of the latter.

For the first time, supermarkets began to challenge department stores in some product segments, particularly expensive cosmetics which had traditionally been the domain of the department stores and their specialized sales staff. A ruling by Japan's Fair Trade Commission barred cosmetics manufacturers from setting retail prices, or from refusing to supply any retailer with goods, and this created the opportunity for supermarkets (and discount stores) to stock luxury domestic cosmetics at lower prices. Abolition, possibly in 1996, of a long-standing Japanese drugs law could permit parallel importers to legally sell foreign cosmetics and perfumes in Japan.[1]

These changes in the retail market present both opportunities and threats to the western luxury goods manufacturers. On the one hand they have become hostages to the US-Japan trade conflict, since US demands for greater openness in the Japanese market threaten to prevent them continuing their exclusive distribution practices (note that within the European Union the right of selective distribution for luxury goods companies is a rare exception to the principle of the common market). On the other hand the restructuring of the Japanese distribution system has allowed the development of newcomers to the marketplace at a speed unthinkable in the 1980s. One European luxury goods company, for example by 1995 had 20 boutiques within department stores compared with none in 1990.

In this environment Japanese consumers have become highly selective in their brand purchases. Some marques that appeared during the bubble economy have almost vanished from sight. Those that remain are being forced to justify the prices they charge. The product must correspond to the price: the myth of the brand has disappeared. People are still enthusiastic purchasers of branded goods, but they must be well-known names and identifiable creations.

Reflecting these developments, branded goods prices began a downward adjustment. In instances where the adjustment was not sufficiently rapid, customers proved themselves prepared to negotiate a discount, based on their experience of prices abroad. On luxury items the discount could reach 40–50%, bringing the ticket down to Paris levels or even lower. '*Le juste*

---

[1] The law requires importers of foreign cosmetics and perfumes to provide the Ministry of Health and Welfare (MHW) with a list of any product's ingredients, and to display the MHW permit number on the product label. These requirements make the retail of parallel imports of these goods illegal, since manufacturers supply the necessary information only to their authorized distributors.

prix' – the right market price – is the rule in Japan in the mid-1990s. 'It is very competitive, the price is controlled by the consumer', says Leymarie. Nevertheless, more and more well-established European luxury goods companies are establishing a presence in Japan.

Case 6

CARTIER JAPAN

When Guy Leymarie arrived in Tokyo in February 1992 the bubble era was over and 'the market was already heading downhill'. Leymarie identified a number of immediate challenges for Cartier Japan: to turn the company into a less Japanese organization; to establish a new product strategy, including repositioning the brand; to redefine the distribution strategy; and to adjust the operations of Cartier to face economic change.

Management reorganization

The Japanese managing director of Cartier Japan in 1989 had established a hierarchical organization which functioned in typical Japanese fashion. It was difficult for people lower in the organization to communicate with their seniors. At first, business was highly successful as Cartier Japan continued to ride the boom. At that time, the Cartier group's strategy department in Paris had relatively limited knowledge of the business environment in Japan. As the economic situation in Japan deteriorated in 1990 and 1991, communication between Tokyo and the headquarters in Paris became increasingly difficult, and an atmosphere of mistrust and mutual misunderstanding developed.

The decision to send a Frenchman to head the Japanese subsidiary ushered in a complete modification of management style. Reflecting the culture of Cartier as a marketing-driven group, Leymarie hired new managers from other firms with a strong marketing culture, such as Procter & Gamble. He intentionally hired older managers, being himself only in his mid-30s at the time and needing senior people to lend weight to his organization.

Luxury goods companies traditionally work on the strategy that the product sells itself (*'le produit se vend'*). Leymarie wanted to add the essential human factor to this formula. He instituted a supervisor system to re-evaluate the working methods of the sales staff, repositioning their status within the company, and emphasizing training as well as their responsibilities to, and relationship with, Cartier.

It was also his idea to introduce an incentive sales programme among the staff, to further motivate them. This was rather a new concept for Japan, and an external Japanese company employed to conduct the feasibility study came to the conclusion that it would not work. Leymarie proceeded with the project anyway – although its implementation was delayed for three months by his failure to communicate properly its function to his staff.

The person selected by Leymarie to manage Cartier's wristwatch distribution was aged 61 and recruited directly from the wholesale industry. A key characteristic of the watch industry is the important role played by specialist wholesalers: intermediaries are critical. Cartier Japan needed someone with the range of contacts and experience of the Japanese market that can only be accumulated over 15 or 20 years, and which Cartier Japan itself sorely lacked.

Leymarie spends two days per week on internal meetings with his staff, building their confidence to communicate directly with him. Through a system of committees, by subject or by department, his goal is to break down the formal organizational structure created by his predecessor. The committees are non-hierarchical, and it took time for junior members of the team to participate actively in front of their seniors. However, the corporate culture is evolving in the right direction. 'We have to communicate as directly as possible between managers and staff', says Leymarie. He attributes the progress of Cartier Japan in the last three years to the motivation of the retail sales staff through this system.

Repositioning of the brand

Under the auspices of the agent Cosa Liebermann, the Cartier brand in Japan had become synonymous during the 1970s and 1980s with high quality leather goods, rather than the distinctive jewellery and wristwatches for which it is famous elsewhere. This positioning did not significantly change during the first years of Cartier Japan's existence, despite the opening of a flagship boutique on Namiki-dori as a showcase for its fine jewellery pieces. A key task for Leymarie was to persuade Japanese consumers that Cartier is first and foremost a fine jeweller, not a competitor to Louis Vuitton handbags. His mission was to make it the leading jeweller in Japan.

The marketing of leather goods was radically reorganized. Somewhat to the concern of headquarters in Paris, three-quarters of the outlets retailing Cartier's leather goods were closed. The strategy was to limit the exposure of leather goods to the Japanese public, while nevertheless maintaining their sales.

For three years not a single advertisement featuring Cartier leatherware was issued. All publicity surrounding Cartier concentrated exclusively on its finely crafted jewellery and watches. Advertising was restricted to quality magazines whose target customer matched the Cartier profile. It appeared in magazines for the more mature sector, geared to company presidents and senior managers, or, like *Kateigaho* and *Fujingaho*, to their wives; and in magazines, such as *25 ans*, which are aimed at trendy, affluent, sophisticated consumers whose aspirations are high. (The French title of this magazine reflects the Japanese reverence for France as the home of the luxury goods industry.)

The staffing of Cartier boutiques was also deliberately conservative. Using an intermediary, Leymarie hired as manageress of the Namiki-dori boutique a Japanese lady some 60 years of age who had never worked before. Her manner reflected the style of presence that Cartier wished to create: the weight of tradition rooted in the image of the family, which plays such an important role in Japan.

Again reflecting the importance of the family in Japanese society, Cartier Japan finally prevailed upon headquarters in Paris to allow them to test market engagement rings. As 'le joaillier du roi', the jeweller of kings, Cartier had never been requested to create engagement rings (a piece of jewellery members of royal families never wear). The products created echoed the craftsmanship of Cartier's other rings: there was no intention to 'Japanize' the offerings for the Japanese market. The success with which the engagement rings were greeted in Japan persuaded Cartier to market the product worldwide.

Timely and effective new product launches contributed to the steady change in Cartier Japan's product portfolio. By 1995 approximately half of Cartier Japan's sales were of jewellery items.

Watches accounted for a further one-third, and leather goods and others the remaining one-sixth.

Distribution

Cartier worldwide uses two separate distribution channels and this system is replicated in Japan. Its boutiques retail Cartier products exclusively: jewellery, jewelled watches, pens, lighters, accessories, and so on. Like most of the best watch manufacturers, however, Cartier's timepieces are for the most part distributed through highly specialized wholesalers operating in a structured, conservative fashion. Japan is no different, and 'to seriously market watches we must enter that system', says Leymarie. Leatherware marketing is also traditionally conducted through a limited number of specialist wholesalers. More selective distribution became a key factor in the relaunch of Cartier Japan's image as a purveyor of fine jewellery and watches.

The wristwatch business

The problem was that when Leymarie arrived in Japan, the distinction between strategies for retail and wholesale trade was unclear – nor was it easy to clarify, because of special Japanese characteristics. The principal difficulty lay in the department store as a channel for distributing watches. Three different locations within a given department store could be selling Cartier timepieces: there could be a Cartier boutique on the ground floor, the traditional location for luxury goods shop-in-shops; on the fifth or sixth floor would be the department store's watch department, operated by specialist wholesaler/retailers; on the topmost floor would be the offices of the *gaisho*, who would market Cartier watches directly to their private clients. The competition between the different locations and the varied pricing strategies they employed caused confusion among consumers and sales staff alike.

As was the case for leather goods, Cartier Japan decided to reconcentrate its watch distribution radically. In early 1992 some 300 watch retailers were selling Cartier timepieces; by 1995 only 160 remained but they were all high quality retailers who could do justice to the company's products and had a sufficiently strong capital base to carry the stock.[2] Cartier Japan also chose to grant exclusivity to a single distributor in some regions, in return for the distributor's commitment to attain a certain level of sales. 'We choose partners who choose us', says Leymarie. 'Our contracts are based on verbal understanding, thanks to the quality of our relationship with our distribution partners. This is the only way to do it in Japan'.

Watch retailers are visited by one of the company's eight salesmen, who advise them which models to take to ensure good stock rotation. As is the case for jewellery, Cartier Japan adopts a highly coordinated push and pull approach, ensuring that the timepieces it advertises nationally are already available in watch shops when customers begin to ask for them. The smallest retailers would stock 50 Cartier pieces (all purchased, not taken on consignment), compared with 70 to 80 pieces at the larger ones. The retailers are arranged in a pyramid according to the products they offer: the Must range of watches and Cartier gold and steel watches are available in all 160

---

[2] The general decline in the role of the wholesaler (as more and more manufacturers supply directly to retail outlets) affected the capital base of many retailers, to whom wholesalers had traditionally lent financial support. A watch retailer might carry Cartier stock worth perhaps ¥30 million (US$300,000) in addition to items from other quality manufacturers.

outlets. Gold watches and some jewellery watches are sold at the leading watch retailers, but the full range of exclusive jewellery and high jewellery watches are sold in Cartier boutiques only.

The boutiques

In 1995 Cartier Japan boasted a network of 22 exclusive boutiques (out of 160 Cartier boutiques worldwide), all displaying the full range of Cartier jewels, watches and accessories (Exhibit CS6.3). Nineteen of these outlets are 'shop-in-shops' within department stores in the main cities of Japan, and two are in hotel shopping arcades: at the Imperial Hotel in Tokyo and at the Royal Hotel in Osaka. Cartier Japan's flagship, however, is a free-standing boutique[3] on Namiki-dori, an exclusive shopping street in Tokyo's Ginza and the only one of its type in Japan. While Cartier is open to the possibility of adding new boutiques, there is no emphasis on expanding beyond the current number.

The Namiki-dori boutique was opened in 1989, the year Cartier Japan was established. Specialist retailers in the USA and Europe have traditionally occupied free-standing sites on luxury shopping streets, but this option is not open to companies such as Cartier in Japan, owing to the dominant position of department stores with long and historic traditions which occupy the prime locations. Many of Cartier's present department store and hotel boutiques were opened in the period when Cartier was still represented by its agent or during the joint venture phase, but the scale of investment required to launch a free-standing outlet was too great and too long term to interest Cartier's partners.

When Leymarie took over as managing director in 1992 he inherited a network of 27 boutiques in department stores and a smaller number of '*coins rouges*' (red corners), which were mini-boutiques selling only part of the Cartier range. He closed seven boutiques in lesser department stores and all of the mini-boutiques. The quality of the host department store is carefully monitored. It is rare that Cartier would choose to close a boutique, but it can happen. In 1995 it withdrew from Seibu in Shibuya (Tokyo), which had remodelled its store to reflect a less upmarket customer target and less prestigious merchandising concept – one that no longer matched Cartier's product offering. Seibu itself is representative of the recent upstarts in the department store sector compared with Takashimaya and Mitsukoshi, which have several hundred years of tradition behind them: it was the epitome of the bubble era, and excelled at avant garde displays.

As far as Leymarie is concerned, department stores remain unquestionably the primary distribution channel in Japan for Cartier jewellery. Hans-Peter Bichelmeier, deputy managing director, concurs: 'Department stores have perhaps remained too stable, their business is being eaten away by the supermarkets and discount stores. They have lost the electronics business already and are losing some of their food business. Luxury consumer goods is the only potential growth area they have, and because of the advantages of their locations they will clearly survive and build this business'.

Adjustment to economic change

Between 1989 and 1991 Cartier Japan had increased its prices each year in order to maintain the

---

[3] A free-standing outlet has its own shop-front and entrance at street level, as opposed to a shop-in-shop boutique which is entered through the department store and does not necessarily have a window on the street.

traditional differential between prices in Japan and those overseas. The renewed appreciation of the yen against the dollar beginning in 1990, however, provoked a dampening of demand for foreign luxury goods among Japanese consumers. In March 1992 total aggregate sales at national department stores fell for the first month in what was eventually to prove a 45-month run of declines which ended only in November 1995. Cartier's products (which at that time were concentrated on leather goods and accessories, and watches but relatively little jewellery) had begun to experience weaker demand in 1991.

In 1993, as the yen continued to rise, Leymarie took an unprecedented decision: Cartier would align the Japanese prices of its jewellery and watches more closely with world levels. This was a potentially dangerous move in a country where received wisdom stated that retail prices cannot fall without destroying the reputation of the brand. On 15 May 1993 full-page advertisements appeared in all the leading daily newspapers announcing the new strategy. They carefully explained that the more attractive pricing policy was to demonstrate Cartier's sense of good citizenship in Japan, in view of the strength of the yen.

Leymarie had visited in advance all the department stores with Cartier boutiques, to explain his actions. Customers who made a significant purchase during the preceding few days were allowed to pay the new prices. Distributors and consumers accepted the argument well. The price of a Cartier piece in Japan became demonstrably the same as the price in Paris. By taking direct action Cartier was able to avoid the negotiated discounting practices that competitors were facing from their customers, and which resulted sometimes in jewels being sold at prices that did not do justice to the product.

On 30 March 1994 Japan's leading financial newspaper, the *Nikkei Shimbun*, published an interview with the president of Mitsukoshi. Mr Itakura stated that the department store would no longer market any imported branded product whose price in Japan was more than 50% higher than in its country of origin, citing research undertaken in December 1993 which showed that 61.7% of imported brands studied (75 brands and 569 references) had a price discrepancy of more than 1.5 times. His goal was also to encourage price reductions for domestic goods, which had been inflated unreasonably to match expensive imported items.

Three months later Rolex reduced the prices of its watches in Japan, using a similar explanation to the one used by Cartier. Thereafter the price reduction momentum increased rapidly among members of the industry association, and it was acknowledged that Cartier had been the initiator. Cartier Japan's market leadership was established.

Consumers' increasing expectations that the price of a product should reflect its value led Cartier Japan to another initiative, this time to establish a market reference price, and therefore price leadership, by issuing Gemstone Industry Association (GIA) certificates for jewellery with diamonds weighing only 0.5 carats. Normally the GIA certificate is given only with diamonds of 5 carats or more. Even so, a Cartier ring would still sell for four to five times the market average in recognition of its artistic and creative value, and the quality of the stones used.

BRINGING THE PRODUCT TO THE CUSTOMER

Mr Perrin, president of Cartier International, maintains strict control over the most important aspect of a luxury goods company: the product. Every item must receive his final authorization for launch. 'There are very few luxury goods companies who retain this degree of control', says

Case 6

Bichelmeier. Some product ranges are modern interpretations of older designs created by Louis Cartier in the early 20th century, and themes continually reappear in new variations.

The marketing department is dominant at Cartier. At headquarters in Paris the product and marketing departments are combined, with one person responsible for a particular item from its development, through the launch phase, and into the final marketing programme. In Japan, marketing personnel are responsible for stock control and ordering, as well as marketing and promotion. A fundamentally important task is to ensure that enough of a product is available in Cartier boutiques in Japan when a promotional campaign is launched.

Cartier Japan works with all department stores, as long as they are the leader in any given area. Thus in the Shinjuku 3-chome district of Tokyo there is a Cartier boutique in Isetan, the undisputed doyenne of the area; in Osaka Cartier selected Hankyu and Takashimaya, each of which have their home base in the city; and Matsuzakaya in Nagoya is the city's most prestigious department store. In this respect Cartier differs from Tiffany, which is to be found exclusively in Mitsukoshi stores; from Louis Vuitton, whose outlets are normally in Mitsukoshi or Takashimaya; and from Hermès, which has a joint venture with Seibu. Like Chanel, who also used Cosa Liebermann as agent, Cartier prefers to remain independent.

The layout of the Cartier boutiques in Japan differs from that of boutiques in Europe and the USA, reflecting differences in shopping preferences. Customers in Japan enjoy browsing and seeing the full range of items on offer, even if they have a clear idea of the piece they wish to buy. Japanese outlets are therefore filled with showcases displaying Cartier watches and jewels, with sales staff available to offer advice as required. In the west, no items are on open display in Cartier shops, but sales staff will exhibit individual pieces on a velvet tray at the request of the customer. This may be a security issue, but even in Japan there is a guard inside the door of the flagship boutique.

Product launches or relaunches are accompanied by advertising campaigns in magazines, in POS (point-of-sales) material and in catalogues. Cartier Japan also uses film advertisements in selected Tokyo cinemas but, unlike in other parts of the world, it never advertises on television: the cost is too great to justify use of a medium which has broad appeal rather than the concentrated focus the company requires. 'People need awareness of our product, so we must concentrate our effort. They won't buy Cartier just because it is Cartier', explains Bichelmeier.

Cartier Japan also draws upon the rich heritage of the company to substantiate its print media campaigns. The Cartier Collection in Geneva assembles a magnificent array of Cartier creations dating back to the turn of the century, which the company claims is unmatched even by the collections of such firms as Van Cleef & Arpels and Louis Vuitton. A major event in 1995 was the presence of the entire collection in Tokyo – only its third journey overseas – for a six-week exhibition at the Teien Museum, a former Japanese royal residence in the 1930s whose art deco architecture echoed the style of jewellery created by Louis Cartier in 1900–20. Cartier Japan held a gala reception at the Teien Museum, to which the press was invited as well as the cream of Japanese society. More than 200,000 people visited the Teien exhibition from all over Japan.

Although the Cartier Collection in its entirety rarely travels abroad (for obvious reasons of security) individual items are frequently used to promote the launch of new Cartier ranges. Every month or two, part of the collection is in Tokyo: perhaps some pens from the early 20th century, or an evening bag, or wristwatch. When a new engagement and wedding ring collection is being presented, for example Cartier Japan may invite young men and women from good families to a party, where the young ladies would be persuaded to try on a tiara from the Cartier Collection. The aura that surrounds the collection is a constant magnet for quality press journalists.

Client interest is also maintained through the launch of limited edition jewellery and watches. In 1995, for example Cartier produced a limited edition Tank watch for the relatively inexpensive Must range. Cartier Japan was allocated 100 men's and 100 women's watches out of the 1,000 pieces available worldwide, at a price of ¥200,000[4] – very reasonable by Japanese standards.

Pricing policy remains a challenge. The across-the-board price cuts in 1993 resulted in a number of pricing anomalies, some of which were rectified later through product relaunches. Having peaked in April 1995 at US$1 = ¥80, the yen rapidly depreciated thereafter by over 25% versus the dollar and the Swiss franc. In late 1995, Cartier Japan raised its prices generally to take account of the weaker yen. Price alignments are calculated as a combination of manufacturing costs (Swiss francs since its watches are made in Switzerland and French francs for the jewellery which is created in French workshops) and exchange rates to the yen.

THE COMPETITION

Cartier recognizes that it was relatively late in establishing a direct presence in Japan. Nevertheless, it was one of the few foreign luxury goods company to invest heavily in the early 1990s while the market was changing. Some key competitors were undergoing a difficult transition phase while others were not yet properly established in the market, and this allowed Cartier Japan to capture some of the business of its rivals. On the other hand, companies such as Tiffany were consistently strong competitors. Since 1994 other jewellers have become more active investors, including some which were well established in their home market but had not yet entered the Japanese market.

Harry Winston – the world's most exclusive fine jeweller has established its only boutique in the Hotel Seiyu Ginza, itself Japan's most exclusive hotel.

Van Cleef & Arpels – Cartier's traditional competitor, offering high quality jewels and enjoying a strong home base in Paris. Its distribution agreement with Seibu department stores was highly successful during the bubble years of the 1980s but proved somewhat less so in the sober 1990s. The jeweller nevertheless retained its links with Seibu, which has been reducing stocks and putting its own house in order.

Bulgari – a recognized competitor in the medium-priced, ¥300,000– ¥1,000,000 segment designated 'affordable' (compared with Cartier's, Harry Winston's and Van Cleef & Arpels' expensive pieces). Its designs are simple and are identifiably Bulgari, and its home base in Italy is strong. In 1993 the Italian company established its first boutique in the New Otani hotel and office complex in Tokyo, and two years later opened outlets in Kyoto (Takashimaya), Osaka (Takashimaya), the Osaka Hilton Hotel and the Fukuoka New Otani Hotel. These are all cities where Cartier is already present.

---

[4] In December 1995 the approximate exchange rate was ¥100 = US$1 or FF4.80.

Boucheron – a strong competitor in Paris thanks to its designs and creations, but less known internationally. Its entry to the Tokyo market is through Bluebell, a privately owned company of French origin which specializes in the import and distribution of luxury items.

Chaumet – headquartered like Cartier in the Place Vendôme in Paris. Its Japanese boutiques are in Mitsukoshi stores.

Tiffany – altered the legal and financial nature of its partnership with Mitsukoshi, which had been highly successful during the 1980s, and established its own company in 1994. Its department store boutiques are all still in Mitsukoshi stores, but a free-standing boutique has been opened in Osaka. Tiffany competes with Cartier at the lower end of the spectrum, in the ¥100,000–¥500,000 range, and enjoys a particularly high reputation for its engagement rings and wedding rings. Its overall image in Japan, however, has suffered since it attracts a young clientele by selling jewellery made of silver costing as little as ¥30,000.

COPING WITH GROWTH

In spite of the new pricing policy and the changes in corporate strategy instituted by Cartier Japan, the company experienced sales growth of 40% in value terms during 1993–95. Although in volume terms sales grew more slowly the average price of products sold remained stable in 1994 and increased by 20% in 1995, reflecting the repositioning of the brand and the consequent higher demand for more expensive jewellery and watches.

The personnel numbered 200 as of December 1995, compared with 220 in February 1992 – an indication of the purges of the system which took place following the change in management style. By March 1996 Leymarie expected to employ 260 people, reflecting the strength of growth.

An operations department now helps the marketing and sales teams to meet their strategies and objectives. Another mission is to facilitate stock management, for example by developing specialized computer programs or instituting a new system for stock deployment in the 22 boutiques. Products are now categorized into best-sellers (specific references within a product range which receive national press and advertising coverage) and harmonics (product references which are representative of the brand but are complementary items, in the sense that they may help customers choose the best-seller in the end). Best-seller items must be available in all boutiques. Since the price of Cartier products is very high, significant sums of money are tied up in inventory at any one time.

The pace of growth at Cartier Japan has placed substantial burdens on the retailers at store level. A current project for the operations department is to simplify the administrative tasks boutique staff must undertake, to allow them to spend more time with their customers. Another project is to improve the after-sales service so that '[we] surprise customers positively and they walk out of here more happy', says Bichelmeier. The company expects to differentiate itself further from competitors by investing substantially in a new service centre in the Ginza, in the same building as its flagship boutique. The new centre, which opens in May 1996, will double the number of watchmakers and jewellers available to attend to customers' needs.

CHALLENGES FOR THE FUTURE

Cartier Japan has undergone substantial change in the last four years, and has reached the point where it is the acknowledged market leader among quality jewellers. One of the results of this achievement is that headquarters in Paris has for the past year been using Japan, together with the French market, as a test ground for new products. The knowledge base about Japan at headquarters has also improved immeasurably, thanks to a steady stream of visitors from there to Tokyo.

The strategy now is to consolidate the Cartier Japan position, while facing an internal and an external challenge.

The internal challenge is to continue to react correctly to market demands and trends, and stronger competition, by properly adjusting the company's internal structure to meet growth. Cartier must develop a service dimension to differentiate itself through customer services, and must inspire the loyalty of its staff. Also at issue is whether the organization should continue along functional lines rather than concentrate on product categories.

The external challenge is to adapt to continuing change in the Japanese marketplace. Competition from other quality jewellers is stronger than at the start of the 1990s. Further, as Japan's rapidly ageing population would suggest, the proportion of office ladies 'who spend their lives away' is in decline. Should there be a repositioning of Cartier to take into account such democratic change?

Thinking long term, what would be the implications of a shift from a consumer society towards a leisure society? Would this require a shift by Cartier towards a new segment of the population, a repositioning, or an extension of the existing product portfolio?

Case 6

Exhibit CS6.1   Vendôme Luxury Group results* (millions of Swiss francs)
(*Source*: Annual Reports)

	1993	1994	1995
Turnover	2,462.9	2,596.0	2,652.9
Cost of sales	993.8	1,024.4	1,038.3
Gross profit	1,469.1	1,571.6	1,614.6
Operating profit	398.9	377.8	453.6
Profit before taxation	455.0	431.5	482.8
Net profit	340.2	336.7	394.3
Earnings per share (Sfr.) (excl. exceptional items)	0.488	0.552	0.565

* The Vendôme Luxury Group was listed in London and Luxembourg for the first time in 1993.

Exhibit CS6.2   Vendôme Luxury Group sales to third parties (millions of Swiss francs) (*Source*: Annual Reports)

	1993	1994	1995
Europe	1,077.7	1,103.3	1,098.8
Far East	827.2	888.5	981.7
Americas	480.4	528.3	499.3
Other	77.6	75.9	73.1
Total	2,462.9	2,596.0	2,652.9

Exhibit CS6.3   Cartier boutiques in Japan (*Source*: Cartier Japan)

Case 6

Case 7

This case was written by Eriko Ishida, Research Associate, under the supervision of Hellmut Schütte, Professor at INSEAD. It is intended to be used as a basis for class discussion rather than to illustrate either effective or ineffective handling of an administrative situation. Copyright © 1990 INSEAD-EAC, Fontainebleau, France

Club Med Japan

In the winter of 1988/89, Alexis Agnello, chairman of Club Méditerranée Asia-Pacific-Indian Ocean was sipping a glass of wine at the Club's ski resort in Sahoro, Hokkaido. He was content with the progress Club Med was making in Japan. Sahoro, the first vacation village opened there, was running at nearly full capacity. The membership growth rate had been far greater than the rapidly increasing industrial average. However, maintaining or enhancing Club Med's position in Japan required various long-term strategic decisions, as many large Japanese companies were entering the leisure industry and expected to offer Club Med-style holidays. The unofficial target for Club Med members in Japan by 1999 was ambitious: 200,000 members, rising from 49,300 members in fiscal year 1989. In order to achieve such an ambitious goal, Club Med had to establish more villages, either in Japan or in other parts of Asia. Other possible sources of growth were new types of Club Med products catering to the manifold aspects of the booming Japanese leisure market and new target groups beyond the young, urban, cosmopolitan clientele Club Med dealt with everywhere in the world.

BACKGROUND

Club Méditerranée was founded as a non-profit sports association in France in 1950 by Gerard Blitz, a former member of the Belgian Olympic Team, along with some of his friends. As the association grew, running it as an informal, loosely organized group became increasingly difficult. In 1954, Blitz invited his close friend Gilbert Trigano to join the association on a full-time basis. Trigano, who saw commercial potential in the concept, became managing director and transformed it into a profitable organization.

As Club Méditerranée grew in size, it became necessary to structure the geographical expansion more formally. In 1972, Club Med Inc. was formed as a US subsidiary which would sell package tours and operate resorts in areas outside the Europe/Africa zone. Over a short period of time, North America became the second largest market for Club Méditerranée. Exhibit CS7.1 depicts the composition of members by nationality. In 1982, in order to manage, market and develop more effectively, the Club established four completely autonomous geographical zones. Club Méditerranée SA headed European and African operations out of Paris, and South American activities were run from a base in Rio de Janeiro. Club Med Inc. managed the group's North American operations from offices in New York and directed the business in Asia, the South Pacific and the Indian Ocean out of Tokyo and Hong Kong. Club Méditerranée regards the European market as mature, the US market as close to mature, and the Japanese and other Asian markets as growing (hence the importance of the Japanese market).

By 31 October 1988 (the end of the fiscal year), Club Méditerranée ran operations in a total of 243 locations with 120,837 beds. In addition to traditional Club Med villages the group manages various forms of holiday villages and residences under different names, some of them acquired over the years. Valtur is aimed at the Italian market. OCCAJ operates and markets vacation villages and rental packages in France. Maeva handles rentals of leisure properties for Clubhotel, Utoring and Locarev. Club Méditerranée's villas are traditional hotels enhanced by the Club's own special *savoir-faire*. City Club combines hotel accommodation in or near a downtown area with conventional premises and fully equipped sports and leisure complexes. There are 96 Club Med villages, 15 Valtur villages, 29 OCCAJ villages and residences, 88 Maeva vacation residences, 12 villas, and one City Club. Club Med is by far the world's largest operator of holiday resorts and in 1987/88 catered to over 1.6 million holidaymakers. It is the leading tour operator in France and ranks third in Europe in terms of both clients and revenue. Club Méditerranée is also Europe's fourth largest hotel chain and holds twelfth place worldwide.

CLUB MÉDITERRANÉE'S PHILOSOPHY AND CLUB FORMULA

The Club Méditerranée's main concept has been 'back to nature': escape from everyday pressures and urban hassles. In advance, the guests pay one price for their holiday, which includes room, air fares, transfers from airports, meals and sports. In order to eliminate the need for carrying or worrying about money, guests wear prepaid necklaces of beads used as currency to cover any spending within the village. Until recently, there were no phones, locks, or TVs in the rooms. Telephones were considered as a means to connect guests with the hassles of the outside world.

What makes the Club unique are the staff called 'GOs', '*gentils organisateurs*' or 'nice organizers', who run the villages. Guests are referred to as 'GMs', meaning '*gentils membres*' or 'nice people'. The GOs, one for every eight GMs, mix with the GMs, teach them sports and present entertainment every night after dinner. The presence of the GOs creates a special atmosphere in the village. GOs are enthusiastic young people who work long hours and are available for GMs most of the day. There are currently 6,400 GOs in the world; because of the nature of the work, there is a high turnover. Still, every year more than 30,000 people apply for 2,000 openings. GOs have to be above all good communicators. They also need to have special skills such as music or sports. Knowing the importance of GOs, Club Med spends substantial resources on training them. To keep GOs motivated, they are moved from one village to another every six months.

Each village is designed to maximize social interaction. The bar is centrally located in order to be a meeting place. GMs and GOs are randomly seated together at meals in groups of six or eight, and single rooms are not usually available. Shy guests will be encouraged, but not obliged, to participate in the various sports and social activities of the Club during the day and may be asked by a GO for a dance in the discotheque at night.

HISTORY OF CLUB MÉDITERRANÉE IN JAPAN

The Japanese market was identified as being attractive as early as 1964, when Gilbert Trigano visited Japan for the Tokyo Olympic Games.

In 1973, the large trading house C. Itoh became the sales representative for Club Méditerranée in Japan. However, this relationship was ended as Club Méditerranée was not satisfied with C. Itoh's commitment to marketing and village development. In 1979, Club Méditerranée K.K. (Japan) was established to market Club Med's products. In 1984, an association was announced with Seiyo Ltd, the leisure branch of the Seibu Saison Group, a major Japanese distributor. Trigano had known Seibu Saison Group chairman Seiji Tsutsumi for 20 years or so. During an interview about the joint venture, Mr Tsutsumi said that his Group had perfected its retail business and would like to concentrate efforts on leisure activities. The Group hoped to gain expertise from Club Méditerranée in resort facility management and the 'art of entertaining', even though Seibu already had substantial expertise in this kind of business. Mr Tsutsumi felt that through this alliance Seibu Saison would be one step ahead of other Japanese competitors, for whom leisure development meant just building nice facilities. The agreement between the two partners foresees, among other items, the marketing of Club Med holidays in Seibu Saison's stores and the opening of vacation villages in Japan.

The relationship is not exclusive for either side and Seibu Saison has numerous joint ventures with other foreign companies, including one with Accor, a French hotel group to introduce 'sea therapy'. It also has an investment in St Andrew's golf course in the UK. Although Club Med has considered various projects with other Japanese companies, the collaboration with Seibu Saison remains a very special one. Not only do Club Med and Seibu Saison cooperate in Japan, but Seibu Saison owns 3% of Club Méditerranée SA's registered shares in France. Mr Tsutsumi is a member of the board of directors of Club Med SA and his sister, who lives in Paris, was invited to join Club Med's President's Special Advisory Committee.

Another large shareholder is Nippon Life Insurance, the largest Japanese life insurance company, which acquired 4.9% of Club Méditerranée SA's registered shares. The role of Nippon Life Insurance is limited to the financial arrangement for the time being.

In December 1987, Club Med opened its first Club Med village in Japan at the ski resort of Sahoro 140 km east of Sapporo as a 'showroom' village in Japan. There Japanese clients can experience first hand what Club Med has to offer. The village operates out of a hotel which was acquired by a subsidiary of Seibu Saison in 1985 but suffered from a low rate of occupancy, especially during the summer season. The village is managed by a joint venture company 50% of which is owned by Club Med Inc. and 50% by Seibu Saison. Club Med's first major move was transforming the interior of the hotel.

Membership has increased substantially since the opening of Sahoro, as Exhibit CS7.2 shows. One year after the village opened the rate of occupancy had doubled: during the winter it reached 96% and in summer 56%. Nevertheless, the opening of other villages has been delayed due to the difficulties in finding other suitable sites and the very high land prices.

Other than the Sahoro ski village, Club Med in Japan has been pioneering new ideas. In the winter of 1989/90, Club Med chartered the cruise vessel Fuji Maru to create a 'floating Club Med

Village' in cooperation with Mitsui OSK, the Japanese liner operator which owns the ship. For 26 days a total of 1,000 Japanese were entertained by GOs brought in from other villages and Club Med's reserve staff. Most of the guests were married couples between 40–60 years of age who had been on cruises before. Hardly any of them stayed on board for the whole trip to Hong Kong, Singapore and Bangkok, but the ship was fully booked at prices ranging from US$1,800 for six days to US$8,000 for 26 days.

Another project currently under consideration in Japan is the construction of a City Club with strong emphasis on corporate use. Several real estate developers have approached Club Med already in connection with such an undertaking located close to Tokyo or Osaka.

RECENT TRENDS OF JAPANESE OVERSEAS TRAVEL

Demand for overseas travel among the Japanese is growing rapidly, and the recent sharp appreciation of the yen has made it economically feasible. In fact, some overseas tours have become cheaper than domestic tours. For example a five-day package tour from Tokyo to Guam costs somewhere around 90,000 yen, while a similar trip to Okinawa, Japan's southernmost island, is closer to 110,000 yen. The number of Japanese travelling abroad has risen from 5.5 million in 1985 to 8.4 million in 1988 and could well reach 10 million in 1989 (Exhibit CS7.3). It seems that the so-called '10 million programme', established by the Ministry of Transport in September 1987 to increase the number of Japanese travelling overseas by 1991, will be attained way ahead of schedule. The figure still indicates that fewer than one in ten Japanese leave the country even once a year. In comparison with other industrialized nations this number is low, and the potential for growth is immense. In the UK, for example 44% of the total population went abroad in 1986. In the USA, 15% of the population travelled abroad in 1987.

Most Japanese go overseas on pleasure trips. In 1987, approximately 83% of overseas travel was categorized as pleasure trips and 15% as business trips.

Exhibit CS7.4 shows the breakdown of overseas travellers by age and sex. A recent phenomenon is the rapid increase of young women travelling abroad. In 1988, 1.3 million of the total 8.4 million travellers were women between 20 and 30 years old. The majority of them are so-called 'OLs', Office Ladies. They usually work for big companies and live with their parents, so they have few financial and family obligations. These young women like to travel as often as possible before getting married. Honeymooners, although they are not classified separately in the statistics, consitute an important segment. The other growing sector is people over 60 years old.

The use of package tours is popular. Some 90% of Japan's honeymooners use them, as do approximately 78% of total sightseeing tourists. The use of well-known brand package tours such as JALPAK, which offer better service but consequently have higher prices, has remained constant. Less well-known, cheaper package tours have been gaining popularity, and all Japanese tour organizers have introduced what they call 'second brand' tours to meet this growing market demand. More and more people are asking their agencies only to arrange round trip air tickets and hotel reservations for the first and last days in destination countries. They prefer to decide itineraries and programmes for the intervening days on their own. An increasing number of young people, among them university students, prefer this type of travel.

The favourite Japanese destinations are also changing, shifting from Southeast Asia to North America, Australia and other more distant regions. The change in destination is somewhat in line

Case 7

with the changing expectations for a vacation. According to the survey carried out by *Mainichi Newspaper*, most tourists spent their time shopping, sightseeing, and eating (Exhibit CS7.5). In this sense, Hong Kong and Singapore were the most popular destinations. On the other hand, the answers to the question about what type of overseas travel people like to do were quite different. Both men and women chose leisure-stay tours first and sightseeing tours second (Exhibit CS7.6). Places such as Australia and the South Pacific Islands were closely associated with leisure-stay tours.

The growth in overseas travel is expected to continue as long as there is no drastic economic change. Airport capacities represent one limiting factor for further growth. Japanese overseas travelling is extremely seasonal, with peak seasons in March and July–August and at the end of the year (Exhibit CS7.7). Although there are other international airports, Narita and Osaka airports bear heavy burdens and are close to full capacity. The new Osaka Airport opened in 1992.

JAPANESE ATTITUDE TOWARDS LEISURE

The Japanese are regarded by westerners as workaholics whose work days are seldom interrupted by holidays. However, according to a recent survey for the Prime Minister's Office, more than half those polled now prefer to have more free time rather than extra payment. They also prefer to spend more money on leisure activities than on consumer durables. Both leisure and work are important in the lives of 39% of the respondents, and only 33% answered that work is more important for them and leisure time is to prepare themselves for work. However, 8% said that leisure is more important than work (Exhibit CS7.8). The survey also demonstrates the fact that there is a considerable difference in attitudes towards work among different age groups. For example, 45% of people in their 50s answered that work is more important than leisure, but only 21% of those in their 20s think that way.

Generally speaking, the younger generation, especially the so-called 'Shin-jinnrui' (new breed), with their more individualistic, western attitude towards corporate life and work, tend to take longer holidays. The young people's attitude towards work is frowned upon by older generations because the former prefer to spend money rather than save and have fun rather than work long hours. Within the same age group women tend to take more holidays than men, as they do not see corporate life as a life-long commitment.

Nevertheless, compared with other societies the Japanese work a lot. The average annual holiday taken by workers was only 7.5 days in 1986. It actually decreased from an average of 8.8 days in 1980, although workers are given 14.9 days annual paid holiday on average.

There are several reasons why the Japanese do not take holidays. First of all, there is a lack of leisure infrastructure in Japan. The long journey to airports, road congestion and the high cost of transport and lodging make all trips very difficult. Secondly, the Japanese are not used to having 'active' leisure activities such as sports. Exhibit CS7.9 shows the breakdown of leisure hours by activity for different age groups and the two sexes. It shows that only 20–30% of leisure time is spent on 'active' leisure such as sports, with the rest of the time spent on 'passive' activities such as reading magazines and watching TV. Thirdly, most Japanese feel guilty when they take a long holiday because it means that their colleagues have to do additional work. Instead of causing friction with their colleagues, they prefer not to take long holidays.

The Japanese government now encourages more holiday taking. The government's new Five-Year Economic Plan approved in May 1988 calls for reducing Japan's annual working hours from an average of 2,111 hours in 1987 to about 1,800 hours by 1993. By comparison, French and German workers only worked 1,650 hours in 1986. Up until recently, only 30% of the total workforce worked a five-day week. In February 1989, the five-day work week went into effect in financial institutions. The government and industries are expected to follow. If the percentage of employees working a five-day week grows by 10% per annum, it will reach 70%, the current level in the USA and Europe, in 1992. Coupled with increased propensity to spend on leisure activities, all of this will create a great demand for leisure industries. The Economic Planning Agency estimates that extending the five-day work week to the remainder of the workforce would boost consumer spending substantially. If salaried Japanese used all of their paid leave, leisure consumption would be even higher.

Bearing these trends in mind, the market opportunities for companies such as Club Med seem to be endless.

MARKETING CLUB MED IN JAPAN

Segmentation strategy

When Club Med was first marketed in Japan, nearly 100% of its customers were honeymooners. The price, the romantic image, the destination (New Caledonia), and the length of stay (two weeks) appealed only to honeymooners.

As overseas travel patterns changed and the number of experienced travellers increased, other customer segments became important. Exhibit CS7.10 shows the breakdown of Club Med members in Japan in 1987/88 as compared with 1984/85 and average stay for each segment. The ratio for honeymooners has come down to 40%. The average length of stay has not increased, mostly due to a rise in short stay package tours to destinations near Japan.

The current major target group is the so-called OL segment, now accounting for 35%. Club Med's image as a young, international, fun-loving organization appeals to most OLs. They are frequent travellers but tend to be quite price sensitive, and their budgets are lower than those of honeymooners. The budget of an average sightseeing tourist is estimated to be around 274,000 yen and that of honeymooners is 387,000 yen. Club Med hopes unmarried young women will become repeat clients as they come back for their honeymoons and then again several years later with their families.

In 1987/88 families with children comprised 15% of the GM population in Japan. Club Med was surprised to find that so many Japanese families travel with their children. Now most of its villages in the region are equipped with Mini Clubs, where children are taken care of by GOs and participate in various activities while their parents enjoy themselves off on their own. Club Med Sahoro opened a Mini Club in summer 1989.

Although corporate business still represents only a small proportion (7% in 1987/88), it is expected to grow rapidly. Club Méditerranée provides conference or training packages in exotic locations in the Club Med ambiance. It also provides meeting facilities and even office equipment. Big companies such as Sony and Toshiba use these facilities. A new village at Opio on the French

153

Case 7

Riviera opened in 1989 is specially designed for such purposes and is strongly marketed towards Japanese corporate clients. This sector will certainly become more important, as the government has extended tax-deductible company trips from two nights to three. Company trips are a common way of rewarding employees and increasing their loyalty. The change from two to three nights means that company trips can take place further afield or even overseas. Club Med Sahoro is focusing its marketing efforts towards corporate clients in the summer season. In summer 1988 corporate clients accounted for 40% of GMs and in summer 1989 it is expected to reach 50%.

Product strategy

In general, Club Méditerranée believes that since the Club Med concept appeals to the French it will also appeal to other nationalities once the language barrier is removed.

In Japan, however, a more flexible approach was introduced by Mr Trigano. He has stated that 'We have tried very hard to improve products for the Japanese. It seems they need an alibi to go on holiday, so we offer them courses on how to use the computer, or speak French or English or whatever they want'.

In order to cater to Japanese demand, Club Med shortened the length of stay as a first step. Club Med's standard packages have been designed on a European basis where four or five weeks of holiday is the norm and a week or more of public holiday can be added. Instead of two-week packages, which are common for the European market, one-week tours were developed for the Japanese market. Recently, three-night package tours to Club Med villages have been launched aiming at the OL segment. The average stay of the Japanese GM is 5 to 5.5 days, whereas the average stay in France is 15 days. This takes into account the fact that long vacations will not take root in Japan even in the long run, as the Japanese prefer to take holidays of three to four days in each season.

Secondly, the utmost care has been taken to arrange the most convenient departure schedule. For example, being able to depart on Monday is essential for honeymooners, as wedding ceremonies are usually held on Sunday.

Thirdly, villages in Asia/Pacific zones were designed to be more luxurious compared with Mediterranean villages, i.e. there is a telephone in every room and rooms are air-conditioned. Nevertheless, the quality of the accommodation still does not fully meet Japanese requirements. Instead of sleeping under thatched roofs in rooms decorated with bamboo and other local materials, they prefer a more neutral and hotel-like environment verging on the antiseptic. All announcements and signs in the villages are in English, French and Japanese.

Club Med has been successful in recruiting Japanese GOs who speak two or three languages and are prepared to work long hours for the standard salary of US$600 per month. There are now almost 200 Japanese GOs, most of them female, who facilitate communication with Japanese GMs and help them to settle into the Club's atmosphere. However, some Japanese guests find Japanese GOs too westernized, while the Japanese GOs want to be assigned not only to villages with large numbers of their countrymen but also to Europe and the USA/Caribbean.

Club Med is known for good eating. Both local food and French cuisine are served in buffet-style restaurants. Japanese dishes are added to the menus in villages catering to Japanese tourists. For those who would like to eat in quieter surroundings, such as honeymooners, there are separate dining rooms.

Club Med makes extensive use of comment cards filled out by GMs. They are analysed and fed back to product development and operational management.

Promotion

Club Med's advertising expenses in Japan account for 8% of sales. About 40% of this goes to the printing and mailing of brochures containing detailed information, as the Japanese like to have extensive knowledge about a tour before departure. Club Med has achieved high awareness in the mind of Japanese tourists, as shown in Exhibit CS7.11. A poll of Japanese holidaymakers by *AB Road* magazine awarded Club Med top marks as the tour operator they were 'most willing to try'.

The present rate of repeat business in Japan is only 20%. This compares with Club Med's worldwide average of 70%. It is partly due to the high number of additional members joining during the year who have not had an opportunity to consider a return visit to Club Med. It is, however, also due to the high percentage of honeymooners for whom their time in Club Med is a very special occasion and not a standard holiday. A regular newsletter and invitations to parties and events given by the Club are designed to promote a Club spirit among GMs and increase the number of repeat holidaymakers. In order to encourage word-of-mouth communication, Club Med is considering offering a free one-day stay at a village for those who successfully introduce a new GM to the Club.

In Japan, Club Med makes extensive use of a 'European' image in its advertising, with photos of beautifully tanned, smiling westerners on the beach. Even for Sahoro, the first Japanese village, the brochure shows a number of westerners, although currently only 8% of Sahoro's GMs are from outside of Japan, mainly from nearby Asia. About half the GOs there are non-Japanese. Club Med rarely uses TV advertising, mainly due to its cost in Japan.

Distribution

As Club Med's holidays appeal to urban dwellers, distribution is concentrated in Tokyo and Osaka. There are about 700 travel agents with 7,000 sales outlets throughout Japan. Approximately 90% of overseas travellers book their trips through these agents. Major tour operators sell their products through either their own sales outlets, independent outlets or their competitors' outlets. In the beginning, Club Med depended entirely on other agents. In order to promote sales more aggressively, it has built up its own direct sales channels. Direct sales in Japan now account for 15 to 17% of total sales.

Club Med's products require a fairly detailed explanation, as they are different from other tour packages. In order to help people understand and to lure them, beautiful video films on Club Med village life are shown at the Club Med sales counters and video tapes are available for home viewing as well. There are Club Med sales points in Tokyo, Osaka, Nagoya, Sapporo and Fukuoka. In addition, there are eight sales points in Seibu department stores, which are staffed by Japanese GOs. Out of the 700 travel agencies 500 deal with Club Med, and 3,000 of the 7,000 outlets sell Club Med packages.

Price

In general, the price is not really considered of prime importance by the Japanese because of the high opportunity cost in the case of vacation failure. They prefer to go for well-proven products.

Although Club Med is a 'European product' with an upmarket image, prices are competitive compared with other well-known Japanese package tours such as JALPAK. The price is determined by the length of stay, departure date/season, and destination. The price of competitors' products and Club Med's internal price structures are carefully taken into consideration in pricing. Usually the price of tours departing from Japan is higher than tours leaving from other parts of the world. According to internal statistics, the average Japanese GM pays US$380 for a day of vacation. This compares with US$140, which the average Australian pays per day, and US$70 paid in Malaysia (these figures include transportation costs). In the case of Sahoro, the price is much higher than average ski package tours offered by Japanese competitors. One night at Sahoro costs about US$200. GMs are still satisfied because this sum includes high quality ski lessons following the methods of the Ecole de Ski Française and unlimited access to the lifts and gondola with no waiting time, which is rare at Japanese ski resorts.

THE FUTURE

While it had taken Club Med many years to penetrate the Japanese market, Alexis Agnello felt very pleased with the recent progress the company had made. He believed that the 'Club Med magic' – the close interaction between GOs and GMs in an informal, pleasant environment cut off from everyday life – had finally been accepted by the Japanese. Moreover, it could not be imitated by others. Sahoro worked well, and so did the other villages in the region such as Bali or Phuket. Club Med did not have any problem finding enough multilingual GOs who accepted to work very long hours for a very low salary. Management was increasingly able to squeeze very favourable terms out of airlines due to Club Med's growing traffic volume. The business was carried forward almost automatically by the leisure and travel boom in Japan.

Nevertheless, 49,300 GMs per annum made up only 0.04% of Japan's population. This hardly compared with the 0.66% of all French going on holiday with the Club. Was it right to stick to a concept different from anything else in Japan, where virtually every local government was drawing up plans to develop resort complexes in accordance with the Law for Development of Comprehensive Resort Areas enacted in 1987? Seventy projects were already underway within Japan. Major private companies were entering the leisure industry in search of growth. Companies in heavy manufacturing, which had gone through rigid restructuring, had started to convert their closed factories into leisure sites and thus utilized their excess employees. Club Méditerranée K.K. (Japan) was taking part in this development, though on a limited scale. Some time ago the firm announced that it was taking a 5% share in a newly formed company called Asahi Kaiyo, which will convert former shipyards into marinas and leisure centres. Other partners were Seibu Saison (35%) and Japan Air Lines, Mitsui and Nippon Steel (5% each).

The overseas travel boom had also accelerated resort development overseas, where land prices and labour costs were comparatively low and government approval came fast. Large-scale leisure facilities such as golf courses and resort condominiums were under construction by various Japanese consortia in Hawaii, Guam, Saipan, Australia, and on the West Coast of the USA. In Australia, some 20 major projects were underway with Japanese capital.

In order to cope with such development, Club Med would have to open up more villages inside and outside Japan rapidly and try to broaden the product range to reach a more general Japanese public. Possible sites were along the sea somewhere in Japan, on Okinawa, in Tokyo, Osaka, the Philippines and Australia. Being unique may be good, Mr Agnello thought, but is it enough to be attractive? Perhaps we should start a Club without international flavour, without informality, without too much activity – a Club exclusively for the Japanese. This would be a Club in which learning and shopping would be of major concern, a Club which would move around, a Club whose purpose would be to get to know five countries in three days, with a duty-free shop in the centre of the resort...

Mr Agnello knew that he was dreaming. Back in Paris, they would never allow him to modify Club Med's recipe for success, the pride of everyone in the organization. And even if he were to be allowed, would he have 200,000 Japanese GMs in 10 years?

Exhibit CS7.1 **Composition of members by nationality (*Source*: Club Med Annual Report)**

	1986/87	%	1987/88	%
Europe/Africa				
France	382,200	38.52	391,100	35.88
Italy	59,100	5.96	76,800	7.05
West Germany	57,400	5.79	66,400	6.09
Belgium	45,400	4.58	53,300	4.89
Israel	23,000	2.32	33,500	3.07
Switzerland	26,800	2.70	29,700	2.73
UK	14,600	1.47	15,800	1.45
Other	44,600	4.50	40,400	3.71
Subtotal	653,100	65.82	707,000	64.87
South America				
Subtotal	26,000	2.62	33,200	3.05
North America				
USA/Canada	215,700	21.74	228,900	21.00
Other	16,800	1.69	17,000	1.56
Subtotal	232,500	23.43	245,900	22.56
Asia/Pacific/India				
Japan	25,100	2.53	37,100	3.40
Australia	21,200	2.14	23,000	2.11
Other	34,300	3.46	43,700	4.01
Subtotal	80,600	8.12	103,800	9.52
Total	**992,200**	**100.00**	**1,089,900**	**100.00**

Exhibit CS7.2   Growth of membership in Japan (*Source:* Club Med)

Year	Number of members	%
1980/81	6,706	38
1981/82	9,300	39
1982/83	12,100	30
1983/84	11,700	−3
1984/85	17,200	47
1985/86	21,100	23
1986/87	25,100	19
1987/88	37,100	48
1988/89	49,300	33

Exhibit CS7.3   Growth of Japanese tourists overseas (*Source:* Ministry of Justice)

Year	Number of tourists
1964	128,000
1970	663,000
1974	2,336,000
1980	3,909,000
1984	4,659,000
1985	4,948,000
1986	5,516,000
1987	6,829,000
1988	8,430,000
1989	9,662,000

Case 7

Case 7

Exhibit CS7.4 Composition of Japanese overseas travellers by age and sex (1988) (*Source:* Ministry of Justice)

Sex	Age	%
Male	Over 50	16.0
Female	20s	15.9
Male	40s	15.6
Male	30s	15.1
Male	20s	12.0

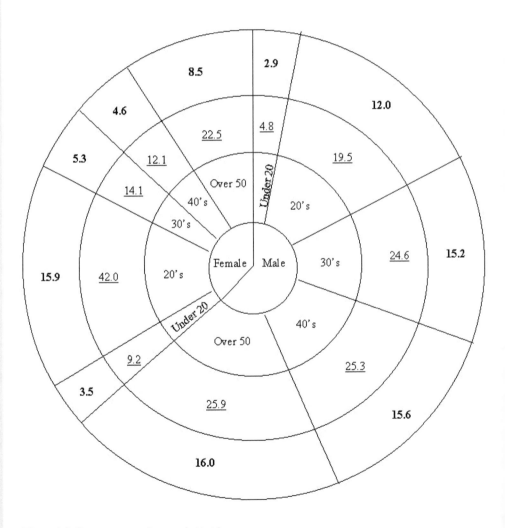

*Outer circle figures are percentages against total.

*Inner circle figures indicate percentages against total by sex.

Exhibit CS7.5   What was done during overseas travel (*Source:* A survey by *Mainichi Newspaper*, 1988)

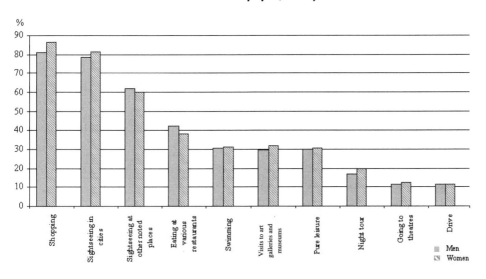

Exhibit CS7.6   Overseas travel one would like to make (*Source:* A survey by *Mainichi Newspaper*, 1988)

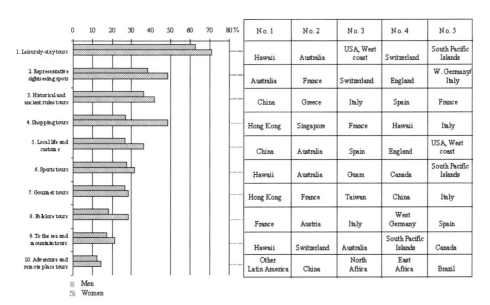

	No. 1	No. 2	No. 3	No. 4	No. 5
1. Leisurely-stay tours	Hawaii	Australia	USA, West coast	Switzerland	South Pacific Islands
2. Representative sightseeing spots	Australia	France	Switzerland	England	W. Germany/ Italy
3. Historical and ancient ruins tours	China	Greece	Italy	Spain	France
4. Shopping tours	Hong Kong	Singapore	France	Hawaii	Italy
5. Local life and customs	China	Australia	Spain	England	USA, West coast
6. Sports tours	Hawaii	Australia	Guam	Canada	South Pacific Islands
7. Gourmet tours	Hong Kong	France	Taiwan	China	Italy
8. Folklore tours	France	Austria	Italy	West Germany	Spain
9. To the sea and mountain tours	Hawaii	Switzerland	Australia	South Pacific Islands	Canada
10. Adventure and remote place tours	Other Latin America	China	North Africa	East Africa	Brazil

Exhibit CS7.7   Number of Japanese travellers by month (*Source*: Ministry of Justice)

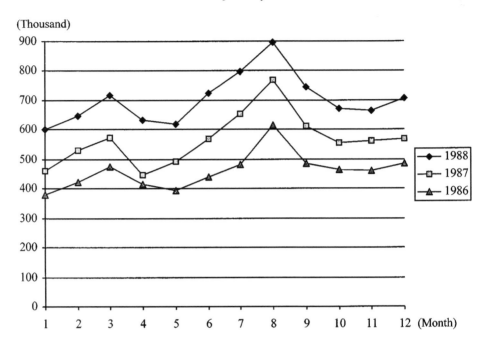

Exhibit CS7.8   Attitude towards work and leisure (*Source*: Prime Minister's Office, Public Relations Section, *Opinion Poll on Leisure Time and Travelling*, January 1986)

Age group

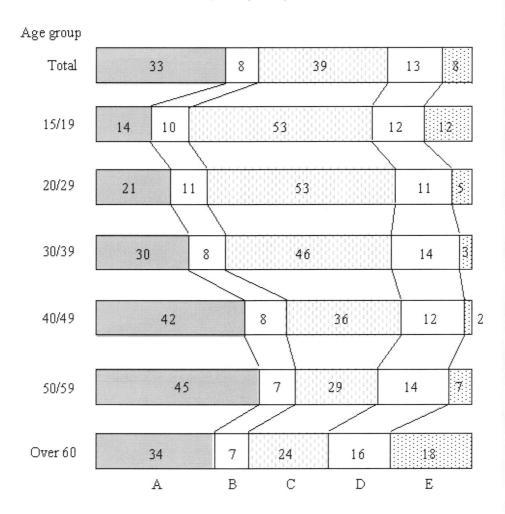

	A	B	C	D	E
Total	33	8	39	13	8
15/19	14	10	53	12	12
20/29	21	11	53	11	5
30/39	30	8	46	14	3
40/49	42	8	36	12	2
50/59	45	7	29	14	7
Over 60	34	7	24	16	18

Case 7

Exhibit CS7.9   Breakdown of leisure hours by activity (*Source:* Somucho, *Basic Survey on Social Life* (interim report), October 1987)

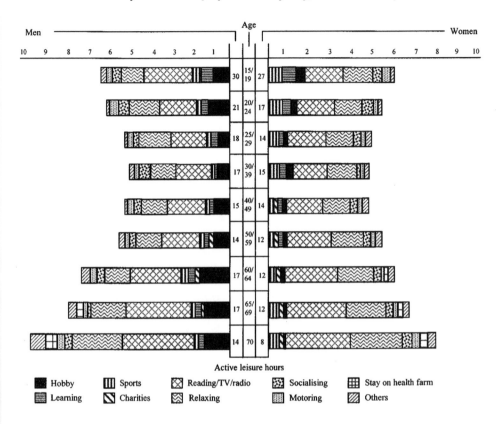

Active leisure hours

Hobby | Sports | Reading/TV/radio | Socialising | Stay on health farm
Learning | Charities | Relaxing | Motoring | Others

Exhibit CS7.10   Japanese members by segments (*Source:* Club Med)

	1984/85	1987/88	Average stay
Honeymooners	72%	40%	7 days
OLs	16%	35%	4.5 days
Families	10%	15%	7 days
Corporate clients	0%	7%	2.5 days
Others	2%	3%	n.a.

**Exhibit CS7.11 Japanese package tours
(Source: A survey by *AB Road* magazine)**

**Percentage of respondents who
recognized the brand name**

Company	%
LOOK	98.8
JALPAK	97.5
HOLIDAY TOURS	90.1
CLUB MED	82.2

**Respondents are asked to name three
package tours they would like to try**

Company	%
CLUB MED	62.9
JALPAK	51.7
LOOK	51.5
HOLIDAY TOURS	25.5

Case 7

Case 8

This case was written by Jocelyn Probert, Research Analyst at INSEAD Euro-Asia Centre, and Hellmut Schütte, Affiliate Professor of International Management at INSEAD. It is intended to be used as a basis for class discussion rather than to illustrate either effective handling or ineffective handling of an administrative situation. The financial assistance of Dentsu Inc. is gratefully acknowledged. Copyright © 1997 INSEAD-EAC, Fontainebleau, France

Goal! Japan Scores in Soccer

Mr Kawabuchi was a man with a vision. Passionately fond of soccer himself, he had played in Japan's epic bronze medal-winning team at the 1968 Mexico Olympics, and dreamed of making the Japanese as soccer-crazy as the Europeans and Latin Americans. He wanted football to appeal to everyone in Japan, and he wanted the national team to play in the World Cup for which Japan had never qualified. He knew that unless the game was rooted in the hearts and minds of the people, the national team would never be truly world class. To breed players of international standing, Kawabuchi had to make Japan's brand new professional soccer league, the J.League, a success.

As chairman of the J.League, Kawabuchi's task was to professionalize soccer. That meant getting the backing of the corporate world, and the support of the civic authorities and the general public. The civic authorities would have to provide the playing facilities, and ordinary people would have to pay to come and watch the games, as they did for professional baseball. Kawabuchi thought there were a lot of latent soccer-lovers in Japan who would come to matches as long as they were packaged properly.

THE J.LEAGUE CONCEPT

Back in 1988, Kawabuchi and other members of the Football Association of Japan (JFA) had started to talk about revitalizing soccer in Japan. The JFA wanted to turn Japan into a great soccer-playing nation. It was a high profile sport internationally, and Japan was hungry for respect and a better national image. Ordinary people worldwide seemed more impressed by sporting achievements than economic success, and Japanese international sports stars rarely won global acclaim.

Some members of the JFA thought Japan stood a better chance of winning soccer world championships than any other team ball game. 'All the best soccer players have the same physique as us', said one. 'Think of Pele, think of Maradonna, think of Eusebio or Keegan. We are not big enough to be the best at rugby, nor tall enough to play basketball'.

The JFA was aware that the major soccer countries had the backing of a strong professional league while in Japan soccer was only an amateur game. 'We concluded that if Japan continued with just its non-professional league, it would never be able to compete successfully internationally and would never get to the World Cup'.[1] South Korea, which was always keen to rival Japan at everything, had set up a professional soccer league in 1983 and already had a record of participation in four World Cup tournaments.

Kawabuchi and the JFA strongly supported the idea of Japan hosting the World Cup in 2002 – and a professional league looked like the only way of making sure Japan had the necessary facilities for it. In 1988, there were only three stadiums in Japan that could hold 40,000 people, and there weren't many even able to hold 20,000. Japan would need 12 new stadiums for 40,000 people by 2002, and that was going to cost US$16 billion. Where would the money come from?

The launch

On 15 May 1993, Japan's first professional soccer matches kicked off around the country amid tremendous fanfare. National awareness of soccer was buzzing after successes in various championships in Asia during 1991 and 1992: in the Kirin Cup (a club tournament), in the Dynasty Cup (which determines the national champion of East Asia), and, the crowning glory, the Asian Cup (when Japan beat Kuwait, the United Arab Emirates and North and South Korea, all of which had previously qualified for the World Cup).

There had been a steady build up of publicity for the league over the preceding months, beginning with the televising of the 1992 Yamazaki Nabisco Cup, which attracted a record 9.9% TV spectator rating. Streams of people began heading for the football stadiums. Professional soccer turned into an overnight success and a hugely fashionable spectator sport.

Soccer in Japan: the background

People only began playing sports beyond school age during the late 1940s and 1950s, when companies started to organize sports teams and cultural activities as part of their workforce welfare programmes. Amateur intercompany and interuniversity competitions created a regional tournament mentality, but national competitions didn't really exist. Baseball was the big sport in Japan, thanks to US influence, and it was the only team sport played professionally. It was also the only team game where talented youngsters could make money from a sporting career. The only other professional sports in Japan were golf and sumo.

Playing sports became much more popular in Japan after the 1964 Olympic Games were held in Tokyo, and the first national leagues for ice hockey, volleyball, baseball, soccer and so on were formed in 1965, all based on 'amateur' company teams. In fact, companies began hiring some youngsters specifically for their prowess at a particular sport, to boost the performance of the

---

[1] Junji Ogura, Secretary General of the JFA, quoted in Varcoe, Fred, 'A league of their own', *Japan Scope*, May 1993.

Case 8

company team. Some companies had already realized that they could improve their corporate image through sports activities. Eight company-sponsored teams from all over the country played in the Japan Football League's first national soccer championship in 1965.

When Japan's national soccer team won the bronze medal at the 1968 Mexico Olympic Games, the country went crazy. This was the first time a Japanese football team had ever achieved such success in any international tournament. All at once, football was the game to watch and play. Four of the ten sporting events drawing the largest audiences to the Tokyo national stadium that year were football matches. Voluntary soccer schools organized by parents sprang up all over the country.

But the fashion faded away. After Mexico, sports gradually became more professionalized within the company system and it was harder to be a part-time sportsperson. Companies gave their sporting staff plenty of time off from their jobs for training, but it was tough for players not to get into the squad of 16 for the next match and to have to go back to their regular work alongside diligent colleagues. Young people who had been the stars of their university teams lost heart if they weren't selected to play in the company team. Parents of skilled high school soccer players discouraged them from thoughts of playing beyond graduation because there was no chance of making a career of it. Players' motivation withered and spectatorship fell.

At junior schools, though, soccer remained popular. The Ministry of Education had endorsed the game during the 1960s as part of the sports curriculum in preference to baseball, because it didn't involve hard bats and balls and the physical exercise in playing soccer was greater. In high schools, though, baseball was a serious sport and the high school baseball championship held in July and August was a national sporting event attracting massive crowds to the Koshien stadium as well as huge TV spectatorship. Any youngster with 'played at Koshien' on his CV was sure to get a good job.

Soccer struggled on as a minority sport in Japan throughout the 1970s and 1980s. Kids playing in the street or park practised pitching baseballs, not kicking a football around. Japan Football League matches still only attracted a few thousand spectators from the companies whose teams were playing. There was no nationwide support for individual teams and there were no players who reached international standards.

GETTING THE J.LEAGUE STARTED

It was in 1989 that Mr Kawabuchi and his friends formally recommended the creation of a professional soccer league to the board of the Football Association of Japan (JFA). They then set up a Professional League Study Committee and between June 1989 and January 1991, they investigated the way that national sports were organized in other countries and looked into methods of financing the new league's development. There seemed to be four main issues: the organizational structure of the new league; the participating clubs; the sponsors; and the 'facilitators', or companies that would handle the non-game aspects of the league.

The organizational structure

The Japan Professional Football League was formally established in November 1991 as a non profit-making association. Kawabuchi was chairman. Mr Mori, brother of one of the other players in the team that had won the 1968 Olympic medal and a long-time member of the JFA, became vice-chairman. The managing director was Mr Kinomoto, another major contributor to the game of soccer in Japan. All the other board members were either directors of the JFA or were elected from among the presidents of the participating soccer clubs.

The new league was quickly dubbed the J.League, a snappier name than its formal title and one that would be much easier to market. The league would operate under the umbrella of the JFA, like all soccer clubs in Japan, and the JFA would represent its interests in dealings with FIFA, football's international governing body. Clubs aspiring to join the J.League would have to work their way up the pyramid of prefectural and regional soccer associations into the amateur Japan Soccer League (JSL), and then become associate members of the J.League by registering their interest and paying a fee. To actually graduate to the J.League, though, a team would have to finish first or second in the annual JSL championship (Figure CS8.1).

The soccer clubs

Choosing the right teams to participate at the start of the J.League was important.

Kawabuchi and his fellow directors strongly believed that the only way to get the general public support which the league needed was to create a true 'home town' system with a close mutual commitment between the soccer club and the local people. They wanted to create the sort of atmosphere found in Manchester or Rome or Mönchen-Gladbach, where local people are passionately involved in the fortunes of the home club. Above all, they wanted to avoid the sort of franchise system used by the American football league, where a team's home depends on the preference of the legal owner. They knew that local communities in Japan were looking for ways to create their own identity. Japanese society is traditionally focused on group membership and

Figure CS8.1   Soccer associations in Japan

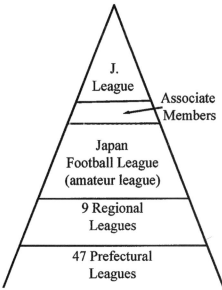

the family remains an important social unit, but many people had left their birthplaces for the cities during the industrialization of Japan in the 1950s and 1960s, and in the countryside, new urban environments had grown up around industrial plants where the inhabitants' loyalties lay with their employer. So the concept of local community feeling in Japan was quite recent.

A home town soccer team had to excite the emotional support of the majority of the local population, not just the few who already enjoyed watching football. The support had to be sustainable too. A club could become a symbol of the town's identity and a measure of its civic pride – there were plenty of clubs in Europe to take as examples. A successful football side could also contribute towards a healthy local economy and a local 'feel-good' factor. Perhaps later, some soccer clubs would be able to excite a national following, like Liverpool in the UK, Ajax in the Netherlands or Flamengo in Brazil.

The J.League management believed that only towns of more than 100,000 people (designated as cities in Japan) would be able to generate enough sustainable support for a professional soccer team. Even so, not just any club from the cities could join the J.League. Clubs had to become independent entities, separately established from their original corporate backers.

Creating a home town team: a profile of Kashima Antlers

In early 1990, a year before the announcement of the first 10 teams to play in the professional soccer league, a small town of 45,000 people in Ibaraki prefecture, north-east of Tokyo began an extraordinary attempt to win the backing of the league selection committee for its football team.

Traditionally a small farming town, Kashima participated in the wave of industrialization that swept Japan in the 1960s and 1970s. Sumitomo Kinzoku (commonly known as Sumikin), Asahi Glass and Mitsubishi Yuka established a plant in the area. As in other prefectures, Ibaraki prefecture offered no entertainment facilities for its inhabitants. The town was also isolated, approximately two hours away from Tokyo, and Sumikin found it increasingly difficult to persuade people to work there. Resorting to desperate measures, Sumikin even began funding half the cost of a night out in Tokyo for its workers.

In the 1980s, the prefectural authorities began searching for ideas to reinvigorate the area, with two aims in mind: to integrate the original farming community more closely with the 'outsiders' who had come to work in the industrial plants, and to create an environment where young people would be happy to live.

The debates in Ibaraki prefecture coincided with preparations for the J.League. Sumikin approached the prefectural office with a new idea: its corporate football team, which played in the JSL from its base at the Kashima plant (rather than near Osaka, where the company's main operations were located), should join the professional league. The notion was welcomed by the prefectural office. Ibaraki prefecture already had a fairly large soccer-playing population, and the relatively low rainfall had created a climate attractive to teams from outside the prefecture, which had come regularly to the area for training camps and high school tournaments.

Mr Kawabuchi was less impressed with the idea. 'He told us we were 99.9999% certain not to be accepted', laughs Mr Kitahata, who was MITI adviser to the governor of Ibaraki prefecture at the time. Kawabuchi was highly sceptical, since the Sumikin team was by no means a star in the JSL and, what was more important, he strongly believed that only places large enough to have city status would be able to give a team the type of support he envisaged.

Kashima set out to prove the strength of its local support. Of the 70 companies with factories in the area, 42 finally agreed to become shareholders in the football club. With such a broad shareholding, the theory was that there should be no problem in ensuring enough tickets would be sold for each match. Even Mitsubishi Yuka, in neighbouring Kamisu, finally agreed to lend support although it had refused initially on the grounds that the Mitsubishi Motors football team also expected to join the J.League as the Urawa Reds. Kashima representatives also elicited the support of the local labour unions for the club as a welfare activity for the workers. Kashima town also took a stake in the new football club. The effort went further. The head of education for Ibaraki prefecture agreed that junior high and high school children be allowed to attend matches as an extracurricular activity, their tickets paid for by the education department.

Kawabuchi, impressed though he was by these efforts, imposed another precondition to his support for the Kashima bid: the town needed a proper football stadium. Although Japan has many multipurpose stadiums, few places exclusively for playing football existed. The governor of Ibaraki prefecture quickly agreed to public funding for a new, US$100 million stadium on the outskirts of Kashima town.

In February 1991, the J.League committee's selection of the 10 teams was announced on the 9 p.m. national news. Nine teams were a foregone conclusion, since they all held city status in Japan. Competition for the tenth place lay between Kashima, Iwata, Hiratsuka and Kashiwa, all relatively small towns. Kashima won the place,[2] and the fame arising from the two-minute interview on the national news accorded to the mayor of the town was sufficient to make him a fervent football supporter.

Since winning the bid, Kashima continues to involve its residents in many ways. For example whereas other football clubs use outside firms at matches for security duties, ticket collection, and so on, many of Kashima Antlers' ticket collectors and ushers are local people known as 'sports volunteers'. Thanks to such high identification of the townspeople with the football team, the 15,000 seater stadium is filled to capacity for every match – which suggests that roughly one in three people in the town is there.

They also had to make a commitment to developing youth teams (under-18s, under-15s and under-12s) in addition to the normal first team and reserve team: long-term development of the game was a key point in the J.League's planning. Of course, they needed adequate facilities too: regular access to a stadium that could seat at least 15,000 people and which was equipped with floodlights for evening matches, as well as proper practice facilities for the youth teams.

---

[2] The other three teams have all been allowed to join the league in subsequent seasons.

Ten teams seemed the right number to play in the J.League's first season. Nine of the company teams playing in the amateur Japan Soccer League (JSL) were city-based and had met the other criteria, so they were obvious choices. The question was, which would be the tenth (see box). The list of teams was announced on 14 February 1991, giving the clubs sufficient time to prepare themselves for professional soccer. Exhibits CS8.1 and CS8.2 show the teams, their corporate backers, the slogans they chose to promote themselves with fans, and their location. Verdy Kawasaki and Yokohama Marinos, playing as the company teams of Yomiuri and Nissan, had for several years been the strongest and the most popular in the amateur JSL. Two new teams joined the J.League from the JSL in 1994 and another two in 1995. When the 10 founder clubs of the J.League became independent, they received up to 1.5 billion yen in capital from their shareholders, who were mostly either individual corporations or small groups of companies.

The players

A primary aim of the J.League was to raise the standard of football in Japan to international levels. That meant bringing in outside talent. Judging by the number of Brazilians playing in the J.League, the Japanese equate success in soccer with Brazil (and a couple of teams have even adopted Portuguese slogans to prove it – see Exhibit CS8.1). The strength of the yen in 1992–93 no doubt also encouraged world class foreign players to consider a career in Japan. Zico, and several players in the Brazilian 1994 World Cup-winning team (Jorginho, Dunga, Leonardo and others), Argentina's Medina Bello and Bisconti, Germany's Littbarski, England's Lineker, Italy's Schillaci... all have made their mark with J.League clubs. Respected players also play for the associate members of the J.League (those clubs hoping to soon join from the JSL).

The newness of the J.League means that many Japanese club players are in their late teens or early 20s, much younger than in the long-established overseas leagues. At first, they stood in awe of the great foreign players and struggled to overcome feelings of veneration and deference at the prospect of tackling, for example the captain of the Brazilian national team (Dunga). Nevertheless, apparent success and the adulation of thousands of young fans have gone to the heads of some Japanese players. Their aspirations have changed from the desire purely to be a good footballer, to wanting to drive a Mercedes and enjoy the trappings of the rich and famous – not normally available to the young in seniority-conscious Japan.

The paradox is that although soccer is essentially a team game, it provides a theatre for individualistic performances. The opportunity for a player to stand out from the rest of the team is what makes football so exciting for the spectators and the players themselves. Their biggest motivation is to play for the national team in the World Cup and in international matches overseas, not just to be a star in Japan.

The Japanese footballer closest to attaining national hero status is Kazu Miura, who plays for Verdy and the Japan national team. He spent six months in 1993 with Genoa Football Club in Italy, which raised the considerable interest of fans at home, before returning to Japan. Other teams have local heroes, like Masahiro Fukuda of the Urawa Reds, who can fill the home stadium for every game.

In a repeat of history, foreign managers, particularly Brazilians and some Europeans, were taken on to train the teams to international standards of play. Back in the 1960s, a West German had coached the Japan national team to its bronze medal success in Mexico. However, managers don't always have the same degree of control over their teams as they do in their home countries. Club general managers tend to interfere in the footballing affairs of the team. One manager for example, returned from a holiday to find that a player had been signed during his absence and others have been fired despite a series of successful seasons with a club for 'not following the Japanese way'. A foreign manager coached the national team to various regional successes in the early 1990s, but he was removed in 1996 in favour of a Japanese to prepare the team for the 1998 World Cup qualifying rounds.

The sponsors

Sponsorship was a key element in Kawabuchi's plans. An official sponsor would lend its name to the league championship, in return for substantial sums of money. In the professional soccer world this is actually quite rare, even though it is very common in other sports. In Europe, only the English teams play in sponsored leagues.

The J.League was trying to find sponsors in 1991–92, just at the end of Japan's bubble era. Still, Kawabuchi and his team didn't expect problems in finding corporate backing because of the appeal of soccer as an international sport, unlike professional baseball in Japan which was basically sponsored only by the companies owning the teams. Having the J.League handle all sponsorship contracts centrally, rather than letting individual clubs cut their own deals, would help them raise the money. The J.League also insisted that firms sponsoring the league had national brand coverage. Around 120 companies became involved in league sponsorship (see Exhibit CS8.3 for the main categories), raising some 2,000 million yen for 1995.

Clubs could arrange their own sponsorship contracts over and above the overall J.League deals, but the limits of what they can do are defined centrally. Up to three companies, for example, can contract to display their logo on players' shirts (front, back and sleeve). Nestlé paid several hundred million yen per year for the right to display various brand names (Nestlé, Buitoni, Kitcat) on Júbilo Iwata shirts. The main corporate owner of a club may pay a sponsorship fee to put its name on the teams' shirtfronts.

Individual clubs keep the money they raise from their own sponsorship contracts but J.League sponsorship fees are portioned out equally between the clubs.

The second round of contracts (1996–98) was negotiated in 1995. Some of the original sponsoring teams renewed their contracts for a second term, beginning with the 1996 season, but the complete list of sponsors now (Exhibit CS8.4) is substantially different from the opening season. Potential financial backers were better placed to evaluate J.League sponsorships in 1995, based on the league's ability during its first couple of seasons to attract spectators to live games and generate TV audiences. The second period of sponsorship contracts was expected to raise revenue of 4,160 million yen for the J.League.

The facilitators

The J.League didn't want to adopt the team franchise system used in the USA, but it was very interested in the way that the US sports associations organize their marketing. European soccer

---

[3] In December 1995   ¥100 = US$1 approximately.

leagues don't have centrally organized marketing machines, and in Japan, professional baseball teams do their own individual team promotion. Kawabuchi reasoned that if the soccer clubs were to act individually, the promotional scope of the game as a whole would be limited – but it could be limitless if done on a national basis. Kawabuchi and his colleagues decided to copy the US pattern and create a coherent, focused strategy to market soccer in Japan. It wouldn't only involve advertising the matches, though, it would be a full package including associated product marketing.

The J.League's thinking on centralized merchandising neatly matched the ideas of Sony Creative Products (Sony CP), a subsidiary of Sony Music Entertainment. Sony CP approached the J.League to propose a marketing plan covering the design, manufacturing, distribution and licensing of products to develop the image of the J.League and its constituent members. Sony CP would also design team mascots and logos, and create an overall J.League logo to appear on a range of products. Such a marketing concept was practically unheard of in the world of soccer, especially among the 'old' footballing nations.

The J.League management team also wanted to try another idea new to Japan: the mass marketing of replica kits (shirts, shorts, socks and so on). Among professional baseball teams, only the Yomiuri Giants and the Seibu Lions made any attempt to reach the mass market, although other teams sold uniforms to spectators at the stadiums. (The potential for kit sales for sumo is rather limited and the only merchandising effort is at tournament events.) Team strips for the soccer clubs were chosen by a J.League committee, and the colours were deliberately jazzy in order to appeal to supporters: bright orange for S-Pulse, lime green and yellow for Bellmare, pink and pale blue for Cerezo, and so on. Japanese baseball uniforms were dull in comparison. The effort put into developing J.League team colours was part of the drive to encourage fans to identify with their teams.

Agreement between the J.League and Sony CP was reached in September 1991 and the two parties signed an exclusive five-year contract in February 1992. Mizuno, competing fiercely against other sports goods makers, won a contract to manufacture and supply all team uniforms and replica kits for the first two seasons. Later, it renewed its contract for another two years.

The unified marketing system allowed 'consistent pricing, design and quality, ensuring responsible trademark management and equal exposure for each club'. One of Kawabuchi's fundamental principles was that all teams should have an equal chance of exposure and an equal share of the merchandising revenue.

Several affiliates of the J.League were created to handle other activities, including J.League Pictures (which controls the rights to video recordings of J.League matches and supplies publicity videos of the league) and J.League Photos (which maintains a library of still photographs of matches).

MARKETING THE J.LEAGUE

Positioning

During the planning phase of the J.League, the management fully expected their main audience to be soccer fans. That meant mostly people who played and enjoyed football in their schooldays – the oldest of them would be in their late 30s by now – and children who were still playing or had been playing until very recently. Because of smaller family sizes in Japan, children were usually indulged by their parents. If soccer promotion was focused clearly at the youth market, the J.League could become a hit.

Spectators at the average baseball game were very different from the J.League's target market. Baseball was a very male-oriented game, and most people in the crowd were men over 40 years old who liked to go along and relax with beers and their business friends. Watching the game itself didn't always seem to be the main reason for going. Kawabuchi and his colleagues didn't expect to convert baseball fans into soccer fans, they were going for a different market altogether.

When the league was launched, he seemed to be right. The crowds became passionately involved in the action on the field. It was real family entertainment. Mums and grandmas were just as keen to come and watch as dads and grandpas. Going to soccer matches quickly became a new leisure time amusement in a country where there weren't many other possibilities for family recreation.

What really surprised Kawabuchi and the rest of the J.League management was the huge number of young women (office ladies, or OLs) at matches. For them it was a new craze. They represented the 'fashion' aspect of the J.League, enthusiastically getting tickets for all the matches and buying the accompanying merchandise. They didn't mind paying up to ¥5,000 for the best seats, or shelling out ¥11,000 for a shirt in their team's colours. It didn't matter that they didn't know much about soccer itself, they came along to cheer the cute young men chasing the ball around. Teenage girls came to cheer individual players, often boys they had been at high school with. Alongside these women were the families: there's not a hint of the hooligan tendency that keeps young women and children away from European football matches.

So where were the real football fans, the young men who had played soccer at junior school? Kawabuchi figured there must be grassroots support out there somewhere. The J.League needed them, it couldn't survive on the whims of the OL crowd. The problem was the relatively small capacity of the stadiums and the OLs' single-minded pursuit of the available tickets. The more laid-back serious fans were simply squeezed out in the rush. By the second and third seasons, the fashion aspect of the J.League was beginning to fade and there were more male fans in the audience. Spectators were more knowledgeable about football by then as well, and could recognize and applaud skilful play by the opposing team, rather than simply react to a good move by a player on their own team.

The delivery

Some sports in Japan are content to rely on income from televised events, but Kawabuchi and his colleagues actually wanted spectators to go to soccer matches. Still, the J.League knew how important TV is to consumers in Japan. They also had to market a lot of goods associated with the J.League.

The match: a live event

An early decision had been taken to organize the season from the point of view of the spectators, to maximize live match spectatorship – a key factor in the desire to create close connections between the teams and their home towns. Television viewers also needed the visual appeal of fresh grass instead of mud baths. That meant reducing to a minimum the number of matches played in the coldest, dampest part of the year and allowing games to be played during the evening in the heat of the summer. The season would therefore begin in March and continue, with a mid-season break, until early December.

Also to maintain spectator interest, every game would have a clear result. At the end of the normal 90 minutes of play, if the scores were level, the teams would play up to 30 minutes of extra time and whichever side scored the first goal would win the match; if neither side scored, a penalty shoot-out would decide the result. This system is not used by the leagues of other footballing nations.

The J.League wasn't interested in knowing how many tickets were sold for each match (the critical measure at other sports events); they wanted to know how many people were actually present. A problem had emerged because some soccer club sponsors were buying large numbers of tickets and giving them away as promotional incentives to their customers. People who weren't interested in soccer ended up with these tickets but didn't use them, while true supporters were left frustrated and ticketless outside the ground. All the J.League could do to curb sponsors' promotional use of tickets was point out that for the long-term good of the league, it was better for clubs to sell tickets to their fans. Now the no-show problem is largely restricted to the VIP boxes. In the second half of every match, the size of the crowd was announced. Exhibit CS8.5 shows spectator numbers for the first three seasons.

The televised event

Japanese consumers are avid trend followers, so TV coverage was crucial to the success of the J.League. The general feeling is that 'if it's on TV, it must be good'. Knowing that a particular game will be televised is likely to boost live spectatorship – exactly the reverse of the European experience, where football clubs now don't allow live broadcasts of their matches because they are afraid all their fans will stay at home to watch.

Dentsu, Japan's leading advertising agency, was the sponsor of the main soccer events in Japan before the launch of the J.League, including the Toyota Cup (played between the best South American team and the best European team) and the national high school soccer championship. The latter didn't win much interest among spectators until Dentsu persuaded the NTV television channel to broadcast it. But Dentsu gave the thumbs down to the idea of professional soccer in Japan, and at first refused to become involved in the J.League. That opened the way for Hakuhodo, another advertising giant in Japan, to seize its chance. The immediate success of the J.League in its first season soon had Dentsu regretting its decision. By 1995, it had managed to claw back 30% of the J.League advertising spend from Hakuhodo, by handling negotiations for TV broadcasting rights on behalf of the J.League. European soccer leagues also normally negotiate the TV rights for their clubs. J.League clubs, though, could arrange their own regional TV contracts.

During the 1993 and 1994 seasons, televised matches were rationed by the J.League among the five national networks. All teams were guaranteed a minimum of two games broadcast nationwide. The huge popularity of the league in its first year meant that TV companies were keen even to televise matches between sides that were playing poorly. By the second season, national TV companies preferred to show only the more popular teams and TV spectatorship declined. There was, however, extensive television coverage of the 1994 World Cup.

In 1995, it was decided to restrict national TV coverage to one game per match day, to be shown in prime time. The J.League asked TV companies to indicate in advance the matches they were interested in showing, and made selections from the submissions to allow even distribution of airtime among the teams and an equal share of matches for the TV networks. Local TV stations submitted their choices directly to their local clubs.

True football fans would be frustrated by the Japanese way of televising matches. Advertisement breaks happen at regular intervals, whatever might be happening in the game, and because the games don't necessarily end after 90 minutes (if the scores are equal) the final result might not even be shown.

Associated products

Target groups and product range

Children's parents are by far the biggest purchasers of J.League merchandise, splashing out for themselves as well as for their offspring. The OLs have also been big buyers, especially in the first couple of seasons. Many spectators at matches wear at least one piece of J.League merchandise, and some entire families are kitted from head to toe in their team's colours.

Each J.League soccer club could choose up to 10 Sony CP-designed products to be manufactured with its team colours and logo. The selection ranged from mascot puppets, hats and scarves through flags, towels, calendars and pens to kit bags, knapsacks and signed footballs. Clubs choose which products they want, depending on the profile of their fans: the average Urawa Reds supporter is relatively old, and likes to buy suitcases and sweaters with the team logo; Kashima Antlers fans range in age from small children to grandmothers, and hats with antlers are popular.

The range of items of replica kit and the selling prices are the same for all teams, for example ¥11,000 for a shirt with team name and logo and ¥4,800–5,200 for shorts in the team colours. A windbreaker jacket with matching trousers costs more than ¥30,000.

Sony CP also took care of the licensing of many other products, most of which had nothing to do with football: bicycles, walkmans, batteries, underwear, socks, food (potato chips, candy) and drinks (J-Water – an isotonic drink – and beer in a special J.League can). Fuji Bank, one of Japan's largest retail banks, even issued a J.League passbook.

Distribution

By autumn 1992, Sony CP was ready to begin selling to the general public club mascots and individual team products as well as J.League-badged merchandise. To keep control and coordinate the marketplace, products would be sold through an independent distribution network rather than through established retail channels.

'Category-1' outlets sold only items related to the J.League and its member clubs, including replica kits. The first shop opened in October 1992 in Kobe and by the end of 1995, 120 Category-1 stores were in place. Most of the shops were franchises, but five are owned by Sony CP. Twenty Category-1s are in Tokyo, either in the form of free-standing shops or as boutiques inside department stores such as Mitsukoshi in Shinjuku.

A second distribution channel for J.League merchandise is the 'J-Station' chain of outlets, which is Mizuno's responsibility. J-Stations sell replica kits made by Mizuno but they also stock some Sony CP-devised goods. There are around 700 of them dotted throughout the country, mostly within existing independent sports shops although Mizuno operates 20 itself (10 in Tokyo and 10 in Osaka).

The third channel for J.League goods is the exclusive team shop: clubs are allowed a maximum of five shops, but most have only one or two, at the home ground and perhaps in the town centre. Revenue from team shops naturally belongs directly to the team concerned. A subsidiary channel is the mail order system available to official supporters clubs. These fan clubs have been able to buy merchandise by mail order since 1993, but from the 1996 season the general public have been able to send off for goods. Initially clubs didn't think team merchandise would be popular with their fans, and so didn't focus on that side of their activity. Later they put in much more effort.

Approximate sales (wholesale value) of J.League merchandise in the first three years ranged from ¥20–30 million.

Mizuno sold 600,000 pieces of replica kit to fans in 1993–95. As a 'serious' (rather than fashion) sports goods company, Mizuno only targeted soccer players at first, and was amazed to find teenage girls and children buying soccer uniforms. In the first three years, 90% of sales went to supporters (and only 50% of these to men) and just 10% to soccer players. Even people who didn't like soccer were attracted by the bright colours of the kit – nothing like it had been seen before in Japan. Although the first flush of enthusiasm is wearing off among OLs, who bought the kit as a trendy outfit to wear on their fashionable outings to soccer matches, Mizuno sees a steady and reassuring 5% growth in purchases by the true player market.

Mizuno's soccer division now represents 7–8% of its total sales, from practically zero at the start of the 1990s. It was much more familiar with selling baseball items, but the popularity of baseball was hit by the launch of the J.League in 1993. Baseball staged a comeback in 1995, when Hideo Nomo shot to stardom as the Los Angeles Dodgers' pitcher after an undistinguished career in Japan, while a youngster called Ichiro playing for the Orix Blue Wave was topping the Japanese batting averages. Although absolute yen figures are not available, an index of Mizuno's football-related sales gives an idea of growth (Table CS8.1).

Table CS8.1 Mizuno's football-related sales

	Soccer division sales	Non-J.League soccer items	Baseball division sales
1992	100	100	100
1993	300	120	95
1994	250	125	100
1995	200	128	110

A significant outcome for both Sony CP and Mizuno of their experience with the J.League has been the high profile they have gained in the world marketplace. Sony CP was selected by ISL, the marketing arm of FIFA, to handle the worldwide merchandising rights for the 1998 World Cup in France, thanks to the success of its J.League campaign. It beat off competition from such giants as Disney Products for the contract. An office will be established in Paris for Sony CP (handling the business in Japan, Asia and Africa) and its Los Angeles-based sister company Sony Signatures (for the American and European side). The corporate image of Mizuno has been raised worldwide by the exposure of the J.League teams to international TV audiences, and the company is moving into football markets in Latin America and the UK to challenge the dominance of companies such as Adidas. It has also been contacted by Japanese non-soccer teams for uniform designs.

THE FINANCES

The J.League itself is a non-profit association. It covers running costs by taking a percentage of sponsorship fees and collecting membership dues from clubs and fees from candidate (associate) members. It receives no share of merchandising royalties or TV rights.

3% of what Sony CP and Mizuno make in merchandise sale goes to the J.League as royalties, which are then distributed to individual clubs according to their share of the total. Royalties on merchandise carrying the J.League logo are split evenly between the teams.

Clubs have three principal sources of income: ticket sales; revenue from their own merchandising and the sale of regional TV broadcast rights; and a share of the sponsorship, national television rights and merchandise sales distributed through the central J.League system. Discussions about a football lottery to raise more revenue for clubs and finance new stadiums came to nothing.

At the start, there was no great difference in the wealth of the various teams because of the J.League policy on equal distribution, but over the long term, a club's financial fortunes will be determined by its income from ticket sales – itself a factor of the home ground's seating capacity and the ability of the team to keep its fans loyal. Clubs are working with their local governments to increase the size of their stadiums to accommodate the demand for tickets. Júbilo Iwata, for example began with a ground capacity of 17,500, raised it to 19,000 by 1995 and plans to have 23–24,000 seats in 1996. Ticket prices (controlled by the J.League) range from ¥2,000 to ¥5,000.

Exhibit CS8.6 shows the budget for the J.League in 1996, agreed shortly before the 1996 season began.

THE LOCAL COMMUNITY EFFECT

There is no doubt that the smaller towns – Kashima, Iwata, Urawa – are the best at inspiring their fans, whatever the match results. In any case, the impact of 20,000 supporters in little towns such as Kashima or Iwata is far greater than 60,000 Verdy supporters in Kawasaki, a city of over a million people. Júbilo Iwata has a supporters club of 25,000 people, even though its stadium holds fewer than 20,000 spectators, and they turn out in their thousands even for end-of-season matches against non-J.League. Forget any ideas of supporters only following successful teams: 'the Urawa Reds have amazing support, the best in the league, even though they finished bottom in the first four series', says one observer. At Urawa, the crowds are reputed for their singing; at

Verdy Kawasaki matches the fans prefer samba-rhythm drumming – and 70% of the spectators are young women, attracted by the strong Brazilian influence of the team. (The Yomiuri media group, which is Verdy's main shareholder, doesn't hesitate to promote the team, and that helps to explain its popularity with the OLs.)

Tokyo doesn't have its own team, partly because there's no overall identity to the city, but also because there aren't the necessary facilities. Only one stadium in Tokyo meets the minimum J.League requirements, but it's too close to a hospital for floodlights to be used for evening matches. Verdy Kawasaki was rumoured to be planning to cross the Tamagawa River and build a new stadium in Yoga in the Tokyo district of Setagaya, but its plans were blocked by the Kawasaki municipal council which had already agreed to pay for the rebuilding of its existing stadium.

In Osaka, support for the city's two teams (Gamba and Cerezo) is less fanatical than in the smaller towns. Gamba's support base is rather weak, which some say is because the team is too strongly identified with a single company (Panasonic). It's also the only team whose home ground (the Expo '70 commemorative stadium) isn't financed by the local community. The J.League tries to insist on the 'home town' concept by refusing to allow the names of the companies owning the clubs to appear in team names, but some have tested the limits. JEF United Ichihara, for example is jointly owned by Japan East (Railways) and Furukawa, and Verdy Kawasaki, the Yokohama Marinos and Gamba Osaka all feature the names of their corporate backers in their logos.

The two essential elements of previous sports booms, according to the J.League, are TV coverage and heroes. Psychologically, Japanese seem to need to find a hero even more than others do. In the run-up to the J.League and during the first season or two, Japanese soccer had to rely on the drawing power of imported foreign heroes in the absence of any real domestic stars. There weren't even any Japanese playing for European soccer clubs like there were in the late 1980s, when Japanese TV coverage of foreign football matches was switched from the UK to Germany because Okudera began playing for a West German team.

Japanese players who join overseas clubs have huge fan clubs – because fans think the status of foreign leagues is much higher than the domestic league, and because they want to see Japan internationally famous. It's the same for baseball in Japan. Unfortunately for the Japanese, there's been a real shortage of national soccer heroes playing overseas in the 1990s – none at all in 1995. If Japan had gone to play in the 1994 World Cup in the USA, instead of losing as they did in the last seconds of the final qualifying match, several players would probably have been signed to play for European teams and would instantly have earned hero status.

THE RESULTS... AND THE CHALLENGE

In 1992, before the J.League was launched, the Japanese national soccer team was ranked #62 in the world according to FIFA. Three years later it was ranked #33. Since 32 teams now qualify for the World Cup championships, up from 24 previously, Japan stands a fair chance of participating in forthcoming tournaments. It knows it won't be a serious contender to win the cup until it ranks among the world's top 10 teams.

As time passes, Japan's pool of skilled professional players will broaden. It expects to be clearly the #1 team in Asia within 10 years, compared with being roughly equal now with several others. The performance of its youth teams in the World Cups played in 1995 was encouraging.

Popular enthusiasm for soccer in Japan is still tied to the success of the national team. The national team will be good if the local teams are good, the local teams will be good if they are well supported locally, and local support will be strong if the national team does well. Kawabuchi and the J.League hope local teams will win the fervent support of local supporters, come what may. How much would a failure to qualify for the World Cup in France in 1998 affect the popularity of the J.League?

The J.League has to keep its matches interesting to maintain support, or the mass media might abandon soccer. What would happen then to sponsorships and advertisers? Is the expansion of the league – to 16 teams in 1996, rising to 20 by 1998 – a threat to the overall quality of soccer in Japan? Another potentially serious issue for the long-term standing of the J.League is the standard of refereeing of matches. Foreign match officials have been brought in to raise standards but Japanese referees have to be more authoritative and stand up to the 'heroes', and the linesmen must learn to disagree with the referee's decisions if necessary.

The J.League board believes a split in the J.League into first and second divisions would motivate the clubs (the winners of the lower league would be promoted to the upper one, and the worst performers in the upper league would be demoted). Professional soccer leagues elsewhere in the world operate on this principle, but is it a good idea for Japan? No decision has been made on the timing of such a split. What are the advantages and disadvantages?

The merchandising campaign was directed very successfully at children during the opening seasons, and through them their parents became soccer supporters as well. Japan is a rapidly ageing society and the percentage of children in the overall population will decline. Also the profile of soccer supporters is shifting from the young females, who are fans of individual players, towards true lovers of the game. What impact could these changes have on the way that soccer is marketed in Japan?

In the 1995 season, baseball produced two new heroes for Japan, Nomo in the USA and Ichiro at home. Would Japan revert to baseball as its favourite game?

The USA, meanwhile, was preparing to launch its own professional soccer league, following the national team's strong showing in the 1994 World Cup. Inaugural matches between the ten teams of Major League Soccer (MLS) kicked off in April 1996, backed by a unified marketing effort, licensed merchandise, and sponsorship deals worth over US$50 million to give the league the financial security which earlier attempts at professional soccer had lacked. This time the stars would be home-grown: even the participation of stars such as Pele, Cruyff and Beckenbauer hadn't been able to prevent the North American Soccer League, MLS's predecessor, from going bankrupt. Average attendance during the MLS's first season was predicted to be 12,000 per game, mostly children and their parents, but the key to success was seen to be television coverage and audiences.

In 1995, Japan launched its formal bid to host the 2002 World Cup after several years of preparation and unofficial lobbying. Advertising giant Dentsu acted as campaign manager and a parliamentary committee, including former premier, Miyazawa, actively engaged in the process.

Case 8

The only other contender to stage the championships was South Korea, which had already qualified four times to play in the World Cup. Both countries became locked in bitter and expensive rivalry to court FIFA officials, with national honour at stake. In June 1996, FIFA decided that the two countries should co-host the 2002 tournament. In July 1996, the whole of Japan went beserk when its national team beat Brazil in an opening round of the 1996 Olympic Games in Atlanta, its first appearance at the Games in nearly 30 years.

Exhibit CS8.1   Teams in the J.League (1995 season) (*Source*: J.League)

Teams	Principal ownership	Slogan
Kashima Antlers	Sumitomo Kinzoku	Dashing beauty
JEF United Ichihara	JR East (50%), Furukawa Denko (50%)	The mighty front
Kashiwa Reysol*	Hitachi	Heat it up
Urawa Red Diamonds	Mitsubishi Motors	Red in Urawa
Verdy Kawasaki	Yomiuri	Com a bola no pé
Yokohama Marinos	Nissan	Sail on to victory
Yokohama Flügels	ANA, Sato Kogyo	Take to the skies
Bellmare Hiratsuka**	Fujita	Winning waves
Shimizu S-Pulse	TV Shizuoka (8%) plus many local companies	Pulsing with excitement
Júbilo Iwata**	Yamaha	Fleet elite
Nagoya Grampus Eight	Toyota	Here we go
Gamba Osaka	Panasonic	The swift attack
Cerezo Osaka*	Yanmar Diesel, Nippon Ham, Capcom	Los lobos victoriosos
Sanfrecce Hiroshima	Mazda, Ford	Pour the heat on

Note: Avispa Fukuoka and Kyoto Purple Sanga joined the J.League in 1996.

* Joined the J.League in its third season (1995).

** Joined the J.League in its second season (1994).

Case 8

Exhibit CS8.2   Geographical dispersion of J.League teams (*Source*: J.League)

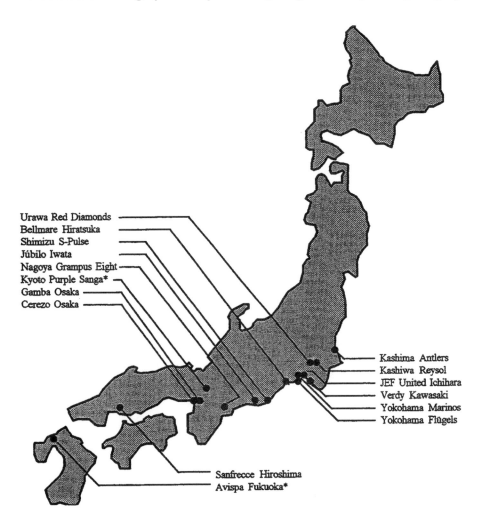

Urawa Red Diamonds
Bellmare Hiratsuka
Shimizu S-Pulse
Júbilo Iwata
Nagoya Grampus Eight
Kyoto Purple Sanga*
Gamba Osaka
Cerezo Osaka

Kashima Antlers
Kashiwa Reysol
JEF United Ichihara
Verdy Kawasaki
Yokohama Marinos
Yokohama Flügels

Sanfrecce Hiroshima
Avispa Fukuoka*

*New to the J.League in 1996.

Exhibit CS8.3   J.League supporting companies (1992–95) (*Source:* J.League)

Capacity	Company	Content
Series sponsors	Suntory	Leading sponsor for official league matches. Can erect advertising placards at all official league matches and use the series sponsorship mark
	Nippon Shinpan	
Official sponsors	NTT Mobile Communications Network	Can erect advertising placards at all official league matches and use the official sponsorship mark
	Okasan Securities	
	Calbee Foods	
Shiseido		
	Shogakukan	
	Japan Energy Corporation	
	Nissin Food Products	
	Nippon Life Insurance	
	Bobson	
	Mizuno	
	Daiei Convenience Systems	
Licensed advertising and public relations sponsors Japan	Citizen Watch	Can use J.League-approved campaign mark and campaign slogan (a part of the 'We love J.League' campaign) in advertising and public relations
	Sekisui Chemical	
	Kentucky Fried Chicken Japan	
	Fuji Bank	
J.League data centre sponsor	Dai Nippon Printing	Company name included on records of official J.League matches and other bulletins. Credit is given in advertisements and when data is used for secondary purposes

185

Case 8

Exhibit CS8.3 *Continued*

Capacity	Company	Content
Man-of-the-Match sponsor	Suntory	Company or product name included in the phrase, J.League – 'Man-of-the-Match')
Official suppliers	Suntory	Supplier of official sports drink (J. Water)
	Kodak Japan	Supplier of film for records of official matches
	Mizuno	Supplier of team kit for league matches
	Menicon	Suppliers of contact lenses for J.League players, managers and coaches
Other suppliers	Crix Yasuda	Supplier of corner posts and flags, and linesmen's flags for official J.League matches
	Cosa Liebermann	Supplier of boots for referees of official J.League matches
	Hit Union	Supplier of kit for referees of official J.League matches
	Seiko	Supplier of wristwatches for referees of official J.League matches
	Molten	Supplier of official balls for official J.League matches
Merchandise licences	Sony Creative Products	Production and sale of goods using team names, logos, mascots, etc. and J.League designs and commercial marks
	Cemic	Production and sale of TV game software using team names, logos, mascots, etc. and J.League designs and commercial marks
	Dai-ichi-Display	Production and sale of medals and accessories using team names, logos, mascots, etc. and J.League designs and commercial marks
	Mizuno	Production and sale of kit and other sports goods using team names, logos, mascots, etc. and J.League designs and commercial marks
Others	Nippon Broadcasting system	Radio broadcasting of official J.League matches on AM, FM, short-wave and satellite audio services

Exhibit CS8.4   1996 J.League sponsors (*Source*: J.League)

Capacity	Company	Content
Official sponsors	Calbee Foods Canon Sales/Canon Daiei Convenience Systems Daiichi Kangyo Bank Japan Energy Corporation Nippon Shinpan Nippon Life Insurance Suntory	The top category of sponsors, contributing to the J.League through the sponsorship of league matches
Fair play campaign	Citizen Trading/Citizen Sekisui Chemical	Support the J.League's efforts to promote the spirit of fair play. May use the slogan 'J.League Fair Play Campaign'
Official suppliers	Dai Nippon Printing Kodak Japan Mizuno Suntory	Support the J.League through the provision of products or services
League cup sponsor	Yamazaki Nabisco	Contributes to the development of the J.League through the sponsorship of league cup matches

Exhibit CS8.5   J.League attendance (*Source*: J.League)

Full season attendance

Year	Total	Average
1993	3,235,750	17,976
1994	5,173,817	19,597
1995	6,159,691	16,922

Note: In the 1993 season 10 teams each played 18 games in the first half season and 18 in the second half; in 1994 12 teams played 22 games in each half; and in 1995 14 teams played 26 games in each half.

Case 8

Exhibit CS8.6   The J.League budget 1996 (*Source: Nikkei Shinbun*, 21 February 1996)

Income

Sponsorship	¥4,500 million	(+¥1,500 million)
Merchandising royalties	¥1,330 million	(-50%)
TV broadcasting rights	¥1,120 million	(-¥500 million)
Entry fees and club memberships	¥2,031 million	
Total	¥8,981 million	(broadly unchanged)
Expenditure	¥8,954 million	(broadly unchanged)
Balance		
Surplus	**¥27 million**	

Case 9

Unilever's Wall's Ice Cream in China

SUCCESSFUL LAUNCH IN BEIJING

Unilever Wall's first factory in China was established in 1994 in Beijing, following the pattern of its strategy for manufacturing and marketing ice cream in Thailand and other South East Asian countries. The large modern US$30 million factory, in which Unilever had an 85% stake, was based in Yizhuang. The business was regarded as one of the city's major manufacturing and distribution successes.

The basis of this success lay in the building up of a proprietary distribution system, bypassing the existing Beijing distributors to create a more flexible and efficient network. Having learnt in other parts of the world that ice cream is rapidly spoiled by any inefficiencies of transport or storage no matter how good the product when it leaves the factory, Wall's was resolved to distribute its product directly throughout China. Half a dozen Beijing concessionaires were therefore selected in different parts of the city to distribute the ice cream on an exclusive basis. These distributors received extensive training – some had no previous experience with ice cream or even low temperature goods, but were deemed suitable on grounds of business credentials. Large trucks carried ice cream from the factory to six distribution points around Beijing, from where the products were transferred in small vehicles to some 2,500 shops and kiosks by means of boxes filled with carbon dioxide. In addition, Wall's salespeople toured the retail outlets to ensure they were continuously well stocked. Freezers bearing the Wall's logo were provided 'on loan' (for stocking Wall's products only) and proved an invaluable way of gaining entry and immediate shelf space.

During the summer of 1995, big store front promotions were launched and Wall's ice cream posters and umbrellas were prominent all over the capital. At the end of the first year, sales had outstripped expectations by a considerable margin, with sales reaching over 10 million litres. Expansion was therefore quickly decided upon, with a new extension to the factory already under construction by late 1995.

THE SHANGHAI MARKET

Seeking to build on its success in Beijing, Unilever then turned its attention to the Shanghai market. Competition in selling goods in Shanghai was fierce, and the problems particular to the city – crowded streets, high cost of space, long credit terms, powerful local wholesalers – provided major challenges.

In 1993, Watson's, a division of Hong Kong's Hutchinson Whampoa, entered the Shanghai ice cream market as the first foreigner with its brand Mountain Cream, the current market leader. In July 1994, Fuller Foods of Taiwan began to sell ice cream; Wall's commenced operations in spring 1995, while other foreign brands included Bud's of San Francisco (made in Beijing), TCBY, Danone and AB Profetti. The rest of the market was held by local brands, primarily flavoured ices, supplied by some 200 small manufacturers.

All Wall's competitors in Shanghai were dependent on the same 150-200 state-owned, but individually operated, wholesalers for distribution. Product protection was poor, both in transport, with most operations using bicycles or insulated but not refrigerated trucks, and at retail level, with freezer temperatures often not correctly maintained. Consequently the ice cream sold was not of the best quality and was often half melted.

WALL'S ARRIVAL IN SPRING 1995

Building up an independent distribution network in Beijing proved expensive but more reliable than the existing system, Wall's only contact with which was the leasing of space in some of the city cold stores. In Shanghai, Wall's attempted to duplicate this successful strategy. It quickly encountered difficulties.

In Beijing, the streets are wider, competition is less intense and retailers have more space. In Shanghai, a number of problems became immediately apparent.

The first obstacle was Shanghai's chronic traffic congestion. To attempt to combat this, there were stringent and complicated bureaucratic restrictions on the movement of delivery trucks; expensive and difficult-to-obtain licenses required, time and vehicle number restrictions imposed within the inner ringroad. Other streets were completely inaccessible due to construction work. Regulations changed frequently, and paperwork needed constant updating, with additional confusion as to which of the many different authorities had ultimate jurisdiction. While in other cities Wall's independent distributors had responsibility for licensing their own vehicles, it became evident that in Shanghai its distributors would require assistance.

In contrast to the welcome it had received in Beijing, in Shanghai Wall's experienced both retailer and wholesaler resistance. 60% of Shanghai's retail outlets already had freezers provided by ice cream or drinks manufacturers such as Coca-Cola. With outlets generally small, most had no room for more. Competition for shelf space was intense, and Wall's salespeople did not find it easy to get cabinet placement. Intense competition also meant long credit terms, with major retailers demanding the accustomed 30 days rather than the three imposed upon its distributors by Wall's. These distributors were therefore forced away from the big downtown areas, where Wall's had intended to establish a strong presence, toward smaller stores which would accept

Wall's credit terms, and peripheral areas where traffic was less constricted and wholesalers less aggressive.

Wholesalers in Shanghai wielded considerable power: particularly since the arrival of the foreigners, manufacturers who once had no need to sell themselves to the wholesale trade were having to prove each product in terms of speed of movement and advertising back-up. Agents regularly exercised their power to reject any product considered insufficiently interesting, wrongly priced or not well-enough advertised. Having attained this position of power, wholesalers regarded Wall's independent methods as a threat to their livelihood, and articles appeared in the Chinese press at the time of Wall's launch suggesting that its distribution strategy would force people out of work. The strength of retail/wholesale relationships in downtown Shanghai meant wholesalers were able to persuade retailers to decline to carry Wall's products. Furthermore, the traffic restrictions in Shanghai meant that Wall's simply could not deliver into certain streets, and was therefore going to be forced to compromise and use wholesalers.

Problems were also experienced with pricing: the income profile of Shanghai showed its inhabitants to be more affluent than those of Beijing. Nevertheless the proven Beijing pricing strategy failed in Shanghai, due to the greater competition and greater range of brands. In comparison with its rivals, Wall's was seen as expensive. Furthermore, its line of flavours, successful in the north, was less so in the south, where the hotter summers had led to preference for ices over ice cream.

Despite the problems, Wall's remained undeterred: the company's Shanghai factory was in operation in February 1996. In the summer of 1995, Fuller Foods' statistics put Watson's Mountain Cream as number one brand, with around 30% market share, followed by Fuller's own brand with 11%. It placed Wall's and AB Profetti at joint third with 5%. Wall's own figures ranked its product sixth, behind both foreign and local competition, but at number three in brand recognition. Attributing its low market share to the mistake of trying to treat Shanghai like Beijing, Wall's devised again, ambitious plans for 1996.

ADJUSTING THE STRATEGY FOR SHANGHAI

As a result of the delivery problems encountered, Wall's enlisted a major wholesaler to distribute in areas of the city where only delivery tricycles with special passes were permitted, while still retaining control of the distribution network: its own employees did the selling and payment collection, and it provided insulated boxes, so that the wholesaler was responsible only for supplying the hawkers and a downtown cold store.

Pricing strategy was adjusted, and with two factories operating, the range of products was expanded to include ices (cheaper than ice cream) and more Chinese-favoured flavours to complement its core group of global products.

COMPETITOR REACTION

Wall's arrival in Shanghai in spring 1995 provoked jitters both among its competitors and the ice cream wholesalers. Despite its problems, Wall's demonstrated persistence, and had the benefit of considerable expertise abroad. In response, Watson's Mountain Cream and Fullers re-created their products for the Chinese market and sought to leverage their local relationships which were perceived as a counter to Wall's greater financial muscle. In 1995, Mountain Cream attributed a big increase in market share to the enormous growth in ice cream advertising in general in Shanghai. Wall's had advertised heavily (in 1995, it spent about RMB14 million[1]) and Mountain Cream was forced to spend more to defend its position – around 70% of the amount poured in by Wall's. In the same year, Wall's installed 2,600 freezers, against about 1,560 supplied by Mountain Cream.

WALL'S FUTURE GOALS

By the end of 1996, Wall's planned to have 11,000 freezers in place, with a further increase in advertising. Whether Mountain Cream could continue to compete, or whether it would be ousted as market leader by Unilever's multinational leverage remained the critical unknown.

---

[1] Equivalent to US$1.7 million at prevailing exchange rates.

Business-to-Business Marketing

Part

4

Japan

In the 1980s, when Japan took steps to lower tariff and non-tariff barriers in response to Western criticism, it became clear that there were other obstacles to Western exports: networks of Japanese firms buying from each other; subtle administrative guidance that favoured local firms; a complex distribution system; closed-door bidding for construction contracts; bureaucratic and regulatory obstacles, especially in high technology sectors.

The Japanese government has gradually removed these obstructions. For example the Japanese telecommunications company NTT has been persuaded to purchase part of its equipment abroad. Japanese science institutions have acquired US supercomputers, and the Japanese electronics industry is buying a sizeable number of US semiconductors. Even US software suppliers have established viable operations in Japan in the 1990s. Also, Japan can now claim to be the only country which officially exhorts its citizens to buy imported goods, which provides special loans for imports and which has set up a government agency (JETRO) specifically to help foreign exporters find a Japanese market for their goods.

To succeed in Japan, however, requires more than just exporting: foreign firms must make substantial direct investments over a long period. In Japan, as a rule, relationships matter more than a good price: transactions are carried out after a relationship has been established, and price is only one ingredient in a mix of expectations and interactions. This, of course, is also true in Europe, and, to a lesser degree, in the USA. But, by and large, in the West pricing has been and still is the most important ingredient in the conclusion of a business deal. In Japan, on the other hand, this rarely holds true, particularly when selling to industrial customers. Saying that while the Japanese market is open, Japanese society remains closed, is still a valid description.

Keiretsu, or enterprise groups, are the best-known example of industrial cliques. Understanding the links between the various members of these groups and the way they grant preferential treatment to each other is vital for calculating an individual foreign firm's chances of success in a given market. But close relationships do not guarantee the conclusion of a contract, even within the *keiretsu*. Business links are becoming looser, and selling to and buying from competitors is becoming more common, even on an OEM basis. But Japanese buyers will continue to define the quality of relationships with existing suppliers, customers and other partners as a competitive advantage that matters more than an outsider's ability to offer the right product at the right price.

The ASEANIEs

Growing demand from the transition and traditional segments, coupled with steady foreign demand for manufactured exports, has caused sales of raw materials and semi-manufactured goods to grow rapidly. New plants and equipment are needed to replace existing equipment and to expand capacity (either because of import-substitution policies, or because exports are increasing throughout the region). Large-scale turnkey projects in extractive industries and the processing of raw materials are further opportunities to sell capital goods. Road construction equipment, power plants, telephone systems, port facilities are required to urgently develop and upgrade infrastructure. Demand for industrial products is far greater in the ASEANIEs than in industrial countries of similar size.

Four market segments

Governments and state-owned enterprises

Governments play a major role in the purchasing of industrial products, either directly, or through state-owned enterprises. In most ASEANIEs the public sector still dominates the industrial scene, despite some attempts to privatize. Political considerations often influence purchasing decisions, and as a rule preference goes to local suppliers, although competitive bidding also exists. Successful bids are often prepared by gathering extensive information well before a tender is officially announced. Consultants who determine the technical specifications of projects will play a major role.

Because Asian governments formulate policies, set standards, grant licenses, provide foreign exchange and credit, they also have a major influence on purchasing decisions in the private sector. Industry associations and chambers of commerce can be of help to the foreign firm.

Leading local firms and non-Japanese multinationals

Leading local or regional firms, and the subsidiaries of Western multinationals, have similar purchasing processes: in both cases local technical staff act as gatekeepers, specifiers and influencers. However, in local firms, important purchasing decisions are made by the chief executive (often the owner), while Western subsidiaries may have to refer to their headquarters or regional office; when expatriate staff are involved in the decision, they may introduce a slight bias toward suppliers of their own national origin, although not to the exclusion of others.

Japanese firms

Several thousand Japanese subsidiaries are actively operating in the region – an important but problematic segment for Western suppliers. By and large they prefer to deal with proven suppliers – usually Japanese. This is due to several reasons:

- close relationships with subcontractors at home, and the strong influence of headquarters on subsidiaries;

- the closed nature of Japanese communities abroad;

- most Japanese manufacturers in the region are joint ventures with local firms and with one of the large Japanese trading houses (*sogo shosha*), whose enormous product portfolio and geographic spread enables them to supply practically anything that is not delivered by suppliers in Japan.

There is not much room left for non-Japanese suppliers except in niche products, such as special chemicals. They should direct their marketing efforts at headquarters rather than at local units.

Backyard operators

These local companies, with little technical expertise and purchasing power, also represent a challenge for the Western firm. They play a useful role in the domestic economy, manufacturing simple consumer goods aimed at the traditional segment on a small scale. While overall they form a major economic factor, they must be targeted individually, which is difficult and expensive – especially since many operate outside major cities. This segment is an attractive market for sellers of second-hand machinery or suppliers of commodity products from Taiwan and Korea; it is less relevant for firms selling sophisticated or expensive product lines.

Service expectations

Over the years Asian managers have developed technical expertise in buying industrial products. Despite comparatively low labour costs, they often select capital-intensive, rather than labour-intensive, processes. Often-cited reasons are a search for quality, the fact that machines are easier to manage than workers, and fears of higher labour rates or impending labour shortages. The desire to impress customers and suppliers is also a factor.

In many industrial sectors, the services provided are at least as crucial as the price and payment terms: many Asians see service as a strong indicator of commitment, and expect suppliers to provide sufficient information and show a willingness to adapt products. This requires extensive local representation, local warehousing for fast delivery, and after-sales service on the spot.

Manufacturers in the ASEANIEs are at different technological and developmental stages, each requiring different marketing strategies:

- *Implementors*, at the first phase of the learning process, assemble a limited product range. They are looking for new product and production opportunities and generally prefer a complete package that includes raw materials, components and capital equipment. (A typical example would be Sumatra Tobacco, a medium-sized cigarette manufacturer in Indonesia, which diversified into instant coffee.) Western firms must learn to bundle their offer and emphasize marketing technology rather than products.

- *Assimilators* are assemblers who have learned fast, and moved toward producing first components. They expect quality and specific technical know-how, and require advice on products and processes that need upgrading,

196

rather than technical expertise across the whole product range. To offer better solutions, the supplier will have to analyse the customer's operations (this is not as essential in industrial countries). The Filipino brewer San Miguel, for instance, wants advice on improving its bottle production – not on brewing.

■ *Improvers* manufacture more sophisticated products. To boost productivity and become world-class producers, they need expert advice on developing new products to extend their product range. Improvers such as Taiwanese PC-manufacturers Acer and Mitac look for advanced technologies such as those in industrial countries, and expect suppliers to offer both expertise and full service. Competitive bids are the rule for any re-buy.

Table 4.1 Buying decision criteria

	First buy	**Modified rebuy**	**Repeat order**
Implementor	Packaged technology	Reliability Training	Reliability Price
Assimilator	Specific technology	Quality Service	Value
Improver	Advanced technology	Delivery Price	Price

All ASEANIEs have manufacturers at all three stages, although Korea and Singapore tend to have more improvers, while Indonesia and the Philippines have more implementors. Table 4.1 shows the main buying criteria for each category of firms. Depending on the foreign parent company's willingness to transfer technology, subsidiaries and joint ventures set up as implementors can quickly become assimilators; they are less likely, however, to upgrade to improvers. Local or regional firms will move through the three stages more slowly.

China

Industrial products in China are purchased either by the government or by producers of other industrial or consumer products; what is crucial for foreign suppliers is to assess their dependence on the government and their ability to finance the purchase (see Figure 4.1).

China's import substitution policies put foreign suppliers at a disadvantage for two reasons: Western firms need to be paid in foreign exchange, and imports are usually subject to high import duties. (These constraints can be overcome when the government, army or party hierarchy has identified their product as a strategic priority.) Western firms that target the government or state-owned firms must not only identify potential customers, and evaluate the urgency of their need, but also estimate how willing potential competitors are to sell on credit.

Figure 4.1   Industrial customer segmentation in China

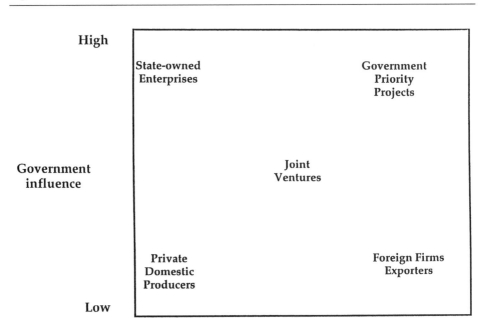

As central planning gradually disappears, it is harder for Western firms to identify customers. Buyers in China can be at the national, provincial or city levels. However, since most Chinese industries have a vertical structure, decisions made at one level may be influenced by bureaucrats at another level. Having to deal through state import and export companies adds to complexity and cost. In electronics, for example, several ministries, departments and bureaus are involved, often with overlapping and ill-defined responsibilities. In the experience of many Western firms, power is where the money is, and that is increasingly in the provinces. As state-owned enterprises become responsible for profit, their managers increasingly take purchasing decisions, but they still need approval from higher authorities. This is particularly true when payments are made in foreign exchange and in cases of major, long-term deals. In any case, foreign suppliers need persistence and a good understanding of the relationships among the various players to deal successfully with a multitude of contacts.

Chinese bureaucrats and managers try to eschew risk when making decisions. They prefer to deal with well-known companies, or individuals with whom they are already familiar. For Western firms the first step is therefore to create awareness of their products before they start to develop personal relationships (*guanxi*) with individuals in the various bureaucracies. The next stage is often a seminar in China where more technical details are provided. If the Chinese partners are still interested, they are likely to ask for an invitation to visit the supplier's overseas plant or headquarters. Only afterwards will serious negotiations begin (see Figure 4.2).

Figure 4.2   Typical industrial marketing procedure

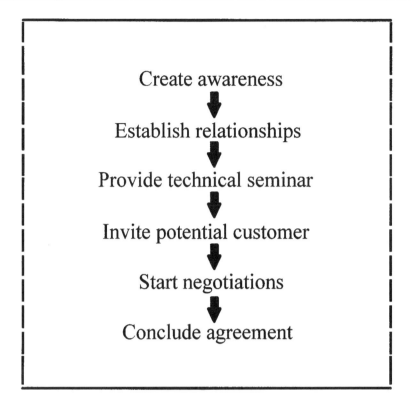

Except for essential staples, China has phased out price controls, so that the seller can set the price. However, foreign firms who take advantage of product scarcity to set high prices should beware of government retaliation. For industrial products, low prices do not guarantee high sales: political arguments may weigh more than economic considerations when making purchasing decisions. In bids for major projects, financial terms are becoming more important. China is less reluctant to becoming indebted to foreigners, and some Western governments support their companies by offering cheap finance.

There is a general aversion in China to paying for software and for services such as training and consultancy. As a result, foreign suppliers often try to bundle the various parts of their offer. Such all-inclusive packages, disliked in other parts of Asia, are appreciated by the Chinese, whose motivation is both to get a discount and make a single request for funding or approval to the bureaucrats in charge.

Because of a long-time emphasis on mass production, product quality in China is generally poor. For several decades, service hardly existed. Progress has been made since 1979, but the quality gap with the rest of Asia, especially Japan, remains huge. Foreign products are expected to be of better quality and carry an image of some prestige; this is highly valued, even in industrial markets. Satisfaction with the product and good manufacturer or brand reputation can result in very high customer loyalty. This may explain why the Chinese often purchase advanced machinery when less sophisticated equipment would be cheaper and easier to handle. Service is expected as a matter of course, normally free of charge or for a low fee.

Distribution agreements in Asia Pacific

Because intermediaries play an important role in Asia, many foreign firms use distributors when entering markets in the region. Although larger, more experienced companies now tend to take charge directly, especially in promising markets, distribution agreements remain crucial for smaller, less experienced firms in lesser markets. In countries such as Indonesia, the Philippines, China and Vietnam, which restrict distribution activities, foreign firms are forced to join up with a local partner or to appoint a local distributor that will act as importer, wholesaler, or retailer, or combine several of these functions. In some cases, distributors take sole responsibility for a given market including logistics, inventory control and financing; in others they merely facilitate sales by establishing contacts. In some cases, large multinational firms are still living with – and bemoaning – the consequences of distribution agreements made dozens of years earlier.

Using a distributor is convenient for firms that lack the experience, contacts and resources to enter a new market. Since sales are low at first, it is also cost-efficient. Besides, in some countries contacts are vital, especially in dealing with governments and state-owned corporations, or in heavily-regulated markets. The appointment of a distributor also makes it easier to pay commissions when the local context requires it, without attracting the attention of internal auditors. For similar reasons distributors in Singapore or Hong Kong are used to import products on which Indonesia, China or Vietnam levy high customs duties: the foreign firm is not directly involved in the import process and avoids problems with customs clearance. Thereafter, it may leave local distribution to the importer, appoint another distributor, or take charge itself.

The greatest disadvantage of distribution agreements is that they cut off the principal from the market. Appointing a distributor will not help a firm gain any market insight or experience. Pre-selling support, price setting and after-sales service are especially difficult to control. Having a distributor in each country in a region which is increasingly integrated also makes it difficult to coordinate activities across borders. Most distribution agreements are structurally flawed and problematic: multinationals which pursue regional or global strategies often see market share and competition as more important than immediate profit while distributors, on the other hand, look at the products of one multinational firm as only a small part of their portfolio, which may contain many similar, sometimes competing, products. For them sales, margins and payment terms matter more than long-term market share.

There is another serious concern related to market dynamics and to the two partners' expectations about the agreement's duration. Distribution agreements are generally made when sales are small or non-existent: the business at this stage cannot support the high fixed costs of setting up and running a marketing or sales subsidiary; a distributor represents no more than a variable cost. If the distributor succeeds in promoting the product and gaining market share, sooner or later the manufacturer will find it more profitable to cancel the agreement and to set up a fully owned subsidiary (see Figure 4.3). This may be natural enough; the danger, however, is that the distributor will then avoid increasing sales volume in order to keep the business, either deliberately underperforming, or by setting a higher price per unit (and therefore his own profit) to make up for lower volume.

The Japanese car importer Yanase is a case in point. For dozens of years it imported Mercedes, BMW and Volkswagen cars into Japan, selling them at inflated prices. Due to the low volume of sales, the German manufacturers did not consider it worthwhile to set up their own import business and distribution network. When they finally decided to, the link with Yanase was difficult to break. Mercedes took over the import business but kept Yanase as one of several distributors. When Volkswagen followed suit in the 1990s, Yanase, which had imported and sold 600,000 Volkswagen cars, balked and walked away, leaving the German firm with a handful of outlets in Japan. Yanase also decided to distribute Opel cars, taking sales and market share away from Volkswagen.

Figure 4.3   Breakeven in distribution

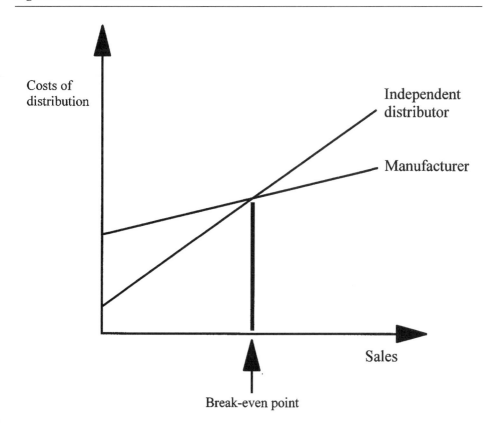

This case illustrates the difficulties of evaluating distribution alternatives and of foreseeing the reaction of the distributor to a proposed change. Understandably distributors argue that market success is the result of their efforts, or contacts. They try to protect themselves by working with several different manufacturers, offering additional services which are difficult to replace, withholding important information and showing an interest in taking over the business of competing manufacturers. Because the potential for conflict is high, when an agreement is signed, attention should be paid to the manner in which it could be terminated later on. Distributors are key external resources that require years of constant, attentive management. Agreements with them represent major commitments. Changes are usually much more difficult and time-consuming to carry out in distribution than in other elements of the marketing mix. Successful distribution partnerships require a fit in strategies, resources, culture and organization. Two broad types of partners can be considered:

Local distributors

They have better local contacts and maybe better local sales forces, but many do not complement well a Western principal. 'Local' in ASEAN and Vietnam often means Chinese; while Chinese entrepreneurs usually work hard and efficiently, using them entails a political risk; when dealing with the state sector in Indonesia and Malaysia, they can be a disadvantage.

International distributors

They are of Western, Japanese and increasingly Asian origin. Some Western distributors have been in Asia since colonial times; once trading outposts, they have become modern marketing firms. Others, unable to adapt no new times, are disappearing. Diethelm, East Asiatic, Hagemeyer, Liebermann, Inchcape, Jardine and Swire are among the best-known survivors. Foreign manufacturers will find it fairly easy to establish a fit with them. However, some local distributors may offer better business connections and resources. The strength of the old houses also varies geographically: British firms, for example, are strong in Hong Kong but weak in Indonesia; Diethelm is successful in Thailand, less so in other countries. This basically rules out appointing an international distributor for the whole of Asia Pacific.

The Japanese *sogo shosha* are the exception. They have well-staffed offices throughout the world, and particularly in all Asia Pacific countries. Itochu, Mitsui, Mitsubishi, Sumitomo or Marubeni are in a class of their own: they are several times larger than any non-Japanese trading company in the world. Their strength lies more in industrial goods, commodity trading and project management than in final distribution or marketing of fast-moving consumer goods. Because of their size and enormous product range, the *sogo shosha* do not offer exclusivity; this makes Western manufacturers uncomfortable. (Some Western multinationals have had good experiences, however, particularly when targeting Japanese companies operating in Asia Pacific, or in projects initiated and financed with development aid from Japan.) Choosing a *sogo shosha* as an importer for Japan, on the other hand, can be disappointing: a Western firm with limited sales is too small to command full attention.

In Japan the solution is either to go into a major, more complex arrangement with a *sogo shosha* aimed at increasing business volume, or to go it alone, or to appoint a smaller distributor.

References

Schrage, Michael, *Old Assumptions, New Markets: Doing Business in a Changing Japan*, Japan Society, New York, 1991, pp. 5–8.

Wortzel, Lawrence H., 'Marketing to Firms in Developing Asian Countries', *Industrial Marketing Management*, No. 12, 1983, pp. 113–123.

Case 10

Case 10

This case was developed by Professor Wilfried R. Vanhonacker as a basis for class discussion rather than to illustrate either effective or ineffective handling of an administrative situation. Financial and administrative support was provided by the Hong Kong University of Science and Technology (HKUST) and the China-Europe International Business School (CEIBS) in Shanghai. Copyright © 1995 INSEAD-EAC, Fontainebleau, France.

Shanghai Honggong Advanced Instrument Co., Ltd (SHAIC): Marketing Electromagnetic Flowmeters in China

Looking out of his office window, Mr E.J. Broekers, general manager of Shanghai Honggong Advanced Instrument Co., Ltd. (SHAIC),[1] a Sino-German joint venture (JV) in the Minhang Economic and Technological Development Zone (ETDZ) of Shanghai, noticed the two smokestacks of the main Shanghai electric power station. His eyes followed the large clouds of smoke that shot out of the smokestacks into the hot summer air. 'Despite continued growth in revenue and profits, some clouds have appeared on SHAIC's horizon as well', he thought to himself.

SHAIC was established in 1986 as an equity JV between the Shanghai-based Honggong Instrument Works (HIW) with 60% equity and the German company Krüger with 40% equity. Since its establishment, the JV had developed a profitable business in China. Selling electromagnetic or magnetic inductive flowmeters of various sizes, turnover in 1994 had reached ¥48 million[2] (including VAT) with a 17% net profit. But market development had been a rollercoaster. Since 1993, orders had come increasingly from the southern part of China (primarily Guangdong Province) and from sectors other than steel which had represented the bulk of business in the early years. With this shift, the role of the Ministry of Nuclear Energy (MNE) (to which HIW belonged administratively) in opening up markets had waned. As new opportunities found themselves outside of the ministerial sphere of MNE, Broekers felt that the Chinese partner would face increasing difficulty in executing its sales and marketing responsibilities. A more aggressive market development approach was needed.

---

[1] Company names and some confidential data have been disguised.
[2] ¥ or RMB stands for Renminbi, the Chinese currency. In October 1995, the Renminbi was semi-convertible at about ¥8.4 = 1 US$.

However, due to (a) lack of liquidity in the economy because of the central government's tight monetary policy since August 1993, (b) complex differences in the industrial ministries to which clients reported (particularly the extent of central control and information exchange), and (c) the general lack of experience with electromagnetic flowmeters among potential Chinese customers, questions arose on where to focus next. Broekers specifically wondered how to access and develop virgin application areas, how to secure an efficient entry, and how to pre-empt foreign competitors who were in the process of getting their own JV operations off the ground. With 60% of the installed flowmeters being from SHAIC, Broekers also questioned how to maintain the motivation among the Chinese employees. The enthusiasm and aggressiveness they had shown during the initial years of the JV would have to be maintained, if not increased, to successfully tackle the new market opportunities.

COMPANY BACKGROUND

SHAIC is a Sino-German JV located in the Minhang ETDZ, southwest of Shanghai (see Exhibit CS10.1).[3] After two years of negotiation with the central government in Beijing, the JV was established in 1986 between Honggong Instrument Works (Shanghai) and Krüger (Germany). Honggong Instrument Works is a centrally-controlled state-owned enterprise (SOE) based in Shanghai which administratively belongs to the Ministry of Nuclear Energy (MNE), one of China's smaller industrial ministries.

Krüger is a family-owned German company headquartered in Duisburg, Germany. It was established more than 70 years ago and has grown to become an international force in the field of measurement technology. In the field of flowmeters, Krüger had become synonymous with quality and reliability. In 1994, worldwide turnover was about 500 million DM. In the early 1980s, as China opened its door for foreign direct investment, Krüger saw enormous opportunities in the China market. Although electromagnetic flowmeters were new to China, many of its overseas clients (e.g. Bayer, BASF, Ciba-Geigy), required flowmeters installed in their Chinese production facilities. To enable broader penetration in the local market and to educate potential customers in its advanced technology, Krüger decided to set up an equity JV and transfer flowmeter product and production technology to China. Initial contacts were made with the central government in 1984, and the JV contract with Honggong Instrument Works was formally signed in 1986.

Under the JV agreement, Krüger contributed technology and an equity investment of 11.7 million DM. In return, it obtained a 40% equity stake in SHAIC. The majority stake of 60% was with Honggong Instrument Works. Where Krüger took the responsibility for production, HIW took responsibility for marketing and sales. By September 1995, SHAIC occupied two production sites in the Minhang ETDZ of Shanghai and a sales office in the centre of Shanghai. One of the facilities in Minhang was equipped with a large flow calibration rig capable of handling a wide range of flowmeters up to 3 m diameter – the only flow calibration system in China. In 1995, a total of 122 people were employed at the three sites. Mr Broekers and the production manager were the only expatriate managers in the JV. The organizational structure of the joint venture is depicted in Exhibit CS10.2.

---

[3] Shanghai has currently four special economic zones: Caohejing Hi-Tech Park, Hongqiao ETDZ, Minhang ETDZ, and Pudong.

In terms of administrative structure, SHAIC – through its Chinese partner HIW – belonged to the Ministry of Nuclear Energy (MNE). Being located in Shanghai and working in the field of instrumentation, it also had to report to the Shanghai Measurement Instrument Bureau (SMIB) of the Shanghai Municipal Government. In essence, SHAIC was required to periodically report performance statistics to MNE in Beijing (the central government link) and to the SMIB in Shanghai (the municipal government link). The latter link had increasingly become a concern as it was well known that SMIB had recently established its own JVs (at the local, Shanghai Municipal Government level) with two of Krüger's international competitors.

In addition to the JV, Krüger continued to import electromagnetic flowmeters from abroad and it occupied a representative office in Beijing.[4] Although Krüger's products were typically of a more advanced design than the flowmeters manufactured by SHAIC, the JV had been known to compete with them on orders originating from outside China.

In 1994, SHAIC attained a turnover of ¥48 million. With a cost of goods sold of 67%, net profit on turnover was 17%, 2% higher than the average for the 112 foreign-funded enterprises operating in Minhang at the end of 1994.[5] The 17% net profit figure represented a 3% drop from the previous year. By September 1995, Broekers believed that 60% of the installed flowmeters in China were SHAIC products. The remaining 40% were imported products, as SHAIC was the only producer in China at that time. Of the imported products, about 8% were Krüger flowmeters.

In September 1995, Krüger was negotiating with MNE and HIW to increase its equity stake to over 50% and to transfer more advanced technology to SHAIC.

THE MARKET

Product

Electromagnetic (or magnetic inductive) flowmeters measure mass flow in pipes. They are installed and used as process control instruments in a wide range of industrial applications including water cooling systems in the steel industry, drinking water supply, mining, chemical industry, power industry, beverage industry, etc. SHAIC manufactures flowmeters for pipes ranging in diameter from 10 mm to 3 m. The design and compactness of the flowmeters are adapted for different applications. For example in the dairy industry, the flowmeters are designed with sanitation in mind; for installation in hazardous areas, other design adaptations have to be made.

The meters are typically included in new plant designs. With the major overhaul and upgrading of existing production facilities in many industries together with the construction of many new production operations (often involving foreign direct investment) in China, the market potential for electromagnetic flowmeters was believed to be very large.

---

[4] Under Chinese government regulations, representative offices are not entitled to do business in China and, hence, cannot solicit orders (i.e. they have no business license).
[5] As a high-tech company, SHAIC had preferential status with an income tax rate of 10% relative to the normal 33% corporate tax rate.

Customers

SHAIC's actual and potential customers were primarily SOEs. With a growth in the number of wholly foreign-owned enterprises (WFOEs), it was possible that in the future some of the customers would fall outside of the direct administrative control of the Chinese government. For the immediate future, however, understanding the administrative control mechanism operating at different government levels and identifying the important actors and gatekeepers in it remained paramount to successful marketing and selling to the state-owned sector in China.

Under the old system of a planned economy which was in place in China until the late 1970's, all enterprises belonged administratively to a central government ministry and/or a more local (provincial or municipal) government bureau. The central government link often involved administrative reporting to, and control by, a central ministry, provincial authorities, and local representative organizations or administrative bureaus. Given that SOEs were essentially manufacturing sites responsible for production output and the social welfare of all employees, the decision-making authority on many important managerial decisions (e.g. distribution) fell outside of the SOE and rested (or was shared) with one or more administrative units in this complex government control mechanism.

With industrial reform starting in 1984, the Chinese government's objective was to separate ownership from management. Although progress had been made, the objective had not been fully reached by 1995. More importantly, with the plight of many SOEs (two-thirds of them were reportedly loosing money in 1995) and the central government's concern about social stability (and the state-owned sector remaining the largest industrial employer), there was often a sense of a reversal of that policy and a tightening of government control. With government decentralization and reorganization (including restructuring of ministries) started in 1984 and partially (and to varying degrees in different sectors) achieved by 1995, expatriate managers – and often Chinese colleagues – were often at a total loss to identify the logic of the decision-making authority in this complex and evolving government control mechanism.

In 1995, SOEs (and hence JV partners) continued to report to local, provincial, and central government authorities. Such reporting and supervision had often created the impression among foreign JV managers that a shadow management structure was operating and influencing JV operations. For companies such as SHAIC selling to SOEs, it remained difficult to identify where the decision-making authority rested and with whom. The latter was important as bureaucratic control was often exercised at the discretion of government officials within the context of vague regulations (often without clear implementation rules or publicly unknown – the so-called *neibu* regulations). Cultivating personal relations with such officials at various levels was critical to develop an understanding of the system and to potentially influence it. Mr Broekers, as some of his foreign colleagues in other JVs, had come to realize that China 'was governed by men, not by laws'. In this context, Mr. Broekers understood the critical importance of design institutes and their engineers to SHAIC's business.

Design institutes

Design institutes were typically responsible for the technical design of all new plants in China. They specified the technical specifications of the equipment to be installed. Historically, design institutes had been part of state-owned enterprises. However, with industrial reform starting in

Case 10

the mid-1980s, they were gradually separated. By 1991, most of them had become 'engineering bureaus' no longer dependent on nor directly supervised by either the industrial ministry or the enterprise to which they had belonged. Finding overnight that they had to fend for themselves had drastically changed the way they operated. Understanding the critical role the design institutes played, enterprises and industrial ministries had recently begun to rebuild their relations with them.

SHAIC understood the critical role the design institutes played in their business. If the design institute included electromagnetic flowmeters in the technical drawings and specified SHAIC as the preferred supplier, the likelihood of clinching the order was greatly improved. Given that flowmeters were relatively new and Krüger's advanced technology was unfamiliar to Chinese customers, they typically followed the design institute's recommendations in building new production facilities.

SHAIC paid particular attention to the design institutes. Understanding the critical importance of *guanxi*[6] it had spent a lot of time and effort to cultivate good relationships with the design institutes (as well as with the industrial ministries and enterprises themselves where strong links or influence existed). SHAIC had developed a system where it hired as 'advisors' key decision makers in the design institutes (and other influential government units). It negotiated an annual contract with those advisors, and if they turned out to be useful and helpful, the contract was extended. A fixed advisory fee was provided; advisors working for design institutes received a 1–1.5% commission on clinched orders.

In greenfield operations involving foreign direct investment, the Chinese design institutes played an insignificant role. Big multinationals making plant investments in China had in-house engineering bureaus which executed the plant design. These bureaus were familiar with flowmeters and flowmeter technology and typically specified equipment they used in their plants elsewhere in the world. European multinationals such as Bayer, BASF, and Ciba-Geigy would use Krüger technology; US multinationals such as Coca-Cola and Johnson and Johnson and would use US technology; Japanese multinationals such as Marubeni and Itochu would use Japanese technology. In this area, SHAIC was often quoted by Krüger as a reliable and quality domestic supplier but conflicts had occurred as Krüger sales reps in Beijing preferred to import equipment from outside China for US dollars. In general, however, if plant investments were partially financed in ¥ (RMB), then SHAIC stood a chance of getting orders.

Application industries

Electromagnetic flowmeters have a broad range of application. In terms of industry breakdown, direct orders in 1995 came from the following industries:

- steel 18%
- drinking water 19%
- sewage 0.4%
- chemical 5.5%
- petrochemical 5.0%

---

[6] *Guanxi* is the Chinese term for network or relationship.

Another 30% of SHAIC's orders came from instrument companies which functioned as either distributors or original equipment manufacturers (OEMs). In 1995, the average order size was four flowmeters with orders ranging from ¥10,000 to ¥200,000. The average list price for a flowmeter was about ¥20,000. To help customers in their budget proposals and design institutes in cost estimates, specific list prices for all equipment had been developed. Competitors had relied on these list prices as reference points for the domestic market.

The domestic order cycle was highly seasonal. Typically, no orders came in until late February or early March; in subsequent months orders picked up and would peak in July, August, or September. As of October, orders fell rapidly up to the end of the year.

The *steel industry* in China was dominated by very large SOEs such as Shougang (also known as Capital Iron and Steel), Magang and Baogang, some of which had ministerial status. Steel was considered a backbone industry and was tightly controlled by the central government. Because of their historical heritage, many of the steel giants suffered from a 'planned economy' mentality which came to haunt them in 1993. With their huge production capacities, they had found themselves going for wider and wider geographic penetration to get rid of their steel output. This pressure pushed them into markets where they had no contacts (or *guanxi*, which they relied upon primarily to develop orders) and which were dominated by smaller competitors who were more aggressive and flexible, and controlled a strong local *guanxi* network. With the central government's economic retrenchment programme (which primarily eyed the rapid expansion of capital construction projects by SOEs) shaking the market and steel imports driving prices down, the steel giants ended up in the doldrums short of cash and highly indebted. By 1995, for example Shougang was SHAIC's largest customer but also its largest debtor. With a continued tight monetary policy to control inflation, the central government had not allocated any funds to the steel sector.

Endemic of the mentality plaguing the steel giants was the reaction to SHAIC's 1995 request to Shougang to settle its outstanding debt. By the end of 1993, accounts receivable from Shougang stood at ¥6.7 million. Orders continued to come in but Shougang did not pay and SHAIC stopped delivering. It was at about that time (and as the triangular debt problem worsened with the tight monetary policy) that SHAIC instigated a policy of cash on delivery, unheard of in the industry at that time. To avoid having to write off the debt (which eventually happened in 1995), SHAIC approached Shougang to settle the outstanding debt with a steel delivery. However, Shougang's production and sales department could not agree on the payment in part because the size of the delivery was rather small relative to the orders Shougang was traditionally used to.

As deliveries to the steel sector dropped, *drinking water* became a new and promising area of application. Under the administrative control of the Ministry of Water Resources (MWR), local water supply companies had been traditionally quite independent and essentially operated local (regional) monopolies in water supply. Recently, as the central government (and MWR) became concerned about drinking water, a process of re-centralization had been taking place with the objective to bring the water supply companies under central coordination and control. Water supply companies were now meeting three times a year to exchange information and discuss development plans (including infrastructure investments). Recognizing opportunities in this sector, SHAIC had bought 'speaking time' at those meetings, and had recently engaged two 'advisors' from the MWR.

Opportunities in the *sewage industry* (also under MWR) had until recently not been aggressively pursued because they required a radically different approach. Sewage projects were typically quite big and often involved financing through international institutions such as the Asian Development Bank (ADB), the World Bank, Japanese funds, etc. As such, they involved international tendering, a process relatively new to both China and SHAIC. In early 1995, SHAIC had received a very large tender order (indeed the largest order ever received for flowmeters) for a project in Chongqing. Inexplicably and surprisingly, the order came in six months after the official granting date. In a recent Shanghai project, SHAIC was listed as the preferred supplier in the tender document, a highly unusual practice in tendering.

Developing opportunities in the sewage industry had required a lot of personal involvement by Broekers. Despite the efforts, Broekers still felt uneasy and unsure about the tendering process in China, and had questions about who controlled it, and who made the decisions. Practices such as the requirement in the Chongqing project to pay an 8% commission before the order was in concerned him about how to efficiently and effectively pursue opportunities in this sector.

The *chemical* and *petrochemical industry* formed great opportunities for SHAIC. In 1995, each was responsible for about 5% of the orders received by SHAIC. The chemical industry, administered under the Ministry of Chemical Industry (MCI), was vast and quite decentralized. Some sectors were expanding very rapidly (e.g. dyestuffs for the textile industry). The huge number of enterprises in the chemical industry constituted a great potential, and only small inroads had been made mostly through the many JV projects in this sector. Apart from those projects involving foreign direct investment and production expertise, SHAIC and its products and technology were unknown in the chemical sector.

With increased use of water in oil refining, the petrochemical sector had begun to show interest in flowmeters as well. In contrast to the chemical industry, the petrochemical industry was highly concentrated in a number of large petrochemical sites most of which were majority-owned and controlled by SINOPEC, a ministry-level organization in charge of petroleum production. SHAIC felt that with some effort, more orders could be obtained in this sector.

Potentially new market opportunities were opening up in 1995 as well. The *paper industry* (which uses large amounts of water) was listed in the ninth five-year plan (1996–2000) as a priority sector. A number of projects in this centrally controlled sector – some involving foreign direct investment – were under negotiation. Noting the dismal quality of paper in China and the low usage levels (25 kg per head per year relative to 195 kg in Germany and about 400 kg in the USA), Broekers saw this market as containing a lot of potential but requiring educational efforts because of the lack of knowledge and use of flowmeters.

The *food industry* offered opportunities as well. The dairy industry was small but concentrated. The beer industry had great potential as China was rapidly becoming the largest beer market in the world. In 1995, Broekers estimated that there were about 860 breweries in China. Most of them were small, regional breweries needing substantial upgrading in production equipment and technology. Process control measures such as flowmeters were clearly needed since, according to SHAIC's estimates, about 20% of the beer was lost in the production process. Somewhat unique for an industrial sector in China, the beer industry was extremely competitive. Qingdao was the only national brand with substantial exports worldwide. Some small, repetitive orders had come in from breweries, but Broekers felt that JVs – bringing in their own technology – were increasingly taking control of this sector. To begin exploring the potential in this sector, Broekers had instigated a policy that SHAIC's travelling sales people could drink a beer on company expense provided they wrote down the name and address of the brewery marked on the bottle.

With Chinese consumers beginning to develop a liking for Coca-Cola, the soft drink industry was another big and growing market. However, SHAIC saw little immediate potential for their product as the industry was dominated by US multinationals working with US technology.

SALES AND DISTRIBUTION

SHAIC sold flowmeters through various channels. One important channel was instrumentation companies. They functioned both as wholesalers and OEMs, and were typically involved in large projects. In 1995, 30–40% of SHAIC's orders came from those companies. Their people were trained engineers who knew flowmeter technology. SHAIC considered selling to them rather easy. The instrumentation companies claimed a 4–6% discount off the price which SHAIC gave in the form of a credit note.

SHAIC had also been developing a direct sales channel. Mr. Broekers had increasingly emphasized the use of a direct sales force to keep 'the channel as short as possible'. In 1995, there were six sales engineers and three service engineers who had direct contact with customers. All of them worked out of a sales office located in the centre of Shanghai. They were paid a salary and commission which pulled them above the level of other JVs. Salary had been a concern given the high turnover rates for personnel in foreign-invested enterprises. Sales and service engineers enjoyed travelling and developing new contacts across China. Sales people generally followed up on leads often established by the general manager, but Mr Broekers complained that they were hesitant to make 'cold calls'. Particularly with JVs, Mr Broekers used his expat contacts to open up new accounts. The service people were primarily involved in installation help and support.

The sales engineers were supported by locally based representatives. In 1995 there were seven regional reps and two foreign reps (one in South Korea and one in Hong Kong) as SHAIC was also actively developing export opportunities. Initially, there had been some reluctance to use reps. As the Chinese side had taken responsibility for sales and marketing, it felt that its *guanxi* network within MNE's ministerial sphere was more than adequate to clinch orders. However, as MNE was one of the smaller industrial ministries, its network was quite limited; furthermore, SHAIC increasingly realized that MNE could not keep up with the various opportunities as they were developing. As SHAIC found itself operating in a broader and broader geographic market, its native Shanghai sales engineers with their own dialect and customs had more and more difficulty in cultivating contacts in remote, regional markets. In response, SHAIC had decided to supplement its direct sales force with reps.

The representatives signed a one-year contract with SHAIC and received a 6% commission. The JV provided them with technical support and conducted all invoicing. The reps had exclusivity in product but not in territory. In selecting new reps, careful attention was paid to product expertise, financial soundness, and market access.

As a result of the split in responsibilities determined during the JV negotiations, Honggong

Instrument Works (HIW) also functioned as a selling organization for SHAIC. As an established instrument manufacturing company, HIW had good contacts and Krüger had been determined to capitalize on them. HIW received a 12% commission for the orders it generated. Some sales engineers and reps had recently complained that HIW was undercutting their efforts by selling at 6% below the SHAIC list price.

A final sales channel was the Shanghai Measurement Instrument Corp. (SMIC) which was part of the Shanghai Measurement Instrument Bureau or SMIB (part of the Shanghai municipal government). SMIC had developed its own sales and distribution network all over China selling a broad range of instruments to industrial clients. SHAIC had viewed SMIC's network as a quick and efficient way to gain national presence. For its efforts selling SHAIC flowmeters, SMIC received a commission of 8%. It was know that two competitors of Krüger recently had established JVs directly with SMIB.

DEVELOPMENTS IN 1995

Despite all the opportunities, Mr Broekers was becoming concerned about a number of developments. The continued tight monetary policy by the central government had created some havoc in industry. Lack of liquidity in the economy and triangular debt problems were becoming serious. To maintain cash flow, Broekers – against the objections of the sales engineers – had instigated a cash-on-delivery policy in late 1993. More recently, he was forced to require pre-payments which in 1995 stood at 30–50% of the order. Such policies, new to China, had taken the wind out of domestic sales particularly with existing customers. In September of 1995, SHAIC warehouse was almost filled completely with finished orders waiting to be paid and shipped.

To maintain turnover, new opportunities had been pursued aggressively. As a result, the geographic mix of orders had shifted as shown in Table CS10.1.

Table CS10.1 Geographical spread of orders

	1993	1995
Beijing	20%	8%
Guangdong	0%	16%
Shanghai (including export)	25%	25%

Furthermore, big projects in areas such as sewage were increasingly being specified from outside China. This resulted in Broekers spending more and more time on sales development (as the deputy GM was responsible for domestic sales and market development). In particular, projects involving tenders required more and more of his involvement and attention.

Although the Krüger name stood for quality and reliability, Broekers also felt at a disadvantage competing for orders originating from outside China relative to Krüger and other international competitors. Chinese enterprises typically preferred to import equipment despite difficulties in obtaining foreign exchange.[7] Although the excuse was quality assurance, Broekers felt it had more to do with pocketing commissions. For a JV, it was difficult to hide cash payments in the books or inflate invoices, practices importers resorted to more easily. He recalled a recent instance at an US JV next door to SHAIC where an equipment invoice for US$1 million was increased by a ¥1 million 'fee' which only came to light in a board meeting after the assistant GM raised suspicion about the invoice amount given the nature of the delivered equipment.

With competitors starting up their own JVs, Broekers became concerned about future domestic competition. Two international competitors were already engaged with SMIB, which was the local parent of SMIC as well as the local government link to which SHAIC had periodically to report financial performance results. Such links also worried Krüger as it was contemplating transferring more technology to SHAIC.

Internally Broekers felt that the Chinese employees had become somewhat relaxed about the JV's performance and showed signs of losing the eagerness and aggressiveness they had demonstrated in getting the JV operations off the ground. With continued profitability and controlling a large share of the market in 1995, he felt motivation slipping at a time when the new opportunities would require an even more aggressive approach than before.

---

[7] All import and export has to be done through Chinese import/export companies. SOEs are typically not allowed to have foreign exchange (forex) and need to apply to the government for a forex allocation.

Exhibit CS10.1   China/Shanghai and Minhang ETDZ

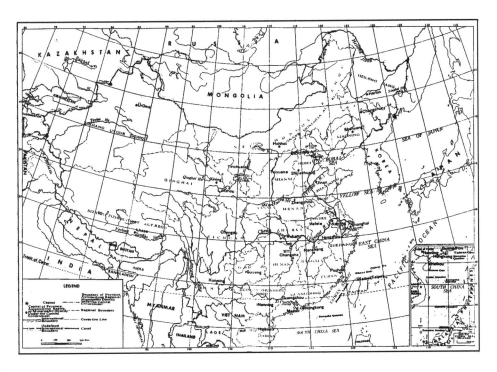

Exhibit CS10.2   Organizational chart of SHAIC

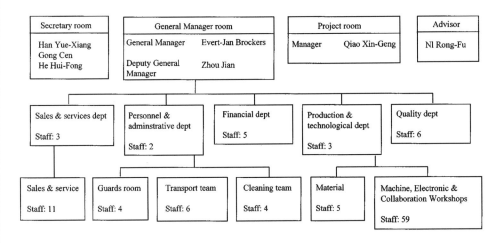

Secretary room	General Manager room		Project room		Advisor
Han Yue-Xiang Gong Cen He Hui-Fong	General Manager Deputy General Manager	Evert-Jan Brockers Zhou Jian	Manager	Qiao Xin-Geng	NI Rong-Fu

Sales & services dept Staff: 3	Personnel & adminstrative dept Staff: 2	Financial dept Staff: 5	Production & technological dept Staff: 3	Quality dept Staff: 6

Sales & service Staff: 11	Guards room Staff: 4	Transport team Staff: 6	Cleaning team Staff: 4	Material Staff: 5	Machine, Electronic & Collaboration Workshops Staff: 59

Case 11

Case 11

*This case was written by Jocelyn Probert, Research Analyst, and Hellmut
Schütte, Affiliate Professor of International Management at INSEAD. It is
intended to be used as a basis for class discussion rather than to illustrate
either effective or ineffective handling of an administrative situation.*

SKF in Vietnam

By mid-1995 SKF had been developing business for four years in Vietnam through a
representative office in Ho Chi Minh City. As the world's largest ball-bearing company, its goal
was to win a commensurate share of the nascent Vietnamese market. Under existing Vietnamese
regulations, however, the activities of trading companies – which was how SKF Vietnam was
classified, since it had no manufacturing facilities in the country – were severely limited. With
these constraints, how could Jean Jacques Schwindling, general manager of SKF Vietnam, establish
SKF as the dominant supplier of bearings? Two top executives of SKF were visiting Vietnam in
November for the first time – a signal of the interest being shown in this market's potential.

BACKGROUND

In 1990 and 1991, as Vietnam began to open its economy to the outside world, Fredrik Jonsson
began to visit the country from SKF Thailand where he was based. During his frequent visits he
contacted prospective major customers of SKF bearings and investigated market potential. It
seemed that there would in future be a market for bearings, though current activity was limited.
His proposal to establish a representative office in Ho Chi Minh City was accepted by SKF in
1990, and in April of the following year the Vietnamese authorities approved the application.
Jonsson moved to Ho Chi Minh City and opened the office in June 1991. In 1993, after the initial
'pioneer' phase was complete, Schwindling took over as general manager from Jonsson.

The office was in the Textimex Building on Nguyen Hue, one of the main thoroughfares in the
centre of what used to be called Saigon. The building was owned by Textimex, the central
Vietnamese import–export organization for the whole textile industry. A good relationship had
been built up between SKF and Textimex over the years since Jonsson had begun visiting, not
least because textile mills were important potential customers of SKF's textile machinery
components. Textimex was also able to introduce SKF to customers in other industries. The
Vietnamese state-owned company became SKF's importer for all bearings, not just those suitable
for textile machinery, and provided valuable help to SKF in navigating through the maze of
regulations to establish its office. SKF also persuaded Textimex to open a showroom on the
ground floor of the building.

Case 11

SKF AND THE WORLD BEARINGS INDUSTRY

SKF is the world's leading ball and roller bearing company, with a market share of approximately 18%. This gives it a strong edge over its nearest competitor, the Japanese company, NSK. The roller bearings and seals business constituted 93% of group sales in 1994. Recession is quickly reflected in the results of bearings manufacturers, and the impact of the slump in demand in 1990–93 is apparent from the losses faced by SKF (Exhibit CS11.1), although by the end of 1994 production was 30% higher than at the nadir in 1992 and had recovered further during 1995. Restructuring of the global ball-bearings industry since the late 1980s has left a handful of companies dominating the world market.

The bearings industry serves two fundamentally different types of market:

- The original equipment manufacturer (OEM) customer, to whom the bearings supplied are crucial components of their end products. Examples of OEM customers would be the car and truck industries, aerospace, general machinery and heavy industry. Exhibit CS11.2 shows SKF's sales breakdown by application.

- The aftermarket, for whom bearings are no more than spare parts. Aftermarket sales, to both industrial users and automotive repair services, tend to be made to dealers and distributors, who sell the product to the end-user.

OEM customers are price-sensitive, since their costs of production are reflected in the final price of their product, whereas aftermarket users are more concerned by product availability and the speed of delivery than price. Particularly in the industrial aftermarket, customers are significantly more concerned by the cost of machinery standing idle than by the price of a replacement bearing.

SKF bearings are manufactured and sold throughout the world. Eighty factories in 20 countries manufacture 25,000 different items, ranging from high volume standardized bearings to custom production of a single, highly specialized bearing. The company's reputation is built on an unrivalled global distribution network, which allows it industry leadership in price setting. In recent years SKF has concentrated on improving lead times, for example in reducing the time between the order of the raw material and the delivery of finished spherical roller bearings, from 110 days in 1989 to 29 days in 1994.

An Asia Pacific strategy for the group was developed in the mid-1980s and, in the five years to 1994, sales in the region doubled to 12% of the group total. (The geographical breakdown of SKF sales is shown in Exhibit CS11.3.) The specific objective of SKF in the Asia Pacific region, stated in the 1994 annual report, is to enhance its direct presence by increasing the number of wholly owned sales companies, and thus to bring SKF closer to its end-customers, thereby gaining greater insight into their needs as well as increasing the potential for offering them technical and other services.

At present, SKF's Asian region produces approximately 40% of the bearings it sells and is thus partly dependent on exports from Europe, which has excess production capacity, to meet sales demand. (The American region's self-sufficiency ratio is 80%.) A new state-of-the-art plant went into operation in Malaysia in 1992 and now supplies OEM customers in Japan, among other countries. SKF has also established joint venture production facilities in China (Shanghai) and Korea.

THE OPENING OF VIETNAM AND THE REGULATORY ENVIRONMENT

The introduction of *doi moi* policies in 1986 began a reorientation of the Vietnamese economy away from communist-style central planning and towards market-based principles. The communist economic system, combined with near-total isolation from the world in the wake of its 1979 invasion of Cambodia, had left Vietnam a deeply impoverished country with estimated GDP per capita of less than US$250 and a shaky physical infrastructure, cobbled together from remnants of the French and US presence and Soviet equipment. Since the late 1980s, Vietnam has moved from a rice-deficient country to become the world's third largest exporter of rice. It has reintegrated itself into the world economy through trade and investment links, reacquired borrower status from the World Bank and other multilateral organizations, and achieved average GDP growth of 8% in the 1991–94 period. A foreign investment law was passed in 1987, and by mid-1995 over US$13 billion of foreign investments had been approved although perhaps only one-quarter of this sum has actually been invested.

Vestiges of central control remain, however. Prior to 1988 a small number of central trading monopolies dominated foreign trade activity, each conducting business for its own government agency or industry. Liberalization in 1989 introduced competition between state-owned companies through the granting of new import–export licences, and later manufacturing firms producing goods for direct export – including foreign-invested joint ventures – were also allowed to import and export goods, as long as they had the requisite licence. Very few private companies have met the additional criteria demanded to qualify for an import–export licence. Further, foreign trading companies – a classification which embraces all companies not manufacturing in Vietnam – are barred from establishing a subsidiary or branch office and may only operate under representative office status. Representative office activities are therefore confined to market research, relationship building and business coordination with offices in other countries. Direct business activity is forbidden, and the authorities have closed down several representative offices deemed to have overstepped the boundaries.

The concept of a national distribution network barely exists in Vietnam. Prior to economic reform there was little trade between different regions of the country, and barriers to the free movement of goods remained in the form of military or customs checkpoints at provincial boundaries even after formal restrictions were lifted.

SKF VIETNAM

The SKF representative office in Ho Chi Minh City is small. The staff of 10 is headed by Schwindling, the only expatriate, who is also the general manager of the Hanoi branch office. The Hanoi office reports to the Ho Chi Minh City office. Exhibit CS11.4 shows the SKF Vietnam organizational chart. Until recently the Vietnamese authorities imposed strict limits on the number of staff a representative office could employ, arguing that since companies were not allowed to conduct business through representative offices they had no need for many employees. Current regulations allow the hiring of an unrestricted number of Vietnamese nationals but severely restrict the number of expatriates employed.

The four service engineers based in Ho Chi Minh City, led by Nguyen Phuong Dong, are responsible for identifying and meeting potential customers of SKF products, discovering their needs and developing the relationship. 'They are very important for the success of SKF in

Case 11

Vietnam'. Each engineer has a separate geographical area to cover as well as responsibility for an industry segment. Mr Dong, for example covers Ho Chi Minh City and northwards as far as the coastal city of Nha Trang, in addition to the big end-user customers wherever they may be based. Another engineer covers the big OEM customers as well as a geographical region. The three engineers in Hanoi work on the same principle, but face a different set of problems in tackling the customer base.

By 1995 SKF Vietnam expected sales of several million dollars, from zero four years earlier. Growth in 1993 was 40% and in 1994 was 20%. In 1995 sales growth was conservatively estimated at 29%, compared with Vietnamese industrial growth of 15–20%. Three-fifths of SKF Vietnam's sales are made in the south, and two-fifths in the north of the country. The cement industry is its largest customer, accounting for nearly 15% of turnover; steel accounts for a further 8–10%, and the paper and sugar industries for 5–10% each. The cement and steel industries are expected to increase capacity substantially in the coming years, through local and foreign investment, to supply the construction industry.

SKF Vietnam reports directly to SKF Asean Bearing Division, the company's regional headquarters in Hong Kong, but supplies are normally imported through the large warehousing operation in Singapore. Technical support is also provided via Singapore. SKF Vietnam may also contact specialists worldwide for additional technical assistance.

In the first phase of activity, SKF Vietnam devoted its efforts to contacting big end-users in the aftermarket. This meant building links with the cement plants, steel mills, paper mills and other industrial customers. In the second phase, the challenge has been to create a nationwide industrial distribution network through which SKF products can be channelled. A third phase, much further down the line, will be to develop access to small customers who currently look after themselves. Exhibit CS11.5 shows this pyramid of customers.

THE CUSTOMERS

In the south, the potential customer base is highly fragmented. Greater familiarity with the concept of private business and a more dynamic business environment has, among people in the south, spawned a huge number of small, private and household businesses which are open to new ideas and new opportunities. In this environment it is hard for the SKF team of engineers to identify targets and to keep their lists of prospective customers up to date. Few of the more than 500 registered SKF customers in the south are large-scale concerns, the main exception being the two state-owned Ha Tien cement companies. Most industrial customers are concentrated in the steel, paper and sugar businesses in Bien Hoa province, while farmers in the Mekong delta area are big users of rice-processing equipment and other agricultural machinery. Marine-use bearings are also important products for a region with so many rivers and a long coastline. Few customers in the south are as yet familiar with the SKF brand.

By contrast, industry in the north of the country is concentrated at a relatively small number of large state-owned enterprises. The principal customer base has so far been fairly easy to identify, but purchasing patterns in northern enterprises are dominated by high cost-consciousness. Given the availability of cheap Russian-made bearings costing as little as one-third the price of an equivalent SKF product, it has proved difficult to convince customers working with cheap

Russian-made machinery of the long-term benefits of using high quality but more expensive bearings.

Most of SKF Vietnam's customers are in the aftermarket, requiring spare parts to repair existing machinery. Over time, the company intends to develop an OEM customer base as well, but this requires a different marketing approach. OEM business is less profitable than the aftermarket (because original manufacturers are highly cost-conscious) but it is a means of developing SKF's image and brand name in Vietnam and, more importantly, it generates the future aftermarket. Obviously, since OEM customers are, by definition, manufacturers of machinery for other industries, OEM business requires a country to have a reasonably-sized manufacturing base – and this is not yet the situation in Vietnam. However, it is an important long-term investment for SKF to make, since aftermarket customers are likely to automatically replace a worn-out bearing in a machine with a new one of the same brand. OEM business represents approximately 20% of current SKF Vietnam sales.

THE ROLE OF THE IMPORTER

SKF Vietnam has one-year contractual relationships with four state-owned importers, reflecting expansion of its Distributor/Dealer network (known as the D/D network).

In the south, Textimex, which is an SKF distributor as well as importer, has been joined by Machino-Import, which acts purely as an SKF importer. Imports to the south are divided roughly 50/50 between these two companies. Elmaco and Vinametal have been appointed as importers and distributors for the northern part of the country. Occasionally SKF Vietnam uses other importers for special situations. The importer is the conduit for SKF bearings to reach Vietnam. Shipments arrive at New Port or Saigon Port in Ho Chi Minh City in the south, and at Haiphong in the north.

Bearings normally carry 0% import tax since there is a strong demand for them in Vietnamese industry but locally produced supplies are not available. However, 40% duty is charged if customs declares them as automotive bearings. Import licences are granted to authorized importers on an annual basis for unspecified quantities of bearings. (In contrast, a licence to import many other goods has to be acquired on a case-by-case basis.)

Customs clearance – the responsibility of the importer – at present can take a week or more, longer in the north. Troublesome details may hold up incoming shipments, as for example if the country of origin of the bearings does not match that shown on the bill of lading. (The SKF warehouse in Singapore sources bearings from SKF plants around the world, depending on their availability.) One of the strengths of SKF is its ability to ship stock quickly to its various subsidiaries and offices. Including the time taken to prepare the shipment and the actual shipping time from Singapore (three to four days each), new stock reaches customers or distributors in Vietnam in three to six weeks at best. Unlike wholly owned sales offices in other countries, SKF Vietnam itself is not allowed to maintain stock in Vietnam.

REACHING THE CUSTOMER: THE DISTRIBUTION NETWORK

In 1993, SKF Vietnam began to put in place its D/D network. Industrial distribution networks of this type have been created by SKF throughout the world. No similar sales organization exists in

Vietnam, whether for bearings or for any other industrial product. According to Schwindling, 'If we have the leading distributor network, we will be the market leader'.

There were no experienced distributors of bearings in Vietnam, and SKF Vietnam has had to find and train them from scratch on SKF bearings. Particularly in the south, entrepreneurial individuals with little or no previous knowledge of the bearing business and limited financial resources present themselves as prospective SKF distributors. Mr Tran To Ha, who today runs SKF Vietnam's largest distributorship, was one of these. Already the owner of a paper mill – and therefore an end-user of bearings – in late 1992 he was looking to diversify his activities and established a separate company, Nguyen Xuong, in Ho Chi Minh City's Chinatown,[1] to handle SKF business.

The distributors selected must agree to handle SKF products exclusively, and one distributor has already been sacked for breaking this agreement. Exhibit CS11.6 shows the network of SKF distributors operating by mid-1995. Five are based in Ho Chi Minh City, with another seven scattered throughout the southern part of the country, up to and including Danang. Only four distributors, all state-owned, cover the whole of north Vietnam. Larger distributors, particularly in Ho Chi Minh City, typically stock 1,000–1,500 types of bearing, while provincial distributorships stock 300–400 items.

Although customers are harder for SKF to identify in the south, the southern distributorship network is stronger since most distributors (nine out of twelve) are privately-run businesses and are generally more flexible in their attitudes than the northern state-owned dealers. Despite the relative availability of good private distributors, 'hard currency is limited, therefore they need our financial support – which is a costly and sometimes a high risk business.'

SKF Vietnam gives its distributors one-year contracts, during which time their progress is regularly monitored. Distributors receive deferred payment terms of two months on their stock, while normally receiving cash for bearings sold. (Frequent customers may be invoiced by the distributor on a weekly basis.) SKF's receivables in Vietnam are some of the highest in Asia, according to Schwindling, reflecting the lack of familiarity among distributors – especially in the north – with the concept of paying for goods. SKF Vietnam first tries to establish why distributors' payments are late, and, for example helps them solve over-stocking difficulties. Repeated late payments without good reason may result in customers being channelled to other distributors or in the temporary halt of shipments. This is seen as a learning curve problem, however.

Below the tier of distributors is the dealership network. Each distributor has between one and three dealers to handle, as well as customers who come directly to them. Any financial relationship between distributor and dealer is arranged between themselves and not with SKF Vietnam. Dealers do not have an exclusive relationship with SKF but stock a limited range of products that they buy to trade. Only in special circumstances do dealers receive special training from SKF Vietnam, for example if they seem to have good long-term potential as vendors of the product, or as part of an SKF image-building exercise.

---

[1] Mr Ha of Nguyen Xuong is one of an estimated one million people of ethnic Chinese origin in Vietnam, the majority of whom live in the south. Cholon has easily the largest ethnic Chinese community in Vietnam and is the location of many Chinese-Vietnamese companies.

On the other hand, SKF Vietnam invests significant time and money in the development of its distributors. It teaches them about SKF products and how to identify customer problems, and provides help with stock planning and computerization. Distributors also attend the seminars that the company lays on for its customers, which are taught by local SKF engineers. Heavy emphasis is placed on developing the technical skills of the distributors and their sales engineers. Says Mr Ha of Nguyen Xuong, 'We are still limited in our knowledge. We can explain 50–60% of our customers' problems but we need the help of SKF for the rest. For Vietnam, the response time is quick but the SKF team is very small. Maybe SKF Vietnam contacts SKF in Singapore, and then we get the answer in two to three days'.

Nguyen Xuong currently represents 25–30% of SKF Vietnam's sales and itself employs three engineers, who not only respond to customers' difficulties but also sometimes visit large customers together with an SKF Vietnam engineer. This is one means for a distributor to better understand customer needs, but relationship visiting itself – the process of developing a business relationship – is the responsibility of SKF Vietnam. As the D/D network develops, the role of SKF Vietnam will shift further away from marketing and sales, to technical advisory services and customer relationship building.

The customer profile of Nguyen Xuong is typical of southern distributorships. Because of the location of its three shops around the industrial goods market of Cholon, there is frequent contact with the customer base. Employees of small and medium-sized companies come nearly every day, to buy one or two bearings. 'There is a long tail of small customers which SKF doesn't see.... Time is not expensive in Vietnam, our customers have the labour available to do the shopping', says Mr Ha. Among these customers, the relationship grows naturally. Larger companies, such as Ha Tien Cement, keep in touch by telephone. For big orders or emergencies Nguyen Xuong will arrange delivery – typically by regular bus service, at a cost to the customer of perhaps 5–10,000 dong.[2] It would not be cost-effective to arrange delivery of the average purchase.

Customers often contact SKF Vietnam directly in the first instance. SKF Vietnam then introduces them to the distributor most appropriate for their needs, depending on their size and the availability of stock. Smaller potential clients tend to be allocated geographically. They are first and foremost SKF product customers, not the customers of the distributors. So far, the market is large enough to easily accommodate all the distributors appointed although SKF Vietnam must sometimes adjudicate between two distributors trying to sell to the same customer. Nguyen Xuong is the biggest distributor in southern Vietnam for non-automotive sales, but a potential automotive customer in Ho Chi Minh City would probably be directed to another distributor specializing in automotive parts. On the other hand, Nguyen Xuong has some customers as far away as Danang.

Mr Ha has managed to transmit the message that although customers may be paying more for an SKF bearing they also get more than a bearing for the price. 'We follow the customer's order history very carefully', he says. 'In the first year he may buy only some special bearings; in the second year he buys common bearings too; and now some customers come for 100% of their needs'. And again, 'Every day we have new customers and the old ones, they never go away'.

---

[2] In September 1995, the approximate exchange rate was US$1 = 11,000 VN dong.

It is the role of SKF Vietnam to establish initial pricing policy, credit terms, delivery terms and so on for new large customers. Thereafter the distributor takes over the order handling, import procedures and despatching the goods to the customer. The customer will contact the distributor directly to place subsequent orders, but SKF Vietnam continues to monitor the relationship to check customer satisfaction.

SKF Vietnam has direct contact with 80% of its registered customers in the south (i.e. those businesses identified as active customers), but is not able to sign purchase contracts with them because of its status as a representative office. Formalities require the customers to work through an importer for SKF or to use the D/D network. It does, however, sign service 'agreements' with core customers, guaranteeing after-sales and emergency services.

Large customers, such as Ha Tien Cement, have two separate routes to buy SKF bearings: directly from overseas, or through the local distributors. In the past they have tended to place a bulk order comprising perhaps 60–70% of their anticipated needs for the year with SKF overseas (in Singapore) and have imported the bearings directly (either using their own import licence or going straight to the importer). The remaining 30–40% is obtained through SKF Vietnam, via the D/D network. Recently, however, some customers have begun to buy considerably more through SKF distributors. The advantages of this include greater flexibility (it is hard for the customer to plan for a whole year ahead), less capital being tied up in stock (they can rely on SKF Vietnam distributors to hold the stock instead), and their being able to pay in Vietnamese dong (direct imports require payment in dollars).

COMPETITION

Until the arrival of SKF the supply of bearings in Vietnam was dominated, in the north of the country, by Russian producers such as GPZ and, in the south, by NTN of Japan which had been importing through a Japanese trading company for the past 10 years. Three other Japanese companies – NSK, Nachi and Koyo – and the German FAG are also marketing their bearings. A range of bearings from Romania, the Czech Republic, Poland, China and Korea are also available. Finally, there is one Vietnamese manufacturer of bearings – Pho Yen – in the north, but its product range and quality are hindered by the age of its machinery and it is not expected to survive.

SKF is, so far, the only international bearing company officially represented in Vietnam. Competitors send in visitors from time to time, as SKF itself had done until 1991, but without an established distribution network they can only sell on a spot basis to individual customers, or to market-based traders. Vietnamese traders, however, are becoming more reluctant to buy products from Japanese trading houses, which require them to order in volumes too large for their needs. Instead the traders prefer to group together and purchase directly from Singapore.

By 1995, market share between the major players was divided roughly as follows:

Four Japanese, combined	40–50%
SKF	20–25%
GPZ	10–20%
FAG	5–10%

SKF has built its market share from zero over a four-year period, while the combined Japanese share has declined. The four Japanese companies compete between themselves but, among them, Nguyen Xuong's Ha sees NSK as the strongest and most direct competitor. It is trying to replicate some of what SKF has achieved in Vietnam. In his view, all four Japanese companies sell standard bearings in the retail market, rather than specialized bearings like SKF Vietnam, so the market they each serve is very different. Exhibit CS11.7 shows the approach SKF Vietnam takes to its customers, compared with the approach of its competitors.

In the major end-user segments such as cement, steel and paper, SKF Vietnam claims a share of nearly 60%, and its share of the OEM market is approximately 50%. Its weakness lies in mass-market sales. SKF has also become the price leader. Newcomers such as FAG have tried to buy their way into the marketplace by offering bearings at prices lower than SKF's, but have not been able to sustain the effort for long. SKF still has the highest prices, but offers organizational support and services that others cannot match.

THE SKF OFFERING

'We never discuss the price first, we talk about the customer's problems', says Mr Dong. SKF Vietnam believes it has several strengths that help justify its prices which are higher than those of international competitors:

- *Product quality.* 80% of all bearings made and used are standard items, which generally makes product differentiation difficult. Some SKF bearings are of higher quality than equivalent competitors' bearings thanks to continuously improved design as well as the quality of steel used. Further, SKF has only one quality of bearing which it supplies worldwide. Some competitors have different quality levels which are inconsistently supplied to Vietnam, and customers have noted the quality variation.

- *Reliability of service and availability of supply.* Stocks held within the D/D network ensure that major items are always available. Although there is no computer system linking the individual distributors with the SKF Vietnam office, telephone calls can rapidly track down in-country supply. In Ho Chi Minh City, for example it may be possible for a customer to collect the required bearing from an alternative location in as little as an hour.

- *Broad range of bearings.* SKF Vietnam can satisfy 80–90% of customers' needs immediately, whereas a competitor would be able to meet perhaps only 50% of their requirements. Customers do not have to spend all day completing their list of purchases.

- *Forward planning of supply.* Regular customers are assured of supply even if they need only a single bearing once a year. In an emergency SKF Vietnam can try to source the item first from the Singapore warehouse, second from an SKF factory, and finally from a competitor. Over the last two to three years, SKF Vietnam has learned the critical needs of its main customers. If it can persuade them to buy an extra unit of the critical bearing, SKF Vietnam will supply a replacement as soon as the standby is used.

- *Competence.* SKF Vietnam engineers are thoroughly trained and can provide an analysis of bearing failures (for example incorrect or insufficient lubrication), to help customers identify avoidable problems. 'We have to be applications engineers, too,' says Mr Dong.

- *Vietnamese language catalogue.* In 1994, SKF Vietnam distributed a detailed handbook for end-users of all major bearings (see Exhibit CS11.8), allowing them to identify worn-out bearings by weight, size and picture, and giving internationally recognized classification codes alongside to facilitate new orders. This catalogue is an important marketing tool, since Russian bearings are not marked, and very old bearings may have classification numbers worn off. The handbook is also adapted to the needs of Vietnamese engineers trained in Russian terminology. Since ball-bearing technology is new to Vietnam, the technical terms are also new and vary between the north and south of the country. Competitors have so far produced only English language marketing materials.

- *Emergency services for core customers.* Big customers have very specific machines requiring non-standard bearings that can be air-freighted from Singapore in an emergency.

- *Complementary products.* SKF Vietnam is able to supply non-bearing items commonly used by industrial customers, for example textile machinery components, lubricants, mechanical tools, etc. These are not always SKF products, and represent only a small portion of total business.

SKF's bearings are on average 20% more expensive than those of its competitors. Moreover, the company uses a fixed-price system, i.e. all distributors are told the price at which they may sell each bearing, which is similar to SKF prices elsewhere in the region. (In the markets, where competitors' bearings tend to be sold, prices may vary considerably.) Transparent pricing has simplified SKF's business relationships, as the customer knows that the price on the invoice is the real price paid.

CHALLENGES FOR THE FUTURE

Until now, SKF has been the only international bearing company in Vietnam. Mr Schwindling and Mr Dong, however, are keenly aware that their international competitors are testing the market and visiting state-owned enterprises. 'We need to be fully established before the others set up their representative office', says Mr Dong.

A Joint Action Programme is in place to strengthen the SKF Vietnam D/D network. This is a continual process of providing support, visiting distributors' areas, helping them to identify customers, and improving stock turnover. More distributors would be added in the future to improve country coverage, but this would require rapid growth in the business. Financial support would have to increase commensurately. Mr Schwindling and his team also want to see a broader dealer network, but this would be the responsibility of the distributors. Some distributors such as Nguyen Xuong have ambitions to reach further down the distribution chain to lower levels of retail customer in the provinces, but this would probably require special discounts that SKF Vietnam would have to finance.

The main thrust of the D/D network is currently towards the aftermarket, but there are growing signs of activity from Japanese competitors in the OEM market. What more can SKF do, under the existing rules of operation in Vietnam, to improve service to customers and raise market share? How best can it block the competition from capturing a share of the market in Vietnam?

Exclusive dealerships and close customer relationships have been the preferred method of operation so far, but competitors (especially the Japanese) are likely to follow Japanese OEM business from Honda, Toyota and others.

Mr Schwindling also needed to consider what would happen if the rules of the game changed. If the government were to change its regulations to allow non-manufacturing companies to set up importing operations, should SKF Vietnam set up a warehouse in Ho Chi Minh City from which to manage its own stock? What if it were to be allowed to distribute as well as import?

Finally, there was another competitor-related issue to address: would the government maintain a zero rating on import duties for bearings if an international producer proposed to establish a manufacturing operation in Vietnam? Should SKF Vietnam make a counter-proposal in these circumstances? And if it did decide to manufacture, should it form a joint venture to do so, even though the SKF preference overall is for wholly owned operations?

Case 11

Exhibit CS11.1   SKF group results (*Source*: Annual Report)

	Swedish kronor, mllions					9 months to
	1990	**1991**	**1992**	**1993**	**1994**	**Sept 1995**
Net sales	27,766	26,302	26,649	29,200	33,273	28,232
Operating income/loss	2,023	−56	−1,347	251	2,121	3,065
Income/loss before tax	1,858	−221	−1,939	−515	1,817	2,586
Net income/loss	1,014	−1,177	−1,704	−491	1,248	1,660
Key ratios (%)						
Return on assets	8.0	1.9	−2.6	2.3	7.8	
Return on capital employed	13.3	3.0	−4.4	4.2	14.7	
Return on shareholders' equity	8.5	−10.3	−17.5	−5.6	13.3	
Profit margin	8.7	2.2	−3.1	2.7	8.0	
Earnings/loss per share (kronor)	9.00	−10.40	−14.60	−4.35	11.05	
Average number of employees	49,305	45,285	46,672	39,439	40,072	

Case 11

Exhibit CS11.2   Sales by application field, 1994 (*Source*: Annual Report)

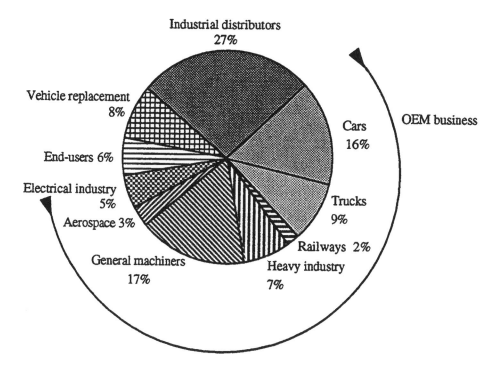

Exhibit CS11.3   Sales by geographical area, 1994 (*Source*: Annual Report)

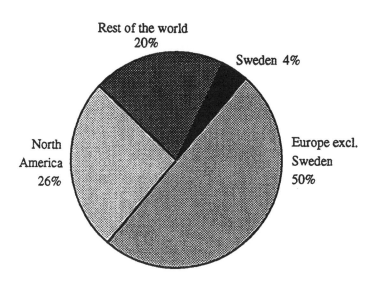

Exhibit CS11.4   Organizational chart of SKF Vietnam

```
                        ┌─────────────────────┐
                        │   General  manager  │
                        │  (J-J Schwindling)  │
                        └──────────┬──────────┘
                                   │
                                   │       ┌──────────────────┐
                                   ├───────│  Secretary HCMC  │
                                   │       └──────────────────┘
                                   │       ┌──────────────────┐
                                   ├───────│   Secretary HN   │
                                   │       └──────────────────┘
              ┌───────────────┐    │
              │  Driver HCMC  │────┤
              └───────────────┘    │
              ┌───────────────┐    │
              │   Driver HN   │────┤
              └───────────────┘    │
```

Finance	Logistics	Sales manager HN	Sales manager HCMC
EDP	Logistics	Service engineer	Service engineer
		Service engineer	Service engineer
			Service engineer

Exhibit CS11.5   The SKF pyramid of customers

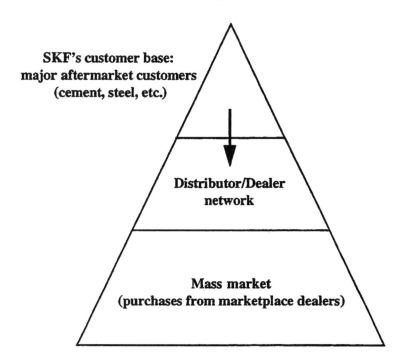

SKF's customer base:
major aftermarket customers
(cement, steel, etc.)

Distributor/Dealer
network

Mass market
(purchases from marketplace dealers)

Case 11

Exhibit CS11.6   The SKF Vietnam distribution network

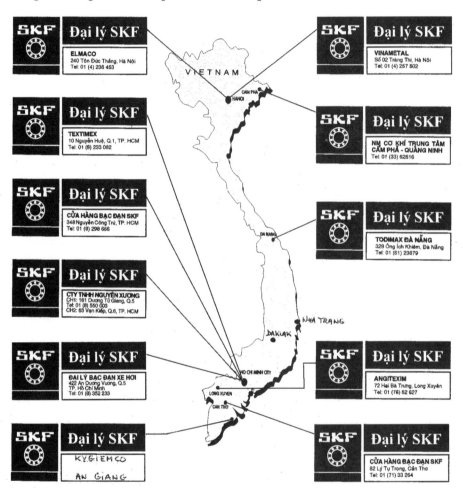

Exhibit CS11.7   Reaching the customer

The traditional way

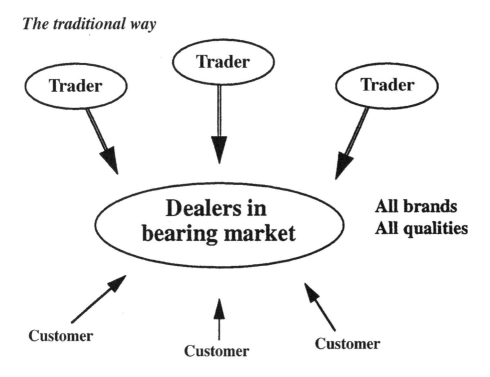

The SKF distribution network

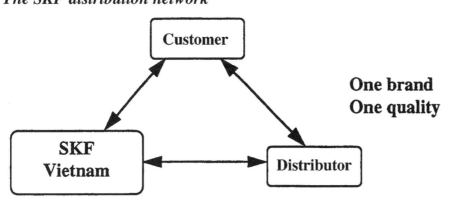

Exhibit CS11.8   The SKF Vietnam product catalogue

SKF Việt Nam

CẨM NANG TRA CỨU
BẠC ĐẠN

SKF - Bạc đạn được tin cậy nhất thế giới

Case 12

This case was written by Jake Vigoda, MBA INSEAD, under the supervision of Hellmut Schütte, Affiliate Professor at INSEAD. It is intended to be used as a basis for class discussion rather than to illustrate either effective or ineffective handling of an administrative situation. Some figures have been changed to maintain confidentiality. Copyright ©1991 INSEAD-CEA, Fontainebleau, France

Gilman Office Automation Bangkok, Thailand

'Now that we have successfully rebuilt the business from the poor image it had assumed under the previous distributor, we need to move from number three to number one in market share ...' (29 June 1990).

Chamchai Leelawatanasuk, 41, chief executive of Gilman Office Automation (Thailand), believes that gaining the market lead is the only answer for his business – the distribution of Ricoh copiers in Thailand. His colleague, Julian Fryett, marketing manager, agrees: 'With new companies continuing to enter the market, gaining market share is difficult. However, we are expected to achieve at least the market share Gilman has reached in Hong Kong for Ricoh copiers. On top of this, Ricoh is the market leader in Japan'. At the same time, Chamchai must define the overall strategy for his company in the Thai market: 'We have to decide in which product lines we will be, with which principals we will work, and which network of agents and dealers we will use ...'

'We are approaching a B250 million[1] company. Within five years, we must be B1 billion', Fryett and Chamchai stated independently, both knowing that their promotion within the Inchcape Group will depend largely on their ability to create such a profitable company. Chamchai can expect a more important role in Inchcape Thailand, while Fryett can expect to continue to receive high profile assignments in Hong Kong and throughout Asia Pacific with Inchcape Pacific.

RICOH IN THAILAND

For over 20 years, Ricoh copiers had been distributed in Thailand by Fantaract Ltd, a tightly held, Chinese family-owned firm. Through the early 1980s, under Fantaract distribution, Ricoh was the market leader. However, as both Fantaract's business and the copier business expanded, and the Thai market became more competitive, certain Fantaract management practices were no longer sustainable. Most notable was the inability of the family patriarch to trust outside family members,

---

[1] 25 Baht is roughly equivalent to 1 US dollar.

Case 12

to accept distribution of power, or to share information about the company with non-family associates.

Unknown to Ricoh, in addition to picking up the distribution of Canon cameras, in itself a business which had grown to sizeable volume, the company was also distributing Minolta copiers through a wholly owned subsidiary company. There are indications it may have been involved in a number of other questionable business distributorship arrangements. Under these sorts of conditions, good management and good staff did not stay. Subsequently, although Fantaract handled import logistics, it was never able to add real value to the distribution arrangement. Ricoh was the market leader only because of recurring advantages from early entry in the marketplace and the technical leadership of Ricoh copiers over competitors. As both of these advantages eroded, so did market share. The Fantaract family began to lose control over its staff and business procedures. By 1984, accounts receivable had grown out of control; often, the company could neither find the buyer nor collect the invoices. Apparently, 'hiding buyers' was a service being offered by some sales staff. Technical service staff had begun selling parts and related consumables to Fantaract customers from non-Fantaract distributors for personal profit. Many were selling imitation parts but charging the higher cost demanded for Ricoh parts and consumables produced in Japan. By 1985, Fantaract was facing bankruptcy. The number of copiers sold had declined from 608 in 1982 to 273 in 1985.

Gilman Office Machines (Hong Kong), a fully owned subsidiary of the Inchcape group, had been successfully selling Ricoh copiers in Hong Kong for almost 20 years. Ricoh contacts alluded to the declining sales in Thailand and to the deteriorating financial position. Company representatives from Inchcape, aware of Fantaract's declining sales in Thailand and their deteriorating financial position, approached the firm and offered to buy the distribution rights for Ricoh copiers in Thailand. Fantaract refused. In the first 10 months of 1986, Fantaract failed to sell a single machine, and in October 1986, Fantaract filed for bankruptcy. In November 1986, Gilman acquired the distribution contract free of charge. Peter Bond, an expatriate manager from Hong Kong, was moved to Thailand to build up the business.

GROWTH OF GILMAN IN THAILAND

In November 1986, Gilman Office Automation was formed, specifically to take over the distribution of Ricoh copiers in Thailand. Although legally set up as a subsidiary company of Anglo-Thai, itself a fully owned subsidiary company of Inchcape Thailand, Gilman Office Automation reports to Inchcape Pacific in Hong Kong, through the Business Machines Group. Affiliate companies include Gilman Office Machines in Hong Kong, Dodwell Business Machines in Hong Kong, Japan, DBE in Australia, and Repromac, also a distributor of office machines, in Hong Kong. Inchcape plc is an international services and marketing group with its headquarters in London. It is the largest European trading company. Organized into 10 business streams and regional sectors, Business Machines is one of Inchcape's smallest business streams. The Business Machines group has its headquarters in Hong Kong, and operates in the Asia-Pacific region, marketing and distributing office equipment. The director reports to the chairman of Inchcape Pacific Limited, Inchcape's regional subsidiary (Exhibit CS12.1).

Inchcape corporate philosophy is to use local management wherever possible. However, in this case qualified Thai management was not available when Gilman took over Ricoh in Thailand. For this reason, Peter Bond was brought in. Gilman believed that it could capitalize on Bond's previous experience in copier products and shorten the time required to bring the company on line and to profitability.

In January 1987, Gilman sold the first Ricoh copier in Thailand in over a year, and in the following 12 months, they averaged an impressive 40 machines per month.

Most of the new staff were recruited from Fantaract. Needing to build the business rapidly, Bond decided to leverage the already developed contact with customers and experience with Ricoh machines from the previous sales and technical service staffs. At the same time, they benefited from the introduction of a completely new line of Ricoh dry toner copiers. Ricoh had been late in matching competitors' switch to dry toner copiers. In the last years of Fantaract's contract, Fantaract had been forced to sell Ricoh's liquid type toner machines against competitors' dry toner machines.

Charnchai had been with Inchcape (Thailand) since 1971 and ran the Fuji Film distribution business for another Inchcape (Thailand) subsidiary, Borneo (Thailand) Co. Ltd. In June 1988, Charnchai was promoted to the position of chief executive of Gilman Office Automation. Bond returned to Hong Kong, since Inchcape now felt that the company could be run under local management. In June 1989, Julian Fryett was recruited from Inchcape's management training programme. Although Fryett, half Thai and half English, had been raised in England since the age of three, he had visited Thailand with his parents on a number of occasions. At the time he joined the company he could not speak or read Thai. However, within one year, he could speak well and read marginally. Charnchai's initial strategy was to build up the leading service organization in the Thai market believing that service reputation sells machines, and that service contracts, including spare parts and machine maintenance, adds turnover. As business growth slows, service should represent a growing percentage of total revenues. In his first 18 months, Charnchai added Pitney Bowes facsimile machines, GBC binding machines and 3M overhead projectors to the product portfolio. He expanded his staff to 28 salespeople, 45 service engineers, and opened a sales and service outlet in Had Yai (approximately 800 km south of Bangkok). He has been rebuilding a network of agents throughout the country by improving communication and contacts with company staff, increasing the availability of spare parts and consumables inventory, faster delivery, improving point of sale and promotional support, and faster response time to service requirements. With Fryett, he met regularly with dealers, seeking to anticipate the evolution of distribution channels in Thailand. Many of these same agents had previously sold Ricoh machines in affiliation with Fantaract. However, in the later years of Fantaract's tenure, they had switched to other suppliers, because they had been unable to get spare parts, service or reliable deliveries. Charnchai and Fryett began to keep a close eye on shipments per dealer and accounts receivable. They actively supported those dealers who could move machines and pay their bills on time, paying close attention to their delivery, promotion and service requirements.

Charnchai and Fryett have been closely studying the performance of the sales force and technical service staff. They have charted the performance of the sales force, in unit and Baht sales per month, and that of the service staff, by the number of daily service calls, time per call, and the time to next machine failure after the service call. They release sales people and service engineers who consistently underperform, regardless of tenure with the company. At the same time, they have been trying to instil a service and 'customer first' mentality throughout the organization, through example, training, reminders and reprimands. They are very conscious of targets, and are quick to reward those staff who exceed these targets.

Gilman has also been seeking to improve communications with Ricoh. They are lobbying Ricoh aggressively for lower lead times on orders and lower transfer prices on certain models of machines. With a view to the future, they are looking for unique characteristics of the Thai market which could be better served with modified products, including a high quality/low speed copier for copy service centres.

In 1990, Chamchai estimates that Gilman will deliver an average of over 120 machines per month, taking 14% of the market. He expects Gilman's profit will continue to grow substantially (see Exhibit CS12.2).

RELATIONSHIP WITH RICOH

For the next five years, Chamchai feels in a relatively safe position as regards the Ricoh business. He believes he has successfully rebuilt the reputation of Ricoh copiers in Thailand, and has developed a close network of agents and a dedicated customer base. However, although Ricoh is not likely to revoke the distribution agreement in the short term, he feels he must make Ricoh number one in the market to reinforce sustainability of the contract. Ricoh will remain highly committed to distributors who perform. But to date, Gilman has been unable to win the distribution rights for Ricoh facsimile machines. Under the previous tenure of Fantaract, Ricoh awarded the facsimile contract to a competitor. As long as his competitor continues to perform well, Chamchai does not expect to win this contract.

He knows from experience that a distributor always runs the risk of losing the business. Should Ricoh want greater control and greater stability over their product lines in Thailand, it may look to establish a subsidiary company of its own. If Ricoh seeks to form a joint venture company, Gilman would be the most likely candidate for a local partner. At the moment though, Chamchai prefers the greater independence, flexibility and control over cash flow that Gilman enjoys as an independent company, and he does not want to change the present situation. Should Ricoh opt to start manufacturing locally, it is likely to turn to one of Inchcape's holding companies to act as a local partner. Under current Thai investment promotion law, Ricoh, if deemed eligible by the Board of Investment, could only establish a distribution, sales and service subsidiary, or a manufacturing facility restricted to 49% ownership.

Ricoh has been one of the leading office equipment makers in Japan with the largest market share in both copiers and fax machines. While it has done well in Hong Kong, it has failed to match its domestic performance elsewhere in the world. Of its total 1989 sales of $5.2 billion, 63% is in its domestic market. Of its export sales 50% are to OEMs, although 100% of sales in Asia are of brand-name products.

AFFILIATION WITH INCHAPE LTD

Inchcape subsidiaries have operated in Thailand for over 130 years, and the Group is currently the largest multinational corporation in Thailand in terms of turnover. Because of its long-standing presence there, and its establishment prior to most of the laws regarding foreign ownership of businesses and properties, it benefits from a number of privileges and exemptions under Thai law. Essentially, it operates with both the benefits of a foreign company and the rights of a local company. It also has built up a deep in-house knowledge of the Thai business community and government machinery. Inchcape (Thailand) holds a few key advantages for Chamchai. One is the in-house management expertise. Where appropriate, Inchcape can introduce Western business practices and theory into local businesses, everything from mission statements and customer feedback to work scheduling and working capital management. Where appropriate, it will encourage local and expatriate managers to adapt to local business practices. A second is access to capital. Gilman can turn to short- or long-term funds easily and quickly at the lowest prime rates. This is a significant advantage in Thailand where local money markets tend to be tight.

As part of Inchcape Pacific Business Machines Group, the company benefits from specific business streams expertise. Initially, this was fundamental in setting up the business, training sales and service staff, marketing, product knowledge, administration and compensation schemes. Gilman continues to benefit from Inchcape's ability to reach potential principals from around the world, to train staff at all levels and to share knowledge. At the moment, Inchcape distributes Mita copiers in Hong Kong, Konica copiers in Hong Kong and Singapore, and Ricoh copiers in Australia, Thailand and Hong Kong. They are in continuous contact with their counterparts in these companies, and are open to sharing new ideas and performance benchmarks (market share, profitability, sales per sales person, etc.). New products with which Inchcape has recently approached Chamchai include cheque-handling equipment for banks and letter-handling equipment for post offices and large corporations. As Fryett explains: 'We can benefit from being a part of Inchcape. We get together. They're good lads and we help each other out. In Hong Kong, Gilman also distributes Ricoh copiers, and we can share ideas. Inchcape has other businesses we can take advantage of, like shipping. And they try to use our copiers. Inchcape (Thailand) is one of our biggest rental customers'.

In fact, while the Inchcape Pacific and Gilman philosophy is to support very entrepreneurial and locally driven country groups, they are seeking to bind the different companies in a cohesive, unifocused direction for the Business Machines Group. As Chamchai considers his options, he makes it clear that there are very few boundaries imposed by Inchcape Pacific (Exhibit CS12.3).

THE THAI COPIER MARKET, 1990

Table CS12.1 shows the size and growth of the Thai copier market, from 1982 to 1990.

Market size statistics assume that 100% of all copiers on the Thai market are imported from Japan. Market size estimates are based on export statistics from MITI to Thailand, and are revised upward to account for copiers shipped through Singapore and Hong Kong.

In 1982 Ricoh sales represented a decline from an estimated market share peak of 20%. This decline corresponds to increasing financial and management difficulties at Fantaract and the late introduction of new copier models.

Chamchai attributes the 1984 market decline to a saturation of the copy service centre market and the slow initial growth in the private business market. The Thai economy entered a short recession in 1984 after a devaluation of the Baht.

Table CS12.1 Market size and growth

Year	Export from Japan	Market growth	Ricoh	Market share
1982	3,743		608	16.2%
1983	5,389	44.0%	542	10.1%
1984	4,021	−25.4%	493	12.3%
1985	3,662	−8.9%	273	7.5%
1986	3,736	2.0%	0	0.0%
1987	5,740	53.6%	482	8.4%
1988	8,110	41.3%	926	11.4%
1989	9,300	14.7%	1,148	12.3%
1990 (est.)	10,700	15.1%	1,500	14.0%

In 1987 Ricoh sales corresponded to the initiation of the Gilman distribution contract and the introduction of Ricoh dry toner copiers.

In 1990 estimated sales are projected from estimates of total growth in the Thai industrial sector of 13% and the Thai real GNP growth of 9%. Sales have fluctuated an average of 49% from month to month over the past year, up from the 23% average monthly variation in 1988. Sales forecasting is therefore a very difficult task.

Gilman sells from inventory, and re-orders from Ricoh once a month. Current lead time on orders is five months, including four months' advance orders on shipments from Ricoh and one month to clear customs and port backlogs. Gilman has not yet been able to model sales fluctuations in total or unit sales, or correlate expected sales to supporting data (i.e. previous month's sales calls). Gilman's sales are given in Table CS12.2 and are divided into the various income-generating activities.

Market shares in Japan are Ricoh (35%), Canon (27%), Fuji-Xerox (21%) and Sharp (7%), based on total estimated machines in the field of 2,550,000.

Ricoh's largest market share is in middle range copiers. In Japan, Ricoh dominates the highest end of the market. Most of these machines would have almost no market potential in Thailand.

Table CS12.3 indicates market segmentation.

In 1989 Gilman's Ricoh sales were 56% in Bangkok and 44% upcountry. Most upcountry purchases are made directly from a Bangkok outlet. Thais tend to believe that merchandise can

Table CS12.2 Sales by copier type

Revenue (millions of Baht and % of total)

Product type	1987		1988		1989		1990(est)	
Copier sales	40	62%	75	65%	91	60%	139	63%
Rental copy charge	4	6%	8	7%	14	9%	18	8%
Supplies	13	21%	22	19%	30	19%	47	21%
Service/maintenance fees	7	11%	10	9%	17	11%	18	8%
Total	64		115		152		222	

Market share estimates, by units sold:

Brand	1988	1989	1990	Total machines in the field
Fuji-Xerox	24%	26%	25%	26%
Mita	22%	21%	20%	21%
Canon	16%	14%	14%	14%
Ricoh	11%	12%	14%	13%
Minolta	6%	8%	8%	8%
Konica	6%	5%	6%	5%
Sharp	5%	5%	5%	5%
Toshiba	3%	4%	4%	4%
Panasonic	2%	1%	1%	1%
Others*	5%	4%	3%	3%
Total	100%	100%	100%	100%
Units	8,110	9,300	10,700	30,500

* Primarily includes OEMs, Selex, Gestetner and Rex Rotary.

Table CS12.3 Market segmentation

	1989	1990	1991	1992
Bangkok	50	47	44	40
Upcountry	50	53	56	60

Table CS12.4 End-users

End-user	1989	1990	1991	1992
Private	70%	80%	82%	84%
Government	30%	20%	18%	16%

Table CS12.5 Purchase patterns by end-user

Customer size	Preferred finance mode	Machine size (cpm)*	Estimated market growth
Large corporations	1) rent	20–45	15%
B500m+	2) buy		
Medium corporations	1) buy	15–30	20%
B100m–B500m	2) rent		
Small offices	1) buy	12–20	15%
<B100m	2) lease		
Copy service centres	1) lease	30–45	5%
<B100m	2) buy		
Government sector	1) tender	12–20	5%

* CPM – copies per minute. As machine capacity increases, other features tend to increase as well, including size, image clarity and job processing capabilities.

always be purchased cheaper in Bangkok and will often order directly from Bangkok without even checking local prices or whether a local agent is available. Gilman policy is to quote upcountry customers as per rates set by Gilman agents in provinces in which agents have been established. However, Gilman has not yet decided on how to credit sales made directly by Gilman sales people in an agent's territory. At both extremes, Canon allows sales people to quote rates in competition with local agents. Fuji-Xerox directs all sales through the authorized Xerox branch outlet for each customer's region.

Gilman currently uses a network of agents/dealers in the north (9), north-east (10), central (8), south (7) and east (4).

The annual dealer sales per agent vary from 5 to 40 copiers for agents located in major cities, and from 3 to 20 copiers for agents located in smaller provincial towns. The agents do not carry only Ricoh machines, and may represent from two to five different manufacturers.

Mita is the dominant competitor in government sales, which in turn are made by tender offer. Price usually represents the most critical purchase decision factor. Service quality is not considered significant. Table CS12.4 illustrates the end-user profiles and Table CS12.5 shows end-user purchase patterns.

- ■ *Rental* – There is no installation and service charge. However, machines are installed with a meter and charged by number of copies per month.

- ■ *Lease* – The machines are purchased by a finance company and lent to the customer. Payments are monthly.

- ■ *Sale* – The machines are bought outright by the customer and the financing is arranged independently.

Competitors believe Fuji-Xerox has an advantage in the rental business. As a joint-venture company, it is easier to finance the inventory holding costs of rental machines and it has more flexible evaluation criteria than Gilman, as Fuji-Xerox is not as concerned with maximizing return on average business assets (ROABA).

Table CS12.6 illustrates competitive profile.

Table CS12.7 indicates the sales and distribution channels.

Gilman sales force salaries are roughly 30–50% salary and 50–70% commission and bonus, averaging approximately B15,000 per month. Gilman technician salaries are roughly 50–70% salary and 30–50% commission and bonus, averaging B10,000 per month.

Average monthly sales per sales person are three units per month in Bangkok and nine units per month upcountry. Gilman believes it leads the Thai market in sales force efficiency. Thai Xerographic is estimated to average two sales per month per sales person. Charnchai plans to continue to increase targets. In Hong Kong, Gilman has achieved 15 sales per month per sales person.

Gilman averages six hours' response time to emergency maintenance calls, with 80% of calls dealt with between two and eight hours. This is believed to lead the market, and matches Fuji-Xerox. However, Fuji-Xerox has successfully differentiated its customers, allowing it to offer varying grades of service. Class A customers have access to standby service capability and will be served in one to four hours; class B in four to eight hours; and class C in six to 12 hours. The customers do not choose a service class; rather Fuji-Xerox selects it, presumably based on the price sensitivity, service requirements, and importance of the customer. Charnchai believes he needs to continue to reduce service response time. However, he has yet to decide whether he will seek to build capacity to reduce total average service time or differentiate customers as Fuji-Xerox does.

With the exception of Fuji-Xerox, all companies sell in the Bangkok area directly from a central office location. Fuji-Xerox has four fully owned sales and service outlets throughout Bangkok. These outlets are set up as upscale copy service centres, with an open receiving area to display models. They carry large inventories of consumables and spare parts.

For upcountry sales, Fuji-Xerox is building a network of fully owned outlets, identical in structure to those in Bangkok. Sharp and Matsushita are selling via established electric appliance stores

Case 12

Table CS12.6 Competitive profile

Brand	Distributor and product portfolio
Fuji-Xerox (26%)	Thai Xerographic System Ltd.: joint venture company between Fuji-Xerox (49%) and local partnership (51%). Incorporated in 1978. Previously a fully owned subsidiary of Fuji-Xerox. Fuji-Xerox has never used distributors in Thailand. Distributes all Fuji-Xerox products, predominantly copiers and fax machines. Dominates the high end of the copier market, measured by copy quality and speed, with perhaps as much as 70% of the high end market.
Mita (21%)	Mita (Thailand) Ltd.: Joint venture company between Mita (49%) and partner from previous distributor (51%). Established in 1984. Previously used local distributor. Distributes all Mita products, specifically copiers and fax machines. Dominates the low end of the copier market. Poor service reputation.
Canon (14%)	FMA Corporation: Fully independent Thai distributor of Canon for over 20 years. Won contract from previous Ricoh distributor. Exploring joint venture with Canon. Distributes all Canon business machines, including copiers, typewriters, computers, printers, fax machines and calculators. Dominates the personal copier market.
Minolta (8%)	Bangkok Business Equipment Ltd.: Fully independent distributor of office equipment. Believed to be currently exploring joint venture company with Minolta.
Konica (5%)	Inter Far East Engineering: Public company, major shareholders are Saha Patanapibul Group of Companies, a major Thai conglomerate with holdings in computer and telecommunications companies.
Sharp (5%)	The Bangkok Trading Company Ltd.: Joint venture company since 1987 between Sharp (49%) and previous distributor of same name for over 60 years (51%). Distributes all Sharp consumer electronics (excluding white goods).
Toshiba (4%)	Chevalier Office Automation: Fully owned subsidiary of Chevalier Office Automation (Hong Kong). Distributes most Toshiba business and office machines. Handling Toshiba copiers since late 1988.
Panasonic (1%)	Siew National Sales & Service Ltd: Joint venture company between Matsushita (49%) and previous distributor of National products (51%). Established 21 years ago. Distributes all Matsushita products, including Panasonic, National and Technics brand names.

Table CS12.7 Sales and distribution channels

Brand	Number of offices	Sales staff	Service staff
Fuji-Xerox	10	45	120
Mita	2	50	75
Canon	1	30	65
Ricoh	2	28	45
Minolta	1	25	35
Konica	1	20	25
Sharp	1	15	30
Toshiba	1	10	20
Panasonic	1	8	10

throughout the country, where inventory and display space are usually tight. All the other companies are selling through a combination of dedicated upcountry salespeople for direct sales, limited branch networks and independent agents. Independent agents carry a number of competing models. However, they can offer an intimate knowledge of the business community and provide customers with easier and quicker access to service and consumables.

1989 ESTIMATED MEDIA SPENDING

Mita makes the most extensive use of the media, accounting for 36% of total advertising expenditure in print, radio and television. Minolta, Ricoh, Toshiba and Sharp spend from one-third to one-half as much. Mita also uses paste-up advertising: stickers and A4 size posters can be found on telephone booths, light poles, rain shelters, above urinals and on construction faces.

The Thai media responds well to press releases, although Fuji-Xerox and Mita are the only companies known to make routine use of this opportunity for copiers. Fuji-Xerox is widely cited in the local press for new product releases, exhibitions, promotions, appointments, training, seminars and release of financial results. As a result, it has become recognized as one of the best run local operations of a multinational.

Mita makes periodic donations of copiers to the Royal Family and selected government groups. These donations are widely covered by all television networks on primetime news programming.

Table CS12.8 show that the officially quoted list price is far above the prices at which the copiers are actually sold to business, dealers or the government. The contribution margin per copier is 45%, based on a commercial price of 57.0 Baht, and goes down to 33% for sales to the

Table CS12.8 Tax and cost data per machine

Line item	Copier cost
FOB	¥98.5
Freight charge	¥1.5
CIF	¥100.0
Import duty	¥40.0
B&M taxes	¥28.9
Clearing charge	¥1.0
Landed cost	¥170.0 = B31.4 (100 Yen = 18.5 Baht)
List price	B115.0
Commercial price	B57.0
Dealer price	B52.0
Government price	B47.0

government. These margins are roughly the same for all models. However, service costs decrease and sales costs increase, as a percentage of total cost, as machine size increases.

The contribution margin on spare parts averages 46%, on rental machines 60%, and on machine service 44%.

THE THAI OFFICE AUTOMATION MARKET, 1990

Paralleling double digit growth in the economy for the past three years, and close to a 9% average over the decade, office automation equipment sales in Thailand have been booming. The largest categories of office automation (OA) equipment have included electronic machines (calculators, key punches, typewriters, computers, key telephones, mobile telephones, computer systems, facsimile machines, data processing, data support services and local communications exchanges) and accessories (stands, furniture, binders, laminators). Growth in office automation equipment sales is expected to exceed 20% for 1989–90. This corresponds to projected growth in the USA, Europe and Japan of under 10%. On personal computers and related products, growth has exceeded 40% per year in recent years. In fact, Thailand is often referred to as the fastest growing OA market in the world.

Analysts expect this growth rate to continue for at least the next three years, and perhaps through to the end of the decade. These optimistic forecasts are based on projections drawn from the new office space and plant construction planned to come on line over this time, anticipated steady demand, and the ability of Thailand to continue to absorb this new investment.

All major principals are represented, either by distributors, joint-venture companies, or fully owned subsidiaries. Some, like Kodak, IBM and Philips, have been active in the Thai market for over 20 years through fully owned subsidiaries. Thailand has long-standing ties with the business communities of South Korea, Taiwan, Hong Kong and Singapore. Companies from these countries, especially in personal computers and telecommunications equipment, are well represented. As a result, in addition to being one of the fastest growing markets in the world, it is also one of the most competitive.

The government has yet to resolve issues surrounding protection of intellectual property rights, subscription to international copyright agreements and breach of faith contract disputes. Pending resolution of government policy, a number of principals have avoided direct investment leading to technology transfer. At the same time, firms are pressing for the easing of government regulations on data communication.

A number of infrastructure problems, most notably the lack of available exchanges for both cellular and key telephones, is, to some extent, holding back development of the market. The waiting list for telephone lines is measured in years, not months. The government is taking a leading role in these latter concerns and is currently installing a nationwide network of fibre optic cable and microwave transmission/receiving towers, as well as state-of-the-art satellite data communication capabilities, in order to make Bangkok the service and information centre of the Indo-Chinese subcontinent, and to match many of the telecommunications features of Singapore.

Taxation on fully built-up electronic machines, running from 35 to over 70%, has restricted buyers to larger firms and to firms involved in international transactions. Following current GATT negotiations, analysts expect the government to lower taxes, possibly from between 20 to 35%. This will broaden the market, in all segments, most significantly in small- to medium-sized internationally competitive firms.

The industry suffers from a serious lack of skilled staff. Companies must be willing to invest in the use of expatriates (i.e. programmers, software and data support system developers) and overseas training of technicians, maintenance and repair people, as well as systems and applications installers.

A number of local firms have sought to build well-entrenched positions in the distribution of office automation equipment, through the development of applications and service staff, binding contracts with principals, extension into local manufacturing, and captive retail outlets.

The most powerful, Sahaviriya, although only eight years old, is projected to reach a turnover of B1 billion in 1990. Its total estimated market share in computers, peripherals and data communication devices is 15 to 20%. The company has taken a leading role in the development of standards for the Thai market, it has increased support staff to its 400 personnel and is currently building an extensive upcountry distribution network.

THE THAI ECONOMIC OUTLOOK, 1990

Economists predict that the current economic expansion will continue, with Bangkok Bank, the largest local bank, releasing mid-year estimates placing total increase in the economy at 10%, with growth in the manufacturing sector of 14% and the agricultural sector of 4%. Inflation has not yet emerged as a significant concern, nor has pressure on wage rates, although land prices have started to increase dramatically. The consumer price index is expected to increase by 6% in 1990, up from a historical average of 2.2% for most of the previous decade.

The government has managed foreign debt well, and despite a historically low savings rate, the current account deficit is only 3.5% of GDP, the debt service ratio is 13.8%, and external debt 39.6% of GDP. The government has run a balanced budget for the fiscal years 1987, 1988 and 1989, and is projected to run a small budget surplus in the fiscal year 1991. There is therefore no external pressure for structural reform of the economy, or for a revaluation of the currency. Exchange rates are fixed to a basket of currencies, predominantly the dollar and the yen. The Bank of Thailand has been noted for maintaining a consistent policy, and exchange rates have only moved within a marginal band around the dollar, mostly in response to changes between the dollar and the yen. Interest rates on deposits have been controlled, leading to an effective cap on commercial lending rates of approximately 16 to 17%.

The most serious threat to the economy is the strain on the existing infrastructure, including rail, road and port facilities, industrial and municipal facilities, wastewater disposal and telecommunications. Of equal concern, is the lack of skilled labour and educational facilities.

However, foreign investment remains strong. Recent polls of Japanese business indicate Thailand is the number one destination for foreign investment in southeast Asia. Over 1,000 foreign investment projects in new industries were approved by the Board of Investment from 1988 to 1989, with only a few hundred having begun implementation. Total foreign investment in new projects is expected to grow by 150%, with net direct investment in existing projects expanding by 45%.

THE TACTICAL PLAN FOR COPIERS, JULY 1990

'Be better than our competitors' is what Chamchai wants his staff to aim for. He has laid out a tactical plan to 'encircle them' and 'pick at their business, one copier at a time'. Chamchai evaluates his opportunities for competitive advantage over the market leaders in Thailand. Gilman has little control over its hardware: the price, availability, features and brand name of Ricoh. It has greater control over the consumables, namely the availability and breadth. It has complete control over service and maintenance, and this is where it must choose to excel and distinguish its distribution network and retail concept. Many ideas come to mind, and Chamchai has to decide which activities should have priority.

THE STRATEGIC QUESTIONS FOR GILMAN, JULY 1990

Whereas the first goal of the company is to achieve the number one market share in copiers, the company must continue to consider the long-term development of its product line and position in the marketplace. It may lose the Ricoh business at any time since it cannot influence the competitiveness of Ricoh machines. At the moment, Ricoh represents over 90% of Gilman turnover, a precarious position for a distributor.

Chamchai has therefore developed a long range vision for Gilman: 'To be the best office equipment supplier in Thailand for service, quality-distinguished by exceptional responsiveness to customer needs'. He has broadened his description of the potential product mix to be 'anything that goes into an office'. He will consider typewriters, printers, computers, key telephones, even office furniture. He expects to look into the possibility of acquiring a computer distribution business within two years.

None of the company's growth outside of Ricoh has been worked out in detail. Chamchai seems to be struggling most with the copier business: what niche it will fill in the marketplace, how it will build upcountry sales channels, who its dealers/agents will be, how the company will bind them to Gilman, what they will look like, what their range of products and services will be. Long-term strategy may evolve in a number of directions. The company could get involved in the distribution of a number of unrelated products through Inchcape (i.e. check-handling and mail-handling equipment). It could move further into retail.

Fryett, like Chamchai, has as his first priority the mission to overtake the firm's competitors. However, he, too, is continually examining the long-range vision of Gilman and the formula for the entire Business Streams Group. Should it invest its resources to dominate the copier business, and plan on an eventual joint venture with Ricoh? Should it build a flexible distribution and retail network that will allow it to pick and switch among principals, as the dominant player in business machines marketing and distribution in all of the Inchcape Pacific countries?

Chamchai concludes: 'First we beat our competitors, then we beat Sahaviriya...'

Exhibit CS12.1   Organizational chart of Inchcape

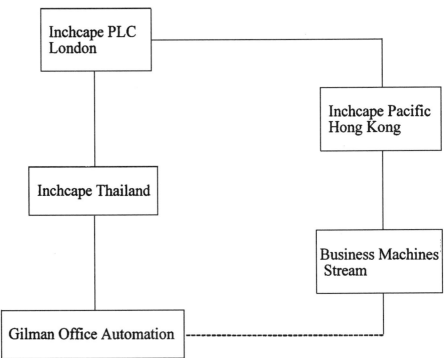

Exhibit CS12.2   Profit and loss statement, Gilman Office Automation

	1987	1988	1989 (Jan–June)	1990
			(millions of Baht)	
Sales	59.3	124.9	165.6	110.0
Cost of sales				
Cost of goods	37.1	77.0	94.7	59.4
Warranty costs	0.1	0.1	0.2	–
Stock depreciation	0.4	7.8	5.9	3.0
Others	0.1	1.2	1.1	1.1
Total	37.7	86.1	101.9	63.5
Gross profit	21.6	38.8	63.7	46.6
Overheads				
Staff commission	2.3	4.6	7.3	5.8
Direct overheads	20.3	26.3	33.0	22.0
Depreciation	2.4	3.4	5.6	4.6
(Fixed assets)				
Total	25.0	34.3	45.9	32.4
Trading profit	(3.4)	4.5	17.8	14.2

Exhibit CS12.3 Inchcape Pacific: mission and goals

Statement:

1   Inchcape Pacific will be the clear market leader in specialized marketing and services in the Pacific region.

2   We shall be judged to be the most successful organization in our chosen markets by our customers, our principals, our staff and our shareholders.

3   We shall differentiate ourselves as a successful organization, by the value we add to our products and services and by the quality of our people.

Our goals:

4   To consolidate our leading position in Hong Kong and to expand each of our business streams regionally, to achieve a significant position in all of the other major markets.

5   To be recognized as a highly commercial organization which creates market opportunities, achieves above average growth and enhances value within our five core businesses.

6   To respond to new markets, products and technology in our core businesses so that change and improvement is synonymous with the Inchcape style.

7   To achieve success through individual and team excellence rather than the application of added cost.

8   To be known for the high calibre, dynamism and integrity of our people. We shall encourage and develop their talents, recognize and reward our people's achievements, and ensure that they share in the company's success.

9   To develop decentralized and accountable business unit management thus reducing the reliance on central controls.

10 To listen to our customers, principals and employees and seek to satisfy their needs as they relate to our business.

Our core values:

1. We care about our customers and the way in which we satisfy their needs.

2. We care about our principals and the way in which we represent them.

3. We care about our people and the way in which we manage them.

The Players

Part

5

With a large number of business players and a variety of strategies, Asia Pacific is a dynamic, highly competitive arena. As Figure 5.1 shows, competitors include both global and regional players across a large range of technologies and markets. Firms in Asia have developed unique management styles, shaped by different cultures and political/economic environments – often an eclectic mix of Confucian values, entrepreneurship and Western professional management. They can be divided into distinct groups: Japan's global *kaisha*, the diversified *chaebol* conglomerates of South Korea, and Overseas Chinese family-owned and managed groups, with additional players such as *hongs* (former colonial trading houses) and state-owned enterprises.

Japanese kaisha

Devoted employees and patient capital

Very few firms in Asia can match Japanese companies (usually referred to as *kaisha*) in terms of size and sophistication. Three-quarters of the largest companies in Asia Pacific are of Japanese origin, and one-third of all 'Fortune 500' companies are Japanese. Many

Figure 5.1   The players in the Asia Pacific competitive arena

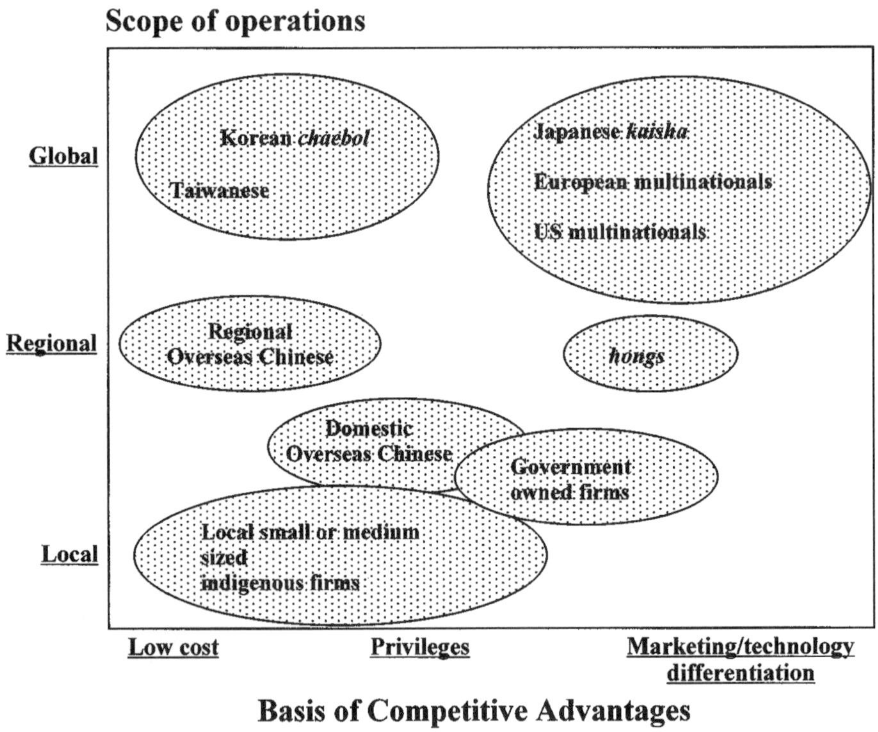

are 100 years old and more, compete in world markets and spend a considerable amount on R&D.

Much has been written about Japanese firms. This chapter focuses on understanding their competitive behaviour, inside and outside Japan. While individual firms may differ, Japanese companies by and large base their strength on devoted employees and patient capital.

The devotion of Japanese employees to their *kaisha* results from two factors:

■ a strong desire to identify with a group rather than striving for individual achievement;

■ an employee who joins a company implicitly pledges commitment and loyalty in exchange for life-long employment; his own future is closely tied to the well-being of the firm.

Japanese managers have converted this group spirit into strong commitment to corporate objectives. This ambitious 'strategic stretch' is a key feature of all globally successful firms. Life-long employment and loyalty also make it worth while to invest in learning and in developing the skills of employees; this, combined with a willingness to share information, develops the work force's overall competence which can be exploited in a variety of ways.

Patient money is another major advantage. An estimated 70 per cent of shares in large quoted Japanese companies is held by long-term investors, often affiliated to the companies themselves, including banks. The direct influence of shareholders is negligible. Boards of directors consist of senior managers whose whole career has been with the firm and who see their job as serving the interests of all stakeholders.

Since long-term investors do not insist on high financial returns, the *kaisha* do not need to worry about dividends, share price or the opinion of security analysts to the extent that US firms do, and can concentrate on pursuing long-term, sometimes risky strategies to develop new products and enter new markets. Shareholders nevertheless do expect rewards, usually in terms of long-term capital gains in the share price, or in gaining business: purchasing orders if they are manufacturers, agency representation for trading houses, loans for banks, and so on. As a result Japanese firms enjoy low costs of equity as well as low-cost debt (interest rates in Japan are consistently lower than in the rest of the world).

Economies of scale, scope and speed

Japanese firms have rigorously applied economies of scale, scope and speed over the last decades. After the Second World War, their main asset was cheap labour. By the 1960s, however, labour costs had increased so much that the *kaisha* invested in large, capital-intensive facilities, substantially increasing output. This produced enormous economies of scale that restored and increased Japan's competitiveness: in the 1970s, the *kaisha* made major inroads into world markets by offering limited ranges of standardized products. Less focused Western competitors found it difficult to muster an adequate response.

By the early 1980s, demand was becoming more sophisticated and differentiated and Japanese firms saw the need to reorganize their factories with flexible manufacturing systems. Without losing the benefits of mass production, they increased the variety of their products, adding economies of scope to economies of scale.

At the end of the 1980s, the *kaisha* further boosted their competitiveness by speeding up response to customer demands. This produced economies of speed (the benefits from shorter development and production cycles). Success in the 1990s requires offering a wide range of products at the lowest possible cost and as quickly as possible. Japanese firms are well positioned in this respect: just-in-time systems have been in place for years, and the sharing of information within the organization, the emphasis on action rather than analysis and highly competent employees at all levels make the *kaisha* highly responsive to time-based competition. Other Japanese traits are extremely useful as competitive weapons, such as customer service orientation and attention to detail. This has enabled Japanese department stores, supermarkets and hotel groups to make major inroads into Asia Pacific markets.

In the 1970s and 1980s, the Japanese *kaisha* became convinced that success depended on high growth. Growth became a dogma: survival and victory required developing faster than competitors by continuous investment to build up capacity or develop new markets and products. Financial indicators such as return on investment (ROI) played a secondary role: what mattered was the markets' judgement in terms of sales and market share. In hotly contested markets, such as consumer electronics, an obsession with tracking competitors led to constantly launching new models at any cost, even in the tiniest segments. Time-consuming market research and long-lasting analyses were discarded in favour of market experimentation, and the inevitable failures were seen as opportunities to learn.

Kaizen not restructuring

When Japan's 'bubble' economy burst in the early 1990s, the *kaisha* found themselves burdened with overcapacity, overstaffed offices, costly and unmanageable acquisitions abroad. Overvalued assets called for large write-offs and depreciation. As export markets declined too, profits began to deteriorate. (The yen rose from 260 yen to the US dollar in 1985 to 80 in 1995, an increase which few Western export-orientated firms would have survived.) In addition, relationships with suppliers and customers had become too cosy, and Japan's offices were no way nearly as efficient as its factories.

Instead of Western-style radical restructuring, re-engineering, downsizing, delayering, Japanese firms pursued *Kaizen*, the continuous effort by everybody to improve everything. Cost-cutting began with early retirement, hiring freezes, bonus and overtime cuts. (Overall, though, large-scale lay-offs were avoided in an effort to preserve the reciprocal loyalty between firm and employee.) Pressure was exerted on suppliers to cut costs, resulting in moving some manufacturing capacity abroad, a reduction in the number of components, and the sharing of models between competitors. (Cars made by one manufacturer, for example, are now sold under its competitor's name.) While some less competitive suppliers had to close down, the overall industrial structure and the *keiretsu* system was retained.

While cost-cutters gained the edge, it is unclear whether this will lead to a major reorientation, or whether the all-pervasive dream of being number one, *ichiban*, will resurface. Production processes continue to improve through *Kaizen* with shorter product development cycles, longer product life cycles and fewer product varieties. Flexible pricing, once shunned, is now acceptable (although outright discounting is not). R&D spending remains high. It seems that for the rest of the decade the *kaisha* will focus on core activities rather than diversification and acquisitions, channelling foreign investment to the markets that promise the highest growth and highest returns – Asia Pacific. By the end of this century, Japan may well invest more in the region than in the USA.

The *keiretsu*

The Japanese firm defines its role and status through its relationship with other firms; most large companies form a *keiretsu* system of long-standing business ties – sometimes cemented by cross-holding of shares – with a large number of affiliates. The largest *keiretsu* dominate Japan's industrial landscape: Mitsubishi, Mitsui, and Sumitomo, successors of the pre-war family-dominated *zaibatsu*; Fuyo, Daiichi-Kangyo and Sanwa, formed after the Second World War (see Table 5.1). In one way or another, 60 per cent of all companies quoted on the Tokyo stock exchange are affiliated with these six groups.

All consist of a large number of firms operating in key industrial sectors and fiercely competing with the affiliates of other *keiretsu*. Because they are spread across various industries, these industrial groups are called 'horizontal' *keiretsu*. The older pre-war *keiretsu* are structured around a core of a main bank, a general trading firm or *sogo shosha*, and one or two major manufacturing firms. The other three are dominated by financial institutions. A sense of common purpose is created from even small shareholdings or cross-shareholdings. Exchange of personnel, monthly meetings of the heads of the largest affiliated firms or the use of a common name (especially in the most closely knit group, Mitsubishi) foster a community of spirit.

'Vertical' *keiretsu* are groupings of small and medium-sized firms under the umbrella of a major manufacturer; the Toyota production system, with over 10,000 subcontractors, is a good example. Other companies form vertical *keiretsu* to organize their distribution systems. As a rule the smaller firms are almost entirely dependent on the umbrella firm, which favours partners that show long-term commitment. This vertical affiliation system fosters exchange of information and joint product development; delivery procedures are faster and simpler, with lower transaction costs.

Because many vertical *keiretsu* also belong to a horizontal group, Japan's industry forms an integrated network of firms. Some US writers see this as indicative of

Table 5.1 Horizontal *keiretsu*

	MITSUBISHI	MITSUI	SUMITOMO	FUYO	DKB	SANWA
Group Members (FY 92)	187	154	173	154	135	124
Council Members (Sep 93)	28	26	20	29	48	44
Finance and insurance	Bank of Tokyo–Mitsubishi Mitsubishi Trust & Banking Meiji Mutual Life Tokio Marine & Fire	Sakura Bank Mitsui Trust & Banking Mitsui Mutual Life Miksui Marine & Fire	Sumitomo Bank Sumitomo Trust & Banking Sumitomo Life Sumitomo Marine & Fire	Fuji Bank Yasuda Trust & Banking Yasuda Mutual Life Yasuda Fire & Marine	Dai-Ichi Kangyo Bank Asahi Mutual Life Taisei Fire & Marine Fukoku Mutual Life Nissan Fire & Marine[1] Kankaku Securities Orient	Sanwa Bank Toyo Trust & Banking Nippon Life Orix
Electronics and electrical equipment	Mitubishi Electric	Toshiba	NEC	Oki Electric Industry Yokogawa Electric Hitachi[1]	Fujitsu Fuji Electric Yasakawa Electric Mfg. Nippon Columbia[1] Hitachi[1]	Iwatsu Electric Sharp[1] Nitto Denko Kyocera Hitachi[1]
Transportation machinery	Mitsubishi Motors Mitsubishi Heavy Industry	Toyota Motors[1] Mitsui Engineering & Shipbuilding Ishikawajima-Harima Heavy Industries[1]		Nissan Motors[1]	Isuzu Motors Niigata Engineering Iseki Ebara Furukawa	Daihatsu Motor Hitachi Zosen Shin Maywa Industry
Trading and retailing	Mitsubishi Corp	Mitsui & Co Mitsukoshi Hokkaido Colliery & Steamship	Sumitomo Corp	Marubeni	Itochu Nissho Iwai[1] Kanematsu Kawasho Itoki[1] Seibu Department Stores[1]	Nissho Iwai[1] Nichimen Iwatani International Takashimaya
Food and beverages	Kirin Brewery	Nippon Flour Mills		Nisshin Flour Milling Sapporo Breweries Nichirei		Itoham Foods Suntory[1]
Construction	Mitsubishi Construction	Mitsui Construction Sanki Engineering	Sumitomo Construction	Taisei	Shimizu	Toyo Construction Obayashi Sekisui House Zenitaka

Industry						
Iron and steel	Mitsubishi Steel Mfg	Japan Steel Works	Sumitomo Metal Industries	NKK	Kawasaki Steel Kobe Steel[1] Japan Metals & Chemicals	Kobe Steel[1] Nakayama Steel Works Hitachi Metals[1] Nisshin Steel
Non-ferrous metals	Mitsubishi Materials Mitsubishi Aluminium Mitsubishi Cable Industries Mitsubishi Shindoh	Mitsui Mining & Smelting	Sumitomo Metal Mining Sumitomo Electric Industries Sumitomo Light Metal Industries		Nippon Light Metal Furukawa Electric	Hitachi Cable[1]
Real estate	Mitsubishi Estate	Mitsui Real Estate	Sumitomo Realty & Development	Tokyo Tatemono	Tokyo Dome	
Petroleum and coal	Mitsubishi Oil	Mitsui Oil		Tonen	Showa Shell Sekiyu[1]	Cosmo Oil
Rubber and glass / Chemicals	Asahi Glass Mitsubishi Chemical Mitsubishi Gas Chemical Mitsubishi Plastics Industries	Mitsui Toatsu Chemicals Mitsui Petrochemical Industries Denki Kagaku Kogyo[1]	Nippon Sheet Glass Sumitomo Chemical Sumitomo Bakelite	Showa Denko Kureha Chemical Industry NOF Corp	Yokohama Rubber Kyowa Hakko Kogyo[1] Denki Kagaku Kogyo[1] Nippon Zeon Asahi Denka Kogyo Sankyo[1] Shiseido Lion	Toyo Tire & Rubber Ube Industries Tokuyama Corp Hitachi Chemical[1] Sekisui Chemical Kansai Paint Tanabe Seiyaku Fujisawa Pharmaceuticals
Fibre and textiles	Mitsubishi Rayon	Toray Industries		Nisshinbo Industries Toho Rayon	Asahi Chemical Industry[1]	Unitika Teijin
Pulp and paper	Mitsubishi Paper Mills	New Oji Paper		Nippon Paper Industries[1]	Honshu Paper	
Mining and forestry		Mitsui Mining	Sumitomo Forestry Sumitomo Coal Mining			
Machinery	Mitsubishi Kakoki	Mitsui Kakoki	Sumitomo Heavy Industries	Kubota NSK	Kawasaki Heavy Industries Ishikawajima-Harima Heavy Industries	NTN
Precision machinery	Nikon			Canon	Asahi Optical	Hoya
Cement	Onoda Cement	Onoda Cement	Sumitomo Cement	Nihon Cement	Chichibu Cement[1]	Osaka Cement
Shipping and transportation	Nippon Yusen Mitsubishi Warehouse & Transportation	Mitsui OSK Lines[1] Mitsui Warehouse	Sumitomo Warehouse	Showa Line Keihin Electric Express Railway Tobu Railway	Kawasaki Kisen Shibusawa Warehouse Nippon Express[1]	Navix Line Hankyu Nippon Express[1]
Service industry	Mitsubishi Research Institute					

[1]Companies are strictly speaking independent or have affiliations with more than one group.
Source: *Industrial Groupings in Japan*, Dodwell Marketing Consultants.

collusion, and charge the *keiretsu* system as just another entry barrier to the Japanese market. This needs qualification. While the provision of preferential buying and selling opportunities to affiliated firms is collusive behaviour, it is not clear that it gives Japan unfair competitive advantage:

- not all large and successful Japanese *kaisha* belong to a *keiretsu*. Sony, Honda, Kao are not part of a horizontal *keiretsu*, though due to their sheer size they have started to build up their own vertical group;

- cooperative behaviour does not rule out competition within the *keiretsu*; besides, outsiders grossly overrate inter-*keiretsu* contracting, whose importance in fact is relatively modest.

- granting each other privileges or having to buy from each other does not necessarily give firms a competitive advantage, and the Japanese appear to see more clearly the disadvantages of a system that uses relationships to cover up a lack of competitiveness. Flexibility in the relationships between *keiretsu* is increasing; so is competition within individual *keiretsu*.

Mini-Japans and *sogo shosha* abroad

The *keiretsu* system is not limited to Japan. Three aspects of Japanese cooperative behaviour abroad are increasingly apparent:

1. Leading manufacturer/assemblers tend to buy only from their own network of suppliers. When companies such as Matsushita or Toshiba moved assembly operations offshore, they continued to rely on shipments of parts and components from their usual suppliers in Japan. Once local sales became important, forcing the Japanese firms to increase local content, instead of turning to local suppliers they asked their suppliers to move to Asia too. As a result, the vertical *keiretsu* are replicated in most of the ASEANIEs and in China.

2. The horizontal *keiretsu* can draw on its affiliated companies to bid for even the largest or riskiest projects (energy systems in China, exploiting raw materials in Siberia), offering complete packages backed up by Japanese development aid. The packages are then parcelled out to the affiliates: industrial firms provide the technology, engineering firms the construction, and so on. Nevertheless, affiliates from other *keiretsu* or foreign firms are increasingly included in the consortia.

3. The *sogo shosha* trading firms play a central role as traders, providers of information and project organizers, spearheading many of the international activities of the *keiretsu* they belong to. Itochu, Mitsui and Co., Mitsubishi Corp., Sumitomo Corp., and Marubeni all are among the world's five largest companies. Each employs about 10,000 people in more than 200 offices around the world. Their increasingly diversified activities cover every conceivable product and service, from commodity trading to satellite leasing. Much of their strength lies in their ability to collect and disseminate information.

The Korean *chaebol*

A *chaebol* (a term that means 'financial clique') is a large business group, originally created by a talented entrepreneur and still largely family controlled, with operations in many diversified areas. The 10 largest *chaebol* have total turnover equal to 58 per cent of Korea's GNP (Table 5.2).

Table 5.2 The 10 largest Korean *chaebol*

Group	Business sectors	Turnover (1996 US$bn)	Total assets (1996 US$bn)
Hyundai	Motor vehicles, electronics, oil, heavy industries, engineering, machinery, construction materials	63.3	59.6
Samsung	Electronics, aerospace, chemicals, semiconductors, food, textiles, services	58.7	57.4
LG	Electonics, chemicals, oil, insurance, telecommunications, engineering, instruments	37.2	42.6
Daewoo	Motor vehicles, machinery, electronics, distribution, shipbuilding, construction, finance	33.9	39.4
Ssangyong	Motor vehicles, cement, oil	17.4	18.3
Sunkyong	Energy, chemicals, distribution, shipping	15.5	25.5
KIA	Motor vehicles, machinery, steel	10.0	15.9
Hanjin	Airline, shipping, machinery, construction	8.5	15.9
Hanwha	Energy, petrochemicals, distribution	9.1	12.2
Hyosung	Chemicals, synthetic fibres, machinery, leather goods	4.3	4.6
Total 10 largest chaebol		258.0	291.4
Korea GNP 1996		490	
% Turnover/GNP		53	

Source: Korea Money, May 1997

The *chaebol* were born of Korea's forced industrialization: in the 1960s, the government offered preferential credit, import licenses and tax advantages to talented, export-orientated entrepreneurs. Thanks to a liberal financial policy and astute financial engineering, the *chaebol* grew by about 30 per cent annually during the 1970s and the 1980s, winning competitive advantage in labour-intensive manufactured products. The cash flow from these activities, amplified by leveraged financing, was reinvested in modern equipment; aggressive pricing generated enough volume to achieve global economies of scale. From the mid-1980s, the *chaebol* developed their own technology and promoted their own brand on world markets. Today they are global players in shipbuilding, construction, steel, consumer electronics, semiconductors and cars.

The *chaebol* initially enjoyed access to managerial talent and to a low-cost, disciplined, hard-working labour force. A crisis erupted in the late 1980s when labour costs shot up and the Korean currency, the won, rose sharply. The conglomerates responded by setting up offshore plants in southeast Asia and investing in higher value-added sectors. Because of competitive pressures, they are slowly rationalizing to concentrate on fewer sectors.

Managerial culture

The *chaebol*, a hybrid of Confucian values and Japanese group loyalty, is run as an extension of the feudal family network, providing life-long employment in return for loyalty and devotion from employees. With the Chinese firm it shares top-down authoritarianism and paternalism. Employees are expected to glorify the beliefs and actions of the chairman, or *Whoe-Jang*, either the founder of the group or his direct descendent.

Top executives are relatives of the *Whoe-Jang*; his sons will inherit the company. Cohesion at the top is enhanced by elitist recruitment among alumni from prestigious institutions such as the Seoul National University or the Military Academy who share common values and social practices. The *chaebol* relies on concepts such as harmony and challenge, as well as nationalism. Samsung's corporate motto ('We do business for the sake of nation-building') reflects this.

As *chaebol* such as Hyundai and Daewoo become more institutionalized, they strive to provide more visible symbols of corporate culture, such as uniforms, to their employees. A critical management challenge may come from the new generation of Western-educated Korean managers, who are frustrated and demoralized by the authoritarian culture, as high rates of voluntary turnover indicate. The Samsung group is already promoting a managerial style based on the Western concepts of rationalization, delayering and re-engineering. Lee Kun-He, son of the company's founder, has rationalized activities by concentrating on three core sectors, and cut down the size of the chairman's office to push decision making down the chain of command.

The very diversification of *chaebol* causes problems of identity. With a business ranging from ships to shirts to microchips, Samsung clearly lacks the focus of Toyota, a name synonymous with cars. Even concepts such as self-sacrifice or harmony are no longer enough to cement the corporation. Lucky-Goldstar's 30-year-old slogan, *Inhwa* ('Harmony among the people'), seen as too insular, is now criticized for serving as a shield to cover up personal mistakes.

The Korean *chaebol* in Asia

The international strategy of Korean firms has long focused on exports; foreign investments were largely aimed at circumventing trade barriers or controlling distribution channels. Target export markets are now Asia Pacific countries (which double as low-cost manufacturing bases), rather than North America. As comparatively late entrants, the *chaebol* either focus on key sectors across the region (construction, heavy engineering, electronics) or enter emerging new markets: Vietnam, northern China, Mongolia, Myanmar. They use their traditional low-pricing strategies and their marketing approach emphasizes the fact that they are not Japanese.

The Overseas Chinese conglomerates

Some 50 million *hua qiao* (Overseas Chinese) are scattered across Southeast and East Asia (Table 5.3). Far wealthier than the indigenous population, they attract great resentment; some estimates put their collective GNP at US$700 billion, the equivalent of the entire People's Republic of China's. The Overseas Chinese share a common cultural background, and even if they are citizens of their country of residence, they keep their language and traditions.

Table 5.3 The Overseas Chinese in Asia

Country	Millions of Overseas Chinese		GNP (US$bn)	
Hong Kong	6	(98%)	114	(80%)
Singapore	2	(76%)	61	(76%)
Taiwan	21	(99%)	247	(95%)
Malaysia	6	(32%)	48	(60%)
Indonesia	7	(4%)	105	(55%)
Philippines	1	(1%)	29	(40%)
Thailand	6	(10%)	88	(55%)
Vietnam	1	(1%)	4	(20%)
Total	50		696	
PRC	1200		745	

Source: Based on data from the World Bank, 1997

Historical origins

Emigration, which started in South China in the seventeenth century, accelerated in the nineteenth century, when many Chinese fled the poverty and political convulsions of the Manchu empire to establish large communities throughout Southeast Asia. Confident of eventually returning to the Chinese mainland, they avoided investing in illiquid assets and set up trading networks which grew so much they became an alternative to the colonial powers' companies. The communist revolution in China triggered another wave of immigration; many Chinese capitalists fled to Hong Kong and Taiwan where they invested into industry and manufacturing (see Table 5.4).

Generally barred from farming and public administration, Chinese immigrants concentrated on trade, finance and services. In most Southeast Asian countries they became middlemen, traders and financiers. Accused of abusing their economic power, they have often been the target of public outbursts, sometimes violent, especially in Muslim countries such as Indonesia or Malaysia. This has given the Chinese a sense of insecurity and reinforced their desire to keep their capital relatively liquid and easily transferable.

The Overseas Chinese have used their capital, business networks, entrepreneurial spirit and mastery of marketing information to gain control of industrial activities, often in partnership with Western and Japanese investors. They yield much influence over the private sector in Southeast Asia, often controlling manufacturing, banking and distribution, even in countries where they are a small minority. This has reinforced popular resentment against them and served as pretext in Malaysia for forced redistribution of wealth in the 1970s. While resentment against the ethnic Chinese business community emerges from time to time in Indonesia and is latent in Malaysia, regional governments increasingly see it as a strategic asset for economic development. While attempts at political consensus among ASEAN countries have largely failed, the ethnic Chinese network is weaving powerful, albeit informal links between the region's disparate economies.

Characteristics of the Chinese family business

Six distinctive features characterize Overseas Chinese firms:

1. Patriarchal leadership: ethnic Chinese firms retain an extended family structure, probably in response to an uncertain environment. The patriarchal founder-owner is surrounded by an internal network of clan members at all key positions; the main financial and legal posts often go to family members or trusted outsiders, regardless of technical competence.

2. Autocratic and centralized management: as in most Asian societies, important decisions require a consensus at the highest level. The director of the enterprise is surrounded by a few trusted advisers without defined positions who oversee the operations of a vast array of subsidiaries. Virtually all decisions are filtered through these advisers.

Table 5.4 Major Overseas Chinese groups in Asia Pacific

Group name (person in charge)	Activities
Indonesia	
Salim (Liem Sioe Liong)	Cement, automobiles, flour, foods, chemicals, banking, property, insurance
Sinar Mas (Eka Tjipta Wijaya)	Paper, pulp, chemicals, agribusiness, finance, property
Astra (founder W. Soeryadjaya)	Automobiles, heavy equipment, office equipment, agribusiness, property, finance
Malaysia	
Kuok Group (Robert Kuok)	Plantations, edible oils, flour, shipping, hotels, mining, computer services, retail, film distribution
Hong Leong (Quek Leng Chan)	Banking, insurance, car distribution, construction, building materials, manufacturing
Genting Group (Lim Goh Tong)	Hotels, casinos, resorts, plantations, property, paper mill, power generation
Thailand	
Charoen Pokphand (Dhanin Chearavanont)	Feedmils, poultry, chemicals, automobiles, telecommunications, textiles, property
Bangkok Bank (Chartsiri Sophonpanich)	Banking, insurance, financial services
Siam Motors (Khunying Phornthip)	Automobiles, musical instruments
Philippines	
Fortune Tobacco (Lucio Tan)	Cigarettes, beer, banking, hotel, pig farming, airline
J.G. Summit Holdings (John Gokongwei)	Food, textiles, hotels, property, power generation, telecommunications, media, banking, airline
SM Prime Holdings (Henry Sy)	Retailing, banking, property
Singapore	
Hong Leong (Kwek Leng Beng)	Finance, property, hotels, trading, manufacturing
United Overseas Banking (Wee Cho Woo)	Banking, insurance, property, trading, manufacturing
Oversea-Chinese Banking Corporation (Lee Seng Wee)	Banking, insurance, hotels, shopping centres, property, trading, manufacturing, media
Taiwan	
Formosa Plastic (Wang Yung Ching)	Chemicals, plastics, fibres, yarn, textiles, plywood
President Enterprises (Kao Chin Yen)	Food, retailing, banking, property, pharmaceuticals
Acer Group (Stan Shih)	Computers, semiconductors, chips, publications
Hong Kong	
Hutchison Whampoa & Cheung Kong Hong Kong Electric (Li Ka Shing)	Property, construction, cement, container terminals, manufacturing, telecommunications, media, energy, finance
Sun Hung Kai (Kwok Brothers)	Property, engineering, finance, insurance
New World (Cheng Yu Tung)	Property, hotels, container terminals, telecommunications, broadcasting, construction, power plants, highways

3. Informal management structures: planning and control are seldom used. The decision-making process often boils down to seizing an opportunity that arises. This requires capital reserves; hence the obsession with staying liquid. The Chinese entrepreneur likes to seal a deal almost immediately and reap a short-term profit.

4. Activities are compartmentalized as a protection against take-overs, bankruptcy or expropriation. Because the history of Chinese communities in Southeast Asia is rife with persecution, the logic of the enterprise recommends losing a piece of the patrimony rather than putting all one's eggs in the same basket.

5. A network of family and personal contacts: it is the main channel for getting crucial business information. Their networking skills enable the Overseas Chinese to enter a variety of business ventures with different local partners, government officials and foreign companies.

6. Financial management skills: Chinese entrepreneurs are generally highly geared, and pay close attention to cash management. They make up for the lack of government backing by helping each other out. Traditionally, ethnic Chinese conglomerates deliberately blur the distinction between public and private assets, grouping their family holdings in what has been described as a squat pyramid where a handful of publicly listed companies form a broad base, but the most profitable enterprises still belong to, and are controlled by, the family.

Strategic development

The Overseas Chinese's initial fortune is often built on an accumulation of 'deals', taking advantage of an opportunity arising through privileged contacts or non-publicly available information. The entrepreneur provides the initial financing, often highly leveraged, and reinvests the cash flow in another deal. Since most of their business development is based on taking advantage of scarcity and market imperfections, Overseas Chinese groups have rapidly moved into a wide range of business activities following the pattern described in Figure 5.2.

The driving force of these conglomerates is not the valuation of shares on the stock exchange, but the entrepreneurial energy of their leaders. It is difficult to assess the absolute size of these sprawling family businesses (they don't publish figures or annual reports) or draw their exact boundaries: they rarely consolidate accounts.

The private conglomerate structure is found in many developing countries. In Indonesia, most of the great Chinese family fortunes were built on exclusive licenses to import or manufacture certain goods. The Salim Group started with a monopoly for the trade of cloves used to make Indonesia's fragrant *kretek* cigarettes; today it controls the domestic flour and cement industries. The Astra Group dominates the car and motorcycle market behind a wall of high tariffs; Sinar Mas has expanded through its monopoly on producing cooking oil.

Figure 5.2   Typical evolution of an overseas Chinese group

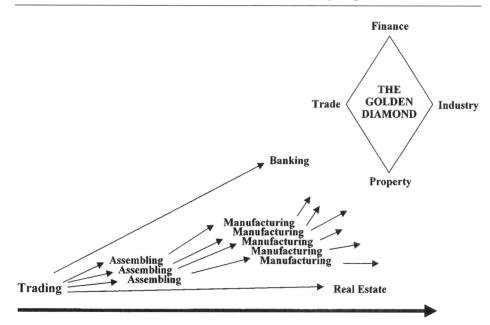

Encouraged by Jakarta's technocratic government, the conglomerates have diversified away from their monopolistic roots. The Salim Group has interests in banking, automobile assembly, processed foods, steel and other areas; Astra is investing in agribusiness, and chemical and glass exports; and Sinar Mas is involved in banking, pulp and paper production, and pig farming. In Thailand, the Charoen Pokphand Group has diversified from agriculture into many other areas, such as telecom services.

The regional activities of Overseas Chinese firms

Several Overseas Chinese firms have become regional players in the 1980s. The Taiwanese were the first to expand, setting up offshore manufacturing plants in ASEAN countries when labour costs went up at home. As China opened progressively, the Overseas Chinese became by far the main investors, ahead of Western and Japanese multinationals. Arguably the most active investor in China is the Charoen Pokphand Group from Thailand, involved in many manufacturing and agribusiness joint ventures. The Overseas Chinese increasingly offer their services as partners to Western and Japanese firms for regional strategic development.

The other players

The former colonial trading houses

Many of the former European colonial trading houses – once major commercial links between European powers and their Asian colonies – continue to operate from Hong

Kong, Singapore, Malaysia and Thailand. Their strengths are still in the traditional areas of trading, agency representation, transportation, insurance and property.

In most countries, however, previously well-known trading houses from Denmark, the Netherlands, Germany and Switzerland have lost former prominence or become local trading and marketing companies. The British colonial houses (*hongs*) remain influential in Hong Kong, but their number is dwindling. The most prominent, Jardine Matheson and Swire, are large conglomerates with 200,000 and 85,000 employees respectively, scattered throughout the world. They are still largely controlled by the founding families and most of their assets remain invested in Hong Kong, although Jardine has delisted its shares as a sign of distrust. Swire banks on China's future and has entered into numerous joint ventures with state-owned Chinese companies.

Some of the former colonial houses have kept one of their major traditional strengths: an ability to recruit, train and motivate bright young managers. The Swire group operates hundreds of businesses ranging from trading, distribution, manufacturing, cold storage, shipping and air transportation to insurance across Asia Pacific. Other firms, such as Inchcape, have become global marketing and services companies with widely spread shareholders. Hutchison, Sime Darby and Hagemeyer have been taken over by local groups, losing their European management style.

State-owned enterprises

In most parts of Asia, except Hong Kong and Japan, the state has played an essential role in industrialization, although it is perhaps most pervasive in Malaysia, Indonesia and China. State-owned enterprises operate mainly in industries that require large investment outlays: plantations, exploitation of natural resources such as oil, steel plants, public utilities, airlines, construction and heavy industrial machines and equipment.

In Malaysia the government set up new firms in order to implement economic policies, control strategic resources or engage in heavy industries. Indonesia created state enterprises mostly by nationalizing existing businesses. In China, until recently, all enterprises of significant size were owned either by central or local government, but this situation is rapidly changing. In other countries, such as Singapore, the government used to control several industrial and services sectors through holdings such as Temasek or Singapore Technology. In Taiwan, state companies which develop computer hardware and software and laser technology are major know-how suppliers to local firms. The same is true in Korea, where the state participates in steel, construction, shipbuilding and banks.

State enterprises are commonly perceived as hulking, inefficient machines which abuse public funds, but many have passed the acid test of market success and bottom-line profitability. In most cases, they have been a vehicle for industrialization. In market-minded Singapore, state-owned firms are managed by professional executives evaluated mainly on profitability criteria. Singapore Airlines is an excellent example of a well-managed government-controlled firm. So is China Steel Corporation of Taiwan. Increasingly, governments in Asia are privatizing some of their firms (Renong in Malaysia, Singapore Airlines) or deregulating the economy by letting private competitors enter monopolies, particularly in telecommunications and banking.

Chinese state-owned enterprises

Until 1979, state-owned enterprises were pure production units which did not distribute their output; their main task was to implement the state's mandatory Five Year Plan. Profits were turned over to the state who subsidized any deficits. Since the economic reforms of 1979, the government has taken steps to make state-owned enterprises more competitive and market orientated. They have been progressively given limited freedom in areas such as production, marketing and finance, and allowed to develop their own plans, including long-term objectives. The companies now receive capital investment loans rather than outright grants, and have the right to hire workers and retain part of their profits.

Changes affect all aspects of management: market mechanisms direct the allocation of resources, enabling managers to set their prices and calculate their return based on market forecasts and on market-based evaluations of the cost of capital, thanks to the modernization of the banking system and the introduction of stock exchanges. They are responsible for their results and bankruptcy has become possible, at least in theory. Employees are increasingly recruited on the basis of professional skills. Rewards are attached to performance and job flexibility is encouraged, while the government is trying to remove from enterprises their obligations to provide free health insurance, housing and schooling.

This transition will take time: an estimated one-third of the 105 million people employed in state-owned firms would have to be laid off if state-owned firms were run productively. However, the role of state-owned firms in the Chinese economy is declining: they produced less than 50 per cent of total output in 1992 and this is expected to drop to 30 per cent by the end of the century.

References

Abegglen, J.C. and G. Stalk, *Kaisha – The Japanese Corporation*, Basic Books, New York, 1985.

Business Week, 'Samsung: Lee Kun-Hee's Management revolution', 28 February 1994, pp. 34–37.

Ernst, Dieter, 'What are the limits to the Korean Model? The Korean Electronic Industry Under Pressure', A.B.R.I.E. Research Paper, University of California, Berkeley, 1994.

Hamel, Gary and C.K. Prahalad, 'Strategic Intent', *Harvard Business Review*, May/June, 1989, pp. 63–76.

Imai, M., *Kaizen: The Key to Japan's Competitive Success*. Random House, New York, 1987.

Institutional Investor, August 1991, p. 30.

Jones, K. and T. Ohbora, 'Managing the "heretical" company', *The McKinsey Quarterly*, March 1990, pp. 20–45.

Kotler, P., L. Fahey and S. Jatusripitak, *The New Competition*, Prentice-Hall, Englewood Cliffs, NJ, 1985, pp. 156.

Lasserre, Philippe, 'Strategic Management and the Overseas Chinese Groups', *Asia-Pacific Journal of Management*, Vol. 5, No. 2, January 1988.

Mackie, J.A.C, 'Overseas Chinese Entrepreneurship', *Asia Pacific Economic Literature*, Vol. 1, No. 6, 1992, pp. 41–64.

MacMurray, Trevor and Jonathan Woetzel, 'The Challenge Facing China's State-owned Enterprises', *The McKinsey Quarterly*, No. 2, 1994, pp. 61–73.

Montgomery, D.B., 'Understanding the Japanese as Customers, Competitors, and Collaborators', *Japan and the World Economy*, March 1991, pp. 61–91.

Redding, Gordon S., *The Spirit of Chinese Capitalism*, Walter de Gruyter, Berlin, 1990.

Redding, Gordon S., 'Overseas Chinese Groups in Pacific Asia; Their Origin and Influence', *Long Range Planning*, Vol. 28, No. 1, 1995, pp. 61–69.

Schütte, Hellmut, *Corporate Governance in Japan*, INSEAD Euro-Asia Centre Research Series, No. 30, Fontainebleau, July 1994.

Stalk, G. and T.H. Hout, *Competing Against Time*, The Free Press, New York, 1990.

Tanaka, Yozo, Minako Mori and Yoko Mori, 'Overseas Chinese Business Community in Asia: Present Conditions and Future Prospects', *RIM, Pacific Business and Industries*, Vol. II, 1992, pp. 1–24.

Whitley, Richard, *Business Systems in East Asia: Firms, Markets and Societies*, Sage Publications, Newbury Park, London, 1992.

Yoo Sanjin and Sang M. Lee, 'Management Style and Practice of Korean Chaebols', *California Management Review*, Summer 1987, pp. 95–110.

You, Zhong Xum, *Seikai no Chainisu (Ethnic Overseas Chinese: Their Expanding Economic Power)*, The Simul Press, Tokyo, 1991.

Case 13

This case was written by Deborah Clyde-Smith under the supervision of Professor Peter J. Williamson. It is intended to be used as a basis for class discussion rather than to illustrate either effective or ineffective handling of an administrative situation. Copyright ©1997 INSEAD-CEA, Fontainebleau, France

The Acer Group: Building an Asian Multinational

The Taipei-based Acer Group had just celebrated its twentieth anniversary. From small beginnings, by the late 1990s Acer was producing personal computers, motherboards, peripherals, fax machines, dynamic random access memory (DRAM) microchips, application specific integrated circuits (ASICS), hybrid microelectronics and software. It was also seeking to develop new products for the consumer electronics and communications fields. Under the dynamic and inspired leadership of its chairman and CEO Stan Shih, Acer had grown to be the number five computer company in the world, Taiwan's leading brand-name exporter and the largest PC-compatible manufacturer in south-east Asia. Acer was a leading brand name in more than 30 countries, holding top position in 13 markets including Indonesia, Malaysia, the Philippines, and Thailand, as well as in Latin American countries such as Chile, Mexico, Panama and Uruguay. Standing at eighth position in the overall US market, it was the third largest supplier to US retail channels. Acer also ranked among the top three companies globally in the monitor business and in the top five worldwide in mid- and high-end PC servers and CD-ROM drive production.

Over the last three years, Acer had set industry records, with over 50% growth in 1993, more than 70% in 1994 and more than 80% in 1995. By 1995, PC shipments had reached 4 million units, plus an additional 1.7 million CD drives, 3.5 million monitors and 52 million memory chips. Net income in 1995 was US$413 million on sales of US$5.83 billion (see Exhibit CS13.1). Pre-audit results showed Acer Group revenues for 1996 would exceed last year's sales figure with PC shipments projected to hit 5.5 million. By 1996 the group was operating 80 offices in 38 countries around the world, employing more than 16,700 staff from 50 different nations. As well as establishing overseas branches, Acer's practice was to form joint ventures with local partners and promote local shareholder investment to increase its share in strategic markets, thus aiming to develop into a publicly traded local company in various different countries while maintaining a global brand.

As the year 2000 approached, Acer planned aggressive action to consolidate a position as a leading provider of world class products and components for a new information technology age. Its strategy of encouraging local investment and expanding overseas joint ventures, based on current rates of expansion, aimed at reaching its '21 in 21' goal of 21 publicly listed companies by the beginning of the 21st century, to become a consortium of borderless networked companies, a US$10 billion 'company of companies'.

ACER'S HISTORY: 20 YEARS YOUNG

Stan Shih, realizing the money-making potential of the microprocessor and microcomputer industries, teamed up with four partners to found Multitech International in June 1976 (the name was not changed to Acer until 1988). The partners dropped out, but Shih in the following years built the company from a US$25,000, 11-employee beginning into a world player. The firm began by importing electronic components, publishing trade journals and consulting on high tech issues. Up to 1980, Multitech trained engineers for Taiwan's information industry, and designed products for local manufacturers (including the Dragon Chinese language CRT terminal, winner of Taiwan's most prestigious design award) plus CRT terminals for export.

Growth through the 1980s

In 1981, the Multitech Industrial Corporation, precursor to Acer, was established. Since the company first began building micro-based equipment in its early years, constant emphasis on R&D had led to the introduction of many innovative products, and 1981–90 were growth years. In 1982, the firm launched an eight-bit Apple clone successful in Taiwan and exported to the UK, Germany, Hong Kong and Singapore. In 1983, Acer was a pioneering developer of PC-compatibles with its XT/PC, and in 1984 switched to production of IBM compatible PCs which used the same microprocessors and ran the same software as the original IBM machines, and were very successful. On this basis, net profits grew by 43% per annum from 1984–88. In 1988, the company name was changed to Acer and it went public, coinciding with an all-time high on the Taipei stock market.

The firm had achieved a reputation for innovation. Leveraging its close cooperation with the dominant US microprocessor Intel, Acer was repeatedly among the first companies worldwide to market computers on the basis of newly developed chips. In 1986 it beat IBM and was second only to Compaq to announce a 32-bit 386 PC based on Intel's 386 microprocessor, leading to considerable media attention and fanfare in the computer press. Acer was one of the first Taiwanese firms to develop own brands for international markets, and subsequently moved more of its business away from supplying established computer companies (original equipment manufacturing or OEM) to sales of its own brands. In 1991, Acer set an industry standard by designing the world's first chip CPU upgrade technology, 'ChipUp'.

Storm clouds

All was not smooth sailing, however. Shortly after becoming a public listed company in 1988, Acer had suffered a significant 'brain drain', with many employees selling their stock and leaving. After 1988, profitability began to decline and Shih became concerned about the company's heavy dependence on the PC business. In response, the decision was taken to broaden the product range by moving into more sophisticated segments of the computer industry, a move which ultimately contributed to the company's first loss-making year in 1990. In 1987, Acer had acquired Counterpoint, a US producer of multi-user systems, for US$6 million; by 1989, however, poor performance meant that most of Counterpoint's factories had to be closed and its products discontinued. In 1990 came the acquisition of Altos, another US multi-user system producer, for US$94 million: in 1992, Altos was still unprofitable.

Alliances and joint ventures had been formed with a number of Western companies, the most significant being with the US firm Texas Instruments in 1989 for production of four-megabit DRAM chips. Acer put in 58% of the capital, US$71.9 million, while Texas Instruments provided the technology. TI-Acer commenced production in March 1992, coinciding with a price drop for DRAM chips to about a quarter of the 1989 level. This was a risky venture which was nearly disastrous: the market for DRAM chips traditionally suffers huge swings of over and under supply, and for two years Acer poured millions into the scheme. The venture did eventually prove successful, generating 80% of Acer's profits in 1993, and a third in 1994, while also guaranteeing Acer a steady supply of competitively priced DRAMs for its PC manufacturing operations.

In addition to problems with its US operations, Acer was trying to survive intense price cutting in the highly competitive PC market – PC prices slumped by 25–40% in 1991, and continued to fall at much the same rate in 1992. These factors combined to give Acer in 1992 its third annual loss in three years. It posted a US$2.8 million loss after tax on sales of US$1.26 billion, and the following year the Taipei stock exchange downgraded its stock, since its earnings-to-revenue ratio was not sufficient to maintain blue-chip standing. Despite the problems, however, Shih succeeded in keeping his team of experienced Acer executives, and in retaining his reputation as one of Taiwan's entrepreneurial visionaries. The challenge now was to transform Acer into one of the industry's leaders despite its slim resources.

Re-engineering the company

To succeed Acer had to enhance efficiency, cut costs and scale down the organization to strengthen competitiveness. This was achieved through setting up independent business units, planning a new global business model, downsizing, diluting shareholdings, and the development of the 'fast food' style logistics and assembly structure. The company shed about 8% of its work force (400 employees) including several layers of management at head office. Other overhead reductions included cutting inventory from a 90- to a 45-day supply – the difference between current and obsolete technology. Conventional wisdom might have dictated that Acer should close the North American operations that were proving a drain on the whole company, but senior management wanted to hold on to the dream of becoming 'a leading global high tech company'. Dependent upon outsiders to run his North American operation, Shih had hired Leonard Liu (formerly chairman of IBM's software development laboratories in California) as president. It was Liu who organized the acquisition of Altos, which rather than giving Acer the hoped for firm foundation in the USA, drained the company of US$100 million. Liu resigned in early 1992, and was replaced with Ronald Chwang, who had moved to Acer in 1986 from Intel. At this time, Shih began his re-engineering of Acer, and his willingness to try the introduction of new and innovative management strategies and to take risks succeeded in turning the company around, with rapid growth between 1992 and 1996 propelling it into the top ranks of the global computer industry and positioning the company for continued expansion in the years ahead.

GLOBALIZATION: OVERCOMING THE INITIAL HURDLES

The image problem

In many respects, Acer had been typical of Taiwanese high tech companies: it had benefited from Taiwan's aggressive technology programmes, such as cheap government loans, and had a factory in Hsinchu science-based industrial park, created by the government in the early 1980s and where companies enjoyed tax advantages and government funding for innovative R&D. Yet Taiwan retained an image problem, and for this reason Shih often tried to disassociate the company from its origins in the public mind. 'Taiwan's reputation is for low-end products', he commented once, 'even bankrupt companies in Silicon Valley have a better image than companies from Taiwan'. Even within Asia, Taiwan suffered from a poor reputation, with many consumers not believing a Taiwanese company capable of sophisticated technology.

Shih admitted problems did exist: 'Our (Asia's) quality is not consistent, and we have not known how to communicate our brand names effectively to the market. At Acer, we are aggressive in trying to change this image'. His contention was that the best Asian companies had lower cost structures and were better prepared than the big US companies to deal with rapid change. The IT industry in Taiwan was dynamic and cost effective, with much US educated and local Chinese talent, and tremendous production capability to support new technologies. (About 60% of Taiwan's university population consisted of science and engineering students, compared with 44% in Korea and 32% in Japan, but Taiwanese engineers earned about half their US counterparts.) Yet the perception of low quality, low price that the 'Made In Taiwan' label carried continued to affect Acer's efforts to penetrate world markets, despite the fact that its plants around the world were certified compliant with ISO 9000, the world's foremost quality assurance standard.

Acer pursued a two-pronged strategy to create a global brand image. On one level, the company contributed to government-supported campaigns to improve the perception of Taiwanese products, and to joint efforts with private enterprises. Acer cofounded the Brand International Promotional Association, and joined such government promotion efforts as Taiwan's Image Enhancement Programme (of which Shih was chairman) and brand-name advertising campaigns which did enjoy some success.

The second prong of Acer's strategy was to promote its own brand image. When Acer's name was changed from Multitech in 1987, this was partly due to the company's desire to adopt a name suitable for expansion into a worldwide marketplace. Multitech was considered too long and not original enough. 'Acer' comes from the Latin for 'active, sharp, incisive', qualities on which the company's corporate culture was built. It also carries the connotation of winner or ace, and the name was intended to pave the way to a new corporate identity. It is short and easy to remember: it needed to be registered in over 100 different countries and have no negative implications in any of them.

Without the resources of its big rivals, Acer needed to keep the cash coming in, and Shih concentrated on the company's strengths as a small, flexible and aggressive local manufacturer while it progressively invested to build its brand. It looked for the most cost-effective routes to brand building. The foundation for Acer's brand-building strategy was a consistent commitment to supplying high quality, innovative merchandise. Acer deployed its R&D capability towards being first on the market with technological breakthroughs which, in turn, helped the company win media attention. It used its strategic alliances with overseas companies to raise awareness of the Acer name. Contrary to the low-profile adopted by many of its Asian competitors, Acer continually used PR channels to promote its goals and achievements. As more financial resources became available, high profile advertising (such as the displays on the luggage trolleys in international airports around the world) was stepped up. In Europe in 1991, for example, Acer's average brand-name recognition rate was only 5%, so a massive advertising campaign was launched in 1992, with a shift from computer to more general publications. By 1995, Acer budgetted $150–170 million on advertising worldwide, the total being split 25% for Central and South America, 25% for Asia, 33% for North America and 17% for Europe. In late 1995, still suffering from low brand awareness in the USA despite its top 10 position, Acer had determined to double its media budget, and begin broadcast advertising in addition to print campaigns.

Scarcity of international management experience

A further hurdle to globalization of the company came in the shape of lack of managers with international experience. Shih conceded that Acer's top management remained too technically oriented, and needed to learn more about the market. 'This is the weak point of Taiwanese companies – they are not able to exploit their technical capability to the level where it reaches their market potential...global expansion and decentralisation demand many qualities from managers – business sense, understanding of corporate mission, the ability to control operations and adjust to change. It is very difficult to develop such people, especially foreign managers in overseas operations', Shih noted.

Localizing management abroad proved a big challenge, while cultural differences also posed communication problems. Outsiders sometimes found it difficult dealing with the intricacies of Acer's organization, where the spreading of responsibility among several people at headquarters made decision making slow. Also, the Taiwanese practice of job rotation, in which personnel moved around frequently in order to gain experience, hindered the formation of relationships with overseas colleagues. Acer began therefore to concentrate on sending more Chinese managers overseas to train the local executives gradually in preparation for greater deregulation at a later stage. While it was not difficult to motivate Chinese managers (or those in developing countries) it was found that people from the advanced countries tended to feel they knew better than headquarters, thus hindering the development of team spirit and mutual trust.

Inadequate access to distribution and market intelligence

In the early days, by Shih's own admission, Acer lacked presence in foreign markets and had little understanding of what was needed to establish a sound presence overseas, as well as a lack of knowledge of legal systems in various countries. Following his early successes, Shih recruited managers from outside the company to oversee Acer's rapid growth in the late 1980s, thus precipitating an excessively rapid expansion which he later admitted had been 'beyond our capacity' and which took the company into the red between 1990–92. These people – in particular Leonard Liu, from IBM, chairman of Acer America – operated in a different fashion from Acer traditional culture, causing internal warfare and the loss of many good employees. Shih came to understand that Liu's appointment was a mistake, and that he had delegated too much too early. Moving back into control (after offering his own resignation, which the board refused) Shih stopped trying to emulate IBM and instead began to shape Acer in his own distinctive fashion.

Outside the USA, Acer's infrastructure was built more gradually. In Europe, for example, Acer began selling its products to distributors in 1984, after making contact through trade fairs and advertising. It was then decided to establish a European office to improve distribution and its understanding of the rapidly expanding market. This office was set up in 1985 in Dusseldorf by Teddy Lu, previously in charge of managing relations with European customers in Taiwan, with three local employees. In the early years, the team concentrated on establishing relationships with the most efficient European distributors, and developing OEM sales. Acer Europe grew rapidly, and after three years contributed almost a third to group sales, though market share varied considerably from country to country. By 1988, it was decided that Acer should set up its own subsidiaries in markets where the potential size could justify them, thus hoping to better understand local particularities, and establish direct links to dealers and corporate accounts. By 1992, Acer had subsidiaries in Denmark, France, Italy, Germany, Holland and the UK. Direct sales to dealers meant higher margins and brought Acer's management closer to the market.

Problems in the USA at this time were forcing most Taiwanese manufacturers to rethink distribution techniques: hence in 1991 Acer introduced the 'Acros' microcomputer range to be sold through mass distribution channels including computer supermarkets. 'Acros' rapidly accounted for almost half Acer America's sales, and was introduced in Germany to be sold via a big consumer electronics chain.

REASSESSING PROFIT POTENTIAL IN THE CHANGING COMPUTER INDUSTRY

By 1995, Stan Shih believed the personal computer was at the centre of the computer, communications and consumer electronics products mainstream, and the industry was much different to that of the 1980s, having become an open environment, an industry based on the use of standard components to create various types of systems. This Shih referred to as the 'disintegrated' mode, being the opposite of the vertical integration mode used by companies such as IBM or Digital Equipment Corporation in the early days. At that time, there were no accepted industry standards for components: under the disintegrated business mode, each standard component represented an industry segment. As a result, customers benefited from a much better performance-to-cost ratio, as open systems led to greater competition in the industry. Competition had also provided opportunities for new players to find a niche in the market. Systems were relying more and more on modular open standard components, and the industry becoming increasingly disintegrated.

In the new IT age, a change had also occurred in the infrastructure: rather than being defined by industry giants, the infrastructure was created by third parties including hardware, software and component suppliers, the media and end users. A further development was in the way businesses competed: technology and manufacturing leaders were now spread around the world, making technological competition increasingly global. With markets divided into segments along regional or national lines, a new environment of global cooperation and competition had emerged, with competitors forming alliances aimed at strengthening each other's business models. The large investment required to develop new products meant many companies could not survive without cooperating with rival manufacturers. As their overseas operations matured, many multinational corporations were becoming increasingly 'borderless' in way they operated their businesses.

STRATEGIC INNOVATION AT ACER: REWRITING THE RULES OF THE GAME

The smiling curve

According to Shih's philosophy, the key to success in the new age was providing value: by succeeding in value-added business segments, companies could do well in the disintegrated mode. To explain the trend, he created a chart he called his 'smiling curve' (see Exhibit CS13.2).

Value is added, Shih argues, in component production on the left side, and marketing/distribution on the right. The dotted line represents the traditional computer industry value-added curve. In the early days, companies such as Acer started from the centre, sourcing the components, assembling the system and then marketing the product. By the mid-1990s, there was no longer any value added in assembling computers, which could be done by anyone, and to succeed in the new IT age, it was necessary to gain a top position in component segments such as software, CPUs, DRAM, ASICs, etc. as a distribution leader in a country or region.

Since universal standards meant global competition, to succeed on the left side, a company needed technology and a strong manufacturing capability, and in some areas a lot of capital. On the distribution side, success required a good image, brand-name awareness, well-managed channels and effective logistics. For both sides, however, it was essential to be a leader of the segment, and Shih believed the chief factors for success in the disintegrated mode to be speed, cost, volume and value. Speed meant fast response to changes, and fast time to market with new products; cost comprised overhead management, inventory reduction and minimizing risks. Companies with access to strong R&D, engineering and manufacturing resources were best equipped to enter volume production quickly. Effective channels for distributing high value products were also necessary for building a strong brand-name image and generating more value. On the component side, Acer was in the top five worldwide for all the segments currently pursued, and in distribution was the leader in developing countries and targeting a top five position in the USA and top 10 in Europe.

The fast food business model

One of the keys to Shih's re-engineering of Acer was his concept of the 'fast food' model of computer supply, based on the example of the uniform quality with which McDonald's produces hamburgers worldwide: the approach being to assemble Acer products locally while still maintaining consistency. The assembly process was consequently spread to 35 sites around the world, while tight controls were prescribed to ensure workers everywhere followed the same testing procedures. Components were prepared in large mass manufacturing facilities, then shipped to assembly sites close to local customers. Retail buyers of Acer computers were guaranteed the 'freshest' ingredients – the latest technology – because Acer made them itself and sped them from Taiwan and Malaysia to its assembly sites: motherboards were flown in directly, while CPUs, hard drives and memory were purchased locally to fill individual user requirements (Exhibit CS13.3). This provided for economies of scale, plus the ability to tailor individual products to suit the needs of individual customers, the result being standardized quality, customizable products and lower inventory costs. 'We serve fresh PCs everywhere, not stale models'. Rather than marketing computers based on six-month-old ideas and specifications, the turnaround time from idea to market dropped to only one or two months. Acer was turning over its inventory more than seven times per year, making it one of the most efficient PC manufacturers selling through retail channels. The high turnover aided Acer in achieving a 34% return on equity, as against an industry average of 15–20%. Without this decentralization of operations, many analysts believed Acer could not have met the price-cutting challenge of industry leaders such as IBM and Compaq. By 1995, Compaq had realized the advantages of local production, and had opened a few offshore sites, but Shih was dismissive: 'Acer is the only company doing the fast food business right now'.

Case 13

Local touch, global brand: a network of joint ventures

The use of joint ventures to build international capability, conserve capital and help raise awareness of the Acer brand name was a further important element of Shih's strategy: the most successful joint ventures were with Texas Instruments on the TI-Acer semiconductor plant, and with MBB, a subsidiary of the German Daimler Benz group, on a hybrid electronics firm. In 1995, Acer also had joint ventures with partners in Thailand, Indonesia, India, Mexico, Brazil, Chile, Argentina and South Africa.

Shih regarded his 'local touch, global brand' philosophy – the formation of joint ventures with local partners and encouragement of local shareholder investment – as a 'key to corporate good citizenship'. Since competition on the distribution side was local, alliances with strong local partners were needed to achieve eventual leadership. Acer consequently formed alliances with local partners to leverage its competitive edge in components with its partners' leading position in local markets. The philosophy also served as a means to integrate global talent and capital reserves to compete with the big names for market share.

Local touch empowered the management team in each market to decide on product configurations, pricing strategies and promotional programmes that were right for its particular territory. These managers were mainly local to the area or country, with in most cases a single Taiwanese joining them to aid communications with headquarters in Taipei. Thus Shih's re-engineering of Acer sought to overcome its competitive weaknesses by rendering them irrelevant: 'Taiwan doesn't have enough people who are really skilled in foreign languages and familiar with foreign cultures to enable us to direct a global marketing effort from Taipei...I turned this weak point into a great strength, a core competence'. 'Local touch' meant more for Shih than just local assembly – through local management and shareholder majorities, Acer aimed to become a true local identity in markets around the world, while maintaining its world-class global identity.

Pioneering frontier markets: Acer in Mexico and South Africa

Another way in which Acer sought to rewrite the rules of the global game was to pioneer frontier, and often distant, markets early, rather than the more traditional pattern of expansion which emphasized starting either with large, established markets or successively expanding outward from home base. Acer's approach in Mexico and South Africa provide good examples of this strategy at work.

In 1996, one in three PCs sold in Mexico was an Acer, giving it a 32% market share, way ahead of that of competitors such as IBM, Compaq or Hewlett Packard, and Acer and its Mexican partner Computec Co. operated to establish a new venture to handle assembly, marketing and distribution for all Latin America. When Computec formed in 1989 to distribute Acer computers, it discovered a gap between the high priced PCs being sold to the corporate market by IBM and HP, and the low quality clones aimed at the private consumer, and zeroed in on the small business and home PC market. The joint venture, formed in 1992, invested heavily in marketing, and by 1993 when the price wars hit Mexico, the company had begun assembling its products in a suburb of Mexico City.

This gave Acer a crucial edge: local assembly enabled Acer to keep prices down and keep pace with rapidly developing technology – the local plant substituted components which became obsolete quickly, rather than waiting to import finished computers with up-to-date components. The Mexican management continually revised tactics (with considerable latitude from Taipei) to deal with problems such as the peso crisis of December 1994. Acer broke with the custom of quoting dollar prices and listed in pesos; while the computer market shrank by 40% it launched a new model, continued to buy TV time and targeted new customers, winning contracts to supply the state-owned power company and the main public university. 'We had great flexibility to make decisions and respond quickly to the market' to quote the company's general director. The next step was set to be the manufacture of components and sub-assemblies such as motherboards and monitors, probably on the US border, for the North American market.

Cooperation with local markets also paid off for Acer in South Africa, where many multinationals shied away from a potentially unstable market during the transition from apartheid to majority rule. Acer's manager/investors took the risk of moving forward in their coverage of the country, which in late 1995 consisted of five branches, 16 distributors and a network of 1,800 dealers, giving the brand tied second place in the market.

The client-server organization

The flexible 'client-server' business model – which sought to harness basic human motivation for mutual support while responding to the trend towards disintegration – stressed the need to achieve independence simultaneously with cooperation among Acer group members. Following its re-engineering, strategic business units (SBUs) were formed to take primary responsibility for R&D, manufacturing, product management and OEM sales, while regional business units (RBUs) took the lead on distribution, service and marketing. This new structure allowed for faster decision making based on changing conditions in each region, while independent ownership and responsibility provided added motivation and incentive. Yet the objective was not to recreate a 'multi-domestic' structure comprising largely independent, national businesses linked to headquarters primarily through a system of financial control (the model traditionally adopted by many European multinationals). Instead, drawing the analogy from a PC network, Acer sought for each business unit to act as both a 'client' and a 'server' within the global network (see Exhibits CS13.4 and CS13.5). Thus, in addition to acting as clients for the SBU's products, the RBUs also act as 'servers', providing local market intelligence and 'best practice' to SBUs and other RBUs. The quasi-independent SBUs meanwhile, also act as both clients and servers to each other through joint purchasing, design and manufacturing of common components and shared R&D.

BUILDING THE CULTURE OF AN ASIAN MULTINATIONAL

Leadership and vision

In any discussion of Acer's development, the force of character of Stan Shih as leader and motivator comes over as the tremendous driving power behind the company's success. Yet Shih, a modest man of humble origins, unlike many of the prosperous businessmen from Taiwan, did not inherit a successful business or a fortune to start one, nor did he have the political connections which facilitate such an enterprise. He always stressed his modest beginnings, but his dream was the creation of a Chinese multinational firm. In the words of Ronald Chwang, president of Acer America, 'Stan is one of the few leaders in the industry with a vision. He believes in the role he wants Acer to play. He sees opportunities ahead of others'.

Acer's dream in the 1970s was to popularize microprocessor technology in Taiwan, in the 1980s to move into the top 10 players in the world PC industry, in the 1990s to be in the 'top 5 in 1995, 21 in 21 and 2000 in 2000'. As a talented engineer, Shih always maintained his involvement with technical product development, but at the same time possessed the ability to steer his growing high tech company through some very turbulent years in the PC market. 'Technically he is very much in touch with the industry, even though he delegates a lot' (Chwang) and it was Shih's own attitudes which were largely the inspiration behind the tirelessness of his engineers, always willing to rise to the challenge of any new technology which might take the company to the front.

At the same time, Shih was deeply rooted in tradition, deriving inspiration from the ancient Chinese board game 'Go', or wei chi, in which players have to follow certain strategies and consider the long-term effects of every move. 'In Go, you always play from the corner, then the side, the main reason being that you need less resources to occupy the corner. As we don't have the kind of resources that Japanese or US companies have, Acer started its business in smaller markets. That gives us the advantage, because these smaller markets are becoming bigger and bigger, and the combination of many small markets is not small', said Shih. The 'Go' strategy was set to become ever more as growth in smaller emerging markets took off.

Shih won considerable acclaim over the years for his success with Acer, with many media and other citations and awards for his individual and corporate contributions to the computer industry and to world trade and commerce. These included being named an International CEO of the Year by Financial World magazine in 1995, the same year in which he received the Emerging Markets CEO of the Year, presented in Washington DC during a joint annual meeting of the International Monetary Fund and the World Bank, for being a CEO whose 'vision and company performance has best shown the pattern that can be offered as a model to other emerging markets companies around the world'.

Values and corporate culture

Up to the mid-1980s, Acer's management motivated employees with the theme of the 'Dragon Dream': Chinese children are repeatedly told of the country's former glory, and Shih's dream was to resurrect some of this greatness. (While successful and well received, it was later felt that perhaps too much patriotism was not a good thing for an aspiring multinational.) Shih introduced a flat hierarchy, with middle management involved in decision making, although this hierarchy was in fact still fairly rigid. The philosophy behind the culture was one of equality and frugality (with Shih himself setting the example). He believed 'human nature is essentially good' and the firm invested more than was usual on employee training, while exercising less control than normal over its workers. While wages were fairly modest, Acer did offer other benefits, including a potentially lucrative stock purchase plan.

Shih was not a typical all powerful Chinese chief executive: 'We don't believe in control in the normal sense. We feel there is another way to succeed. We rely on people, and build our business around them'. He always listened carefully to others' views, and did not object to his top executives having a high public profile. His employees called him by his English first name, and he professed to treat every employee as his boss, as they were his shareholders and thus all equal. (Employee ownership in the company in 1995 accounted for about 30%.)

Corporate slogans were considered by Shih an integral part of Acer's corporate identity system for their ability to convey a company's business philosophy. Acer began with the slogan 'The Microprocessor Gardeners', progressing to 'Bridge the Gap for a Better Tomorrow', 'Global Vision through Technology', 'Technology for Everyone', and then 'Fresh Technology Enjoyed by Everyone, Everywhere'.

Shih felt that in general Chinese companies were infused with too much family influence, and strongly disagreed with the traditional philosophy that businesses should be handed down to sons rather than capable managers. Acer offered opportunities for committed talent from anywhere, regardless of background. Talented people, he believed, would not necessarily be happy working for a foreign company without real participation – hence the Acer vision of a progressive global partnership, with local management and local shareholder majority. 'We are demonstrating a new way to run a business. It is not just new for Taiwan, it is new for the world. It is truly a 21st century approach'. People in the local operations of Acer companies could be proud to contribute to their society and be a local company, and there was a common goal to become part of a world-class IT company.

There is an old Chinese saying that it is better to be the head of the chicken than the tail of the ox – it is better to run your own shop than be an employee in a large enterprise (and better to be a leader in a small segment than an also ran in the mainstream.) Hence the plan to make a lot of Acer employees heads of chickens – Taiwanese people like to be their own boss, and have a strong entrepreneurial spirit. Acer had always pursued a decentralized management model, upon which the client-server structure was built, and a management philosophy stressing that fast decision making, direct communication and a reliable organization were the keys to success. At the heart of the client-server organization lay a closely linked team of mature and experienced managers committed to the success of their own 'piece of the Acer group' as well as to ensuring Acer's overall long-term growth. Acer's top managers were loyal and had worked together closely for a long time: through regular summits, strategies were continually outlined and new possibilities explored for contributing to overall group success.

Mutual understanding and trust, communication and consensus were the cornerstones of Acer's management strategy: thinking and dealing in a human way, cultivating an easy working environment, providing the right motivation, setting competitive but achievable goals. 'Acer's success depends on teamwork between managers with business sense. Corporate performance is based on people'.

LEVERAGING THE MULTINATIONAL NETWORK

In June 1995, Acer unveiled its new mission statement: 'Provide Fresh Technology to be Enjoyed by Everyone, Everywhere'. Fresh, for Shih, meant more than just 'new', which could carry connotations of unproven, expensive and risky – it meant the best high value, low risk, user friendly and affordable technology. Moreover, the 'fresh' concept applied not just to technology; fresh ideas were equally important for business strategy, and the key to survival in a rapidly changing industry. Shih foresaw a shift in focus, as consumer electronics and related markets became the target for Acer brand products, his policy being to rely on the core PC technologies that Acer had always specialized in, using them in products for the home that were 'digital, interactive and smart'.

Case 13

In September 1995, Acer launched the Aspire line of stylish multimedia home PCs. Acer America, working closely with the California design company Frog Design, created the revolutionary Aspire look and crafted the overall design concept, while Acer Inc's powerful PC product expertise developed the tooling and internal PC technology. Acer Peripherals Inc. added innovative monitor and keyboard technological assistance, and much of the creative work behind the global promotion campaign was supported by Acer operations in the USA, Singapore and South Africa – a good example of the group's combination of a deep resource base plus flexible strategic design and organizational structure. The sleek grey Aspire, a radical departure from the bland look of the PC for the last 15 years, was an immediate huge hit in the USA, the key selling point being the innovative award-winning design, which attracted rave reviews and caused the then troubled Acer America's sales to nearly double in the fourth quarter of 1995. Having previously had an uninspiring image in the USA and with nothing to lose, Acer was able to take a gamble on something radical which the market leaders were perhaps too risk-averse and complacent to attempt.

At the same time, Acer was also designing a computer aimed at markets in the developing world, the Acer Basic, a 'monitorless' budget computer 'for the masses' to be launched in summer 1996, on which construction costs were slashed by the use of a 100 megabyte 'zip' drive instead of an expensive hard disk, and by incorporating less expensive chips and software. In 1996, Acer also planned the launch of the AcerKids and AcerEden computers aimed at families with children, 'monitorless' boxes able to play a host of IBM compatible games and education programmes on audio and video disks. From these, Shih hoped to spawn a host of future information appliances to carry Acer higher up the industry's ranks. By the turn of the century, he hoped to see Acer offering everything from Internet services and software to manufacturing cellular telephones, wide-screen TVs and digital video disc players as well as PCs and microchips, a leader in a new market of intelligent consumer products.

Some saw this as ambitious: shipment growth in the USA cooled from 75% in the fourth quarter of 1995 to 25% in the first quarter of 1996, despite cutting the price of the Aspire in the autumn, and earnings from its chief profit maker, chips, had fallen. Shih admitted the company would fall short of its forecast of US$217 million net profit due to the fall in memory chip prices. Acer planned to boost its name recognition with a new ad campaign – despite the Aspire's success, Acer was still outflanked in brand awareness in the West by the industry giants such as Sony, Compaq, IBM and NEC – to expand its distribution by the end of 1997 from mass market chains to office supply and computer stores, and to renew its assault on the corporate market. At the same time, Acer was continuing its push into markets everywhere – number one in Asia, Africa and the Middle East, number two in Latin America, number three in India. In Russia, Acer was delivering computers from a new plant in Finland, 20 km from the border, in five days (instead of five weeks) with sales rising from $3.4 million to $42 million in 1995. Thanks to intensive advertising, Acer had higher name recognition in Russia than Compaq or Toshiba.

While US companies were turning increasingly to Taiwan's cheap, highly skilled labour, Acer was already moving to even lower cost manufacturing bases, opening plants in the Philippines and Malaysia, and with plans eventually to move into China. In March 1996, an IDC report released in Boston predicted that by the year 2000, the top three players in the PC market would be Hewlett Packard, Compaq and Acer.

However, there was also the possibility that Acer might confuse consumers with too wide a range of products, that the new products required high investment but had low margins, and might not sell. Moreover, a simple design like the AcerBasic was easily copied, and Acer might itself end up competing with low cost imitators. But Shih believed that by steadily building a low cost manufacturing base and accumulating skill in all digital technologies, Acer always retained the option, if necessary, of returning to being a behind the scenes supplier of components and systems sold by the big brand names. (At this time, half the PCs Acer manufactured were still under OEM agreements for other brand names, and a good deal of its global clout had been gained through strong OEM relationships with the big US and Japanese manufacturers.) One way or another, he was determined to be a major player in the digital age.

LOOKING TO THE FUTURE

'21 in 21'

The initial public offering in August 1995 of Acer Computer International (ACI), the regional business unit responsible for marketing and services in the Asia Pacific, Africa, the Commonwealth of Independent States and the Middle East, and 75% owned by Acer Inc., met with overwhelming response and was 19 times subscribed at its close, with the 9.43 million shares available for public subscription and the 3.17 million reserved for ACI management, employees and associates all snapped up, confounding the popular belief that US dollar offerings on the Singapore stock market tended to elicit a lukewarm response. In September, Acer announced that Acer Peripherals had applied to the Taiwan stock exchange to offer 32.3 million shares, intending to launch its IPO in March the following year, and Acer Sertek successfully followed suit in late 1996.

Shih's plan to break Acer into 21 public companies listed around the world would open investment in the company to foreigners, as Taiwan enforced strict protectionist barriers against outside capital, with no foreign institution permitted to own more than 7.5% of a listed company in Taiwan. Under his grand design, Acer's Latin American marketing company went public in Mexico in late 1996, and Acer America and TI Acer were to be floated within two years. These being core subsidiaries, Acer kept a 40% stake, but in less crucial subsidiaries, Acer's ownership might be as little as 19%. 'Eventually Acer will have a majority of local ownership in each country, and no one will be able to say that we are a Taiwanese company'. Ultimately the spin-offs would halve Shih's own stake in the group to about 5%.

Shih stood to gain new sources of financing and new opportunities to motivate managers with stock ownership: without majority control, however, some questioned whether he could maintain his hold over the group. 'Some people talk about control with 51% ownership. But I control through an intangible approach, common interest'. Naturally independent units would face investor pressure to protect their own interests: 'To meet their requirements, we will have to provide value added'. It was unheard of for the founder of a Taiwanese company to relinquish so much control, as he acknowledged: 'US and Japanese companies would never do this. To them, risk is losing control. My answer is that I am willing to lose control, but make money'. Once Acer was broken up, however, the group would no longer be able to use profits from units such TI-Acer and Peripherals – which together accounted for 60% of the group's 1995 earnings – to subsidise losses overseas, which might affect the marketability of the companies.

Case 13

New frontiers

Shih believed that Acer's strong foundation making PCs put it in an excellent position for capitalizing on the anticipated convergence of the computer and consumer electronics markets in the late 1990s. 'We believe the industry is on the verge of a transition to new usage platforms'. By the turn of the century, he wanted 15% of Acer's revenues to come from a line of 'information appliances'. Acer planned the launch of a wide-screen TV able to double as a computer monitor, with DVD players, high speed CD-ROM drives, set-top boxes for cable and satellite TV and a combined fax, scanner and colour printer to follow the next year. Acer Peripherals was to begin work on a plant to make plasma displays for flat screen monitors and TVs, and Acer was investing heavily in telecommunications to develop wireless and integrated services digital network (ISDN) modems and video phones.

Reflecting on these developments and their future implications, Shih noted: 'Revenues may be limited in the warm up stage, but the potential lies in the future. Even so, our resources will not be defocused by these efforts, as we will commit even more to the server, notebook and many other software and peripherals technologies. We believe these are long-term investments today for securing our position in emerging markets'. With the boost from these products, Acer expected to reach $10 billion in sales by 1999, and to become a 'household brand name' around the globe. 'Because we are from Taiwan, people do not appreciate our strengths yet. But we have patience. We have a very long-term plan: affordable fresh technology to be enjoyed by everyone, everywhere. That is our mission statement'. Shih reiterated.

Exhibit CS13.1   Acer group's performance

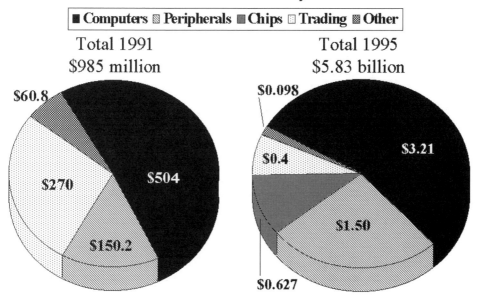

Where Acer makes its money

■ Computers ▨ Peripherals ▨ Chips ▨ Trading ▨ Other

Total 1991
$985 million

$60.8

$270

$504

$150.2

Total 1995
$5.83 billion

$0.098

$3.21

$0.4

$1.50

$0.627

Case 13

Exhibit CS13.2 The 'smiling curve'

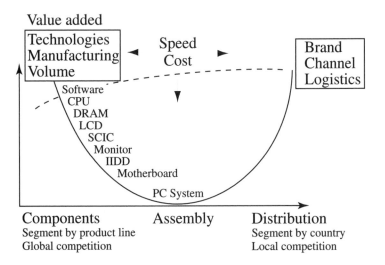

Notes to the smiling curve
- The dotted line indicates the growth path of traditional IT industries
- Computer system manufacturers used to provide nearly all 'value added'
- In the new IT age, there is no 'value added' in assembling a computer – anyone can make a PC today out of standard off-the-shelf components
- 'Value added' is manufacturing key components and marketing brand-name products

Exhibit CS13.3   The 'fast food' model

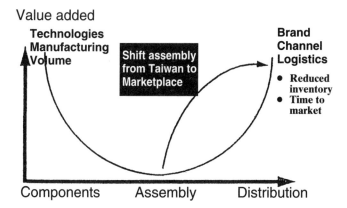

Key words in the new IT age
- Speed: time to market; time to volume; time to phase out; inventory turnover times; no idle time
- Cost: low overhead; low material cost; low manufacturing cost; high productivity; no idle assets
- Volume: economics of scale; purchasing power; marketing efficiency
- Value: new technology; lower prices; better quality; easy to purchase/use/get support

Exhibit CS13.4   Client-server relationships

Interaction in Acer's Client-Server Organisation

	RBU	SBU
RBU	Share market intelligence and marketing "best practice"	Traditional interaction: SBU provides product to RBU
SBU	Communicate market needs to SBU (sensing)	Joint purchasing, development and manufacturing of common components; shared R&D

Client (left axis) / *Server* (bottom axis), RBU and SBU columns

Case 13

285

Exhibit CS13.5   The client-server organization

Acer Regional Business Units (RBUs)

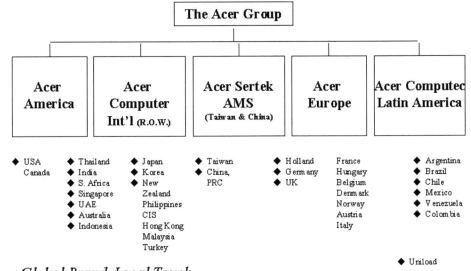

The Acer Group				
Acer America	Acer Computer Int'l (R.O.W.)	Acer Sertek AMS (Taiwan & China)	Acer Europe	Acer Computec Latin America

Acer America
- USA
- Canada

Acer Computer Int'l (R.O.W.)
- Thailand
- India
- S. Africa
- Singapore
- UAE
- Australia
- Indonesia

- Japan
- Korea
- New Zealand
- Philippines
- CIS
- Hong Kong
- Malaysia
- Turkey

Acer Sertek AMS
- Taiwan
- China, PRC

Acer Europe
- Holland
- Germany
- UK

- France
- Hungary
- Belgium
- Denmark
- Norway
- Austria
- Italy

Acer Computec Latin America
- Argentina
- Brazil
- Chile
- Mexico
- Venezuela
- Colombia

- Uniload

Global Brand, Local Touch

Acer Strategic Business Units (SBUs)

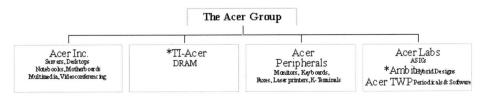

The Acer Group			
Acer Inc. Servers, Desktops Notebooks, Motherboards Multimedia, Videoconferencing	*TI-Acer DRAM	Acer Peripherals Monitors, Keyboards, Faxes, Laser printers, K-Terminals	Acer Labs ASICs *Ambit Hybrid Designs Acer TWP Periodicals & Software

* Joint Venture

Global Brand, Local Touch

Case 14

This case was prepared by Professor Peter J. Williamson and Qionghua Hu as a basis for class discussion rather than to illustrate either effective or ineffective handling of an administrative situation. © 1992 P.J. Williamson.

The Beijing Matsushita Color CRT Co. Ltd

The president of Beijing Matsushita Color CRT Co. (BMCC) had just returned from addressing the regular Monday morning meeting of staff (numbering over 1,500) in the main square which formed the centre of BMCC's plant complex. His message was by now a familiar one:

> BMCC is like a boat in the ocean. Never feel complacent because it is big and sailing well. It can sink at any time because of just a small hole. Small mistakes in day to day operations are like small holes.

He pondered on where the small holes might be opening up. BMCC had grown quickly to become a large ship. But was it appropriately designed and constructed to withstand the competitive and political storms ahead?

THE COLOUR TV BUSINESS IN CHINA: GROWTH AND COMPETITION

In the early 1980s Philips of Eindhoven, with the support of the Chinese government, sent a team of experts to investigate the potential market for colour TV sets in China. After visiting several major cities and provinces, this group reached the conclusion that the product would long remain out of reach of the mass-market consumer. At the time, the cost of even a modest colour TV set was equivalent to more than one year's total earnings for an average Chinese worker.

Sanyo of Japan took a different view. They reasoned that even if income was low, expenditure was also low. There were few outlets for consumer spending and many Chinese had a tradition of thrift. There was also a deep-seated tradition of family-based leisure life and a shortage of suitable leisure activities. Sanyo's local managers reported that people would postpone their marriage until they could afford to equip a new home with a colour TV set. The Sanyo investigators also observed that people would travel right across China to the southern provinces to buy sets smuggled in from Taiwan or Hong Kong.

Sanyo had been a pioneer in China, entering with a representative office, followed by a number of small ventures in the early 1970s. In the late 1970s Sanyo's audio division had established a subsidiary to market and later to assemble radios and simple tape recorders in China. In the early

287

1980s Sanyo established colour TV assembly line in China, exporting used equipment from Japan into a wholly owned subsidiary in China. It was based entirely on kits supplied from Japan. After 1985 when Sanyo established Sanyo Semiconductor Shekou Co. Ltd, a limited proportion of parts, specifically transistors, were supplied from this sister plant located adjacent to the colour TV set assembly operation. The vast bulk of components, however, continued to come from Japan. Demand for the finished TV sets was strong and the company saw little need for heavy expenditure on advertising and brand promotion.

Hitachi also entered in the early 1980s. It constructed a large assembly plant for colour TVs. Unlike Sanyo, however, it chose to form a joint venture with a state enterprise, creating the Fujian Hitachi Television Company. Hitachi believed that, despite some additional management complexity, a joint venture would help to secure continued access to local services such as power and water and help to maintain the flow of imported components at times of shortage of foreign exchange or import authorizations. Hitachi also believed that, while it did not need to spend heavily on marketing and advertising to sell its product in the short term, it should make this investment from the beginning. It saw a unique, never-to-be-repeated opportunity to establish its brand by heavy advertising and promotion at a time when it could obtain a very high 'share of voice' in a market starved of appealing, professionally presented marketing messages.

Between 1984 and 1986 the Chinese market for colour TV sets entered a period of explosive growth. Finished sets imported from Japan flooded in. Towards the end of this period, however, competition intensified. At the same time the government, having become alarmed at the drain on foreign exchange created by the huge volume of imported TV sets coming into China, imposed tough restrictions on imports. As a result, more and more local plants for assembling colour TV sets were established. By 1990 there were over 100 colour TV assembly plants in China and the government began to refuse applications for the establishment of additional enterprises devoted to this activity.

BMCC: COMPANY BACKGROUND

Beijing Matsushita Colour CRT Co., Ltd (BMCC) was established in the north-east outskirts of Beijing on 8 September 1987 with registered capital of RMB500 million – approximately US$95 million at official exchange rates. The Chinese investors were Beijing Electronics Tube Factory; China National Electronics Import & Export Corp., Beijing Branch; The Industrial & Commercial Bank of China, Beijing Branch and Beijing CRT Factory. The Japanese partners were Matsushita Electric Industrial Co. and its sister company Matsushita Electronics Corporation. The Chinese partners together held 50% of the total equity and Matsushita the remaining 50%. Although the Beijing organizations borrowed to make their investment, these debts remained on the balance sheets of the partner organizations so that BMCC did not directly take on any debt.

The joint venture began production with one line on 1 July 1989 after 22 months of construction work. This first line still produces 21" flat-square (FS) picture tubes for colour TV sets. A second production line was brought into operation in May 1990 producing 14" tubes and 19" FS tubes. The total capacity reached 1.8 million units per annum by November 1990, requiring a staff of 1,450.

BMCC was one of the four new CRT projects in China. But it was by far the largest, figuring as a key construction project in the government's Five-Year Plan. In fact, at the time, BMCC represented the largest cash investment into a Sino-Japanese joint venture. In contrast to many other ventures in China at the time, BMCC did not rely on conversions of existing (often obsolete) plant and machinery. The construction engineering was monitored by the mayor of Beijing who was responsible in the municipal government for the establishment of BMCC.

BMCC's CRTs have since reached the international quality level obtaining certification against all four major, international safety standards (UL of USA, BSI of UK, VDE of Germany and CSA of Canada).

ORGANIZATIONAL STRUCTURE

The chairman of the board of directors of BMCC was a former deputy mayor of Beijing and now advisor for the Beijing People's Government. The vice-chairman of the board is the president of Matsushita Electronic Industrial Co. Each of the four Chinese investors appoints one director. This board meets once a year to discuss critical issues such as the expansion of lines and introduction of new products, distribution of profits, process of local content and the changes of senior personnel.

Both the president of BMCC (a Matsushita appointee) and vice-president are also board members. The vice-president was the former director of the Beijing Electronics Factory and then the chairman of the Electronics Industry Office of the Beijing Government and widely recognized in China as an expert in the electronics industry.

The Japanese hold the directorships of five out of seven departments below the main board. These include manufacturing, engineering, planning and finance, equipment and power, materials and supply. Chinese directors head the personnel and general affairs department and the marketing department. In those departments headed by Japanese, a Chinese deputy takes the primary responsibility for external relationships and training of Chinese managers. The manufacturing department accounts for 80% of the total staff.

Formal meetings of these department heads are held once or twice per month, chaired by the president who is considered directly responsible for the entire operation. In the meetings each department presents its proposals for the operations both in Chinese and Japanese and circulates information on production and personnel changes. Then they discuss future plans and initiatives.

Below the departments the structure includes sections (25), divisions (55) and shifts (67). Managers below the department level do not have deputies and white-collar employment is kept to a minimum through multitasking. BMCC uses temporary staff to provide services and logistics, including cleaners, cooks, and some drivers and manual workers.

Specific targets are set for volume and quality. These form a detailed plan prepared by the planning and finance department which states exactly what every individual section and division is expected to achieve.

MANAGERIAL STYLE

The Matsushita management style is very much in evidence. Every employee carries a handbook which outlines the specific procedures to be followed for his or her job. It begins with 10 broad principles that are continually reinforced through training:

1. Making contribution to the nation by developing industry;

2. Seeking truth from facts;

3. Developing through reform;

4. Cooperating in a friendly way;

5. Depending upon fairness and honour;

6. Working with unity and solidarity;

7. Working hard and aiming high;

8. Showing courtesy and modesty;

9. Abiding by laws and regulations;

10. Serving and devoting to society.

The layout of the offices plays an important role in reinforcing culture and control. The seven departments share two large, open-plan offices. Manufacturing and engineering are in one and the remaining departments in the other. In such office rooms shirking is easy to detect and communication convenient. More importantly, this structure gives people a sense of unity, working together for the same objectives. In Japanese style, the managers are located at the back of the room overseeing their staff.

TRAINING AND EMPLOYEE INVOLVEMENT

Every staff member undergoes extensive and detailed training. In early 1988, BMCC sent 250 staff to Japan for six months' study and on-the-job training. The majority of these workers were transferees from the Chinese partners' existing operations. Back in China the BMCC culture is continually reinforced. There is a morning meeting of each unit every day. Each Monday the entire staff meets in the square around which the plant is constructed. At the daily meetings, staff recite the objectives and principles. Monday meetings include ceremonies such as raising national and company flags and singing the national anthem and company song. Senior managers in turn greet the staff every Monday morning at the entrance of the factory, and then preside over the Monday meeting and hold briefings on the production levels and company performance.

Every month there is also a so-called 'sincere talk meeting'. During this time people exchange opinions and raise concerns with fellow workers and managers that would normally remain below the surface.

From the base of 'core' workforce trained in Japan, BMCC began to grow its labour force by recruiting in the open market. Its new recruits begin with three months' on-the-job training. The programme is extensive. It includes language, morality, general knowledge and physical fitness. This emphasis on employee development is captured in another BMCC slogan:

> Every good quality CRT justifies the hard work of every staff and worker of the company. And we make high quality personnel before we make products.

In practice, the BMCC president asks his managers to devote half of their energy to building a high quality staff team.

THE COMPENSATION SYSTEM

Many state enterprises operate employee incentive or piecework systems with the aim of improving motivation and enhancing productivity. BMCC does not do so: it requires its staff to be 'nuts and bolts on the big BMCC machine'.

Instead of piecework, BMCC has designed a unique wage system. The basic wage is the largest part, topped up with a 'bonus' and access to company welfare provision. Each employee receives a basic wage made up of three components:

1. Age allowance accounts for 20% and increases at a higher rate for the 25–36 age group, eventually reaching a ceiling for those 50 and over.

2. A wage award specific to each 'post' accounts for 40% and is decided by the nature of the job. This increases through examinations and promotions.

3. The 'contribution' component accounts for 40% depending on one's education and experience and increases based on merit.

4. A bonus is awarded twice a year and is decided by the board.

The wages to individuals are confidential and credited directly to their accounts by the personnel department through the 'Great Wall' credit card system.

The pay is about 50% higher than state enterprises, but the jobs are much more demanding. The average productivity per employee in BMCC is about 20–30 times more than that in the state enterprises. It also ranks at the top of the range among foreign joint-venture companies.

Even with this formidable wage system, however, BMCC has found that wages alone are insufficient to attract and retain high productivity staff. So BMCC also provides other services to its staff. For example the company has built two residential buildings for its workers and provides some leisure entertainment facilities. BMCC also has a sophisticated health insurance system and is planning a pension scheme – despite the fact that most of its staff are very young. Pension is usually a major concern for Chinese employees to work in joint-venture companies: the state's responsibility to provide for these workers, in effect, lapses when they choose employment with a joint venture or foreign company. Yet, many wholly owned foreign subsidiaries do not provide such schemes, leaving workers feeling insecure about their retirement.

But above all else, the most important factor is the company's first-rate reputation and the fact that workers perceive that BMCC 'has a bright future'.

There are seven Japanese in BMCC and all paid by the company. Their salaries are higher than those for equivalent responsibilities in Japan. BMCC also provides its expatriates with accommodation as part of their compensation package.

THE ASSESSMENT SYSTEM

Workers are employed on the contract basis, usually three years with six months' probation. The contract can be extended indefinitely if the worker continues to perform well. But it can also be terminated anytime if the employee violates the regulations.

Case 14

The assessment of the performance of the employees is carried out twice a year. Every staff member is classified to one of five levels: AA (Super-excellent), A (Excellent), B (Normal), C (Need some effort) and D (Definitely need effort). The five levels must adhere to a 'normal' distribution ('forced curve grading'). For operators, the assessment criteria include: technical knowledge, skills and productivity; discipline; unity and sense of cooperation; and effort. For managers, assessment is based on the following criteria: technical knowledge and quality of planning; leadership; coordination and cooperation; and success in educating subordinates. The results of the assessments are not published but passed onto the individuals by their immediate superiors at a confidential feedback session.

PRODUCTION AND QUALITY

Both production lines have round-the-clock operations of three shifts. Both began with a single shift and reached full operations at the end of 1990.

The operations management department comprises a cluster of four sections: quantitative management, quality management, 'major problem management' and materials management. Four technical manuals dominate life in this part of the company: product specifications, production technology instructions, quality standards and operational regulations. Each manual was introduced directly from Matsushita. Together they form a complete system of operations and management standards.

Day-to-day quality management is primarily the responsibility of line workers. The concept of quality control at BMCC is simple, yet powerful: 'quality' says the company 'does not come through checking finished products'. Instead it results from the rigorous contribution of every individual. On the production lines that means substandard parts must not be passed on to the next section. 'Every employee needs to treat the next stage in the production process as a customer'. These internal 'customers' will not accept substandard goods from a previous stage.

Employees also know that, contrary to common Chinese practice, BMCC does not dispose of substandard products by discounting them in the market. A reject is just that. It continually reminds staff that a substandard product represents a 100% defect rate to the individual customer who receives it, even though it may be only one out of 10,000 for BMCC.

Quality management includes four stages: checking of materials and parts on delivery to the factory, production process management, final inspection prior to shipment and after sales service. BMCC constantly sends technicians to the users of their products – the TV assembly factories. These technicians help BMCC's customers solve their assembly line and product design problems and collect information on product performance.

PROCUREMENT

Following the wave of colour TV assembly lines installed using new and used equipment from Japan, parts supply continues to present a major problem for all of those involved in the industry. Most of the components and sub-assemblies necessary to feed these lines still have to be imported. The rising cost of imports and a lack of hard currency have threatened the survival of many assembly operations. In recent years industry observers have noted that joint ventures seem to have clear advantages over wholly owned 'screwdriver' subsidiaries in obtaining supplies.

As China's major supplier of a critical sub-assembly – the picture tube – BMCC occupies a pivotal role in the industry. While it must also rely on a proportion of imported components it is also the single most important local supplier to 40 of the 100 or so colour TV assembly plants now in China. In 1989 and 1990 BMCC drew most of its parts and raw materials from Japan through Matsushita. But in 1991 BMCC set itself three targets:

1. To enhance the overall quality of the products and services and therefore competitiveness of the company.

2. To develop local sources for a 'substantial proportion' of its inputs.

3. To start the installation of two new lines.

A substantial increase in local content is by no means an easy target to reach. Local suppliers' existing quality usually falls well short of BMCC standards. Current designs are often a poor match with BMCC's requirements. However, the Japanese president is a very active promoter for the supply of local content. He emphasizes the importance of this goal to his staff 'again and again' and has made it a central feature of the company's long-term plan. Local content, he believes, will not only improve BMCC's currency balance, but also assist the development of local industry. The president's stance on this issue has played a key role in the process of building a climate of trust between Matsushita, its Chinese partners and other Chinese authorities.

MARKET STRATEGY AND PERFORMANCE

Most of the BMCC's CRTs are sold domestically to assemblers of colour TV sets. BMCC was the first to manufacture FS (flat-square) CRTs. Its strategy was to sell these FS CRTs at the same prices as ordinary CRTs of similar quality. Since assemblers can sell their TV sets at higher prices if they are equipped with FS CRTs, this policy rapidly established BMCC in the market. By 1990 demand exceeded BMCC's capacity with sales revenue of RMB650 million (US$124 million). In 1991 sales exceeded one billion RMB.

The company showed profit in the first year of the production, reaching RMB190 million (US$36 million) by 1990, placing it in China's 'top 500' ranking of enterprises for sales and profits.

These results were based on production lines embodying mid-1980s' vintage technology. Matsushita has now decided to introduce the next generation of technology for a 29'' FS CRT which will take its production to four lines. This additional investment will take the total funds invested in BMCC to RMB1.9 billion (US$360 million) but this will be financed from the retained earnings of BMCC. Each of these new lines will add to the sales of RMB500–600 million.

BMCC currently restricts its sales to 40 of a potential customer base of over 100 colour TV assemblers in China. In part, this reflects BMCC's desire to keep the problem of providing service to its customers within manageable bounds.

The 14'' CRTs are bought by Matsushita and resold in eastern Europe. Margins on this export business are razor thin. Rather than direct profitability, the main role of these exports is to help maintain the company's hard currency balance. The plan is to maintain exports at between 20 and 30% of the total production.

LOOKING TO THE FUTURE

The Chinese Premier Li Pen made two visits to BMCC. As is the custom of Chinese leaders, he left the company an inscription. It asked BMCC:

> To become an internationally first class enterprise and a model for Sino-foreign joint ventures.

BMCC had developed a successful operation quickly and was now earning good profits. The senior management wondered, however, how well it had positioned itself for future development. Should it, for example, have forward integrated into the supply of finished TV sets? What role should distribution, service and marketing play in its future? How should it go about developing reliable, quality local suppliers? And, in an increasingly competitive environment, would its major customers themselves begin to integrate backwards? Where might small holes start appearing, holes that could cause the good ship BMCC to take in water – first a trickle, but potentially a flood?

Case 15

This case was written by Elizabeth Withell, Research Analyst, under the supervision of Professor Hellmut Schütte, Affiliate Professor of International Management at INSEAD. It is intended to be used as a basis for class discussion rather than to illustrate either effective or ineffective handling of an administrative situation. Copyright © 1997 INSEAD-EAC, Fontainebleau, France.

Daewoo's French Affair

In 1996 Daewoo Corporation was South Korea's fourth largest conglomerate, or *chaebol*. Its founder, Kim Woo-Choong, had overseen its growth from a small clothing exporting company in 1967 to a group of 22 companies in 1995 with sales of US$51.4 billion, 125,000 employees and a presence in 130 countries. Kim took up residence in Vienna in December 1995 in order to concentrate on Daewoo's worldwide auto strategy in the wake of several acquisitions of automobile factories in eastern Europe. Yoon Young-Suk, a colleague with whom Kim had attended high school, was promoted at the same time to share Kim's post as Daewoo chairman. Yoon's task was to carry on with internal campaigns to improve management and product quality within the group, and to steer the Daewoo companies through a highly ambitious phase of overseas expansion, in which total group sales were expected to reach the giddy heights of US$186 billion by the year 2000. Kim would continue to concentrate on external affairs.

Part 1 of this case provides a brief introduction to the Daewoo Group, while Part 2 details the bid which its subsidiary, Daewoo Electronics, made for the French state-owned company Thomson Multimédia in 1996.

PART 1: THE DAEWOO GROUP

Chairman Kim

Described as a workaholic, an authoritarian and impatient boss, a super-salesman, an indefatigable traveller, and a wizard of industrial enterprises, Kim Woo-Choong was part of the South Korean generation that grew up under Japanese rule and learnt first-hand about war and economic deprivation. Born in 1936, Kim passed the highly competitive entrance exam at the elite Kyunggi High School in Seoul after the Korean War had ended and later studied economics at Yonsei University. While a student, he made many friends who later became vital business contacts.

After serving for a year on South Korea's Economic Development Council, a government organization, Kim joined a trading firm, Hansung Industrial Company. At the age of 26, he started

Case 15

South Korea's first significant textile export business for Hansung. In 1967 he resigned from Hansung and started a joint venture with a friend from Daetoe Textile Company. They named their company Daewoo, taking the 'Dae' from Daetoe Textile and the 'Woo' from Kim's name; in Korean, Daewoo literally means 'great universe'.

Although Daewoo quickly became an extremely successful conglomerate, Kim eschewed the common Korean practice of using his *chaebol* to build a super-rich family dynasty, believing this to be unacceptable in a nation where annual per capita income was still low. He believed in the virtue of hard work and felt that he had a mission to help establish a viable industrial base for South Korea which would lead his country into the twenty-first century. Proud of his heritage, he was committed to patriotism and Confucianism. His dream was to: 'show people around the world that South Korea can produce the highest quality products at the lowest price'. He travelled 200 days in the year and had taken only half a day's holiday in his life to attend his daughter's wedding.

Despite corporate financial setbacks and government bail-outs, Kim was considered one of the most popular and successful businessmen in South Korea and was practically a cult figure at Daewoo. In 1989 he published a best-selling book in South Korea, *It's a Big World and There's a Lot to Do* (later published in the USA as *Every Street is Paved with Gold*), which he addressed to South Korea's young people, who were growing increasingly anti-business. In it, he again stressed the spirit of sacrifice and hard work: 'There is no limit to perfection'. At one stage, he apparently considered standing against current South Korean president, Kim Young-Sam, in the 1992 elections.

Kim was an extraordinary leader, whose authority was not often challenged by those around him. Despite having the usual boards of directors and hierarchies that you would expect to find in a diversified conglomerate, Daewoo's command structure was, in practice, rather simple. 'I make the decisions', said Kim. As Jerzy Wozniak, president of the Solidarity labour union at Daewoo's car assembly plant in Warsaw commented: 'Kim has the sort of charisma that makes you want to follow him, even with a sabre against tanks'. It was generally considered that the Daewoo Group would be in chaos if anything happened to Kim. He had not appointed relatives to succeed him, as had the founders of the Hyundai and Samsung groups.

By 1996 Kim had received a great many awards and honorary degrees in a wide range of countries, and frequently represented South Korea on international committees (see Exhibit CS15.1).

The building of an industrial giant, 1967–92

Daewoo, like the other major *chaebol*, was the offspring of South Korea's forced industrialization. In the 1960s the South Korean government identified talented, export-oriented entrepreneurs such as Kim Woo-Choong and systematically sponsored them by granting them preferential credit, import licenses, tax advantages and domestic protection. The *chaebol* had privileged access to resources including talented managerial staff from the best South Korean universities and a low-cost, disciplined, and hard-working labour force. The *chaebol* were quickly able to generate cash flow from labour-intensive manufacturing, which, amplified by highly leveraged financing, was reinvested in the equipment needed to create significant economies of scale.

In the mid 1970s, under pressure from the South Korean government, Daewoo began acquiring troubled companies, establishing a formula for expansion which has persisted to the present day. Kim quickly became known for his ability to successfully turn around failing enterprises. The group's four largest companies were formed in this way: Daewoo Heavy Industries in 1976, Daewoo Shipbuilding and Heavy Machinery and Daewoo Motor in 1978, and Daewoo Electronics in 1983. A more detailed history of the group's development is provided in Exhibit CS15.2.

The overseas push

Daewoo's first foreign investment was a joint-venture tyre plant in the Sudan in the 1970s. Daewoo later entered into numerous construction projects in places such as Iran, Libya and Nigeria; Kim was attracted 'to work in the jungles and deserts because of the possibilities of high profits. If we're successful half the time, we make money'. He chose places shunned by most Japanese and Western rivals.

In its early days, Daewoo's job was simply to produce, while its foreign partners would look after market research, after-sales service, financing and technology. For Kim, however, surrogate manufacturing was only a step towards something bigger and better: developing new products and boosting Daewoo's own brand name.

Kim travelled to North Korea in 1992 as the first businessman from the South to receive an official invitation. There he made a commitment to invest US$10–20 million in nine light industry factories. Kim saw an important historical mission in his commitment, saying that: 'I am going to develop the final market in the world'. Although delayed by the North Korean nuclear issue, by March 1996 Daewoo had finally secured both South and North Korean government approval for Daewoo Corporation Trading Division to establish the first factory in the port city of Nampo.

In 1993 Daewoo took a major step towards the fulfilment of Kim's dreams by launching VISION 2000, a campaign designed to guide member companies towards becoming global industry leaders in the next century. The theme for the campaign was 'Daewoo Globalization Through Daewoo Technology'. The programme included various numerical targets for the year 2000. For example the total number of overseas trade, production and sales subsidiaries was due to reach 660, covering 150 countries. The group's total sales, which amounted to $42.5 billion in 1994 and $51.4 billion in 1995, were due to reach $72 billion in 1996 and $186 billion in the year 2000.

As part of the campaign, the group designated three strategic business areas: telecommunications, motor vehicles and electronics. Daewoo was to capture 10% of the world market in each area with a 'top product family' by the year 2000. These products, including automobiles, commercial vehicles, televisions, washing machines and refrigerators, were to account for over 30% of total group sales by the turn of the century. In parallel, technology development would focus on automobiles, six major electronic products, diesel engines, satellites, very large double-hull crude carriers and high-speed ferries, among others. The globalization plan would ideally involve: a greater ratio of goods produced overseas; non-Korean executives on the fast track to top management; multinational board members overseeing operations; decentralized decision making; flexibility in research and development programmes; successful management of multiple identities and loyalties; and a global, rather than national, image.

The group companies' roles in 'Vision 2000'

Trading and construction

Daewoo Corporation, the lead company and trading/construction arm of the Daewoo group, held its first-ever company-wide managerial strategy meeting in January 1996 in the manner of an investor relations conference. At this conference, Daewoo Corporation announced plans to concentrate efforts in the three major areas of trading, distribution and multimedia. The Trading Division's executives outlined plans to accomplish new targets of $74 billion in total sales by the year 2000. Strategic markets included the CIS, Eastern Europe, China, India and Myanmar (for example plans were announced in March 1996 to establish a chain of at least 15 'Daewoo Mart' small department stores throughout Myanmar.) At the beginning of 1996 Daewoo Corporation took over Daewoo Electronics' multimedia business and promptly announced plans to achieve annual sales in the industry of $1.3 billion by the year 2000 and to be one of the world's top 10 multimedia groups by the year 2015.

Daewoo Corporation's Construction Division had plans for 1996 that included a 30% increase in new orders. Examples of the types of projects it was involved in include the construction of a $192 million dam in Laos to be operative by late 1998 and a railroad in Australia linking Alice Springs with Darwin.

Shipbuilding and heavy industries

In 1994, Daewoo Shipbuilding and Heavy Machinery merged with Daewoo Heavy Industries to form South Korea's largest integrated manufacturer of heavy machinery and equipment, ships, mini vehicles and commercial vehicles. The merged company accounted for 31% – the largest single portion – of the Daewoo Group's profits in 1995, and planned 28% growth in total sales to $6.4 billion in 1996. By 2001 Daewoo Heavy intended to be one of the world's top five manufacturers in the areas of excavators, lift trucks, rolling stocks, machine tools and engines. At the end of 1996 its global coverage was limited to three overseas facilities: it had an excavator plant in Belgium, a construction equipment plant in Shandong Province, China, and a skid loader production plant in Georgia, USA.

Telecommunications

Daewoo Telecom, growing in parallel with the Daewoo Corporation companies, signed a $25 million build-operate-and-transfer contract with the Bangladesh Rural Telecom Authority in December 1995 for the establishment and operation of telephone offices in Bangladesh. At home in South Korea, it formed an alliance with Motorola to sell the latter's cellular phones bearing Daewoo's name in South Korea.

Securities

Daewoo Securities was also in full expansion mode and completed the establishment, for example of the Daewoo (Hungary) Investment Fund Management Co., Ltd in Budapest in January 1996. Daewoo Securities had been present in Hungary since 1990 when it had established a joint venture, now named Daewoo Bank (Hungary). Other overseas subsidiaries were located in Hong Kong, New York, London, and Bombay. Revenues for 1994 totalled $564 million, making it the largest securities firm in South Korea.

Automobiles

Daewoo Motor grew rapidly after ending a 14-year joint venture with General Motors in 1992. According to Lee Sung-Sang, director of Daewoo Motor's planning division: 'Our independence is the core reason for our recovery. GM's meddling was overwhelming. After its departure, we could make our own decisions regarding investment, development and marketing strategies'. In 1995 Daewoo Motor (an unlisted company) made profits of $12.7 million on sales of $4.6 billion, representing a major turnaround from former losses. Much of the 1995 profit came from sales in Europe, which had been restricted under the agreement with General Motors.

Daewoo had begun building its own global network of plants to produce 2 million motor vehicles annually by the year 2000, half of them in South Korea. South Korea's two other large automobile manufacturers, Kia and Hyundai, were targeting 2.2 million and 2.4 million vehicles, respectively. Although most executives at the world's largest automobile manufacturers recognized that the big growth in their business would be outside the US-Western Europe-Japan triad, it was Kim who was actually willing to take the risks in investing in developing countries. 'You have to find places that people have never been to, and you have to do things that people haven't done yet. We will go everywhere'.

Adding to existing motor vehicle plants in India, China and Indonesia, Daewoo Motor started its expansion in Eastern Europe in January 1994 when it signed a joint-venture agreement with Automobile Craiova of Romania to form Rodae Automobile. Setting a precedent for future cooperative agreements, Daewoo began renovating Automobile Craiova's existing facilities and sent upwards of 1,000 Romanian engineers and production workers to its South Korean facilities for training.

Later in 1995 Kim invested $340 million in the Polish state-owned car manufacturer, Fabryka Samochodow Osobowych (FSO), and pledged a further $1.1 billion investment over seven years. GM had spent five years negotiating to buy parts of FSO and retain less than one-third of its work force. Kim, however, proposed to keep all of the 21,000 workers for three years. 'I figured that if we increased production three to four times, then we'd need all those people. This is the difference in our way of looking at things'. FSO was set to be a strategic assembly facility for sales throughout Europe. In 1995 Daewoo had also taken a 61% equity interest in Fabryka Samochodow Lublin, the Polish national truck manufacturer. In September 1996 it was reported that Daewoo was threatening to pull out of its Polish investments after Hyundai applied for a licence to begin car assembly in August. Kim sent a letter to the Polish prime minister saying he was extremely worried by the activity of certain groups such as Hyundai in Poland. The Polish industry ministry subsequently said that it was against awarding the license to Hyundai.

Also in 1995, Daewoo Motor committed to invest in the truck producer, Avia, in the Czech Republic, and agreed to spend $658 million on a new auto factory in Uzbekistan. Daewoo expected to put these plants, plus assembly or production plants, in Vietnam, the Philippines, and Iran into full operation by 1998. Thus by the end of 1996 Daewoo Motor had a total of 11 overseas production plants, most of which were in operation.

Elsewhere in Europe, Daewoo was concentrating on car sales rather than production. In the UK, for example Daewoo launched its Nexia and Espero cars (both based on an outdated GM model) in April 1995. At the time of the launch, Kim declared that he wanted to sell 6,000 units in 1995 and, by the end of 1997, obtain 1% of the UK car market. The launch was unique in two respects. Firstly, Daewoo sold the cars from 32 fully-owned showrooms staffed by Daewoo personnel who were not paid on commission, eliminating both dealers and car sales people. Secondly, it offered three years of free warranty, maintenance and membership in the Royal Automobile Club, and promised no hidden prices. Its ad campaign described Daewoo as: 'the biggest car company you've never heard of', and won multiple British advertising industry awards in 1996. Daewoo became the fastest-growing car brand on record in the UK, with registrations for 1995 totalling 13,169 units, or 0.93% of the market, far exceeding Kim's targets. In 1996 Daewoo also began linking up with the supermarket chain Sainsbury's to offer full car sales services inside supermarket complexes. Daewoo's sales of automobiles in France were doing almost as well.

Daewoo Motor put increasing emphasis on research, and to that end, bought the Worthing Lab in the UK in 1994. The company also established Daewoo Motor Engineering GmbH in Munich, Germany to support engineer technical training, collect technical information and develop product programmes. In May 1996 Daewoo Motor and the Siemens Automotive Group of Germany signed a joint-venture agreement to conduct research, development, production and sales of electronic controls and low emission components. Kim was also interested in buying the British sports car designer and automotive consultancy, Lotus Group.

To support Daewoo Motor's expansion, Kim had been quoted as saying that the group was considering acquisition of steel mills and banks, as well as the construction of an oil refinery.

Electronics

Daewoo Electronics was led by Bae Soon-Hoon, a US-educated, soft-spoken man with a PhD in thermodynamics, 10 years' experience in the USA, and a love of classical music. He twice left positions at Daewoo to teach at Stanford and MIT. Returning to head Daewoo Electronics in 1991, he launched a quality campaign called 'Tank' to promote an image of durability and reliability to internal and external audiences. Bae himself appeared in television commercials in South Korea, quickly becoming a popular figure and role model. 'Tank' was also a manufacturing campaign to design and produce home appliances and consumer electronics that were of high quality, durable and simple to operate. Daewoo Electronics' sales growth reached nearly 30% annually over the 10 years to 1996. Net profits rose 35.6% in 1995 to $61.4 million on sales of $4.05 billion (see Exhibit CS15.3). In contrast, Samsung Electronics had 1995 sales of $19.5 billion, and LG Electronics had $7.9 billion.

Bae saw the electronics industry's cut-throat pricing as an opportunity for his company. US companies had abandoned the industry to lower-cost Japanese producers in the 1970s, in Europe all competitors except Philips and Thomson had sold out of the business or lost their independence, and Japanese companies were subcontracting production of simpler goods to manufacturers in places such as China and India. His objective was to concentrate on the low end, high volume segment of the market.

In 1996 Daewoo Electronics was the world's largest exporter of washing machines, and had television, VCR, microwave oven, washing machine and refrigerator production projects planned or in operation in such diverse nations as Northern Ireland, France, Uzbekistan, Malaysia, and Myanmar. The company also had integrated production complexes which in most cases doubled as strategic investment bases for a different region in each of France, Mexico, Poland, Vietnam, and China. A new European headquarters was opened in Frankfurt, Germany in January 1996 (prior to this, Europe had been managed from Seoul). Typifying Daewoo's international outlook, Daewoo-Hanel in Vietnam made its maiden export of 10,000 colour televisions to the UAE in late 1995. Exhibit CS15.4 provides an overview of Daewoo Electronics' existing or planned production facilities in 1996.

Daewoo Electronics' ambitious plans included:

■ Becoming one of the world's top 10 producers of home appliances by the end of the century, and one of the top three producers by 2010.

■ Increasing global sales from $4.1 billion in 1995 to $5.2 billion in 1996, $10 billion in 2000, and $50 billion in 2010.

■ Achieving a 10% share of the global market by the year 2000 in six core products: televisions, refrigerators, washing machines, VCRs, microwave ovens and vacuum cleaners. By 2010 Daewoo Electronics expected a 20% share of the global market, of which 40% would be in the six core products, 30% in components, 20% in new business areas such as multimedia, automotive electronics, batteries, etc. and the final 10% in miscellaneous business.

■ Increasing global brand sales from 42% of all sales in 1995 to 75% in the year 2000, with a corresponding reduction of sales to other manufacturers from 58% to 25%. In Europe, brand sales accounted for 50% of sales in 1995 and were hoped to reach 70% in 1996. (Daewoo Electronics expected to have a total of 15 production and sales subsidiaries and three design centres in Europe by the year 2000. In 1995, the company's sales in Europe totalled $830 million, more than for any other region.)

■ Increasing the number of local employees at overseas locations from 5,000 personnel in 1995 to approximately 30,000 by the year 2000.

■ Investing $10 billion over 1997 to 2001 to expand the overseas R&D and design network from 7 to 30 facilities, with the aim of localizing product development capabilities. In the process, Daewoo Electronics would increase R&D personnel from 200 to 1,000 by the year 2000.

■ For 1996, Daewoo Electronics was also planning a number of reductions: a 30% reduction in the cost of materials through fewer, more compact components; a 30% reduction in line work as a result of greater automation; a 50% reduction in storage; and a 50% reduction in its number of products, by homing in on 'hit' products. In quality control, it expected to reach the goal of only 100 defective parts per million.

■ One 'hit' product was the 'Tank' refrigerator, which featured multilevel cooling and freezing systems. Daewoo Electronics planned total investments of $700 million so that by the year 2000 it would have nine overseas production bases, annual production capacity of 6 million units (72% of which would be outside South Korea), and a 10% share of the worldwide refrigerator market of an anticipated 58.8 million units.

Daewoo Electronics had accelerated its research activities in the 1990s. Its first international

Case 15

design centre was the Tokyo Design Centre founded in 1989. In 1995 it set up a Television Research Centre in Fameck, France and a European Design Centre in Paris. In Russia the company had established a joint venture, the Orion Plasma Research & Production Co. for production and R&D of flat panel displays. In April 1996 the company opened the Daewoo Electronics Research Center in the USA, and planned to invest a total of $30 million over a five-year period for the development of next generation non-memory semiconductors, digital broadcasting systems, multimedia software and hardware, and futuristic consumer electronics, including HD and digital VCRs. In November it signed a contract with the Sarnoff Research Institute of the USA to jointly develop next-generation multimedia technology. Daewoo Electronics also planned to open a VCR research complex in Northern Ireland.

In 1996 Daewoo Electronics' television production capacity stood at 6.8 million units. With the purchase of Thomson (see Part 2) it would become the world's largest television producer (see Exhibit CS15.5a). It would also gain a presence in important Southeast Asian markets such as Singapore, Malaysia, Indonesia, Thailand, Taiwan, and Australia/New Zealand, where it currently had no Daewoo-brand sales activity.

The financial perspective

In May 1996, Kim commented on Daewoo's ability to finance its prolific expansion activities as follows: 'In fact, the capital required for initial investments is not particularly large. We can easily meet these initial investment requirements from the international finance market, where we have an established reputation for excellent planning and total reliability. Daewoo has a long track record in turning failing or failed enterprises into profitable ventures. After a certain fixed period, we will retrieve much of the capital investment by going public with stocks on local capital markets. And we will reinvest this capital'. Kim also made use of the group's cross-shareholdings to fund projects, a strategy that was questionable from a legal point of view in South Korea.

Daewoo had grown largely on borrowed capital and had been trying, since 1970, to expand its off-shore financing by establishing foreign subsidiaries with access to local bank credit. The group's debt-to-equity ratio at the end of 1994 was 261%, compared with 253% for Samsung and 382% for Hyundai. Group companies had much higher ratios; Daewoo Electronics' ratio in 1995 was 347.5%. In the past, Daewoo had had some loan repayment difficulties: in 1970, its main banker, the South Korea First Bank, had refused to extend further credit; and four years later, during the first international oil crisis, the Chase Manhattan Bank had had to rescue Daewoo with a US$7 million loan.

Kim was renowned for masterfully playing the politics of trade and investment. Before signing the joint-venture agreement with Automobile Craiova, for example he persuaded the Romanian government to pass a law granting Daewoo tax concessions and duty-free privileges for bringing in components from South Korea to assemble cars. Similarly, Kim persuaded the government of Uzbekistan to put up half the money in exchange for half-ownership of a new $658 million car factory (and the Uzbeks were paying with cotton, which Daewoo's trading arm sold on the world market). Both car ventures were given tax holidays for five years.

Some observers thought it unlikely that Daewoo would ever face severe financial difficulties while Daewoo Securities remained a strong investment house. Daewoo financiers were generally recognized by their South Korean peers as being financial wizards, and Kim's personal expertise in mergers and acquisitions was legendary (so much so that Daewoo was often criticized for never having actually built a factory). Faith in Daewoo's solvency was also derived from the group's critical role in South Korea's economy and a general belief that the government would stand behind it. However, the South Korean government had shown itself in recent years to be less inclined to support the *chaebol* when they were in trouble; in January 1996 it did not intervene to save the construction arm of the Woosung *chaebol* from bankruptcy. In late 1995 the government also introduced a new requirement aimed at preventing the *chaebol* from taking on too much foreign debt: South Korean companies were now obliged to finance at least 20% of their foreign investment from domestic sources, either from retained earnings or by selling assets.

At the beginning of 1996 the Daewoo group had 168 recently announced or planned projects requiring a total of $20 billion in investment (see Exhibit CS15.6), and during the year both figures continued to rise. In 1995 Daewoo Corporation's combined long- and short-term debt rose 20% to $5.8 billion, with further debt of $17 billion carried off-balance sheet in the form of loans to affiliates and subsidiaries. While it was acknowledged in South Korea that the essence of Daewoo's financial strength was the powerful personality of Chairman Kim, it was also in South Korea that Kim faced charges of bribery and risked imprisonment for paying bribes to former President Roh Tae-Woo, who was at the centre of a $650 million corruption scandal.

PART 2: DAEWOO ELECTRONICS' BID FOR THOMSON MULTIMEDIA

In early 1996 Daewoo Electronics joined forces with the French Lagardère Group to bid for Thomson SA, a French government-owned holding company about to be privatized. The heavily indebted Thomson SA possessed a consumer electronics subsidiary, Thomson Multimédia, which interested Daewoo, and a defence electronics business, Thomson-CSF, which interested Lagardère. The Daewoo-Lagardère combination were bidding against another large French group, Alcatel Alsthom, for the purchase of Thomson.

This section provides an introduction to each of the parties involved in the bidding process, followed by a brief chronology of the events in 1996.

Daewoo in France

Daewoo first established a trading office in Paris in 1976. Twenty years later, France was the centre for much of Daewoo Electronics' production in Western Europe, with investments totalling $350 million since 1988. In an interview with *Le Monde* newspaper in 1988, Kim said: 'We're ready to co-operate with the French. They have a sound technological base, but are not very developed in the marketing sphere. We have set up a joint venture with Thomson (a Thomson subsidiary, LCC, had joined up with a Daewoo subsidiary to manufacture ferrite in South Korea) and we're ready to discuss defence projects with them. But the question is whether the French will be receptive to Daewoo's management style'.

In 1996 Daewoo Electronics had three factories in the Lorraine region in the east of France, producing microwave ovens, colour televisions, and cathode ray tubes. In Lorraine, Daewoo was only 300 km from Paris, Brussels and Frankfurt, which minimized transportation costs in Europe.

The factories employed a total of 1,400 people. Daewoo had received substantial subsidies from the French government and the European Commission to establish these sites.

The first of the three factories to be built was a $32-million microwave oven production plant established in Longwy in 1988. Originally a joint venture with JCB of France, Daewoo Electronics France SA became a wholly owned venture in 1994 with Daewoo Electronics' purchase of JCB's equity share. Following the take-over, Daewoo Electronics boosted annual production capacity to 1.5 million units, creating Western Europe's largest single microwave oven plant.

Colour televisions were produced by Daewoo Electronics Manufacturing SA in Fameck, which was established in August 1992 as a $40 million investment. In 1996 the company was expanding the assembly lines for the fourth time. Daewoo Electronics Manufacturing, in concert with the company's colour television plant in Poland, had the goal of making Daewoo Electronics Europe's leading television manufacturer, accounting for 10% of the entire European colour television market.

Daewoo Orion SA, also in Lorraine, was a joint venture between Daewoo Electronics and Orion Electric (which was itself another Daewoo subsidiary). The project was started in 1993, and production would commence in mid-1996. The company expected to be assembling two million cathode ray tubes a year by 1999, and would achieve this by employing five around-the-clock shifts all year long. A total of $45 million, or a third of the $137 million invested in the plant, was provided by public subsidies.

Daewoo Electronics had plans to expand its presence in Lorraine by building a semiconductor plant for $1.2 billion as well as a $150 million factory to produce glass for cathode ray tubes, both due in 1998. It also had a research centre near the Fameck plant and a design research centre in Paris.

Daewoo Electronics was not the only Daewoo group company to have activity in France. As previously mentioned, Daewoo Motor had commenced car sales in the country in March 1995, with an office in Roissy, and was achieving excellent results: 1995 sales had reached 7,000 units, surpassing all expectations.

In January 1996 Daewoo Corporation signed a cooperative agreement with the Cogema Group of France to sell nuclear fuel manufactured by Cogema to Asian nations, including South Korea and China. Daewoo planned to generate a turnover of more than $500 million from the fuel by the year 2000. In addition, Daewoo intended to participate in uranium mine development projects with Cogema. And in February 1996 Daewoo Heavy Industries signed a cooperative technology agreement with an affiliate of GEC-Alsthom of France, one of the world's leading suppliers of power generation facilities, for the production of large turbine generators. GEC-Alsthom was a joint venture between GEC of the UK and Alcatel Alsthom, the French company which was the competing bidder for Thomson.

Thomson SA

Thomson, although heavily indebted, was one of France's 'national champions'. It had been nationalized in 1982 and reorganized as a holding company, Thomson SA, with two principal subsidiaries: Thomson-CSF, which produced defence and commercial electronics, and Thomson

Multimédia (TMM), which made consumer electronics. The group's home appliance manufacturer, Thomson Electroménager (which made products such as washing machines), was sold off in 1992. The group's ownership structure is illustrated in Exhibit CS15.7.

Thomson-CSF

Thomson-CSF was Europe's leading defence electronics group and the third largest worldwide, representing more than 160 companies. The group was also a world leader in a number of commercial markets, including air traffic control and simulation. 75% of its work force was based in France. It made losses of $173 million in 1994 and $160 million in 1995 on revenues of $6.6 billion and $7.1 billion, respectively. (All French franc amounts used in the case have been converted to US dollars using year average exchange rates given in the bottom row of Table CS15.1.) A large source of Thomson-CSF's losses was a series of transactions related to its holdings in the state-owned bank Crédit Lyonnais, itself a big loss-maker.

Thomson Multimédia (TMM)

TMM was the second biggest consumer electronics company in Europe after Philips, and the fourth largest in the world. TMM had a broad spectrum of middle- to upper-range products covering televisions, video, audio and digital equipment (such as telephone sets and satellite broadcast receivers), as well as tubes and components. 42% of its 1995 revenues came from the sale of 8.5 million television sets (compared with 63% in 1992). TMM held the number one position in the USA in the television and VCR markets with well-known RCA, GE and ProScan brands, and the number two position in the same products in Europe with the Thomson, Telefunken, Saba, Brandt, Ferguson and Nordmende brands.

TMM was leading the field in several emerging high-growth product markets. In 1995 it sold more than 1.5 million DSS (Digital Satellite System) decoders for televisions in the USA and was developing and producing decoders for the impending launch of digital television in Europe. It had secured a deal with three US telephone companies for the delivery of three million digital decoders for MMDS (Multi-Channel, Multi-Point Distribution System) microwave broadcasting. It was developing technology for interactive television and the production of colour plasma screens, and in October 1996 it launched the DVD (Digital Video Disc), the first true multimedia product. TMM had invested considerable resources (over $200 million a year) in the development of 17 television, video and audio 'dream products' which, although not yet commercialized, demonstrated its expertise in state-of-the-art technologies. With regard to its other products, however, its technology was generally considered to be behind that of the leading Japanese electronics manufacturers. It was also regarded as weak in sales and marketing.

TMM's sales in Asia had commenced in the late 1980s and grew 50% in 1994 and 30% in 1995. The position of vice president for Asia, located in Singapore, was created in July 1995. TMM had established production facilities in China, Taiwan, the Philippines, Thailand, Malaysia and Singapore, and more recently India, with distribution and sales offices in a further four countries. Capacity was being expanded at the Singapore video plant, a joint venture established in 1987 with Toshiba, to produce kits for assembly at factories in France.

TMM employed 49,500 people in some 45 locations around the world. A mere 10% of its employees worked in France at nine factory locations, two research laboratories, and at its world headquarters in Paris. A further 46% of employees worked in the Americas, 22% in the rest of Europe, and 22% in Asia. In contrast, 64% of 1995 sales were in the USA, 33.9% in Europe, and only 2.1% in Asia.

In the 1980s TMM (then called Thomson Consumer Electronics) bought a succession of electronics companies including the German Telefunken, Nordmende and Saba, and the British Ferguson. In 1987 the chairman of the Thomson Group, Alain Gomez, clearly expressed a desire to sell TMM and concentrate his energies on Thomson-CSF, and was rumoured to be negotiating to sell TMM to either Daewoo or Toshiba. The French government, however, vetoed any sale of TMM. Instead, Gomez negotiated with Jack Welch, the head of the US giant, General Electric, to buy the latter's profitable consumer electronics firm, RCA, both to strengthen TMM and to provide a cash-cow with which to feed Thomson-CSF. Gomez swapped $800 million in cash and Thomson's loss-making medical electronics group for General Electric's RCA television division (minus RCA's prestigious David Sarnoff Research Center, with which Daewoo signed an agreement in November 1996).

In 1991, Gomez renegotiated that part of the agreement reached with General Electric which concerned patents. When TMM had bought RCA, it had taken RCA's brands and industrial assets but not its cash-earning patents. These had been placed in a holding company jointly held by TMM and GE. Each year, TMM was to add its new patents to this company, and over 1993 to 1999 TMM would gradually acquire ownership of the company and, with it, the rights to the patents. These arrangements were changed under the 1991 renegotiation. Under the new agreement, Gomez immediately received a cheque for $210 million, equivalent to the present value of the revenues coming from the patents over five years, and in return deferred the process of acquiring the patents by five years. Gomez argued that the operation was financially neutral, but he used the $210 million for Thomson SA, not TMM. As a result of this deal, TMM would not receive any patent income until 1999; from 1999 onwards, it expected to earn an annual sum of $250 million in patent royalties.

In 1990 TMM had begun a research programme, in conjunction with its main competitor, Philips, with the aim of creating a European standard for high definition television (HDTV). The research programme was due to cost $3.7 billion, of which TMM would contribute $1.7 billion and Philips $2 billion. The French government agreed, in 1990, to subsidize TMM's part of the research deal to the tune of $550 million over five years. Unfortunately, the European standard was not widely accepted, even in Europe: the European Commission was unable to impose the European standard on European broadcasters. In January 1993 Philips suspended plans to make HDTV sets because there were no European programmes for them.

Beset with such disasters, TMM's debts rose steeply, reaching $1.9 billion in 1993 and $2.8 billion in 1995. The French government had not injected capital into TMM since the 1987 purchase of RCA. Debt servicing costs consistently pulled it into the red. It did not register a profit in the six years to 1996, as shown in Table CS15.1.

TMM explained the fall in operating income in 1995 as being the result of a weak dollar, plus a pronounced decline in the US television market (down 5% in volume, coupled with a 6% fall in prices), and a further decline in the European market (down 1% in volume, coupled with a 5% fall in prices), combined with especially tough conditions in France and Germany towards the end

Table CS15.1 TMM's losses, 1991–95 (billions of US dollars)

	1990	1991	1992	1993	1994	1995	First half of 1996
Consolidated revenue	6.09	5.51	5.78	5.91	6.87	7.31	N/A
Operating results	0.14	−0.04	−0.06	0.03	0.11	0.07	−0.20
Net profit/loss	−0.50	−0.44	−0.33	−0.17	−0.11	−0.22	−0.59
Year-average exchange rate: US $1 =	FF5.45	FF5.65	FF5.29	FF5.67	FF5.55	FF4.99	FF5.09

Source: TMM company records

of the year. TMM's costs of production were also high. Sales in the emerging new digital markets, which accounted for 15% of TMM's turnover, were far from able to offset these trends.

Lagardère Group

The Lagardère Group was formed in 1992 upon the merger of two corporations, Matra (a producer of missiles, cars and cellular phones) and Hachette (which was involved in publishing, magazines such as *George* and *Elle*, broadcasting and newspaper distribution.) The group was tightly controlled by the entrepreneur Jean-Luc Lagardère and his son. Its revenues in 1995 totalled $10.5 billion.

Matra Défense Espace had a turnover of $5.2 billion in 1995, 50% of which came from exports. Matra had joint ventures with British Aerospace and GEC of the UK. The merger of Matra with Thomson-CSF would create Thomson-Matra with a turnover of around $12 billion. It would be the second largest weapons system and electronics group in the world behind Lockheed Martin Loral of the USA (see Exhibit CS15.5b).

Alcatel Alsthom

Alcatel Alsthom, the other bidder for Thomson, was France's largest industrial firm and the government's premier partner in power plants and high-speed trains (TGV). It had joint ventures with GEC of the UK among others. Although previously very profitable, with record profits of $1.3 billion in 1992 and 1993, it made a loss of $5 billion in 1995 which included significant restructuring costs.

Alcatel stated that it expected synergies between its huge telecommunications business and Thomson-CSF, although the move was commonly perceived as a step towards further diversification. Bae, Daewoo Electronics' head, had been quoted as saying that: 'Alcatel is not a consumer business. Television is a keen competition area, and you need some expertise'.

Although Alcatel made no promises of significant job creation were it to purchase the group, both the media and Thomson employees anticipated that Alcatel would win the bid for Thomson.

The French government

President Jacques Chirac's stated aims were to privatize Thomson in line with his government's ongoing privatization programme, and to rationalize the bloated French defence industry in line with world defence trends.

Thomson was one of a series of companies that had been nationalized in 1982 with the coming to power of the socialists in France. However, since 1986, successive governments had reversed the trend, and begun fully or partially privatizing industrial giants such as Rhône Poulenc, Elf Aquitaine, Renault and Seita, as well as banks and insurance companies.

In 1996 the government was in the process of privatizing a number of loss-making French public companies including Thomson, using the largely untested 'over-the-counter' method. This method contrasted with the more traditional and transparent process of selling the state's shares by public tender. For this reason, the government would assign an independent observer to survey and prepare a report on the fairness of negotiations held with the bidding companies. Having received and reviewed several bids, the government would then submit them to the French Privatisation Commission, an independent body comprising eight bureaucrats. The independent observer would submit its report to the same body. The Privatisation Commission would then make a decision on which bidder would be given permission to buy the company. The government found itself in the awkward position of having to inject money into the loss-making companies in order to reduce their debt and thereby render them more palatable to companies that might want to buy them.

In 1996 unemployment in France stood at 12%, and the French government was, in general, very sensitive to criticisms that its own actions would lead to increased unemployment.

The French government had another concern, that of its relations with South Korea, which had not been particularly smooth during the 1990s. For example in 1991 the French company, Dassault, was awarded a contract to build eight submarine-detecting aircraft for the South Korean army. Arriving in Seoul to sign the deal, the French secretary of state was informed that the deal had been re-assigned at the last minute to Lockheed. A year later, the same pattern of events was repeated when Dassault and Thomson, this time in partnership with the US companies, TRW and Cessna, were usurped at the last moment by two other US firms, Loral and Raytheon, for the contract to build electronically protected planes.

In September 1993 President Mitterrand visited Seoul, the first French head of state to make the journey to South Korea. He brought with him a 78-member delegation to discuss bilateral political and trade relations, and finalize the recently concluded agreement between the South Korean government and GEC-Alsthom regarding the provision of trainsets and equipment for the construction of a high-speed railway (TGV line) in South Korea. The remaining sticking point was the extent to which the French company would transfer technology to the South Koreans; it took until June 1994 to complete negotiations for the $2.1 billion project. As an expression of goodwill, Mitterrand promised the return of nearly 300 South Korean manuscripts and documents which had been seized by the French navy in 1866, and which the South Korean

Case 15

government was anxious to re-acquire. As of the end of 1996, however, the French government had still not returned the documents.

Daewoo's bid for Thomson Multimédia: a brief chronology

1996

21 February	The French government announced the privatization of Thomson SA specifying that Thomson-CSF and TMM would be sold as one unit. Marcel Roulet was appointed by decree to the position of chairman and chief executive officer of Thomson SA. and charged with the preparatory work needed for the privatization.
28 May	Daewoo Group chairman Kim Woo-Choong received France's highest Medal of Honour bestowed upon a civilian, 'Les insignes de Commandeur dans l'Ordre de la Légion d'Honneur' (Legion of Honour Commander Medal) from French Prime Minister. Alain Juppé, at the prime minister's office in Paris. A number of other leading government officials and business leaders. including GEC Alsthom chairman, Pierre Bilger, and Siemens Automotive president, Jean Fayet, attended the ceremony. In his remarks, Prime Minister Juppé lauded Kim for his positive investments and efforts to promote economic and cultural cooperation and exchange between France and South Korea. He also said that the govermnent of France had selected Kim to receive France's highest civilian honour for his efforts in contributing to global economic development through his outstanding managerial capabilities. Kim noted that Daewoo's projects in France were the most diversified of all programmes in Western European nations, and that Daewoo was committed to working in cooperation to realize France's visions for the future. He mentioned Daewoo Electronics' plans to invest an additional $530 million in the Lorraine region and a promise to create 1,800 more jobs.
12 June	At the opening ceremony of the Daewoo-Orion cathode ray tube plant in Lorraine, Bae Soon-Hoon, head of Daewoo Electronics announced that he had informed the French government of his company's interest in buying TMM on the condition that the French government restructured its debt.
End July	The joint bid between the Lagardère group and Daewoo Electronics had been publicized. The Lagardère Group had approached 35 firms in order to find a partner who would bid for TMM, but only Daewoo had been interested. Of the 35, 18 were financial services companies and 17 were industrial companies. Philips, Samsung and Toshiba were known to have been among those consulted; Philips apparently turned down the offer because of competition concerns.
31st July	Bae announced Daewoo Electronics' plans to invest $2.6 billion in Europe by the year 2000, of which $1 billion would be spent on TMM, creating 5,000 jobs. Bae committed Daewoo to preserving all TMM's current jobs in France.
3 August	The government called for bids for Thomson SA, and assigned an independent observer to monitor the bidding process.

21 August	Two hundred workers at TMM's plant in Angers. France stopped work for an hour to protest against a visit by Daewoo executives. Union officials said they planned to provide a similar welcome for representatives of Alcatel Alsthom.
26 August	Kim Woo-Choong was sentenced to two years in jail by a South Korean lower court for bribing former South Korean president. Roh Tae-Woo, with regard to national construction projects. Roh had received $650 million in 'donations' from businessmen while in office from 1988 to 1993. Kim was one of nine top business tycoons to be sentenced, although five. including the chairman of the Samsung group, were given only suspended sentences. The Daewoo Group announced they would appeal the conviction, and Kim would remain free until the Supreme Court ruled on the appeal. Kim left South Korea two days after the sentencing to attend the opening of a Daewoo-built hotel in China. Kim commented that he was 'sickened' by the idea of being sentenced after building such an important business group for South Korea. He had, in fact. already been convicted in 1995 of offering a bribe for the construction of a nuclear power project in the early 1990s.
15 September	*Le Monde* newspaper revealed that TMM had made plans for internal restructuring ahead of the privatization. The plans involved the closure of eight commercial and industrial sites in the USA, Germany and Southeast Asia, but not in France. involving the loss of 5,000 jobs. TMM's loss of $590 million for first half of 1996 included provisions of $240 million for the reorganization.
16 September	Both Alcatel Alsthom and the Lagardère-Daewoo combination submitted formal offers to the French government for Thomson SA. *Le Monde* newspaper estimated that Thomson SA's debt stood at $1.95 billion, and TMM's totalled $2.73 billion.
End September	TMM union members visited their counterparts at Daewoo Electronics factories in Lorraine. They discovered that turnover rates were very high. South Korean managers did not speak French. and security regulations were not well respected. Turnover was high because Daewoo had mainly employed cheap and inexperienced young people. In the beginning, before a union had been established, sick employees had been fired. At the time of the visit, there were 14 suits pending from employees against Daewoo. French employees also experienced cultural shocks: managers at Daewoo took over on production lines when the workers took breaks.
2 October	Alcatel Alsthom announced that, in order to raise the capital needed to smoothly manage TMM, it intended to merge its nuclear engineering subsidiary, Framatome, with one of its existing joint ventures, GEC Alsthom. This sparked debate since Framatome held vital French nuclear technology and GEC was a British company.
10 October	The Japanese firm JVC announced that it would terminate production at its audio equipment factory in Lorraine in January 1997, sell off the factory for one symbolic franc, and shift production to one of its factories in Scotland where it would gain $480 million in subsidies from the European Commission. JVC had

opened the factory, which employed 240 people. in Lorraine in 1988 after receiving subsidies of $3 million from the French government and $1.5 million from the European Commission. The move caused some anger among French trade unions.

16 October   Prime Minister Alain Juppé announced President Jacques Chirac's preference to sell Thomson SA to the French Lagardère Group, chosen to the surprise of observers over the other bidder Alcatel Alsthom. The rival bids had been identical in financial terms.

The government proposed to inject $2.1 billion (FF 11 billion (converted at the October 1996 rate of US$1 = FF 15)) into the Thomson group, and then sell the entire group to Lagardère for one symbolic franc. Lagardère, in turn, would sell TMM to Daewoo Electronics for one franc.

The French government sent a letter to the French Privatisation Commission. asking it to consider the offers presented by Lagardère and Alcatel Alsthom. It was against protocol for the government to have declared its preference for a candidate prior to submitting such a dossier to the Privatisation Commission. A similar dossier would be submitted to the European Commission, which would want to ensure that any aid given by the French government to Thomson represented the normal provision of equity capital by a (government) shareholder acting under normal market conditions.

The government commented that: 'Daewoo Electronics, having real expertise in controlling production costs of mass market products, will endow TMM with the competitive gains required for its recovery and its future development'.

TMM union officials commented that: 'Tax-payers are going to pay $2.1 billion so that Daewoo, a dwarf South Korean company, can grab their technologies of the future'.

17 October   From Seoul, Bae reiterated that Daewoo Electronics planned to invest $2.6 billion in Europe in the coming five years, of which $1.5 billion would be in France. It would create 9,000 jobs in Europe and 5,000 in France (the latter would include the 1,800 additional jobs already announced in the Lorraine region). Daewoo would also repay or take on the portion of TMM's debt which remained outstanding after the government's $2.1 billion injection.

Daewoo Electronics' share price. which had been underperforming the South Korean stock price index by approximately 14% since the beginning of 1996. rose 6% after the announcement, but security analysts in Seoul predicted that at Daewoo Electronics' purchase of TMM would almost double Daewoo Electronics' debt-to-equity ratio to approximately 800% on a consolidated basis.

Les Echos newspaper said it had discovered that Daewoo Securities was negotiating with the French government to buy the troubled state-owned bank, Marseillaise de Crédit which was due to be privatized using the over-the-counter method at the end of the year.

17 October   Employees at TMM's Angers plant demonstrated against Daewoo Electronics' acquisition of TMM. In an interview with *Le Monde* newspaper, a representative of TMM's unions declared: 'Daewoo is only interested in our market shares and our brands. The 5,000 jobs promised. that's rubbish. Who can make us believe that a private South Korean company wants to produce televisions in France?' TMM's workers did not trust Bae's promises to increase production at the Angers plant to three million televisions: 'The potential of the factory is one million. Where will we make three million? This year. we won't even make the planned 750,000!'

19 October   Lionel Jospin, head of the opposition Socialist Party, complained in parliament that the French state was financing a bid by Daewoo to corner the promising market for next-generation digital televisions.

21 October   Lagardère's share price rose 6%, having already risen 23% on the day following the 16 October announcement. This added fuel to accusations that the state was selling off assets too cheaply. The Lagardère group complained that a serious communication error had been committed in saving that Thomson was to be sold for 'one symbolic franc'. resulting in accusations that Lagardère and Daewoo were to be recipients of a 'lavish gift'. In general, the French public did not understand the financial engineering behind the decision to sell the debt-laden Thomson SA to Lagardère for one franc.

22 October   Bae indicated that within two years of privatization of TMM, Daewoo would turn the company around and might then allow the entry of other partners. He also stated that he envisaged maintaining 20% annual growth in TMM's television sales, maintaining TMM's brands, and keeping TMM's headquarters in Paris, although he would review the current management while also asking their advice on possible site closures around the world. Daewoo would increase the number of production sites in France, although TMM's partnership with Toshiba in Singapore would undoubtedly be broken off.

Daewoo Electronics and Lagardère announced that they would create three joint ventures to conduct research and development into next-generation consumer electronic products such as plasma and liquid-crystal displays, which were some of TMM's key research areas. In this way France would retain an interest in these high-technology sectors.

23 October   TMM unions stepped up criticism of the government's non-transparent decision process. The mayors of approximately 30 of the 80 communes in France in which a Thomson-CSF or TMM plant or office was located, also expressed their condemnation of the decision. While the opposition party challenged the legality of the government's decision, Prime Minister Juppé described Thomson-CSF and TMM as 'badly managed' companies.

24 October   Daewoo Group chairman, Yoon Young-Suk, as well as the 1995 president of Daewoo Heavy Industries and the current Daewoo Heavy vice-president, were questioned by South Korean state prosecutors over a $362,000 bribe from

Daewoo Heavy to an ex-defence minister in connection with a South Korean government purchase of military helicopters.

25 October   South Korea became a member of the OECD.

27 October   Alcatel Alsthom announced that, had it been selected, it would have set up a joint venture between TMM and a foreign partner.

28 October   A week before he was due to present his group's proposal to buy Thomson SA to the French Privatisation Commission, Jean-Luc Lagardère announced in *Le Figaro* newspaper that a suit had been filed against him by French judicial authorities. The Lagardère Group later explained that the suit concerned misuse of corporate funds in 1992, but that the charges had nothing to do with the proposed purchase of Thomson, and would not lead Lagardère to prison.

29 October   The French government promised a full parliamentary debate before a definitive decision, due before the end of the year, on the sale of Thomson to the Lagardère group in response to mounting controversy over its handling of the sale.

3 November   Yang Jae-Yeol, vice-president of Daewoo Electronics, said in an interview with the French newspaper, *Libération,* that: 'there are 350 people doing nothing at TMM and we will need to simplify the organization. Management is top-heavy and it will only be by getting rid of this burden that we will be able to produce high quality products at competitive prices'. The following day Bae declared that this was not Daewoo's position, and that the quote must have arisen from a misunderstanding.

4 November   *Les Echos* financial newspaper reported that the true total of the Thomson group's debt was $5.4 billion, of which the government would pay $2.1 billion. Daewoo would take $1.4 billion and Lagardère $1.9 billion.

6 November   Daewoo placed advertisements in French newspapers to try to counter growing resentment (see Exhibit CS15.8).

7 November   Approximately 400 employees of Thomson Television Components France went on strike to protest against the sale of their parent company, TMM, to Daewoo. They carried placards which read: 'No to the privatization', and 'At Thomson, we don't want little dwarfs who say we're worth nothing'. They explained that they wanted the majority of TMM to rest in French hands.

17 November   On a French television programme, Bae stated that Daewoo Electronics' European headquarters would be transferred from Germany to France. He explained that Daewoo Electronics had 22 factories in 15 different countries. and tried to determine specific management policies in each. He confirmed that he wanted to conserve the rights and work patterns of French employees and did not want to transform them into South Korean workers, since: 'a Frenchman who tries to become South Korean is not productive'.

20 November   One in three Thomson group employees, including 80% of TMM personnel, marched in Paris and several other French cities to protest against the privatization of their companies and, in particular, the sale of TMM, a company with world-first technology, to a smaller, less reputable South Korean company. Some employees carried placards showing a picture of one symbolic franc. Employees felt betrayed by the government, which had refused to recapitalize Thomson prior to the 16 October announcement, and seemed prepared to sacrifice them in order to restructure the French arms sector. They were dubious of Daewoo's promises to maintain their jobs.

On the same day. a second suit was filed against Jean-Luc Lagardère concerning the terms of the merger of two key group companies, Matra and Hachette, in 1990.

26 November   Alcatel Alsthom declared itself ready to make a new offer for Thomson.

4 December   The French Privatisation Commission presented its conclusions on the sale of Thomson. The Commission was highly critical of the government's handling of the privatization, and rejected the government's decision, giving the following reasons:

- One of the bidders had submitted only one copy of its report, instead of the required 20, and had submitted it 20 minutes late with no proven significant reason for being late. The Commission disagreed with the independent observer's judgement that both bidders had been fairly treated in the bidding process.

- The Commission thought the government should have investigated in greater depth the future prospects of Thomson-CSF and TMM given that the reduction of TMM's debt would enable it to realize gains from its technological capital, its research teams and its large portfolio of patents. Among other factors, the government should have given further consideration to the employment aspects, the cross shareholdings between the Thomson companies and the French state-owned bank Crédit Lyonnais, and the fact that the French tax bureau owed these companies money (since taxes in a given year in France are based on anticipated profits for the coming year).

- Even if Daewoo Electronics, with its low market capitalization and high debt. were to bring financial and commercial resources to TMM, it was not clear that, in the medium term, the result of the sale would be positive. For the French state, the sale of TMM would mean the renunciation of a first-rate portfolio of technologies in the areas of digital televisions, flat screens, decoders and components which had been developed as a result of long and substantive research financed in part by public subsidies. (This ambiguous statement was widely interpreted in the international press to mean that the sale would lead to the unwanted transfer of technology from France to South Korea.)

- Neither the French government nor Lagardère could place Daewoo

Electronics under any legal obligation to deliver on its promises regarding financing, location of new investments. and job creation. For example, Daewoo Electronics had promised to produce a guarantee from a first-rate bank, but could delay providing such a guarantee until the last moment. The Juppé government, finding that its preference for the Lagardère-Daewoo combination had been overturned by the Privatisation Commission, announced that it was postponing the privatization of both TMM and Thomson CSF.

The decision represented a major setback for Daewoo Electronics. Without TMM, its brand names and its technology, how would Bae, and behind him, Kim, achieve their ambitious plans for international expansion?

The French government was also in a difficult position. Its decision was received very badly by the South Korean public, and the South Korean government threatened to retaliate through measures which could materially affect the French economy, mentioning nuclear power plants, the TGV project, etc. What could be done to preserve French-South Korean relations?

Case 15

Exhibit CS15.1   Kim Woo-Choong's personal achievements as of March 1996

Personal

■ Born 19 December 1936, Taegu, South Korea

Married Chung Heeja in 1964. Chung Heeja studied at Harvard and is the chair of a Daewoo subsidiary which owns the Seoul Hilton Hotel. They have three children: Sunjung, Sunhyup and Sunyong.

Education

■ BA in Economics from Yonsei University, Seoul, South Korea (1960)

■ Graduated from Kyunggi High School, Seoul, South Korea (1956)

Business-related activities

Chairman, South Korea-Germany Association (Since 1993)

Member, The South Korea-America Friendship Society (Since 1992)

Honorary Chairman, South Korea Federation of Textile Industries (Since 1989)

Vice Chairman, Federation of South Korean Industries (Since 1979)

Vice Chairman, South Korea Foreign Trade Association (Since 1979)

Vice Chairman, South Korea-Japan Economic Association (Since 1981)

Vice Chairman, SOUTH KOREA-ASEAN Business Club (Since 1978)

Member, Board of Directors, South Korea-US Economic Council (Since 1978)

Member, South Korea-US Business Council (Since 1988)

Member, International Board of Advisors, Republic of Malta (Since 1990)

Other activities

Chairman, South Korea Baduk (Go) Association

Chairman, Alumni Association, College of Business & Economics, Yonsei University

Vice Chairman, South Korea Amateur Sports Association

Member, Board of Directors, South Korea Institute of Modern Society

Member, Board of Directors, South Korea Science & Engineering Foundation

Member, Board of Directors, Yonsei Cancer Centre, Yonsei University

Member, The Board of Directors of the Associates, Harvard Business School

Member, The Board of Governors, The Joseph H. Lauder Institute of Management and International Studies, The Wharton School, University of Pennsylvania

Member, Board of Trustees, South Korea University

Member, Visiting Committee, University of Michigan School of Business Administration

Honorary Consultant, Peking University

Social contributions

Donated US$3.5 million to the Seoul National University (1986). Of the donation, named the 'Daewoo Academic Research Fund,' more than 70% is to be spent for research and studies on such basic sciences as mathematics, physics, chemistry and biology.

Established the Daewoo Medical Foundation, which operates a 300-bed general hospital in South Korea (1981). Daewoo also established and operates four additional general hospitals providing medical facilities and services to local residents for whom adequate medical services had previously been available. A total of US$14.2 million previously had been provided for the enhancement of medical facilities and other medical service programmes.

Established the Jisung Foundation, which operates a middle school and a high school (1980). The Foundation later established and now operates three additional kindergartens and a primary school, and also manages a foreign school.

Donated US$10.3 million to establish the Daewoo Foundation, a non-profit public service organization for the promotion and enhancement of social welfare (1978). An additional endowment of US$30.3 million was made to the Foundation with the express hope that the fund be used for the cultivation and advancement of basic arts and sciences.

Donated US$2 million to establish the Seoul Press Foundation, a non-profit service organization aimed at the development of South Korean journalism (1978). Activities of the Foundation include providing scholarships to South Korean journalists to study at Western universities. Twenty-two journalists have received scholarships since the overseas study programme was launched.

Donated US$10.3 million to establish the Daewoo Educational Foundation, an independent unit aimed at the realization of industrial academic cooperation and the cultivation of elite scholars/students (1977). The Foundation operates Ajou University which is located near Seoul. The university has 6,550 undergraduate students and 27 departments with 300 graduate students at two speciality schools. Since its establishment, the Foundation has contributed about US$38 million to the university.

Honours and awards

'Les insignes de Commandeur dans l'Ordre de la Legion d'Honneur' (Legion of Honour Commander Medal), France's highest Medal of Honour bestowed upon a civilian (1996)

Honorary Degree from Romania Craiova University (1996)

Honorary Degree from Universidad Santiago de Cali and Universidad del Valle, Colombia (1995)

Case 15

'Honour Al Merito Grando Gran Cruz' from Colombian President H.C. Dr. Ernesto Samper (1995)

Honorary Degree of Doctor of Humane Letters from South Carolina University (1994)

'Commander's Cross of the Order of Merit of the Federal Republic of Germany' from German Federal President Richard von Weizsaeker for contributions to development of South Korean-German Relations (1992)

Honorary Doctor of Science from the Russian Economic Academy for contributions to economic co-operation between the Russian Republic and South Korea (1992)

'Commandeur de l'ordre de la Couronne' (Commander of the Order of the Crown) from His Majesty Baudouin, King of the Belgians, for contributions to improved and expanded relations between Belgium and South Korea (1991)

'Sitara-i-Pakistan' (Star of Pakistan), the highest award bestowed by the government of Pakistan on a foreigner, for valuable contributions to closer economic cooperation between Pakistan and South Korea (1989)

'Manager Grand Prize' from the South Korean Association of Business Administration (1988)

Honorary Doctor of Public Service from George Washington University for many outstanding accomplishments and qualities of perseverance, innovation, intelligence, vision and unselfish sacrifice (1988)

'Marronnier Corporate Culture Award' from the Supporting Council of Art and Literature Promotion in South Korea, for contributions to the development of national culture and art (1987)

Honorary Doctorate in Business Administration from South Korea University for contributions to the economic development of South Korea (1986)

Honorary Doctorate in Economics from Yonsei University for contributions to the economic development of South Korea through entrepreneurial activities (1985)

Second 'International Business Award' from the International Chamber of Commerce (1984). Given triennially, the award goes to 'an entrepreneur who has contributed to the idea of free enterprise by creating or developing his own company'.

'Order of the Two Niles', the highest award bestowed on a foreigner, from the Sudanese government (1979). The order recognizes contributions to the economic development of the Sudan.

'Manager Prize' from the Alumni Association, Yonsei University Business School (1976)

'Manager of South Korea Prize' from the South Korea Management Association (1973)

'Citation for Superior Business' from the Business Management Research Institute, South Korea University (1972)

Source: Company records

Exhibit CS15.2   A brief history of the Daewoo Group's development

Daewoo started out in 1967 as a garment and textile exporter and importer, and soon became a leader in sales to Southeast Asia and Africa. Success in the US market resulted in a doubling of Daewoo exports in 1970. Predicting that the US government would impose a quota on textiles and that allocation would be based on recent exporting performance, Kim pushed his textile sales in the USA at all costs. Exports to that country quintupled, and when the quota was imposed in 1972, Daewoo was awarded 30% of the South Korean share.

Kim expanded into related light industries such as leather goods by buying local manufacturing firms which lacked overseas marketing competence. In 1975 Daewoo became a 'general trading company' which gave it preferential access to export financing and enhanced its international standing.

In 1976 Kim was asked by the South Korean Development Bank to take over Hangkook Machinery, Ltd., one of South Korea's largest producers of diesel engines, rolling stock, construction equipment and machine tools. This company had never made a profit in the 38 years of its existence, and its debts were twice Daewoo's equity. Daewoo's executives were opposed to the project, but Kim accepted. Renaming the company Daewoo Heavy Industries, Ltd, he personally supervised its turn-around. He quickly noticed that workers were putting in overtime to enhance their wages, but producing little. Instead of cutting back hours, Kim generated more business through aggressive marketing and improved quality. Production costs were lowered and break-even was achieved in the first year.

In 1978 Daewoo took over the nearly bankrupt Okpo Shipbuilding Company, again at the government's request, and created Daewoo Shipbuilding and Heavy Machinery (DSHM). Daewoo injected about US$500 million into DSHM. Through hard selling and aggressive pricing, including selling ships on which DSHM made no profit, Kim succeeded in turning the company into a leading shipyard in terms of orders. However, by the late 1980s the DSHM was crippled by debts stemming from the world shipbuilding recession and faced bankruptcy. Since various Daewoo affiliates had guaranteed DSHM's debt, bankruptcy could trigger cross-defaults and endanger these other companies which themselves suffered from severe cash-flow problems. Kim turned to the government for help.

Kim was strongly criticized in political circles. 'Kim ... cannot escape responsibility for his political adventurism', said one opposition party member in 1988. The government was very sensitive to accusations that it continued to grant special treatment to large business groups and was anxious to have the rescue plan publicly debated before approval. Kim threatened to resign as head of the Daewoo group if a satisfactory solution could not be reached. The government finally assisted Daewoo by injecting cash, but also forced the Daewoo group to give it equity in some of its most profitable subsidiaries and to sell various companies. In the years that followed, Daewoo managed to bring the shipbuilding operations back to profitability. Kim actually took up residence in the shipyard to oversee the revitalization process. In 1993, DSHM received $3.8 billion in new orders, more than any other shipyard in the world.

In fact, 1978 was a big year for Daewoo, as it saw not only the creation of DSHM but also that of Daewoo Motor, which has become one of the most important companies in the group.

Case 15

Daewoo took the place of a financially troubled South Korean firm (Shinjin Automotive) as partner in a 50-50 joint venture with General Motors. Since Daewoo believed that South Korean companies were not yet big enough to manage US sales networks, its products appeared in the USA under GM's name. In the South Korean market it competed with its own-branded vehicles. Daewoo also relied on GM for technology and marketing channels, including after-sales facilities.

Disagreements between GM and Daewoo began to surface over marketing strategy and commitment, as Daewoo wanted to invest aggressively in South Korea's booming domestic market, especially in the minicar sector, but GM disagreed. Daewoo turned to Suzuki for technological assistance and launched production of minicars at DSHM, the shipbuilding unit (in order to fill unused capacity). The partnership with GM ended acrimoniously in 1992, and, among other penalties, Daewoo Motor was barred from the USA and Western European markets until 1995.

In 1983, Daewoo Electronics was created, again through the acquisition of a troubled firm. At first the new company produced major home appliances, but it soon began to move into higher technology in line with government directives. Believing that: 'the future of Daewoo, and of South Korea, lies in high technology', Kim again undertook to alter his portfolio of businesses by building capabilities in telecommunications, computers, robotics and their underlying electronic components. Daewoo Electronics entered into technology licensing agreements with firms such as Northern Telecom (Canada) and Siemens. It also became a major subcontractor to General Dynamics, Boeing and Dornier as a builder of aircraft fuselages. In 1984 it took over a California-based PC maker, but results were disappointing, involving only the manufacture of banking terminals for IBM. A venture with Leading Edge was initially successful. In 1986 it began trade with NEC, making its first shipment of a 14-inch colour television in 1988, and proceeding to export over 2 million units to NEC in the eight years up until 1996. By the late 1980s, despite heavy investments, Daewoo Electronics was still a distant third in the local market, with much lower brand recognition than the leaders, Goldstar and Samsung. Following the merger of Daewoo Telecom and Daewoo Electronics in 1991, however, Daewoo became the largest South Korean exporter of PCs.

Needless to say, the Daewoo Group had significant financing needs that drove it, over the years, to develop a substantial presence in the South Korean financial sector. As of 1983, it controlled three financial companies and had a direct interest in several others, such as First Bank of South Korea and South Korea Merchant Banking Corporation, through stock ownership and personal relations with management. It had been one of the leading partners in the creation of the KorAm Bank, a joint venture between the Bank of America (49.9%) and 11 South Korean companies. In the early 1980s, when the stock market was booming, Daewoo Securities, the largest broker in South Korea, served as one of the group's main cash cows.

Technology was an issue which concerned Kim. In an interview with Le Monde in 1988 he stated: 'We're very poor in basic technologies and are too dependent on the United States and the West. Our research isn't developed enough. We lack scientists and we need to buy our technology and licenses and create joint ventures'. In the early 1990s Daewoo executives initiated an internal campaign called 'Daewoo Technology', under which, among other measures, they established Daewoo's own academic-industrial think-tank, the Institute for Advanced Engineering (IAE) in Seoul in 1992. The IAE acted as both an educational institution – offering full doctoral programmes – and as the focal point of Daewoo's global research and development efforts.

In late 1989, the Group announced the beginning of an internal restructuring programme. Although Daewoo counted among its most valued assets its highly motivated, self-sacrificing, young white-collar workers, critics had often contended that there was a lack of support and coordination within the ranks. By 1992 the group had completed a large-scale managerial reform aimed at preparing itself for a decade of rapid international expansion.

Exhibit CS15.3   Daewoo Electronics' rapid expansion (*Source: Business Week*, 16 September 1996)

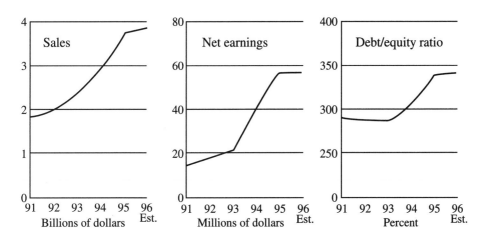

Exhibit CS15.4   An overview of Daewoo Electronics' production facilities in 1996 (excluding South Korea)

Country	Product	Production*	Production beginning	Investment
ASIA				
CHINA				
Tianjin integrated production complex	Microwave ovens	0.4	Due 1997	$15 million
	Car stereos	1.0 world's largest	1993	$10 million
	Vacuum cleaners	1.5	1995	$30 million
	Refrigerators		Due 1997	
	Air conditioners	0.3	Due 1997	$35 million
INDIA				
Noida	Washing machines	0.5	Due 1998	JV, $100 million for 2 plants
	Refrigerators	0.5		
	Colour televisions	0.6		
INDONESIA				
West Java	Colour picture tubes	2.3	1995	$110 million, Orion Electric has 15% equity interest
Jakarta	Washing machines	0.1	1995	$6 million (Daewoo 60%)
MALAYSIA				
Kuala Lumpur	Washing machines		1994	$1.6 million (Daewoo 51%)
MYANMAR				
Yangon integrated production complex	Refrigerators	0.7	1991	
	Colour televisions	0.2	Due end 1996	$20 million by 1999
	VCRs	0.2		
	Components			
THAILAND				
Rayong Industrial Estate	Non-CFC refrigerators	0.1	1996	Daewoo 30% of JV with Distar

VIETNAM

Saidong integrated production complex	Colour televisions	2.0	1995	$170 million: JV with Hanel Electronics
	Washing machines	0.2		
	Refrigerators	0.1		
	Core components	1.0		

THE AMERICAS

MEXICO

Sonora integrated production complex	VCRs	1.0	1996	
	Monitors	1.0	1996	
	Components	3.6	1996	$25 million
	Colour televisions	2.0	1991	$57 million
	Microwave ovens	0.6	Due 1997	
Baja California	Picture tubes	4.0	Due 1997	$260 million
Queretaro	Washing machines	0.2	1996	$38 million
	Refrigerators	0.2		

BRAZIL

	Home appliances		Due 1997	

EUROPE AND THE CIS

FRANCE

Longwy	Microwave ovens	1.5	1988	$32 million
	Glass for CRT's		due 1998	$150 million
Fameck	Colour televisions	0.8	1993	$40 million
Lorraine	Cathode ray tubes	1.2	1995	$137 million
	Semiconductors		due 1998	$1.2 billion

KAZAKHSTAN	Colour televisions	0.1	1994	$17 million

N. IRELAND

Antrim	VCRs	1.3	1988	$7 million, plus $22 for capacity upgrade
Carrickfurgus	Electronic tuners	1.2	1995	$12 million

POLAND

Pruszcow integrated production complex	Colour televisions (assembly)	0.4	1993	$28 million
	Components		1995	$4 million
	Refrigerators			

Case 15

Warsaw	Washing machines	0.1		$6 million

SPAIN

Vitoria, Basque Country	Refrigerators	0.5	Due 1997	$87 million over 5 years, 100% ownership

UZBEKISTAN

Tashkent	Colour televisions	0.1	1993	$60 million JV with local government
	Components	1.5	1993	
	Cordless phones			
	Vacuum cleaners			

* Expected production in 1996, or expected production in first year of operation; millions of units.

Source: Company records, media reports

Exhibit CS15.5   Doubling their size: (a) Daewoo with Thomson Multimédia; (b) Matra with Thomson-CSF

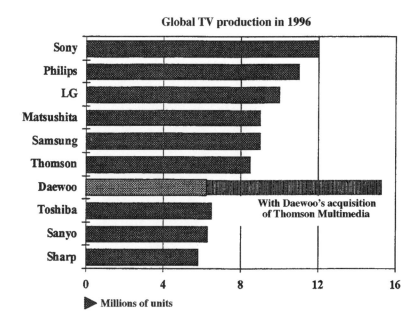

Global TV production in 1996

With Daewoo's acquisition of Thomson Multimedia

▶ Millions of units

Source: Business Week, 16 September 1996

Sales revenues in 1996

(+ Unisys)

(+ E-Systems)

With Matra's acquisition of Thomson-CSF

(+ Westinghouse)

Acquisition in process

▶ $ Billions

Source: "Les Echos" Newspaper, 17 October 1996

Case 15

Exhibit CS15.6   Daewoo's planned foreign investments, January 1996

	Recently announced			Still under negotiation		
	Projects	Total costs $m	Daewoo's contribution $m*	Projects	Total costs $m	Daewoo's contribution $m*
Asia	41	6,903	1,529	52	4,425	676
Africa/Middle East	7	277	68	7	355	136
CIS/Europe	14	3,452	587	26	3,753	392
America	11	396	83	10	71	9
Total	73	11,028	2,267	95	8,604	1,213

* Paid-in-capital.

Exhibit CS15.7   Structure of the Thomson Group

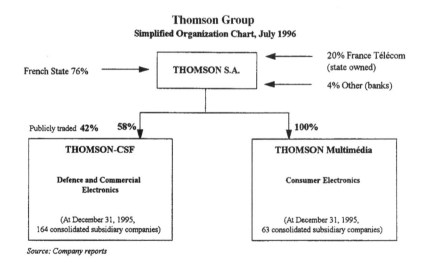

Source: Company reports

Right: Exhibit CS15.8   Advertisement placed by Daewoo Electronics in *Le Figaro* newspaper, 6 November 1996

CONNAISSEZ-VOUS LE NAIN DAEWOO?

34ᵉ GROUPE MONDIAL

Case 15

■ **Un groupe diversifié**

Notre nom ne vous est sans doute pas inconnu. Mais peut-être souhaitez vous mieux savoir ce que nous représentons vraiment?

Daewoo est un groupe diversifié, dont les activités recouvrent l'automobile, l'électronique, la construction navale, l'industrie lourde, le bâtiment, la finance et le négoce. Le magazine américain Fortune, dans son dernier classement des 500 premières entreprises mondiales, place Daewoo au 34ᵉ rang, avec un chiffre d'affaires de 260 milliards de francs.

■ **Une croissance soutenue dans l'électronique**

Notre branche électronique, qui devrait tout particulièrement vous intéresser, est en passe de porter son chiffre d'affaires de 34 à 40 milliards de francs sur la période 1995/1996, soit un chiffre comparable à celui de Thomson Multimédia. Dans le même temps, son résultat net augmentera de plus de 30%; de 790 millions à plus d'un milliard de francs.

Cette dynamique incontestable représente, sur le plan des volumes, un poids équivalent à celui de Thomson Multimédia. Daewoo Electronics produira en effet 7 millions de téléviseurs, 4 millions de magnétoscopes et 12 millions de tubes cathodiques en 1996. Notre taux de croissance, supérieur à 25% sur la période 1992/1995, nous place loin devant nos compétiteurs.

■ **Une présence internationale et des compétences multiples dans l'électronique**

Daewoo Electronics dispose d'un réseau global dans les domaines du marketing, de la Recherche et Développement et de la production. Nous avons construit un ensemble de 39 unités de production très compétitives dans 14 pays à travers le monde, notamment en France, Grande-Bretagne, Pologne, Mexique, Vietnam et Chine.

Nos technologies de fabrication, de niveau mondial, ont constitué le moteur de notre compétitivité dans les domaines de la qualité et des coûts. Daewoo Electronics a également renforcé ses capacités en termes de Recherche et Développement puisque, avec des dépenses de 1,8 milliard de francs et des équipes de 2 800 chercheurs, nos efforts dans ce domaine sont également comparables à ceux de Thomson Multimédia.

La mise au point et le développement de téléviseurs pour Internet et d'un des écrans plats les plus prometteurs démontrent notre savoir faire dans les technologies de l'affichage et du numérique. Dans le domaine des ventes et du marketing, Daewoo electronics dispose d'une solide présence dans les marchés en forte croissance tels que l'Asie, l'Amérique Latine, l'Europe de l'Est et la CEI. Il est également présent, bien que dans des proportions moindres, en Amérique du Nord et en Europe de l'Ouest. En ce qui concerne le Japon, où Daewoo Electronics a concentré ses ventes dans le segment des produits haut de gamme, il détient des parts de marché équivalentes à celles des principaux groupes japonais.

■ **Daewoo croit en la France**

Pendant des années, la France a été au cœur de notre stratégie de développement. Nous avons établi des liens étroits avec l'industrie française : de l'électronique grand public aux projets TGV. Depuis 1988, nous avons investi en France. Bien avant le projet de privatisation de Thomson, nous avons engagé un plan d'investissement de plusieurs milliards de francs intégrant la création de plusieurs milliers d'emplois, dont 1 400 sont d'ores et déjà effectifs dans trois sites en Lorraine. Pour s'en tenir à un seul exemple, la capacité de notre usine à micro-ondes a été triplée depuis son ouverture.

Contrairement à tous ses autres compétiteurs qui se sont installés ou déplacés vers des pays voisins, Daewoo a donc choisi la France.

Tout simplement parce qu'il y croit.

Exhibit CS15.8 Advertisement Placed by Daewoo Electronics in *Le Figaro* newspaper, 6 November 1996

English Translation

Have you heard of the dwarf Daewoo?

34th largest group in the world

A Diversified Group

Our name is surely not unknown to you. But perhaps you would like to know more about what we really represent?

Daewoo is a diversified group, whose activities cover automobiles, electronics, shipbuilding, heavy industry, construction, finance, and trade. The American magazine Fortune ranked Daewoo 34th in its latest classification of the top 500 companies in the world, with a turnover of FF260 billion ($52 billion).

SUSTAINED GROWTH IN ELECTRONICS

Our electronics arm, which should be of particular interest to you, is in the process of boosting its turnover from 34 to 40 billion francs over the period 1995/1996, a result comparable to that of Thomson Multimédia. Over the same period, its net profit will grow by more than 30%; from 790 million to over a billion francs.

This undeniable dynamism represents, in terms of volume, a weight equivalent to that of Thomson Multimédia. Daewoo Electronics will in fact produce 7 million television screens, 4 million video recorders and 12 million cathode ray tubes in 1996. Our growth rate, which was greater than 25% over the period 1992/1995, places us far ahead of our competitors.

AN INTERNATIONAL PRESENCE AND MULTIPLE COMPETENCIES IN ELECTRONICS

Daewoo Electronics possesses a global network in the areas of marketing, Research and Development, and production. We have built a group of 39 highly competitive production units in 14 countries across the world, notably in France, Great Britain, Poland, Mexico, Vietnam and China.

Our world-standard production technologies have been the engine of our competitiveness in the areas of quality and costs. Daewoo Electronics has also reinforced its Research and Development capabilities as, with expenditure of 1.8 billion francs and teams of 2,800 researchers, our efforts in this area are also comparable to those of Thomson Multimédia.

The conception and development of television screens for the Internet and of one of the most promising flat screens serve as testimony to our expertise in display and digital technologies. In the area of sales and marketing, Daewoo Electronics has a solid presence in the high-growth markets of Asia, Latin America, Eastern Europe and the CIS. It is also present, although on a lesser scale, in North America and Western Europe. With regard to Japan, where Daewoo Electronics has concentrated its sales in the upmarket segment, it holds market shares equivalent to those of the principal Japanese groups.

DAEWOO BELIEVES IN FRANCE

Case 15

Over the years, France has been at the heart of our development strategy. We have established close links with French industry: from consumer electronics to TGV projects. We have invested in France since 1988. Well before the project for the privatization of Thomson, we committed to an investment plan totalling several billion francs including the creation of several thousands of jobs, of which 1,400 are already in place in three sites in Lorraine. To give a single example, the capacity of our microwave plant has tripled since opening.

Contrary to all its other competitors who have installed themselves in or shifted to neighbouring countries, Daewoo has therefore chosen France.

Quite simply because it believes in it.

Case 16

Case 16

This case was written by Lizabeth Froman and Marc Canizzo, under the supervision of Hellmut Schütte, Affiliate Professor at INSEAD. It is intended to be used as a basis for class discussion rather than to illustrate either effective or ineffective handling of an administrative situation. Copyright © 1992 INSEAD-EAC, Fontainebleau, France.

The Salim Group

Liem Sioe Liong has been remarkably industrious. After leaving his native province of Fukien in China in 1937 and starting with nothing in Indonesia, he built an empire that had a US$8 billion in turnover in 1990. Luck was also on his side. When he began supplying peanut oil and staples to the Indonesian army during the fight for independence in the 1950s, Liem forged a bond with the chief supply officer of the Diponegoro division, Lieutenant Suharto, who later rose through the army ranks to become president of Indonesia. This early friendship helped Liem to prosper during a period when then President Sukarno was promoting businesses run by the indigenous population at the expense of those run by the Overseas Chinese living in the country.

As in many Southeast Asian countries, the ethnic Chinese who migrated to Indonesia have become an economically powerful minority, representing less than 5% of the population but controlling over 40% of the country's wealth. Their success has been attributed to growth in the Asian economies, the immigrant status of the Chinese which motivated them to succeed in their new country and the social values and organization of the Chinese culture.

By making aggressive use of his contacts and his negotiating skills, Liem has built a network of businesses that dwarfs other Indonesian groups and is, in fact, the largest Overseas Chinese conglomerate. Liem's Indonesian businesses today represent 5% of the country's GDP. In 1990, 40% of Group sales and 25% of Group assets were located outside Indonesia. Liem, now 75 years old, is handing the reins of the Salim Group over to the youngest of his three sons, Anthony Salim (Salim is the Indonesian name of Liem).

Anthony's mission is to focus the company's businesses and strengthen the Group's competitive position. Like his father, he has been described as a 'clever, gutsy operator... loyal to friends and... outwardly unassuming.' The elder Liem is 'famous for driving a hard bargain', but his son is reputed to be even tougher. In addition, Anthony is more internationally minded and more committed to the art of professional management.

BACKGROUND ON THE INDONESIAN POLITICAL SYSTEM

At the end of the Second World War, Indonesia declared its independence from the Dutch. Over the 20 years of President Sukarno's leadership, Indonesia was united as a country but suffered economic decline. President Sukarno replaced the elected House of Representatives with an appointed Assembly that zealously pursued domestic politics and waged foreign policy feuds with the Netherlands and Malaysia at the expense of the country's economic prosperity.

Following what was claimed by the government to have been a communist-led coup attempt in 1965, Major General Suharto assumed executive power in March 1966 and has served as Indonesia's president ever since. A new political order was established based on a constitutional republic. Two political parties remain – the Indonesian Democratic Party (PDI) and the Islamic United Development Party (PPP). A third political group, Golkar, is dominated by the military and has won substantial majorities in elections to the House of Representatives since 1971.

Indonesia has been politically stable since 1968. Tensions still arise, however, due to some Muslim integrist circles and the discontented intelligentsia. The antipathy toward the economically prosperous Chinese minority has also caused violent outbreaks. Because of his long reign, Suharto has created a succession problem. In order to unite the various factions in the country, the president of Indonesia needs three qualifications: he needs to be from an operating unit of the military, from the central island of Java, and a Muslim. For many years, no one was properly groomed for the position.

Demands for political reform continue. Suharto has come under increasing criticism for allowing the Overseas Chinese to dominate the business scene and for the growing gap in income distribution in the country. He recently announced plans to encourage businesses to sell 20% of their equity to employees or to cooperatives.

Indonesia has achieved economic stability through a series of five-year plans setting specific sectoral growth targets. The first five-year plan (1969–74) focused on agricultural production and infrastructure. Further plans set goals to increase social welfare benefits and generate adequate employment opportunites, primarily with private sector investment. Indonesia is the fifth most populous country in the world with 180 million people, 40% of whom are under the age of 15. To achieve the latest plan's goal, 5% real growth is essential. This growth is expected to come from the manufacturing sector. Local manufacturing has been encouraged through tariffs and quantity restrictions, looser monetary policies and the free convertibility of the rupiah, which has led to a boom in foreign investment. However, high interest rates and the current credit crunch in Indonesia are obstacles to the attainment of the government's goal.

THE LIEM INVESTORS

The Liem investors are the shareholders of most of Liem's businesses. They include Liem himself; Djuhar Sutano, a friend from Liem's Fukien province in China; Sudwikatmono, President Suharto's foster brother; Ibrahim Risjad, said to have close ties to the military; and Anthony Salim, Liem's son. In 1990, the Liem investors took four of the top six spots in the list of Indonesia's highest personal taxpayers. Government officials and other Suharto relatives figure prominently among the other investors in Liem's companies. Liem is but one of a number of beneficiaries of the Suharto regime's practice of granting monopoly rights to insiders. The government has shielded

Liem from losses through substantial equity infusions and, by allowing Liem in many cases to own the competition too, through artificial competition. Liem has enjoyed privileged access to capital and preferential buying arrangements for his goods.

ORGANIZATION OF THE GROUP

The Salim Group is made up of over 350 companies of varying sizes that are operationally separate. About 100 are centrally administered, while the rest are more passive investments. As Anthony admits, 'The formation of the Salim Group was by accident, not design. [Our growth] was driven by opportunities available to us'. The new Group leader is looking to divest smaller holdings and to take greater control of key businesses. The Group currently employs 135,000 people.

Liem influences operations in his disparate companies through resource allocation, particularly that of intangible resources such as information and connections. Cohesion among business units is accomplished in part through the small numbers of managers rotated around different companies in the Salim Group, whose loyalty is therefore to Liem and not to the individual businesses. This level of trust allows subsidiaries' operations to be decentralized while cash flow is allocated centrally. A small group of executive directors oversees the strategy of all the affiliates. Equity not held by the Liem family is placed in friendly hands (either with trusted individuals or with management). Entrepreneurship is strongly encouraged and is rewarded in managers and younger family members, as demonstrated by the many start-up businesses run by the top team.

LIEM'S DEVELOPMENT

Commodity monopolies

Through the 1960s Liem concentrated on businesses in cloves, coffee, rubber and soybeans. In 1969 Liem gained access to new capital through his relations with Bulog, Indonesia's logistics agency for commodities. Bulog had been run by Suharto and was later managed by Bustanil Arifin, who is related to Suharto by marriage. The monopoly arranged for Liem's Bogasari Flour Mill (BFM) provided the capital to fuel the growth of his holdings in the 1970s. BFM contributes 20% of its profits to political and charitable organizations run by Suharto-related shareholders.

Government support

In the 1970s, Indonesia encouraged import substitution industries by guaranteeing sustainable profits through price fixing. Liem built strong concerns in cement, steel, assembly and distribution of foreign cars, and banking. Forestry products, chemicals and agribusiness were opportunistically expanded. Real estate became a prime focus in Indonesia and in the 'Golden Triangle' of the Riau Islands, Singapore and Malaysian Johor.

Government support of Liem's investments is best exemplified by the history of Indocement, one of the star performers on the Jakarta Stock Exchange (JSE) and a credit deemed worthy of European bond investors. By 1980 Liem owned five cement companies and was being encouraged to expand capacity through above-market government pricing. By 1985 Liem could boast of the largest production complex in the world. However, the recession in the early 1980s in Indonesia, prompted by the fall in oil prices, led to cutbacks in government infrastructure spending. Liem was losing a lot of money and was granted a government-supported restructuring. His five companies were merged into Indocement Tunggal Prakarsa with the government taking a 35% stake for US$325 million. Expensive US dollar loans were refinanced with rupiah credits issued by state-owned banks. Two years later, profit requirements were waived so that Indocement could once again list its shares on the JSE. In 1990, Indocement earned 47% gross profit margins.

A similiar story of consortia, artificial competition, government buying arrangements and equity injections can be found in the steel industry.

Cross ownership

Through cross ownership arrangements with other Indonesian-Chinese tycoons, Liem has been able to control his markets and his competition. Such shareholding agreements include Liem's friends Ciputra and his Metropolitan Group in properties, Eka Cipta Wijaya and his Sinar Mas Group in chemicals and agribusinesses, and Robert Kuok in commodities trading.

Liem's first attempt in banking came in the early 1950s with Bank Windu Kentjana. This was not a success, despite strong links with the military. In the late 1950s Liem purchased the Bank Central Asia (BCA) in Indonesia, which languished for 15 years. In 1975 Liem brought in Mochtar Riady, owner of the most successful private bank in Indonesia, Panin Bank, to aid the ailing BCA. The merged group flourished. Riady was recently bought out, his Lippo Bank being a formidable competitor. BCA is owned 32% by two of Suharto's children. Liem still holds 15% of Lippo.

International growth

In the 1980s, Liem established offshore holding companies and aggressively grew his investments outside Indonesia. Primarily through the First Pacific Group in Hong Kong (discussed in the next section), Liem controls banking and property in Hong Kong, real estate development in Singapore, drug stores in the Philippines, a US Savings and Loan, a Dutch trading house and an Australian communications firm. Liem uses the banking division of First Pacific to tap new sources of capital – it arranged private financing for Indocement – and to scout out and review international acquisitions.

The company has also turned its attention to Vietnam, where it has engaged in commercial real estate and coal mining. The latter project is a US$27 million venture embarked upon with two other Indonesian industrial groups (Astra, Gemala) and entails a long-term commitment (30 years).

Joint ventures with foreign partners

Building on his skill in finding solid business partners and investors, Liem established a number of joint ventures with foreign partners. In Indonesia, the Group is discussing a US$240 million chemical production facility with Amoco Chemical and already has a joint venture with Henkel from Germany. More recently, the group entered into partnership with Dow Chemical to produce polystyrene resin. Liem is teaming up with Japanese companies in a wide range of industries. Working with Japan's largest general contractor, Taisei Corp., Liem is developing an industrial park. He is expanding the range of cars marketed for Mazda Motor Co. and Nissan Motor Co. Bank LTCB-Central Asia was set up with the Long-Term Credit Bank of Japan and Nikko Securities Indonesia, and joint ventures are being negotiated in the soft drink industry with Yakult Honsha Co. and in wire harnesses with Sumitomo Electric Industries Ltd. First Pacific is expanding its telecommunications business through agreements with British Telecom.

Ever open to new opportunities and an extended geographic reach, the Group entered into a partnership with a Swedish firm (SKW Trostberg) to buy an East German company producing agrochemicals. This acquisition comes in addition to the outright purchase of a fatty alcohols company in the former East Germany, which cost the Group $40 million.

THE FIRST PACIFIC GROUP

First Pacific Group, located in Hong Kong, was founded in 1982 and is listed on the Hong Kong, Dutch and US stock exchanges. The Liem investors retain 65% ownership and tight management control. First Pacific is run by Manuel Pangilinan, a Filipino educated in the USA. While he was with American Express, he became the trusted advisor of Liem and Anthony and was asked to start up a vehicle for international expansion. The company's stated goal is the 'increase of shareholder value' (1990), which has largely been accomplished through opportunistic acquisitions. Performance is measured by growth of per share earnings and net asset value. The current business divisions are marketing and distribution (trading); banking; real estate; and telecommunications. Each division manages its own portfolio of businesses.

The 1990s are stretching the limits of the group's capital. Despite grumblings from First Pacific's treasury staff about the need to digest the current businesses, all divisions are looking at new growth opportunities. These opportunities are analysed within First Pacific's merchant bank. First Pacific has been kept relatively cash tight for its expansion plans, which require direct investment (and some control) from Indonesia.

THE GROUP'S ACTIVITIES

Trading

In 1983 First Pacific acquired the ailing Dutch trading company Hagemeyer with roots in Indochina. The company now operates in 21 countries, represents thousands of branded consumer products and generates US$1.4 billion in sales. Hagemeyer is increasing its international presence through acquisitions of specialty products companies in Europe, North America and Asia.

In June 1991, First Pacific proposed a merger between Hagemeyer and Internatio-Mueller NV in the Netherlands after First Pacific announced in May that it had already amassed 43.2% of the shares of the underperforming conglomerate; this investment amounted to about US$100 million. The proposal was rejected in August with Internatio pledging to focus on two main businesses – engineering and wholesaling of pharmaceuticals. Discussions continue and First Pacific has been offered representation on Internatio's board. This year, Hagemeyer is also completing the acquisition of a German trading company that it is financing through the private placement of new shares worth 60 million guilders.

Banking

First Pacific launched its banking division with: (a) the purchase of Hong Nin Bank, a small Hong Kong-based retail bank; (b) a new brokerage unit, First Pacific Securities; and (c) the acquisition of Hibernia Bank, the twelfth largest bank in California. In 1988 the poorly performing securities unit was divested, as was Hibernia Bank. Proceeds were used to expand the Hong Kong retail-banking network through the acquisition of Far East Bank. First Pacific has continued in US banking with United Savings Bank, a savings and loan catering to Chinese clients in the San Francisco area. All current banking operations worldwide (outside Indonesia) have been consolidated under First Pacific Bancshares, a separately listed company on the Hong Kong stock exchange and Hong Kong's sixth largest banking group.

There is no clear commitment to this sector despite its usefulness as a source of new capital. Stock analysts predict the sale of the division, but new opportunities for growth are constantly examined. First Pacific made a bid for the Hong Kong branch of the scandal-shaken BCCI in the summer of 1991. Instead, the Lippo Group made the final bid but withdrew at the beginning of 1992.

Real estate

First Pacific Davies, purchased in 1985 from founder and chairman David Davies, is one of Hong Kong's leading real estate agencies involved in property brokerage, valuations and project management. The group has associations with major real estate agencies in the UK, the USA and Australia. David Davies is a long-standing and very well-respected Hong Kong real estate expert, having previously served as CEO of Hong Kong Land, a Jardine company.

Another Liem offshore company, KMP Pty of Singapore, purchased Singapore's largest commercial real estate company, United Industrial Corp. (UIC) in 1990. KMP is mainly owned by Anthony and his brother Andre. KMP was dormant for 10 years, but its recent activity shows a clear attempt by Anthony to gain more family control of the expanding business. There is talk that UIC and its 75%-owned subsidiary Singapore Land could be merged with First Pacific's real estate holdings in Hong Kong to create the largest pan-Asian real estate company.

Management of a merged company would be sensitive, as FP Davies is run by David Davies and UIC is run by Leong Chee Whye, a member of the Singapore Parliament, with executive chairman Lee Kim Yew, brother of former prime minister Lee Kwan Yew. Neither group is likely to relinquish operating control. There are also financial obstacles to a FP-UIC merger; First Pacific's capital constraints may not allow it to assume UIC's high debt level.

One of the largest projects is the conversion of 19,000 hectares of Bintan island, in the Indonesian archipelago located close to Singapore, into a leisure resort area. The Bintan Resort Development Company plans to invest US$600 million over the next three years with total investment rising to US$3 billion by 1998. UIC is trying to have Bintan declared a trade zone free from import restrictions. Anthony is putting together a consortium of private and public sector investors to complete this master plan.

In February 1992, First Pacific entered into a 50/50 joint venture with the Keppel group (of Singapore) to build a US$75 million commercial complex in Ho Chi Minh City (former Saigon). This represents one of the largest foreign investments in Vietnam to date.

Case 16

Telecommunications

First Pacific agreed in August to buy the 50% of Pacific Link Communications currently owned by a Luxemburg affiliate of US-based Millicom Inc. for US$150 million. This is expected to increase FP's earnings tenfold. Private minority investors (from Indonesia) will provide a portion of the capital.

The company has also found a very profitable niche in the mobile phone market and is expanding its telecommunications division through trunked radio lines and distribution of equipment.

Other

First Pacific has purchased and divested operations in New York catering, Hong Kong retail operations, and manufacturing plants.

MANAGEMENT STYLE

First Pacific is known in Hong Kong as an aggressive organization when it comes to opportunistic new investments. Top management includes the heads of each division (two Europeans) but is dominated by a small group of Filipino bankers all educated in the USA or Britain and recruited from Western financial institutions by Manny Pangilinan. FP has been described as a one-man show, and Manny himself as a financial genius and a visionary by his admiring management and employees.

The company tries to strike a balance between relationship-driven transactions (either from Indonesia, the Philippines or elsewhere) and long-term growth opportunities such as telecommunications. Top managers have important equity positions in the companies they manage (and possibly in others within the Salim Group as well) and therefore share 'the increase of shareholder value' as the company's goal.

VISION FOR THE FUTURE: HOW CAN IT BE REALIZED

Anthony Salim is working toward building a pan-Asian company by: (a) streamlining the Group's holdings; (b) consolidating the family's control at the expense of the other Liem investors, and (c) strengthening his companies' balance sheets. Anthony is perceived as a very capable manager and negotiator who could work comfortably anywhere in the world. He is trying to gain international credibility by professionalizing management and using new, non-Indonesian holding groups as acquisition and growth vehicles. He has purchased reputable and traditional companies such as Hagemeyer, Hibernia and Shanghai Land, and the Group has engaged top-name advisors – Price Waterhouse, Jardine Fleming, Citibank and Goldman Sachs, among others – despite having some of these firms' capabilities in-house.

Through opportunistic expansion, the Salim Group has successfully established itself as an Asian company, not just an Indonesian one. It has moved into Europe and North America with centralized decision making but decentralized operations management. It is well positioned to become Indonesia's first truly multinational company.

Case 16

RESEARCH SOURCES

1. Dodwell, David, 'First Pacific pauses to re-group', *The Banker*, October 1984, pp. 28–32.

2. First Pacific Group, Annual Report 1985–90.

3. Gardini, Anne, Analyst Reports: 'PT Indocement Tunggal Prakarsa' and 'PT Unggul Indah Corporation', 22 January 1991.

4. Hagemeyer, Annual Report 1988–90.

5. Hagerty, Bob, 'Dutch firm vetoes First Pacific merger plan', *The Asian Wall Street Journal*, 12 August 1991, p. 1.

6. 'Indonesia Country Profile 1989–90'. *The Economist Intelligence Unit.*

7. Lasserre, Philippe, 'Les Groupes Prives Indonesiens', INSEAD – Centre Euro Asie, 1990.

8. Lasserre, Philippe, 'Corporate strategic management and the Overseas Chinese Groups', *Asia Pacific Journal of Management*, 2 January 1988; pp. 115–131.

9. Limlingan, Victor Simpao, *The Overseas Chinese in ASEAN: Business Strategies and Management Practices*, Manila, Vita Development Corp., 1986.

10. Owens, Cynthia, 'Hong Kong clears a proposal for BCCI unit's sale to Lippo Group', *The Wall Street Journal Europe*, 3 September 1991, p. 12.

11. Redding, S. Gordon, *The Spirit of Chinese Capitalism*, Berlin/New York, W. de Gruyter, 1990.

12. Schwarz, Adam, contributing article to 'Empire of the Son', *Far Eastern Economic Review*, 14 March 1991, pp. 46–53.

13. Schwarz, Adam, contributing article to 'Focus Indonesia 1991', *Far Eastern Economic Review*, 18 April 1991, pp. 24–30.

14. Stine, Stephen F., 'First Pacific builds its telecom business', *The Asian Wall Street Journal*, 22 August 1991, p. 3.

15. Sito, Peggy, 'First Pacific pays HK$1.17b in takeover', *South China Morning Post*, 22 August 1991.

Case 16

Exhibit CS16.1   Liem Holdings

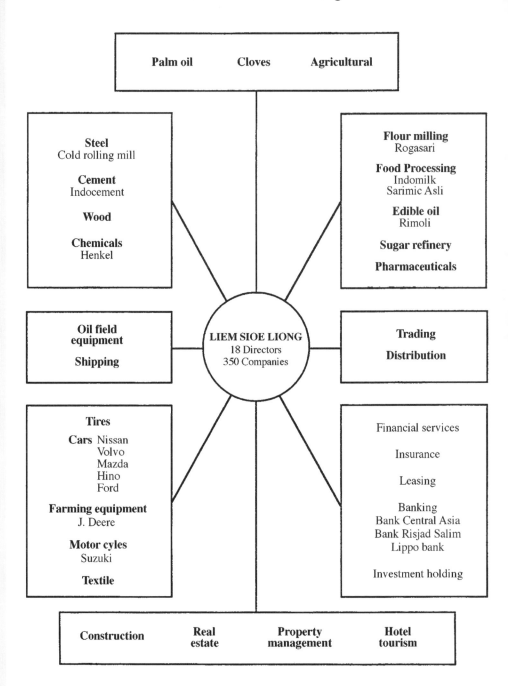

Exhibit CS16.2 First Pacific Group structure

First Pacific Company

Marketing and Distribution
- 69% — Hagemeyer N.V.
- 40% — First Pacific Metro Corporation
- 38% — Berli Jucker Company Ltd
- 67% — Malaysia Pharmacy SDN BHD
- 34.3% — Thai Pacific Foods Ltd

Commercial and Investment banking
- 33.9% — F.P. Special Assets Ltd

First Pacific Bancshares Holdings Ltd — 47%
- 100% — United Savings Bank
- 100% — First Pacific Bank
- 40% — First Pacific Capital Corporation

Communications
- 50% — Pacific Link Communications Ltd
- 73.5% — First Pacific Telecom
- 45% — Personal Communications
- 42% — Imagineering Technology
- 100% — Asia Link

Real estate consulting and investment
- 96% — First Pacific Davies (Holdings) Ltd
- 60.5% — First Pacific Land (Bermuda)

Case 17

This case was developed by Professor Peter J. Williamson and Dr Hongmin Chen as the basis for class discussion rather than to illustrate either effective or ineffective handling of an administrative situation. Copyright © 1996 by China Europe International Business School

China Eastern Airlines
Building Competitive Advantage

Mr Wang Li An, chairman of the board of China Eastern Air Group and president of China Eastern Airlines, and his board were meeting to review the future plans of the company. Over the past eight years, China Eastern's management and staff had made enormous progress in modernizing the business. From its home base in Shanghai and with a fleet of 44 McDonnell Douglas and Airbus and Fokker aircraft, the company had expanded rapidly both in Chinese domestic and international routes while making big strides forward in reliability, punctuality and service standards. It was looking forward to the forthcoming flotation of its shares on the New York stock exchange led by Mr Xiao Liyan, vice-president and director of the Privatization Office, and to the delivery of new, state-of-the art Airbus 340s during 1996.

Optimistic about the future, the management was also aware that the competitive environment in China's aviation industry was changing rapidly. While carriers such as China Eastern, Air China and China Southern Airlines had prospered, others were having difficulties. Indeed, one of the decisions facing China Eastern was whether it should make an approach to acquire the ailing China North Western Airlines, based in Xian. Would such a move help to strengthen China Eastern's competitive position and underpin its ongoing growth, or would it instead divert the attention of the company from its primary goals? What other policies and initiatives should China Eastern be adopting to build on its success to date in the Chinese market and prepare for expansion in the challenging international aviation industry – a business where losses were all too common and former giants such as Pan Am had disappeared altogether?

THE EMERGENCE OF CHINA'S CIVIL AVIATION INDUSTRY

Before liberation in 1949, the industry was divided between two organizations: China Airlines and China Central Airlines. During the collapse of the nationalist government dozens of aircraft were sent to Taiwan from where today's China Airlines was re-established. With the aged fleet that remained and pilots trained by the new People's government in northern China, CAAC (the Civil Aviation Administration of China) was formed. CAAC combined control of flight operations, airport management and administration of the industry (such as traffic rights and other regulations) under the umbrella of a single operation. In 1953 the Shanghai Division of

CAAC was established for administration of the CAAC fleet based in Shanghai, local support operations and the Hongqiao airport.

Strictly speaking, air transportation in China up until the 1980s could not really be regarded as an industry. It developed very slowly from 1949–78 under the control of the army (firstly the air force, then the military commission) and the Department of Transport. Accordingly, there was little evidence of a 'business mentality'. Employees were treated like military personnel and the passengers were high-ranking officials rather than business people or ordinary citizens. As a result, air transportation developed in response to political rather than economic needs, thus contributing little to economic development.

The real development of an industry started in the early 1980s, after the 3rd Session of the 11th Party Congress. The Civil Aviation Administration of China (CAAC), which was running at a heavy loss and had no real control at local level, recognized the need to adopt a more business-like approach. To achieve this, the local CAAC organizations were given the responsibility of managing their own revenues and costs, and by 1983, the CAAC authorized international borrowing for the purchase of aircraft. In spite of the fact that key decisions were still made by central government, these reforms saw the industry expand from 1.8 billion passenger kilometres in 1977 to 18.2 billion passenger kilometres in 1987, with average annual growth reaching 25.8% (compared to a rate of 8.5% from 1949–77).

It became clear, however, that the traditional, semi-military airline industry could not meet the demands of China's rapid expansion. In 1987, the CAAC announced that each of the six local bureaux (Eastern China, North China, South China, Northeastern, Southwestern and Northwestern) were to establish their own airlines which gradually would be accountable for their own revenues and costs under the 'complete responsibility system'. Simultaneously, the CAAC's administrative levels were also reduced from four to two: the national administration and the local bureaux.

DEVELOPMENTS SINCE THE LATE 1980s

In 1988, the local bureaux of CAAC were split into three separate entities. Thus the Shanghai Administrative Bureau was split into China Eastern Airlines, East China CAAC and Hongqiao (Shanghai) airport. However, although the industry had certainly progressed since the strict central control of the CAAC, the so-called 'complete responsibility system' did not mean that the airlines operated as independent entities. Most aspects of their operation were tightly regulated and decisions on domestic and international routes, aircraft selection, major capital investment, foreign exchange management and pricing were still made by the CAAC.

By the end of 1992 the government had authorized the formation of 55 corporate groups that would form a vanguard of the next phase of China's economic development. These groups were given increased freedoms including special rights to manage their finances through a corporate holding structure that held interests in subsidiary companies (which, in the case of four of these groups, included a bank). The China Eastern Air Group (CEAG), along with the Air China Group and the China Southern Air Group were among these 55 corporate groups. This afforded China Eastern Airlines a key opportunity to diversify its interests and to obtain more operating freedom. The core company of the CEAG is China Eastern Airlines which accounts for half of the seats on the Group board (including that of chairman). The remainder of the Group is made up of 16 subsidiaries operating in real estate, imports and exports, advertising, hotels and tourism, air catering, and the China Eastern Air Group Finance Co. – a non-banking financial organization approved by the headquarters of the Bank of China. CEA controls the majority of the voting stock in most of these companies. The formation of the Group allowed CEA important rights not normally afforded to state-owned enterprises, which afforded it greater flexibility in running its business. Specifically, as one of the designated corporate groups, CEA was awarded the following special rights:

- to import aircraft and other transport equipment (after consultation with CAAC);

- to borrow money from domestic or international markets as an independent legal entity;

- to approve overseas postings for its staff (a discretion normally restricted to senior administrative levels such as provincial governments);

- to appoint managers to most of the key posts (with the exception of the presidents and vice-presidents of CEAG and its major subsidiaries);

- to set pricing levels in accordance to market demand conditions, subject to maintaining a 'base price' on average (as explained in more detail below).

At ministerial level in the central government, CAAC, now administers the regulatory framework of the industry, including safety standards, in much the same role as civil aviation authorities around the world. In addition, CAAC is involved in government-to-government negotiations over purchase of aircraft from alternative international suppliers and the allocation of international routes. Domestic route allocations also require final approval of CAAC. Domestic and international route allocations allowing airlines to fly from outside their regional bases are shown in Exhibit CS17.1). East China CAAC now acts as the local administrative arm of CAAC which regulates all players in the industry in eastern China, which now includes new competitors such as Shanghai Airlines. The Hongqiao airport, meanwhile, is managed by an independent government organization providing services to domestic and international carriers operating to, and from, Shanghai. Frequency of flights and 'slots' (i.e. takeoff and landing times within the total number of aircraft movements allowed in a day) are negotiated with local airport authorities.

THE AIR TRANSPORT MARKET IN CHINA

By 1995, the total size of China's air transport industry had passed 18 billion RPKs (Revenue Passenger Kilometres – an industry standard measure equivalent to flying one fare-paying passenger one kilometre), equating to 7 billion RTKs (Revenue Tonne Kilometres). These totals were flown over more than 780 routes serving 134 cities in China and 56 international destinations across 39 countries. Industry growth over the past two years had been 26.3% and 22.4%, respectively (see Exhibit CS17.2).

Although China was already the 11th largest aviation market in the world, expansion was expected to continue at a rapid pace. Relative to her huge population and vast land area, China's aviation industry still had a great deal of untapped, potential demand by world standards. The top five US carriers, for example, flew a total of over 600 billion RPKs between them, while British Airways (the largest carrier on international routes) alone flew over 75 billion RPKs. One estimate by foreign bankers forecast that China would spend about US$90 billion on more than 1,200 new passenger aircraft before 2010.

In 1995 there were 41 airlines established in China of which 28 provided passenger and cargo services. The major players, part of the CAAC, were Air China, CEA, China Southern Airlines, China Northern Airlines, China Northwest Airlines and China Southwest Airlines. These accounted for 80% of the market. The first three – Air China, CEA and China Southern Airlines between them shared 63% of the market (see Exhibit CS17.3). The second type of carrier was funded by regional government – Shanghai Airlines, Xiamen Airlines and Sichuan Airlines are the largest and most profitable. The third type of carrier was jointly owned by the CAAC, regional government and a large corporation, e.g. Zhejiang Airlines which is owned by CEA and the government of Zhejiang Province. Fourthly, Hainan Airlines is the first foreign equity joint-venture company in the airline industry into which overseas investors injected some US$25 million. The final player is the market is Xinhua Airlines, created as the commercial arm of the airforce. It uses military transport planes and airfields as well as two Boeing 737s.

Customer profiles

Surveys suggested that between 40 and 50% of total passenger traffic was accounted for by business people, with a further 35 to 40% holiday travellers. The mix of passenger nationalities varied between airlines. Air China, with a large number of international routes, had a high percentage of foreign passengers. Citizens of Hong Kong, Macau and Singapore made up 30% of the total passengers, Japan a further 25% and North Americans 13%. Approximately 70% of China Eastern's passengers were citizens of the PRC (People's Republic of China), while Shanghai Airlines carried around 50% PRC passengers, a further 25% Hong Kong and Macau and 25% citizens of foreign countries (see Exhibit CS17.4).

Distribution

Before 1988 more than 60% of tickets were issued directly by the local offices and branches of CAAC. Most of the remaining tickets were distributed through a few, large government-owned travel agents such as China Travel Service and China Youth Travel Service. There were few computer terminals set up for ticketing and service was often indifferent.

In response to the rapid growth in the air transport market, private ticket sales agencies began to be established from early 1988. Faced with a slump in sales in the wake of the Tiananmen Square disturbances in 1989, airlines paid increasing attention to mobilizing these new travel agents in the quest to sell their seats. Initially requests for flight booking were received from agents and subsequently confirmed by telephone or facsimile. From 1992 computer reservations systems were expanded allowing more agencies to be added and tickets to be ordered and issued via computer screens. These innovations, combined with the continued growth in demand for tickets and attractive sales commissions (3% on the domestic ticket price and 7% on international tickets) stimulated entrepreneurs to set up new agencies. In fact the number of agents grew by as much as 100% per annum during the early 1990s.

There were now over 2,000 sales agents operating on the computer reservation system (CRS) developed by the CAAC. Some 60% of the major airlines' total sales income was generated by sales through private agencies. In Shanghai this figure was even higher, with agencies selling around 80% of all tickets. Airlines actively solicit the help of agencies in promoting sale of their tickets with various incentives (such as an allocation of free tickets for each 100 seats sold).

To become registered as a new travel agent, entrepreneurs now require minimum capital of RMB500,000 plus the cost of investment in a terminal. They must obtain approval from the local branch of the CAAC by establishing their credentials and require at least three staff who have successfully completed a training diploma.

Pricing and price competition

The 'base price' of airline tickets in China was set by CAAC, but changes in this base price required the approval of China's State Council. Airlines were allowed to vary the average ticket price 20% above or below this base price, to take account of 'local conditions'.

As competition to sell tickets had become more intense, however, airlines had gradually introduced more and more complex discount structures for individual tickets. Off-peak fares, for example might be sold at little more than half the standard fare as carriers sought to fill up under-used capacity on certain flights. Fares also varied in response to seasonal variations in demand. Deep discounts were also available for 'students', 'teachers', various 'group bookings' and so on. It was not clear that all airlines applied the rules for deciding which passengers qualified for discounts in a consistent and systematic way leading to what some observers described as 'non-standardized' pricing.

The emergence of this type of price competition had greatly complicated the task of sales, creating new pressures for proper training for sales staff and provision of the correct information to sales outlets. It also creates new pressures on the CRS (Computer Reservations System) which could handle only a limited number of fares on the screen for any particular route.

Price competition and proliferation of fares also meant new and challenging decisions in the area of what airlines called 'yield control' – in other words getting the right mix between full-fare tickets and various discounted fare so as to maximize the 'yield' or revenue from any flight. If too few discounted tickets were made available on less popular flights, the plane was likely to go out with many empty seats, reducing the yield from the flight. On the other hand, if too many discounted seats were sold, the flight might fill up early so that no space was available for passengers willing to pay full fare who tried to book on the flight in the last few days. In this case the plane would fly out with every seat full, but at a poor yield due to the high proportion of discount tickets.

Airlines in markets such as the USA and some European countries were very familiar with the yield management problem. They used sophisticated computer systems to monitor the rate of ticket sales on particular flights and to decide how many discounted tickets to sell, at what prices, in order to maximize the potential yield. Various airlines, such as American Airlines, had approached CEA to discuss the possibility to selling or licensing their 'expert system' for yield control.

Non-price competition

Price was not the only way in which airlines competed for customers. In fact, for many segments of the market (such as business travellers) price was not the most important factor in deciding which flight to take. Airlines therefore competed on the basis of 'non-price' factors including:

- *the timing of their flights* – airlines tried to set their schedules to offer the most convenient departure and arrival times on competitive routes, scheduling less popular routes at off-peak times;

- *better types of aircraft* – some aircraft were more spacious and comfortable than others, travellers often preferred newer aircraft, and using more reliable planes could reduce the chance of inconvenient delays through breakdown;

- *service quality* – which covered a wide range of aspects from the efficiency and accuracy of bookings and check-in, to reliability of luggage transfers, how helpful and courteous were the staff, through to whether customers 'felt at home' on the aeroplane;

- *punctual departure and arrival* – while sometimes delays were inevitable due to factors such as bad weather, an airline's punctuality depended importantly on the efficiency of its systems, procedures and staff; flights could be delayed, for example if maintenance was not completed on time, aircraft cleaning were delayed, or the catering was late or incomplete, and so on.

Supply of pilots

The CAAC estimated that Chinese airlines will take delivery of between 700–800 new aircraft over the next decade. To operate one aircraft on a normal schedule, an airline requires between five and seven pilots (given a maximum ceiling of 100 flying hours per month that a pilot should not exceed). Based on these calculations, somewhere between 3,500 and 5,600 new pilots will be needed (equivalent to between 350 and 560 per annum). But China's Guanghan Civil Aviation College graduated only 160 qualified students per year. Despite an expansion of training capacity by the industry, pilot shortage was expected to be an important constraint on future expansion.

Airport infrastructure

Between 1980 and the early 1990s, China opened 24 new airports and upgraded further existing ones. Over the next five years, CAAC estimated that investment in airport infrastructure would be US$5.2 billion.

Despite this massive investment, of the 140 airports in use in China, it was estimated that more than one-third were handling more passengers than they were designed for. Therefore, infrastructure shortages and competition for a limited number of flight slots were also expected to present continuing problems for expansion.

THE MARKET POSITION OF CHINA EASTERN AIRLINES

CEA operated a core fleet of 47 aircraft with a capacity of 7,299 seats (see Exhibits CS17.5 and CS17.6). This main fleet was based in Shanghai where CEA had the largest aircraft maintenance and engineering department in the industry. In addition, the CEA Anhui Branch (based in Luogang, Hefei city) operated 16 aircraft; the CEA Shandong Branch (based at airports in Qingdao and Jinan) operated 14 aircraft; and the CEA Jiangxi Branch (based in Nanchang, Jiangxi Province) operated a fleet of six aircraft). CEA also held minority stakes in three regional airlines serving areas in eastern China (Zhejiang Airlines, Qi-Lu Airlines and Jiang-Su Airlines) which act as feeder services to CEA's trunk and international routes. Excluding its regional branches, CEA flew 90 domestic, 11 international and 10 regional routes (see Exhibit CS17.7).

Since 1992, CEA had been the most profitable Chinese airline. By the end of 1994 the company's total revenue was RMB5,700 million with profits of RMB670 million. Other dimensions of its performance versus the industry has been equally impressive. CEA was number two in RTK with 15.3% national market share (894 million ton-km); number three in passenger volume (with a 13.9% market share or 5.61 million passengers) and number two in mail and cargo volume (18.2% share or 149,000 tons). It has achieved a flight safety record of 86,000 hours with no serious accidents since its formation in 1987.

Having its principal base in Shanghai is clearly of benefit to CEA's development as Hongqiao International Airport in Shanghai is the largest airport in eastern China, where CEA holds 36.9% of flight departures, 38% of passengers and 49.4% of mail and cargo volume. The airline has also opened domestic offices in Beijing, Xiamen, Guangzhou, and Shenzhen and 14 international offices including Japan (5), the USA (3), Bahrain, Belgium, Korea, Singapore, Spain, and Thailand.

Growth of the airline had been dramatic: its RTKs flown had tripled between 1988 and 1994 (growth of almost 20% per annum); revenues had grown by an average of 39% per annum over the same period, while annual profit growth averaged 15.4%.

CEA recognized the importance of in-flight service and focused on certain measures to close the gap between its standard of service and that of the international competition: combining experienced cabin staff with younger staff to improve the composition of the team; promoting an attitude of 'if I were a passenger', and standardizing and implementing training at all levels. For three years running (1993, 1994 and 1995) CEA won CAAC's award for high service quality. It was also one of 50 firms to be listed by the Customer Committee of China's Association of Quality Management for customer satisfaction. Not content to rest on their laurels, cabin service managers had recently visited Japan Airlines and Singapore Airlines to gain a better knowledge of the competition.

MAJOR COMPETITORS

Despite its excellent performance to date, CEA faced a highly competitive market. Increased capacity in the industry had forced load factors (the average percentage of seats sold per flight) down from around 75% in the 1980s to 65% in the 1990s. Since a high percentage of an airline's costs were fixed, falling load factors severely impacted profitability. Management of the less successful airlines had typically bid for approval for new aircraft from CAAC with the objective of increasing their power and prestige rather than whether they profitably sell the extra seats. The weaker airlines also had poor records for safety, punctuality and service, so many passengers were discouraged from using their flights where they could choose to fly with a better managed carrier. As a result, they were faced with high costs, excess capacity and low load factors, leading to heavy losses.

These trends, combined with rising fuel prices and widespread discounting of tickets had plunged many Chinese airlines into loss by 1994. Concerned about this development and fearing the loss of economies of scale, the CAAC announced a ban on new entry into the airline industry. It has also begun to encourage horizontal mergers and cross-shareholdings between airlines with the aim of reducing the fragmentation of the market between small, inefficient carriers.

Among the stronger airlines against which CEA had to compete were Air China, China Southern Airlines and its associate Xiamen Airlines, Shanghai Airlines and Hainan Air Line (see Exhibit CS17.8). On international routes Dragon Air (a Chinese joint venture with Cathay Pacific Airlines) and a large number of international carriers from Asia, Europe and the USA also competed for the business. Indeed, it was estimated that international carriers controlled more than 50% of the international air traffic market to and from China.

Air China

Air China is the largest Chinese carrier, formed out of the international division of CAAC. Based in Beijing, it inherited most of the international routes (since, for many years, the major international routes had been concentrated in Beijing). In addition, it was awarded rights to a number of domestic routes into and out of Beijing and neighbouring Tianjin. Overall, Air China operated 50 major domestic routes and 34 international and regional routes to 26 countries.

Air China was equipped with a fleet of 61 aircraft. Many of these were large aeroplanes, including 13 Boeing 747s, seven Boeing 767s, 11 Boeing 737s, five Boeing 707s. It also has four British Aerospace 146s, two Lockheed L-1011 and a number of other aircraft. Air China's safety record remained unblemished since it was established.

Although profitable, Air China had lower operating margins than some of its main rivals such as CEA. In part, this reflected lower load factors and competition from established foreign carriers on many of its long-haul international routes. Air China was reportedly eager to expand its operations further, particularly to increase its market share in the high-growth regions of southern and eastern China. It was also preparing for the listing of its shares on the New York stock exchange.

In addition to its own operations, Air China held an interest in the newly created Shenzhen Airlines, based in the Shenzhen SEZ (Special Economic Zone) near the border with Hong Kong.

China Southern Airlines

Based in Guangzhou, capital of the high-growth Guangdong province, China Southern operated 122 domestic routes and 35 international routes, including Hong Kong, Manila and Bangkok. Its fleet included seven Boeing 767s, 14 Boeing 757s, 31 Boeing 737s and 52 smaller aircraft. Of the six major CAAC airlines, China Southern had grown fastest, but prior to implementation of 'stricter controls and rectification of procedures' by CAAC in mid-1994, China Southern's safety record had been poor.

China Southern also controlled a 60% stake in Xiamen Airlines, based in Xiamen an important SEZ (Special Economic Zone) in Fujian province from which it flew 42 routes. In addition, one of its divisions operated out of Shenzhen airport in the Shenzhen SEZ from which it flies three

Boeing 757s, three Boeing 737s and four other aircraft. China Southern had ambitious expansion plans for its Shenzhen division having ordered six Boeing 777s, three Boeing 767s and a further Boeing 737 for its base there, with plans to fly routes to Bangkok, Kuala Lumpur, Seoul and possibly Moscow.

China Southern was profitable (although its rate of return was lower than China Eastern) and it had sought permission to list its shares on the New York stock exchange.

Shanghai Airlines

Founded in 1985, Shanghai Airlines was the first local airline created outside the ownership of CAAC. It was part owned by the Shanghai Municipality and a large, regional commercial group, the Jinjiang Group (ultimately state-owned) and other investors. During its start-up phase it obtained technical advice through an agreement with Singapore Airlines.

Shanghai airlines operated Boeing 757 and 767 aircraft on 30 routes including Shanghai to Beijing and Guangzhou. It was reputed to be planning significant expansion of its fleet to 13 Boeing 757s and five Boeing 767 by the year 2000, equivalent to a 150% increase in capacity over five years.

Hainan Air Line

Hainan Air Line was currently the only foreign joint-venture company in China's aviation industry. It was established in May 1993 by a consortium of 13 investors including the provincial government of Hainan Island and an investor from the USA. The core of its fleet is two Boeing 737s and three smaller, modern aircraft. It planned to add four more Boeing 737s during 1996. It held a 78% share of flights out of Haikou, the capital of Hainan Province, and international routes were under consideration.

Hainan Air Line had established 13 offices in other Chinese cities and a network of 600 booking agencies. Its strengths included a clean safety record, excellent punctuality (with two years without flight cancellation or significant delay) and high standards of service (including free door-to-door transport for full-fare passengers).

Dragon Air

Dragon Air was established by Hong Kong shipping magnate the late Sir Y.K. Pao based at Hong Kong's Kai Tak airport. Beginning life as a charter airline, its performance floundered in the 1980s as it sought to introduce scheduled services and became embroiled in a complex struggle for international route rights involving powerful interests in China, the UK and Hong Kong. Access to the major trunk routes from Hong Kong to Beijing and Shanghai were particularly hotly contested between Dragon Air and Cathay Pacific, controlled by Swire Pacific, part of one of the oldest and largest British *Hongs* in the territory.

In 1990 Dragon Air was restructured under a deal brokered by Larry Yung Chi Kin, chairman of CITIC Pacific, the Hong Kong arm of the Chinese government investment company China International Trust and Investment Corporation (CITIC) chaired by Yung's father Rong Yiren, vice-president of China. Under this agreement, the majority of Dragon Air's shares were acquired by CITIC Pacific and Cathay Pacific on the condition that Cathay would give up its rights to fly into China (Cathay also received a contract to manage Dragon Air for two years). In 1996 Dragon Air was 46% owned by CITIC Pacific, 43% by Cathay and Swire and 11% by other investors.

Dragon Air held routes from Hong Kong to Beijing, Shanghai, Nanjing and 11 other cities in China. It had recently renewed its entire fleet with advanced Airbus A-330 and A-320 aircraft and was regarded as offering excellent service.

Air Macau

With the opening of an airport in the Portuguese enclave of Macau in 1996 (the colony was scheduled to return to Chinese control in the year 2000), a new airline 'Air Macau' was established. In addition to a number of foreign shareholders, Air Macau was 40% owned by CAAC. Plans for its further development were as yet unclear. However, Air Macau had a significant advantage in serving the large market for air travel between Taiwan and Chinese cities. No direct services between Taiwan and mainland destinations had been authorized. But a large number of passengers flew from Taiwan to Hong Kong where they transferred to flights into China with China Eastern, Air China, China Southern, Dragon Air and other carriers. Air Macau was in the unique position of having rights to flight both to and from Taiwan and mainland China. This allowed it to carry passengers from Taiwan to mainland Chinese cities via Macau without requiring them to change aircraft en route (although the flight numbers changed in Macau) as well as the possibility of convenient connections through Macau using a single ticket.

CNAC

In 1995 the China National Aviation Corporation, a subsidiary of CAAC had applied to the Hong Kong government for permission to establish a new airline based out of Hong Kong. Although still in the early stages of discussion, this approach could lead to the establishment of an important, new competitor in the Chinese market after Hong Kong became a Special Administrative Region of China on 1 July 1997.

While CNAC's long-term objectives were still unknown, on 1 May 1996 it was announced that CNAC would acquire 36% of Dragon Air for around US$250 million to be used 'as the vehicle for expansion of airline operations from Hong Kong'. In a related deal, Cathay Pacific Airlines announced that it would issue around US$350 million of new shares to be taken up by CITIC Pacific taking its stake in Cathay from 10% to 25%. Swire Pacific's share in Cathay would fall from 52.6% to 43.9% as a result.

BUILDING COMPETITIVE ADVANTAGE

In the early 1990s China Eastern's senior management made a number of important strategic decisions in order to build a base for further expansion and competitive advantage. The goals of these changes were 'Safety, Punctuality, Service and Profitability'.

Renewal of its fleet

Top management of the newly established CEA moved aggressively to retire its old-fashioned, small aircraft and replace these with large, modern aeroplanes from leading international manufacturers. Between 1988 and 1990 CEA leased or purchased three Airbus A300's and nine McDonnell Douglas MD82s. During 1991–92, the airline leased a further five, long-range MD-11 aircraft, allowing it to enter the market for intercontinental routes.

Restructuring its route network

CEA began by restructuring its network of domestic routes. The focus was on building Shanghai, Hangzhou and Nanjing as major bases for the fleet and increasing the frequency of flights on major trunk routes from these cities. New routes were opened to coastal cities enjoying rapid economic growth and where new airports were being opened. To make these changes possible, CEA's management took the decision to cease operating some routes with less demand or where competition from local airlines was considered 'cut throat'.

While the number of domestic routes operated by CEA was reduced from 111 to 78 between 1990 and 1993, CEA's total number of flights was increased by 50%. In addition to offering its customers greater frequency on its trunk routes, CEA used its new capacity to open up international routes. Prior to 1990, Japan and Hong Kong were the only areas outside mainland China where CEA operated. During 1991/92 CEA opened long distance intercontinental routes between Shanghai and Los Angeles, Shanghai-Seattle-Chicago and Shanghai-Brussels-Madrid. This represented a doubling of its international flights. RTKs on international routes grew at an average rate of 36.5% p.a. between 1990 and 1993.

Safety

Safety was adopted as the number one goal of CEA's flight operations. The airline's motto was 'Putting Prevention First to Assure Flight Safety'; in others words, to establish a set of procedures and checks that would prevent safety problems from arising. Two of the most critical elements here were pilot training and maintenance procedures.

Despite a national shortage of pilots, CEA required that each pilot undertake refresher training for a full week every six months. Following CEA's lead, the CAAC had asked other Chinese carriers to adopt this creative method of safety assurance.

In the area of maintenance, CEA had established the largest maintenance base in the country. Its maintenance division had 2,500 staff, including 800 technical professionals. Central to safety was the extensive total quality control system that had been implemented, backed by advanced maintenance testing equipment. CEA had also entered into a technical cooperation agreement with Swissair for training of its maintenance staff. Under this cooperation agreement, aircraft were flown to Switzerland with a team of more than 20 CEA maintenance technicians for practical training. By 1996, CEA's maintenance base had achieved certification to carry out all maintenance on its MD-82 fleet, including 'grade D' (or heavy) maintenance. As part of the development of CEA's maintenance capabilities, grades A and B (lighter maintenance) for MD-11 and Airbus aircraft was carried out in Shanghai with C and D grade, heavy maintenance, of these aircraft taking place in Switzerland as of 1995–96.

Service quality

Given the history of China's civil aviation industry described above, improving service quality was one of the most important challenges CEA had accepted. Major improvements in service quality required a fundamental change in company culture which management described as changing people's thinking from 'facing south (with their back to the customer and the market) towards facing north'. Critical determinants of service quality were punctuality, ground handling, on-board service and the computer reservation system (CRS).

Punctuality

CEA's operations department had adopted punctuality as its most important priority after safety. Management regarded punctuality as one of the key ways an airline could differentiate itself in the Chinese market. CEA had therefore established a special, new department – Flight Operations Dispatch – to coordinate the complex set of activities required to ensure each flight departed on time. Using a computer network linked to all relevant departments, Flight Operations Dispatch was able to monitor potential delays and act immediately to rectify potential problems as well as to communicate the status of flights to passengers when unavoidable delays caused by weather or air traffic control (generally associated with congestion in Hong Kong or Beijing) did occur.

Other improvements had been made by learning from the experience of foreign airlines, including Singapore Airlines (SIA) and Japan Airlines (JAL). One cause of delays, for example, was the failure of a passenger to show up at the boarding gate after checking in. In this case the passenger's luggage would need to be off loaded before the flight could take off. Historically this had meant unloading every bag and asking passengers to identify their luggage. By adopting a new, four part tagging baggage tagging system used by leading international airlines, CEA was able to identify exactly which container contained the missing passenger's luggage. This enabled the offending bag to be unloaded quickly without disturbing other passengers, avoiding a delay of anything up to two hours that would have been caused under the old system.

When a flight did fail to leave on schedule, CEA's flight operations division conducted an investigation into exactly which department was responsible for the delay so that the system could be improved in the future. The contribution of each department in ensuring punctuality was important factor considered when appraising the department's performance. Punctuality performance therefore affected the size of the annual pay bonus staff in each department received. Exhibit CS17.9 shows the comparative punctuality of major Chinese airlines during May 1996.

Ground handling

The service that passengers received on the ground from ticket sales through to check-in and boarding was just as important as service standards on board the aircraft. CEA were developing their systems and procedures for reducing waiting times and managing queues at check-in, accommodating passengers seat preferences, checking and tracing luggage, and smoothly releasing seats of 'non-show' passengers (those not turning up for a flight) to standby passengers on heavily booked routes such as Hong Kong. Intensive employee training and upgrading of computer support systems were two of the most important areas where CEA was taking initiatives to improve its ground-handling service.

Staff were trained to greet passengers appropriately, to solicit their requirements and to observe carefully, and to anticipate potential problems and respond as quickly as possible. CEA ground-handling staff visited other airlines once per month as part of CEA's contract to act as ground-handling agents for foreign airlines such as SIA and JAL. On these visits staff worked to understand the requirements of their foreign airline customers as well as looking for new ways of doing business which CEA could learn from.

Improvements to the computer support system were allowing CEA to offer 'through check-in' so that a passenger connecting to a flight through another airport could be issued with boarding passes for their entire journey in Shanghai and have luggage checked right through to the final destination. Currently, through check-in services were only available on flights via Hong Kong. Other procedures were also being improved to allow CEA to offer more 'customer-oriented' service. Historically, for example when luggage had been delayed or incorrectly routed, Chinese airlines had telephoned the customer requesting them to come and pick it up at the airport once it had been recovered. CEA had replaced this procedure with a service to transport delayed luggage direct to the customer's door by express delivery.

On-board service

Key to improving on-board service was to impress upon cabin staff the importance of service quality in competing effectively in a market economy against both local and international rivals. This required that customers felt positive about the service offered on board CEA flights and 'at home' on CEA aircraft. The goal was to become passengers' preferred choice of airline and to build a loyal customer base.

Extensive training for cabin service staff began by building knowledge of techniques and procedures, appropriate deportment, and correct and incorrect behaviour in serving customers (including eye contact, smiling, polite and respectful language, gestures and body language). The training then built on this base with a series of exercises designed to help staff think through on-board service from the perspective of different types of customers. By 'standing in the customers shoes' staff were encouraged to understand the special needs of business customers, children, women, older people, etc. and to anticipate their needs 'even before they ask'.

Equally important was a focus on the role of the cabin supervisor or 'cabin chief'. As the front line manager of the cabin, it was important that this individual managed his or her team effectively, giving encouragement and correcting inappropriate behaviour where necessary. One challenge was to ensure the cabin chiefs 'managed bravely' putting customer needs and service excellence first, rather than simply avoiding unpopularity with staff. In addition, CEA had effectively strengthened its on-board service teams by combining experienced flight attendants with younger, less experienced staff. This was especially important to ensure practical knowledge was passed on as the airline expanded rapidly and recruited many new employees. Examples of the regular reports on service quality completed by inspectors from cabin service departments and direct feedback surveys to be completed by customers are shown in Exhibits CS17.10 and CS17.11, respectively.

CEA had already won awards for service excellence from CAAC in 1993, 1994 and 1995. Its new slogan was to 'catch up with the best international standards'.

The CRS

CEA was quick to adopt the CRS that had been developed by CAAC since 1992. All of its registered travel agents were required to purchase CRS terminals so that flight information could be retrieved, bookings confirmed and tickets issued immediately. In addition, CEA provided training to its agents prior to them becoming registered.

A new service was being introduced to allow customers with a 'touch tone' telephone to reconfirm their tickets and obtain a confirmation number directly by responding to recorded instructions rather than waiting to speak to an operator. Similarly, CEA were testing a service to deliver tickets and collect payment directly at the customer's office or home. These policies enabled the airline offer its passengers increased convenience.

Brand building

CEA sought to reinforce its growing reputation for safety, punctuality and service quality by developing its brand image. The airline's logo depicted the red sun rising over the sea (a reference to 'east') behind a 'silver swallow' in flight. This symbol was widely recognized inside China and increasingly overseas.

CEA's annual budget for direct advertising amounted to around RMB3 million (approximately US$350,000) and was expected to increase in the future. Most of this was targeted at point-of-sale material displayed in travel agencies. In addition, CEA sponsored various sports and cultural events.

FUTURE PLANS AND CHALLENGES

By 2000, CEA was forecasting an RTK of 1.86 billion (representing growth of 13.2% p.a.); a passenger volume of 12 million (13.4% growth p.a.), a mail and cargo volume of 350,000 tons (15.5% growth p.a.) and an annual increase in the number of available seats of 11.8%. The company was looking forward to the delivery of its new Airbus 340 long-range aircraft in 1996 as well as the expansion in its MD-82 fleet; the establishment of a new, US$100 million base at the new Shanghai airport in the Pudong development zone scheduled to open in 1999; and the further expansion of its route network. An important part of this expansion strategy was the plan to float up to 25% of the shares in CEAG on the New York stock exchange. CEA saw this as a way of tapping into a new source of capital, improving the company's image and allowing it to more easily form new relationships with international partners in the future.

Management made no secret of its desire to 'go to the world' and operate as an international rather than a regional carrier. CEA was ideally placed to benefit from the economic boom in eastern China and looked forward to Shanghai becoming an important international gateway in the Far East. In order to compete successfully in the international market, however, CEA recognized that it has to focus on further improving its technology, skill base and service quality. Although its service quality is high compared to the competition in China, the airline still had further to go to match the best international standards. Likewise it would have to pay close attention to reducing its administrative and operating costs and improve productivity in order to succeed in the very competitive international aviation industry. It may also need to reorganize its network into a more efficient hub and spoke system.

Case 17

Asked about the major challenges facing CEA for the future, one senior manager replied: 'to further build the skills and capabilities of our people and learn advanced technology, management and techniques; training people and changing their thinking takes longer than acquiring new aircraft'. It was in this context that senior management had to decide whether to make an approach to acquire China North Western Airlines (CNW), a loss-making sister CAAC company based in Xian in Shanxi province. CNW operated 74 routes, mainly domestic, with a fleet of 42 aircraft (including two Airbus A300s, three Airbus A310s and 10 Russian Tupolov TU-154s) and over 4,000 employees. Despite 250 million RTKs and serving over two million passengers per year, CNW had substantial excess seat and cargo capacity so that its costs had far outstripped its revenues. Further aggravated by endemic discounting of ticket prices and a questionable service reputation, CNW was on the verge of bankruptcy.

Sooner or later CEA could probably acquire CNW at an attractive price. But as they planned CEA's development the question for senior management was how such an acquisition might fit into their strategy for the future? Did the CNW situation represent an opportunity or might it prove a damaging distraction from CEA's long-term goals?

Exhibit CS17.1   Competition between China's airlines outside their regional bases (*Source*: Official airline guides)

Routes	Competing airlines
Beijing to:	
Bangkok	Air China, China Southern
Brussels	China Eastern
Chicago	China Eastern
Hanoi	China Southern
Hong Kong	Air China, China Southern
Los Angeles	China Eastern
Kuala Lumpur	China Southern
Madrid	China Eastern
Guangzhou to:	
Melbourne	Air China
Singapore	Air China, China Southern
Sydney	Air China
Shanghai to:	
New York	Air China
Osaka	Air China, China Eastern
San Francisco	Air China
Tokyo	Air China, China Eastern
Vancouver	Air China
Shenzhen:	
Bangkok	China Eastern, China Southern
Jakarta	Air China
Singapore	Air China, China Southern
Xiamen to:	
Jakarta	Air China
Singapore	Air China, China Southern

Case 17

Exhibit CS17.2   Growth of China's air transport market

**Passenger volumes
1988–94**

Year	China domestic routes (million passengers)	China international routes* (million passengers)
1988	11.71	2.72
1989	10.52	2.31
1990	13.46	3.14
1991	17.46	3.81
1992	23.94	4.92
1993	28.05	5.78
1994	34.45	5.94

* including Hong Kong

Exhibit CS17.3   Market shares of major Chinese airlines

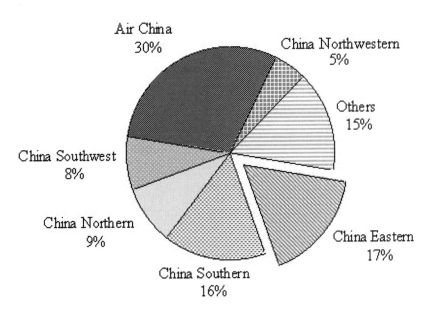

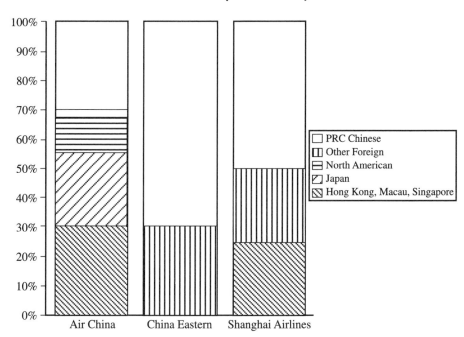

Exhibit CS17.4   Customer profiles of major Chinese airlines

Legend:
- ☐ PRC Chinese
- ⊞ Other Foreign
- ⊟ North American
- ▨ Japan
- ▨ Hong Kong, Macau, Singapore

X-axis: Air China   China Eastern   Shanghai Airlines

Exhibit CS17.5 The China Eastern Airlines Fleet

Aircraft type	Number	Seats
MD-11 Passenger	5	1,700
MD-11 Freighter	1	N/A
Airbus A300-600R	8	2,192
MD-82	13	1,885
FK-100	10	1,080
Dash-8	3	162
YN-7	7	280
Total	**47**	**7,299**

Case 17

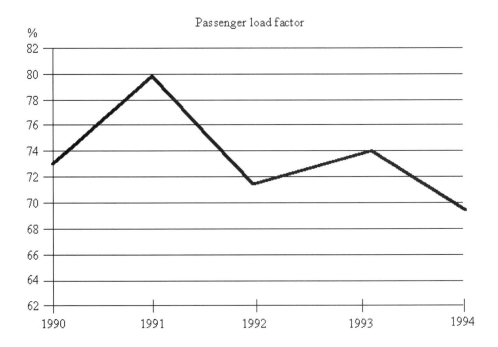

Exhibit CS17.5   The China Eastern Airlines Fleet (contd.)

Passenger load factor

Exhibit CS17.6   China Eastern Airlines financial performance 1988–95

Year	RTK (RMB Yuan)	CTK (RMB Yuan)	Total asset (RMB 10,000 Yuan)	Fixed asset (RMB 10,000 Yuan)	Revenue per employee (RMB 10,000 Yuan/ person)	Available seats
1998	2.83	1.99	176,005	156,630	35.42	
1989	3.17	2.33	257,427	175,414	29,98	
1990	3.83	2.50	283,178	193,189	29.72	4,134
1991	4.35	2.99	527,463	413,014	41.00	4,513
1992	3.99	3.09	760,471	632,454	51.39	5,817
1993	4.69	3.36	1,223,752	633,377	59.47	6,738
1994	7.30	4.32	1,790,541	646,623	81.94	6,788
1995	7.28	4.78	2,090,541	1,201,939	76.38	7,299

RTK – Revenue per ton-kilometer

CTK – Cost per ton-kilometer

Exhibit CS17.7   China Eastern Airlines route network

Exhibit CS17.8   Basic information on selected competitors

Competitor	Number of aircraft	Main aircraft types	Sales revenue (1994) (RMB million Yuan)	Profit or loss (1994) (RMB million Yuan)
Air China	Approximately 60	B747 (16) B767 (10) B737 (18) YN7 (4) YN5 (6)	8,326	431
Southern Airlines	Approximately 98	B767 (6) B757 (20) B737 (34) YN7 (5) YN5 (18)	5,907	503
China North-West Airlines	Approximately 35	A3000 (4) A310 (3) Tu-154 (9) BAE 146 (9) YN7 (1) YN5 (9)	1,210	−541
Shanghai Airlines	8	B757 (7) B767 (1)	600	10

Exhibit CS17.9 Punctuality performance of major Chinese airlines

During May 1996, there were 43,531 scheduled flights reported by CAAC. Among them, 33,169 flights were on time and 10,362 flights were 'delayed', including 2,178 that were cancelled. Punctuality was therefore 76.2% raised.

Airlines	Total scheduled flights	% of flights	Number of flights delayed for 'human reasons'	% of flights delayed for 'human reasons'
Air China	4,847	77.8	215	4.4
Northwest	2,377	76.9	180	7.6
Southern	9,092	67.8	1,348	14.8
Southwest	4,455	82.1	210	4.7
Eastern	5,282	82.9	365	6.9
Northern	3,583	75.6	350	9.8
Xinjiang	1,322	81.6	81	6.1
General	839	78.4	75	8.9
Yunnan	1,771	78.2	101	5.7
Xiamen	2,166	80.3	141	6.5
Great Wall	350	72.3	44	12.6
Shanghai	952	76.8	45	4.7
Shichuan	1,072	72.0	81	7.6
Wuhan	715	62.9	51	7.1
Central	535	82.4	43	8.0
Guizhou	292	74.2	40	10.2
Hainan	1,226	76.8	182	14.8
New China	920	71.5	94	10.2
Shenzhen	567	66.5	59	10.4
Chang'an	288	87.9	19	6.6
Nanjin	422	65.2	47	11.1
China	69	65.2	24	34.8
Shandong	289	83.4	15	5.2

Exhibit CS17.10   On-board service quality inspection form

| Supervisor | Work unit | Flight No. | Flight route | | | Case 17 |

Items	Good	Fair	Poor	Remarks
Uniform neatness, numeral badges worn				
Appearance standardization				
Appearance procedure standardization				
Service normativeness				
Service attitude (e..g. amicable, with smile)				
Conversation politeness				
Response to any inquiry with patience				
Taking special care of customer in need				
Phone announcement fluency and normativeness				
Staff always available in cabin				
No gossip				
Toilet cleanness				
Service appropriateness under unforeseeable situations and emergency				
Publicity and confirmation of safety regulations on-board				
No provision taken without permission				
Food and drink supply				

Brief
comment

Att. Give a tick to every item in its evaluation column to your opinion, please.

CEA Cabin-Service Dept.

Case 17

Exhibit CS17.11 Customer service feedback forms

DATE OF FLIGHT ———————— FLIGHT No. ———

	Items	Evaluation	Good	Fair	Poor
Reservation & Sales	City of the sale___	Service Attitude			
		Ticketing Quality			
	Place of the sale___	Environment & Order			
Check-in Service	Service Attitude				
	Check-in Efficiency				
	Flight Regularity				
	Service in case of FLT Irregulrity				
Departure Airport	Service Attitude				
	Limousine Service				
	Inquiry, Broadcast & Information				
	Service Facilities & Equipment				
	Environment & Order				
	Guide Signs				
	Food & Drinks, Hygiene				
	Hotel (Hostel) Srvice				
	Shop Service				
	Security Check				

	Items	Evaluation	Good	Fair	Poor
Cabin Service	Service Attitude				
	Food & Drinks Quality				
	Cabin & Lavatory Hygiene				
	Pamphlet, Newspaper & Magazine				
	Cabin Equipment				
Arrival Airport	Service Attitude				
	Inquiry, Broadcast & Information				
	Guide Signs				
	Service Facilities & Equipment				
	Speed of Luggage Delivery				
	Restaurant Service				
	Hotel (Hostel) Services				
	Environment & Order				
	Limousine Service				

Which aspect of the evaluated airline are you most satisfied with?

Which aspect of the evaluated airline are you most dissatisfied with?

Your hopes for the evaluated airline.

Passenger's Name _____   _____

Guest Supervisor's Name & Work Unit

Note: Please mail the card to us immediately after filling it up.

Asian Business Logic

Part

6

A sian behaviour and values in business often differ significantly from Western norms. Western expatriates must learn to decode and understand this behaviour to operate effectively. This chapter looks at four essential traits of the Asian business environment: the role of governments, the central importance of relationships, the role of ethical and religious cultures, and their implications for competitive and business logic.

The role of government

Except in Hong Kong, Asian governments have intervened in economic development. They have tried to create a business-friendly, market-led environment, without shying from taking a more directive role in some cases. To use the World Bank's terminology, governments have used two sets of policies:

- 'fundamental' policies aimed at promoting macro-economic stability, investment in human capital, stable and secure financial systems, limited price distortion, and a receptive attitude to foreign technology;

- 'selective intervention': directed credit, sectorial industrial promotion, trade policies.

The context of development

A consensus for growth

A popular consensus about economic objectives and the shared belief that economic growth is good and must take priority over egalitarian or social welfare goals have played a key role in supporting the efforts of Asian governments to stimulate growth. Asia Pacific is often seen as the most growth-obsessed region in the world. In Korea, the 'sacrificed generation' of the 1970s and 1980s deferred immediate enjoyment to build up competitiveness. In Indonesia, President Suharto, the self-styled 'father of development', has made economic growth the national priority. In China, it has precedence over democracy and individual freedom.

A high degree of cooperation between government and business

Cooperation between business and government is either institutionalized, or informal, or a mixture of both. High performing Asian economies usually have formal institutions to foster communication between the state and private sector. Japan has 'deliberation councils' where cabinet officials and business leaders discuss policy projects. Japanese ministries do not hesitate to put pressure on business by issuing notifications, informal hints, invitations and direct pressures. Japanese bureaucrats can benefit personally from successful cooperation, obtaining *amakudari* – lucrative positions on the board of a corporation – after they retire. They remain in close contact with former ministry colleagues, thereby ensuring the continuance of close cooperation.

Because laws are vague in Asia, government ministries often have great leverage over firms. In Korea, Malaysia, Singapore and Thailand, cooperation between government and business is close and institutionalized, while relationships are less formal in Indonesia and the Philippines. In China, contacts are maintained through informal networks. A culture of economic nationalism (as in Korea or Japan), and 'old boy' or alumni networks (in Korea or Singapore) reinforce these links. Relationships may be strained in countries where top government officials and leading businessmen belong to different ethnic groups.

Pro-business bureaucrats

Skilled, business-orientated state bureaucrats help foster economic development. Singapore, Korea and Japan all have well-educated, well-remunerated civil servants aware of the needs and constraints of business. (Singapore uses management-by-objectives and tried to align salaries of civil servants with those in the private sector; business-school training is increasingly popular among civil servants.)

Development orientations

The role of government in Asia is often compared to the coach of a football team: instead of managing the economy, pragmatic governments have emulated market forces. This applies even in Vietnam and China, which embraced market policies although they retained control in the political sphere. China's late leader, Deng Xiaoping, is famous for saying, 'It does not matter whether the cat is black or white as long as it catches mice'. Some Asian countries have chosen import-substitution policies to promote development; others, more open and outward-looking, have privileged exports.

The import-substitution countries

In the 1950s, most countries in the region adopted import substitution to accelerate industrialization; this involved selective trade protection for domestic producers and incentives to localize production. Japan and the NIEs began to deregulate and dismantle import-substitution regimes in the 1960s and 1970s; southeast Asian countries only did so in the mid-1980s.

- Indonesia, with a history of large-scale government intervention, state ownership and regulation, still retains an overall import-substitution orientation, although it began to deregulate selectively in the late 1980s.

- Malaysia combined import-substitution policies with its quota-based New Economic Policy to redistribute wealth in favour of the Malay population (the *bumiputra*), and at the expense of the more entrepreneurial Overseas Chinese, in the early 1970s. In some cases it has imposed local content in manufacturing, as for the Proton Saga car, made by state-owned HICOM.

- Thailand and the Philippines, less reliant on state-owned enterprises, nevertheless implemented classic import-substitution policies through tariffs and quotas, and the control of production licenses.

- Since Deng's 'open door' policy was launched in 1979, China has been moving away from a central planning and gradually introducing market forces and elements of free enterprise. The share of ailing state-owned enterprises in the economy falls year after year.

Export-led countries

Export-led economies fall into two subgroups:

Japan, Korea and Taiwan are **middle of the road**. In the 1950s and 1960s Japan used a combination of import substitution, export stimulation and fierce internal competition. The two main government departments, MITI (International Trade and Industry) and the Finance ministry, encouraged successful companies and tried to discourage others. MITI, once empowered to channel investment and working capital to companies whose activities conformed to national policy, has seen its role considerably curtailed by the increasing clout of leading Japanese firms.

Korea's industrialization policy initially targeted heavy and chemical industries. Large private business groups (the *chaebol*) were the prime engines of growth.

In Taiwan, the government funded major infrastructure investments and created favourable conditions for exporters: lower exchange rates, removal of import controls for exporters, low interest rates. The goal was to sustain export-led growth by increasing the output of standardized products such as calculators, watches, colour televisions, apparel, plastics, synthetic fibres. By the 1980s, the target had switched to high-technology industries, which were offered various incentives.

Wide-open-door countries Singapore and Hong Kong had to open their economies because they had such small markets. Singapore, which adopted free trade policies at independence in 1965, still promotes industrialization and export expansion, mainly through tax concessions to exporters and foreign investors. A big attraction for foreign investors is Singapore's huge investment in infrastructure such as housing, transport and telecommunications. Since the mid-1970s, the government has encouraged more capital- and skill-intensive manufacturing, instead of traditional labour-intensive activities.

Hong Kong always practised minimal government intervention to preserve its competitiveness as an industrial, financial and export centre. Its economic policies featured balanced budgets with no public debt, fiscal reserves, and interest rate management.

Attitudes towards foreign investment

Many Asian countries expect foreign firms to contribute to economic development by bringing in technology and capital, and by creating jobs. Import-substitution countries require that foreign firms must produce locally, usually in association with a local partner, in order to gain access to the domestic market. Export-led economies such as

Singapore or Hong Kong welcome Western firms in the expectation of production platforms, employment, technology transfer and export income. Korea (and Japan in the past) are more reserved: foreign investors are welcome provided they share their technology with local partners. By and large, restrictions on Western ventures depend on the nature of the investment project: in general, the more a foreign firm is geared toward exports, the fewer the restrictions. Pressure on foreign firms to sell a percentage of shares to local business or to government remains strong in Indonesia, and in the Philippines for some large-scale projects.

Direct government participation

Most Asian governments play a direct role in the economy through owning or controlling enterprises and through targeting public procurement, though the extent varies:

- The economies of China and Vietnam are still dominated by state-owned enterprises.

- Indonesia nationalized most foreign firms in the 1960s, especially in the plantation, oil and petroleum industries.

- The Thai government still controls sectors such as fertilizers, commodities distribution, air transport, steel.

- Malaysia has set up state companies to carry out its ambition of becoming an industrialized country by the year 2020.

- Singapore controls many firms through state holdings (for example Temasek and Singapore Technology).

- Korea and Japan rely on targeted procurement rather than state ownership.

- Hong Kong has few state enterprises (the Mass Transit system is one exception) and rarely uses targeted procurement.

While most of Asia Pacific moved towards deregulation and privatization in the 1980s, state enterprises will not disappear overnight. In China, the proportion of industrial production controlled by state enterprises has fallen to 48 per cent in 1992 from 56 per cent in 1985. Malaysia, the Philippines and Singapore have all launched privatization drives.

The role of relationships

Building and cultivating relationships is crucial to business development in Asia Pacific. While every society is built around relationships, the need to network is greater in Asia. The depth and quality of relationships matter more than their number; personal and reciprocal connections are also valued more than contractual, transactional connections. Personal relationships are mutually binding and permeate all aspects of the firm. In any situation – whether applying for a visa, finding information, getting an investment proposal approved or cutting through a maze of red tape – Asian managers will turn to the individual most likely to help them effectively. The Asian business environment is best described as a series of interlocked networks: family and relatives, ethnically based connections, alumni connections, social clubs, industrial connections and lastly government-business connections.

Family and blood ties

Figure 6.1 shows the various levels of relationships in Chinese society:

- The nuclear family, where relationships are hierarchical, strictly codified: father/children, husband/wife, elder/younger brothers and sisters. Because trust and loyalty are taken for granted, Chinese entrepreneurs appoint family members to top management positions. There is no reciprocity, though respect for the hierarchy and obedience are automatically rewarded with protection. Appointments based on family ties, business undertakings and networks between family members also dominate in non-Chinese societies such as Korea, the Philippines, Indonesia and Thailand.

- The extended family, which includes cousins, uncles, in-laws. Their loyalty is expected, but on the basis of reciprocity. One relative will enter a business deal with another if he can expect a return, either immediately or in the future. Just as powerful as nuclear family relationships, business networks among relatives form a web of reciprocal obligations.

- Friends and connections. Life-long *guanxi* result from shared experiences in early or formative years. Growing up in the same village or province, attending the same school or military academy, creates lasting bonds. Major networks bind alumni from the same secondary school or university,

Figure 6.1   Chinese relationships hierarchy

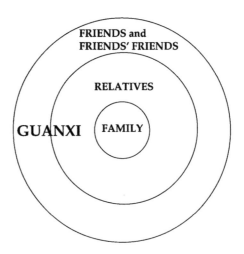

particularly in Japan and Korea (where they play a key role in recruitment) much more than in the West. Membership of the same clubs or sponsorship of the same charities also creates close links. In Japan and the ASEANIEs, senior civil servants often become senior executives; this creates a direct channel of communication between government and business.

To enter a network, one needs to be connected to someone who already belongs to it; loyalty relies on a web of mutually binding obligations and dependencies, cultivated through regular personal contacts. In a purely contractual transaction, mutual commitment is not as strong. Many Westerners have trouble understanding the network culture. Building relationships is more time-consuming in Asia than in the Western world: it involves frequent visits, socializing, exchanging small presents... Westerners tend to dismiss this as nepotism. The patient Western manager can penetrate a network and develop his own web of *guanxi*; this will require far more sensitivity and experience than is usually expected in Western firms.

Corruption

In the West, Asia Pacific has the reputation of encouraging corruption. There is no empirical evidence that this region is more corrupt than others; there are, however, differences in definition. Customs that most Westerners define as corrupt are acceptable, even indispensable in many Asian countries. There are also differences in usage: in developing Asian societies, very few civil servants or ordinary citizens think in terms of conflict of interest, or the separation of public and private concerns. Since civil servants in many of these economies are poorly paid, emoluments regarded as corrupt elsewhere are seen as simple perquisites – a sort of social subsidy which keeps them above the poverty line.

In the past, few Asian societies sanctioned corruption. In China and the Philippines, elaborate systems of patronage make investigation difficult, and in Japan the nature of the political system ensured that little social stigma was attached to bribery. Asian societies tend to be regulated by shame (public humiliation) rather than guilt, which is often a private or individual matter, as in Judeo-Christian societies. Few Asian civil servants will feel guilty about accepting a favour; indeed, this will often be seen as a tribute, something essential to maintaining the social fabric. For this reason anti-corruption campaigns in Asia are less successful (Singapore is an exception). In East Asian politics, reciprocity is at the root of most relationships; past favours must be returned, and the ritual practice of gift-giving plays an important role.

Cultures and business in Asia Pacific

Asia Pacific is at the crossroads of many cultural and religious traditions: Confucianism, Taoism, Buddhism, Hinduism, Islam and Christianity. Western political philosophies (such as liberalism and communism) have also had a major impact. Instead of becoming a cultural patchwork, the region has developed unique norms and values reflected in the behaviour of economic players. Although Malaysia is more influenced by Islam, China by Confucianism, two dominant cultural contexts have an impact across the region: a homogeneous concept of social organization and pervasive Confucian values.

The Asian concept of social organization

All Asian countries share a common pattern of work-related values: they score high on power distance, low on individualism; countries in Northern Europe, North America, Australia and New Zealand are the exact opposite. In high power distance societies, people are considered unequal; this translates as a strong respect for hierarchy and autocratic leadership. Individualism is low when groups rather than individuals are seen as the nucleus of society: individuals exist only as members of groups, and their duty is to provide for other, higher status, group members, who in turn will offer their protection. These differences are visible in the way Asian corporations are managed. Asian group orientation is the foundation for networking.

Saving face is another dominant feature. In business dealings, it often entails avoiding humiliating the other party in public, or making symbolic concessions. Another consequence is that conflicts are often settled out of court, through informal mediation by a third party. Attention to face-saving is particularly important in managing local personnel. High power distance in business is evidenced by punctilious protocol and extreme deference to hierarchical status. In Asian societies, formalism and due process must be respected.

Confucian ethics

Confucian values – which emphasize hard work, thriftiness, obedience, benevolent leadership and harmony, as well as strict respect of traditional hierarchical relationships and the importance of education – are highly correlated with economic growth. Western scholars have argued that some of these values, particularly respect for tradition, are not particularly conducive to economic progress. It is clear, however, from what happened in Korea in the early 1970s and in China in the early 1990s, that economic development gathers momentum when Confucian ethics meet Western technology.

Competitive and business logic

Competitive or business logic refers to the premises and models used by top management to formulate strategy. It includes the definition of objectives, the way a firm approaches competition, and the criteria it uses to make decisions. The rules in Asia Pacific differ quite substantially from those in Europe or the USA, especially in three managerial domains: goal setting, competitive behaviour and decision making.

Goal setting

The objectives of businesses vary according to the economic system in which they operate, the society which has created them, and the values of the dominant coalition which controls them. In some, but not all, Asia Pacific countries, goal-setting differs from the West in three aspects essentially:

■ In terms of *time orientation,* Asian businesses tend to be either very long-term orientated or short term and opportunistic. The political context and financial incentives provided by government in Japan and Korea encourage a long-term outlook, while the Overseas Chinese, who are an ethnic minority, tend to operate in volatile, adverse political contexts. Even in a context where local firms have a short-term orientation, foreign firms must adopt a long-term view: acquiring experience and cultivating relationships both take time.

■ In terms of *outcome orientation,* Asian firms place more emphasis on marketing objectives, in contrast to US and British companies which stress financial targets. This does not mean that Asian firms neglect financial performance: however, stable ownership and long-term stakeholders (whether they are state-owned or family-owned) free them from the worry of quarterly returns.

■ *Social orientation.* Asian societies believe that firms must fulfil social, even nationalist functions before pursuing individual wealth. There is therefore greater acceptance of government intervention in business. In Singapore, for example, teams from companies parade right after the armed forces on National Day.

Competitive behaviour

In most Asian countries, local businesses receive preferential treatment, particularly when bidding for government contracts. This can take the form of preferential terms of credit, access to business licenses, restrictions on employment and protective regulations; it is viewed as an acceptable form of government intervention and economic nationalism.

With the exception of Japan, most Asians bargain in business transactions. This does not mean that they sacrifice quality for price: their usual strategy is to first determine the level of technological performance and quality they need, then select suppliers on that basis, and finally take advantage of competitive rivalry to negotiate lower prices. This approach does not conflict with the need to cultivate relationships: loyal long-term suppliers are expected not to overprice products or services. Bargaining is particularly common in competitive bidding situations. Western suppliers, who tend to emphasize technological sophistication and guarantee margins in their bids, are surprised to lose out to bidders whose strategy is to offer a lower base price and leave additional features for future negotiations.

Although not limited to Asia, imitation is indisputably part of Asian business life – whether illegal copying, counterfeiting of trademarks, or simply attempts to replicate the success of a competitor through 'me-too' products. First mover advantages do not last long unless they are supported by a unique product or competence. The absence of protective regulations or the lack of effective enforcement do not help. Although legislative protection is being introduced gradually, enforcement remains largely ineffective. Reverse engineering (copying competing products by learning the technology and disassembling the product itself) is still common in China, Korea, Taiwan and Hong Kong.

Decision making

Western and Asian business logic also differ in decision making. Unlike Westerners, Asians often use an incremental approach to planning, inductive decision making, and a reliance on personal interface and commitment rather than on formal systems and written contracts.

There are many reasons why Western-style long-term business planning is not widely practised in Asia Pacific. First, in developing economies, local entrepreneurs tended to seize opportunities as they present themselves – an approach that makes planning irrelevant; also, databases only recently became available. In highly developed Japan, where data are obtainable and economic planning exists at government level, businesses prefer to rely on incremental planning – a series of short-term operational plans guided by a set of business principles and inspired by a long-term vision. While Westerners privilege abstraction and deductive reasoning, Asian managers at all levels resist abstract management theories; they prefer more inductive decision making, proceeding from concrete situations.

Where Western managers have an engineering approach to building and regulating organizational behaviour, Asians see their enterprises as organic, living entities where various individuals and groups gain from cooperation. This basic difference has a considerable impact: Western managers tend to favour systems for decision making and mechanisms for problem solving. Their formal or legalistic approach is abhorrent to many Asians, who value paternalistic, informal relationships between employer and employee. Significant cultural misunderstandings can arise in situations between Western managers, confident of being fair in using contracts and well-defined procedures, and their Asian colleagues or business partners, who value the quality of interaction defined in terms of loyalty, trust and dedication and see recourse to legal contracts and procedure as a failure of human interaction.

The Asian business context: an overview

The profile of organizational behaviour in Asia Pacific differs significantly from that of Europe or the USA. This distance is depicted in Figure 6.2, based on a survey of 294 European and American managers in October 1996.

Figure 6.2   The Asia Pacific competitive context

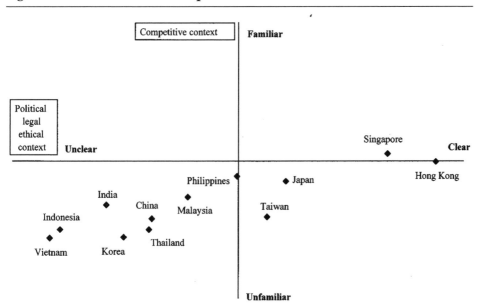

It comes as no surprise that, according to the survey, the rules of the game are most familiar in Singapore and Hong Kong. Vietnam and Indonesia are the countries whose business environment Western managers find the most puzzling. In between lies a cluster of 'moderately accessible' countries: Japan, Taiwan, the Philippines and Malaysia; all four occupy a reasonably clear position on the political, legal and ethical dimension, but challenge Western notions in the competitive context. Compared with a previous survey in 1992, both China and Japan have improved their position. The results confirm the idea that, except for Singapore and Hong Kong, Asia appears as complex and unfamiliar to many Western managers. This perception may be due to lack of experience. With time, Asia will undoubtedly lose some of its mystery.

References

Benedict, Ruth, *The Chrysanthenum and the Sword*, Meridian, New York, 1976.

Cyert, Richard and James March, *A Behavioral Theory of the Firm*, Prentice-Hall, Englewood Cliffs, NJ, 1963.

Hamel, Gary and C.K. Prahalad, 'Strategic Intent', *Harvard Business Review*, May/June, 1989, pp. 63–76.

Hayes, Robert and W.J. Abernathy, 'Managing our Way to Economic Decline', *Harvard Business Review*, Vol. 58, No. 4, 1980, pp. 67–77.

Hensley, Matthey and Edward P. White, 'The Privatization Experience in Malaysia', *Columbia Journal of World Business*, Spring 1993, pp. 71–82.

Jenkins, David, *Suharto and his Generals Indonesia Military Politics 1975-1983*, Cornell Modern Indonesia Project, Cornell University, Ithaca, New York, 1984.

Joon, Bae, 'Ex-bureaucrats and Ex-military Men in the Financial World', *Sin-Dong -A*, August 1986, p. 403, quoted in Steers, Richard, Yoo Keun Shin and Gerardo Ungson, *The Chaebol: Korea's New Industrial Might*, Harper & Row, New York, 1989.

Lasserre, Philippe, 'Strategic Planning in South East Asia: Does it Work?', *Euro Asia Business Review*, Vol. 2, No. 2, April 1983, pp. 37–41.

Lasserre, Philippe and Jocelyn Probert, 'Human Resources Management in the Asia Pacific Region: A Comparative Assessment', *INSEAD Euro-Asia Centre Research Series* No. 25, Fontainebleau, January 1994.

Lasserre, Philippe and Jocelyn Probert, *The Asian Business Context: A Follow-Up Study*, INSEAD Euro-Asia Centre, March 1997.

MacMurray, Trevor and Jonathan Woetzel, 'The Challenge Facing China's State-owned Enterprises', *The McKinsey Quarterly*, No. 2, 1994, pp. 61–73.

Palmier, Leslie, 'Corruption In the West Pacific', *The Pacific Review*, Vol. 2, No. 1, Oxford University Press, 1989.

Prahalad, C.K. and R.A. Bettis, 'The Dominant Logic: A New Linkage Between Diversity and Performance', *Strategic Management Journal*, Vol. 7, November–December 1986, pp. 485–501.

World Bank, *The East Asian Miracle: Economic Growth and Public Policy*, Oxford University Press, New York, 1993.

Case 18

This case was written by Charlotte Butler, Research Assistant, under the supervision of Philippe Lasserre, Professor of Strategy and Management at INSEAD. It is intended to be used as the basis for class discussion rather than to illustrate either effective or ineffective handling of an administrative situation. Copyright © 1991 INSEAD-EAC, Fontainebleau, France. Revised 1997. Financial support from P.T. Inti Indorayon Utama is gratefully acknowledged.

P.T. Indorayon: A Strategic Vision 1980–85

'Gentlemen, we are now on our own. What shall we do? Go on? Or not go on? Are you confident we can do the project?' As he put the question, Mr Sukanto, head of Indorayon, looked around the table at the sombre faces of his inner cabinet. They were gathered together in a restaurant in Medan, North Sumatra on a hot and humid evening in July 1986. Two years before at a meeting of the same group, he had taken the decision to go ahead with his plan to build a US$200 million pulp and rayon plant on a greenfield site in North Sumatra. The intervening period had been spent trying to find an experienced engineering firm to act as consultant to the project, working side by side with the Indorayon team to translate that plan into reality. Three successive failures to find such a partner had brought them all to the restaurant, and to another momentous decision. Should they now go on and try to build the mill without a consultant, or should they abandon the project altogether?

THE IDEA

The idea of building a pulp mill had first come to Mr Sukanto in 1980. An ethnic Chinese entrepreneur from the port of Belawan in North Sumatra, he had begun a career 15 years earlier when his father's ill health and the closure of schools during the alleged Communist coup combined to put him to work. As the eldest of seven sons, he had taken over responsibility for his family at the age of 16. Starting as one of many contractors selling spare parts to the state-owned Pertamina Oil Corporation, he had shown himself to be a quick learner, rapidly becoming a major supplier. Taking full advantage of the oil boom years of the 1970s, he had amassed US$10 million by the age of 23. During those years 'in the real world out on the streets', he had gained vast practical experience of 'people, technology and business'. He absorbed the trading mentality and learnt 'how to compete by doing something different'. He also built up the networks and made the connections necessary to be able to succeed in the Indonesian business environment.

Judging that the Pertamina bubble was soon to burst, in 1974 Mr Sukanto broke away from contracting and supply and, with the financial future of his family secure, looked round for 'a new challenge'. The result was the construction of a plywood and timber mill, PT Raja Garuda Mas (RGM – King Golden Eagle). RGM was built with Sukanto's own money at a time of economic recession in a record eleven and a half months, using all his contracting know-how and connections. It was to be the foundation of his business empire, the RGM Group. Impressed by this performance, the Minister of Industry arranged the attendance of President Suharto at the opening ceremony, and Mr Sukanto gained a solid reputation with the Indonesian government as a man who could deliver. In the succeeding years he went on to build up a successful agri-based business, and entrenched his respectability by becoming the owner of a bank.

In retrospect, Mr Sukanto's entrance into the pulp industry could be seen as a logical progression from this beginning. Involvement in the highly competitive plywood business led on to further exploitation of forests, expansion into the plantations business and, by 1979, investments in palm oil, rubber and cocoa. But in 1980, embarking on a new, high-risk business such as pulp was by no means the next obvious move. While subconsciously aware that he was ready to move on to 'a new game', Mr Sukanto had no preconceived map in his head of where he wanted to go next. As at several junctures in his career, he was merely aware of an entrepreneur's desire to expand his forest-based interests.

Mr Sukanto had for a time been a shareholder in one of the rayon manufacturing companies in Java, Viscose Far East. Dissatisfaction with the company's management had eventually led him to withdraw his investment, but attracted by the possibilities offered by rayon production in Indonesia, he was drawn to the idea of starting a rayon pulp project. In 1981, his brother Mr Polar Yanto and another close associate, Mr Ridwan, were dispatched to visit one of the biggest pulp mills in Finland and their report sharpened his interest. In 1982, Mr Sukanto visited the Finnish mill himself and began his learning apprenticeship. From rayon pulp the trail led to the possibilities of paper pulp. Slowly the concept began to take shape as his instinct told him he had found the right business, one where he could do better than others.

He proceeded to do what he always did when contemplating a new project: learn anything and everything he could about the industry from the experts. Together, he and his brother toured the world during 1982 and 1983, meeting people involved in the pulp business, making initial contacts and following up suggestions to increase their knowledge. The tour became virtually a 'who's who' of the industry. Meanwhile, in Java there were meetings with the Cellulose Research Institute at Bandung to learn about pulp, the different kinds and the advantages of one over the other, their uses, and demand for them in the world market.

The philosophy of the pulp business was, Mr Sukanto concluded, very simple, and hinged on the length of time it took to produce the raw material, wood. Thus in Finland, where it takes 70–100 years to grow a tree, 'you plant a tree for your grandson. In Spain or Portugal where it takes 20–25 years, it is for your son'. In these countries, the dominant species grown is the pine tree, which produces long fibre pulp. However, in tropical Indonesia the climate favours cultivation of the eucalyptus tree. Eucalyptus produces short fibre pulp and has a much shorter growth cycle. Consequently, in Indonesia 'you can grow a tree for yourself in 7–10 years'. Brazil was the main producer of eucalyptus which, as Mr Sukanto further discovered, was becoming widely used as a renewable resource for the production of high quality pulp. From that pulp either paper or rayon products could be made, and the latter would give him the opportunity to enter the textile industry.

An initial estimate of likely production costs convinced Mr Sukanto that he would be the lowest cost producer of short fibre pulp in the world, with a guaranteed renewable resource (Exhibit CS18.1). This advantageous position was likely to be reinforced in the future if and when, as widely forecast, US, Scandinavian and Canadian producers of long fibre pulp began to experience rising costs because of the depletion of their timber resources and the implementation of stricter environmental controls.

A look at supply and demand of forest-based products in the Asian region confirmed his instinct that here was a feasible project with a huge ready-made market. Indonesia, Korea, Thailand, Taiwan, the Philippines and Japan all imported wood fibre, mostly from North America and Europe, and demand was growing. Moreover, he already visualized a planting programme that would ensure a long lead-time over any new domestic competitors trying to follow him later.

By 1983, Mr Sukanto had learnt enough to be convinced that the business had potential. PT Inti Indorayon Utama ('Indorayon') was incorporated in April 1984. The next stage was 'the fine tuning of the concept' by gaining a thorough understanding of the business in order to be able to assess the risks and advantages before making the final decision to go ahead.

THE INNER CABINET

Planning and decisions were in the hands of an inner cabinet consisting of Mr Sukanto, Mr Polar Yanto and their close financial advisor Mr Ridwan Hartono, 'a very cautious man'. Mr Polar Yanto, then 28 years old, was appointed project director in charge of building a pulp mill. A mechanical and electronics engineer by training, he had started work in his brother's plywood mill straight from school, beginning on the maintenance side and working his way round every aspect of the business at a junior level. In 1979 he had been assigned to handle the forestry operations, and had also attended business courses held in the region to learn the theoretical side of management.

Other members of the RGM group, notably Mr Sutrisno and Mr Linardi, were co-opted and consulted on an ad hoc basis. Mr Sutrisno had joined the Group in 1983 to expand the agri-business. As an engineer with experience of building processing plants, he was asked to join in the early stages of the project to assess the relative merits of the engineering firms which might become involved in the project. Mr Linardi was another longstanding and loyal associate of Mr Sukanto's. He had recently taken charge of setting up a procurement office for RGM in Singapore.

Mr Newton Luas had joined the Group straight from school in March 1980. His role was to prepare financial feasibility studies for internal management so that they could assess risks, and for the banks in order to raise external funds for the project. At the end of 1983 Mr Samantra, who had worked for Far East Viscose, joined the team to add his knowledge and experience. He was responsible for a prefeasibility study of the market for internal discussion and a detailed market survey, based on his previous experiences in Jakarta and Bandung. However, the dominant force throughout remained Mr Sukanto, and it was he who took the final decisions.

Case 18

THE CRITICAL AREAS

Mr Sukanto concluded that there were three critical areas to consider. The first covered all factors relating to timing and market projections, the second all factors concerning resource availability and environmental issues, and the third all factors affecting the size of the necessary capital investment. Mr Sukanto did not consider financing when making the decision whether to go ahead or not, as he knew that domestic financing would always be available to him.

Timing and market projections

There were a number of factors for the team to consider, such as the general economic situation in Indonesia, the likely evolution of the pulp market, and the timing of market entry by competitors.

The economic context

In the mid-1980s, Indonesia was in the grip of a deepening recession. The oil sector, the prime source of income for over a decade and the basis of its economic activity and development, had been hit by the world oil shocks and the subsequent collapse of oil prices. The government was desperate for new projects and investment. On 1 April 1984, President Suharto stated that the government would encourage private investment by 'simplifying investment procedures, removing unnecessary levies and providing concessionary credits for investment in priority sectors'.

The mill would be just the type of project the government wanted, and officials gave assurances of support in case of trouble. Some problems were readily foreseeable, such as opposition from the operators of a high-profile Japanese hydroelectric power plant that shared the waters of a lake adjacent to the proposed mill site. The power plant, inaugurated in June 1983, was a huge project. It was intended to serve the east coast of Sumatra, an area which the government aimed to open up and develop. At a cost of US$3 billion, the plant was a symbol of Japanese-Indonesian friendship.

The market for pulp

The Indorayon team concluded that Indonesia offered a ready-made market for the pulps used to make either paper or rayon products. Their feasibility study estimated that Indonesia's demand for bleached softwood pulp would rise from 120,000 tons per annum ('tpa') in 1990 to 210,000 tpa in 2000, while for the same period demand for dissolving pulp, used in the production of rayon, would grow from 75,000 tpa to 110,000 tpa (Exhibit CS17.2). The potential in the Indonesian market was brought home by comparing the annual per capita pulp consumption of 7 kg in Indonesia in 1985 with the 20 kg consumed in Thailand, the 55 kg consumed in Malaysia and the 230 kg consumed in Japan. Being one of the only domestic producers of these pulp types, Indorayon could 'secure a major share of the domestic market'. An integrated project was planned, so that eventually the mill would be able to produce both paper and dissolving pulp.

Prospects for exports in the region also appeared sound. 'A small 10% market share in China, Japan and Taiwan would enable Indorayon to sell 85,000 tpa of paper grade, and 30,000 tpa of dissolving pulp in 1990'. It was anticipated that demand for bleached kraft pulp would grow faster in Asia, and Southeast Asia in particular, than in any other region in the world. Pulp-producing capacity in the region was also expected to lag behind demand.

At the time of the feasibility study in 1985, the paper pulp price was starting to decline from US$500 to $400 per tonne (Exhibit CS17.3). This made prospects for servicing any loans 'very dim'. However, Mr Sukanto was convinced that prices would begin to rise again, and aimed to start production to coincide with this upturn.

The competition

In the mid-1980s, there were approximately 14 pulp producers operating in Indonesia, with an aggregate capacity of 0.97 million tpa. Of these, 13 were integrated non-wood pulp producers. There was only one competing softwood project, the Cilicap project in Central Java. However, it was not expected to be in a position to begin production until 1991 at the earliest.

Resource availability and environmental issues

A critical factor in Mr Sukanto's decision was, of course, the forest. Indonesia had the world's second largest tropical rain forest after Brazil: an estimated 100 million hectares of forest covered approximately two-thirds of Indonesia's total land area. The forests represented one of the country's most important economic assets and, according to Indonesian law, came under state administration. The government was not directly involved in their exploitation, but assigned rights to private companies operating under its supervision. In the 1980s the government banned the export of logs, and encouraged downstream processing by local companies, at the same time insisting on reforestation programmes.

As a local group, and in view of Mr Sukanto's previous performance in building the plywood mill, Indorayon was a favoured candidate when it came to obtaining a concession from the Ministry of Forestry. The mill would be a prestige project for the government, and the minister was keen that it should be a success. Despite a lack of experience in pulp manufacture, Indorayon leap-frogged the rest of the competition and was granted two licences by the Ministry of Forestry. The first, a utilization licence expiring 1 April 2004, permitted Indorayon to harvest the existing pinus merkusii resource on an area of 86,000 hectares in North Sumatra. The company was obliged to replant this area, and could not then log the concession again. The second, a forest exploitation licence, was a 20-year concession starting in 1984 covering a further 150,000 hectares of land. This licence gave the company the right to cut trees and undertake replanting on a continuous cycle.

Indorayon thus had access to 236,000 hectares of forest, containing tree varieties capable of producing both long and short fibre pulp, in one of only three places in Indonesia where softwood (pine) was found. A detailed survey established that this would provide enough wood for 10 years of operation. The original projected annual capacity of the mill was 112,000 tonnes of dissolving pulp or 165,000 tonnes of bleached paper pulp.

The concessions were located within an average radius of 60 km from the proposed plant, which was to stand near the town of Porsea on a 150-hectare site adjacent to the Asahan river. This river flowed out of Lake Toba providing a plentiful supply of clean water for the mill. Porsea had an ideal climate for growing eucalyptus, but no electricity or drainage. The infrastructure between

Porsea and the main local town of Medan was very poor; an asphalt road already existed but this, and various bridges on the route, would have to be strengthened. There were no electricity or telephone links. However, from Medan to the port of Belawan a much faster road link existed. In all, the distance from Porsea to Belawan was approximately 250 km. From Belawan, which was located on the east coast of Sumatra, 600 km from Singapore, there was easy access to North Asia, Europe and Oceania.

One of the greatest threats to the mill was the possibility of trouble over environmental issues. From the beginning Mr Sukanto was clear that the mill was to be designed to the highest standards required by the government, and emission controls 'were to follow Scandinavian air pollution control practice'. He also hoped to ward off criticism by implementing a reforestation programme using fast-growing eucalyptus seedlings from Indorayon's own nursery. Until the eucalyptus was ready for harvesting in 1994, the company would use the existing pine trees and some mixed tropical hardwood. They would plant 16 seedlings for every tree felled, and aimed to be 'one of the greenest companies in the world' within 10 years. Also planned was a nucleus estate scheme in association with the government whereby trees would be planted on land owned by local residents. Indorayon would provide the seedlings and government grants would finance the planting. Indorayon would buy the mature trees from members of the scheme.

Capital investment

The capital investment required was estimated by Mr Sukanto to be US$200 million. In contrast, a similar project recently completed in Malaysia with a smaller capacity had cost US$500 million, and another project in Indonesia built on a turnkey basis by a Japanese contractor had cost US$425 million.

After careful analysis, Mr Sukanto had decided to reject the turnkey approach as he viewed it to be the most expensive option, and one that would not result in any transfer of learning that would be valuable to Indorayon in the future. He had also noted a surprising phenomenon about the implementation of a turnkey contract. The actual installation of the machinery was done by a foreman or welder, working under the local foreman. The foreman himself was supervised by a small subcontractor working for the main contractor, and he in turn was hired by the project team of the company holding the turnkey contract. In other words, concluded Mr Sukanto, it took one man actually to do the job and four layers of management to supervise him.

Mr Sukanto had also observed that there was a tendency for contractors to follow the same building pattern year after year. The standard structures, though admirably suited to the climatic conditions of the West, contained many features that were superfluous in the tropical Indonesian climate. Despite this obvious difference, mills built in Indonesia had been given the same strong roof structure as those designed for the snows of Canada or Finland.

According to Mr Sukanto, a turnkey project designed to withstand Western northern climatic conditions and costing $1 in Canada would end up costing $1.57 in Indonesia because of the contingency factors that the various operators would add to cover all uncertainties. He was convinced that a project designed for tropical climatic conditions and managed according to local practices would cost only $0.80. But no turnkey contractors would accept this price. The only solution was to run the project himself, using an external consultant to provide the expertise he lacked. This would be risky, but he decided that the costs justified it.

The financial calculations were the final pieces of the jigsaw (Exhibit CS17.4). For Mr Sukanto, they were very simple. Based on a forecast pulp price of US$450 per tonne, the project would pay back in six to seven years. The key factor would be the ability to run the mill at US$200 per tonne of pulp produced, which depended on maintaining low wood and operating costs (chemicals, energy). Labour costs were insignificant. The main financial risk would be any delays that occurred in the construction of the mill, which would be expensive.

One crucial asset was a tax holiday of five years from the day the mill began commercial production, granted to Mr Sukanto in December 1983. Introduced by the Indonesian government in order to encourage investment in certain industries, it was the last such licence to be granted.

THE DECISION TO GO AHEAD

Having weighed up the risks and advantages and found the project viable, Mr Sukanto decided to go ahead. He was putting his own money into it, and had a very firm idea of how he wanted to proceed. There would be no waste, no superfluous overheads, and no inflated margins for error. To Mr Sukanto it seemed quite simple: he wanted to build a state-of-the-art mill in the shortest possible time, at the lowest possible cost. His final summary to the team was brief but to the point: 'OK, that is the risk we are taking on a quantified basis. I am a practical man, I am an entrepreneur. We can do it'.

So it was that in November 1984 the Indorayon team began the search for an experienced consultant to work with it to design and construct the plant. They required services which fell into four stages (Exhibit CS17.5). First would come the design development phase, which included design criteria, tender documents for the supply of machinery, a construction budget and a feasibility study. After this came the detailed design phase, followed by construction management and finally, the training of personnel and operation of the plant. The team approached several international consulting firms reputed for their engineering services.

In the end, the choice was narrowed down to four candidates: Lone Star Inc., a large US firm of engineering consultants specializing in pulp; John Smith Engineering Corp. and Tom Brown Corp., both Canadian consulting companies with worldwide reputations; and Lars Corp., a Finnish company with a strong base in pulp plant construction. Representatives from these four firms visited the group's headquarters in Medan and the site in Porsea to discuss the scope of the project, and subsequently submitted their proposals. The Indorayon team painstakingly evaluated the proposals on the basis of both subjective and objective criteria, such as knowledge and experience, the project team, scope of services offered, back-up facilities, guarantees and corporate character.

From the perspective of the consultants, of course, Mr Sukanto was an unknown entrepreneur from Indonesia whose company had no track record in the pulp production business. Those who visited Indorayon's head office often left unsure of the company's financial stability. They entered the office via an anonymous entrance in a busy commercial street in downtown Medan. For many, it was a strange experience to climb an uneven staircase – tripping on steps added at random to avoid an unlucky number – and walk along a narrow passage to sit around an old wooden table in a bare, utilitarian room through whose thin walls could be heard the clack of

Case 18

typewriters and the loud shouting of Medanese voices, and be served tea by people who could occasionally be seen shuffling round in carpet slippers.

On 3 January 1985, the John Smith Engineering Corp. ('Smith's') was awarded the contract for the design development phase. Mr Sukanto's team felt that the firm had experienced engineers and operations staff, and an impressive training record. On the whole, communications were good, and the consulting team gave an impression of honesty and openness.

THE EXPERIENCE WITH SMITH'S: THE DESIGN DEVELOPMENT PHASE

The Smith's team began work quickly and efficiently, and the early good impressions were confirmed when Indorayon staff went to work with them in Vancouver. 'The rapport', said Mr Samantra, 'was excellent. They treated us as personal guests, and we did the same when they came to Jakarta'.

The first ripples of disturbance appeared when a team of specialists from Smith's travelled to Indonesia for an on-the-spot investigation. In Indorayon's judgement, some of these specialists were mediocre. There were several sources of friction, particularly when it came to settling out-of-pocket expenses. When Indorayon looked at Smith's costings, they found they were 'way out – they were engineers, not commercial people'. However, Mr Sukanto carried on, and invested in the education of some of the specialists by giving them a tour of other plants in Indonesia and India to provide examples of economically constructed mills. Eventually, the specialists submitted details of their observations and recommendations to Indorayon.

The next step was the drafting of tender documents for major equipment packages, and a team from Indorayon flew to Vancouver to participate. During their stay in Vancouver, however, Smith's did not organize a single coordination meeting, nor prepare an activity schedule setting out target dates for completion. Smith's project manager did not appear to be fully in control of events: they had to force him to prepare a consolidated list of suppliers, and meet with him daily to ensure status reports were prepared. To Indorayon, the entire project seemed to be 'floating in the air, without any centralized control'. The team returned to Medan convinced that if they had not gone to Vancouver, the tender documents would not have been sent out by the targeted date.

Four rounds of meetings were then planned with the bidders for each equipment package required. The first round of meetings went well, and both the bidders and technical specialists from Smith's and Indorayon were satisfied. Then one of Smith's senior executives arrived, and after brief preliminary discussions he turned to the subject of payment. Specifically, he raised the issue of cost over-runs, and stated that his company was losing heavily on the assignment. To Indorayon, it appeared that to talk of cost over-runs and then ascribe them to delays for which Smith's refused to bear any responsibility had 'become an obsession' with the consultants.

The relationship finally foundered over such budget disagreements. Indorayon found itself challenging many of the figures produced by Smith's. They were also critical of Smith's insistence on doing things the Western way rather than adapting to local circumstances. They were not surprised when, in discussions about meeting Indorayon's target budget, Smith's revealed that there was 'no way we can do it for that amount'.

CONSULTANT NUMBER TWO: LARS CORP.

The design development phase of the project was coming to an end. For the next phase, detailed design (engineering, implementation and procurement), Indorayon decided to opt for a different consultant. On 1 September 1985, the two brothers, Sukanto and Polar Yanto, and the 25 other people who would be most concerned with the project met in Medan. Their agenda was to discuss the lessons of the Smith's experience and work out a strategy for selecting and dealing with the next firm of consultants. They analysed the causes of the problems with Smith's, including faults of their own. For example, since they wanted to learn, their most frequent contribution had been 'why?', a question not always appreciated by Smith's engineers. The team compiled a list of those issues they thought should be decided in advance next time (Exhibit CS17.6).

The same four consulting companies again showed interest in undertaking the next phase and two of them, Tom Brown Corp. and Lars Corp. had already submitted detailed offers. Lars Corp. appeared to have the most potential, so, armed with the list of important issues, two European business consultants (one of whom had been present at the 1 September meeting) visited Helsinki to sound them out.

The consultants produced a lengthy report which concluded that 'given Lars' level of competence, commitment and experience, we believe that they have the skills to implement the project effectively, provided that a relationship based on trust is built at an early stage. They are ready for it'. Impressed by Lars' references, and after discussions to clear up any lingering problems and make it clear that the contract would have nothing to do with Lars' Jakarta office, Mr Sukanto and his team decided to award them the contract for the detailed design phase. At the end of November 1985, draft contract in hand, Mr Samantra and Mr Linardi flew to Helsinki to finalize negotiations.

The two Indorayon men found that the negotiations were carried out in a very different manner from the way they had anticipated. While they were negotiating with the aim of reaching a basic understanding, the emphasis on the Finnish side was on finalizing legal aspects and setting down tight clauses. The Lars Corp's legal advisor was present at every meeting. Mr Samantra recalled that 'every time we started getting somewhere, he would intervene to protect his client'. Negotiations were 'not conducted in the spirit of give and take we were used to'; Lars Corp. played 'a power game'. In spite of these problems, the negotiators concluded after a week that there was enough common ground to work together, and the final draft of the contract was completed to everybody's satisfaction.

On a bitterly cold December day, with 'the sun just looming up like a thief', Mr Sukanto landed in Helsinki, ready to sign the contract. He had kept in touch throughout the negotiations, had met the company's president on several occasions, and was satisfied with the final document. That evening, although the contract was not yet ready for signing, a celebratory dinner was held. The next morning, Mr Sukanto discovered that Lars' president had left for the USA. However, before leaving he had drawn up a letter of understanding, signed it, and sent it to the hotel. Inserted in this document, Mr Sukanto found a clause concerning performance guarantees that was 'totally against the spirit of everything we had discussed'. The clause, which had not been previously seen or discussed by the Indorayon team, had 'turned a fixed price contract into an open contract'.

Other clauses, already agreed, had also been changed. To Mr Sukanto, the message was clear; it indicated a lack of trust in himself and his company.

Utterly frustrated by this development, Mr Sukanto refused to sign the document. Lars' Jakarta representative, the architect of the agreement, was stunned by the sudden turn of events and asked Mr Sukanto to wait for 24 hours while he contacted Lars' president. Mr Sukanto refused, and flew directly to Vancouver to begin discussions with Tom Brown Corp. They were back to square one.

CONSULTANT NUMBER THREE: TOM BROWN CORP.

Shortly after Mr Sukanto's visit to Brown's, a meeting was held between staff from both companies. On Indorayon's side, anxiety centred on the juxtaposition of low cost and high quality and how to achieve the right balance. Those present went through every remaining stage of the project and discussed potential problems. It was decided to prepare a list of questions and problems for a cross-cultural seminar, planned for Vancouver. At the end of the meeting everyone felt drained but optimistic. This time it would work out.

The director of engineering at Brown's was 'a polished, very polite and persuasive gentleman'. In Vancouver he and Mr Samantra discussed the project and the distribution of responsibilities between the two parties for two weeks. Shortly afterwards Brown's president, Mr Tom Brown, flew to Medan to see Mr Sukanto. In a small hill station where a training programme was being conducted, they signed a letter of understanding governing the detailed design phase.

Back in Vancouver, Brown's prepared their team and examined all the earlier documents relating to the project sent to them by Indorayon. A team of seven including Mr Polar Yanto, Mr Samantra and Mr Sutrisno, plus three engineers from Taiwan and one from Indonesia went out to work with them. The team was pleased to find that Brown's had provided half a floor especially for them, with offices partitioned off and tea- and coffee-making facilities. Work was to begin with a series of meetings with the suppliers.

In February 1986, the planned cross-cultural seminar took place in Vancouver. Divided into groups, the participants were asked to identify their respective strengths and weaknesses, the tasks to be performed, and their perception of the problems that might threaten the smooth working of the two teams. The practical outcome, it was hoped, would be to resolve some of the problems before they arose and to forge a team spirit.

Despite these efforts, 'a feeling of uneasiness' began to surface on the Indorayon side during the early meetings to prepare for the supplier negotiations. Indorayon found that Brown's was 'building in safety after safety, which gave us serious doubts about the eventual cost of the project'. For example, where Indorayon wanted 500 tonnes per day pulp production capacity, Brown's specified 650 tonnes 'to be sure'. Mr Samantra sent a letter to Brown's project director objecting to the extra capacity and action was taken to reduce it. But doubts had set in.

The breaking point came over a much more important issue. Brown's had agreed to give Indorayon two almost unconditional bank bonds which they could cash if the project failed. Brown's had signed the letter of understanding and so, even though the main contract had not yet been signed, Indorayon had begun operations and 'paid bills in good faith'. Unfortunately,

Brown's appeared to have second thoughts about the bank bond. Each time Brown's representative was tackled about it, he gave a different answer. The Indorayon team took a decision: no bank bond, no further discussion. The outspoken Mr Sukanto made his views clear: 'If you want your fee as a consultant, you must perform'. Brown's representative offered to issue the bank bond against a certified cheque from Indorayon. Indorayon said no, the bond should be issued without any such conditions.

Indorayon then withdrew their team and sent Brown's a letter noting that 'under the circumstances, we feel we cannot work together. Thank you very much'. Tom Brown himself flew to Indonesia with further proposals, but it was too late. Even the offered intervention of a former Canadian ambassador was politely refused. Enough was enough. It was the end of another brief encounter.

Case 18

Exhibit CS18.1   Regional average cost estimates for bleached softwood papergrade pulp

(Costs levels for second quarter 1985, average of producers in each region)

	USA South	USA North-west	Canada West	New Zealand	Chile	Sweden	Indo-rayon
Wood							
Consumption, m³ (s)ub	4.90	5.85	5.90	5.40	5.50	5.15	4.92
Cost per tonne of pulp, US$	147	199	136	181	88	206	87
Energy							
Purchased power, kWh	380	600	670	280	250	160	—
Cost per tonne of pulp, US$	16	18	12	7	5	3	—
Purchased fuel, kgoe	260	260	320	140	150	110	57
Cost per tonne of pulp, US$	32	36	35	17	28	25	13
Total energy costs, US$	*48*	*54*	*47*	*24*	*33*	*28*	*17*
Personnel costs							
Man hours per tonne of pulp	3.5	4.6	4.1	4.5	6.5	3.9	7.2
Cost per tonne of pulp, US$	55	77	65	31	20	44	15
Other manufacturing costs, US$	90	105	94	75	75	60	73
Total manufacturing costs, US$	*340*	*435*	*342*	*211*	*216*	*338*	*192*
Distribution costs, US$	100	85	85	70	90	85	35
Total costs before capital charges, US$	*440*	*520*	*427*	*281*	*306*	*423*	*227*
Capital charges, US$	104	106	85	70	90	55	231*
Total, before import duties, US$	**544**	**626**	**512**	**351**	**396**	**478**	**458**

* Interest costs assumed to be US$13.8 million in 1990. Amortizations: US$16.6 million per year; dividends: US$4.2 million a year.

Exhibit CS18.2   Projected demand for bleached softwood market pulp and dissolving pulp in selected Asian countries, 1983–2000

Bleached softwood market pulp

Country	1983 ('000 t)	1990 ('000 t)	2000 ('000 t)	Growth 1983–2000 (% p.a.)
Indonesia	50	120	210	+8.8
Thailand	20	70	110	+10.5
Philippines	47	60	90	+3.9
China	390	530	660	+3.1
Taiwan	73	110	180	+5.5
South Korea	94	140	200	+4.5
Subtotal	*674*	*1,030*	*1,450*	*+4.6*
Japan	940	1,100	1,400	+2.4
Total	**1,614**	**2,190**	**2,850**	**+3.4**

Dissolving Pulp

Country	1983 ('000 t)	1990 ('000 t)	2000 ('000 t)	Growth 1983–2000 (% p.a.)
Indonesia	43	75	110	+6.0
Thailand	20	22	30	+2.6
Taiwan	135	145	150	+0.7
China	33	55	125	+8.7
South Korea	19	23	25	+1.7
Subtotal	*250*	*320*	*440*	*+3.6*
Japan	523	480	415	−1.4
Total	**773**	**800**	**855**	**+0.6**

Source: Indorayon Feasibility Study, 1985

Case 18

Exhibit CS18.3   NBSK pulp prices and inventories

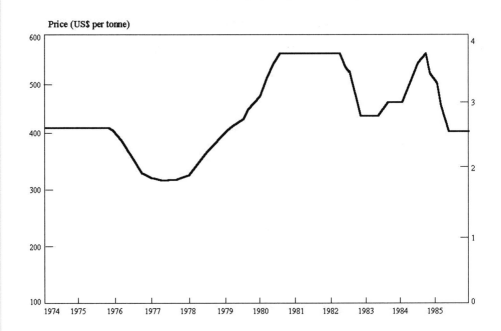

Exhibit CS18.4   Tentative financing budget

'000 US dollars

	1985	1986	1987	1988	1989	1990	1991	1992	1993	1994	1995	1996	1997	1998	1999
Uses															
Mill, fixed investment	15,857	47,572	79,286	15,857											
Reinvestments							1,586	1,586	1,586	1,586	1,586	1,586	2,378	2,378	2,378
Change in working capital				4,280	938	1,104	−26	−20							
Plantation estab.	25,000	2,300	5,800	2,160											
Total investments	**40,857**	**49,872**	**87,686**	**22,297**	**938**	**1,104**	**1,560**	**1,566**	**1,586**	**1,586**	**1,586**	**1,586**	**2,378**	**2,378**	**2,378**
Total interest	0	1,620	6,505	15,252	16,053	14,623	12,584	10,540	8,496	6,454	4,410	2,406	784	137	57
Fees		117	311	272											
Financing charges	**0**	**1,737**	**6,816**	**15,524**	**16,053**	**14,623**	**12,584**	**10,540**	**8,496**	**6,454**	**4,410**	**2,406**	**784**	**137**	**57**
Loans amortization	**0**	**0**	**0**	**0**	**10,252**	**16,940**	**17,030**	**17,030**	**17,030**	**17,030**	**17,030**	**15,700**	**6,950**	**700**	**528**
Total uses	**40,857**	**51,609**	**94,502**	**37,821**	**27,243**	**32,667**	**31,174**	**29,136**	**27,112**	**25,070**	**23,026**	**19,692**	**10,112**	**3,215**	**2,963**
Sources															
Operating profit			−920	22,503	30,760	42,650	43,270	43,750	43,750	43,750	43,750	43,750	43,750	43,750	43,750
Equity	35,000	23,000	12,000												
Debts	5,857	28,608	83,421	18,423											
Total sources	**40,857**	**51,608**	**94,501**	**40,926**	**30,760**	**42,650**	**43,270**	**43,750**	**43,750**	**43,750**	**43,750**	**43,750**	**43,750**	**43,750**	**43,750**
Financing balance	3,106	3,518	9,983	12,097	14,615	16,637	18,681	20,725	24,059	33,637	40,533	40,787			
Net income statement															
Total production	0	0	0	106	124	150	150	150	150	150	150	150	150	150	150
Total sales income	0	0	0	50,119	60,072	72,376	72,376	72,376	72,376	72,376	72,376	72,376	72,376	72,376	72,376

Case 18

389

Case 18

Exhibit CS18.5   Phases and scope of services

1. **Design Development Phase**

   Project procedures

   Site visits and data collection

   Process selection

   Design criteria

   Flow diagrams

   Civil engineering

   Mechanical equipment and purchase enquiry

   Instrumentation and electrical

   Project schedule

   Construction budget

   Manufacturing cost estimates

   Banker's report

2. **Detailed Design**

   Project management

   Civil and structural design supervision

   Purchasing assistance, inspection and expediting

   Interconnection design

   Scheduling

   Cost control

3. **Construction Management (Civil and Erection)**

   Construction pre-planning

   Contract management

   Construction management

   Materials management

   Construction management team

4. **Training and Operation**

   Detailed personnel planning

   Implementation

   Results measurement

   Operations management team

Source: Indorayon archives

Exhibit CS18.6   Issues to settle in advance with consultant

1   To convince the consultant about the need for Indorayon engineers to be closely associated with the consultant engineers on information sharing and decision making at all phases of the project.

2   To convince the consultant that the 'why' philosophy of Indorayon is not to threaten/question them but is a learning device.

3   To work out in depth a proper transfer/training programme.

4   Protect Indorayon interests.

5   Define the scope of the work.

6   Establish a mutual understanding.

7   To build good team-work

8   To discuss philosophies (compatibility)

9   To have a 'flexible' way of resolving issues.

10 To explain the local situation to the consultant.

Source: Indorayon Archives, dated 1 September 1985.

Case 19

This case was written by Professor Hellmut Schütte, Affiliate Professor of International Management at INSEAD.

Chicago Truck and Diesel, Philaysia

For decades Chicago Truck and Diesel Ltd (Chicago TD) had marketed its products in the USA and Europe, but it was not until the late 1980s that the company started to have a closer look at the markets of Asia. Chicago TD belonged to a conglomerate which was one of the world's leading enterprises in the mechanical engineering sector and one of the biggest firms in the USA, with turnover of more than US$25 billion and approximately 100,000 employees in 1995.

Within the conglomerate, Chicago TD was the largest and most important company with share capital of US$1.2 billion, sales revenue of US$8.2 billion and 49,000 employees in 1995. Within Chicago TD, there were several product divisions which operated rather independently. The biggest was the Commercial Vehicle Division, which was responsible for the production and sale of trucks, buses, public service vehicles, and diesel engines for automobiles. Larger engines such as those used as the main propulsion systems in ships were manufactured by another division.

Turnover of the Commercial Vehicle Division reached a record US$4.1 billion in 1995, but year-to-year volatility was high due to the cyclical nature of the business. Chicago TD thus tried to assure steadier growth in revenues by globalizing its activities. This strategy assumed that a recession in the USA would probably be counter-balanced by a concurrent boom in Europe or Asia, or vice versa. Chicago TD's largest project abroad was a bus business in the UK which had achieved a considerable market breakthrough but also accumulated large losses. Chicago TD also had fully owned truck assembly and manufacturing plants in Australia, Brazil and South Africa, was a minority shareholder in a truck assembly plant in Turkey, and was constructing a new factory for the manufacture of diesel engines in Turkey in 1996. In Asia it had entered licensing agreements in Korea and Japan, and had recently started to negotiate a joint venture for the assembly of trucks in China. Another project was under consideration in India. Its most strategically important yet troublesome project, however, was in Philaysia.

INTEREST IN ASIA IN THE EARLY 1990s

At the beginning of the 1990s, business in Asia was limited to the occasional sale of trucks, buses and engines by local agents. Chicago TD management, however, were aware that the rapid market changes and the prospects for continued high growth rates in Asia could no longer be neglected. The Japanese and the Koreans already dominated the local auto industries: Japanese competitors had set up several truck assembly plants in the region and the Koreans had surfaced in several markets as aggressive newcomers. Second-hand trucks flooded in from Japan and made sales efforts by local agents difficult.

One of Chicago TD's closest competitors, a German truck and diesel engine manufacturer, had begun the licensing of diesel engines in Indonesia. Chicago TD, on the other hand, had run into difficulties with its Indonesian sales agent which it was unable to overcome due to a long-term contract. In Malaysia, road regulations made the introduction of standard Chicago TD trucks problematic, although sales of military vehicles were satisfactory. Fusuki of Japan had gained an almost monopolistic position in heavy trucks and buses in Thailand making it impossible for Chicago TD to win a bid in 1991 for the local assembly of engines.

Charlie Miller, who in the early 1990s was Chicago TD's director in charge of foreign manufacturing operations, had been searching for further opportunities in the Asia Pacific region for some time. However, no results had been achieved so far, as Chicago TD considered any diesel engine project feasible only in connection with the assembly of vehicles, a view not shared by either potential partners or their respective governments. In order to explore market opportunities more systematically, and to prepare for better market penetration of Chicago TD's commercial vehicles, Miller opened a regional office in Singapore in 1990, which was staffed by Pete Sanders as representative for Asia. Sanders had spent some years in Tokyo, was married to a Philaysian lady, and seemed capable of establishing and developing relationships with local organizations in Philaysia and other Asian countries.

At the beginning of the 1990s Philaysia was perceived by Chicago TD as a second-tier country in Asia: not as large or as promising as China and not as booming and stable as Singapore, but still enjoying good growth rates and a reasonably large market. As a member of ASEAN, products manufactured in Philaysia would eventually enjoy reduced import duties when exported to other ASEAN member states.

The government of Philaysia had received mixed reviews in the US press, particularly concerning the widespread corruption, and the tendency of the government to change its rules frequently. Nevertheless, the inflow of foreign investment had been steady and many foreign firms reported healthy profits. No dramatic change in the political or economic arenas was expected for the next few years. In the medium and the long term a bright future for Philaysia was predicted by economists.

It was on one of his first exploratory missions to Philaysia that Sanders managed to meet the well-known local industrialist, Tom Risingstar.

TOM RISINGSTAR

Risingstar was one of Philaysia's glamorous business stars, whose comet-like success was not unrelated to the president's rise over the preceding two decades. Born into the family of a rice-trader, Risingstar made his first money by selling imported clothes and textiles to his compatriots in the late 1960s. In the 1970s he learnt by chance that Toyota was trying to export cars to Philaysia, but their first large shipment had been blocked at customs. Risingstar bought the shipment from Toyota for a token price and started bringing Toyota cars into the country and selling them, though initially without great success. Risingstar therefore used the Toyotas as taxis, gained a good reputation for them, and succeeded consequently in selling more and more to the public. He quickly became the owner of Philaysia's largest taxi fleet.

To meet demand for spare parts, Risingstar started to produce some components locally with the help of associates. Unable to boost his annual intake of cars because of a government preference for local assembly, he soon switched from the import of finished cars to the import of completely knocked-down Toyota kits for cars and later for light trucks, which were assembled at his new car company, Romeo Motor – though with difficulty at first.

Within a few years Risingstar had built up a conglomerate of companies, the largest being Romeo Motor. Romeo's Toyota cars held a steady market share of around 40–45 per cent at the beginning of the 1990s. Other ventures included: the assembly of air conditioners, refrigerators, and home appliances; tableware; an airline; a logging and a mining company; a bank; and an insurance company. Cooperative agreements existed with a number of foreign firms which provided the appropriate technology for his ventures. Despite financial constraints connected with the tremendous growth of his empire, Risingstar did not allow the Japanese to take an equity participation in Romeo Motor. He was proud of having been one of the first Philaysians to enter into various cooperation agreements with foreigners without being swallowed.

The success of Mr T. Risingstar was admired. His links with the president were close, and it was known that he had been able to influence government decisions in his favour. The president had come to power through what was locally understood to be a democratic election, but he had accumulated substantive power since his victory by alternately suppressing and co-opting opposition forces.

AN AGREEMENT BETWEEN CHICAGO TD AND RISINGSTAR

Pete Sanders' market research showed that in the late 1980s an average of 1,200 new heavy-duty trucks and large buses above 15 tons, requiring diesel engines above 150 hp, were sold per annum in Philaysia. He estimated that about three times as many second-hand trucks and buses were imported each year. He felt that the market for new vehicles of this type could expand to about double the size within the next 5–7 years provided that in the future the government applied more rigid import restrictions for used vehicles. Sales of new vehicles in the market for smaller 9–15 ton vehicles, powered by diesel engines of 90–150 hp, were expected to grow by about 10 per cent per annum over the next few years. If Chicago TD were to join forces with Romeo Motor, Sanders estimated that Chicago TD could reach a market share of 30 per cent of both categories of new vehicles by 1995.

When approached by Sanders, Risingstar showed an immediate interest in the distributorship and assembly of Chicago TD commercial vehicles, on the condition that Chicago TD also entered into a cooperative agreement with Romeo Motor for the production, at some future date, of diesel engines. Such a commitment raised potential conflicts for both parties. Risingstar had earlier started discussions on a similar project with Daetoo from Korea. Chicago TD, on its side, felt under some obligation to another Philaysian group although it was known that the latter was negotiating at the same time with MMM from Germany.

None the less, in June 1992 both Chicago TD and Romeo Motor agreed to work together and to discontinue negotiations with other partners. Contracts were signed in Chicago covering a distributorship and local assembly agreement for Chicago TD commercial vehicles, a licensing agreement for the local production of diesel engines in the 168–320 hp range, and the appointment of Chicago TD as consultant for the design and construction of the diesel engine manufacturing facilities.

Risingstar was keen to start marketing his new product lines immediately. On the occasion of the signing of the various agreements in Chicago, he ordered the first 16 commercial vehicles to see how the Philaysian market would respond. They were presented to the public during the official opening, in December 1992, of the new 'Chicago TD Division' within Romeo Motor, and were sold immediately.

To meet Risingstar's expectations regarding adequate Chicago TD support, Sanders moved the regional headquarters from Singapore to Philaysia in the beginning of 1993. He was given an office in the Romeo Motor building along the same corridor as Risingstar, acquired a Toyota car for himself, and in the capital's best residential area rented a large house which belonged to Risingstar.

BIDDING FOR THE DIESEL ENGINE PROJECT

Romeo Motor had no problems in obtaining permission for the assembly of Chicago TD commercial vehicles since, through its assembly of Toyota cars and light trucks, it was already part of the Philaysian government's Progressive Truck Manufacturing Programme (PTMP) which was designed to lead eventually to the creation of a fully independent truck manufacturing industry in Philaysia. When concluding the various contracts with Chicago TD, Risingstar had already known, through inside sources, of the government's intention to introduce a similar programme to encourage the local manufacture of diesel engines. Risingstar would be well placed indeed if his company was already producing diesel engines when the government started, as he predicted, to force all truck assemblers to put locally manufactured diesel engines in their vehicles.

Risingstar felt that he could influence the government's forthcoming regulations by moving ahead with his own ideas on diesel engine manufacture before the decision-making body, the Board of Investments, finalized their new programme. He therefore asked Chicago TD to rush the preparatory work on the planned joint diesel engine project.

In May 1993 the Board of Investments (BOI) announced the details of the Progressive Manufacture of Automotive Diesel Engines Programme (PMADE), and invited bids for the local assembly of diesel engines ranging from 50–200 hp, with a possible extension up to 320 hp (see Exhibits CS19.1 and CS19.2). The production of diesel engines was to be included under a separate Investment Priority Plan, which provided preferential treatment and various tax incentives for those firms which complied with the PMADE requirements. The BOI specified that bids for PMADE, accompanied by detailed feasibility studies, were to be submitted by interested parties by 7 September 1993. In the event, almost all of the world's leading diesel engine manufacturers applied, most of them associated with local partners. Chicago TD submitted a bid in which it specified itself as a foreign licenser and Romeo Motor as its domestic licensee.

The Board of Investments had originally intended to announce their decision within one month. However, the surprisingly large number of contenders and various technical questions requiring supplementary information delayed the evaluation process considerably. In November, the BOI eliminated several firms from further consideration, leaving Chicago TD, Purkin of the USA, MMM of Germany and Fusuki of Japan.

To further evaluate the project proposals, the shortlisted companies were asked by the chairman of the Board of Investments, who was also the minister of industry, to submit additional data concerning the costing of locally produced components, as well as the extent to which the engines could be exported.

At the end of 1993, rumours indicated that the engine range would be extended above 200 hp and that Chicago TD would be selected for the range above 150 hp. Discussions regarding the manufacture of smaller engine sizes were still open, and further changes were in the making with respect to the ownership of the diesel engine plants. In January 1994, the BOI announced rules requiring:

- Direct investment by the foreign licenser in a 100 per cent owned diesel engine manufacturing subsidiary in Philaysia for a period of five years. During this time, no licensing fees or royalties could be paid by the subsidiary to its parent company. This rule was created in order to prevent foreign licensers taking funds out of their Philaysian ventures via transfer pricing during the initial five-year period when all the feasibility studies had shown that the ventures would be relying heavily on imports of parts and components from their licensers, and would also be losing money.

- Transfer of ownership of the subsidiary to the citizens of Philaysia beginning after five years, commencing with sales of at least 20 per cent of the shares to individuals or individual organizations. At least 60 per cent of the shares had to be in the hands of Philaysians after 20 years.

All four shortlisted competitors hesitated but finally agreed to the new terms. Chicago TD now had to allocate substantial investment funds to Philaysia and replace Romeo Motor (formerly its licensee) with a fully owned Chicago TD subsidiary as its domestic operator. One possible solution for the future transfer of the subsidiary's shares to Philaysians would be a swap of shares between the subsidiary and the Romeo Motor vehicle assembly plant's Chicago TD division.

NEGOTIATIONS WITH THE BOARD OF INVESTMENTS

On 16 February 1994, the BOI's vice chairman announced the BOI's decision to enter into final negotiations with Purkin for the lower horsepower engines, and with Chicago TD for the higher horsepower range. The final awarding of the project would depend on the outcome of these negotiations. While Purkin was likely to cover the range from 50 to 150 hp, Chicago TD would probably be allowed to produce engines from 168 to 320 hp. Furthermore, the BOI specified that local assemblers of commercial vehicles would not be obliged to use locally manufactured engines in trucks and buses above 15 tons. This would mean that there would be no secure domestic market for engines larger than 150 hp. The Board did not envisage an import ban on diesel engines either, although restrictions were promised.

These arrangements were unacceptable to Chicago TD, particularly since the highest sales were expected in the range below 150 hp. After protracted negotiations between the BOI, Purkin and Chicago TD, an agreement was reached in April which would allow Chicago TD to produce a smaller engine as well, thus creating an overlapping sector from 90–150 hp corresponding to

9–15 ton vehicles. Detailed discussions on the local content requirements led to solutions acceptable to all concerned, leaving only the questions of export commitments and market protection open for further negotiation.

Meanwhile, Mr T. Toughline became the new chairman of the BOI and minister of industry. A former Harvard MBA and consultant in the USA, Toughline was particularly keen to set up industries in Philaysia which could manufacture products competitive with those coming from abroad. To ensure that the foreign licensers would bring the latest technology, he asked Purkin and Chicago TD to export a substantial percentage of their production, and expressed reluctance at giving government protection against imports. He did not, however, immediately impose new regulations on the two prospective investors, preferring instead to be flexible and ask them for their views.

Both Chicago TD and Purkin knew that the quantities they would produce in Philaysia would not enable them to compete cost-wise on international markets, and tried to convince Toughline to either refrain from imposing any export obligations on them, or to reduce the extent of the obligations. They also asked the BOI not to allow the import of engines for completely knocked-down vehicles, and to restrict the import of stationary diesel engines, in order to at least be able to fully exploit the local market. Chicago TD asked the government to ban the import of second-hand commercial vehicles to protect its assembly operations; Purkin, in turn, insisted on the banning of imported second-hand engines since it manufacturered only diesel engines.

While the BOI agreed to consider import restrictions, it did not loosen its stance regarding its requirement for the foreign investors to export. It specified that exports during the first five years should amount to US$40 million from the manufacturer of the smaller engines and US$20 million from the company producing the bigger engines. If these export commitments could not be fulfilled, the manufacturers would have to pay in cash to the Philaysian government the difference between the appropriate export target and their actual exports. A sum equivalent to 10 per cent of the export commitment had to be submitted to the government in advance in the form of an export performance bond, or letter of guarantee from a financial institution, to ensure strict adherence to the contract. Failure to achieve agreed local content requirements would also be subject to a heavy penalty.

The new rules dramatically changed the outlook for Purkin and Chicago TD, and it seemed prospects would be dim even if the government were to accept some escape clauses and ban all imports of diesel engines between 50–320 hp. As a result, both companies were reluctant to make any commitments, and adopted a wait-and-see stance.

FUSUKI'S ENTRY INTO THE NEGOTIATIONS

At about this time the Japanese company Fusuki, which had been left out in the first bid, re-entered the negotiation scene. Fusuki already had a dominant share of the Philaysian market for new commercial vehicles in the imported second-hand sector. Fusuki had obtained the support of current Philaysian diesel engine users; so much so that mini-bus drivers, bus operators and trucking companies had placed advertisements in the newspapers demanding the inclusion of Fusuki in the diesel engine programme. They had, in fact, a strong case. The majority of diesel engines in the country were from Fusuki, and many of them needed replacement. The action of the Philaysian diesel engine users was followed by political pressure from Japan. The Japanese government was not keen for Japanese companies to be left out of a sector which was seen to be so important, and one in which the USA, which was otherwise less engaged in Philaysia, seemed to have acquired a very strong influence. Also, Fusuki let it be known to the public that it was prepared to accept all the conditions set by the government.

Purkin was abruptly told by the BOI to withdraw from the diesel engine programme and Fusuki was asked to take over production of the Purkin range. Less than two months later, in January 1995, Fusuki signed a contract with the Philaysian government for the local production of 50–150 hp diesel engines and accepted conditions such as the US$40 million export commitment within five years and local content requirements ranging from 30 per cent at the beginning to 60 per cent after five years. For the BOI, it was their first success in the long process of negotiation.

For Chicago TD, Fusuki's participation in the diesel engine programme meant the presence of a much better established competitor in the overlapping 90–150 hp range and a weakening of Chicago TD's bargaining position with the government. Furthermore, Fusuki was not only a manufacturer of diesel engines, but also of commercial vehicles: 40 per cent of all new 9–15 ton trucks and buses powered with engines up to 150 hp came from Fusuki, as well as 80 per cent of all imported second-hand vehicles in that class.

Naturally, the BOI and Risingstar began to put pressure on Chicago TD's local representative, Pete Sanders, to follow Fusuki's example and accept the BOI's terms and conditions. It was obvious that the BOI also wanted to go ahead with the larger diesel engine project, with or without the US investor. Pete Sanders had been involved in all the negotiations so far, and felt like an intermediary between the BOI, Risingstar and his own headquarters in Chicago. Together with one of his colleagues from the USA he finally accepted and initialled the BOI's terms and conditions and sent them to Chicago for approval by Chicago TD's board. The board, however, had objections and was not prepared to accept the entire package of terms and conditions, and in the middle of 1995 sent Charlie Miller to Philaysia to re-negotiate the project.

RECONSIDERATION OF THE DIESEL ENGINE PROJECT

Miller's discussions with the BOI were far from easy. The government, for reasons of fairness, could not offer Chicago TD better terms than those accepted by Fusuki. Chicago TD, on the other hand, argued that fewer economies of scale could be achieved in the bigger engine range, so that local content as well as export requirements would have to be adjusted accordingly. Chicago TD also asked for a delayed production start for the smaller-sized engines in the overlapping range. Finally, in August 1995, the government and Chicago TD reached a compromise on the terms and conditions, and agreed on a timetable for production.

According to the timetable, a Philaysian subsidiary of Chicago TD had to be formed not later than February 1996. Commercial start-up for the larger engines was scheduled for 1 April 1997. The BOI assured Chicago TD that, subject to the president's approval, local vehicle manufacturers would be obliged to use domestically produced diesel engines in trucks up to 18 tons gross weight, equivalent to 200 hp and over, by mid-1996. This would mean a larger secure market for Chicago TD's bigger engines. A formal project agreement was not signed, as Chicago TD first had to review its plans and prepare an up-to-date feasibility study.

After weeks of internal discussions, Charlie Miller came up with a new plan for the development of Chicago TD's Philaysian diesel engine project, which fell into in three phases:

- Phase 1 (1997) About 1,250 bigger engines were to be produced by Chicago TD making extensive use of Romeo Motor's personnel and capacities which were not fully utilized at the time, but found capable of producing good quality products. Investment in assets and working capital would amount to US$6 million. A certain percentage of the output would be exported.

- Phase 2 (1998) Production of all engine sizes would start, requiring utilization of both Romeo Motor's foundry and machining facilities and of new machinery to be set up by Chicago TD. An additional investment of US$12.5 million would be required. A total output of 2,750 engines was planned, of which a certain percentage would be exported.

- Phase 3 (1999–2001) Production would reach the target of 4,000 engines per year, of which a certain percentage was to be exported.

The export of engines in Phases 1 to 3 would make up about 50 per cent of Chicago TD's total export commitment. The additional 50 per cent would come from the export of parts, specifically crankcases. The production of crankcases on fully automatic transfer machining lines would be started during Phase 3. Suitable production facilities were currently in use in Chicago, but could be converted and transferred to Philaysia; alternatively, new machines could be ordered. The production of crankcases would reach 2,500 in 1999 and 5,000 per annum in the following years. The additional investment was substantial and amounted to about US$25 million.

While details of the Miller's plan were still under discussion at Chicago headquarters, another development in Philaysia gained momentum and became increasingly alarming.

RISINGSTAR'S DOWNFALL

Chicago TD's sales of completely knocked-down trucks and buses to Philaysia had increased rapidly since Romeo Motor and Chicago TD had signed the distributorship and local assembly agreements for commercial vehicles in 1992. By 1995, sales to Romeo Motor had reached more than US$40 million, a spectacular success bearing in mind that Chicago TD had been a latecomer in the market and was exposed to heavy competition. Risingstar had invested heavily in a brand new plant for his Chicago TD division, with a covered floor space of 30,000 square metres. As in all his other industrial undertakings, Risingstar had acquired only first class equipment of recent or the latest technological standard.

In 1995, it became apparent that the over-ambitious sales targets of Romeo Motor and overselling by Chicago TD had resulted in substantial stocks of completely knocked-down vehicles in Philaysia. The fast economic growth of 1993 and 1994 had slowed down considerably, causing a serious decline in passenger car sales. In 1995, the number of vehicles sold by domestic makers decreased by 19 per cent in comparison to 1994. Romeo Motor's turnover fell by 15 per cent, and production was down by 27 per cent. At the same time Philaysia was suffering from a high inflation rate. Romeo showed the first signs of trouble in paying for deliveries of parts and components from the USA. By the end of 1995 the company owed US$10 million to Chicago TD.

Case 19

For the first time in its history, Romeo Motor recorded a loss of about US$3 million in 1995. Its cash flow decreased considerably, and its debt/equity ratio increased to 12:1. Managing the mostly short-term borrowings at interest rates of about 25 per cent became extremely difficult. Sales forecasts for 1996 were not promising.

Early in 1996, a financial debacle in Philaysia was precipitated by the flight of Dewey Twinkle, a respected Philaysian entrepreneur whose business empire had collapsed. He left behind more than US$60 million in unsecured debts. His disappearance caused temporary panic in the financial community and a tightening of credit. Companies which had been short of cash for months suddenly could no longer roll over their short-term loans.

Risingstar's own finance house, Philyfinance, was badly hit by the financial turmoil and almost collapsed. Two insurance companies belonging to Risingstar also got into trouble. Risingstar had no choice but to ask the government to bail him out. As his group represented a major force in Philaysian industry, the government was committed to rescue it and established an industrial loan fund which would infuse new capital into the ailing ventures. It was known, however, that government technocrats such as Minister Toughline – who in addition to his other positions was also a member of the Central Bank Monetary Board – would attach tight strings to such aid to ensure fast recovery.

Chicago TD hoped that a loan to Romeo Motor would enable the company to repay, among other items, its long overdue and by then substantial supplier credits. Meetings with Risingstar and Toughline in May encouraged such expectations, although it had already become clear that Chicago TD would have to restructure at least some of its short-term credits into a longer term loan with some years grace.

In the meantime, the BOI had become increasingly impatient with Chicago TD's reluctance to sign the diesel engine project agreement. A new legal entity had been incorporated on 27 February 27 1996 with the name of Chicago TD Diesel (Philaysia), Inc., but in Spring 1996 it was obvious that it was unlikely to start commercial operations by 1 April 1997. Although Fusuki had started actual construction work for its plant, the BOI extended the deadline for both companies until September 1997. Rumours spread that Fusuki had offered to go into the production of the larger range of engines, too, in the case of Chicago TD's withdrawal.

In August 1996, Chicago TD was informed that loans extended to Romeo Motor from the government's Industrial Loan Fund could not be used for the repayment of accounts with suppliers such as Chicago TD. At the same time Risingstar asked Miller for a restructuring of his entire obligations to Chicago TD.

The government, the public, and the local and foreign press began to speculate about a Chicago TD decision on its future in Philaysia

Exhibit CS19.1   Invitation for submission of proposals

Republic of Philaysia
Office of the President
Board of Investments

The Board of Investments invites the submission of proposals for the PROGRESSIVE MANUFACTURE OF AUTOMOBILE DIESEL ENGINES. Proposals should be submitted to the Office of the Chairman not later than 11:00 a.m. 7 September 1993.

The proposals shall cover the manufacture of automotive diesel engines in sizes ranging from approximately 50 hp up to 200 hp and indicate capability of the project to manufacture automotive diesel engines up to a maximum size of 320 hp. The manufacturing programme to be presented in the proposal shall be based on increasing progressively the number and value of engine components sourced domestically, and shall cover a period of not less than five years from start of commercial operation of the project.

The Government intends that the automotive diesel engines, to be installed in all domestically assembled commercial vehicles, trucks and buses under the Progressive Truck Manufacturing Programme, shall be of domestic manufacture once the automotive diesel engine project has been placed in full commercial operation. The vehicle units to be assembled under the Progressive Truck Manufacturing Programme are estimated by the truck assemblers participating in said Programme to be as follows, in 1995:

Category 1: up to 2,045 kgs (4,500 lbs) GVW	20,000 units
Category 2: 2,046–4,545 kgs (4,501–10,000 lbs) GVW	4,000 units
Category 3: 4,546–13,636 kgs (10,001–30,000 lbs) GVW	7,000 units

The foregoing figures represent the projected number of vehicles to be assembled and sold in the domestic market in 1995; the proportions of the vehicles in each category that will be fitted with gasoline and with diesel engines should be estimated by each proponent, on the basis of their experience and assessment of engine trends.

It is expected that only one diesel engine project, but in any event no more than two, shall be authorized, and if there shall be two authorized projects the horsepower range of engines to be manufactured by each project shall be limited and specified to avoid overlaps or duplications between the projects in engine sizes manufactured.

The submitted proposals shall include, but not be limited to, the following elements:

1. The engine models and series proposed for manufacture, providing specifications, performance characteristics and other information which would enable comprehensive evaluation of the suitability of the engine for domestic manufacture and use in domestically assembled trucks and commercial vehicles for the Philaysian market.

2. A schedule of the present prices, FOB in export boxing, and overseas freight, for the engine models and series proposed for progressive manufacture in the Philaysia.
    – In fully assembled form
    – In completely knocked-down form
    The present import C & F prices of individual engine components which are proposed for domestic manufacture during the submitted program period shall also be submitted.

Case 19

3. The proposed programme for progressive manufacture which shall provide information on intended sources of domestic supply for each of the components to be sourced locally, and on the estimated costs of domestic sourcing against imported procurement for each component proposed for domestic sourcing. The submitted programme shall cover at least a five-year period from start of commercial operations. The proposal should provide supporting data which would enable evaluation of the practicability of the respective elements of the progressive manufacturing programme.

4. The financial programme, which shall estimate the capital required to carry out the project, distinguishing between equity and long-term debt capital, and between foreign and local currency capital. The sources of each of the elements of capital shall be specified in as much detail as possible, as well as the terms and conditions under which they are expected to be raised.

Evaluation of the proposals shall be guided by existing laws and industrial policies and take into account, among others, the following criteria for selection:

1. Suitability of the engine for domestic manufacture for the use in domestically assembled trucks and commercial vehicles, and for other applications.

2. Extent and pace of achievement in engine local content, and minimization of cost to realize such achievement.

3. Contribution of the project to the development of the Philaysian engineering industry.

It is expected that evaluation of submitted proposals will be completed and announcement of award of the project will be made in early October 1993. Proponents should have technical representatives available in the second half September 1993 to provide such clarifications and additional information that may be required for the thorough evaluation of their submitted proposal.

Additional information that may be required by parties intending to submit proposals may be obtained from the Machinery and Transport Section, Fabrication Industries, Board of Investments.

> 11 November 1992
> Chairman
> Board of Investments

Exhibit CS19.2 Timeline of steps in the negotiation of Philaysia's diesel engine programme

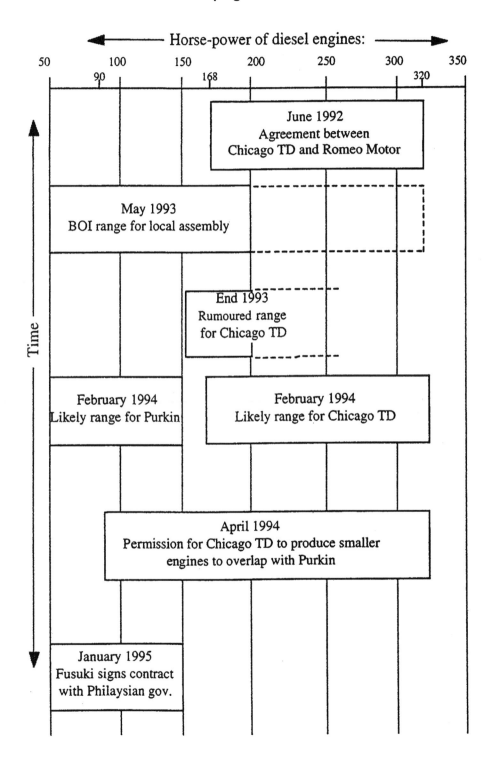

Case 20

This case was prepared by Hellmut Schütte, Affiliate Professor at INSEAD. It is intended to be used as a basis for class discussion rather than to illustrate either effective or ineffective handling of an administrative situation. Copyright © 1986 INSEAD-EAC, Fontainebleau, France.

Peter Clausen

THE ADVERTISING AGENCY

It was 8:30 on a Monday morning and Peter Clausen was going through his mail in his office located in a modern building in Bigtown in Indolandia. He had just returned from a lovely weekend spent with his wife and two children on a beach not too far from the city.

Peter was the managing director of McKintosh, the leading advertising agency in Indolandia, which was set up 10 years ago as a joint venture between a small local agency and McKintosh, New York. McKintosh had 70 subsidiaries and affiliated agencies in 56 countries and prided itself as being among the top 10 advertising agencies in the world.

Peter, who was born in Denmark, joined McKintosh in Copenhagen 11 years ago as an account executive in the client service department. On his own initiative he was transferred to New York from where he was sent to Indolandia two and a half years ago. At the age of 36 he was in charge of 55 members of staff, one being his British creative director, Dick White.

As the workload increased, he tried to have another expatriate brought in to act as head of the client service department. However, his request for a work permit from the government had been turned down. Since most of McKintosh's clients were multinational firms with expatriate directors or marketing managers, they expected an expatriate on the agency side to be their main contact. It was for this reason that Peter had to spend a substantial amount of his time in meetings with clients, a task he felt was rather superfluous since he had full confidence in his local client service staff. Instead of discussing the conceptual and main creative work with the agency's team before it was presented to the client, he often found himself seeing the material at the same time as the clients and then selling it to them regardless of whether he liked the output or not. To overcome this problem he brought in additional expatriates on tourist visas from offices in the neighbouring countries for short periods whenever major advertising campaigns had to be developed.

BUSINESS PRINCIPLES OF MCKINTOSH

McKintosh's reputation in the market was that of an agency with good creative work, coupled with the best quality final products locally available such as artwork, photography, typesetting, films. The latter was due to the fact that the majority of the advertising material was brought in from the USA or Europe only to be adopted locally. McKintosh also had the image of a reliable and trustworthy partner – highly appreciated in a country such as Indolandia where media rates (prices for space in print media or time on air on radio and television) were practically never fixed and where it was possible to obtain agency commissions from so-called 'official' rates of up to 70%. Most agencies in town charged their clients the full 'official' rates or offered them a small discount, pocketing the rest for themselves. As this business was very profitable and the purchase of space and time in the media made up the bulk of advertising budgets of almost all clients, agencies were able to offer development work on advertising campaigns either very cheaply or free of charge.

Peter Clausen's predecessor had decided to implement a different system. He had asked his media buyers to bargain very hard to obtain the lowest rates of all agencies in the country, based on the fact that they placed more orders than anyone else. He then slapped a standard agency commission of 20% on top of this and charged the total to his customers. As a result McKintosh could claim and prove that in terms of media buying they were the cheapest agency in Indolandia. To make up for lost revenue, however, McKintosh's fees for creative services and artwork were higher than those of most of their competitors. Most of McKintosh's clients not only accepted, but also appreciated, this more open pricing policy.

CONTROL MECHANISM

Peter Clausen happily went along with this system which had even enabled him to attract new clients into the agency. He did this by comparing the amount of money clients of other agencies spent for a given media plan with the proposal his own media buyers would give him. Peter also considered this a useful control mechanism for his own staff in the media department which under the given rate system could find it rather easy to divert funds into their own pockets in the form of kickbacks from the media owners.

Another substantial part of McKintosh's business was the printing of advertising material such as brochures, labels, cartons, point-of-sale material, posters, etc. Almost each job was somewhat unique. Differences in paper quality, size, quantities, colour scheme, delivery schedule and so on made it necessary to request quotations from printers for each new job. These differed substantially, even for similar work to be done, due to a variety of factors, one of them probably being the printer's lack of knowledge of his own costs.

This situation necessitated quotations from at least three printers for each job, a time consuming, but, as Peter felt, worthwhile effort. It forced printers who knew that their prices would be compared with their competitors to quote realistically. Peter also assumed that it would reduce the opportunities for the print buyers to give out favours to certain suppliers, since all quotations had to be delivered to the office in closed envelopes and would be opened only in the presence of himself or his financial director. Over time Peter Clausen had visited the most important printers in Bigtown to look at their facilities and at the same time to explain to them their purchasing procedures. He also became personally involved in negotiations with both printers and media from time to time. During those meetings, Peter tried to demonstrate to suppliers as well as to his own print and media buyers that it was he and not his staff who took the final decision. He hoped that this would reduce the temptation of suppliers to offer special incentives to his buyers in exchange for attractive orders.

AN UNEXPECTED VISITOR

Peter Clausen had gone through all of his mail and had just stepped out of his office when he met Mr Chan, the representative of one of Indolandia's biggest printers, in the corridor. He knew him quite well and somehow liked him – probably because his company had always delivered on time and also produced good quality material. Mr Chan was Chinese and probably part of the family who owned the company. He was a tough negotiator, knowledgeable and self-confident and his relationship with the buying department was apparently good.

That morning Mr. Chan seemed to be quite irritated. When Peter invited him into his office for a chat he gladly accepted, especially since the chief buyer he wanted to see was not around. Mr Chan immediately started to talk about his business relationship with McKintosh. He stated that gradually the volume of jobs he received from the agency had steadily diminished, despite the fact that he had never let his customers down and delivered the best quality in town. Peter admitted that he had been unaware of this and promised to look into the matter. Mr Chan further explained that it was McKintosh's chief buyer who was pushing him out of business and who might gradually squeeze the whole agency out of business by making it uncompetitive.

It was at that moment that Peter realized that the discussion involved him in much more than exchanging pleasantries. Mr Chan continued to accuse his chief buyer of having forced him not only to include in his quotations, 'the usual 10%', but then 15% and even 25% lately, to be paid to him as soon as the agency had paid the printer. Mr. Chan felt that the chief buyer had not asked the other printers to increase their percentages. As a result his quotations had probably become so high they were no longer considered.

After listening attentively to Mr. Chan's accusations, Peter Clausen asked Mr Chan how to solve the problem. Mr. Chan shrugged his shoulders and advised him to get rid of his chief buyer. Then Peter asked whether he would repeat his accusation in front of the chief buyer and other witnesses. Mr. Chan smiled and said, 'Do you think I want to kill my business? Do you think I want to kill myself? Even if you repeat what I have told you I shall always deny having made those statements. It is your problem, and my problem, but I can try to get orders from other sources while you might price yourself out of the market'. With those last words he stood up and walked out of the door.

MR TANI'S COMMENT

The nice weekend was soon forgotten. Peter realized that he had to do something. Probably the whole agency knew about 'the usual 10%'. His staff might even laugh about his control procedures, his closed envelopes and visits to suppliers.

Would there be any way to confront his chief buyer with some hard facts? Was there any way of firing him? Peter suddenly remembered that his secretary had once told him that the chief buyer was closely related to somebody in the immigration department of the government and had even helped Peter to obtain the first extension of his work permit, which was very difficult to obtain without special connections, or a substantial amount of money.

Peter called in his financial director, Mr Tani, a man who had worked for over 30 years for a European multinational, had an impeccable track record and had joined the agency six years ago after he had reached the retirement age in his former firm.

To Peter this man was the only person in the agency he could trust and whose advice he highly appreciated, mainly because of Mr Tani's maturity and fatherly attitude toward him and everybody else in the agency.

After having recounted the discussion with Mr Chan, Peter asked him how the agency could stop fraudulent activities in the agency and how to get rid of the chief buyer and anybody else involved in 'illegally taking money which belonged to the company'. The more Peter actually talked about it the more desperate, frustrated and at the same time, aggressive he became towards Mr Tani who patiently sat listening to him. When Peter finally stopped talking and invited Mr Tani to comment, he replied with a question. 'Peter', he said, 'How long have been in this country?' And before Peter could react, he added, 'Have you never realized that you work in Indolandia?'

Partnerships

Part

7

STRATEGY AND MANAGEMENT IN ASIA PACIFIC

D
uring the 1950s, industrial partnerships proliferated between Western companies in Asia Pacific and local firms, mainly as equity joint ventures or licensing agreements. Asian firms on the look-out for technology joined up with large Western multinational firms. While Asian governments encouraged foreign firms to invest, they took care to protect local business and enforce fair prices for technology transfers. Much has changed since then. Asian companies have become stronger, financially sounder, technologically more advanced, their management more sophisticated. In Japan and Korea, where many firms are now global players, alliances with Western companies have become partnerships between equals rather than one-way transfers of technology or exploitation of local market expertise.

Partnerships in Asia are set up either to capture opportunities in a particular market or to exploit local resources such as raw materials and labour, although it is sometimes difficult to make a clear distinction: Shell and BP, who cooperate with local oil companies for exploration and production, also sell the oil they extract in local markets. Cooperative agreements cover not only the Asian partner's home country, but also other countries in the region: the US sports shoe maker Nike uses Korean firms to produce its shoes in Indonesia, a Japanese trading house provides working capital for the venture, and Nike's long-term partners in Taiwan supply it from China.

Partnerships take various legal forms:

- long-term supply or management contracts, such as licensing and franchising operations;

- consortia set up to carry out joint research and marketing;

- equity joint ventures, which are separate legal entities in which two or more partners invest tangible and intangible capital.

Legal agreements should not be taken at face value in Asia. Even with a 51 per cent equity stake, the Western partner can never be sure that the joint venture is managed according to its wishes; the local environment, the partners themselves, and the joint venture's managers all are influential factors.

Partnerships in Asia

Rationale for partnering

Three major forces seem to drive foreign investors to enter joint ventures.

The political imperative

Because Asian governments want their own people to benefit from industrialization, they often push foreign investors to ally with local firms before granting access to markets or resources. This concern is strongest in countries with import-substitution policies: in Indonesia, Malaysia and, to a lesser extent, Thailand and the Philippines.

Asian governments with large and attractive domestic markets – such as Japan – have been most successful in imposing partnerships on foreign investors. China, which endorsed wholly owned foreign ventures in March 1992, still encourages Western companies to choose joint ventures. However, since the early 1990s, governments have been more flexible and have accepted in some cases 100 per cent foreign ownership.

Some Western firms choose to enter into partnerships to win contracts for important government infrastructure projects. Even in Singapore, which has no protectionist regulations, the government has a policy of positive discrimination towards foreign contractors with local joint ventures.

The competitive imperative

The need for a foreign company to access critical resources, assets and competencies has also favoured joint ventures. In most cases, the Western partner looks for a local firm with capabilities in distribution, sales, local market know-how, local production expertise or, more importantly, contacts with decision makers and business networks. Managerial and human resources are often the most critical resources provided by a local joint venture partner.

Successful multinational companies will be less inclined to tie up with a local partner for competitive reasons: they assume that the market adjusts to them, so they don't need to adjust to the local market. Companies with strong international brands entering newly developing markets may need less local support than late entrants with unknown brands.

The risk sharing imperative

Some Western firms seek to reduce risk, especially when the financial investment is high, or the ROI uncertain. They usually have one of three motivations:

- the complexity of a project;
- uncertain market acceptance of a product or service;
- country risk in terms of macro-economic and political stability.

Extremely risk-adverse Western firms use agents or importers to sell products locally, or a license production locally. This considerably limits their influence and carries its own risks: market potential may be insufficiently exploited, and their own image may suffer if the local partner provides low quality products.

Western firms often have strong views on how they should enter a new market. Some prefer joint ventures and give up if they cannot find the right partner. Others are determined to go it alone. Japanese companies, used to operating in their home market through an extensive network of cooperative agreements, have a higher propensity to enter partnerships than US firms. European companies fall somewhere in between. Whether the firm is self-sufficient enough to begin activities by itself is also a consideration.

Some Western firms want to have a government partner, others have strong preferences for certain ethnic groups, such as the entrepreneurial Overseas Chinese. Companies fearful of cultural barriers may want to consider European or US partners which have the legal status of local firms, such as Inchcape, the East Asiatic Company, Diethelm or Italthai in Thailand. Japanese trading houses have the advantage of having a presence throughout the region. In politically sensitive areas, it is better to stick to a partner with local roots.

Partner selection

The selection process

The selection of a potential partner has crucial, long-term consequences. It is important to find a partner with compatible objectives, and with whom it is possible to communicate and build a stable, lasting partnership; the foreign firm's success will depend on the partner's capabilities, willingness to cooperate, and the climate of mutual trust. Most Western firms conduct far too little advance planning. While the Japanese usually set up a representative office far in advance and staff it with at least one full-time expatriate manager, in general, Western multinationals simply approach their local agent or another existing contact. They conduct little or no screening and in many cases, end up choosing a long-time local agent or distributor without searching for alternatives. The partner's past track record in their mutual dealings reassures the Western firm – although it knows little about the local company competence in manufacturing or other crucial activities.

To thoroughly investigate potential partners, the foreign firm should:

- require information;
- interview in depth the owner, top managers, operating staff in manufacturing and sales;
- ask for financial data (although these may be of limited value);
- interview the local firm's other joint venture partners, bankers, suppliers, customers and competitors, as well as diplomats and established foreign investors.

The importance that Asians attach to personal relationships often facilitates the gathering of information. Consistent probing, cross-checking and sufficient time will allow the Western firm to put together a reliable profile of potential partners. Before embarking on a joint venture, they should try to have some sort of 'pre-marital' arrangement: a manufacturing contract, a limited distributorship or a licensing agreement allow to test the working relationship on a small scale and detect misfits.

Even if government pressure or legal obligations prevent the Western partner from selecting a partner independently, a thorough inquiry is necessary – particularly for late entrants in an established market, who may find only limited choice.

Companies forced into partnerships by government regulations can, provided they already have the necessary operational capabilities, retain managerial control by sharing their subsidiaries' capital with 'sleeping partners' who are usually banks, insurance companies, or government departments with no expertise to actually run the business; sometimes they are wealthy Asian individuals.

At best, sleeping partners simply provide support and finance, if the Western firm is capable of running operations and producing results, few problems will arise. Others, however, turn out to be opportunistic political partners looking for a free shareholding and healthy dividends, or other advantages such as procurement from a sister company or employment for friends. In this case, they create operational headaches without contributing to the business.

The selection criteria

The most important consideration is the degree of fit (see Figure 7.1).

Strategic fit exists when the two partners have compatible long-term objectives. They will pool some of their resources to reach goals which they cannot attain alone. Assessing strategic fit involves analysing the partners' implicit or explicit motives for joining forces, as well as the benefits they expect to gain. There are three main types of motives:

- To develop the potential of a given market by creating a new business activity. In this case, the primary intention is to join forces rather than to take advantage of the other partner.

- One partner wants to acquire a key resource, asset or competence from the other. Asian partners typically seek either product or process technology, hardware and software from foreign joint ventures; they may also want to gain access to international markets. Foreign partners often use joint ventures to build relationships and win market access, or to make up-front profits through high transfer pricing on equipment, components or management services; sometimes they are interested in access to raw materials or low-cost labour rather than in promoting the business of the joint venture itself.

- Some motives are opportunistic or passive: the local partner may want to capitalize on citizenship and political contacts, or seek a financial return. The foreign partner may be complying with regulations, or want to enter into a short-term 'deal'.

A classic example of conflicting goals would be a Western partner who wants to acquire marketing expertise and a local partner looking for technological expertise. Figure 7.2 assesses the chances of success of joint ventures according to the partners' original motives. The most favourable fit is when both partners want to build and develop a new business.

The degree of commitment to the joint venture is particularly important: the moment of truth comes when unexpected problems arise in day-to-day operations.

Figure 7.1   Partner analysis

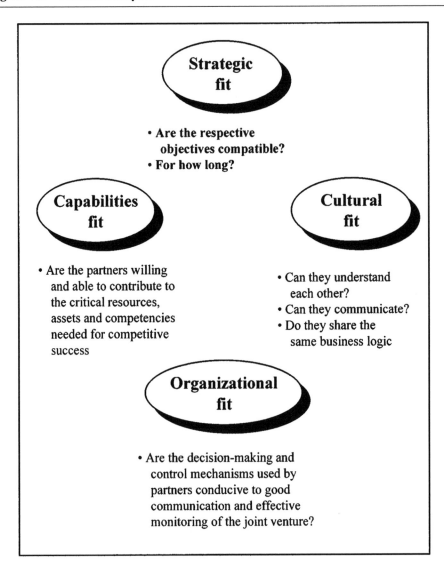

Even if individual managers assigned to a joint venture are committed, the two parents (for instance, a Western multinational and an Asian conglomerate) may give it relatively low priority. When a cooperative agreement is purely opportunistic, commitment is problematic; this is why many opportunistic partnerships end in failure.

A good **capabilities fit** means that both partners must be able to contribute to the resources and competencies needed; they must identify and solve potential gaps in contributions. Gap analysis (illustrated in Figure 7.3) involves:

Figure 7.2   Analysis of strategic fit

		BUILD NEW BUSINESS (Venturing motive)	EXTRACT MARKET KNOWLEDGE (Extractive motive)	COMPLY WITH LAW MAKE A 'DEAL'
		Foreign partner		
L o c a l	**BUILD NEW BUSINESS** (Venturing motive)	Child strategy Basis for long-term success is present	Stable in the short term Potential conflicts arise very rapidly	Asian partner may feel frustrated by lack of clear vision support from partner
	EXTRACT TECHNOLOGY (Extractive motive)	Stable in the short term Potential conflicts arise very rapidly	Short-term stability Conflicts will arrive when a 'learning' period is over	Conflicts
p a r t n e r	**BENEFIT FROM POLITICAL RENT** (Opportunistic motive)	Can be successful if the Western partner is self-sufficient High risk of frustration	Western partner may feel frustrated by lack of operational support from partner	High risk of frustrations and misunderstanding
	FINANCIAL INVESTMENT (Opportunistic motive)	Can be successful if the Western partner is self-sufficient	Chances of failure are high, especially if the Western partner is not familiar with the environment	Chances of failure are high, especially if the Western partner is not familiar with the environment

- identifying the resources (people, financing, contacts, raw materials), assets (tangible and intangible) and competencies needed to be competitive at each stage of the value chain;

- listing the respective contributions of each partner;

- identifying any gap that may require corrective action.

A classic mistake is to overestimate one's partner's contribution to the joint venture. Westerners (particularly newcomers) tend to exaggerate the local company's marketing capabilities; Asian partners frequently idealize Western allies as technological masters. Problems also arise when initial resources, assets and competencies become insufficient to sustain competitiveness over time. New funding will be needed; profits will have to be reinvested into the business. A short-term orientation, opportunism or simply inconsistency by one or both partners may aggravate a potential resource gap.

Valuing contributions which don't have a market price, because they are either not traded or intangible, can cause conflict. Intangibles and technology are often the most valuable contributions brought to a joint venture, and can become a key element in the negotiation.

Establishing a **cultural fit** requires personal involvement from the Western partner's managers. Cultural differences can create many problems and conflicts. Asia, because of the heterogeneity of its peoples, has no monolithic business culture. To assess cultural fit, partners should ask the following questions: can we understand each

Figure 7.3   Analysis of capabilities fit

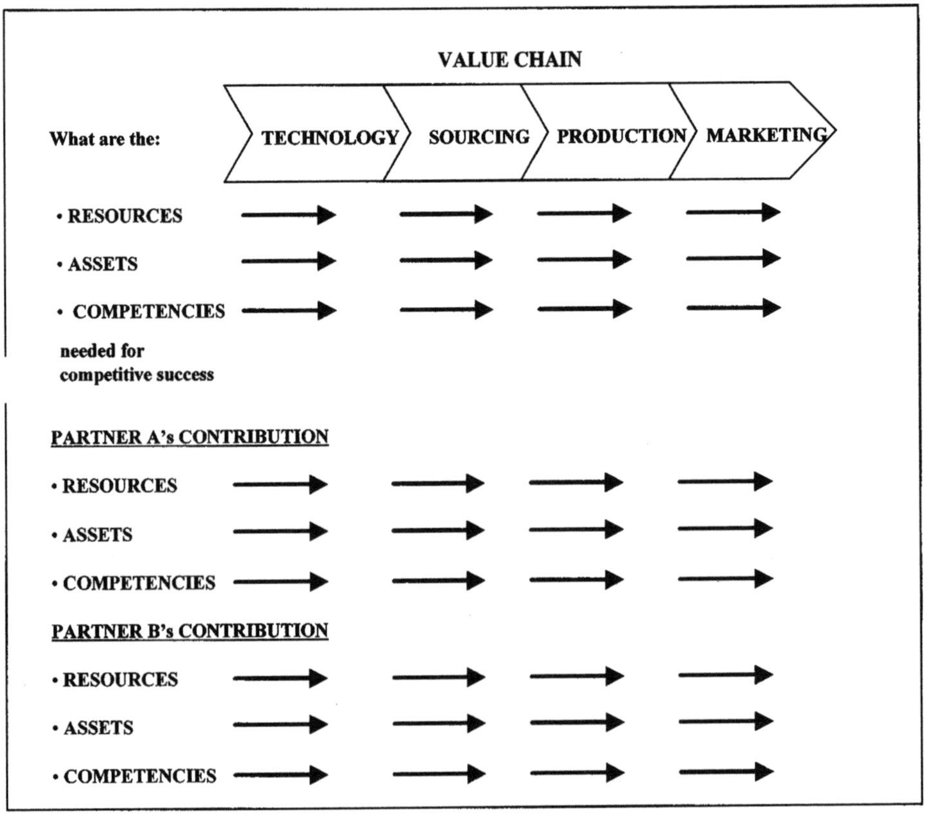

other? do we speak the same business language? do we share a common logic? can we communicate with each other?

In an international joint venture cultural differences are likely to influence three major aspects of management (Table 7.1): business objectives (what are the priorities of the venture, over which time horizon?); competitive approaches (how do we compete, what critical capabilities should we invest in?); management approaches (how should authority be defined and exercised, and what type of control should be used? what kind of people management?).

There are three possible types of cultural differences:

■ **Corporate culture** is shaped by the firm's history, the imprint left by past leaders, and the ownership structure (private, public, family). A Western partner will find in Asian corporations markedly different traditions and habits. Generally speaking, there are two major differences: in Southeast Asia in particular, many firms remain overly dependent on the decisions of the man at the top, often the founder or owner. This entrepreneurial culture

Table 7.1 Assessing cultural fit: the three dimensions of culture

Management issues	Potential cultural differences
Objectives	
• Role of business in society	• Social role: shareholders' satisfaction
• Time horizon	• Long term versus short term
• Criteria emphasis	• Profit versus growth
	• Shareholders' value versus stakeholders' value
• Use of cash flow	• Reinvestment versus dividend
Competitive approaches	
• Role of government	• Market price versus 'managed' competition
	• Price versus value
• Advantage factors	• Economic versus political
	• Competition versus monopolies
	• Competition versus 'relationships'
• Role of expansion	• Organic versus acquisitions and alliances
Authority/Interaction	
• Power	• Autocratic versus democratic
	• Hierarchy versus technostructure
• Formation	• System-led versus people-led
• Performance	• Individual versus group
• Individual relations	• Paternalistic versus contractual

contrasts sharply with the 'checks and balances' culture of Western firms. In East Asia particularly, local firms have a strong nationalist orientation and emphasize the duty to contribute to society.

■ Differences in **industry culture** will also be felt. If the two partners come from the same industry, there is greater potential for understanding. However, Western firms often team up with trading-based Asian companies. Rapid economic growth has given many Asian firms a short-term orientation, concentrated on closing a deal quickly. There is a marked difference between this opportunistic trading mentality, and the Western outlook which favours analytical, long cycle investments. (In this respect developing Asia differs from Japan, where long-term orientated companies find it difficult to find a cultural fit with potential Western partners whom they see as impatient and shortsighted!)

- **National and ethnic cultures** are shaped by the differences in sociological conditions and philosophical or religious beliefs. Asian partners will have very different value systems depending on whether they are Muslim Malay, Overseas Chinese, or Japanese bureaucrats.

The success of a joint venture largely depends on **organizational fit** – the way in which management systems and procedures shape communication between the two partners. A small Asian firm with no procedures may have trouble cooperating with a big, bureaucratic Western multinational. The entrepreneur who heads a large Asian conglomerate will resent having a Western middle manager as a counterpart. Headquarters accountants at Western multinationals often require a variety of monthly reports which the Asian partner considers as unnecessary. While Western firms should avoid imposing their strict internal procedures, Asian partners should try to be more formalistic. Both parties must agree on details of various interfaces, discuss operational issues openly, and set minimum standards for decision making and financial reporting. Organizational fit is hard to achieve when it comes to integrating the local joint venture into the two parent companies' network of subsidiaries. Transfer pricing can be a major cause of disputes if no clear guidelines have been established. The transfer of technology also needs to be carefully structured.

Negotiating partnership agreements

While many approaches used in Europe or the USA to negotiate and structure a partnership agreement can also be used in Asia, certain peculiarities deserve special attention:

- Asians are patient negotiators who enjoy bargaining. Compromise is part of a successful negotiation: one usually gives in to some extent in order not to let the other party lose face. Bargaining on credit, a technique of giving away an advantage to morally oblige the other party to give something back at a later stage, is a sophisticated way to build relationships.

- Because relationships are personal and cannot be transferred from one individual to another, once they have been established Western firms should keep the same team.

- A good relationship implies trust. It forces both parties to be reasonable, act in good faith and respect each other's opinion. This does not mean that written contracts and lawyers should be dispensed with; however, there should be a general agreement on principles before lawyers look at the details.

- Negotiating is much more time-consuming in Asia than in the West. Often the need to clear issues with the government slows down the decision process.

While to the Western mind time is money, it usually counts less for the local partner. The Western partner should remember that efforts to close a deal quickly, without clarifying technological and operational aspects, may be self-defeating: many joint ventures fail over operational issues such as the implementation of the transfer of technology, the organization of marketing responsibilities, or transfer prices.

■ Negotiating a joint venture involves more than just agreeing on financial and legal clauses. A strategic business plan should be drawn up, forcing both parties to spell out their expectations. Partners should test whether they share a common vision for the joint venture, and try to identify potential sources of future misunderstanding.

■ The two partners would be well advised to conduct joint feasibility studies and market surveys. This encourages active communication, reduces risks, reassures both parties, and establishes relationships among operational managers, which are vital to success. A sort of 'pre-marital agreement' would be even better: a limited trial run to test each other.

Negotiations never end in Asia: local firms emphasize finding the right partner rather than putting the right words on paper. Negotiating joint venture agreements requires unusually high flexibility from the Western partner, who is used to signing a contract and then fulfilling it to the letter. The Asian approach may be better adapted to the region's volatile environment.

Managing partnerships

Organizational design

A joint venture's organizational structure should reflect the two partners' original intention:

■ If it is to build and develop a business, the company should enjoy a high degree of autonomy. The partners should simply spell out the business objectives, appoint a managing director and control performance. The managing director will recruit personnel and organize operations; and can request managers or technical personnel to be seconded from the parent companies to support the venture.

■ If the partners' objective is to learn from each other, they should be more involved in operations. In this case, a 'shadow' structure in which each position is staffed by both partners is not unusual.

The first design, which increases staff motivation and commitment, tends to be more effective.

Staffing

Joint ventures require managers with political and cultural skills as well as technical competencies. Foreign managers unprepared for the cultural complexity of Asia will not handle critical situations properly and will jeopardize their parent company's ability to learn. The most important task of managers assigned to joint ventures, particularly when the strategic intent is to extract knowledge from the local environment, is to synthesize and transmit learning experiences to each relevant department in their parent company. It would be a mistake to assign managers lacking clout or prestige to an Asian joint venture; the local partner may interpret this as a lack of commitment to the partnership. The worst attitude would be to consider such postings as a form of exile for undesirable personnel.

When recruiting local employees, identity and loyalty are critical. Do they feel that they belong to the Asian parent company, or to the joint venture? Most of the time, the local partner will recruit local staff. Western partners should monitor hiring carefully to ensure that the new employees are loyal to the joint venture, not just to the local partner.

Control

Joint ventures are controlled by a board of directors consisting largely of executives, as well as a few non-executive directors; these are usually Asian personalities who can play a useful role as go-betweens in cases of conflict with the local partners.

Western companies tend to prefer having a majority stake in a joint venture, although there is no evidence that this allows them to exert real control. When a firm controls more than 70 per cent of capital, the joint venture can be considered a 'quasi acquisition', in which case the majority partner is in command. Below 70 per cent, it is not necessarily the case. Various studies have failed to demonstrate significant correlation between shareholding and control. Some companies who are in charge of key operational functions can be in control even with a minority stake.

Communication

A 1996 study on joint ventures and licensing agreements in ASEAN countries by INSEAD Euro-Asia Centre shows that cultural and strategic fit are the crucial factors for success (see Figure 7.4). Instead of formal reporting, partnerships should institutionalize face-to-face communication through frequent high-level meetings between top management, annual conferences for licensees or other partners, and joint training seminars for staff.

Of particular importance is regular direct contact between the chairperson (or a top-ranking executive) of the Western firm and the chairperson of the local partner. The expatriate in charge of the joint venture, who is normally the interface between the Western firm and the local partner, should have decision-making power. Local

Figure 7.4   The effect of strategic fit and cultural fit on satisfaction

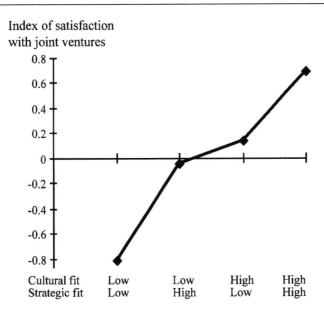

Index of satisfaction
with joint ventures

Cultural fit	Low	Low	High	High
Strategic fit	Low	High	Low	High

entrepreneurs want a certain parity of recognition with their Western counterparts, and may resent dealing with lower-ranking expatriate managers who rotate after a few years.

Joint venture decay and failure

It is typical for joint ventures to experience a rapid deterioration immediately after start up as the partners find out more about each other and make efforts to adapt. This period, dubbed 'Death Valley', creates a lot of tension; to overcome it requires perseverance and a desire to learn. A period of relative stability then follows, which can last three to six years; after that mutual interest suddenly drops. The resulting crisis can lead to a split. This phenomenon, known as joint venture decay, happens when both partners feel that they have acquired whatever advantage they sought from their association; at this moment the impetus for further collaboration can vanish. If both partners want to avert a divorce, they must revitalize their association by increasing the range or broadening the scope of its activities.

The experience of Western companies in joint ventures in Asia has not always been a happy one. Most companies have become disillusioned because of unforeseen problems in setting up and operating their partnerships. There are several main causes of failure or difficulty:

- **The absence of strategic vision.** When a joint venture is launched precipitously, or for purely defensive or opportunistic reasons, the Western firm often fails to evaluate the intentions and capabilities of the local partner.

A classic error in an industrial partnership is to choose a distributor whose corporate culture is likely to be inappropriate to a slow cash-flow cycle, and who will probably privilege a few rapid cash-flow deals instead of investing for the long term.

- **Believing without seeing.** The art of appearances can be highly refined in Asia and many a Western investor has been led into mistaking elaborate ceremony for a real commitment.

- **Failing to understand the local partner's strategic logic.** In most cases a thorough investigation would reveal the real intent: for example, to achieve vertical integration to appropriate technology, or simply to enter into an opportunistic deal.

- **Haste in negotiation.** The desire to conclude a deal rapidly often leads the negotiators to concentrate on financial or legal clauses and neglect technological or operational issues. In Asia, the contractual stage must be preceded by an overall planning session for the project, during which the partners will agree on objectives and strategies. This implies a minimum investment in understanding the logic of the partner. It is a good idea to advance step by step: a licensing contract, for example, can be a good way of testing the capacities of the other party before making a longer term commitment.

- **Insufficiently prepared staff and lack of organizational support.** Unprepared expatriate managers who fail to understand the logic of their partners and employees can exacerbate tensions, and hurt the reputation of both the joint venture and the Western parent. In Asia, local partners are often highly respected businessmen, and when they suffer what they see as improper treatment at the hands of unsophisticated foreign staff, they quickly become disillusioned. Besides, the joint venture is often poorly served by headquarters (delays in technical assistance, delivery of poorly adapted products, exorbitant transfer pricing; exaggerated administrative rules or constraints that ignore local conditions).

These five causes of failure are often interrelated, contributing to a vicious circle of misunderstanding which can degenerate into open conflict and end in frustration, loss of market share, and sometimes legal action. A Western enterprise that seriously considers setting up in Asia through a partnership should devote enough resources and effort to carefully prepare and monitor the selection of a partner and management of the joint venture.

A special case: joint venturing in China

The political and legal context

China's history of colonial exploitation has left it with a deep-rooted mistrust of foreigners. The Chinese see economic reform and business transactions as crucial to political stability, and the vagueness of the legal system gives government and party bureaucrats substantial leeway. Western firms should also be aware that for the Chinese, a contract is a starting point for negotiation rather than a final, binding agreement.

China's foreign investment legislation defines two types of joint venture:

■ the equity joint venture, in which both the foreign and the Chinese partner provide capital and management, and share the risks and profits;

■ the contractual joint venture, which does not necessarily entail forming a legal entity; the partners contract their contribution to a joint activity and profit can be distributed differently than in an equity joint venture.

Entering a joint venture in China

While Western companies increasingly prefer wholly owned foreign enterprises to equity joint ventures, this is not always possible. For Western firms willing to form joint ventures, partner selection will be particularly fraught, since it is a highly politicized issue, and the freedom of choice is severely restricted. Political imperatives are a key consideration: the most important resource of Chinese partners is their close connections with regional or national authorities.

Negotiating a joint venture can take two years or longer. The Chinese are often more intent on learning and gathering information from their counterparts than on making decisions, and their negotiators must usually refer back to higher authorities. China's multi-tiered administration, with various state, provincial and municipal ministries where, as a rule, no one individual has decision-making power, considerably slows the process.

Conducting a joint feasibility study as part of the negotiation process is highly recommended: it will provide the foreign firm with more detailed information on potential markets and cost estimates; it is a good opportunity to test the real intentions and capabilities of the Chinese partner. It is also crucial for the Western firm to understand the role of *guanxi*: in China, personal relationships and mutual obligations often determine the allocation of resources.

Creating and managing the fit

Chinese and Western partners come from very different backgrounds. The Chinese side, usually government-owned, aims at achieving policy objectives, while the Western side, as a rule, comes from the private sector, is not subject to government influence, and pursues profit objectives. This creates substantial room for misunderstanding, as well as four types of misfit:

■ **Strategic misfit.** The Chinese party generally aims at obtaining technology and earning foreign exchange by exporting, while the Western partner usually seeks to tap the domestic market. When attractive local market opportunities emerge, the Chinese government has often favoured local firms. The Western partner is less keen to export from China, since local operating costs are high by regional standards, and is reluctant to transfer technology because the Chinese tend to copy or re-engineer technology, and piracy is rife.

- **Capabilities misfit.** Resources, assets and competencies are difficult to value; contributions with no market price, such as expertise, intangible assets and land, may be sources of conflict.

- **Cultural misfit.** While training can help overcome misunderstanding, creating a shared corporate culture in a Chinese joint venture is problematic.

- **Organizational misfit.** Westerners and Chinese parent organizations are very different: the Chinese often have a broad political mandate representing 'the people' or big bureaucracies, while Western firms have clearly defined objectives and responsibilities. Disagreements over staffing are common: for the Chinese partner, it is a political decision, while Western firms insist on finding the most capable person for the job.

Early entrants' advantage

In contrast to other countries in Asia Pacific, China does not seem to offer any particular advantage to early entrants. During the first half of the 1980s, few joint ventures in China were successful; they had to cope with many operational problems, and both Chinese and Western partners had to learn how to work with each other. This has changed; more and more joint ventures are now doing quite well. Latecomers have found a more refined legal system, better infrastructure and partners familiarized with Western business systems. Many of the more recent joint ventures have turned quick profits (Avon, Pepsi, P&G).

Whether a joint venture is a success or a failure cannot be judged within the first few years. This is especially true when growth is exceptionally high and almost all new ventures prosper. On the whole, Western companies which came to China with a limited investment and a cautious approach to partnerships have done reasonably well. They often took a realistic, firm approach to initial negotiations with the government and potential partners. In most cases, they also had the backing of a senior board member at headquarters.

References

A.T. Kearney Inc., *Capturing The Asian Potential: Insight For Western Multinationals*, 222 West Adams Street, Chicago, Illinois, 60606, October 1992.

Aguilar, Frank and Doug Sung Cho, *The Daewoo Group*, Harvard Business School case study No. 38J-014, 1984.

'The China Connection' *The Far Eastern Economic Review*, 5 November 1992, p. 60.

Fork Contractor, *International Technology Licensing: Compensation, Costs and Negotiations*, Lexington Books, Lexington, Massachusetts, 1981.

Franko, Lawrence G., 'Joint Venture Divorce In The Multinational Company', *Columbia Journal Of World Business*, Vol. 6, No. 3, June 1971.

Gomes-Casseres, Benjamin, 'International Trade, Competition, and Alliances in the Computer Industry', Working Paper 92-044, Harvard Business School, 1991.

Graham, John L. and Yoshikuro Sano, *Smart Bargaining*, Ballinger, Cambridge, Massachusetts, 1984.

Harrigan, Kathryn Rudie, *Strategies for Joint Ventures*, Lexington Books, Lexington, Massachusetts, 1985.

Hendryx, Steven R., 'The China Trade: Making The Deal Work', *Harvard Business Review*, July–August 1986, pp. 74–84.

Lasserre, Philippe, 'Training: Key to Technology Transfer', *Long Range Planning*, Vol. 15, No. 3, 1982, pp. 51–60.

Lasserre, Philippe and M. Boisot, 'Transfer of Technology from European to ASEAN Enterprises: Strategies and Practices in the Chemical and Pharmaceutical Sector', Euro-Asia Centre Research Paper, No. 2, Fontainebleau, 1980.

Lasserre, Philippe and Elisabeth Fouraker, *Thai Polyester Company*, INSEAD Euro-Asia Centre case study, 1989

Laurent, André, 'The Cross Cultural Puzzle of Global Human Resource Management', *Human Resource Management*, Vol. 15, No. 1, 1986, pp. 91–102.

Mann, Jim, *Beijing Jeep: The Short Unhappy Romance of American Business in China*, Simon and Schuster, 1989.

Pye, Lucien, *Chinese Commercial Negotiating Style*, Oelgeschalge, Cambridge, Massachusetts, 1983.

Pye, Lucien, 'The New Asian Capitalism: A Political Portrait' in Peter Berger and Hsin-Huang Hsiao (eds), *Search of an East Asian Development Model*, Transaction Books, New Brunswick and Oxford, 1986, p. 76.

Schneider, Susan, 'National vs. Corporate Culture: Implications For Human Resource Management', *Human Resources Management*, Vol. 27, No. 1, 1988, pp. 133–148.

Teece, D.J., *The Multinational Corporation and The Resource Cost of International Technology Transfer*, Ballinger, Cambridge, Massachusetts, 1976.

The Financial Times, Industry Survey, 15 December 1988.

Tung, Rosalie, *Business Negotiations With The Japanese*, Lexington Books, Lexington, Massachusetts, 1984.

Vanhonacker, Wilfried, 'Entering China: An Unconventional Approach', *Harvard Business Review*, March/April 1997, pp. 130–141.

Wagner, Cecilia L., 'Influences on Sino-Western Joint Venture Negotiations', *Asia-Pacific Journal of Management,* Vol. 7, No. 2, 1990.

Weiss, S.E., 'Creating the GM-Toyota Joint Venture: A Case in Complex Negotiation', *Columbia Review of World Business*, Vol. 22, No. 2, 1987, pp. 23–37.

Case 21

This case was written by Philippe Lasserre, Professor of Strategy at INSEAD.
It is intended to be used as a basis for class discussion rather than to
illustrate either effective or ineffective handling of an administrative
situation. Copyright © 1995 INSEAD-EAC, Fontainebleau, France.

Siam Polyester Company

Jacques Lanvin, Director of international business in the textile division of the Chimie du Sud group in France, was considering the opportunity of getting involved in a joint venture with Mr Yipsoon of Thailand. The proposal was to set up a polyester fibre plant with a capacity of 20,000 tons per year for a total cost of 1.5 billion baht (60 million US dollars). He had to make up his mind quite rapidly in order to present his recommendations to the Board of the company in two weeks time.

CHIMIE DU SUD

Chimie du Sud was one of the largest chemical groups in France, operating in various product lines (basic chemicals, fine chemicals, pharmaceuticals, textiles, agrochemicals and fibres), as well as in many countries. Approximately half of the turnover of the group came from exports and foreign subsidiaries located mainly in the northern hemisphere and Latin America. The group had no major investments in Asia and even among its small projects in the region, none was in textiles.

The group was very loosely organized with a lot of autonomy was given to the divisions which, in most cases, were separate legal corporate entities. The textile division, which produced raw materials for the textile industry, (rayon, nylon, polyester), was facing serious difficulties in Europe due to fierce competition coming from Southeast and East Asia; in addition products such as rayon were progressively being substituted by other fibres. Restructuring of production obliged the division to close factories. The textile division had recently developed a new 'continuous' process of polymerization which offered the advantages over the 'discontinuous process' of being less labour intensive and more productive in raw material consumption. To develop its international operations, the division was trying to sell its new process through technical agreements, licences equipment supply and services, in association with one of its suppliers of spinning equipment.

ORIGIN OF THE PROJECT

A few months earlier, the expatriate representative of the Banque Française du Commerce Exterieur, Mr Degas, met with a local Thai entrepreneur who was considering the possibility of entering into a joint venture with a foreign partner to produce polyester fibre. Mr Degas conducted a market survey and his conclusions were extremely positive. The key elements which emerged from the study included the following:

- There was only one producer of polyester fibre in Thailand, Teijin, a Japanese firm which used the discontinuous process. Its domestic sales of 15,000 tons/year which covered only 70% of the market needs;

- The market was growing fast, doubling every five years since the Thai textile downstream industry was very active on the domestic and export markets;

- Labour in Thailand was abundant;

- The Thai government looked favourably at non-Japanese investment and was ready to give pioneer status to an investment in the upstream sectors. Pioneer status would imply a tax-free position for at least five years.

Degas convinced the French Trade Commissioner in Bangkok that it would be a good opportunity for a major French company to get a foothold in this very dynamic region.

Support from the French authorities would entail the granting of a COFACE (export insurance) guarantee that would allow the export of French equipment financed at a preferential rate of 4%. Degas, through his office in Paris, approached Chimie du Sud and the project arrived on Lanvin's desk.

PROJECT DEFINITION

During several visits to Thailand, Lanvin met with Yipsoon and his sons and was convinced that the Thai partners would not consider any other solution than a 49/49 joint venture, the remaining shares being in the hands of Thai minority partners. The joint venture company, to be known as Siam Polyester Company, would be constituted for the manufacturing and marketing of polyester staples and threads, with a capacity of 20,000 tons per year (one third thread, two thirds staples). This plant would consist of two major parts: the polymerization part which would use the continuous processing method to produce polyester staples, and the spinning area which would use equipment supplied from France to transform the staples into thread. The raw material for this plant was DMT, a petrochemical product which was an international commodity and so its supply would not raise any problem. The total investment would be approximately 1500 million baht divided into 500 million of equity, 700 million in COFACE guaranteed export credit and 300 million of debt at a commercial rate of 7%.

YIPSOON GROUP

Mr Yipsoon, a Thai of Chinese origin, was one of the few textile magnates in Thailand. He was involved in weaving, spinning, knitting, dyeing and also some final products. He owned and controlled more than 15 companies, some of them with foreign partners. He controlled approximately 40% of the Thai market and was in contact with the Chinese diaspora in Southeast Asia, as well as with some PRC officials. Yipsoon could not speak English. He managed his companies through various members of his family, keeping a very personalistic, family style direct control over his empire. He had a 5% share in Teijin Thailand.

OTHER CONSIDERATIONS

While preparing his presentation to the board, Lanvin was very much aware that certain aspects of the project presented risks and opportunities. The profitability prospects seemed to be positive. The price of polyester staple in Thailand at 40 baht a kilo had always been 30 to 40% higher than world prices; this was because the Thai government practised an import substitution policy, seeking to protect domestic production from imports. With its modern equipment the new plant could possibly achieve world cost standards.

Furthermore, and in spite of the official reluctance of Chimie du Sud to enter into joint ventures, the Thai project had the advantage of offering a foothold in the Asian region. On the other hand, Thailand was known for its frequent '*coups d'état*' which could possibly result in a complete change of government policies.

Other question marks referred to the project itself. What would be the future attitude of Yipsoon in this venture? How to figure out what he really wanted out of this project? Would Chimie du Sud be capable of setting up a new plant 10,000 km away from the parent company? What were the major risks? How to anticipate them? Lanvin knew that the Board would basically follow the course of action that he recommended.

APPENDIX I

Thai Textile Market

The market throughout the textile sector is extremely price sensitive. Independent thread and fabric merchants serve as price-volume brokers, and seem to exhibit no supplier – or brand – loyalty. (See Exhibit CS21.1). The operation of the typical industrialized firm requires trading with as many as 200 local suppliers of goods and services. Spinning and weaving firms that buy synthetic materials require that their suppliers maintain their machines and train their operators. (Substitution of man-made fibres for natural fibres necessitates slight adjustments in the speed of spinning and the tension exerted on the threads.) There is currently only one polyester thread and fibre producer in Thailand, Teijin Polyester Company Limited, in which Yipsoon holds a small interest. The Teijin plant has about 17 local institutional customers for its polyester thread, and about 12 customers for its polyester fibre, located in Hong Kong (5), Indonesia (2), the Philippines (2), Malaysia, Singapore and Thailand (1 each). Approximately 80% of the Teijin Plant's output is sold in Thailand.

The Board of Investment has awarded the textile industry 'priority status' which brings the following advantages:

1. guarantees against nationalization or creation of state operations in the same sector

2. reduction or elimination of customs duties on imported raw materials and equipment

3. profit repatriation rights for foreign investors

4. levy of import duties on products in the same sector

5. discounts on water, electricity, transportation costs

6. discount of company profit tax of up to 90% for the first 5 years

Case 21

In order to protect the textile industry, the Thai government levies taxes on imports as follows:

- 20% on synthetic threads

- 20% on cotton threads

- 40% on cotton cloth

- 60% on other cloth

- 60% on ribbon, hats, stockings and other accessories

- 60% on ready-to-wear clothing

But if the import of raw material is for a final product which will be exported (if, for example, rayon thread is imported to be woven and fashioned into shirts for sale in China), these import duties are lifted. This tariff structure is more severe than Malaysia's but milder than that of the Philippines.

Exhibit CS21.1   Interdependencies in the Thai textile market

Case 22

Case 22

This case was prepared under the supervision of Hellmut Schütte, Affiliate Professor at INSEAD and written by Eric Dugelay. It is intended to be used as a basis for class discussion rather than to illustrate either effective or ineffective handling of an administrative situation. Copyright © 1990 INSEAD-EAC, Fontainebleau, France

Tianjin Merlin Gerin

On Monday 4 June 1990, at 6.30 a.m., a group of young pioneers prepared to compete in a kite contest in Tiananmen Square, watched by their parents and under the discreet but efficient 'protection' of soldiers. In Tianjin, 100 miles away, Michel Collonge, general manager of Tianjin Merlin Gerin Company Ltd, hurried out of the lobby of the Tianjin Hyatt Hotel and got into his Peugeot 505 ('Made in China') to be driven to the factory. One year after the Tiananmen Square 'incident' (as the 'New China' news agency baptized it), life had returned to normal in the Empire of the Middle Kingdom. As the driver blew his horn to scatter a group of cyclists, Michel Collonge caught a glimpse of the China Daily. 'One year later, our successes are many', the newspaper said. The picture was not too bad for Tianjin Merlin Gerin either, Michel Collonge thought to himself. If everything went as expected, the joint venture would be profitable by November, which would be quite an achievement after having had three consecutive years of losses.

But problems still remained. Since its creation, Merlin Gerin's joint venture had achieved only modest sales in the Chinese market, had not generated any profits and had run into problems regarding their balance of foreign exchange. On the other hand, Merlin Gerin was now in China on a long-term basis and had acquired some goodwill from which it had started to benefit.

MERLIN GERIN SA

For the last 15 years Merlin Gerin SA has consistently been described as an outstandingly dynamic and successful French enterprise. Since its foundation in Grenoble in 1922 by two young electrical engineers, Paul Merlin and Gaston Gerin, it has developed rapidly in the field of electrical protection devices. In 1989 it made a profit of FF706 million with a turnover of FF14.6 billion. By June 1990 it had 29,000 employees. In the 1960s Merlin Gerin was viewed as a specialist in circuit breakers. It manufactured circuit breakers from the low voltage (220 V) up to the very high voltage range (800 kV). But Merlin Gerin SA products also included switches and capacitors. In the 1970s it acquired a number of small- to medium-size companies in related businesses and built up a core competence around the 'mastering of electrical power'. Its acquisitions, enabled in the 1980s, helped it to become a major player in the world industry of

Case 22

electricity distribution and also in some electronic goods, namely UPSs (uninterruptible power supplies) and PLCs (programmable logical controllers).

Schneider SA is the principal shareholder of Merlin Gerin SA. In the 1980s Didier Pineau Valenciennes, chief executive officer and general manager of Schneider, successfully restructured the group. Merlin Gerin became its most prominent company, together with Spie Batignolles, a leading French company in the construction field. In 1988 Schneider hit the headlines when it acquired Télémécanique (a company which specializes in the related contactor business) in a highly contested public battle against Framatome, the leading French nuclear power plant builder.

Merlin Gerin's development over the past few decades stems partly from the convergence in Grenoble in the early 1960s of a generation of young graduates and executives who came from different parts of France to partake of the 'Grenoblois' way of life: the city of Grenoble (380,000 inhabitants in 1990) is only half-an-hour away from many skiing resorts and is not much further from the Mediterranean coastline. Its universities are considered among the best in France. Merlin Gerin employs 7% of the active population of the city.

In the 1970s, Merlin Gerin was considered an international pioneer in France with operations in 20 countries on five continents. The 1980s saw its turnover outside France multiply sevenfold. Today, the company has 49 subsidiaries and affiliates outside France and its products are sold in 100 countries.

Since 1966 Merlin Gerin has become well known for its technological experience in the field of SF6 technology for medium voltage circuit breakers (SF6, i.e. sulphur hexafluoride, has a breaking capacity of electrical arcs much higher than vacuum.)

During the 1980s, most circuit breaker manufacturers progressively replaced oil and air technologies with the SF6. Merlin Gerin's reputation as a technical innovator was reinforced by the development of its low voltage security equipment. The firm emphasized the miniaturization of its range of low voltage products and in 1980 started manufacturing a complete range of miniature circuit breakers, contactors and switches known under the brand name 'Multi 9' which was soon valued for its flexibility, its low surface area and its reliability. The Multi 9 formula offers two main circuit breakers: the C45 and the C45N. The C45 has a breaking capacity of 3 kA while the C45N can cut electrical arcs of up to 6 kA.[1] Both are used as a protection device to break short circuits occurring during over-utilization of an electrical network, and support overvoltage during thunderstorms, etc. In industrialized countries these products are already installed in every household. With the homogenization of international laws regarding the security of electrical networks, the potential for development in less developed countries is high.

MERLIN GERIN'S CHINA STRATEGY

In the 1970s, when the Asian markets started attracting more European companies, Merlin Gerin SA was already selling circuit breakers in a number of Asian countries through a network of distributors. In 1978 the company decided that a distribution centre in the area was needed to

---

[1] The breaking capacity is the capacity to cut short circuit arcs. The intensity of accidental short circuit currents that result in the formation of arcs is much higher than the nominal intensity that normally flows in the circuits. For instance, the C45 receives currents of 5–45 A under normal conditions, but is able to cut short circuit currents as high as 3 kA, i.e. 3,000 A.

cut down transportation costs and improve delivery schedules; and so Merlin Gerin Far East Pte. Ltd opened in Singapore in November 1979. In Hong Kong, Merlin Gerin SA first acquired a subsidiary of the French Immunelec company through which it sold its UPSs, and then opened a representative office in February 1986 to be responsible for direct sales of the whole range of products in the Hong Kong market.

In China, Merlin Gerin had been represented since the beginning of the 1970s by SOPROMO, a trading company owned by Alfred Moller, a German with a French passport. He had established an office in Beijing during the 'Great Leap Forward' in 1958, six years before Charles de Gaulle decided to establish diplomatic relations with the People's Republic of China. Through SOPROMO, Merlin Gerin sold mainly very high voltage equipment for the lines connecting major Chinese cities.

In 1979, when China started its 'four modernizations' policy and began to favour foreign investment, Merlin Gerin promptly set to work. Its strategy was to achieve a presence in the Chinese market via local manufacturing and sales so as to gain acceptance and recognition of its technology. In the long term, Merlin Gerin would then benefit from its acquired 'Chinese goodwill' and increase its direct sales in the People's Republic of China.

Merlin Gerin signed a 10-year technical licence agreement with Ping Ding Shan switchgear factory to allow the manufacture of very high voltage circuit breakers under the company's name. However, technical problems were encountered in their mastering of the SF6 technology and the 1984 production had to be shipped to France for repair because of leaking circuit breakers. The root cause of this problem was the Chinese party's lack of respect for the manufacturing process as specified in the agreement with Merlin Gerin. In 1985, because of the poor results of the Ping Ding Shan factory, Merlin Gerin was discredited and consequently started to detach itself from its Chinese counterpart. In 1989, when the licensing agreement came to an end, it was not renewed.

In 1985 the increase in direct sales and the prospect of a wider market opening with a potential of one billion users led Merlin Gerin to replace SOPROMO with a representative office which opened in Beijing in July 1986. Three expatriates recruited four Chinese staff including two engineers. Though the Beijing office had no legal right to undertake sales activities, it prepared sales contracts that were signed by Merlin Gerin's representatives in Grenoble.

At the same time Merlin Gerin decided to try and find a second and more reliable Chinese partner to establish a joint venture. This venture would conform to the 'Law of the People's Republic of China on Joint Ventures Using Chinese and Foreign Investment' which had been adopted on 1 July 1979. The underlying strategy was to put a foot in the opening door and gain a long-term 'observer' position. By going for a co-production agreement, Merlin Gerin would benefit from Chinese recognition which would eventually lead to an increase in direct sales of other products in this market through the Beijing representative office.

THE JOINT VENTURE PROJECT

In June 1985 a task force of six departmental specialists from Merlin Gerin conducted a survey of the Chinese market to investigate the validity of establishing a joint venture. The survey took three weeks, during which time 26 factories were visited in most of the Special Economic Zones

(SEZ) and coastal cities (a map of these SEZ and coastal cities is displayed in Exhibit CS22.1). Mr van Eeckhout, the marketing director of the low voltage division visited 12 factories manufacturing low voltage circuit breakers and found that the miniature technology was greatly appreciated by the Chinese managers.

The market for low voltage circuit breakers, as observed by the task force, was served by six Chinese manufacturers and some Japanese exporters, all of which used the outdated QL technology introduced by Westinghouse in the 1950s. The market size was estimated at three to five million poles[2] per year and was expected to develop quickly to reach 10 to 15 million poles within the next five to 10 years. The C45 circuit breaker seemed the best prospect. It was decided to further investigate low investment, low risk joint venture opportunities in this field. The two partners most capable of integrating Merlin Gerin's technology were Tianjin Switchgear Works and Guangzhou Switchgear Factory.

In January 1986 during Mr van Eeckhout's second trip to China, a third factory, the Tianjin Aviation Electromechanical Corporation, approached Merlin Gerin. Known as the '105 factory' because of its registration number with the Chinese authorities, this factory showed signs of greater commitment and possibly more local authority support than the two previous partners.

Thus a feasibility study for a joint venture agreement between the '105 factory' and Merlin Gerin was launched. Merlin Gerin based its evaluation of the joint venture prospects on its previous experience of manufacturing the C45 and C45N circuit breakers in Spain, South Africa, Morocco and Indonesia. Neither the C45 nor the C45N would require any adaptation since Chinese regulations had long conformed to international standards in electricity distribution. The '105 factory' collected information on the Chinese market for these products, as well as information on potential suppliers of parts required for assembling the circuit breakers.

THE NEGOTIATION OF THE CONTRACT

In December 1986 negotiations started in Tianjin, between Merlin Gerin SA, '105 factory', the China National Aero-Technology Import & Export Corporation (CATIC) and the Industrial Investment Corporation of Tianjin Economic Technological Development Area (TEDA). An industrial consulting firm attended the negotiations in an advisory capacity on Merlin Gerin's behalf.

CATIC is a corporation owned by the Ministry of Aviation. It deals with foreign investment in corporations attached to that ministry and is structured on the model of the powerful CITIC (China International Trust and Investment Corporation), founded in 1979 to promote foreign investment in the People's Republic of China.

Founded in October 1984, TEDA is the authority in charge of one of the most developed Chinese Economic Technological Development Zones (ETDZ), located 50 km east of Tianjin's city centre on Bohai Bay (see the map of Tianjin municipality in Exhibit CS22.2). The development of an ETDZ in this area was decided upon for several reasons: it was close to the Tanggu urban area, which, with its total population of 400,000, could provide labour for the

---

[2] Production capacity of circuit-breaker manufacturers is measured in poles: one tri-phased circuit breaker contains three poles.

enterprises in the ETDZ; it had direct access to the sea via a newly developed port; and it was only at a 45–60 minute drive from Tianjin, China's third biggest city, and approximately 2½ hours from Beijing by car.

In the first phase of negotiations, the four sides reached a general agreement on mutual goals. The feasibility study was used as the basis for the second phase of the negotiations in which details of the agreement were discussed. Three weeks of 15 to 18 hours' work per day were needed to reach detailed agreements (on the participation of each party, the production process, the distribution system, training and salaries, etc.). A month later, another three-week session resulted in the ironing out of the 'difficult' problems: the purchasing price of parts by Merlin Gerin, the selling price on the Chinese market, the percentage of production to be exported and the local content growth schedule. The joint venture contract (as well as a purchase and export sales contract, a local sales contract, a technical licence contract, a trademark and trade names licence contract) were signed on the eve of the Chinese New Year at the end of January 1987.

THE TERMS OF AGREEMENT

The joint venture agreement leading to the creation of Tianjin Merlin Gerin Company Ltd (TJMG) was signed for a period of 15 years. The investment totalled RMB14.8 million[3] (US$3.85 million). Merlin Gerin had a total investment share of 45% in the form of cash in foreign exchange and equipment, while '105 factory' had a 35% share in cash in RMB and equipment. TEDA and CATIC contributed cash in both foreign currency and RMB, amounting to 10%, respectively.

Although negotiations had already started on the production of C45, an agreement was finally reached on the production of C45N circuit breakers. The move towards a circuit breaker with a breaking capacity of 6 kA was made at the request of the Chinese parties, who estimated that the prospects of profit and sales volume were more attractive for this product than for the 3 kA breaking capacity circuit breaker. This move was accepted by Merlin Gerin whose estimation of the Chinese market relied mainly on the judgement of the Chinese.

The forecasted volume of production assumed a steady growth from one million poles in Year 1 (July 1987 to December 1988) to two million in Year 4 (1991). Forecasts of exports relied primarily on agreed purchase quantities by Merlin Gerin SA: 150,000 poles for Year 1, 125,000 for Year 2, 175,000 for Year 3 and 200,000 for Year 4 (1991). (Details of the forecasted production levels and sales breakdown can be found in Exhibit CS22.3). The joint venture was to be profitable from Year 1 with a net profit of RMB950,000 forecasted, assuming sales of RMB10.3 million. Profits and sales would rise steadily to reach RMB2.9 million and RMB20.4 million respectively in Year 4.

A quick start in manufacturing by the Chinese parties was expected with a view to as much as 86% being produced locally from Year 1. The remaining 14% of the content consisted of special devices (copper electrical junctions and some plastic moulded parts) and was due to be imported from a Merlin Gerin factory in Alès in the South of France.

The PA6.6 plastic required for the moulding of the frame of the circuit breaker was said to be already available on the Chinese market.

---

[3] RMB stands for Ren Min Bi, the People's Money, also called Yuan. In January 1987, RMB1 = US$.26.

The joint venture itself was a production-only facility. The marketing of the C45N fell under the responsibility of '105 factory' for sales in the Chinese market, and Merlin Gerin for sales in foreign markets. The breakdown of sales on both local and foreign markets (Exhibit CS22.4) relied heavily on sales in the local market.

100 employees were to work for the joint venture in Year 1, including two expatriates – the general manager and the production manager. After the factory installation phase, the production responsibility would be transferred to a Chinese national, leaving the general manager as the only expatriate. Production staff would be increased regularly to reach 105 workers in 1991, while the number of administrative staff would remain at the initial level of 42.

THE JOINT VENTURE IN PRACTICE

As expected, in March 1987 TEDA provided TJMG with a rented building. André Christin and Michel Dulfour were released by Merlin Gerin and hired by TJMG to become general manager and production manager, respectively. Their first task was to organize the reception of plastic moulds, cutting machines and tampographic printing machines shipped from France. At the same time, Mr Xu, the vice general manager, hired by '105 factory', purchased the remaining machine tools required for the production of the C45N.

Mr Christin was a former watchmaker who had been with Merlin Gerin for 10 years and had become a house engineer. He moved from Indonesia, where he had been responsible for Merlin Gerin's joint venture manufacturing of C45s and C45Ns. Michel Dulfour, a technician, had been responsible for setting up Merlin Gerin's manufacturing unit of C45 in South Africa.

Mr Xu had trained as an engineer and had previously worked as a production manager of '105 factory'. Since the housing and recreational facilities offered by TEDA were minimal, André Christin and Michel Dulfour were commuting everyday from Tianjin where they had rented two suites in the four-star Hyatt Hotel. The expatriate manager of Wella, the German hair cosmetic manufacturer with a plant virtually next door, had the same arrangement. Mr Xu and the Chinese employees were also commuting since TEDA's rents were much higher than those of the state-subsidized housing available in Tianjin. There, a worker paid approximately RMB5 to RMB10 per month for an apartment, whereas dormitories for three persons offered by TEDA cost RMB150 per person.

In December 1987, TJMG was officially inaugurated in the presence of Li Rui Huan, the famous mayor of Tianjin, Mr Vaujany, president and chief executive manager of Merlin Gerin, a representative of the French Ambassador in Beijing and the French commercial counsellor. Attendance by such high-level people and coverage by the local television network helped to promote the newly born joint venture. Mao Tai[4] flowed freely in the reception room of the Hyatt Hotel and 10,000 years of prosperity were wished on the venture.

A few days later in Tianjin, at the second board of directors' meeting, TEDA announced that it was leaving the project. Unofficial leaks said that the decision had been taken on the grounds of poor profitability forecasts due to the lack of knowledge of the distribution channels on the

---

[4] The national drink, made out of sorgho, and served at traditional banquets.

Case 22

Chinese market by '105 factory'. Merlin Gerin and '105 factory' agreed to take over the 10% share previously owned by TEDA, giving final investment shares of 43% to '105 factory' and 47% to Merlin Gerin.

SALES IN THE CHINESE MARKET

Actual sales in the Chinese market are detailed in Exhibit CS22.4. In 1987, 1,869 poles were sold in this market and 55,000 poles in 1988. They represent less than 7% of the forecasts specified in the joint venture contract. Due to the low volume of sales and the limited storage capacity, production was gradually reduced in 1988 and was virtually at a standstill in October of that year.

The low sales volume in the Chinese market confirmed fears that '105 factory' had, in fact, little knowledge of the distribution channels for circuit breakers. Dependent on the Ministry of Aviation, '105 factory' had gained some experience from the manufacturing of its DZ6 circuit breaker in the 1970s, but on the commercial side, they had had virtually no experience. Their production of DZ6 was purchased by the Ministry of Aviation on a guaranteed quota basis, and consequently '105 factory' had no incentive to extend its sales to other clients. The products of the joint venture, on the other hand, were aimed at panel builders and corporations dependent not only on the Ministry of Aviation and the Ministry of Machine Building and Industry (MMBI), but potentially on any ministry. The Ministry of Aviation was of little help in selling TJMG products to panel builders depending on the MMBI.

In view of '105 factory's' inability to attain its sales objectives in the Chinese market, it was proposed and accepted that responsibility for distribution in the local market should be given to TJMG itself. TJMG was assisted in this task by its industrial consultant.

SALES IN FOREIGN MARKETS

The foreign exchange issue had been a subject of intense debate during the negotiations: in addition to the initial input of roughly RMB3 million in foreign exchange by the partners. The joint venture was to generate further foreign exchange to fulfil the following obligations (given in order of priority as stipulated in the joint venture contract):

1. 'pay salaries and expenses to expatriate managers and foreign expatriates who assist in starting and maintaining production';

2. 'pay expenditures for imported raw materials, parts and equipment required for starting and maintaining production';

3. 'pay royalties to Merlin Gerin';[5]

4. 'pay interest, if any, on foreign exchange loans';

5. 'pay dividends to Merlin Gerin';

6. 'pay any other expenditure specially approved by the board of directors'.

Due to the non-convertibility of the RMB against foreign currencies, the possible sources of

---

[5] The royalties are paid to Merlin Gerin during the first 10 years of the 15-year technical licence contract. They are calculated at the rate of 1.5% of the joint venture's net profit after tax.

foreign exchange were sales outside China and, when available, exchange of RMB against dollars on the 'Grey Market'.

Chinese corporations dealing with foreigners sometimes had excess cash in foreign exchange. The Bank of China played an intermediary role and offered to change this foreign exchange for RMB at a rate roughly 40% higher than the 'official' rate.[6] Some companies cash-rich such as the Hyatt Hotel in Tianjin, managed to get a better rate by dealing directly with foreign exchange.

TJMG's sales on the export markets (i.e. non-Chinese) were vital to achieve the balance of foreign exchange. They consisted of direct sales to Merlin Gerin SA as well as sales to panel builders in Asia (Hong Kong, Singapore, etc.).

Exports to Merlin Gerin SA, as stipulated in the joint venture agreement, were to be made at a fixed price of US$1.65 per pole. This price was far below TJMG production costs and was revalued in 1988 to US$2.15 per pole. That year 300,000 poles were sold to Merlin Gerin, as compared to the 150,000 poles forecasted for Year 1. In fact, Merlin Gerin took over the total quantity unsold on the Chinese market.

Exports to Merlin Gerin were shipped from Tianjin to Marseille (France). They were then directed to Merlin Gerin's storing and distribution facility, SERVILOG, in Lyon (France) to be quality checked. From there, they were redistributed to the markets where the specifications of electrical networks met those of the C45N (breaking capacity of 6 kA, for a nominal current of 45 A). These markets included the Middle East as well as Southeast Asia. In the first two years of the joint venture, the fixed quantities purchased from the joint venture by Merlin Gerin were partly shipped back to Singapore, where Merlin Gerin Far East Pte Ltd was in charge of redistributing them in the region. The total cost of transportation for the circuit breakers' return trip Tianjin-Lyon-Singapore was estimated at around 13% of the production costs, excluding storage costs. From 1989, all quality controls were made in Tianjin and the circuit breakers no longer had to be sent to Lyon.

The objective of export sales to panel builders in Asia was achieved in Years 1 and 2 at the quantity defined in the joint venture contract. These exports were shipped directly from Tianjin to Merlin Gerin Far East Pte Ltd who took care of redistribution in the region.

Even with the increased share of production purchased by Merlin Gerin as compared with the quantity agreed upon in the joint venture contract, the equilibrium in foreign exchange was attained neither in 1988 nor in 1989. In 1989, the situation was artificially stabilized through a FF6 million flexible credit line in foreign exchange provided by a French bank established in Shenzhen. In addition, the use of the 'Grey Market' became common practice that year, allowing further adjustments. In 1990, foreign banks and even some Chinese banks, officially started to offer to change RMB for US dollars.

Several factors contributed to aggravate the disequilibrium of the foreign exchange balance :

---

[6] The 'official' rate applies to the exchange of foreign exchange currencies against 'Foreign Exchange Certificates', abbreviated FEC, i.e. a special kind of Yuan available to foreigners and used by Chinese to pay for imported goods.

- Even after Michel Dulfour had been replaced by a Chinese production manager, the salary paid to André Christin still represented 30% of the foreign exchange generated by the joint venture, a ratio that had been underestimated at the time of the contract.

- The devaluation of the RMB in December 1989, from RMB0.28 to RMB0.21 per dollar provoked mixed reactions in TJMG as well as in most joint ventures experiencing a shortage of foreign currency. On the one hand, exports were facilitated by a devalued RMB but on the other, and more importantly, the import of parts from France was made more costly. A second devaluation was feared for the end of 1990 which would possibly lead to a worsening of the situation.

- By June 1990, parts imported from Merlin Gerin still amounted to 35% of the cost of goods sold. At 65%, the local content ratio was far below expectations. The cost of imports was increased by as much as 42% by customs duties. The PA6.6 plastic represented approximately one-third of the total value of the imports. No plastic with comparable properties was available as yet on the Chinese market. A laboratory in Shanghai, which produced a very high quality plastic at an experimental level, had been approached. The prospect of an affiliate corporation to the laboratory undertaking the plastic production at an industrial level within two or three years would allow TJMG to increase the local content of its circuit breakers by 10%, from 65% to 75%. The chances of finding Chinese substitutes for the remaining parts imported from Merlin Gerin remained low.

A NEW STRATEGY IN 1989

During the spring of 1989, when three-quarters of the world was following the events of Tiananmen Square on television, there was virtually no disturbance at TJMG. Working hours were respected, no increased absenteeism was noticed above the contractual maximum of 4%, the production experienced no major problems. On 4 June Michel Collonge (who had replaced André Christin as the new general manager) was asked to return to France and came back at the end of the month. Spring 1989 was a time when drastic action was taken to increase sales revenues on the Chinese market, and to implement more sophisticated management practices.

As soon as TJMG was given the responsibility for distribution in the Chinese market, it launched a market survey (in close collaboration with the Merlin Gerin Beijing representative office) to identify end users and distribution channels for the C45N. The crucial role of electrical design institutes in defining specifications for electrical boards was recognized. Promotional action was taken to teach electrical board designing to these institutes.

Three salesmen were hired by TJMG to monitor sales in the Chinese market. The recruitment was carried out, through classified advertisements in the national press, with the help of the Merlin Gerin Beijing representative office and an industrial consultant. Over 500 applications were received and several dozen interviews conducted. Such a recruitment effort was regarded as a 'first' in the world of joint ventures in China.

The market survey revealed a price level of TJMG C45N comparable to that of Chinese products. Since the quality of TJMG products was higher than that of competitive products, a price increase was deemed necessary. From a cost of 17RMB, as previously proposed on the

Chinese market, the joint venture raised the price of the C45N to 21RMB, with no improvements made to the product. By the end of 1989, this policy showed signs of success. The low price sensitivity of the corporations, with state subsidies forming most of the customer base, explained the relative stability of sales volume, even at an increased price.

Finally, the market survey revealed that, contrary to '105 factory' estimates, at the time of the joint venture negotiation, there *was* a potential market for the C45 model. TJMG started manufacturing the C45 at the end of 1989. In June 1990, the production of the C45 accounted for one-third of the total production, with the C45N representing the remaining two-thirds.

As a result of the new product development and the new pricing strategy, the sales volume in the Chinese market quadrupled between 1988 and 1989, while sales revenues were multiplied fivefold (see Exhibit CS22.4). The balance sheet of TJMG at the end of 1989 is shown in Exhibit CS22.5.

In a move towards more rationalization in the administration of TJMG, Arthur Andersen Hong Kong was hired to review the accounting and control procedures of the joint venture. Biannual control reports were implemented, using international accounting norms. A cost control system was also proposed. Lastly, special emphasis was put on the control of the foreign exchange balance.

EVALUATION OF THE EXPERIENCE

So, what was the situation in June 1990, Michel Collonge asked himself, as the car approached TEDA? And would the evaluation be the same whether he reasoned as the general manager of TJMG or as an employee of Merlin Gerin? Michel Collonge was more inclined to reason from TJMG's point of view:

- The production itself was not a problem and never had been: the 71 employees were committed and reliable. The experimentation of the Kanban JIT production method implemented in the spring of 1990 was very promising.

- TJMG was expected to be profitable that year for the first time in its existence after an accumulated loss of nearly RMB3 million over the last three years. It would then be able to distribute dividends and pay royalties for the first time.

- Sales were expected to increase further that year by 63% in the Chinese market and 16% in the export market.

- The company would still have difficulties reaching an equilibrium foreign exchange balance in 1990. To reach that equilibrium, sales in foreign markets would have to exceed forecasts and imports of parts from France would have to be reduced.

Then he looked at it from Merlin Gerin's standpoint of view:

- Since no immediate increase in the local content ratio could be foreseen, Merlin Gerin would still be able to ship its components to Tianjin, at a substantial margin over the transfer price. The day Merlin Gerin SA no longer had these profits, the only cash flows coming from its joint venture project would be dividends and royalties. Both were contingent upon the joint venture becoming profitable. Furthermore, after 10 years, royalties would no longer be paid.

- The transfer of technology in which '105 factory' had been so interested had started to show some unwelcome effects. 'Me-too' products were being developed by Chinese competitors and would potentially be sold at a discount.

- Finally, direct costs for labour and materials were not as low as expected and the cost of goods sold in TJMG was comparable to that of other production facilities in which automation was high.

And, Merlin Gerin had shown commitment for a long-term relationship in the 'Empire of the Middle Kingdom' and had gained Chinese goodwill. But figures were difficult to evaluate. As the car was entering the TJMG premises, Michel Collonge remembered the words of Jean Claude Lasaunière, the area manager for Asia: 'Assuming a local content ratio stabilized at 80%, I would calculate a pay-back period for our investment in the joint venture project of several decades! ... Yes, but beyond this oversimplified calculation, our presence in China is now recognized by our clients and we get commercial benefits out of it that are already high and will increase in the near future. Furthermore, our technology is now known and accepted by the Chinese. In the case of a Hungary-like opening of the People's Republic of China, we have our feet in the starting blocks and are ready to run...'.

Exhibit CS22.1   Map of China's four SEZ and 14 coastal cities

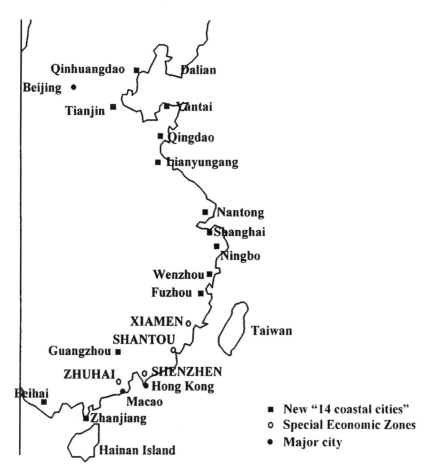

Case 22

Exhibit CS22.2 Tianjin municipality

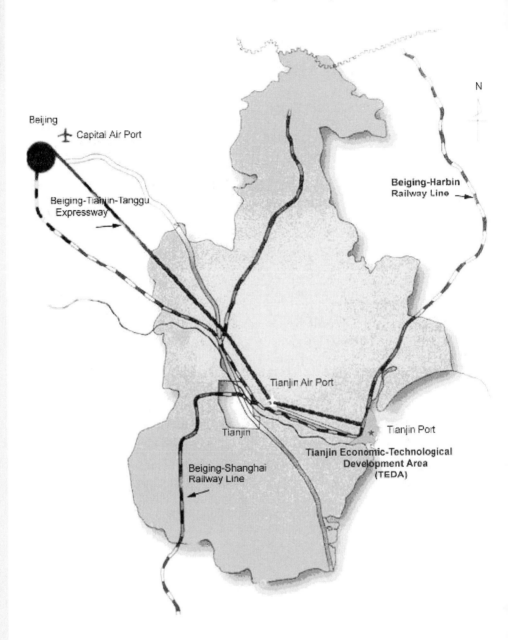

Exhibit CS22.3   Forecasted production level and sales breakdown (*Source:* Feasibility Study)

Sales (in RMB)

Years	Year 1 (07/87–12/88)	Year 2 (1989)	Year 3 (1990)	Year 4
Volumes	1,000,000 poles	1,250,000 poles	1,750,000 poles	2,000,000 poles
Exports to MG 1 pole: 1.65 US$	150,000 poles RMB945,450	125,000 poles RMB787,875	175,000 poles RMB1,103,025	200,000 poles RMB1,260,600
Exports to panelbuilders 1 pole: 1.80 US$	20,000 poles RMB137,520	75,000 poles RMB515,700	175,000 poles RMB1,203,300	200,000 poles RMB1,375,200
Local sales 5% = sales tax 1 pole: 11.7 RMB	830,000 poles RMB9,225,450	1,050,000 poles RMB11,670,750	1,400,000 poles RMB15,561,000	1,600,000 poles RMB17,784,000
Total	RMB10,308,420	RMB12,974,325	RMB17,867,325	RMB20,419,800

Note: 1 US$ = 3.82 RMB

Exhibit CS22.4   Sales situation in 1987, 1988, 1989 and 1990

	1987 Actual	1988 Actual	1989 Actual	1990 Budget
Sales summary				
China		767	3,909	6,389
Export		1,529	2,600	3,032
Sales quantity				
China	1,869	55,000	226,000	300,000
Export	14,456	235,000	325,500	300,000

Exhibit CS22.5   Balance Sheet of TJMG on 31 December 1989

Assets	At end of period	Liabilities and capital	At end of period
Current assets		Current liabilities	
Cash on hand	1,328.20	Short-term bank loans	
Cash in bank	2,380,254.52	Accounts payable	507,182.26
		Advances from customers	42,606.09
Accounts receivable	2,016,201.64	Taxes payable	22,062.69
		Dividends payable	
Prepayment to suppliers	26,944.04	Other payables	98,942.46
Other receivables	23,094.94	Provision for expenses	35,159.11
Deferred & prepaid expenses	4,703.59		
Inventories	3,644,050.69		
Deferred exchange gains and losses			
Total current assets	8,097,573.92	Total current liabilities	786,032.61
Fixed assets			
Costs	7,926,573.90	Foreign bank loans	2,896,208.90
Less: accumulated depreciation	1,423,143.99		
Net value	6,503,429.91		
		Total liabilities	3,684,241.51
		Capital	
Intangible assets & other assets		Total amount per joint venture contract	14,809,000.00
		Paid in capital	14,809,000.00
Proprietary technology & patents	682,465.00	Including Chinese participant	7,842,568,00
		Foreign participant	6,966,432.00
Organization expenses	215,410.08		
Total intangible assets & other assets	897,875.00		
		Retained earnings	−2,944,478.60
		Total capital	11,814,521.40
Total assets	**15,498,762.91**	Total liabilities & capital	**15,498,762.91**

Case 23

*This case was prepared by Philippe Lasserre, Professor of Strategy and
Management at INSEAD, on the basis of a paper written by Claire Chai
and edited by Huong-Giang Nguyen, both from the class of MBA '93. It is
intended to be used as a basis for class discussion rather than to illustrate
either effective or ineffective handling of an administrative situation.*
Copyright © 1993 INSEAD-EAC, Fontainebleau, France

Daewoo and General Motors

At the December 1991 meeting of the Tokyo Motor Show, Kim Woo Choong, chairman of the South Korean conglomerate Daewoo, and Jack Smith, vice-chairman of the US motor giant General Motors talked about ending their 15-year joint venture, Daewoo Motor. Daewoo Motor represented the second-largest foreign investment made in South Korea by a US automaker to produce cars for sale in both domestic and foreign markets. However, mounting losses and deteriorating market shares had plagued the operation. Both partners had for some time been dissatisfied with various aspects of the relationship, the main problems revolving around quality, technology, capital infusion, sales support, market access and, management style.

With so many areas of divergence, the separation was expected, especially after GM asked the Korean government in August 1991 to help it convince another South Korean automaker, Ssangyong Motor, to replace Daewoo as its partner.

BACKGROUND

From GM Korea to Saehan Motors: 1972–78

GM entered the South Korean automobile industry in 1972 when it bought out Toyota's stake in Shinjin Motor, and established GM Korea. As South Korea's first manufacturer of the popular 'Saloon' line, Shinjin enjoyed a 50% share of the domestic car market at the time of GM's capital participation.

Production of Opel-designed passenger cars was started in December 1972, followed by heavy trucks in March 1973 with the technical assistance of GM affiliate Isuzu Motors. Despite this rapid rate of new product introduction, GM was unhappy with Shinjin's management, and asked the US embassy in Seoul to persuade the South Korean government to find it another partner in 1976. Facing increasing financial difficulties, Shinjin finally transferred its 50% stake in the venture to the government-owned Korea Development Bank in 1976, at which point GM Korea was renamed Saehan Motors.

The evolution of GM's venture in Korea is shown in Exhibit CS23.1.

From Saehan Motors to Daewoo Motor: 1978–83

Capitalized at US$50 million, Saehan manufactured compact and family-sized passenger cars, heavy-duty trucks, and buses. The relationship between Daewoo and GM began when Daewoo was asked by the South Korean government to take over the 50% stake in the venture from the bank in July 1978. Under this arrangement, half of the management responsibility in Saehan was transferred to Daewoo, representing the company's 50% equity share in the joint venture.

Over time both partners became increasingly dissatisfied with the joint venture's structure, as each company sought to have a stronger management role. This power struggle, combined with the adverse impact of depressed domestic and overseas markets during the recession of the late 1970s, helped contribute to a severe slump in the joint venture's business.

In 1983, Daewoo finally took over complete operational responsibility for the joint venture and changed its name to Daewoo Motor (DM). Under the agreement, GM would continue to provide assistance in engineering technology, financing, and overseas marketing to DM, who in turn would assume sole responsibility for the vehicle production and domestic sales. Although the US automaker had reduced its appointees within the joint venture from four to three, a GM executive continued to serve as senior vice-president and joint representative director, albeit with diminished authority. GM seemed content with the settlement at the time: 'This is a natural progression for GM in its 10 years of operating in Korea. It publicly demonstrates confidence in our Korean partner and in Korea's economic potential and recognizes the [JV's] role in GM's world car strategy', said one GM official. According to the latter, the agreement illustrated GM's recognition of the value of Daewoo's business skills, aggressiveness, and 'thorough knowledge' of the Korean market and business practices.

DAEWOO MOTOR

Product range

DM produced mid-size (Super Saloon series), compact (Prince and Espero series), and subcompact (Le Mans series) passenger cars, highway and city buses, heavy trucks, and large special purpose vehicles such as concrete mixers, tankers and refrigerator trucks (Exhibit CS23.2).

The first model released after Daewoo took over management responsibility from GM was the Maepsy-Na, a small car based on the rear-wheel-drive Chevette. This model gained a 40% market share in 1983 in the small car segment, making it a worthy competitor to number one Hyundai's Pony.

Buoyed by the success of the Maepsy-Na, Daewoo planned to collaborate with GM for the production of a new, front-wheel-drive, subcompact model to be named Le Mans. The negotiation called for a transfer of GM's technology via its European subsidiary Opel to DM for local manufacturing and assembly in its Pupyong plant. While marketing of the Le Mans in Korea would be carried out by the joint venture's domestic sales force, GM's network of US dealers would have sole responsibility for marketing of the exported models in the USA.

The Le Mans series production started in 1985, and was introduced to the Korean market in July 1986. Exports arrived in the USA in 1987. 'In a very real sense, this vehicle is a product of the best that Germany, Korea and the USA have to offer', said Roger B. Smith, GM's then chairman in Seoul in September 1986. Despite a higher price than the comparable Hyundai model, the Le Mans enjoyed a tremendous success: by the end of 1986, Hyundai's share of the Korean market had declined from 80% to 60%. This was perhaps the best period that the Daewoo-GM relationship had experienced.

However, in 1990 relations between the two partners started to sour when tension mounted over the P500, a spin-off of the Le Mans styled by Bertone of Italy and featuring different ride and handling characteristics with a different drive train. Designed for the more affluent segment of the domestic market, the medium-sized P500 sported a profile similar to that of the Ford Taurus, and was based on an Opel Ascona platform. Despite strong objection by GM, DM planned to proceed with the production of 20,000 P500 in 1990, and an even larger number in 1991.

Seeking to compete against domestic rivals who had been introducing mini-sedans with newer technologies than the Le Mans', Daewoo finally decided in June 1988 to go it alone. It concluded a licensing deal with Suzuki Motor to produce a mini-car 800 cc model in its wholly owned subsidiary, Daewoo Shipbuilding, since its request to manufacture the car in the joint venture was repeatedly spurned by GM.

Technology

Because of the relationship with GM, most of DM's products came from Opel, GM's European subsidiary. The Le Mans was based on the Opel Kadett, chosen 'European Car of the Year' in 1985. Plans for its production, evaluated by an international team of engineers from Daewoo, GM, and Adam Opel, included state-of-the-art technology such as anti-corrosive paint vats and automated spray booths for painting. The influence of Opel engineers was evident in the assembly line that tilted sideways for easier installation of brake, fuel, and exhaust parts.

Furthermore, the one-piece assembly of the driver instrument panel, steering column, and steering wheel was an innovation not found in US plants. The new plant also incorporated robots and other automated equipment to boost quality, including 18 welding robots manufactured by GM Fanuc and Italian robots that positioned body panels precisely during framing operations. Opel provided an engine suited to Korean driving conditions, and Pontiac and Opel adapted it for US emissions requirements.

In 1986, Daewoo also signed a contract with Nissan of Japan for minivan production technology. Exhibit CS23.3 shows a summary of the different links between DM and foreign car manufacturers.

Success with the Le Mans had brought confidence to DM, who started experimenting with its own designs and testing techniques to further adapt its products to the domestic market. The joint venture now committed more resources to developing its own engineering capabilities, and sometimes even relied on outside stylists to design its passenger cars, as was the case with the P500. While emissions testing was performed in-house, DM contracted with various GM affiliates for other design aspects, such as GM Holden for ride and handling characteristics, and Harrison Radiator for the heating and cooling systems.

Production

The four plants, Pupyong (cars and trucks), Pusan (buses), Tongnae (truck and bus frames), and Inchon (foundry) experienced substantial over-capacity problems in the late 1980s as slowing sales in both the USA and Korea forced the joint venture to operate at less than capacity after a peak in 1988. As a result, the German-built Opel Kadett was 5 to 10% less costly than the Korean-built Le Mans. In 1989, against a capacity of 282,000 vehicles, DM's actual output was fewer than 162,000 vehicles, representing an over-capacity factor of 40%.

Exports

Despite a temporary increase in productivity leading to increased exports in the years 1978–80, Daewoo's sales in foreign markets had been lacklustre, stagnating at about only 1.4% of total production at the end of 1986 (see Exhibit CS23.4). The introduction of the Le Mans in the USA in 1987, however, helped to quadruple production and brought the number of exports to 44% of total output. This did not last long, as changing business climates, and the partners' divergent strategies caused DM sales in the USA to tumble again after a peak of 65,600 units in 1988. In 1991, DM only managed to sell 33,220 Le Mans in the USA, little more than half its original exports just three years earlier.

Parts supply

In order to provide local sourcing for the Le Mans engine production, body stamping and final assembly as called for in the joint venture contract, Daewoo Precision Industries and GM's Delco Remy were merged to form Daewoo Automotive Components and Koram Plastics in 1984. Unlike DM itself, Daewoo Automotive Components had always been a success. Even at the time of the dissolution of the DM joint venture the two partners agreed to continue their relationship in the component business.

Management structure

When Daewoo took over operational management of the joint venture from GM in 1983, Daewoo's forceful founder, Kim Woo-Choong, assumed the position of chairman and installed his brother, Kim Sung-Choong as president of the newly renamed Daewoo Motor. Korean nationals occupied all key posts in manufacturing, engineering, sales, marketing and finance. Robert Strammy, previously in charge of GM's operations in Mexico, was also part of DM's management committee; however, he had only a limited advisory role.

At the start of the Le Mans' production in Pupyong, a total of 68 engineers and technicians from Opel were on site installing equipment and doing training, and 93 Daewoo foremen and key workers went to Opel to learn about engine and suspension production, paint and body work, and press operation. Special training was also provided by Opel's equipment suppliers to some 245 Daewoo's workers overseas.

Financing

The Le Mans project involved an investment of US$427 million in total to expand Daewoo's manufacturing capacity. Initially, Daewoo and GM each contributed US$100 million in the joint venture to maintain their equal partnership, with the balance financed externally. In the end, GM had poured nearly US$200 million into the venture. The contract provided for the establishment of engine production, body stamping and final assembly operations to produce up to 170,000 cars per year. The model was to be manufactured from local components, but some components were being sourced from outside South Korea initially.

BUSINESS ENVIRONMENT

The role of government

The South Korean government has had a major influence in shaping the development of the Korean motor industry, which became a strategic industry in 1972 when the government began focusing on heavy and chemical industrialization. Protectionist measures that had the effect of more or less closing the South Korean market to foreign competition were first taken in 1974. This forced the industry to change its status from assembler to manufacturer.

In August 1980, the government decided to restructure the industry. Highly protected from the effects of foreign competition, the South Korean motor industry had developed along fragmented and uneconomic lines during the 1970s. There was under-utilization of capacity and a failure to achieve economies of scale. These weaknesses emerged as the second oil crisis and one of the worst recessionary periods hit the market in the early 1980s. The government actions in 1981 reduced the number of car producers from three to two – Hyundai and Daewoo. The third, Kia, was left to concentrate on light truck production, a sector which both Hyundai and Daewoo were required to leave.

In 1987, Kia was allowed to re-enter the car sector and Hyundai and Daewoo to recommence the manufacturing of light commercial vehicles. However, mindful of the need to build up the strength and international competitiveness of the existing vehicle producers, the government also tried to enforce a limit on the number of firms that could enter the sector. For example Samsung's deceased chairman Lee Byung-Chull had been denied access repeatedly on the grounds that this would mean over-investment and excess competition in the industry.

The relaxation of government restrictions on domestic vehicle production came about in July 1989 and raised potential for new entries into the sector. By the end of 1991, Samsung Heavy Industries Co. had already formed technology alliances with a number of foreign auto manufacturers, among them Nissan Diesel, to build heavy commercial vehicles. While Samsung was assisted by Daf of Holland to produce special vehicles of over 20 tons, the Halla Group had a technology-sharing agreement with Fiat of Italy to produce commercial vehicles. Both groups saw the passenger car market as the next target, although the government turned down their bids. Other aspiring entrants included Pohang Iron & Steel Co., the Hyosung Group (construction, petrochemicals), and the Daelim Group (motorcycles).

Growing Korean market demand

During the 1970s, cars were seen as luxury items. The government discouraged car ownership by imposing high taxes on gasoline. This was reflected in car ownership figures: in the late 1970s, there were only 7 units per 1,000 people in Korea, compared with 32 per 1,000 in Taiwan, 65 in Brazil, 70 in Mexico and 115 in Argentina.

Case 23

Apart from 1980, when the economy encountered a series of setbacks due to the worldwide oil shock, the new car market in South Korea has showed steady growth over the 1980s in line with rising GNP per capita and rising employment levels. The growth was particularly strong at the end of the decade and sales climbed by 46% in 1987. Even so, the Korean market still had substantial growth potential, with modest car ownership levels, at the beginning of 1989: a ratio of one car per 34 persons compared with countries such as Malaysia (14.0) and Brazil (13.5) which have similar income levels. The steady expansion in domestic demand was helped by a general decrease in vehicle prices in 1984 and a decline in the price of oil from 1986. More recently, the reduction of a special excise tax and the introduction of a car loan system have served to maintain the market momentum.

The only real cloud on the domestic market horizon was the expected moderation in the increase in personal disposable income that had fuelled demand. Inflation, together with moderating wage rates, are also likely to slow growth in the future.

Segmentation: more sophisticated consumers

For a long time, South Koreans had no choice but to buy Korean cars. Indeed, South Korea was closed to imports of foreign cars until 1 July 1987. The high duties charged subsequently on the foreign vehicles made it difficult to purchase foreign cars. Under such conditions, Koreans had limited exposure to different car models. In the early 1980s, the question facing the Korean consumer was less, 'Which car should I buy?' but rather 'Should I buy a car?'. Manufacturers had to compete on getting a new car to the market which was affordable for the majority. The small car segment accounted for about one-half of the domestic market.

On the basis of growing affluence, medium-sized cars started to gain in popularity, especially with the launch of Hyundai's Sonata in July 1988. This segment included Daewoo's Royale and Kia's Concord. The luxury segment, relatively small, comprised Hyundai's Grandeur, Daewoo's Super Saloon, Kia's Potentia and imported cars. The upcoming range of down-priced 'public' minicars from Asia Motor, Daewoo Shipbuilding and Hyundai constituted another promising segment.

In general, new models had to be launched to maintain the interest of consumers who were getting more and more sophisticated. The level of advertising rose with a general upsurge in retail incentive bonuses and promotional offers, including, for example, the addition of air conditioning as a 'no charge' extra. To compete successfully in the domestic market, car manufacturers needed more rapid model changes and a more diversified model to mix with more upmarket, niche and high tech products.

Starting in 1986, South Korea began to register trade surplus with the rest of the world principally as a result of the automobile industry's burst of export activities (especially to the USA). This advantage increasingly fuelled growing worldwide protectionist sentiment. The government of South Korea decided to focus on the domestic market and to impose strong competition among the major players as an alternative means to continue strengthening the industry.

Intense competition from domestic manufacturers

Hyundai Motor (HM). HM has been the South Korean motor industry's leader accounting for over 54% of the country's vehicle production volume in 1989 (see Exhibit CS23.5). It was the first to design, develop and manufacture its own compact car – the Pony – with the help of a team of UK engineers. Launched in 1975, the Pony had engines, gearboxes and rear axles produced under license from Mitsubishi. Its success can be seen from the steady build-up in car output during the second half of the 1970s to over 70,000 units in 1979. The Pony succeeded in laying the foundation for HM's future development in the motor industry by allowing HM to sell in a protected home market, as well as in selected export markets where low price provided an entry niche.

Often viewed as a 'one car' producer, HM stepped up its model development programme with the mid-range Stellar family saloon starting in 1978, the front-wheel-drive compact car Excel in 1985, the executive Grandeur series the same year, and the Sonata in 1988. Hyundai was to maintain this acceleration of its new model programme by shortening its products' life cycle from five to four years and allocating 3–4% of turnover to new model development. The most significant addition recently was the S coupé (1500 cc).

Mitsubishi Motors of Japan, with a 15% equity stake in HM, has been the major technical licenser and source for design and engines and other components. This relationship has also given rise to further trading links with companies such as Chrysler. HM supplied Chrysler with Sonata models from 1992, with provision for further cooperation in the future. One of Hyundai's strategic objectives was to reduce its traditional dependence on Mitsubishi Motor for the design of engines and major components. By the early 1990s HM was successful in developing its own engine, its own vehicle design, and its own production of components, including ABS systems and four-wheel steering. This not only reduced royalties and licensing payments but also helped to improve Hyundai's bottom line, signalling HM's intent to compete abroad and heralding the company's coming of age as a self-reliant vehicle manufacturer.

Kia Motors Corporation (KMC). KMC is South Korea's second-largest vehicle manufacturer and the flagship of the Kia Group, a conglomerate of several affiliates, including Asia Motor, manufacturer of heavy-duty trucks, buses and special purpose vehicles. Kia is 8% owned by Mazda Motor Co. and 10% by Ford. This alliance allowed Kia to have access to Mazda vehicle and component designs and manufacturing technology. Taking advantage of Ford's extensive and well-established marketing network in the USA, Kia has also been able to export its subcompact cars on an OEM basis and develop and strengthen its presence in this strategically important market.

After the launch of the small Pride model in 1986, Kia began to complete its range of passenger cars by moving upmarket with customers as their income levels increased and interest in mid-size and luxury models grew. Introduced in October 1987, the 2000 cc mid-size Concord was marketed in the USA by Mazda under the name Mazda 626 and by Ford under the name Probe.

Kia planned to introduce a new J-car model based on proprietary technology. A new medium S-car was to follow in 1992 as well as an M-car also equipped with the company's own engine design. A sports car project was being pursued with partners Ford and Mazda. Kia also closely surveyed Eastern Europe market potential. A proposal with Scala Kupp of Hungary for a JV assembly plant in Hungary recently came under scrutiny and talks had also been held with the truck producer BAZ in Czechoslovakia.

THE PARTNERS AND THEIR INTEREST IN THE JOINT VENTURE

Daewoo: 'Spirit of Challenge, Creativity and Sacrifice'

Daewoo founded in 1967 as a small textile trading company with an investment of US$18,000 and four employees, is now South Korea's fourth largest conglomerate with US$25 billion in sales, more than 120,000 employees, and interests spanning heavy construction and manufacturing operations, shipbuilding, diesel engines and forklift trucks.

Daewoo's success story runs parallel to South Korea's economic success. By the mid-1970s, Daewoo became one of the most profitable firms in Korea thanks to its success in exporting textiles worldwide. Based on this initial success, Daewoo progressively expanded its business to other light industry products, and, by 1975, it had acquired 14 companies and taken major positions in two other firms. At the same time, Daewoo began diversifying into banking and financing businesses. By then, chairman Kim Woo-Choong had earned an excellent reputation as a manager in the eyes of government officials and the public.

As the country's focus shifted from light to heavy industry in mid-1970, Daewoo also started to acquire new businesses in steel, machinery and shipbuilding. Singled out by the government as one of the companies most capable of developing the heavy industry in Korea, Daewoo benefited from generous bank financing. This enabled the company to expand rapidly.

Daewoo's objectives in the joint venture

Given the active role the government took in shaping Korea's industrial policies and the good relationship that Daewoo had always enjoyed in the past with the government, it was not surprising Daewoo could not refuse the joint venture offer from GM after the government had specifically designated it as a partner for the US automaker. This did not mean, however, that Daewoo walked into the partnership unwillingly.

At the time of the joint venture, despite the *chaebol*'s presence in an important number of heavy industries, its business strategy was not quite complete for the conspicuous lack of participation in the automobile industry. Chairman Kim's ambition was for his group to become a major international car maker by joining forces with an already established player in order to learn the much-needed Western technology and enhance production expertise for the future. A joint venture would be much less costly than if Daewoo were to go it alone as there would be capital participation from GM to build up manufacturing capabilities. Additionally, GM was a respected and well-known foreign firm. The prestige of being connected with GM could only enhance Daewoo's reputation and image. Whereas Daewoo would be responsible for sales performance in the local market, it could take advantage of GM's capital and overseas network to promote exports. Finally, the joint venture presented a fit with the diesel engine manufacturing capability of another division within Daewoo, Daewoo Heavy Industries.

General Motors: 'Effective Performance as a Worldwide Corporation'

General Motors founded in the USA in 1908, was a relatively small automobile manufacturer up until the 1920s when it started to acquire young enterprises such as the Olds Motor Vehicle Company (Oldsmobile), Cadillac Automobile Company, Buick Motor Company, Oakland Motor

Car Company (now Pontiac Motor Division) and Chevrolet Motor Company, as well as other manufacturers of components and accessories.

In 1966, GM stated that a 'unified ownership for coordinated policy control of all our operations throughout the world is essential for our effective performance as a worldwide corporation'. It was in this international expansion phase that GM linked up with Daewoo, as it did with other firms both in the USA and around the world.

GM's objectives in the joint venture

When GM entered Korea, it had no other manufacturing capabilities in Asia. Initially seen as a beach head to develop the Japanese and Chinese markets, South Korea was additionally attractive for its cheap labour in the production of inexpensive cars to compete against Japanese models. The Korean enthusiasm for learning and reputation for hard work and skills contributed to GM's decision to manufacture in Korea. Even though personnel in Korea are entitled to three weeks' holiday a year, few take more than three days at a time.

Additionally, GM needed a local partner to gain access and operate in the highly regulated Korean market. Even though this might seem foolhardy given the insignificant size of the Korean market in the 1970s, growing affluence and the government's decision to encourage car ownership starting in 1986 combined to create a boom in the domestic market, rewarding GM for its long-standing presence in Korea.

Finally, for the same reasons as Daewoo had, GM needed a partner to share market and financial risk in this highly capital-intensive venture.

ESCALATION OF TENSIONS

Weak sales, declining market share and poor financial performance

'The (Daewoo-GM) joint-venture has not been a happy one, because they have not done as well as they expected, both in Korea and in America', said Boston University professor Yu Sang Chang.

Except for a brief honeymoon period when the joint venture was unanimously heralded by industry experts as the perfect match, the Daewoo-GM relationship was continually plagued by poor performance. Starting in 1987, DM was unique among South Korea's vehicle manufactures in experiencing a net deficit from sluggish sales and production. US sales of the Le Mans through GM's Pontiac division were running 33% below target in 1988, and collapsed to just 39,081 cars in 1989, a 39% decrease from the already-below-target number in 1988. In the first half of 1988, Daewoo lost US$40 million. Sales nose-dived a further 15% in 1990. At the same time, DM's domestic market share in the passenger car segment dropped from 31.5% in 1987 to 19.3% in 1991, costing the group the number two position which went to Kia Motors.

Furthermore, DM faced growing cash-flow problems. Even allowing for the Korean propensity to favour debts in financing new investments, the joint venture's debts and receivables had pushed the debt-to-equity ratio to an alarmingly high 9:1 level at the end of 1990 three years after introduction of the Le Mans. In the same year, interest payments increased to Won 104 billion from just Won 51 billion three years before.

Conflicts arose when Daewoo decided to introduce a concessionary finance programme in mid-1991 to reduce DM's stock of unsold cars, apparently without the knowledge of its US partner. Potential buyers could finance the purchase of their Le Mans at extremely attractive rates. GM believed that such concessions were foolhardy given the general liquidity squeeze in Korea at the time and DM's already high debt burden. 'We were paying 24% for money and lending it out at zero interest', said a GM source.

Marketing, technology and sales support

Daewoo complained that GM did not provide enough technology and sales support for the Le Mans in the USA. GM virtually controlled Daewoo exports to world markets by means of an unwritten understanding. Under this condition, Daewoo was frustrated by GM's refusal to sell any other Daewoo vehicles than the Le Mans in the US market. Unlike Hyundai, which ran its own dealer network in the USA and sold cars under its own brand name, Daewoo, with its lack of brand identity, had to rely on the GM network and Pontiac. Daewoo officials blamed the Pontiac motor division for not promoting the Le Mans aggressively for fear of drawing sales from GM's other divisions' subcompacts. 'The feeling, and perhaps the fact, is that the Le Mans is not a priority product for GM', said Park Won-Jang, senior auto analyst at the Korea Institute for Economics and Technology.

In addition GM did not enjoy the goodwill of many of DM's Korean workers, who felt that the US automaker meddled in operational decisions in Korea while underperforming its marketing tasks in the USA. Union radicals even advocated severing Daewoo ties with GM completely. 'Daewoo should have as much say in the marketing of cars as GM', said Hong Kwang-Pyo, a union executive.

Moreover, GM refused to allow DM to enter the European market except through GM's marketing channels. Many Daewoo officials came to realize that it would be difficult for DM to become a world-class automaker as long as GM influenced manufacturing decisions and controlled sales in North America.

Diverging views on industrial strategy and commitment

As the domestic market started to take off, absorbing 60% of all Korean-built cars from just 33% in 1987, and US sales continued to skid downward, Daewoo increasingly focused more attention on sales at home. Its policy was to win market shares, even at the expense of bottom-line profits. Daewoo had repeatedly requested GM's agreement to increase capital expenditures in order to improve its outputs, both in terms of quantity and of quality, so as to compete against DM's rivals, who were bringing to market newer models with newer designs and technology. GM's executives chafed at the Koreans' seemingly extravagant strategy of expansion in the face of ever-rising losses and refused to pour more money into the joint venture. GM vice president Barton Brown said his company was not interested in making 'extensive additional investment in Korea at this time'. Daewoo concluded that if it wanted to compete more aggressively in the domestic market, it would have to do so alone.

This tenuous situation eventually led Daewoo to link up with Japan's Suzuki Motor for technology assistance and production launch of a mini-car the Daewoo Tico, and to sign a licensing deal to obtain design, development and production expertise from the Japanese car maker. Although GM owned 4.8% of Suzuki, the Americans were not involved, as Daewoo chairman Kim negotiated the deal. Responsibility for the project was kept separate from GM's control in DM and it was another Daewoo division – a shipbuilding unit – who ended up manufacturing the mini-sedan. DM also had links with Suzuki for two new commercial vehicles. Daewoo looking elsewhere for technology further weakened the Daewoo-GM joint venture.

In addition, Daewoo was disappointed with GM's decision to supply the two-litre engines for the export version of the Le Mans from GM Holden in Australia, although Daewoo had wanted them to be built in South Korea.

Finally, in an effort to diversify its export destinations, Daewoo negotiated with both Hungary and Czechoslovakia for the supply of the Le Mans model to these countries. An agreement was reached with Czechoslovakia, for the delivery of 7,000 cars, beginning in 1989. Exports to China began in October 1988 when 175 Le Mans units under the 'Laser' logo were shipped to Hainam Province. Daewoo Motor's increasing desire to formulate its own export policies added to the friction between the company and GM.

Labour disputes

Korea's advantage as a low-cost export base faded as the country prospered. Korean workers wished to have a fair share of the country's increasing affluence, with militant, newly formed labour unions demanding higher wages. In 1989, union leaders at DM agreed not to exercise workers' right to a year-end bonus in solidarity with the company over difficult times. Daewoo was expected to concede some ground as a return gesture, however, it did nothing. Humiliated, workers staged a walkout that lasted from the end of February until mid-March. Daily losses over the period were estimated at W4 billion. This followed 90 days of disputes in the preceding year when losses totalled W345 billion. GM officials blamed these labour disputes for poor sales performance in the USA. They said interruptions in the Le Mans shipments during these periods of unrest caused headaches for US dealers and hurt sales.

Management clashes and operational disputes

GM's methodical and prolonged decision making had been ill suited to Daewoo, where decisions were made quickly by a few top executives. On the other hand, commenting about Daewoo's autocratic management style, a GM official said that 'an operation [under Daewoo's management] has to meet its target, or it has to face wrath from the top. There is less penalty for not selling the target than for not building it'. He added: 'The problem is their penchant for operating full out without considering the market. That drives operating costs up and increases inventory'.

Sources

1. Joseph L. Badaracco, 'The New General Motors', Harvard Business School, Case #9-387-171, 1987.

2. Joseph L. Badaracco, 'General Motors' Asian Alliances', Harvard Business School, Case #9-388-094, 1988.

3. Francis J. Aguilar and Dong Sung Cho, 'Daewoo Group', Harvard Business School, Case #385-014, 1984.

4. Tom Lowry , 'The South Korean Motor Industry: A Return of Japan?', EIU, July 1987.

5. Ian L. Robertson, 'South Korea's Motor Industry', EIU, September 1990.

6. 'Is the GM-Daewoo Deal Running on Empty?', Business Week, 12 September 1988.

7. 'Can this Tiger Burn Bright Again?', Business Week, 3 December 1990.

8. 'Why GM and Daewoo Wound Up on the Road to Nowhere', Business Week, 23 September 1991.

9. Hellmut Schutte, 'Daewoo', INSEAD, September 1992.

10. 'An Introduction to the Daewoo Group', Daewoo Corporate Culture Series 3, November 1992.

11. 'High Octane Relationship', Business Korea, November 1991.

12. 'Wheels off the Wagon', Far Eastern Economic Review, 23 January 1992.

13. 'A Parting of the Ways', Business Korea, February 1992.

14. 'Daewoo Weds Again', Business Korea, December 1992.

15. 'Focus on the Local Market', Business Korea, March 1993.

Case 23

Exhibit CS23.1 **The evolution of General Motors in Korea**

2/55	11/62	6/72	11/76	1/83	10/92
Shinjin Industry	**Shinjin Motor**	**GM Korea**	**Saehan Motor**	**Daewoo Motor**	**End of J/V**
	'66: Saenara Take-over	GM Capital Participation	'78: Daewoo Capital Participation	Daewoo Management Take-over	Daewoo bought out GM's stake

Exhibit CS23.2   Daewoo Motor's product range

Model	Capacity
Passenger cars	
Le Mans	1500–1600 cc
Racer	1500–1600 cc
Penta	1500 cc
Royal Duke	1500 cc
Royal Prince	1500 cc, 1900 cc, 2000 cc
Royal Saloon	2000cc
Royal Diesel	2000 cc diesel
Royal Super Saloon	2000 cc
Imperial 3000	3000 cc
Buses	
Vanette	9 passengers
Vanette	12 passengers
City Bus	
Inter-City Bus	
Highway Bus	
Trucks	
Vanette	1 ton
Elf-II	2.75 tons
Cargo	8 tons
Dump	8 tons
Dump	10.5 tons
Cargo	11 tons
Dump	15 tons

Exhibit CS23.2   *Continued*

Model	Capacity
Special vehicles	
Refrigerator Truck	
Concrete Mixer Truck	
Concrete Pump Truck	
Crane Truck	
Full Cargo Truck	
Tank Lorry	
Fuel/Water Tanker	
Tractor	39–53 tons

Exhibit CS23.3   Relationships between DM and foreign manufacturers

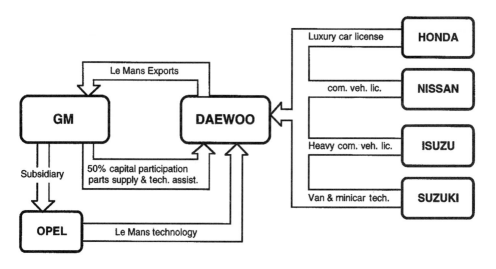

Case 23

Exhibit CS23.4   Production and exports of DM's vehicles (*Source*: EIU)

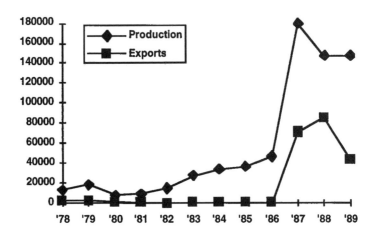

Exhibit CS23.5   Vehicle production by South Korea's top three car manufacturers (*Source*: EIU)

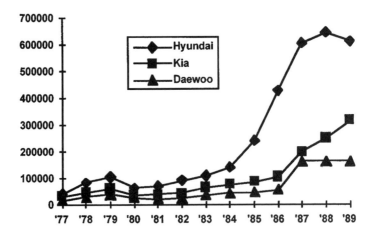

People and Organization in Asia

Part

8

The failure of some Western firms to establish a presence in Asia Pacific commensurate with the region's strategic potential is often due to their inability to adapt to local managerial cultures and competitive climates. Inadequate financial allocation and inappropriate human resource management are the main causes for the weakness of Western companies' presence in the region. In Figure 8.1 they are shown as two interrelated vicious circles. Both relate to Asia Pacific's low internal visibility at corporate headquarters, where influential top executives seldom support the region's perspective. Unless championed by a powerful board member, Asian strategies fail to receive adequate attention; this in turn prevents the firm from developing Asian operations and contributes to the region's poor visibility.

The first vicious circle is about the allocation of financial resources. While projects and plans for planning and budgeting, as well as capital appropriation, are prepared at the operational level, decisions are made at higher levels, and the acceptance of proposals depends on top management's confidence. In fact Asian-related investments are generally perceived as riskier than comparable projects in Europe or the USA, and are therefore given lower priority. This creates another vicious circle: top managers, especially if they are unfamiliar with Asia, have less confidence in Asian projects; consequently, Asian projects are gradually perceived to be less important, an attitude which reinforces the weakness of the Western company. The result is a self-fulfilling prophecy where the uncertainty of future investment is reinforced by lack of support from top management.

The second vicious circle relates to human resources management. Expanding Asian operations would require entrepreneurial managers with the right cultural and political skills, and with enough drive to push projects through the maze of corporate systems and procedures. However, since the region has such relatively poor internal

Figure 8.1   Organizational vicious circles

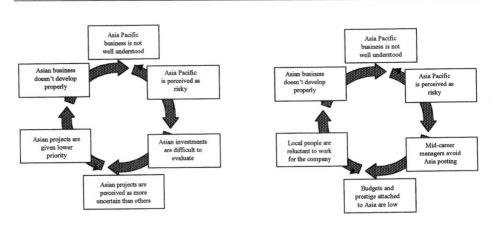

FINANCIAL RESOURCES   HUMAN RESOURCES

visibility and financial support, managers perceive it as risky for their careers and avoid volunteering for posts there. Local graduates feel that Western companies provide limited opportunities for long-term career advancement. This lukewarm commitment translates into mediocre results.

Organizational capabilities

In order to understand how Western companies either perpetuate or break these two vicious circles, in 1992 the Euro-Asia Centre at INSEAD undertook an in-depth study of three companies: Unilever (UK and the Netherlands), L'Oréal (France) and Wella (Germany). All three have achieved a measure of success in Asia Pacific, and the similarity of their approaches highlights five main facilitators for success in the region (Figure 8.2).

Regional legitimization

The three companies each developed an Asian strategy after top executives had recognized the region's strategic importance. Unilever had always seen Asia Pacific as strategically important, but invested only sporadically until the late 1970s. In the 1980s, it decided to expand its presence in the region. This process of 'legitimization' was followed by a reorganization at head office and a considerable investment programme, while board members paid frequent visits to Asia.

At L'Oréal, the appointment of a new president in the mid-1980s provided an opportunity to realize that, in its global strategy, the company was walking on two legs instead of three. A big investment program was launched, largely in defensive response to competitors, sending a strong signal that Asia Pacific had become an area of strategic importance for top management.

Wella's Asian strategy was the result of a search for new growth areas in the late 1960s. A manager was posted in Japan; his success made top management aware that the country had the potential to become Wella's second largest market. A corporate director was relocated to Japan, and there were important repercussions in terms of internal recruitment.

Regional drive

All three companies had similar approaches. Unilever believed in the local power of its operating subsidiaries; L'Oréal developed entrepreneurial managers often referred to as 'missionaries'; Wella sent a newly recruited manager to Japan to start an operation. In all three cases, early business expansion was characterized by a high degree of autonomy; expatriate managers had free rein to accumulate knowledge, contacts and operating experience throughout the region.

465

Figure 8.2 Asia Pacific facilitators

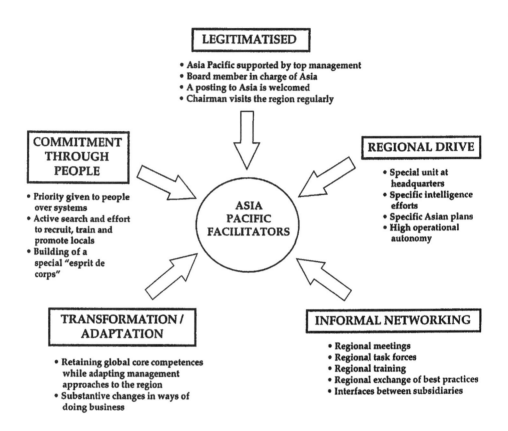

In all three companies, the centre started directing the regional drive more closely in the late 1980s. In one case, administrative structures were set up and attempts made to stimulate synergies among different regional operations. All three companies made efforts to collect information in the region and disseminate it among their subsidiaries. At Unilever, where information gathering was part of corporate procedure, the 12 operating companies in the region were encouraged to share intelligence by circulating reports. There was a feeling at headquarters that learning from past experiences and expertise should be documented and conserved. L'Oréal assiduously collects information on products and competitors' moves, relying on word-of-mouth and personal contacts to pass on expertise. Wella also routinely collects information and encourages the pooling of experience at its home training centre.

Informal networking

None of the three companies sought to standardize the operations of their Asian subsidiaries, or their degree of autonomy. Quite naturally, as their operations in the region expanded, they looked for synergies to reduce their costs and increase their clout, with regard to products, as well as to human and financial resources. They use informal networking between subsidiaries across the region to create a regional identity and to achieve synergies without building layers of bureaucracy.

Unilever, which has the longest presence in Asia of the three, has made the most progress in creating synergies, clearly departing from the usual way in which it runs its regional operations. Its various subsidiaries stimulate a multi-country approach to product launching or to better allocating resources. Regional task forces play an important role in transferring know-how and experience among subsidiaries; regional senior, product and marketing managers meet regularly to exchange information. Top management has encouraged this move, which provides more strategic information, as well as the adoption of 'best practice' throughout the region. The emphasis is increasingly on group-wide coordination, rather than on local autonomy. As country barriers crumble, the central group has actively applied a multi-country approach to organization and management. Comparisons and conclusions are made and transmitted via the network.

Wella has kept its tradition of strong regional coordination through regular regional conferences; a regional director based in Tokyo coordinates product marketing throughout the region.

Commitment through people

The strategies of all three companies were aimed at creating bodies of committed managers, rather than elaborate marketing plans. Unusually, they managed to build corps of talented managers able to generate local initiatives without diluting the corporate identity. Their efforts covered both internal recruitment of home-grown managers, sent out to Asia for three to five years, and the hiring, training and promotion of local managers to maintain continuity.

All three companies had difficulty deciding how many expatriate managers they should appoint, and for how long. In early days, it was hard to find managers of the required calibre; high flyers became available once the three companies had 'legitimized' Asia and recognized it as an important posting. In these companies, Asia is now seen as a good ladder for career advancement, and ex-Asia hands are increasingly prominent among top management.

As the three companies expanded their Asian business, they focused their efforts on attracting and retaining skilled local managers, whom they saw as crucial for sustained performance and future growth in the region. When Wella's first Asia director began to build the business in Japan, assembling a local team was one of his first priorities. He now attributes the success of the business to his ability to recruit such a team.

Since 1991, Unilever has offered special training programmes to attract skilled local managers. The Hong Kong subsidiary made a point of developing as many

467

Mandarin speakers as possible and 'roll them through China' to build a pool of Chinese managers for the future. At L'Oréal, corporate 'missionaries' have the task of recruiting and training local people.

In the long term, opportunities for promotion to top management positions will be important to retain local managers. The best way of training and developing them is an issue. Unilever, L'Oréal and Wella all have strong corporate cultures and operate through networks of personal contacts with a European business style. At Unilever, there seems to be a general acceptance that the style must change, and that Asian managers must be encouraged to 'do it their way'. The Asian director for Wella also believes that companies must build a different, hybrid corporate culture between Europe and Asia. L'Oréal, on the other hand, is determined to retain its culture, and believes it needs to have managers who are 'true company men', steeped in its particular strategic logic. It expects its local managers to be 'vaccinated' in this culture, first through training by its 'missionaries', later by attending courses in France.

Adapting management practices

One manager interviewed in the 1992 survey said: 'One problem that all our divisions face is the degree of difference in the Asian markets that they should take into consideration when formulating their strategies. Are these differences of substance or of context?' This encapsulates the dilemma between making a few adaptations to strategic thinking and approach, or completely changing it. All three companies balanced the need to retain their global core competence against transforming their regional practices. At Unilever, for example, when the Hong Kong subsidiary realized that the market in China did not develop according to the usual models, headquarters decided to re-evaluate its marketing strategy and reinterpret data.

One important issue is the conflict between global integration and local autonomy. How should the company manage the balance of power between the manager who focuses on country strategy, and the global manager who looks at broader product strategy? The three companies began with decentralized, autonomous operations, with a high degree of product adaptation to local market needs. Unilever, which has adapted to local markets to the greatest extent, changed its approach in the late 1980s; for instance, a Southeast Asian concept for personal products was created, and marginally adapted for use in other markets in the region.

The experience of these three companies shows that Asian strategies call for both substantive and contextual adaptation, at least during the learning phase. However, adjustments must be made in a way that does not endanger the company's core technological competence. Such a balance is difficult to achieve and escapes codification; it requires a high degree of flexibility both at headquarters and in the field.

Regional headquarters

Many multinational corporations have established regional headquarters (RHQs) in Asia Pacific. The motivation was either that the region was becoming too complex, too large and too far away to be handled from corporate headquarters, or that it was too different from other parts of the world. At a time when most companies are busy implementing delayering and lean management, RHQs are usually created specifically in order to implement very ambitious strategies for the region.

Regional headquarters actively manage integration and coordination across the region, and provide a link with the corporate centre; in this respect they differ from a representative office, a holding company set up for fiscal reasons, or a regional organizational unit which provides services and a regional infrastructure. Companies typically set up an RHQ when they feel that the benefits of regional integration are greater than the costs of setting up an additional organizational unit and those associated with the loss of independence (and responsiveness) for national units. These costs and benefits, however, are often difficult or impossible to measure.

Location and boundaries

The first move towards regionalization and establishing regional headquarters is to decide how many regions a multinational firm will need to manage global operations. Most MNCs have adopted a 'triadic' structure – Europe, Asia, the Americas – complemented by a fourth region which covers their home market. They usually adopt a pragmatic attitude in defining the boundaries of these regions: Australia and New Zealand may be part of Asia, South Africa may be attached to the European region.

Most multinationals try to operate with a single RHQ for the whole of Asia Pacific, although the broader the geographical area, the harder it is to ensure control. Some firms, however, have appointed regional vice-presidents responsible for sub-regions; others, such as Louis Vuitton Moët Hennessy, have divided Asia into two and have two RHQs instead of one. The cost of managing this additional complexity must be weighted against the potential costs of losing control with only one RHQ. Western multinationals in Asia must address a further issue: should major markets such as Japan, and, one day, China or India, be included into a region which otherwise consists of much smaller countries? The manager in charge of these large countries often prefers to report directly to headquarters. To address this issue, two points must be considered:

- the extent to which the specific country business is linked to the region (differences in technical standards, existence of regional customers);

- the importance of the country operation for the firm's global competitiveness and success.

Japan is seen as strategically important by many Western MNCs, and therefore reports directly to headquarters. Several pharmaceutical firms treat Japan separately from the rest of Asia, on an equal foot with major European countries and the USA; this closely parallels Japan's political membership of the G7. In the case of P&G and IBM, Japan remains closely linked with the region as lead country.

Most Western corporations locate their Asian RHQ in Asia; a few have it at headquarters, where its main task is to secure support for the region at the centre of the organization. Four criteria influence the decision of where to locate an RHQ:

- *Geographic location:* by and large, a central location is preferred; for this reason, few Asian RHQs will ever be based in Australia.

- *Convenience and infrastructure* have a direct impact on operations (facilities and staff, supporting services, legal environment, business mentality) and determine the well-being of expatriates (quality of life, language, schooling facilities).

- *Costs* – including taxation – are a consideration, although cheaper locations may have drawbacks in terms of convenience and infrastructure.

- *Proximity to business:* RHQs may be located either where the main market opportunities lie, or, conversely, where the business is small and vulnerable and needs support.

The role of regional headquarters

Regional headquarters have two main sets of roles:

- Strategy development and implementation, which are directed towards headquarters: budgeting and control, strategic stimulation, intelligence gathering, new business development, and more generally providing a channel for demands from local operations, and ensuring attention from headquarters in competition with other regions.

- Integrative, administrative roles more directly involved with local operations: pooling resources for greater efficiency and effectiveness; benchmarking and spreading best practices; coordinating activities across borders and business divisions. The aim here is to achieve synergies and consistency.

When a RHQ has been set up, its role is frequently challenged at other levels in the company by corporate, business, functional and national unit managers who feel that their power to influence their specific territory has been curtailed (Figure 8.3):

- Corporate managers fear that the region may go astray and therefore try to keep the RHQ in line with other arts of the world.

- Business managers argue that product specific knowledge counts more than regional market know-how.

- Functional managers believe that their expertise is best leveraged across the world without any modification;

- National unit managers maintain that their specific market is different, and is best left alone.

To overcome such resistance, some companies have assigned very senior executives to their RHQs: either main board members, or managers just one level

Figure 8.3   Challengers to the regional headquarters

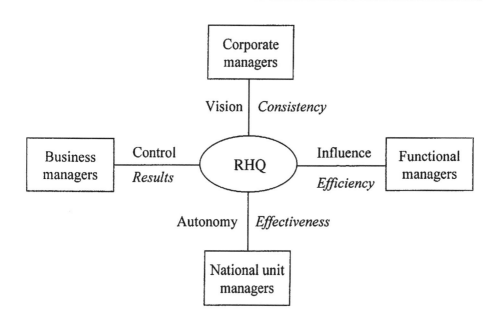

below. In practice, regional headquarters headed by less senior managers tend to be less effective. The actual leverage of an RHQ also depends on the overall organization: when the various businesses dominate at board level, at the expense of geographic entities, RHQs tend to be relatively weak.

There are several ways of structuring RHQs, both in terms of reporting lines and management. Most Western firms so far prefer hierarchically organized RHQs in which all managers in the region report to the regional director who in turn reports to headquarters. Normally reflecting the organizational logic of the firm in general, those directly reporting to the RHQs are either the heads of the divisions in the region (with a dotted line directly to headquarters), or heads of sub-regions. In some cases matrix structures representing divisions and sub-regions have been found useful. In all cases divisions and geographic managers will be supplemented by regional staff, such as a regional human resources manager and a regional finance manager.

Rarely will a multinational find a strategy and organization that equally suits all its businesses: some businesses will be better off pursuing a global, others a regional strategy. Unilever, for instance, ran its chemical division on a global basis while its main businesses (detergents, toiletries and food) were organized regionally.

Two alternative models of organization can be proposed for Asia:

■ The horizontal RHQ, which operates on a consensus basis, and where authority is, to some extent, dependent on the national units. In the extreme, the RHQ becomes the executive arm of the operating units.

- The virtual RHQ, which also relies on input from regional units, does not exist as a separate organization with its own premises and staff. RHQ responsibilities and functions are distributed among the national units, and its tasks are fulfilled by dispersed local managers who take on additional responsibilities as regional or functional managers.

This comes close to what is described as 'federalism' in organizations which combine the autonomy of individual organizational units with the scale benefits of coordination. The horizontal and virtual RHQs guarantee the integrity of the national units and unify their activities for common regional objectives. Local directors become local barons or local heroes, yet their individualism is moderated by collegial mechanisms which enforce close cooperation. Both models, however, lack mechanisms to solve conflicts: difficult or unpopular decisions are rarely made by consensus.

So far few multinationals have adopted a federalist organization in Asia, although some ask their managers to 'wear two hats' – for instance, to work for a local subsidiary, or functional group, or business division, as well as at an RHQ. 'Double-hatting' is harder to achieve for recent regional organizations: the more senior managers in the region should already know and trust each other, and methods of cooperation must be well established. With time, however, an increasing number of Western multinationals can be expected to take this route.

Regional headquarters as change agents

There are three main stages of expansion for multinational firms in Asia Pacific (Figure 8.4):

Figure 8.4   The foreign firm in Asia

Stage	Explorer	Strategic Investor	Global Consolidator
Objectives	• Exploit local opportunities	• Build regional presence • Pre-empt	• Balance global portfolio
Operations	• Limited • Self-contained	• Regional linkages • **RHQs**	• Global linkages
Commitment to the region	• Ambivalent	• Very high	• High

■ As *explorers*, they seek to exploit local opportunities. Their operations are limited and self-contained; they are directed from headquarters, whose commitment to the region is ambivalent.

■ The next stage is that of *strategic investor*: this is where many Western firms are now in Asia, after the need for a more systematic and regional approach became apparent in the 1980s and 90s. RHQs were set up to channel initiatives and turn them into action. Founding an RHQ increases attention to Asia, replaces opportunistic activities with a more systematic regional strategy, takes power away from headquarters and the national units, and is a reflection of a much higher level of commitment to the region.

■ A further step, which few Western multinationals in Asia Pacific have taken as yet, will take them to the *consolidation* stage. Once a sufficient regional presence and efficient regional linkages are in place, the RHQ acts as a decentralized headquarters and enjoys more power. However, as globalization becomes a major driving force, the RHQ's independence starts fading away, and power moves back to the HQ.

People skills

Surveys of Western companies operating in Asia Pacific usually identify human resource management as one of the most difficult challenges. While problems differ from country to country, there are some key strategic and managerial issues that Western firms will have to deal with throughout the region.

Human resource development of local managers

Recruiting local staff

In most Asia Pacific countries, recruiting local staff is problematic, either because of a shortage of qualified technicians and managers (as in ASEAN countries except the Philippines), or because locals are reluctant to work for foreign companies (in Japan).

Scarcity

China has perhaps the most severe shortages of adequate personnel, particularly in managerial positions. Mao's Cultural Revolution in the 1960s completely disrupted secondary and university education. Countries which encourage vocational training, such as Singapore, usually have curricula high in theory with little practical content. Where business education is available, students tend to opt for soft disciplines such as marketing rather than accountancy or engineering. Throughout the developing countries, local universities now offer formal business training, including MBAs, but much of it remains rather academic.

There is a significant gap between the business qualifications of Asians in their twenties or early thirties and those in their forties. Young Asian managers tend to have a solid business education, but lack experience, while senior managers often don't have relevant education or international experience. This problem is acute in China, and to some extent Indonesia.

In order to overcome this problem of scarcity, companies can resort to:

- *Image building* by promoting the company in local university campuses and host communities. Grants and arts or sports sponsorship help to build a positive corporate image.

- Asians highly value *training* opportunities. Large Western companies reputed for their training policies, such as P&G or Shell, find it easier to recruit skilled personnel. Smaller companies which cannot afford such programmes should use personal relationships, teamwork and informal or personalized recruitment.

- A *consistent policy of career development* will establish the reputation of the firm and help recruitment efforts.

Reluctance to work for foreign firms

This problem is particularly acute in Japan, where less than one per cent of the workforce is employed at foreign firms. Most foreign companies are perceived as small and unable to offer attractive career opportunities. Moreover, Japanese managers traditionally do not change employers: those who join foreign firms are effectively forsaking the possibility of working for a mainstream Japanese firm later on. To palliate this disadvantage, foreign companies can resort to three strategies:

- recruit Japanese women;

- offer higher salaries than comparable Japanese firms;

- offer more interesting jobs: foreign postings, working with more advanced technologies, accelerated career paths.

However, these incentives have limits. The answer to recruitment problems is a constant, long-term effort to offer challenging and stable careers.

Retaining local staff

Job hopping is a serious problem in Hong Kong and in some sectors in Singapore, Thailand and Indonesia. Staff leave because they feel that the foreign firm does not offer opportunities for future development, or that compensation for local personnel is low compared with expatriates. Companies which take a long-term view of personnel development, such as Shell or IBM, have fewer retention problems. To retain local staff, foreign firms should:

- *Act fairly.* A thorny issue is the disparity in compensation between local and expatriate personnel, especially if they have the same qualifications. Some

Asian subsidiaries will employ a local engineer with the same degree – in some cases from the same school – as an expatriate engineer. If the disparity in pay is too great, local managers will spread the word that the Western company is not for the locals.

■ *Be tactful in granting rewards and punishments.* Punishment should always take place in private to avoid causing an employee to lose face. Individual rewards should not get too much public emphasis, unless they are part of a company ceremony; the public reward of a team performance, however, is welcome. Local personnel usually prefer to be rewarded for their loyalty and honesty than on quantifiable performance criteria.

■ *Create a sense of belonging.* Asians generally appreciate a family-style work atmosphere, and in nearly all Asian countries superiors are expected to take an active role in solving personal problems: what would be seen as interfering in the West is welcome in Asia as a mark of benevolence and caring. Paternalism is viewed positively.

■ *Have long-term human resources policies.* A consistent, long-term career development policy must show commitment to integrating and promoting local staff. Multinational firms must convince local managers that opportunities are open to them in the firm, and that, with the right skills, they can rise to join the core of international managers.

Expatriate management

Common expatriate problems: motivation and performance

According to survey of 198 European expatriates in Southeast Asia, expatriate managers are more motivated by the challenge of the job than by salary benefits, personal and professional development, or long-term career opportunities. Many Western managers still see a position in Asia as a dead end or retirement posting; their main concern is to reintegrate the main track, and their chief fear is of being forgotten. For certain expatriates, cultural and geographical distances exacerbate a sense of loneliness.

Respondents to the survey said they derived most satisfaction from the responsibilities of managing a business unit, and from feeling independent or autonomous. However, autonomy can have negative connotations, if it means that corporate headquarters undervalues or ignores the subsidiary. According to the respondents, the main sources of failure were the inability to adapt and cope with the job, or the family (or spouse's) inability to adapt to the host country.

Expatriate skills

The kind of expatriate management skills required depends very much on the individual Asian country's stage of development. Table 8.1 illustrates the kind of skills needed by expatriate managers. Figure 8.5 shows different profiles according to the

Table 8.1 Individual skills for expatriate managers

Cultural skills	Relationship Skills	Political skills	Professional skills
Understanding of, and sensitivity, to etiquette, social norms, religions, ethnic characteristics	Ability to build and maintain a network of contacts	Ability to understand the subtleties of the local political context	Knowledge and expertise in product technology
Knowledge and reference to arts and literature	Ability to call on 'friends' when needed	Ability to get close to leaders and high ranking officials	Ability to demonstrate logically the characteristics and performances of products and processses
Language skills can help	Ability to negotiate		
	Leadership and paternalism		

Figure 8.5   Different profiles of expatriates

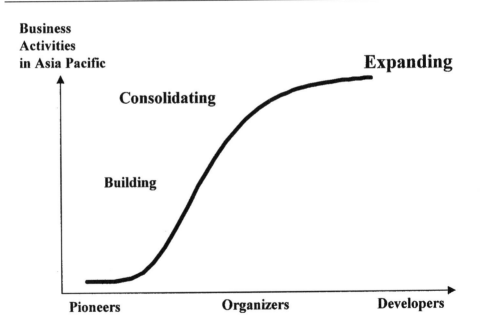

stage of development of the company in the region. The ability to build and maintain relationships is essential almost everywhere in Asia:

- In the early stages of development in Asia, a Western company should have a *pioneering* or *missionary* generation of expatriates with cultural and political skills.

- Once basic contact networks have been established and the Western firm has started to gain experience, *traditional managerial and technical skills* become more important.

- At a later stage, expatriates from head office are gradually replaced by *locals*, or by rotating international managers.

- In the final stages of a Western firm's establishment in the region, it is no longer appropriate to speak of expatriates, but of *international staff.*

Cultural assimilation

In the old colonial days, some Westerners who went to the 'Far East' as expatriates or soldiers fell in love with the local people and culture, and progressively 'went native'. Such extreme assimilation presents the danger of losing credibility, both with local personnel and business partners, and with the parent company. Although Western firms should look for expatriate managers with a degree of cultural sensitivity, they should prevent extreme assimilation through rigorous rotation (except at market entry stage, when time is needed to build relationships.) The length of expatriate tenure will usually vary in line with the need to build relationships.

Cultural differentiation and integration

The religious and civic traditions of Confucianism, Buddhism, Islam and Hinduism have a deep impact on Asian entrepreneurial culture, affecting government policies, social norms, consumption patterns, business transactions, management practices and labour relations. Table 8.2 shows enduring cultural traits that are found across Asia. To organize and manage people in the region, Western managers must thoroughly understand these traits.

Group versus individual identity

In most Asian cultures, the individual is deeply attached to his social group, beginning with the core and extended family. This reflects the monolithic organization of Asian societies, where all organizations, including the state, are seen as an extension of the family. In Asia, a person's membership in a group matters more than individual identity. Compliance with group norms is expected and individualistic behaviour is discouraged. Individual transactions are often based on group membership. This has implications for human resource management: expatriate managers who encourage competition among local staff or reward individual rather than team performance may encounter resistance. This does not mean that individual performance should not be rewarded: in Hong Kong and Singapore, it is expected to earn a pay-off.

Conflict avoidance

Most Asian cultures systematically avoid the overt expression of conflict. Buddhist, Confucian and Islamic societies value harmony, even if it is only superficial. In stark

Table 8.2 A summary of Asian cultural traits

GROUP REFERENCE

- Group belonging is asserted before individual instinct
- Compliance with group norms is expected
- Individualistic behaviour is condemned
- Individual transactions are based on intra-group affiliation leading to networking

CONFLICT AVOIDANCE

- Overt conflicts are perceived as highly disruptive
- Social etiquette prohibits the manifestation of anger
- Harmony is sought

IMPORTANCE OF FACE

- Most societies are regulated by shame, as opposed to guilt
- Public shaming is unacceptable and can lead to revenge
- Stress is often translated by a smile

RESPECT FOR AUTHORITY and SENIORITY

- Leaders are expected to be benevolent and virtuous
- Formal authority is not openly discussed
- High social distance, even in societies where wealth is evenly distributed
- Age brings a fatherly aura

PATERNALISM

- Leaders are expected to be attentive to the personal life of employees

RESPECT FOR ACADEMIC CREDENTIALS

- Hunger for diplomas

ATTITUDE TOWARD WOMEN

- Certain Asian societies do not value the professional role of women

SUPERSTITION

- Belief in cosmology or supernatural forces

EXTENDED FAMILY and NEPOTISM

- Family support is considered the norm
- As an extension of the family support structure, organizations are seen as providers of social welfare
- It is proper to give preference to family members in business dealings

contrast with Western culture, which often encourages overt conflict, avoiding open conflict or the expression of anger is crucial to the reputation of an Asian organization. In Asian cultures, particularly the Chinese, the opposition of elements is seen as symbiotic rather than conflictive: opposites coexist and in some cases cooperate (Yin and Yang). Asian cultures favour indirect conflict resolution (for example, via a third party, or via intense private discussion and lobbying). If an issue is seen as potentially conflictive, public debate will be avoided.

Expressing anger in public is demeaning and undermines one's authority. However, the need to maintain a facade of harmony can cause unexpressed tensions to escalate into accumulated frustration and even violence. The Indonesian have a phrase for this – going amok. In the business context, this could be an unexpected strike or a sudden manifestation of bizarre or violent behaviour. Dormant conflicts must be addressed, although privately and indirectly.

Another way of avoiding conflict is to express negation by making a non-committal answer. In Indonesia, 'maybe' is used to express disagreement rather than a blunt, categorical 'no'. This has the advantage of protecting the feelings and reputation (face) of the other person.

The importance of face

The concept of face – an individual's public reputation *vis-à-vis* his family, company, and society – has important implications for management (Figure 8.6). There is a deep taboo against the public shaming of employees, and a Western manager should never discipline an employee in front of his peers. Negative feedback should be shared with caution, always in private. Face-saving has other implications: Asians blame their mistakes on external causes, or smile to mask their embarrassment. The Chinese regard asking for help as an admission of incompetence; when a problem arises, they try to solve it themselves.

Figure 8.6   Asian employees and conflict resolution

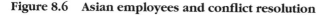

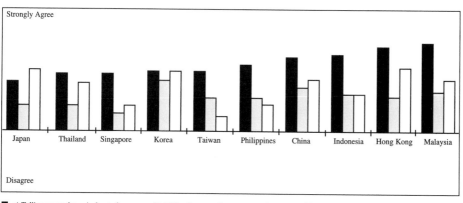

a) Telling an employee in front of others that he has made a mistake is not acceptable

b) Employees and managers prefer to tell stories rather than admit they made a mistake

c) Local employees avoid telling their boss that they think he is wrong

Respect for authority

Formal authority must be respected in Asia; this is part of harmony. Contesting authority is perceived as rebellious, and challenging one's boss is improper. Expatriate managers new to Asia are often perplexed to receive consistently positive feedback despite simmering tensions or an explosive social and political climate. When the problem comes to the surface, generally in a very extreme and unpleasant fashion, and the Western manager asks, 'Why didn't you tell me?', the answer is often an embarrassed smile. A bad leader is corrected or contested through indirect means: pressure directed towards a third party, anonymous letters, passive behaviour and resistance camouflaged with excuses, among others. Feedback is often cryptic and the Western manager must learn how to decode and interpret indirect signs of discontent.

Respect for seniority

This trait is more pronounced in Asia than in other parts of the world. Age is supposed to bring wisdom and gives a natural right to command. Local personnel is more comfortable with mature, middle-aged superiors than with younger ones. This does not mean that young managers are barred from the top: however, they must demonstrate a higher degree of technical competence. One advantage younger Western managers often have is a better command of the local language.

Paternalism

Political and corporate leaders in Asia are expected to embody religious or family values. In terms of corporate leadership and human resource management, employees often expect benevolence and a degree of attentiveness to their personal life and welfare far greater than would be expected, or even deemed acceptable, in the West.

Reverence for academic credentials

Academic credentials and diplomas bring respect but also raise expectations. This is an expression of the traditional respect for education that prevails in Asian societies. It is easier for Western firms to retain their Asian managers if they give them the opportunity to acquire these credentials. Local staff highly value training seminars in reputable foreign institutions.

Attitudes towards women

Although many Asian societies are deeply patriarchal, women, especially of a certain age, command respect. There are advantages for Western firms in hiring or sending Western women to Asia as expatriate managers. In China and Japan, Western women, simply because they are foreigners, are often treated with more respect than local women in similar positions of authority. Korea is an extreme example of male chauvinism, with virtually no women in high management.

Superstition

Traditional mystical or superstitious practices in China and Southeast Asia may surprise the unprepared Westerner. Even in more industrialized societies such as Hong Kong, Taiwan and Singapore, traditional practices still prevail. *Feng shui*, the divination and interpretation of landscape features and sacred sites, is widely practised; real estate purchases and building sites must be approved by a geomancer. Western expatriate managers should be aware that their Asian staff and colleagues see this as an important procedure.

Extended family and nepotism

Nepotism and corruption are a particularly sensitive issue. Due to the importance of the extended family, nepotism, far from being perceived as corrupt behaviour, is part of the moral obligation to support one's family. This means that local managers will often give preference to relatives when hiring, purchasing or contracting. Pressure from government officials, who see it as their duty to place family members in key positions in joint ventures with Western companies, are difficult to resist; they are also difficult to explain to Western corporate headquarters. This is slowly changing, and in Japan and Singapore nepotism has disappeared from modern corporations.

More difficult to handle is the practice of giving commissions to employees who buy services or products. This internal corruption may undermine a Western company's efforts to instil a culture of quality, openness and fairness. Foreign managers need to understand that the borderline between gifts and graft is often blurred. However, if the Western company provides an adequate and fair compensation scheme, it should not tolerate such practices.

References

Adler, Nancy, 'International Dimensions of Organizational Behavior', *PSW*, New York, 1987.

A.T. Kearney Inc., *Trade and Investment in Japan: The Current Environment*, Tokyo, June 1991.

Bartlett, Christopher and Sumantra Goshal, *Managing Across Borders: The Transnational Solution*, Harvard Business School Press, Boston, 1989.

Blackwell, N., J.-P Bizet, P. Child and D. Hensley, 'Creating European organizations that work', *The McKinsey Quarterly*, vol. 2, 1992, pp. 31–43.

Business International, *Managers for Asia Pacific: Recruitment and Development Strategies*, Report No. Q107, Hong Kong, March 1991.

Conway, Bryony, 'Expatriate Effectiveness: A study of European Expatriates in South East Asia', London Guildhall University, London, 1994.

Debroux, Philippe, 'Human Resource Management in Foreign Companies in Japan', paper presented at the 8th LVMH conference, INSEAD Euro-Asia Centre, 5–6 February 1993.

Gersten, Martine Cardel, 'Intercultural Competence and Expatriates', *The International Journal of Human Resource Management*, Vol. 1, No. 3, December 1990.

Goshal, S. and N. Nohria, 'Horses for Courses: Organizational Forums for Multinational Corporations', *Sloan Management Review*, Vol. 35, No. 2, 1992, pp. 23–35.

Handy, Charles. 'Balancing Corporate Power: A New Federalist Paper', *Harvard Business Review*, Vol. 70, No. 6, 1992, pp. 59–72.

Hiltrop, Jean Marie and Maddy Janssens, 'Expatriation: Challenges and Recommendations', *European Management Journal*, Vol. 8, No. 1, March 1990.

Lasserre, Philippe, 'Regional headquarters: The Spearhead for Asia Pacific Markets', *Long Range Planning*, Vol. 29, No. 1, 1996, pp. 30–37.

Lasserre, Philippe, and Charlotte Butler, 'Strategic Development in Asia', paper presented at the 8th LVMH conference, INSEAD Euro-Asia Centre, 5–6 February 1993.

Lasserre, Philippe and Jocelyn Probert, 'Human Resource Management in Asia Pacific: A Strategic Challenge', *Strategic Change,* Vol. 5, 1994, pp. 75–88.

Malnight, Thomas W. and Michael Yoshino, *Otis Pacific Asia Operations*, (A), (B), Harvard Business School, case study Nos. 9-393-009 and 9-393-010, 1992.

Morrison, A.J., D.A. Ricks and K. Roth, 'Globalization versus Regionalization: Which Way for the Multinational?', *Organizational Dynamics*, Winter, 1991, 17–29.

Prahalad, C.K and Yves Doz, *The Multinational Mission: Balancing Local Demands and Global Vision*, Free Press, New York, 1987.

Roth, Kendall, and Allen Morrison, 'Implementing Global Strategies: Characteristics of Subsidiaries Mandates', *Journal of International Business Studies*, Fourth quarter 1992, pp. 715–735.

Schütte, Hellmut, 'Strategy and Organisation: Challenges for the European MNC's in Asia', *European Management Journal*, Vol. 15, No. 4, 1997, pp. 436–445.

Schütte, Hellmut, 'Henkel's Strategy for Asia Pacific', *Long Range Planning*, Vol. 28, No. 1, 1995, 95–103.

Schütte, Hellmut, 'Between Headquarters and Subsidiaries: The RHQ Solution', in: *Multinational Corporate Evolution and Subsidiary Development*, editors Birkinshaw, Julian and Hood, Neil, Houndmills/New York, Macmillan, 1998, pp. 102–136.

Case 24

*This case was prepared by Hellmut Schütte, Affiliate Professor of
International Management at INSEAD. It is intended to be used as a basis
for class discussion rather than to illustrate either effective or ineffective
handling of an administrative situation. Copyright © 1994 INSEAD-Euro-
Asia Centre, Fontainebleau, France*

Henkel Asia-Pacific

It was 9 January 1994. Ulrich Lehner leaned back in his business class seat on a Lufthansa flight from Hong Kong back to Germany. He had lost count of the number of flights he had made over the last two years as chairman of Henkel Asia-Pacific Ltd. 'Too many', his wife would say. 'Not enough,' he thought to himself, given the tasks the board in Düsseldorf had assigned him. In November 1991 he had gone to Asia to set up a regional headquarters in Asia that would strengthen Henkel's position there and to develop new ideas and strategies for the company in the fastest growing region of the world.

The office had been established with a small team of highly dedicated Germans who hoped to make Henkel grow as fast as possible in the coming years. A comprehensive strategy for the company's future in Asia had been developed and adopted in 1992. The first steps toward rationalizing Henkel's diverse activities in the region were taken and a large number of new ventures initiated, mainly in China. Within the company, Asia had moved from relative obscurity into the limelight.

The president and most other board members had travelled to Asia and supported Lehner's work. A recent visit of the supervisory board chairman to China had convinced him that Henkel should spare no money to increase its exposure in Asia. Back in Düsseldorf most of the diversified chemical firm's divisions and strategic business units (SBUs) had suddenly begun to develop new ideas for Asia. On the corporate level the company, after a recent spate of acquisitions, had declared Asia to be the only priority investment area apart from East Germany and Eastern Europe. Following the launch of new projects, expectations about the rewards to be had from the Asia Pacific region had risen significantly. The 1992 strategy paper had targeted an 80% increase of sales within five years. In the meantime this figure had been substantially increased.

For Lehner, leaving Hong Kong this time was not merely a routine trip back to Germany; it was his final departure from Asia as the chairman of the regional office. He was returning to headquarters to take over an important function in the corporate finance department, where he had spent most of his life before coming out to Asia. The company had already announced that he would replace the current finance director on the board of managing directors following the latter's retirement within the next year or two. In fact, this decision was public knowledge within the company at the time of Lehner's appointment to the Asia Pacific post.

Lehner's successor as chairman of Henkel's Asian operations, Mr. Veit Müller-Hillebrand, had already been posted to Hong Kong. Both Lehner and his successor had spent sufficient time together to ensure a smooth transition. Together they had visited all subsidiaries and met with most of the company's important contacts and joint venture partners.

While Asia had gained visibility in Henkel and a good structure had been put in place, Lehner was not sure whether his successor's job would be any easier than his had been. Had the SBUs and the local subsidiaries really accepted the need for a regional strategy? Was the regional office already sufficiently staffed? And how far had the company gone with the implementation of new organizational initiatives and the realization of the new joint ventures in China? Had adequate attention been paid to the growing local competition and to competitors from the USA, Europe and Japan? With China absorbing most of the regional office's resources, had Japan been neglected? What would happen to the regional push if China turned inward again and all the new investments had to be written off?

THE HENKEL GROUP

Henkel was founded in 1876 as a bleaching powder company that over time grew from Düsseldorf, Germany, into a conglomerate of more than 200 companies operating in 56 countries and with business relationships with more than 100 other countries. In 1993 the company recorded a turnover of DM13.9 billion and a profit of DM375 million.

Of the parent company Henkel KGaA the Henkel family owns 100% of the ordinary shares (with voting rights) and one-third of the preferred shares (without voting rights, but entitled to a higher dividend). The other shares are widely scattered and quoted on various stock exchanges. The family is represented on the supervisory board, as are the workers, management personnel, and bankers. Konrad Henkel is the honorary chairman of both the supervisory board and the shareholders' committee. No one in the Henkel family, however, is a member of the management board that runs the group. The management board consists of the president and CEO, five members (each in charge of a business division), a finance director, a director in charge of research and development (R&D), and a personnel director.

Henkel considers itself a specialist in applied chemistry, selling 11,000 products worldwide to industrial customers and end consumers. It is the world's largest producer of oleo chemicals made from natural fats and oils, of metal treatment products, and of adhesives. Research and development are important for the company, which spends DM400 million annually on this sector. All nine managing directors held PhDs, though not necessarily in the natural sciences, and all had risen within the company's ranks. In recent years, Henkel researchers have laid major emphasis on environmental protection issues. This emphasis has made Henkel a leading firm in the industry's switch to the biodegradable surfactants that serve as raw materials for liquid and powder detergents.

In Europe Henkel ranks among the top companies for detergents, cleaning agents, personal care and cosmetic products, and competes head on with Unilever, Procter & Gamble, L'Oreal, Colgate, and others. Persil, a universal detergent launched in 1907 as one of the first branded products in the world has remained Henkel's largest single product and the market leader in Germany. (The brand, however, is owned by Unilever in the UK and France.)

Henkel's product range is split into five divisions and one separate unit, a joint venture with Ecolab in the area of institutional hygiene. In the early 1990s the divisions were further subdivided into SBUs (see Table CS24.1).

Henkel has substantial shareholdings in Degussa in Germany, and in Clorox, Ecolab, and Loctite in the USA, but no direct influence on the operational management of any of these firms.

During the last 10 years Henkel's growth came to a large extent from a very high number of acquisitions, especially in Europe and the USA. Henkel had also been quick to move into Eastern Europe after the collapse of communism. Eleven joint ventures in Russia, Poland, Hungary, the CSFR and Slovenia in 1992 already produced sales of DM500 million in 1992. In this year, the last major acquisition – of Barnängen from Nobel of Sweden – boosted Henkel's position in the cosmetics' field, but put some strain on the company's finances. Henkel's conservative equity ratio had deteriorated to less than the 40% that had been the company's long-standing golden rule. While Henkel management announced the re-establishment of the ratio over the medium term, it did not categorically rule out further acquisitions.

Henkel's diversified product mix had by and large shielded its profit performance from cyclical swings. Profitability was seen as acceptable, but was below that of Unilever or Procter & Gamble in terms of return on investment. This was one of the reasons why Henkel had recently launched a 'cost chase' across all parts of the company. On the personnel side a 'cultural evolution' had been launched to change the conservative and paternalistic attitudes then particularly pervasive in Germany. This was considered necessary in order to make the employees more customer- and performance-oriented, to reduce hierarchy, and to streamline the organization. In line with Henkel's long-standing mission of being an attractive and supportive employer, the company avoided large-scale reductions in the number of personnel – which became common in Germany in 1993 – and opted instead for more socially acceptable measures. At the end of 1993, Henkel employed 40,500 people worldwide, of which 16,700 were employed in Germany.

Table CS24.1 Business divisions

Business	Percentage of sales	Number of SBUs
Chemical products	28	14
Metal chemicals	5	1
Industrial adhesives and technical consumer products	16	8
Cosmetics/toiletries	10	4
Detergents/household cleaners	31	4
Institutional hygiene	10	joint venture
Total	100	31

Case 24

Table CS24.2 Henkel group sales 1993 (total DM13.9 billion): shares by region

Region	Sales by location of customer %	Production by location of company %
Germany	29	35
Rest of Europe	48	47
North America	12	12
Latin America	4	3
Africa, Asia, Australia	7	5
World	100	100

Germany remains Henkel's most important market, although other European countries such as France, Italy and Spain have gained importance. Henkel's US operations which included Nopco, Emery, and Parker+Amchem represent its second-largest single market. Table CS24.2 shows a regional sales breakdown according to the location of customers and the Henkel company that delivers the products.

Given the stagnation in Europe and the prospects of slow growth in the Americas, Henkel became increasingly aware that it had to significantly boost its exposure in Asia if it was to continue to grow and prosper.

HENKEL IN ASIA

Henkel's earliest activities in Asia date back to the 19th century when the company's founder, Fritz Henkel, started to trade with China. Yet it was only after the Second World War that the company began to invest in the region, though its expansion remained limited in comparison with the growth of activities in Europe and the USA.

In the 1980s Henkel found itself involved in a large number of mostly small operations in Asia Pacific. Some of these were only sales offices, while others also had manufacturing activities. Some subsidiaries (in Henkel jargon called 'VU' (*verbundene Unternehmen*)) were 100%-owned, while others had been set up as joint ventures. In addition, Henkel had concluded a number of licensing contracts with a variety of partners in Asia, and certain businesses were represented by agents and distributors, often operating in parallel with the local Henkel organization. This situation was the result of the SBUs, or their organizational predecessors in Düsseldorf pursuing independent strategies in the countries concerned.

The situation became somewhat confusing when Henkel acquired companies that had a number of subsidiaries in Asia and sold its institutional hygiene business in the region. These moves forced Henkel's local operations to integrate certain new businesses while letting go of other parts. This process was not always easy, due to the existence of local joint venture partners.

The overwhelming majority of Henkel's business in Asia was conducted by the chemicals division, and all of the 10 country managers in Asia reported directly to Mr Dieter Ambros, the board member in charge of the chemical division. As Henkel had introduced a matrix organization, Ambros also had responsibility for the regions of Asia and North America.

In 1985 Ambros sent Mr Leonhardt to Singapore to open a regional office that would ensure that the company stayed in closer touch with the region. The office consisted only of Leonhardt and his secretary. Though Leonhardt was Ambros' 'man on the spot', he did not report to him directly, but to one of the directors in Düsseldorf working with Ambros. Leonhardt's task was to represent headquarters in the ASEAN subsidiaries and the operations in Australia and New Zealand. Japan was not considered part of the region and the operations in Taiwan, Korea and Hong Kong/China were not deemed in need of any special attention. Leonhardt took care of the subsidiaries' board meetings, looked after the joint venture partners, and tried to coordinate activities of general concern to the VUs. His involvement in day-to-day operations was limited, not least by long-serving expatriate country managers, who jealously guarded control over their area of responsibility. In 1989 Leonhardt returned to Düsseldorf and the regional office was closed.

During Leonhardt's tenure in Singapore the idea was born and implemented to strengthen product development, adaptation, and technical services in the region. A number of specialists were brought in from Germany for extended periods to support the sales activities in selected countries. The chemical division carried costs for these experts, but their services were not always appreciated. The exception was the Thai subsidiary, to which most of the technicians were assigned and which therefore benefited considerably from their efforts. The last specialist was recalled to Düsseldorf in 1993.

From 1989 on the Asian region was again entirely coordinated from Germany, by the chemicals division, where Ambros was in charge. But the growth in the region, increasing competitive pressures from both local and international rivals, and the need to integrate certain activities regionally rather than linking individual Asian operations with headquarters, made the task of coordination more demanding. It had also become clear that the Asia Pacific region offered excellent opportunities for other businesses as well; the adhesives and the metal treatment divisions, for example, had made major inroads into certain markets. As a result the chemical division was less dominant in the region.

In the fall of 1989, awareness was growing within Henkel that individual SBUs or countries were doing well in Asia, but that few synergies and hardly any trade existed between the various businesses and subsidiaries. In 1989, Henkel achieved a turnover of DM354 million in the region with a profit ratio that was above the company's average. The Henkel board decided to develop an overall Asia strategy and hired McKinsey consultants to lay the groundwork by conducting a study of opportunities in the region. In defining the region, Japan was excluded, since it required the development of a separate strategy. Henkel nevertheless recognized the influence of Japan and Japanese competitors on the region.

The study was carried out and its results presented in 1990, a year during which the attention of German industry had been drawn toward East Germany and Eastern Europe following the fall of the Berlin Wall and the re-unification of Germany. McKinsey was very positive, almost bullish, on the potential of the region for Henkel, noting that the company was presently under-represented

Case 24

in the Asia Pacific region compared to its competitors. The McKinsey consultants, who felt that with better coordination and minimal additional investment substantial profits could be achieved, recommended that Henkel take a closer look at downstream (i.e. branded consumer) products. Up until that point, this type of product had only been sold in very limited quantities in the region.

The McKinsey study identified Taiwan and Korea as the countries with the best short-term potential for Henkel, and Thailand and Indonesia as those with the best long-term potential. China was considered to be of 'less interest to Henkel', though the study reported that the country '…could be of great interest in the long run'.

The study recommended improved technical support (in the form of extensive product adaptation by qualified chemists in several new centres of competence) as well as increased local production (on account of imports from Germany). McKinsey also felt that a number of partnerships needed to be re-evaluated and renegotiated. Finally, the establishment of a regional organization was proposed as a means of overcoming 'the lack of decision-making competence in, and isolation of, the individual VUs…'

During the months that followed, discussions in Düsseldorf focused on the structure of this regional organization, particularly on the question of whether or not to include Japan in Henkel's definition of the Asia Pacific region. In terms of turnover Japan represented by far the largest individual country with about DM150 million. Japan had the best technology, the most critical customers, and faced a very specific problem: the existence of a brand new, expensive and dedicated plant producing sophisticated chemicals for which demand had disappeared.

In Malaysia, the second largest Henkel country in Asia, a new investment in a major fatty alcohol facility in joint venture with Japanese, Korean and local partners was in the pipeline. Some of the output would find its way to other Henkel operations in Asia, including Japan. And opportunities in China appeared too appealing to pass up. After numerous visits by Henkel managers from a variety of SBUs the first projects became more concrete.

In the fall of 1991, the Henkel board appointed Lehner as head of the Asia Pacific region and sent him to Hong Kong to set up a regional headquarters. He was also asked to develop concrete proposals for a regional strategy.

ESTABLISHING HENKEL ASIA – PACIFIC LTD (HAP)

On 1 November 1991 Henkel announced the establishment of a new legal entity as a management holding with headquarters in Hong Kong. In a press release the holding group's objectives were defined as: the centralization of management; the intensification of advisory services; and the re-enforcement of the management of subsidiaries and joint ventures. Lehner became chairman of this holding and all the heads of the subsidiaries reported directly to him, including Japan. The region consisted of 12 countries – Australia, China, Hong Kong, Indonesia, Japan, Malaysia, New Zealand, Philippines, Singapore, South Korea, Taiwan, and Thailand. 1,600 people were employed in 15 subsidiaries that generated sales of about DM450 million (see Exhibit CS24.1).

A small team of German managers surveyed Henkel's activities in the region and generated ideas for the future. Then, in July 1992, Henkel Asia Pacific (HAP) invited board members and other key managers from Düsseldorf and the heads of the subsidiaries in the region for a presentation of Henkel's Asia Pacific strategy.

The presentation was based on the assumption of continued high growth and a tendency towards further integration in the region. Given the importance of Japan in the region, due consideration would be given to that country. On the other hand, China was seen as the country with the greatest potential for expansion. A HAP assessment of the various markets in Asia is shown in Exhibit CS24.2.

As far as new ideas for the various product groups and SBUs were concerned, the HAP team stressed that no separate Asian product strategies would be developed, and that instead they would be considered in the framework of global strategies generated by the SBUs. In fact, all the product-related ideas presented during the meeting had been discussed in advance with both the product groups as well as with the country managers concerned. Not surprisingly, the meeting went very well and most of the proposals were accepted in one form or another.

By classifying their proposals into 'Must do', 'Option 1', and 'Option 2', the team established a priority list. 'Must do' issues mainly concerned the various ill-defined areas of responsibilities that needed to be sorted out before any proper strategy could be implemented. 'Must do' issues also dealt with some pending operational issues. 'Option 1' was concerned with the generation of internal growth, and 'Option 2' with the opportunities for external growth through acquisitions and partnerships.

Most attention was paid to organizational changes and functional strategies. The main points are summarized below.

Organization

1. Business teams will be formed per SBU with members from Europe, the USA, and the Asia Pacific region. These teams will be in charge of coordinating and leading the regional business activities in the specific product category. 'Asian Desks' will be established in some SBUs staffed by managers concentrating their efforts entirely on the region. Twelve of those managers would be immediately assigned to these tasks and become members of the business teams. As a rule, these managers would not be newly hired Asia experts, but rather consist of existing staff within the SBUs who had dealt with Asia in the past, though not exclusively. The business teams would have to look after marketing strategies, resolve conflicts between competing subsidiaries (VUs), allocate technical support and production facilities, etc.

2. The SBUs and HAP would share responsibility for product strategy and profit. They were also in charge of strategy implementation and control. By arguing that profits result from sales to the customer, as opposed to sales from Henkel headquarters, or Henkel VUs to another VU, transfer pricing disputes were to be minimized. The respective VUs would have to implement the SBU strategy, optimize production capacity, maximize contribution through active marketing and sales, and minimize their costs.

3. The various partnerships had to be streamlined and, whenever possible, consolidated

Case 24

under one roof. In some countries wholly owned subsidiaries and joint ventures (both called VUs) existed side-by-side with independent agents selling Henkel products and manufacturers under license to produce other Henkel product lines. The ideal would be to build 'Henkel clones' over a period of time.

Manufacturing

A regional production system had to be established. While some of the existing facilities were under-utilized, production capacity in Asia was inadequate in certain product categories. Economies of scale required the rationalization of some facilities. A first regional production meeting would have to be scheduled and a regional production audit commissioned.

Accounting/Finance

In order to compare costs across the region, Henkel had to introduce a unified and standardized accounting and reporting system that would also facilitate transfer pricing discussions. In the past, the independence of the VUs had led to a variety of different software and hardware systems. Under the leadership of HAP these would gradually be standardized. In addition, there was a call for the optimization of the financial structure of some of the VUs. Better management information systems would improve opportunities for global and regional purchasing.

Technical service

There was widespread recognition that the provision of professional technical services was essential to boost sales in the region. Nevertheless, the establishment of a large regional technical centre was not recommended, since this was likely to lead to a duplication of efforts. All VUs would have to set up technical service facilities sufficient for their own local needs. Moreover, regional centres of technical competence would be established. Japan, for example, would take the lead in chemicals for the leather industry, while Indonesia in those for the textile industry. Singapore would be in charge of metal cleaning chemicals.

Headquarters in Germany would be required to accelerate the development of new products or applications for the region. More staff would be assigned to service the specific needs of the Asia Pacific region. The number of visits by technical experts from Düsseldorf to advise and train local staff, and hold regional seminars, would also be increased.

Human resources

The former emphasis on the development of individual VUs in the various countries had led to a low profile for Henkel as a recruiting organization and to limited career opportunities for local staff. These weaknesses had to be overcome through the establishment of a regional human resource strategy and the development of a regional corporate culture. As a first step, a more systematic assessment of management potential and needs had to be undertaken, and compensation packages brought in line. Local and regional training programmes were also to be launched.

There was also an initiative to institutionalize an internal regional job market for Asian managers that would foster cross-border job rotation. The situation in which most VUs were directed by expatriates would be overcome by a mechanism — referred to as the 'Tandem Principle' - that would oblige the established expatriates to train an Asian manager to take over his position at the end of an assignment. Long-term expatriates would have to accept local compensation packages after eight years. Bonuses for the VUs' managing directors would depend on both the results of the respective VU and its contribution to the region.

EXPANSION OF EXISTING OPERATIONS

From 1991 sales of DM450 million, Henkel aimed to increase the existing business in the region to DM850 million by 1996. (These figures are exclusive of exports from Asia Pacific, Malaysia in particular, to markets outside the region.)

In 1991, 75% of the HAP business came from the chemical side (oleo chemicals, organic specialities, and care chemicals), 14% from adhesives (industrial and consumer adhesives), and 11% from metal chemicals (chemicals for treating metals, in most cases during the production process). Adhesives were expected to grow fastest, representing 20% of Henkel's total sales in Asia Pacific in 1996. The share of chemicals was projected to fall to 69%.

Sales by country in 1991 were as follows: Japan's sales were the largest with 34%, followed by Australia, Indonesia and Thailand each contributing around 10%. In 1996 Japan was still expected to have the highest sales, although its percentage of total sales would drop to 29%. Indonesia, Thailand and Korea would each contribute 10–11%.

Henkel's existing operations in China were expected to grow from DM29 to DM109 million in 1996, then representing 13% of HAP's sales. In 1991 they were small scale and scattered, and consisted of:

1. *Business development*
   Henkel Beijing Representative Office (mainly adhesives).

2. *Trading (indent business and ex-stock)*
   Henkel Chemicals Hong Kong with service offices in China (mainly chemicals).

3. *Local manufacturing and marketing*
   Shanghai Henkel Chemicals (mainly metal chemicals)

4. *Local manufacturing and marketing*
   Guangzhou Henkel Chemical Products (mainly metal chemicals).

Exhibit CS24.3 provides an overview of Henkel's existing activities in the Asia Pacific region.

The operations that sold products of DM450 million in 1991 had by 1993 grown to DM615 million. This pace of development was the fastest recorded by Henkel worldwide during this period.

NEW PROJECTS FOR CHINA

The activities of the HAP office, the visits of board members and major shareholders to China at the beginning of the 1990s began to have an impact on the various SBUs at the Düsseldorf headquarters. There was a dramatic increase in interest in selling into or investing in the country. Of all the 'newcomers', the detergent division was the first to become involved in China with an investment in an existing plant in Tianjin. After a period of search and negotiation that lasted for several years, a joint venture agreement was concluded with HAP's assistance. Henkel took a 20% share, which was complemented by a 10% participation from DEG, the German government-owned investment bank. The operations of the joint venture started in 1993 with 1,000 people. Persil was also among the brands launched and relaunched. Sales in 1993 were DM65 million and a small profit was made. At the beginning of 1994 Henkel increased its share in the venture to 45%.

As Henkel's largest division the detergent group carried a lot of weight. Its decision to invest in China was a major one for Henkel, not least because of the large capital outlay required.

Many years earlier Henkel had decided to concentrate the detergent business on Europe where it held a very high market share. The logic behind this concentration was that Henkel, as an integrated producer, was involved in both upstream and downstream activities. Consequently, companies such as Procter & Gamble and Unilever were at once Henkel's competitors in end products and its customers for raw materials. The strength of Henkel's position in Europe allowed the company to pursue this policy. Outside Europe, however, Henkel felt it would be better to act solely as a supplier. This decision had led, years earlier, to Henkel's withdrawal from the detergents' markets, most notably in Brazil.

In the early 1990s Henkel began to reconsider its policy and to see detergent as a global business. This new attitude was in part influenced by the aggressive strategies of Henkel's competitors in the Asia Pacific region, which was thought to account for 25% of the world demand. In view of this, Henkel felt it could not afford to miss out on the growth in Asia. In fact, after the start of the first venture the division was keen to find further projects in China. A project proposal for Vietnam was also discussed.

The cosmetics division had become equally restive. In contrast to their colleagues from the detergents division they had already established a small presence in eight countries in Asia Pacific through a number of distribution and license agreements with companies such as Inchcape in Thailand and Lucky in Korea. Henkel's main brand was Fa. The cosmetics division had also assigned their own representative to the HAP office in Hong Kong. Investments so far had, however, been limited. Due to recent acquisitions in Europe the division felt it would be difficult to find large funds for a rapid expansion in Asia, even for China, which was seen as a priority country.

Henkel therefore agreed to form a new joint venture with a small Hong Kong agency to which it had previously granted all distribution and licensing rights for China. This company was owned by a former Henkel employee from Hong Kong with good contacts in China. The venture, in which Henkel took a 90% share, was called Henkel Cosmetics China. It would both manufacture and market a variety of products utilizing existing Chinese plants.

The chemical division was in the process of constructing a new major plant in Shanghai. In partnership with four Chinese organizations Shanghai Henkel Oleochemicals would produce surfactants and other raw materials for detergents, shampoos, soaps, etc. as of the end of 1994. Henkel had taken a 70% share in the venture. In light of China's fast growing automobile sector Henkel Shanghai Teroson was founded to market protective coatings, sealants and adhesives for motor vehicles. The adhesives and metal chemicals divisions had further projects under consideration and negotiation.

In early 1994 almost all of Henkel's 31 SBUs appeared to be searching for business opportunities in China.

HAP'S ORGANIZATION AND FUNCTIONS

With so many ventures and partnerships under discussion the coordination of Henkel's activities in China became a matter of concern. Traditionally, Henkel Chemicals Hong Kong had covered China. If anyone could claim some expertise on China it was this VU that employed 44 people. Therefore the idea was born to convert this office into an umbrella organization for China called Henkel China. Although this was quickly realized, the move was opposed by those divisions that, while not yet active in China, were then aggressively pursuing various projects in the country. These divisions argued that Henkel Chemicals Hong Kong only had experience in chemicals and adhesives, but not in their fields. They would therefore rather remain independent from the Henkel China office.

The discussion of the organization of the China activities had a direct impact on HAP's role as a regional office. So far most of the new projects had either been initiated, or supported by the office. However, due to China's unforeseen growth, and Düsseldorf's strong interest in the country, Lehner and his team had, in fact, spent most of their time and energy on that country. Expectations were emerging that in the years to come Henkel's business in China alone could equal that of all the other countries combined.

Should the VUs in China be first of all coordinated within the country and only later integrated into a regional coordination body called HAP? How would Taiwan or a 'Greater China' concept fit into such an organization? What would be the implications in terms of layers and bureaucracy? Alternatively, with all the activities in China and the location of HAP in Hong Kong, was the regional office in fact evolving into a *de facto* China office?

The reluctance of the detergents' division to operate under a China umbrella raised the more fundamental issue of its relationship to HAP, as well as the rationale for the existence of HAP. Because of the size of its projects and their importance, the division was reluctant to share any responsibility with other parts of the organization. Nevertheless, it welcomed the administrative and human resource services that the HAP office could provide. There was also the issue of reporting lines. Under Lehner, HAP still reported to Mr Conrad, the board member who was in charge of both chemicals and Asia. The detergent project in China had been personally championed by the board member heading the detergent division, who did not see a need to have his representative in Tianjin come under the HAP umbrella.

While most VUs were pleased with the establishment of HAP in Hong Kong, the Japanese resisted and stressed that their market had little in common with the region, with the possible exception of Korea and Taiwan. They saw their operation as more in line with medium-sized European VUs, which were not asked to report to a regional office. It was therefore important to assess and redefine the role of HAP at regular intervals as Müller-Hillebrand, the successor to Lehner, had at the beginning of 1994. For Müller-Hillebrand, HAP carried out the following functions:

Integrative function:

- ■ Translation of SBU strategies into an integrated Asia Pacific strategy.

- Promotion of synergies across businesses and countries.

- Provision of services (technical, legal, financial, human resources).

Strategic operative function:

- Direction of Henkel's regional strategies and support implementation.

- Coordination between VUs, SBUs and corporate functions.

- Support for the exploitation of new business opportunities.

Since the opening of the HAP office much had been done to fulfil these tasks for Henkel in the region. An overall regional strategy had been developed, proposed and accepted. A regional production network was beginning to emerge and a regional accounting system had been agreed upon. A regional office for corporate purchasing had been established at HAP.

Key countries in the region were taking over technological leadership as 'Centres of Business Competence'. Not all Asian desks had been staffed as planned, but certain managers concerned had moved from headquarters to Kuala Lumpur, Bangkok, or Singapore. Many operational issues had been tackled such as those related to the new plant in Japan. The decision whether or not to open a representative office in Vietnam had to be made soon.

Due to the enormous workload, the initially small team of a chairman and four managers plus support staff had grown, though only slightly (see Exhibit CS24.4). The HAP's operational costs had therefore remained reasonable. The HAP office was, however, still exclusively staffed with expatriate managers and most of the VUs in the region were still headed by expatriates.

Müller-Hillebrand now reported to Lehner, who would soon be on the board as finance director without representing any specific product division. With Lehner's background in Asia the region would have sufficient backing in Düsseldorf.

HENKEL'S ASIA PACIFIC STRATEGY

But there were more than organizational issues on Müller-Hillebrand's mind as he looked from his office desk over the bustling Hong Kong harbour.

Strategically the region had gained in importance for Henkel, but its total share in its worldwide sales and profits was still tiny. Much of Henkel's growth in the region now depended on progress in China and its future development. What would happen with Henkel's Asia Pacific strategy if a prolonged crisis were to hit the country? Had Japan, Indonesia, or Thailand been neglected as a result of the emphasis on China? Was success in Asia possible – as some would argue – without being successful in Japan?

When in 1992 Henkel's strategy for Asia Pacific was formulated, two objectives were set:

1. To strengthen Henkel's position in the region.

2. To adequately participate in the region's growth.

Both these statements were open to interpretation. Henkel's position certainly had improved compared with past performances, but compared to its competitors there was no evidence that its position had really been strengthened. Competing in so many product areas across so many countries with limited market data made any serious benchmarking exercise extremely difficult. Reports and newspaper articles on competitors' activities in the region, however, had created some fear that Henkel, despite its growth, might, in fact be falling behind.

It was also unclear what was really meant by 'adequate participation' in the region's growth. What was the yardstick by which Henkel's growth was to be measured: GNP growth, industrial growth, growth of the chemical industry, growth in sectors in which Henkel already competed or could compete?

On an aggregate level several surveys had shown that 20–25% of all chemicals in the world were sold in Asia. There was consensus that this percentage would increase considerably over the coming decades on account of declining shares held by Europe and the USA. Henkel still had only 4.4% of its business in Asia.

Incremental moves spread over 31 SBUs would not be enough to rectify this situation. To become a truly global player Henkel would have to come up with alternative strategies. As the new chairman of Henkel Asia Pacific what could Müller-Hillebrand do to launch a second campaign in favour of the region?

Exhibit CS24.1   Employees in Asia Pacific

1991

Henkel Australia	150
Shanghai Henkel	33
Guangzhou Henkel	5
Henkel Peking (Rep. Office)	6
Henkel Chem. Hong Kong	44
Henkel Indonesia	245
Henkel Hakusui (Japan)	321
Henkel Korea	19
Henkel Daesung (Korea)	18
Henkel Oleochem (Group Malaysia)	289
Henkel New Zealand	19
Henkel Philippines	38
Henkel Singapore	26
Henkel Taiwan	57
Henkel Thailand	309
Total	1,589

Exhibit CS24.2   Opportunity matrix for Henkel in Asia Pacific

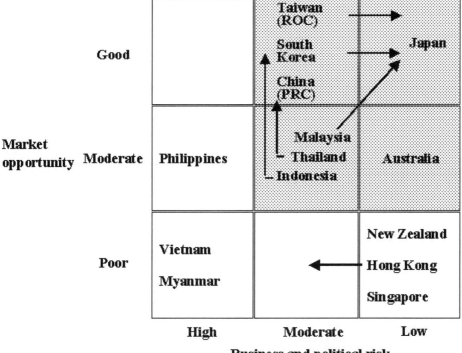

Opportunity matrix for Henkel in Asia Pacific

Case 24

Exhibit CS24.3　Henkel Asia Pacific by product groups

	Henkel Australia	Henkel Shanghai	Henkel Guangzhou	Henkel China	Henkel Indonesia	Henkel Japan	Henkel Korea	Henkel Daesung	Henkel Malaysia	Henkel New Zealand	Henkel Philippines	Henkel Singapore	Henkel Taiwan	Henkel Thailand
Oleo chemicals	X			X	X	X	X		X		X		X	X
Textile auxiliaries	X			X	X	X	X		X		X		X	X
Leather auxiliaries	X			X	X	X	X				X		X	X
Plastics and coating additives	X			X	X	X	X		X	X	X		X	X
Pulp and paper additives	X									X			X	X
Mining/oilfield chemicals	X				X									
Cosmetic and pharm. raw materials	X			X	X	X	X		X	X	X		X	X
Fiine chemicals	X					X								
Food additives	X													X
(Toll-manufacturing for Ecolab)					(X)			X			(X)		(X)	
Metal surface treatment	X	X	X	X	X	X	X			X		X	X	X
Consumer adhesives	X	X		X	X	X	X			X				X
Industrial adhesives	X			X	X	X	X			X	X		X	X

Exhibit CS24.4   Organizational charts of Henkel Asia Pacific: 1992 and 1994

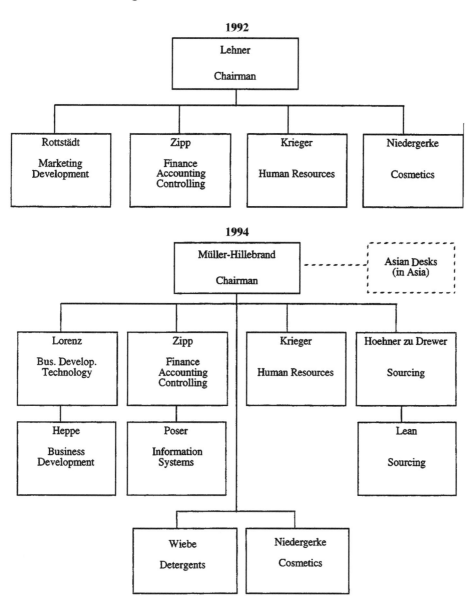

Case 25

This case was written by Charlotte Butler, Research Associate, and Henri-Claude de Bettignies, Professor of Organizational Behaviour at INSEAD. It is intended to be used as a basis for class discussion rather than to illustrate effective or ineffective handling of an administrative situation. Copyright © 1996 INSEAD-EAC, Fontainebleau, France.

The Evaluation

'Why?' To Richard Evans, managing director of the Siam Chemicals Company (SCC) the single word, written in the margin of the company evaluation form, seemed to stare accusingly up at him. The form was densely written, filled out with comments under all the headings that made up the annual assessment process, yet for him, this one word obliterated all the carefully thought out phrases he had composed. For that single word represented a spontaneous and quite uncharacteristic outburst from the subject of the evaluation Mr Somsak, one of his Thai business managers. For Richard Evans it meant that he would now have to take a critical decision which could affect both his authority in the company, and the future standards by which his local managers would be judged.

The ringing of the phone interrupted his thoughts. He picked it up and his secretary, Wilai, put through James Brown, a colleague based in the Singapore office of their mutual parent company, Chimique Helvétique Ltd (CHL), a Swiss chemicals group headquartered in Basle.

'Dick', James' voice echoed down the line. 'I just got a copy of Somsak's evaluation. I was absolutely amazed when I read it. I gave the guy an "A" but you've only given him an overall "C". What's going on? As you know, he's worked with me for the last three years in the polymers side of the business. I know he reports to you as his direct line manager for his activities as a senior manager in SCC, but I am his boss when it comes to his operating performance and his work for us has been outstanding. He has way surpassed all his commercial and financial objectives, moved more product and at higher prices. We consider him exceptional. So what are you trying to do to the guy? Make him quit? You know how sensitive the Thai locals are to the slightest hint of a negative remark, let alone anything as direct and public as this. I told him when we had our assessment interview how pleased I was with his performance. Now, when he sees this he's going to be devastated. This is just a slap in the face. You know the problem we had when you first took over. This will finish things off, for sure. What's going on?'

Evans did indeed remember the problem. He had flown out from Geneva to take over as MD of the company with very little preparation or briefing. Newly promoted to his present grade it was his first time in Asia, and the cultural shock had been enormous. He still remembered those first weeks with a shudder. It had been a nightmare of trying to note all the advice his predecessor, who had stayed on for a few days, was giving him, to absorb the details of the company's businesses in the local market and master the details of its past and current performance, then meeting his exclusively local staff and, at the same time as all this, settling in his unhappy family.

Richard, an Englishman, had joined CHL five years ago, having been recruited from the British chemicals group he had joined straight after graduating. He and his wife, Mary, had welcomed the move to Switzerland and spent four happy years in Basle, their three children well settled in the international school and all of them enjoying the novelty of being able to spend weekends skiing in the mountains. To be then so suddenly uprooted and put down in a strange new world where they spoke not a word of the language or had any notion of its customs, was a terrible and unwelcome shock, especially to his wife. In Bangkok, there were no pavements along which she could take the baby out in its pram, shopping for food was a major expedition and, with the elder children leaving at 7 a.m. for the long bus journey to school, she was thrown on her own resources for the 12, 13 or even 14 hours a day her husband was absent. Coping with their new life imposed a considerable strain on all of them.

It was on one of those exhausting and confusing first days that Somsak, considered one of the senior and longer established mainstays of the company after three years in the job, had resigned. It had happened after a meeting during which Somsak had mentioned that he did not always find the CHL matrix system easy to understand. Thai people, he explained to Richard, found the concept of two bosses impossible to reconcile with their strong sense of hierarchy. They preferred to know exactly who was their senior manager, the man whose approval they should seek. Richard had seized on the opportunity to demonstrate his qualities as the new MD by, as he saw it, helping Somsak function better within the system. In what he considered a constructive way, one that had always previously been successful in dealing with European managers, he had tried to coach Somsak in how to approach his dual responsibilities more effectively. He had been stunned when Somsak had reacted with the words, 'I realize from what you have said that I am not doing a good job. I am not suitable for my post and so the only thing I can do is to resign'. Only the strenuous efforts of Somsak's other boss, Brown, to whom he owed a strong sense of allegiance, had persuaded Somsak to stay.

In the 18 months since this early setback, Evans had undergone an intensive and often tough course in cross-cultural management. His experiences had led him to conclude that some issues were not important enough to bring out in the open and risk undermining the harmony of the company and that more often than not, discretion was indeed the better part of valour. However, the evaluation issue was one that he judged would have to be tackled head-on. Unfortunately, it seemed likely that the first casualty of this intention would be Somsak.

During the last 18 months, Somsak had maintained a very polite and correct but by no means warm attitude towards his MD. For his part, Evans had come to appreciate that Somsak was a hard working and meticulous manager. He was willing to work every hour of the day, was highly intelligent and spoke excellent English, having been dealing with European companies for many years. Richard had made every effort to convey his appreciation of Somsak's efforts and recently, had been heartened by signs of a more trusting, comfortable relationship between them. Now, the evaluation question threatened all the gains Richard had so painstakingly made.

The annual evaluation process was imposed on all the CHL group's subsidiaries and had been in use in Thailand ever since the company's foundation, seven years ago. The same format was used company-wide for all management grades, employees in supervisory grades and below being evaluated by a much simpler, numerical form. The process was designed to measure an individual's input and output, competencies and results (Exhibit CS25.1). The basis for performance appraisal was a set of six to seven key, previously agreed objectives to be achieved by a certain point in time. Objectives could be weighted to show their relative importance, and all were judged according to a grading system ranging from A to E.

The actual process was carried out during two, one-to-one interviews. During the first, a manager's past year's performance was reviewed. The senior manager would encourage his or her subordinate to talk about his or her performance, go through last year's objectives, and assess how well they had been achieved. In Europe, individuals did this without hesitation, enjoying the opportunity to debate their performance as equals and quick to argue their case forcefully if they disagreed at any point.

Such frankness was impossible in Thailand where, as it quickly became clear to Richard, his managers expected to be told how well they had done. It was not for them to make any judgement about their performance, what else was the boss there for? They were not disposed to talk about themselves at all. Moreover, the discomfort with any hint of criticism made the whole meeting a minefield. So instead of a dialogue, Richard found himself spending an hour in which he did most of the talking. He tried in vain to provoke some response, posing open, detached questions such as what did they want out of their job, were they happy or not. The reply was always polite, brief and invariably non-controversial except for any issue concerning their staff or the overall business performance. Their perceived role as middlemen for their staff would prompt them to talk about pay and whether or not it was up to market rates, or about parity between jobs. But to talk about themselves was something they resolutely refused to do.

A second meeting set objectives for the coming year. In the West, managers usually set their own objectives and Evans had had some success in instituting this revolutionary procedure with some of his direct reports. But it was a difficult process, more characterized by verbal suggestions from himself that his managers would go away and write up. If their English was poor, they would return and ask him to write it up for them.

Richard knew that his local managers found the very idea of sitting down with their boss to appraise their performance a threatening and alien concept. Even the most senior, who had a good command of English and had been with the company for some time, found it difficult both to meet Richard for their own assessment, and also to carry out the process with their own staff.

The most contentious part concerned the overall performance rating. The group used a standard A–E grading in which, according to a normal distribution, an 'A' grade would apply only to the top 3–4% of outstanding managers. These would not necessarily be the most senior, but those who had displayed real leadership qualities, for example had perhaps innovated a certain way of doing things, and whose performance was above and beyond the average.

A 'B' grade was awarded to those whose performance was judged to be excellent in all respects, and who had added to the overall improvement of the company (perhaps by serving on one of the committees for safety or an action team). A 'C' grade, into which category 60–70% of managers usually fell, implied a good, standard performance with all requirements fulfilled. A 'D' grade implied that there was scope for improvement and an 'E' grade that there was a real problem.

Looking through the record of previous evaluations, it was clear to Richard that his predecessors had decided it was better not to rock the boat by insisting on adhering to European standards. Over 90% of managers had been awarded an 'A' grade, although some MDs had tried to indicate nuances by giving A-, A+, A++, etc. Richard also had a shrewd suspicion that in interviews with their subordinates, his managers had similarly glossed over any potentially controversial issues. A query he had once made about an 'A' grade awarded to someone who was clearly not pulling his weight had been met with the assurance, 'Oh, it is OK, we all work round him'.

His suspicions were endorsed when he checked the previous year's results. Then, 95% of those evaluated had been given an 'A' grade, with a very few clearly reluctantly given 'B' grades. In part, he had come to realize, the local attitude was associated with the Thai school marking system where a 'B' meant 'could try harder' and a 'C' meant trouble. Only an 'A' grade, therefore, was psychologically acceptable.

This year, however, Richard had decided that he would tackle the issue directly by imposing the norm for the performance rating, and so align SCC with standards in the rest of the group. He himself would make sure that the norm was respected in his own direct reports and, where there were discrepancies in those of other managers, he himself would change the grades.

In part, he was motivated by wider strategic considerations. SCC had been established in Thailand for eight years. The last three years had seen rapid growth and good results. The company was considering implanting itself in other parts of the region, and would expect its successful Thai offshoot, staffed by experienced people familiar with the parent company's organization and trained to the high standards of safety and quality that were a key part of its culture, to provide managers for the new subsidiaries.

This project coincided with a move, initiated by the group human resources director, to identify an international cadre of managers that could be moved between countries in support of CHL's global ambitions. However, this required a common standard in grading job performance and career potential between different parts of the group. Richard therefore decided that this year, he would implement the system as intended by headquarters, and award grades so that anyone looking at the results would be able to make judgements about an individual's potential based on a common language.

Not greatly to his surprise, the whole process had brought nothing but trouble. Faced by this latest problem, Richard was almost tempted to give up and award everyone the 'A' grade they were accustomed to and the same salary increase. However, he knew this would only be a short-term respite that would not be good for SCC in the long run. It would not give recognition for an exceptional performance and so effective SCC managers would probably vote with their feet, confident that in the hectic Thai job market they could walk into another probably better paid job the same or, at the latest, the next day.

With this in mind, Richard had to decide what to do about Somsak. In his own mind, an overall 'C' grade was the correct judgement. For despite his outstanding work for his Singapore boss,

Case 25

Somsak had failed to meet three out of the four objectives Richard had set for him in his wider role as a senior manager in SCC. These had been concerned with building up communications between his polymers business and the rest of the company, and supporting the key safety and quality assurance initiatives.

In the last year, Somsak had put a huge effort into building up his own team but ironically, instead of building bridges he had only succeeded in forming an isolated clique whose behaviour was having a divisive effect on the rest of SCC. The team acted like a family centred on Somsak. While the shared strong identity and bonds made them all work well for each other, it meant they rejected all those outside the group. Consequently, working relations between the polymers team and the rest of the company were very strained. Again, this mirrored Thai society, where the family formed the core that owed no allegiance to anyone outside it. All the energy expended on fostering the inner circle was countered by an attitude of total selfishness towards everyone else.

During the interview, Richard had spent considerable time talking to Somsak about the evaluation process in a bid to explain what he was trying to achieve by introducing the new approach. Going through the four objectives and where he felt they had not been achieved, he had explained that his notion of leadership in a senior manager such as Somsak was to help lead the company by building bridges. He had also emphasized that in the wider CHL group, 'C' was considered a good grade.

Later, after much heart searching, Richard had given Somsak a 'C' grade overall, not the 'A' grade he had so obviously expected. In reaching this decision, Richard felt he had made a big effort to be fair. He believed that he now understood some of the conflict that Somsak felt, the permanent tension caused by trying to please two bosses and the consequences of failure in terms of loss of face. So he had ignored the things Somsak had not done and given him credit for those that he had. After working together for the past 18 months, he felt that he was finally able to communicate with Somsak and that therefore he would understand, and accept the decision in the spirit it was meant.

The reaction had been far worse than his expectations. A visibly hurt and uncomprehending Somsak had asked 'But where did I go wrong?' As far as he was concerned, he had worked incredibly hard for 12 months and at the end, had been awarded a disgraceful 'C' grade. He had returned that day and given back the form on which he had written his single comment. His injured pride and sense of injustice was affecting all his team, and Richard could see only problems ahead.

As he looked through the report one more time, Richard Evans knew he had to make an important decision. Should he compromise his principles and upgrade Somsak, or stick to his guns and risk losing him? Sticking to his principles, it was clear, would make life difficult with his Singapore colleague who would resent the loss of such an effective manager. And after all, he wondered, was it fair to inflict Western standards on Asian managers who worked hard, and did everything right according to their own cultural norms? Whatever the outcome, Richard was determined to find some way of avoiding a recurrence next year. Which raised the question of how?

Exhibit CS25.1   Chimique Helvetique Ltd: Executive Performance Review

Name   Job Title

Division   Company

Age   Years in Service   Years on the Job

1. EXECUTIVE PERFORMANCE REVIEW

a. Review is to be done by the Reviewer and discussed with the Employee.
b. Complete Sections 2, 3, 4, 5 and 6 before completing this section.
c. Highlight most noteworthy areas of performance after taking into consideration achievements against objectives, work-related dimensions and external/other factors. Indicate both achievements and areas for improvement.

OVERALL PERFORMANCE RATING

A Excellent   Reviewer's Name

B Superior

C Competent   Reviewer's Position

D Marginal

E Poor   Reviewer's Signature   Date

RATING DEFINITIONS

To arrive at the overall rating, an 80:20 weighting between objectives and work related dimension is recommended.

Excellent   (A) – Performance that consistently delivers very high quality results, far exceeding expectations.

Superior   (B) – A high quality performance where results exceed expectations

Competent   (C) – Satisfactory performance that effectively meets expectations.

Marginal   (D) – Performance that often falls short of expectations

Poor   (E) – Totally unsatisfactory performance that does not meet expectations.

Source: Company documents

Case 26

This case was written by Professor Hellmut Schütte, INSEAD and Michele
Jurgens from the Academy ACCOR. It is intended to be used as a basis for
class discussion rather than to illustrate either effective or ineffective
handling of an administrative situation. Copyright © 1997 INSEAD Euro-
Asia Centre, Fontainebleau, France

ACCOR in Asia

Sitting down to review the latest proposal for the construction of a Novotel hotel in Indonesia,
Raymond Capdevila quickly found that he could not concentrate. Later in the afternoon he was
due to meet the ACCOR group's vice president Benjamin Cohen, who oversaw the ACCOR
group's relationship with Capdevila's company, ACCOR Asia Pacific Corporation (AAPC).
Capdevila was worried about AAPC's strategy for 1996 and beyond. AAPC had performed very
well in 1994 (see Exhibit CS26.1) and had continued to expand, but could the organization
which he had put into place support ongoing rapid growth and still retain the strong ACCOR
corporate culture? Would there be sufficient demand for the highly standardized hotels ACCOR
excelled in, or would a change in the ACCOR formula be needed for success in Asia?

THE CREATION OF AAPC

AAPC was created in September 1993 as the result of a merger between the Asian operations
of ACCOR SA, the giant French-based service and leisure group, and the Australian company
Quality Pacific Corporation. As a result of the financially complicated merger process, Quality
Pacific Corporation ceased to exist and ACCOR's share of AAPC was set at approximately 34%
(ACCOR was the largest shareholder). Quality Pacific was an Australian company that had
successfully developed a chain of hotels under the US-based 'Quality' franchise label. At the time
of the merger, the company had 24 hotels under its management, which were in good shape and
all well located in Australia.

In the early 1990s ACCOR's resources had been urgently needed in Europe and the USA, and it
had not been in a position to dedicate sufficient capital to fund development in Australia and
Asia. And with only one hotel in Australia and approximately 15 in Asia, ACCOR seized an
opportunity to merge its Asian operations with an existing player in order to attain critical mass
quickly, rather than developing on a hotel-by-hotel basis. By using Quality Pacific's listing on the
Sydney stock exchange, the newly created AAPC had rapidly been able to raise the capital it
needed. An initial Australian issue of AU$90 million had been followed up by a $62 million issue
and a listing on the Hong Kong exchange.

After its creation, AAPC found itself with 63 hotels and had another 34 committed, under construction or under negotiation. Now, in January 1996, the total had risen to 98 hotels with a further 54 on the way (see Exhibit CS26.2). Growth had been very rapid, outstripping that of all major competitors in the region.

THE GROWTH OF THE ACCOR GROUP

The origins of the ACCOR Group go back to 1967 when entrepreneurs Paul Dubrule and Gérard Pélisson set up the first Novotel near Lille airport in northern France. The French were travelling increasingly for business and pleasure and Dubrule and Pélisson saw an opportunity to create a three-star, standardized hotel chain. French legislation in the late 1960s and 1970s also encouraged the construction of new hotels in France. The concept was an immediate success and customers came knowing that Novotel offered convenient locations, reasonable rates and reliable service.

Dubrule and Pélisson soon recreated their success in the two-star category with the introduction of Ibis in 1973, aimed at the price-conscious business traveller. In 1975 they bought the Mercure hotel chain, and five years later they acquired the exclusive four-star Sofitel chain. In 1983 ACCOR was created with the merger of Novotel SA and the Jacques Borel restaurant and service voucher group. In 1985, ACCOR completed its coverage of the hotel spectrum by launching the innovative no-star, no-frills 'Formule 1' hotel in the budget range followed by the Etap chain in the one-star category in the early 1990s. The Formule 1 hotels were built from prefabricated modules, adjacent to highways, and offered their rooms at rock-bottom prices.

Subsequently, through a combination of internal growth and acquisitions, ACCOR grew into one of the world's foremost leisure and tourism groups with activities in the hotel, restaurant, catering and other corporate services sectors. It became a major player in the USA with the acquisition of the well-known one-star Motel 6 chain in 1990, although it was an expensive move since many of the hotels required extensive renovation work at the time of acquisition. In 1991, ACCOR acquired a large stake in WagonLits of Belgium, one of the world's largest players in travel agencies, hotel chains and catering services. In 1994, WagonLits' travel agencies were merged with those of another player, Carlson, creating a 4,000 agent-strong group and one of the top two travel companies in the world.

ACCOR was thus the world's biggest travel and services company with 147,000 employees in 132 countries and with over 50 trademarks. The hotel business remained the cornerstone of the group's activities.

THE ACCOR HOTEL CONCEPTS

The positioning of ACCOR's seven major hotel chains in terms of stars could be summarized by the pyramid shown in Figure CS26.1.

The element of standardization was important to ACCOR, as it had always been strong in the lower-priced sectors and these continued to be its primary focus for development. The 'de luxe' sector – 5-star in the Asian and American context – was not a principal target as the skills required for operating such hotels were somewhat different from those which enabled the group to excel in the standardized chains. ACCOR was reputed for its strengths in positioning, concept

Figure CS26.1   ACCOR seven major hotel chains

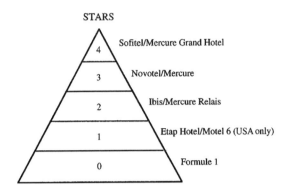

ACCOR'S MANAGEMENT

development and cost-conscious control and management. The positioning of ACCOR's different chains in the hotel market in terms of their degree of chain-wide standardization and the intensity of interaction needed with the customer could be summarized by Figure CS26.2.

In the past, consumers had preferred more standardized service which explained in part the great success of Novotel and Ibis. Recent trends in consumer tastes, however, were towards less standardized service. ACCOR's Sofitel, Mercure and Etap chains emphasized the differences between individual hotels and allowed for adaptation of services to the region in which the hotel was located. Many Etap hotels had in fact been acquired rather than built to ACCOR's specifications.

ACCOR'S MANAGEMENT

In France, ACCOR developed a management style and culture adapted to an environment in which the group, as builder, owner and operator, had complete control over its hotels. The Mercure chain was an exception, as it operated increasingly under franchise agreements in France

Figure CS26.2   The positioning of ACCOR's different hotel chains

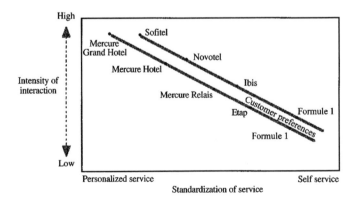

and throughout Europe. Outside France, ACCOR had to develop in largely the same fashion as other major hotel chains: in general, it obtained management contracts from, or occasionally signed franchise agreements with investors or hotel owners/operators.

Management contracts were signed between the owner or investor(s) and the hotel chain (i.e. ACCOR). The contracts gave responsibility for the running of a hotel to ACCOR in exchange for a set fee paid by ACCOR to the owners/investors, generally equal to between 5 and 7% of the revenues generated by the hotel. The agreements were established for periods of about five years. The management staff were brought in by ACCOR, while the non-managerial staff were recruited locally and generally stayed on even if the management contract changed from one chain to another. The investor/owner maintained the right to approve all major investments in the maintenance of the property, and, in most cases, in the training of non-management personnel.

Franchise agreements were in effect the reverse of management contracts. Under a franchise agreement, ACCOR would 'lease' the right to use its reservation network and its brand name to a hotel owner/operator in exchange for 2 to 3% of revenues. Responsibility for managing the hotel rested solely with the owner/operator.

A principal feature of ACCOR's management style was that its decision-making process was highly decentralized. Great effort was made throughout the group to give the greatest possible degree of autonomy to those in the field who had responsibility to the customer. Sales and service were a particularly local affair. Hotel managers and their staff were encouraged to take initiatives to adapt or improve the service of their hotel to meet their customers' needs; these experiences were often generalized throughout the chain to help it evolve in parallel with customer trends. Managers were judged primarily on the basis of financial results for their profit centre or, in the case of administrative staff, according to objectives.

ACCOR's head office in Evry, slightly south of Paris, was relatively small with not more than 80 staff including secretaries. Vice presidents, who were based in Evry, were each designated a sector of activity: hotels, travel, services and car rental, and human resources. Traditionally, strategic marketing was led by Dubrule and the director responsible for an operating company with the help of a very light support staff, although recently two of the operating companies had hired marketing directors who took on strategic responsibilities.

The real power within the group, at least in France, lay with the directors of each of the operating companies. These directors were responsible for developing their brand and for operations in France. There was a great deal of competition between the directors to achieve the best results and fastest growth. Outside France, responsibility for operations belonged to country or regional directors who reported directly to the executive committee. Since they did not report to the directors of the operating companies, they were under no obligation to implement product or service innovations launched in France in their own countries.

Despite the group's fast growth and emphasis on decentralization, Dubrule and Pélisson made every effort to retain a common culture of entrepreneurship and innovation. Training and personal development were priorities. One tool created to promote the group's common culture was the Academy ACCOR, a corporate university for the training of mid-level and top managers. The Academy also operated as a centre for the exchange of management approaches and as a resource for consulting and research in the areas of service management.

ACCOR'S PRESENCE IN ASIA

ACCOR's first presence in Asia in 1978 came as the result of an association with UTH, the hotel arm of the UTA airline company. In 1982 ACCOR operated several hotels in Thailand, Singapore and New Caledonia. The group sent out a skeleton staff to manage these operations and investigate other opportunities.

It became rapidly apparent to that first team that with the limited capital for investment at its disposal and such a large territory to cover, ACCOR would not be able to develop in Asia as it had in France – as owner/operator of hotel chains represented in every city and large town. Another strategy needed to be found.

China with its '1.2 billion stomachs' had just opened up and was considered to be a very attractive target market. In 1985, a landmark joint venture agreement was reached with the Chinese authorities to renovate and manage hotels in China. However, by 1987 only two hotels were up and running. Experience had shown that renovating hotels in China was a challenging task – on average, 240 permits needed to be signed by various local officials before work could even begin. ACCOR's China focus had also had the effect of diverting scarce resources from development in other parts of Asia.

When ACCOR began looking at other Asian countries, it was faced with the difficulty of attracting investors to support the construction of hotels in the mid- and economy ranges in which it specialized. The majority of hotels being built in Asia at the time were top-range 'five-star' hotels that catered to the very rich or to travelling businessmen. Local investors were more interested in these top-range hotels, since the returns on investment in hotels were considered to come primarily in the form of capital gains on the properties themselves and not necessarily from the margins made on running the hotels. A top quality hotel brought a greater return upon resale than a hotel constructed for the mid-range or economy market.

In an effort to attract capital investment, the centre of ACCOR's Asian operations was moved out of Asia to California from 1986 to 1987. While ample sources of capital were available in Los Angeles, the physical distance from Asia created other barriers to development.

BREAKTHROUGH IN BANGKOK

When Raymond Capdevila moved out to head up the region from his previous posting in Dubai, the development of the Asian market had become an important and urgent objective for the ACCOR group. In late 1987, ACCOR had only seven hotels operating in the entire Asian region which stretched from China and Mongolia in the north to New Zealand in the south, and from India in the west to the International Date Line in the east.

Capdevila's first move was to shift the Asian headquarters back to Asia, to Bangkok. His decision reflected ACCOR's belief that in the hotel business, one must be close to one's market, and the Novotel Siam Square in Bangkok – the first ACCOR purpose-built hotel in Asia – was due to open in 1988. Its success was crucial. The 429-room hotel, in which ACCOR had an equity participation of 30%, was located in the centre of the shopping district in Bangkok and not far from the business sector. Above all, it was aimed at the growing number of travelling Asian businessmen and tourists and charged 30% less than five-star hotels in Bangkok while offering many of the same conveniences.

The hotel quickly broke even with almost immediate record occupancy rates of over 65% – a rate new hotels usually take 12 months or more to achieve. Within a year, occupancy reached peaks of 90 to 100%. This success confirmed Capdevila's belief that it was important to have a highly visible local presence. Establishing ACCOR's Asian head office in Bangkok, at a time when most Western companies had their Asian head office in Singapore or Hong Kong, had drawn a great deal of attention and press coverage. Thai business and political leaders, who were anxious to attract foreign investment, were pleased by the move.

Capdevila and his team capitalized on this attention to promote the Novotel as a new, innovative concept for the Asian market. Its subsequent success quickly attracted local investment for other projects throughout Thailand; 10 or so were already under construction or under negotiation within a year and a half. This was ACCOR's first major commercial success in Asia.

WHERE NEXT?

By 1989, Capdevila's attention had turned to markets outside Thailand. He believed that ACCOR had to be solidly established in Asia in order to convince business people to become its partners. A good way to increase both ACCOR's reputation and its capital base in Asia would be to issue stock in Singapore or in Hong Kong, however this threatened to take a long time.

Capdevila saw another good reason not to issue on these stock markets. In his eyes, Hong Kong, Singapore and for that matter Taiwan as well did not have hotel markets in which ACCOR should seek to develop a presence. They were mature markets, with many five-star hotels and independent hotels that catered to local tastes. ACCOR's concept of 'affordable accommodation' (economy and mid-range hotels) was better adapted to countries where a newly affluent middle class travelled for business and for pleasure. Capdevila preferred to target 'high potential' markets such as Indonesia, India and Vietnam, where an emerging middle class was growing rapidly.

ACCOR entered the Australian market in 1989 after winning a tender to build and manage a Novotel in Darling Harbour, a newly renovated site in central Sydney. The Novotel opened in early 1991 and quickly became a success. It was at this time that Capdevila met David Baffsky, a local businessman who had a strong association with Quality Pacific Corporation. They decided to collaborate together and, after a complicated negotiation process, finally merged the two companies to create ACCOR Asia Pacific Corporation (AAPC) in 1993. Baffsky became chairman and Capdevila was the managing director and chief executive officer. Head office was in Sydney, and the Bangkok office lost its role as ACCOR's headquarters in Asia.

AAPC BECOMES NUMBER 1 IN ASIA PACIFIC

AAPC's large-scale development effort made it the biggest operator in the Asia Pacific region with 98 hotels, well ahead of its largest competitor, Holiday Inn. In Australia, AAPC had acquired

12 hotels from another company, Resort Hotels Management, built a new Ibis in Darling Harbour, and successfully bid for management of the Sydney Convention Centre. It had opened the first Formule 1 in Asia Pacific at Campbelltown, Sydney. Although local growth was now slowing, AAPC operated 45 hotels in Australia, slightly more than its major local competitor, South Pacific Hotel Corporation.

In South Korea, AAPC had obtained management contracts or sold franchises for several hotels that were either under construction or already in operation. For example it owned 19% of the very successful Seoul Novotel. In China, it operated four hotels (the plans to renovate 100 hotels had fizzled out). It was looking to increase its activities in China and Korea and was negotiating management contracts for existing hotels or hotels under construction. However, few investors were prepared to put money into hotel projects in China.

Novotel was making good progress in India – with one hotel open, in Agra, and others under construction. AAPC was doing even better in other newly developed countries. In Malaysia, it was preparing a major expansion with the Novotel Kuala Lumpur, a 'flagship' property intended to attract the interest of the local business community. AAPC reached an agreement with a local group for the development of Formule 1 hotels throughout the country.

In Vietnam, where it had operated only one Sofitel in 1992, AAPC was preparing to open seven additional hotels: another Sofitel, one Mercure, three Novotels, and two Ibis. This was despite unfavourable legislation which prevented investors from using hotels as collateral for bank borrowings. In Thailand, Cambodia, Myanmar and Laos, AAPC managed 15 hotels, some of which it also partly owned; 14 more were under construction, or negotiation. AAPC would soon manage over 9,000 rooms in Thailand alone – more than it had had in all of Asia Pacific in 1992, four years earlier.

Development had been strongest in Indonesia where AAPC had managed only three properties in 1992 – all of which had come from the acquisition of WagonsLits. Two of these contracts had been discontinued and the remaining hotel had been given Associate status. In 1993, AAPC successfully opened the flagship Ibis Kemayoran, in which it held 10% of total equity. By 1995, more than 10 Ibis hotels were being built; eight Novotels and three Mercures had also been committed to and were due to open by 1998. Further expansion was planned to come in the area of serviced apartments.

Capdevila had confirmed the effectiveness of the strategy he had first used to break into the Thai market. AAPC entered each new market with a major flagship property that made it possible for local investors to test the ACCOR product. AAPC usually took 10 to 40% of the hotel's equity as a sign of commitment destined to reassure the business community. The success of the flagship hotel enabled AAPC to negotiate management contracts for existing or new properties that would generally be run as Novotel or Ibis hotels. AAPC rarely took a financial interest in existing properties; in new properties, however, it often invested a small amount, primarily to show its commitment. Once a suitable presence had been established, AAPC introduced additional ACCOR brands. In Thailand, for example where Novotel had been developed first, the latest hotels under consideration were Ibis. AAPC generally used the Mercure brand for existing hotels for which it had won a management contract but whose layout did not match the standards of other brands.

SERVICE STANDARDS IN ASIA

Between 1989 and 1995, Capdevila had been obliged to redefine ACCOR's branding strategy in order to adapt it to Asia. Hotel standards in Asia were very high, and AAPC had had to offer a quality of service at least one star above that which was offered in Europe for each brand. In Australia, service standards were between those in Asia and in Europe.

In each market, AAPC was careful to include services considered essential in the country, even if they were not standard for the brand. This was the case for laundry, for example, while it was not a standard service in Europe, it was offered at Ibis hotels in Indonesia. Novotel, often the first ACCOR brand established in a new market, was the most highly standardized. AAPC's efforts to adapt the Siam Square Novotel in Bangkok to local tastes had been viewed with some scepticism at head office in France.

ACCOR's head office warned that an international traveller who stayed at a Novotel in Asia then at a Novotel in France would experience a difference in service that could be detrimental for the brand. In recognition of this, AAPC had tried to apply European standards in the Ibis at Darling Harbour in Sydney – for example regarding room size – but they had received a number of complaints from local customers.

With regard to pricing, Capdevila decided to apply what was known as 'the 30% rule': in Asia, the prices and service of a Novotel would be 30% below those of a Sofitel; an Ibis 30% less than a Novotel, etc.

THE ORGANIZATION OF AAPC

At AAPC's headquarters in Sydney, Capdevila had set up a team working directly for David Baffsky and himself. Aside from the finance group headed by Roger White, head office employed an external communications specialist and, later, a marketing director and team. It also had a large technical assistance and development department that also handled some of the activities of Baffsky's former company, CitiState. This unit continued to be extremely profitable, with higher margins than the hotel management business. It was not, however, considered core income.

The relationship between Capdevila and Baffsky worked well. Capdevila focused on running and developing AAPC while Baffsky was head strategist and financial guide. While Baffsky was responsible to AAPC shareholders as a whole, Capdevila played an important role in AAPC's relationship with ACCOR SA. Back at ACCOR head office in Evry, France, it was vice president Benjamin Cohen who handled the relationship with AAPC.

Soon after he moved to Sydney, Capdevila had created a network of six regional offices, each responsible for developing and managing business in a given market, as shown in Table CS26.1. There was also a representative office in each country for the purpose of establishing links with actual or potential hotel owners. AAPC's organizational chart as of April 1995 is shown in Exhibit CS26.3.

Each regional office had a chief executive plus managers for a number of the following major areas of responsibility:

Table CS26.1   Network of regional offices

AAPC regional office location	Markets covered
Bangkok	Cambodia
	Laos
	Myanmar
	Thailand
Hong Kong	China
	Philippines
Jakarta	Indonesia
Kuala Lumpur	Korea
	Malaysia
	Singapore
	Vietnam
New Delhi	India
	Nepal
Sydney	Australia
	New Caledonia
	New Zealand

- *Human resources*: Only the larger offices (i.e. Sydney and Bangkok) had this function because Capdevila felt it was extremely important and deserved the attention of each chief executive. The group HR director, Sylvie Quesnel, was responsible directly to Capdevila for recruiting and managing expatriate staff and for handling relations with human resources in Paris for AAPC as a whole.

- *Development* involved selecting new hotel projects and negotiating terms with co-investors and owners. The chief executive was also highly involved in this process.

- *Finance and administration*: It was essential to closely control each region's budget, since management contracts in Asia were by and large less profitable than those in Europe. After expenses, including a license fee to ACCOR SA, barely 1% was left to cover corporate overheads. Finance managers helped the regional directors, who rarely had financial management experience, to navigate on that slim margin.

- *Marketing and sales support* managers handled relationships with tour agents and major touring groups and developed business for the hotels in their region.

- *Technical services*: ACCOR's experience in hotel design and construction was a major selling point in negotiating with potential owners and investors. In many instances,

AAPC sold its technical services separately, which generated fee income early in the project and ensured that the hotels could be managed efficiently once they were open.

MANAGING THE RELATIONSHIP WITH OWNERS

It was becoming increasingly important to carefully select hotel owners and investors. Over time, AAPC had learnt the advantages and disadvantages of having local investors as partners. Asian investors took a much more active role than Westerners in the day-to-day running of hotels and occasionally played a role in recruiting or in choosing suppliers. Many had little experience in designing and running a hotel, with the result that many hotels in Asia were difficult to manage or unprofitable. On the other hand, Asian investors actively promoted their hotels to friends and associates. Some were generous with funds for training or for renovating hotel properties; others were stingy.

This high level of investor involvement meant that hotel managers and AAPC corporate staff had to devote a large proportion of their time to handling relationships with owners: at least 30% in Australia, and as much as 60% in Asia. In Asia, the quality of the working relationship between AAPC's representatives and the owners/investors was the key to success; signed agreements carried little weight. Nothing could have been more different from managing an ACCOR hotel in Europe, and AAPC was beginning to find it difficult to recruit experienced ACCOR managers who could adapt.

MAINTAINING THE ACCOR CULTURE

Capdevila felt that it was essential for AAPC's future to guard its links to the ACCOR group and particularly to nurture the 'ACCOR spirit'. AAPC tried to have experienced ACCOR personnel in the number one or number two position in each hotel. In 1995, such personnel numbered 75 out of AAPC's total of 11,000 staff.

In general, the regional chief executives felt confident that they would be able to sustain the ACCOR culture despite the cultural barriers and the high turnover of non-management staff (this was normal in Asia). One executive director said: 'You have to hire an ACCOR profile ... a diamond in the rough, and then you have to give him a chance. If you are lucky, he will become more ACCOR than ACCOR'.

The ACCOR management style in the Asian context was characterized by strong delegation and a 'make it or break it' approach to staff development. ACCOR executives were willing to give a new recruit a chance; if he had the right attitude and the right talents, he would make it in the ACCOR environment. He had to accept to work harder and run faster. Decentralization, an important aspect of the ACCOR culture, was reinforced through the remuneration system. Throughout the group, managers were paid a base salary and a large bonus based on results. Capdevila had made business development a priority for regional chief executives. Thus while the six executives ostensibly cooperated together, the remuneration and recognition system fostered a high degree of competition, and they knew that success in their own region meant greater financial returns, a bigger territory, a larger revenue base and more independence from Sydney. It was estimated that for every new hotel opened, an additional staff function could be created at the regional office.

Since they focused so much on development, chief executives spent relatively little time at the hotels in their region that were already operating. Successful regional executives were developers and marketers who delegated daily management to hotel directors. Hotel directors, in turn, were chosen for their capacity to operate autonomously.

Ironically, establishing a strong ACCOR culture in Australia proved to be a difficult task. Many of the hotels had been fully staffed when they had become part of AAPC, and growth was slowing. Management was willing to train staff in the ACCOR style, but little such training was available locally and attempts to use ACCOR trainers from France had proved too costly. As a compromise, some French ACCOR programmes had been adapted for local use. Despite these efforts, the influence of local culture and management style remained strong. Some managers openly doubted the need for AAPC to retain strong cultural links to the parent company.

THE CURRENT DEVELOPMENT INITIATIVES

In January 1996 development remained a priority in every market except Australia. Capdevila described it as 'a race for critical mass'. Critical mass in a country was attained when AAPC had two or more brands in the major business and tourist locations, and a large enough volume of activity to give it significant leverage in negotiations with suppliers. The number of hotels necessary to attain critical mass varied by brand; it was often in inverse relation to the number of stars. Ibis, for example, needed more hotels to reach critical mass than Sofitel.

The race in Asia Pacific focused on the mid-range segment. The success of ACCOR and Holiday Inn had drawn competitors into this market, so while investment capital was now more readily available, AAPC had to compete against others to obtain it.

Choosing hotel locations was also more of a challenge. When there had been only a few mid-range hotels in the market, selecting a location for a new hotel had been fairly easy. But once the obvious sites had been developed, AAPC had to identify future 'hot spots'. In Indonesia, for example, it carried out a study associating natural resource sites with potential economic expansion to identify promising hotel development sites. A similar effort had been made to identify future tourist resort areas.

By 1996, regional executives were developing projects that went beyond hotel management or ownership. One common activity, in which large-scale growth was expected, was the provision of serviced apartments that were rented by the week or month, generally to business travellers, and furnished, cleaned and maintained by AAPC. A new complex had recently opened in Bangkok, and in Australia a major serviced apartment complex was situated at Darling Harbour, right next to the Ibis hotel and Novotel.

Marc Steinmeyer, the chief executive for Indonesia, had previously worked in catering and was looking to diversify operations in Indonesia into catering by linking up with ACCOR's catering arm Eurest. Other chief executives were following his lead in their regions. AAPC hoped to break into the market through a bid won by Eurest for the concession management of the Oceanpark amusement complex in Hong Kong.

To ensure that regional chief executives made viable investment decisions, they were obliged to present new projects to an investment committee in Sydney and to technical and development managers. Raymond Capdevila and David Baffsky actively participated in this decision process.

OUTSTANDING QUESTIONS

In retrospect, Raymond Capdevila identified three distinct periods in AAPC's development. First were the 'pioneer' days, before development in Asia was considered to be of strategic importance, which had culminated in the move to Los Angeles in search of capital. Next came the move to Bangkok and the 'visible presence' strategy that had launched ACCOR in the region. Finally came 'financial take-off', with the reverse acquisition of Quality Pacific and the stock issues in Sydney. Better access to capital had enabled the company to become the largest hotel chain in Asia Pacific. But, Raymond Capdevila reflected, this period was also coming to a close.

In January 1996, fundamental questions about AAPC's future were what had brought Benjamin Cohen to Sydney. Capdevila knew that during the meeting he would have to comment on each of the following issues:

- From which sources should AAPC seek increased profitability? To date, AAPC had focused on earning management fee income from hotels or related projects. Some within AAPC saw a limited future for the hotel management business, with its set fee structure, competitive environment and restricted leverage opportunities. Other options were available: ACCOR could generate higher fee returns from activities such as technical development and services, or could turn activities in which ACCOR had expertise, such as event handling, services to companies, reservation services, etc. into real businesses.

- Continued expansion required a large, stable source of capital. Should AAPC seek strong financial partnerships with banks, insurance companies or other long-term investors? Or should it create an investment fund specifically aimed at financing ACCOR hotels?

- How should ACCOR's role in AAPC be defined? While AAPC was closely tied to ACCOR because of its brands and the transfer of managers, ACCOR's share of AAPC's capital was relatively low. Should it increase its stake? Would that make AAPC more dependent on ACCOR and restrain its development as in the past, when Asia had not been a priority for ACCOR?

- The emphasis on growth and new project development had turned regional chief executives into a driving force, and their autonomy and their interest in diversification had grown. Since they reported to Sydney, their ties to France were weak. Sydney, on the other hand, was not in the heart of Asia. Did all of this mean that ACCOR's activities in Asia were too fragmented and there was a danger of diluting the brands?

- Would AAPC or ACCOR suffer if the degree of standardization required by head office in France was in fact lowered in Asia? In parallel, what was the value of the ACCOR culture in an environment so different from that in France?

- After establishing a separate organization for Asia, was it necessary to set an explicit regional strategy for Asia? For example, should efforts in China be revived? If so, what could AAPC do to prepare itself for a major entry into China?

Exhibit CS26.1 AAPC financial results (1994)

1 January–31 December 1994	AUD $'000
Managed property turnover	431,159
Operating revenue	97,847
Operating profit before income tax and abnormal items	26,011
Income tax expense	(4,737)
Operating profit after income tax	21,274
Outside equity interests	(368)
Operating profit attributable to members of the group	20,906
Earnings per share:	
– Basic	4.7 cents
– Fully diluted	3.9 cents
Annual dividend per share	3.3 cents

AAPC number of hotel rooms under management (1982–March 1995)

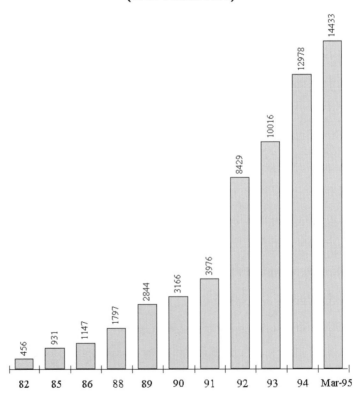

Case 26

Exhibit CS26.2 ACCOR Asia Pacific hotels by brand and country (January 1996)

	Sofitel	Novotel	Mercure	Ibis	Quality	Formule 1	Other	Total
Australia		13 (3,288)	12 (1,656)	4 (724)	7 (487)	1 (72)	8 (398)	45 (6,625)
New Zealand		1 (187)						1 (187)
New Caledonia		2 (272)		1 (58)				3 (330)
Cambodia	1 (254)						1 (49)	2 (303)
China	1 (389)	3 (760)						4 (1,149)
India		1 (142)						1 (142)
Indonesia		3 (480)	2 (418)	4 (688)				12 (1,988)
Korea	1 (450)	1 (330)					3 (402)	2 (780)
Laos		1 (233)						1 (233)
Malaysia	1 (166)	1 (318)						2 (484)
Myanmar		1 (206)						1 (206)
Philippines	1 (500)	1 (340)	2 (385)					4 (1,225)
Singapore		1 (450)	1 (393)					2 (843)
Thailand	1 (195)		4* (1,267)				3 (407)	15 (3,483)
Vietnam	2 (152)	7 (1,614)	1 (104)					3 (256)
Total	**8 (2,106)**	**36 (8,620)**	**22 (4,223)**	**9 (1,470)**	**7 (487)**	**1 (72)**	**15 (1,256)**	**98 (18,234)**

*Includes 41 Mercure villas at Hotel Sofitel Hua Hin.

Note: the number of rooms is shown in brackets.

Accor Asia Pacific hotels scheduled to open 1996–98

	Sofitel	Novotel	Mercure	Ibis	Formule 1	Other	Total
New Zealand		1 (200)					1 (200)
China		3 (797)					3 (797)
India	1 (196)	2 (264)					3 (460)
Indonesia		8 (1,375)	3 (492)	7 (1,156)			18 (3,023)
Korea		1 (240)					1 (240)
Malaysia		2 (494)		1 (200)	1 (80)		4 (774)
Myanmar	1 (270)						1 (270)
Nepal		1 (180)	1 (190)				2 (370)
Philippines			1 (164)				1 (164)
Thailand	2 (831)	3 (574)	2 (760)	6 (960)			13 (3,125)
Vietnam	1 (135)	3 (490)	1 (120)	2 (242)		7 (987)	
Total	**5 (1,432)**	**24 (4,614)**	**8 (1,726)**	**16 (2,558)**	**1 (80)**	**7 (987)**	**54 (10,410)**

Note: the number of rooms is shown in brackets.

Exhibit CS26.3 Organizational chart of AAPC (April 1995)

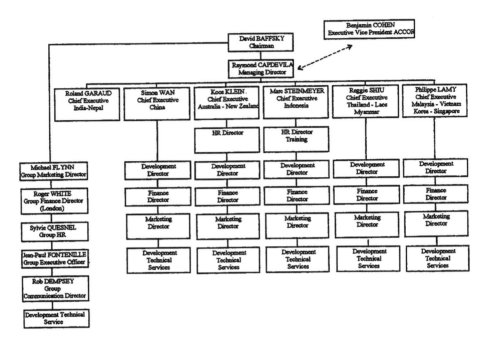